NO DIRECTION HOME

THE LIFE AND MUSIC OF
BOB DYLAN

ROBERT SHELTON
Revised and updated edition edited by
ELIZABETH THOMSON and PATRICK HUMPHRIES

Backbeat
Books

An Imprint of Hal Leonard Corporation

Dedicated to the memory and widows of Geoff Ablett and Ralph J Gleason.
How a twenty-eight-year-old London cop and a fifty-eight-year-old California journalist found
their short lives deeply touched by a writer of songs is part of the mystery this book explores.

For my sisters and brother-in-law, who lent support when it was most needed. And for uncommon
help and inspiration from Gabrielle Goodchild, Liz Thomson, and Clare Pedrick ... deep thanks.
—R S, LONDON, 1986

REVISED AND UPDATED EDITION

Text copyright © 1986 and 2010 by The Estate of Robert Shelton
Introduction and notes © 2010 Elizabeth Thomson and Patrick Humphries
Design/layout © 2011 Palazzo Editions Ltd

Published in 2011 in the United States by
BACKBEAT BOOKS
An Imprint of Hal Leonard Corporation
7777 West Bluemound Road
Milwaukee, WI 53213
Trade Book Division Editorial Offices
33 Plymouth St., Montclair, NJ 07042
www.backbeatbooks.com

Produced by
PALAZZO EDITIONS LTD
2 Wood Street
Bath, BA1 2JQ
www.palazzoeditions.com

Publisher: COLIN WEBB
Art director: DAVID COSTA (Wherefore Art?)

ISBN 978-1-61713-012-0

Library of Congress Cataloging in Publication Data is available upon request.

A CIP catalogue record for this book is available from the British Library.

Printed and bound in China by Imago.

Previous pages: p1 Waiting for the Aust ferry to Wales while touring the UK in May, 1966, and traveling in a limo on loan from the Rolling Stones.
p2–3 Exhaustion in Manchester, May 1966.
Opposite: Dylan's Gibson guitar and harmonicas in Studio A at Columbia Records, New York, the first recording session in 1961.

CONTENTS

Robert Shelton and Bob Dylan caught backstage at the Newport Folk Festival, 1964.

The first publication of *No Direction Home* in September 1986 marked the twenty-fifth anniversary of Robert Shelton's celebrated *New York Times* review of "a bright new face in folk music."[1] This new edition coincides with its fiftieth, and the seventieth birthday of its subject.

Shelton's 400 words, the four-column headline announcing the arrival of "Bob Dylan: A Distinctive Stylist," described a young man "bursting at the seams with talent" whose past mattered less than his future. Its prescience was remarkable, for Dylan's talent was raw indeed and three record companies had failed to spot his potential. The fourth, Columbia, offered him a contract the day after the review appeared, before they had heard him sing a note.

As Suze Rotolo reflected years later: "Robert Shelton's review, without a doubt, made Dylan's career … That review was unprecedented. Shelton had not given a review like that for anybody."[2] In her memoir, *A Freewheelin' Time*, Rotolo describes how she and Dylan bought an early edition of the *Times* at the kiosk on Sheridan Square and took it across the street to an all-night deli. "Then we went back and bought more copies."[3]

Yet Shelton never claimed to have "discovered" Dylan ("he discovered himself") and, when his magnum opus was published, many friends and colleagues realized for the first time that the quiet American in their midst was rather more than simply a regional critic (Shelton was by then, somewhat implausibly, Arts Editor of the *Brighton Evening Argus*, a south-coast city daily). When he died, on December 11, 1995, after a final burst of freelancing, this time as film critic of the *Birmingham Post*, new friends in the Guild of Regional Film Writers, of which he was a founder, were similarly astonished. As Michael Gray noted in his *Guardian* obituary, Shelton "displayed in this final phase of his life the same rare qualities as in his New York heyday: he was gregarious, warm, a good listener, secretive to a fault about his own distinguished past, and wholeheartedly committed to the humane arts."[4]

Gregarious, warm, a good listener. That last quality is the *sine qua non* of any serious music critic, but the first two were no less important in Shelton's quest to seek out burgeoning talent in the clubs and coffeehouses of 1960s Greenwich Village, New York's perennial bohemia, and to bring it to the attention of America at large. Judy Collins remembers him as both a friend and critic "with the intelligence and perception and the ability to get the fact that something rare and wonderful was happening in the world of music and social consciousness" and who wrote about it with "a crisp and unique clarity."[5] For Janis Ian, who has long acknowledged the role Shelton played in her early career, bringing her to the attention of conductor-composer Leonard Bernstein, "Bob Shelton exemplified all the best in music writing — stylistically, ethically, morally. He foresaw trends through the sheer exuberance of listening, and went out on a limb for so many of us."[6]

Robert Shelton Shapiro was born in Chicago on June 28, 1926, the son of a research chemist and a homemaker. Graduating from high school in June 1943, with his parents' permission he dropped the family surname, their shared feeling being that "to be immediately identifiable with any minority group was not an asset." Soon, he was in the Army, shipping to France in the wake of its reclamation by the Allies. So began a life-long passion for French culture in particular and for Europe in general. Back in civvy street at the end of War, he returned to Chicago and Northwestern University's School of Journalism, emerging as a Bachelor of Science.

By February 1951, he was in New York, hired as a copy boy on the *New York Times* and trained as a reader, writing news on the side. His cuttings file reveals short items on voting rights, community affairs, education, and the ending of racial discrimination at the National Theatre in Washington. Soon he was contributing to a range of magazines: an article on a university-led agricultural experiment in New Jersey for *Colliers*, a piece on how we hear for *Modern Hi-Fi* and, in 1959, a long report for the *Nation* on that summer's Newport Folk Festival.

The Shelton byline seems first to have appeared in the *New York Times* on March 18, 1956 on a piece about hi-fi jargon, the first of several items about records and recordings in general. From January 1958, it appeared regularly above articles on such diverse subjects as southern folk songs from prison; Irish, Jewish, and African music; bluegrass and flamenco; a tour by the Soviet Moiseyev Dance Company;

John Lomax; Oscar Brand ("A Civic Troubadour"); tradition versus art in folk music; "Folk Music on the 'Hit Parade.'" On November 17, 1960, Shelton noted: "Folk music is leaving the imprint of its big country boots on the night life of New York in unparalleled fashion, from the grimiest Greenwich Village espresso joint to the crook-fingered elegance of the Waldorf Astoria." Not surprising, then, that come 1960, he was reviewing more and more live music: Theodore Bikel and Odetta at Town Hall, Lightnin' Hopkins at the Village Gate, Joan Baez at the Y and, in April 1961, John Lee Hooker at Gerde's. On that occasion, Shelton famously *didn't* review the support act but Bob Dylan did catch his ear at a Monday night hootenanny in June and, in July, his first New York City concert appearance in a folk marathon at Riverside Church led to a mention in the *Times*.

Beyond reviews, Shelton wrote about music's connections to everyday life—an early piece examined the role of "freedom songs" in the Civil Rights struggle, another pondered how history could be taught through folk song. The *Times* archive lists 408 articles, the last, March 24, 1969, about the Metropolitan Opera's "sturdy new production" of *Tosca*, one of a surprising number of classical music reviews.

Ironically, it appears that Shelton owes his career as a music critic to Senator McCarthy. In January 1956, he was subpoenaed to appear before a Senate subcommittee investigating Communist infiltration of the press. The case was actually one of mistaken identity (the Eastland Committee, as it was called, was in pursuit of a Washington-based journalist named Willard Shelton) but, in any event, Robert Shelton refused to testify, arguing that the Committee was infringing freedom of the press and engaging in a smear campaign against the *Times*. Instead he read out a statement: "No one who knows me would doubt my loyalty to the government of the United States. Because I am a loyal American, I must, as a matter of principle, challenge questions into my political beliefs and associations as a violation of my rights under the First Amendment to the Constitution." The left-leaning *Times* was lily-livered, affirming its commitment to freedom of expression but pledging to dismiss any known Communists—and re-assigning Shelton from news to entertainment and features. Twice convicted, Shelton sued, supported in his fight by the American Civil Liberties Union. Finally, in September 1963, an appeal court ruled two-to-one in his favor. Ultimately, a five-to-two decision in the Supreme Court reversed the convictions.[7]

By then, of course, "Robert Shelton of the *New York Times*" had ploughed his own very distinctive furrow and was, as Jon Pareles wrote in the paper's obituary, both "catalyst and chronicler of the 1960s folk boom."[8] Far lesser critics have made greater claims for themselves. Besides Dylan, and the aforementioned Collins and Ian, innumerable other performers owe him a debt of thanks, among them Joan Baez, whom he reviewed at the 1959 Newport Folk Festival, and Phil Ochs, Buffy Sainte-Marie, Peter, Paul and Mary, Tom Paxton, Janis Joplin, José Feliciano and Frank Zappa.

As Dave Laing notes in his survey of "the folk revival journalism of Robert Shelton," New York was the capital of the revival and "the New York folk scene was centered on the Greenwich Village district and was populated by a volatile group of musicians, journalists, club-owners and music business entrepreneurs who met frequently on a face-to-face basis. Shelton had established himself as a member of this network by the beginning of the 1960s, not least because of his passionate defense of folk music in an article for the *Village Voice* in 1960."[9] Thus, some of his most avid readers, including many of the performers he wrote about, were (or became) friends, simply because they lived and worked in the vicinity of his home, 191 Waverly Place, equidistant from Gerde's and the White Horse Tavern. Nevertheless, Shelton wrote neither for them, nor even specifically for folk music fans, but for the general reader and record-buyer, many of whom (because the *Times* was then the closest the US came to a national newspaper, and anyway much of its content was syndicated) lived a long way from the Village. For the first time, readers "from California to the New York islands" were invited to follow Shelton into a smoke-filled coffeehouse much as the great Harold C Schonberg took them to Carnegie Hall.

The precise moment when he and Dylan finally agreed to proceed with the project is unclear. On New Year's Eve 1965, the two men discussed a proposed biography over dinner at the Clique in uptown Manhattan. By that time, Shelton had a number of reasonably large-scale projects under his belt or in train, among them *Born to Win*—a collection of writings by Woody Guthrie, *The Face of Folk Music* with photographer David Gahr, *The Country Music Story*, plus extended essays in various songbooks and, under the pseudonym Stacey Williams, numerous album notes, including that for Elektra's *Folk Box*, for which he also chose the tracks. Thus, by March 1966, when Shelton joined his subject on the road, he had already built up a significant body of research and writing on both Dylan and the folk movement and he knew the players as well as anyone. From the outset, it seems clear that Shelton's intention was a serious study, not a potboiler, though presumably neither party imagined that it would take twenty years to come to fruition. After a flirtation with Viking, he signed a contract with Doubleday and, shortly thereafter, left New York for Europe, spending time in Ireland before coming to Britain, where he would remain.

In an interview in 1987,[10] he summed up his needs as "money and a sympathetic publisher." His advance had not been ungenerous "but it wasn't sufficient"—and Shelton wasn't good with money. Anyway, the costs incurred were considerable and by his own admission he over-researched, expensive in the pre-internet age. He researched not simply Dylan but everything that had informed Dylan's life and work, socially, politically, culturally. It all had to be contextualized. When he began writing in the early Seventies, what emerged was (as one critic would put it) "fascinating social history," a study of "the American musical scene and Dylan's place in it." But it was long, way too long, and Boswell couldn't keep pace with his Johnson who, by the mid-Seventies, was once again in high gear. In 1976, Shelton had reached 1966, the motorcycle accident. An appropriate place, he felt, for the conclusion of the first volume of what he now hoped could be a two-volume biography, but the suggestion fell on stony ground.

Freelancing in order to pay the rent, he wrote on and, by the close of 1977, Shelton's Dylan was poised to launch Tour '74. New chapters and revisions of old ones were dispatched to his publisher but correspondence suggests they met with a deathly silence, even though the success of Dylan's 1978 world tour made the climate propitious. Furthermore, Shelton's own reputation was enhanced, with high-profile accounts and an interview during Dylan's acclaimed London concert visit. In February 1979, Shelton wrote to Doubleday that, though he'd been amassing material, "I haven't written one further word."[11] He saw "no end to this status quo and status woe" without more money. A year passed, and Shelton was sent "an egregiously poorly edited manuscript,"[12] which convinced him that Doubleday neither liked nor understood the book. Pointing to the public outcry over Albert Goldman's muckraking biography of Elvis Presley, "longer than my edited, mauled manuscript," he charged that Doubleday "encouraged me to invade the privacy of Bob Dylan and Johnny Cash and many other characters in my book," imposing "constant unrelenting pressure for me to sell down the river many of my friends in this book for commercial gain."[13]

By 1983, Shelton had parted from Doubleday and the contract passed to New English Library in London. Still, the financial and legal arm-twisting continued, and the new editors found themselves routinely on the receiving end of Shelton's blistering late-night prose. With the resale of US rights to Morrow, Shelton felt that, at last, the manuscript had a simpatico publisher, a feeling confirmed by a telegram from his New York editor: "I AM OVERWHELMED BY THE MAGNIFICENT JOB YOU HAVE DONE ON YOUR BOOK. CONGRATULATIONS AND GRATITUDE." A few days later, a detailed commentary on the manuscript concluded that the past twenty years had been "wholly justified."[14]

Shelton replied that he could "accept a great many of the suggestions and ideas and queries," though a hapless copy editor seeking confirmation that "Dylan's plane was really eight miles high" during his celebrated in-flight interview drew a vitriolic response. Arguments over length were exacerbated when Shelton was forced to accede to the publishers' demands that the book be brought up to date: with no question of a second volume, vast cuts had now to be found in *earlier* sections of the book. A compromise was reached, whereby Shelton accepted less money in exchange for retaining more words.[15] The prefatory quote to the final chapter revealed his anguish: "a portrait can never be finished; it can only be abandoned." Until his dying day, Shelton regarded his book as having been "abridged over troubled waters."

Finally, *No Direction Home* was published and Shelton took to the road for tours of Britain and the US, a prospect that amused Dylan when the two men met in London during the filming of *Hearts of Fire*. International editions followed: European readers, notably in Italy and France, where it made the front page of *Le Monde*, were especially appreciative of the book.

Shelton's life's work received a good deal of thunderous applause, though, unsurprisingly, given the weight of expectation, some slow hand-clapping as well. In the years immediately following its publication and with Dylan's star having waned, some critics and rival biographers saw fit to denigrate both book and author—disregarding the fact that, without that *New York Times* review, Dylan's career may not have taken off and failing to acknowledge that Shelton was *there*, a witness to all its crucial moments: At Newport '63 and at the celebrated Philharmonic Hall concert on Halloween 1964. At Newport '65, when Dylan went electric. On the pivotal 1966 tour with the Hawks. At the Woody Guthrie memorial in 1968 and the Isle of Wight in 1969. Along the way, the two men spent many hours together, often just hanging out, sometimes with their girlfriends, Rotolo and Baez in Dylan's case. They chatted for hours in New York in 1971, during Dylan's long public withdrawal, and talked long into the night on his 1978 tour.

During those crucial years in Greenwich Village, Shelton was part of Dylan's "gang." Dylan's friends were Shelton's friends. As Rotolo recalls in her memoir, evenings sometimes ended at Shelton's apartment where, on one occasion after a long night that had begun at the White Horse Tavern, Dylan fell asleep on the sofa. Thus, Shelton was given unique access to many of those closest to Dylan, including his brother, David, and his parents, Abe and Beatty, to whom no other journalist ever spoke in depth. When news broke of Dylan's motorcycle crash in July 1966, it was Shelton whom Abe Zimmerman called for more information. Shelton also talked to Dylan's childhood friends from Hibbing, including Echo Helstrom; Bonny Beecher, the "Girl from the North Country"; and fellow students and friends from Minneapolis.

And of course he talked to the musicians closest to Dylan, including Baez, Peter Yarrow, Jack Elliott, and Pete Seeger; to his manager, Albert Grossman; and to would-be Dylan producer Phil Spector, whom he interviewed during the sessions for "River Deep, Mountain High." So many of those witnesses are no longer with us: Dylan's parents, of course, but also John Hammond, Johnny Cash, Mary Travers, Allen Ginsberg, Dave Van Ronk, Richard Fariña, and Phil Ochs have all passed away. Their testimony lives on, thanks to the assiduous work of Robert Shelton.

Despite such access and closeness, Shelton retained a journalist's objectivity, and his move to Europe was as much to put a distance between himself and those he was writing about as it was to escape what he saw as the ugliness of Nixon's America. To those who complained that Dylan remained elusive, that questions were left questions unanswered, Shelton would say that "it's all there, if you know how to break the code." Cries for blood were simply ignored. Bankruptcy was a constant anxiety but no amount of money would have persuaded him to "sell off the relics of a friend."

From the outset, Shelton was determined to establish Dylan as a major figure of twentieth-century culture whose work was discussed alongside that of Picasso, Chaplin, Welles and Brando. It's true that he can overstate the intellectual argument, but if some of the song analysis is overwritten, literary comparisons overwrought, we should remember that Shelton was making his case years before popular music in general, and Dylan in particular, became subjects of academic scrutiny. The times have, indeed, changed—and Shelton and his book helped to change them.

Certainly, Shelton could be difficult, firing off letters that should have remained forever unsent. But sometimes—often—he was difficult for the right reasons, because a principle was at stake. Sadly, he didn't live to see the revival of interest in the 1960s and its music, nor the return to form of the poet-singer-songwriter who defined the era. As he pointed out, Dylan "could have died in 1966, or after, and still have changed the face of popular music, and its metabolism."[16] Neither did Shelton live to witness the reassessment of his study, which every Dylan chronicler since has drawn on and sometimes plundered. Increasingly regarded as a classic of the genre by a man who could be said to be the father of serious music journalism, *No Direction Home* is, as cultural historian Dr Lawrence J Epstein put it, "disorganized but fascinating, filled with wonderful anecdotes … an authentic and valuable portrait for what it is, and what it is is a *great* book."

This new edition is, we believe, better edited and organized, with some twenty-thousand words of authentic anecdote and detail restored from Shelton's 1977 manuscript. The most significant additions are to chapters one, four and ten, each one pivotal: Hibbing and Greenwich Village, and the celebrated 1966 interview *en route* from Lincoln to Denver. The Prelude is previously unpublished. Sections which have dated—bootlegs, the so-called New Dylans—have been excised. So, too, has much of the sketchy and unsatisfactory update: the book now ends in 1978, behind the scenes of the triumphant London concerts.

"Find something that you feel strongly about and just write it," Dylan advised Shelton as they enjoyed some downtime together in the Gaslight one evening in October 1965, four years after that life-changing *New York Times* review. It was advice the critic took to heart. Within a few weeks he had found his subject.

Elizabeth Thomson and Patrick Humphries

Above: Robert Shelton in the compositors' room at the *New York Times*, 1950s.
Right: Dylan reading "How to avoid the draft" in the Berkeley student magazine
The California Pelican. By this time in 1962 he was well into supplying marching
songs for the campus protest against war.

Could there be a more uncomfortable position intellectually than that of floating in the thin air of unproved possibilities, not knowing whether what one sees is truth or illusion?
CARL JUNG, PREFACE TO *I CHING*[1]

Take care of all your memories … For you cannot relive them.
DYLAN[2]

Because he is part Orpheus, the poet … is architect of myth, magician over savagery, and pilgrim towards death …
GEORGE STEINER, *SILENCE AND THE POET*

The truth was obscure, too profound and too pure; to live it you have to explode.
DYLAN[3]

Someone had to reach for the risin' star, I guess it was up to me.
DYLAN[4]

"I am my words." Dylan at work in Woodstock, 1964.

This is a story about a poet and musician who was born and reborn time again, who "died" several "deaths" and yet continued to live. It is the story of a popular hero who denied his own heroism, of a rebel who so eloquently challenged his culture that he helped build a counterculture, and who then turned against the excesses of what he'd helped create. This is a chronicle of change, of challenge to unquestioning tradition, and of the tradition of change itself. This is an attempt to tell the truth about a myth-maker, a myth-taker and a myth-breaker. If myths are public dreams and dreams are private myths, then this story will try to show how a song-poet became a public dreamer who mythologized the dreams and nightmares of a generation.

The quest of Bob Dylan is riddled with ironies and contradictions, shadowed with seven types of ambiguity, scorched with stage-light glare, heightened with scabrous humor and darkened with his pain, and ours. Dylan wore a score of masks, assumed a legion of personas, invented a galaxy of characters we recognize as friends and foes. "There's so many sides to Dylan, he's round," said a Woodstock friend. "He's a dozen different people," said Kris Kristofferson. "Just let me be me," Dylan wrote in 1964, "human me/ruthless me/wild me/gentle me/all kinds of me."[5] In 1966, he said that "it's always lonely where I am," but ten years later he said the only place he could feel alone was on a public stage.

Dylan's career has been a personal search, a constant flight along an endless spiritual highway strewn with debris, gashed by crashes, hedged by ugly billboards, and relieved by interludes of serene countryside. At times, he sang, his flight was "Down the foggy ruins of time … Far from the twisted reach of crazy sorrow."[6] Like every artist, he had a vision of the future: "Someday, everything is gonna be smooth like a rhapsody/When I paint my masterpiece."[7]

Bob Dylan first sang for an audience at the age of five; scribbled inchoate poems at 12; suffered adolescence under a cloud of imminent death; was reborn at 19; outlined his own epitaphs at 22; amassed a fortune and an international following by 24. Then, at 25, he retreated into the vapors of legend until artistic and spiritual rebirth began all over again: "We died and were reborn/And then mysteriously saved."[8] After seven years off stage-center, he was back in the spotlight with a burst of concert, film and recording activity. It was less a revival than a resurrection, before a vast new audience.

Dylan songs have orchestrated our time: "Like a Rolling Stone," "Blowin' in the Wind," "Idiot Wind," "Knockin' on Heaven's Door," "Mr Tambourine Man," "A Hard Rain's a-Gonna Fall," 'It's Alright Ma (I'm Only Bleeding)," "All Along the Watchtower," "George Jackson," "Hurricane," "It's All Over Now, Baby Blue," "Tangled Up in Blue," "Shelter from the Storm," "Chimes Of Freedom," "Gates of Eden," "Subterranean Homesick Blues"—a handful from the hundreds that are known, loved and studied by an army of Dylanites, Dylanologists, Dylantantes, Dylan interpreters, fans, freaks and followers. Among them were two men named Carter—one called Hurricane, who once lived in the jailhouse, and another called Jimmy, who once lived in the White House. The convict Carter called Dylan "a man that was for life and living, not for death and dying." The President-to-be Carter accepted his nomination exhorting America to heed Dylan's line: "he not busy being born is busy dying."[9]

However deeply Dylan is immersed in show business, its glamour, cruelties and shams are only a portion of his landscape. He has entered classic American folklore, pop lore and mythology, (I use "myth" here not as "false belief," but for those archetypal symbols and stories that express a culture's dreams, attitudes and values.) Long before Dylan met or read Robert Graves, he was following the old poet's admonition that a poet must think mythically as well as rationally.

The Dylan lore tells of an arch-rebel disturber of the peace who'd been a "nice boy." He has also been a 12-year-old student of Hebrew; an accident-prone driver long before he crashed his motorcycle into retreat; an apprentice appliance salesman; a magazine columnist and "editor;" a novelist and annalist; an incipient playwright; a film star; a painter; a Bible student; a voracious reader; a preacher; everybody's son, then everybody's father, many people's dream lover, and many people's "enemy."

If reporters asked him *who* or *what* he was, they'd invite his sarcasm. "I'm just a trapeze artist," he'd say, or a "rabbit-catcher and dog-smoother" or "an ashtray bender." Reporters often risked Dylan's scorn. "Does it take a lot of trouble to get your hair like that?" an Australian newsman dared to ask him. "No, you just have to sleep on it for about 20 years," Dylan parried. "What do you think about drugs?" a French reporter asked him. "Brigitte Bardot is the only good one I know." Dylan twitted one impatient reporter: "I'm just trying to answer your questions as good as you can ask them."

As early as 1964, he knew the dangers of defining his views, writing, sardonically: "do not create anything, it will be misinterpreted, it will not change. It will follow you the rest of your life."[10] I think Dylan always wanted to keep his options open. In 1966 he said: "I define nothing. Not beauty, not patriotism. I take each thing as it is, without prior rules about what it should be." In 1976, he said he didn't "comprehend the values most people operate under ... I can't understand the values of definition and confinement. Definition destroys. Besides, there's nothing definite in this world." Despite his ambiguity, defiance and rhetorical flourishes, Dylan *has* defined and redefined himself often and unequivocally, but the definitions were always *subject to change*. Since the day I first met him in 1961, he has come closer to defining the shape, course, moral order and texture of our time than any artist I've encountered. His art and life trace his search for a workable existence as a creative iconoclast seeking his own answers. In 1964, in the notes to *Another Side Of*, he wrote:

> *i know no answers an' no truth*
> *for absolutely no soul alive*
> *i will listen t' no one*
> *who tells me morals*
> *there are no morals*
> *an' i dream a lot*[11]

Yet by 1968, having written the Biblically-infused and moralistic *John Wesley Harding*, he was ready to say that "we are all moralists." Dylan's ability to change was an implicit critique of a rigid educational system that yields "useless and pointless knowledge." Defiantly, he dropped out of college, finding then that the universities and museums were among the institutions where "Lifelessness is the Great Enemy." But in the value-shifting Sixties, he became a hero to collegians and intellectuals. Some named him "Public Writer Number 1." By the beginning of the 1980s, Dylan, the self-taught writer-musician, had become a suitable subject for study. Princeton University gave him an honorary doctorate of music. A man who had long disdained "school," he was a tireless student, albeit a "roads scholar."

A basically quiet man, he's been blisteringly articulate. An international communicator, he has often been unable to communicate directly to those around him. As moods of dark and light colored his personality, silences alternated with pistol shots or geyser blasts of words. What sure aim he had in this line: "I'm helpless, like a rich man's child."[12] His definition of "life, and life only"[13] overflowed in word-flood:

> *Pointed threats, they bluff with scorn*
> *Suicide remarks are torn*
> *From the fool's gold mouthpiece*
> *The hollow horn plays wasted words*
> *Proves to warn*
> *That he not busy being born*
> *Is busy dying.*[14]

Using language elliptically, he wasted few words in writing about pity, terror, release, longing, vulnerability, liberation, responsibility, cages, traps, injustice. He was a quintessential writer of this period. His chief form was the song-lyric. He wrote, often with his extraordinary twist of black humor, about the arrogance of power and authority, utopianism and its deceits, existential freedom and the modern apocalypse, the search for identity, commitment and lack of it, love and its many faces, and about all the false beliefs that hold us prisoner, the truths that can set us free. To counterpoint even his most somber view of the modern wasteland, he could summon up hope for renewal and fulfillment. Always, he asked challenging questions. As he sang of *his* quest for answers and for new questions, *his* search for wholeness and for a sense of himself, the songs set the tempo for *our* own quests. We grew up, or stayed younger, with Dylan. Often misunderstood, he demanded to know: "how come you're so afraid of things that don't make any sense to you?"[15] He new a lot about fear: "experience teaches that silence terrifies people the most."[16] He knew as well as Rimbaud ("I am the master of silence") how to master silence and turn it into a protective fence round wisdom.

As friend, reporter, critic and biographer, I was often able get behind that fence. Sometimes he provided the key, sometimes I found a door myself. It was marvelous when he'd really open up. Once he told me: "Everybody has something to do. I just can't believe that people are born and die without reason." He told me repeatedly how he hated labels: "I don't know what I am, truthfully speaking. When people believe that I am *this* or *that*, already there is a misunderstanding, a barrier, between them and me." He's said a lot to me down the years, but he also says a lot to people who've never met him, if they really *listen* to his songs.

However sardonically, Dylan stressed his role as entertainer, as "song and dance man." He deflated his role as teacher, yet he taught us much about love and loss, society's flaws and powers, alchemy and redemption, the border country between life and death. Dylan's career and work are metaphors and myths, card games, street games and pantomimes, where everything operates on several levels. Like Jung, he was often astounded at the creativity that came out of him, as if he were just a vessel through which insight poured. Of his success he once said: "I'm there only because of time and chance. There are a million me's, all over the United States. And they are all hung up, but they cannot split from where they are."

Almost single-handedly, Dylan took poetry off dusty shelves and put it on the jukebox. Still, he was often uncomfortable at being labeled a "poet." He once exploded at me: "That's such a huge, God-damn word for someone to call themselves. 'A Poet!' I think a poet is anybody who wouldn't call himself a poet. When people started calling me a poet, it didn't make me any happier."

By disdaining the title "poet," he protected himself from those unaware of the grand tradition of folk and popular poetry, those who couldn't see the artistry in his borrowing and reshaping everyday speech, those who rejected the possibilities of a literature of the jukebox. Dylan began with the language of folksay, then he flowered into sophisticated city expression. His determined use of the syntax, vocabulary and rhythms of colloquial speech, his reliance on popular song-form, and his disavowal that he was a poet—all retarded his serious acceptance as a literary figure. Why is Dylan an extraordinary poet? I can call attention here to his concise and memorable formulations and aphorisms, his ability to say several things simultaneously, his audacious use of metaphor, simile and symbol, his evocative imagery, his cunning use of rhyme and near rhyme, of the sounds and colors of his words, the surprising contexts and combinations of felicitous phrases that touch and unsettle the listener, the musical bend and sway of his lines. For many, Dylan's art is an aural/oral expression that needs the nuance and emphasis of song. Yet once known, his lyrics come alive on the page, music resounding in the mind's ear.

As literary acceptance of Dylan grew, he winced less at being regarded as a romantic-visionary poet who'd made vast contributions to modernist poetics. When commentators saw him as a Whitman with a guitar or a Rimbaud with a recording contract, Dylan could stop pretending he didn't know the difference between a quatrain and a freight-train. Definitions of "literature" had to be expanded in new and exciting ways to encompass Dylan's art. It included his stage and page writing, his novel, *Tarantula*, his early "journalism," and his development of all forms of media as valid writer's vehicles. His duels with the press, his famed anti-interviews, were, in themselves, a form of literary performance.

Central to Dylan's nimbus of genius is his art of concealing art. He often gave the impression of being *only* the spontaneous, intuitive, automatic wordsmith, the casual minstrel. He sheltered the purposeful, highly conscious designs that weave throughout his work from the storm of critical overkill. He could not, however, conceal his talent to disturb, a talent that created envy among his peers even as he won their imitation. Because his indictments of social ills and human failings were so severe, his listeners felt guilt, and some were quick to strike back. He was called arrogant, manipulative, ambitious, paranoid and egotistical. He's frequently admitted that his sudden fame threw him, that he wished he hadn't said quite so many harsh things about associates. He often contended that his motives and meanings were distorted, producing an enemy for each convert. Like most self-made men he thought, I suspect, that he could do with a bit of tailoring. His history, I submit, doesn't need "tailoring" as much as it needs sympathetic understanding.

This romantic, angry, passionate, delightful and maddening man, who, many thought, could not maintain any close relationship for long, is, he freely admits, contradictory. Yet, there was no confusion about his compassion for the victims he recognized in all of us—victims of social lies, of deceptions, of manipulations in government, media, the music world. He heard apocalyptic voices and distant bells tolling in the storm:

> *Tolling for the deaf an' blind, tolling for the mute*
> *Tolling for the mistreated, mateless mother, the mistitled prostitute*
> *For the misdemeanor outlaw, chased an' cheated by pursuit*
> *An' we gazed upon the chimes of freedom flashing*[17]

As he matured, his catechism went beyond the simplistics of good and evil. He changed from activist critic to observer to evangelist. He sometimes played the part of visionary and of satanic jester who knew that life was tragic for those who felt too much and an absurdist comedy for those who think too much. His work oscillated between tears and laughter. He often lived to excess. Then, as moderate man he reveled in balance and order. As Blake wrote: "The road of excess leads to the palace of wisdom." Soon, he was back in emotional turmoil again, living to excess, refining it all into song. Ultimately his catechism was the absence of catechism. What he seemed most deeply to accept was the constancy of change itself. "There's nothing so stable as change," he said in 1964.

"No artist can accept reality," Nietzsche wrote. Dylan challenged the larger realities and his own. Because some of his own actualities were too mundane and literal for his romantic vision, he changed them a dozen times. Thinking mythically, he often lived mythically. Yet, here was a most vulnerable, sensitive writer who longed, repeatedly, for obscurity and its blessings, even though the other part of him needed to surpass, triumph and conquer. The two parts of his Gemini personality warred with each other. He tried to protect his inner core by becoming increasingly distant, elusive and unreachable. Yet he repeatedly bared his soul in song. We knew that even if he wrote about he, or she, or them, or it, or any of a large cast of characters, he was never far from himself, or the many selves that roared in debate inside him. In our minds, he became some of the characters he created. Who are the ragman, the lover, "Napoleon in rags,"[18] the armed orphan, the outlaw, the Jack of Hearts, the Drifter, the husband-brother of Isis, the joker and the thief? Who lurked behind the masks of Doctor Filth, Miss Lonely, Mrs Henry, the landlord, Achilles, the immigrant, Mr Tambourine Man? And what do the women-anima figures of Johanna, Marie, Ramona, Queen Jane, Mona, Valerie represent?

So here is a man as elusive as a Garbo or Brando simultaneously exposing to strangers his experiences, thoughts and feelings. He was there—visible and tangible; yet he was nowhere—spectral and hidden. The more the public clamored to know the inner Dylan, the less he revealed. Unless you could break the code to the revelations that lay behind the "Dylanese" of his poems and his talk, the veiled language which was opaque to the squares and carried secret messages to his "friends." He could use words as a screen. As Talleyrand said: "Man invented speech to conceal his thoughts." Dylan developed new forms of popular song in which both to reveal, and conceal, his thoughts. The lonely artist in America is a sad legend. Dylan is part not only of the old tradition that doomed Hart Crane and John Berryman, but he also pioneered a new tradition in which the poet could find larger audiences than ever. Some of his alienation was social, some was that of the writer who agonizes over the discrepancy between the way things are and the way they ought to be.

The power of Dylan's leadership, his stagecraft, the force of his personality and talent, the bardic stance and the self-perpetuating aura of legend—all this led some to try to deify him. Show business tends to elevate even shallow stars to the constellations. At the other extreme, from ancient times the bard was seen to have the potency of the priest, in touch with the gods. Dylan backed away from much of the power the public wanted to bestow upon him, although the temptations were great. Saint or sinner, he discarded the messianic clock and the devil's pitchfork and just sang: "Don't follow leaders."[19]

Despite his efforts to shrug off "mystique" and "charisma," those words seemed coined for him. Those who felt Dylan's strong gravitational pull were often unable to describe his special magic. Some have found him "just very sexy." "Mystic force," others would say, or, "he seems to live out a lot of my dreams." With this gift, or curse, of magnetism, Dylan became one of the most influential artists of his time. If he recorded a song one day, it was sung the next in Prague or Tel Aviv, discussed at Oxford, disputed at Antioch, imitated in Los Angeles, or copied in Nashville. Of course, the influence was centered in pop music. He made the topical-protest song "respectable." When he sired "folk rock" and other styles, the whole music world followed him. Groups named Blonde on Blonde, Judas Priest and Starry-Eyed and Laughing echoed his titles, characters. Critics, novelists and poets echoed Dylanisms in book titles such as *Something Happened*, *Hard Rain Falling*, *Busy Being Born*, *Outlaw Blues*, and *Gates of Eden*.

Dylan is typically ambivalent about his pre-eminence. "I never said I was the king. Others said that. The media said that, I didn't," Dylan told me while he was enjoying being off the throne. Yet his mid-1970s return to the stage and a gush of brilliant recordings put him right back on a throne he had only verbally abdicated. He knew if he acceded to his place on a pedestal, detractors would point to his feet of flesh. Beneath his many public faces, Dylan has always been an easy mark for critics. How effortless to deflate, lampoon, satirize and mock him. It became a vicious game of contradicting his "fables," rather than appreciating why he wove them. What fun they've had saying: "Even if he didn't always write great poetry, he always acted like a great poet." In those early years, his voice baffled those it didn't overwhelm. That affecting rugged singing voice was ridiculed, called "tubercular," like that of an animal in a trap. "It makes me think I'm not being heard," Dylan once said. Yet those who loved that distinctive voice felt it was the perfect vehicle for the anguish, wit and anger it articulated. (When he unexpectedly turned country crooner, fans demanded he return to rough, raspy singing again.)

Even granting his errors, excesses and contradictions, the case can be made for placing Dylan among important and innovative creative artists. Dylan arguably did for the popular song-form what Picasso did for the visual arts, Stravinsky for "serious" music, Chaplin for film, Joyce for the novel. Dylan lived up to the artist's greatest tasks—growth, exploration and change. Those unable to savor the heights to which he took popular song-poetry might regard such homage as a biographer's myopia or tunnel vision, a friend's hyperbole. Theirs is the loss.

Some Dylan detractors link his admirers with the groupies and shriekies of pop. There's been Dylanmania, of course, but his ranking must be assayed more seriously. Those who lionized him were not just star-struck "kids," but seasoned "cultured" commentators, as well. I was scoffed at in 1963 when I dubbed Dylan "the singing poet laureate of young America." Since then, a chorus of assent has grown steadily. John Clellon Holmes: "No one, years hence, will be able to understand just what it was like to live in this time without attending to what this astonishingly gifted young man has already achieved." Charles Reich saw Dylan in *The Greening of America* as "a true prophet of the new consciousness." John Peel regarded him as "the single most important force in maturing our popular music," Allen Ginsberg as "a space-age genius minstrel."[20] The acceptance of Dylan as a literary voice has grown enormously. Professor Christopher Ricks: "A great amuser, a great entertainer, who belongs with the artists who've looked for the widest popular constituency, like Dickens and Shakespeare." Frank Kermode thought him "a virtuoso" with "no close rival." Dylan's work has been compared to Whitman, Yeats, Eliot, the Kabbalah and the Bible.

Conversely, some would argue that Dylan was a flawed genius, an unfinished musician, an erratic songwriter, a bewildered surrogate-messiah, an uneven performer. This book will try to show Dylan as a very human being, but equally an artist of transcendent historical importance. He is, I submit, a threshold-figure to our grasp of the contemporary fabric of American ideals and society. I see him as a new type of artist and entertainer, a new breed of superstar, a new species of poet remarrying speech and song. He is a new culture hero and anti-hero who tested the strengths, limits and failings of the several worlds through which he traveled. I find his self-education and quest that of an archetypal American Dreamer. He is an incarnation of the Young Man from the Provinces, who fought to gain recognition in the city. He is a born combatant, opposing everything that looks untrue, unfair or distorted to his vision. Embodying a little of all of us who have ever dreamed of influencing, changing and conquering, his journey became emblematic of the Sixties. Yet, we're still caught in the echo of songs he wrote decades ago. Dylan's "Hard Rain" is still falling on our thirsty deserts.

For all the lionization and emulation, for all the riches he earned, or spurned, Dylan has been mistreated often by the public and press. Joe Hill, the radical union singer, was executed while, fifty years later, Dylan sang his way to being a millionaire. "A lonely man with money is still a lonely man," Dylan once said. Must the American artist, even the vastly popular one, still be cursed with isolation, lacking the fully aware audience he or she needs? Dylan made his voice heard, against all odds and critics, as he kept moving abrasively against the tides. He was luckier than Joe Hill, of course: luckier than those 18th-century Scots protest singers hanged for their defiance. Dylan fared better than poet-balladeer Wolf Biermann, forced into exile in November 1976 by East German communists who didn't like his dissident tune. Dylan prospered better than Prague rock stars put on trial for their anti-Big Brother independence. And, he's luckier than those "subversive" singer-poet-dissidents in the Soviet Union who faced jail or psychiatric hospital for their underground tapes. Yet, for all his wealth and honor, Dylan, surrounded by aides, buffers and myrmidons, was often denied the acceptance and respect his work deserved. For a lot of us, the time since 1960 will be etched in memory as "the age of Dylan." Many others still don't know who he is, what he signifies, except, perhaps, "that crazy hippie who sang 'Blowin' in the Wind.'"

We start, then, with a controversialist—just a songwriter and pop star to some, but the "hero with a thousand faces" to many others. Some wanted Dylan to be *Time*'s "Man of the Year," *Rolling Stone* talked of "Dylan for President." Slowly, even grudgingly, the academy, the politicians and the media acknowledged Dylan's signature on these changed times. Dylan personifies the spirit of his period in the way Byron and Fitzgerald represented theirs.

There is scarcely a popular music form (blues, country, topical, folk-rock, ballad, prayer, even a waltz) Dylan didn't infuse with new possibilities. A master-politician as well as influencer, he befriended and affected the Beatles, Peter, Paul and Mary, Joan Baez, the Band, the Byrds, Johnny Cash, and a roster of singer-writers often referred to as "new Dylans." He wouldn't stand still, or lock himself into a single pander-to-the-audience style, so he was always losing admirers as he turned elsewhere and gained others. His 1960s work seemed to categorize itself into early, middle and late "periods," but he kept turning in new directions and soon there were many more "periods." He is still changing and growing, and proving just how much that change disturbs.

Dylan's life-style and death-style were so widely imitated that he became the precursor of nearly every major youth-culture trend for two decades. Often, the influence ran far beyond his command. A sub-industry in his bootleg tapes and records sprang up around the world. The self-destructing Weathermen took their name from his line: "You don't need a weather man/To know which way the wind blows."[21] Demonstrators at the Chicago Democratic Convention in 1968 chanted, "The whole world is watching," a paraphrase of another Dylan line. Admen, copy editors, headline writers, columnists borrowed or adapted his lines and titles: "My Back Pages," "Bringing It All Back Home," "Visions of Johannesburg." Classified property ads in *The Times* of London were once sold under the heading "Subterranean Homesick Blues!"

Every cult figure stands on the shoulders of those who came before. Dylan, the great assimilator, amalgamated a legion of types and styles—Dean and Brando from the films, Woody Guthrie and a dozen ballad-makers and bluesmen and others from music. His image in our mind is connected to great and little mythic figures. He is the Alchemist brewing knowledge out of commonplace things. Changing form and style, changing his looks, changing his expression, Dylan is Osiris one day and Proteus the next. One moment he was the Magician from a Tarot pack, the next, Pierrot in whiteface singing "Life is pantomime." The style of it all was cool and mysterious, for to *explain* just what he was doing would violate the part left unsaid that we, the listener, had to complete. As Oscar Wilde wrote in *The Picture of Dorian Gray*: "He knew the precise psychological moment when to say nothing."

Dylan's rhythms, cadences and images have re-entered our everyday speech from which he refined them: He moved the carpet under us. We know Mister Jones as the arch-Philistine who's unaware that something is happening. Even though we're afraid we're stuck inside Desolation Row, we keep on keeping on. There may be blood on the tracks and nothing is revealed, yet he's told us there must be some way out of here. There's no direction home, but with one foot on the highway and the other in the grave, we try to get outside the empty cage. Desperation and hope fight in the captain's tower. Although it's all over now, we renew ourselves to leave the dead behind us. We're younger than that now. Death and re-birth, endlessly with seven people dead, but "Somewhere in the distance/There's seven new people born."[22] Dylan has so affected the loam of our speech, we can forget where his lines end and our own begin.

Even though he said he was not "in the teachin' business," he entered our "cavity minds"[23] and demanded response and explanation. That was how it all began, in our old circle of friends in Greenwich Village when Bob got off the subway from America's heartland. We were all looking for answers, only he asked the most probing questions. He knew the question itself might hold the answer. We turned to him—those younger and many older than he—for his vision, wit, fresh ideas, his daring to try what hadn't been tried. He "spit fast/with weapons of words/wrapped in tunes."[24] We soon sensed what he meant when he said: "I am my words." Find your own answers, man, and you'll value them more, he said to us, man and woman, time and again. He wouldn't play guru, even when we insisted. He was too skinny to carry a cross, and too wary to let his manager carry it for him.

From 1961 on, Dylan spoke to us in riddles and paradoxes, epigrams and metaphors. Even when he spoke volubly, there was a sense of control over what he said. We often wondered about his long and palpable silences, as he watched with such intense focus that you sensed he was memorizing a scene and a conversation. He loved to make us laugh, at first, and then he seemed to love to mystify us. There was always that mixed sense of nearness and distance in which one Dylan was beside us and another was outside watching each drama unfold. He seemed, at first, aching to be recognized. "I was hungry and it was your world,"[25] he later wrote. What really impressed us most about him was that he wouldn't compromise. As a friend of his from Minneapolis later described those times: "It wasn't a question of selling out as much as it was a question of who was willing to buy." He not busy selling was busy buying—but Dylan fought concessions fiercely.

Often, he seemed to accept chaos, using its swirling energy to reshape his artist's sense of internal order. He moved so dizzyingly fast, we couldn't keep up with him. He seemed part of us and yet always detached, always elusive, sometimes even to himself. We envied his drive, yet we knew about the loneliness of the long-distance runner, and we didn't envy him that loneliness.

Then, from mid-summer of 1966 until late 1973, he stopped running. He built up to an incredible three-year onslaught of concert, film and recording activity. Then, he stopped running again. Each time, he'd outdistanced all the other runners. During the first hiatus, he did what he always said he'd wanted to do—sit with a big family in a big house and write. The second pause, that family life in disarray, he pondered his next moves. The pauses gave me a chance to catch up, to assimilate his achievements. Dylan troubled us, haunted us like a lost part of ourselves. Whether in action or repose, in front of me or distanced, Dylan astonished me with his sense of intense life, and astonished me further by not burning himself out. He cheated the undertaker. On the way to the cemetery, he got out of the hearse and hitchhiked back home. We saw him dying young, like poets and stars are "supposed" to do. He beat the rap, a writer who decided he'd rather be read than dead.

Where can I begin his story? I'd need a movie camera to show the flashing chains of visual images: Dylan at Chicago starting Tour '74 to a thunderclap ovation? Or at London's Albert Hall and Paris's Olympia in May, 1966, resisting audience hostility to his new music? Dylan's playing to 250,000 at Blackbushe, England in 1978, or way back at Folk City in 1961, in his black Huck Finn corduroy cap, galvanizing us with his intense singing, his jokey stage games? Or shall I begin with him sitting near Jack Kerouac's grave in 1976, improvising a tribute to one of the writers who opened new roads to him? A turban-headed image on national TV, in 1976, looking oppressed and singing oppression? Jamming on Sunday afternoons in his home town, Hibbing, with a scruffy rock band? Tumbling through the New Orleans Mardi Gras madness, demanding to know why blacks can't drink in white bars? Delighting or shocking the audiences at the Newport Folk Festivals? Contemplating a house that wasn't a home on the Pacific Coast, or strumming his guitar on the streets of Woodstock? A magnetic performer in so many settings, his whole life seemed a performance. Perhaps the camera should focus first on a 1966 college pad where raggy students sprawl, turning on to *Blonde on Blonde*. Or, ten years later, those students now respectable middle-class parents, playing *Desire* for the first time?

Or, do I begin at the midpoint, with the turbulent 1960s behind him and the unexplored 1970s still ahead? About a decade after I'd befriended him, he came to visit me at the Henry Hudson Hotel on Manhattan's West Side. I hadn't seen him since he appeared at the Isle of Wight Festival eighteen months earlier. I'd been living in England, sifting and assembling the facts and the truths-behind-facts of his career. I'd been seeking absolute truth, though I knew relative truth was the best I could hope for. I wanted to unlock the door of his creative mysteries. I told him that he held the key but didn't own the lock. He is often not his best explicator. He had written his masterpieces, told his turbulent tale piecemeal in songs, poems, interviews and arguments. I wanted to piece it together partly because I thought he was a far more remarkable character than any novelist could invent. I had interviewed scores of people who thought they knew him. Virtually no one had told me: "I know what he is all about." Usually, they said they knew only a part of the picture, and they would give me a jagged piece of experience, insight or anecdote to fit into the mosaic. Nearly everyone I interviewed had as many questions for me as I had for them, including his parents and brother. I had felt like the reporter in *Citizen Kane*, looking for Rosebud. But there were *dozens* of Rosebuds.

As he came up the hotel corridor, he looked different again—very healthy, with even a bit of color in his cheeks. Fringe beard, heavy workman country boots, cord slacks, an old country undershirt peeking out beneath his leather jacket. Would the meeting be an anti-climax, I wondered, or would it be like all the other times—a few jokes, sense of imminent drama, a dash of mystery, a flash of anger? No man is a hero to his biographer, nor is he an anti-hero, either. Why did this man I knew so well always intrigue me? After all, he was off-stage now; why should I be keyed up as if the curtains were parting? How would he be today—mercurial, chimerical, tense or gamey? Which of his many pseudonyms would he be wearing—Elmer Johnson, Tedham Porterhouse, Bob Landy, Robert Milkwood Thomas, Big Joe's Buddy, Blind Boy Grunt, Keef Laundry or Judge Magney? After Princeton, Dr Bob Dylan? "How're you doin'?" I asked, and he said with a warm smile as we shook hands, "Oh, gettin' along, I guess."

Bob entered my room and began a minute examination of every detail of it. "The things that must have gone on in this room," he remarked, as if he'd never been in a dingy hotel before. A piece of wall plaster was missing. He tried to guess whether a whiskey bottle or an ashtray might have been thrown in some lovers' quarrel years ago. Bob had repose written all over his face. I recalled his brother's remark: "He was like a fifty-year-old man. So calm, so peaceful and so dignified." He looked like *New Morning* that morning.

We compared experiences about where we were living. "Woodstock turned into a bad joke. Why, they were running tours up there. There were people up there trying to pick up a piece of the earth, a piece of the lawn or of the shrubs." His "Eden" had turned into a zoo, he made that clear. Why had he returned to the Village? "I'll be able to let you know about that better after we're not living in the Village anymore. We're just passing through. A lot of time, you just have to go down many roads to get where you are going. The important thing is to keep moving. Or else to stop by the side of the road every once in a while and build a house. I guess that's about the best thing anyone can do." Was it a question of finding some place to hide from the notoriety and fame? "No," Bob replied, "I really don't want to hide from anything." The speaking voice was so calm, its tempo matching the serenity of his mood. But soon he was telling me he was embattled again.

One self-styled "Dylanologist" had been systematically plundering his garbage pail for "clues" to the "real Dylan." "Yes, it's true," Bob said with a sigh. "I guess that's just part of the price of fame. We all kept loading up the garbage pail with mouse traps, then all the dog-shit we could find, but he kept going through the garbage, anyway." Not every superstar had to pay *that* price of fame. Why was he still so worshipped or castigated? "The media created the trouble for me. They blew me out of proportion. My thing was just for a crowd of people who were on the same wavelength that I was on. What I was doing wasn't really for a mass audience. The mass audience was all shuck, all hype. I'm not a Shea Stadium type of performer, I never was. The slogan that was going around was 'the Beatles, Dylan, and the Stones were the kings.' I never said that. I never called myself the king, or anything like it. The promotion men did all that. The media did all that. I never rejected the title of 'king' because I never accepted it in the first place." That's how it looked to him then, before he was ready to go back into the market-place with Tour '74. If he wanted to blame the media, which he could play like a harp, one just listened.

I told him how depressing it was, after he'd stamped intelligence on to pop music, that there was still such a lot of trivia being hawked. How could top-forty radio continue with such poor quality when he had actually changed the face of pop music? Dylan replied: "Changing the face of pop music is not necessarily changing its metabolism. I didn't change the metabolism. All I did was just open up a whole lot of doors. But, you have to admit, the influence—*my* influence—is there, all over, even in country music. Now you can hear the street sound in pop music almost anywhere. The influence is there."

We talked about some old mutual friends we didn't see much anymore. Bob could be nostalgic about those old times, then, and he would, later try to bring it all back home with the Rolling Thunder Revue. "Those were wonderful days, all right. It was a movement then, a *real* movement. But it was probably the last movement. Say," he exclaimed, "that would make a good song title wouldn't it?" Bob resumed, sadly:

"The dream is gone. That feeling is gone now. It's meaningless to try to grasp what's passed. I see no similarity between what the people are trying to do today and what happened in the early 1960s. Those early days in the Village were great, and the days in Dinkytown were even greater. Now, things are depressing. The Village is depressing. Neon and cheapness. Today, it seems as if thousands of years of experience are being compressed into a year. What is going on now doesn't surprise me. Do you see the sort of books and records and junk they are rushing out every day? It's unbelievable."

Couldn't he find any encouragement in the activities of the New Left? "The New Left has no policy, no program, no philosophy, really, when you come right down to it. There really isn't a New Left. Those people who march for peace are just interested in peace, but that doesn't make them part of any New Left. It is not like the Old Left, or what we had in the early years. The Old Left had a program and a policy and a place, and things like that. The Old Left had some reason behind it. When you come right down to it, there is no youth culture, and there is no New Left, and, as far as the music business is concerned, it's just a toy, nothing but a toy."

The words seemed cynical, but his tone wasn't. It was his quiet estimation of the situation, at that moment. I asked him what he'd been reading lately. It was the sort of question he wouldn't have answered when he arrived in New York, when he was devouring everything he could lay his eyes upon. Even in the late 1960s, when he kept a large open Bible on a reading stand in Woodstock, he would have thought it pretentious to tell anyone. (In early 1977, the *Times Literary Supplement* asked Dylan, among a roster of literary heavies, which he regarded as the most under-rated and over-rated books of the century. To both questions he puckishly answered: "The Bible.")

Bob told me: "It's a very heavy responsibility for me to say what it is I'm reading, because too many people would regard that as some kind of endorsement. Some of them would run right out and start reading the same thing and I don't want to do that. That happened once when I said I was interested in the *I Ching*." He relented, and told me he was reading novels by Isaac Bashevis Singer and Chaim Potok. "They make a lot more sense to me these days than all that Maharishi stuff or the Indian mystic thing." Bob was about to go on a private visit to Israel but, again, beyond his command, it was to be publicized out of shape "I went to a Hasid wedding last week," he told me, weighing, I thought, my reaction. "The Jewish thing in this city is becoming very heavy," he said.

Bob knew I'd spent years contacting old friends of his to piece together a comprehensive biography. I told him I'd finally tracked down a good Hibbing friend, John Bucklen. Bob smiled. "Where in the hell did you find him?" I told him he was a disk jockey in Wisconsin. "John was really my buddy, my best buddy." He regretted that when he'd last seen Bucklen "I was terribly rushed, terribly busy. I went back to Hibbing for the class reunion." That tenth anniversary of high-school graduation had been a moment of elation. He continued: "When I was 15, I said to myself: 'They treat me pretty low down here now, but I'll be back one day and then they'll all run up to shake my hand.' It's true, that I said that to myself. I said: 'I'm gonna come back here and have people look up to me.' I made that deal with myself. And it actually came true, in the summer of 1969. I sat there in Hibbing and signed autographs for an hour, more than an hour … Yes, Echo was there, too. You've seen Hibbing," Bob continued. "You've seen that great ugly hole in the ground, where that open-pit mine was. They actually think, up there, that it's beautiful. They think it is a scenery place. Well, they are doing that now to the whole country. I didn't really look at Hibbing, when I went back. I just went for the graduation party. I don't need to be reminded of what it was like. I'll never forget it." His face was impassive, but a shudder seemed to run through him. It reminded me of his book *Tarantula*, where he said he'd make a Faustian pact with the devil to get away from the wasteland vacuum of Middle America. "I'm sick of cavity," he wrote, and the big hole in the ground in Hibbing was a metaphor for all the sickening cavities he saw around him.

We talked about his recordings. I told him that I often regretted that journalism pressurized me to analyze some of his albums before I'd lived with them. We came to *Self Portrait* and his eyes narrowed as they always used to when he thought he was on the defensive. I told him I'd have to listen to that controversial album again. Dylan was embattled then, and since, by bootleggers, scavengers and by the writers he didn't know or respect who'd threatened their way into his life. Bob clearly was ambivalent about the honors some had shown him, but he disdained the sales-mill approach toward instant popular culture, the grinding out of posters, bootleg tapes, pseudo-biographies, magazine pieces, ill-considered reviews. It was an old wound to him. I remember his lines from "11 Outlined Epitaphs" of 1964:

I don't like t' be stuck in print
starin' out at cavity minds
who gobble chocolate candy bars
quite content an' satisfied
their day complete
at seein' what I eat for breakfast
the kinds of clothes I like t' wear
an' the hobbies that I like t' do[26]

I tried to assure Dylan that I could end up with a portrait in which he could retain dignity and respect as an artist. He had known me long enough, I hoped, not to bracket me with the reporters who think denuding celebrities is a respectable way of earning a living. Dylan suggested some people I might try tracking down, such as Philip Saville, an English TV director with whom he had once worked. A name or two from Minneapolis came up and I asked how they might be helpful. Bob smiled and said: "It's just a clue."

Did he want to comment on the question of drugs? "What sort of drugs?" he riposted. "I never had anything to do with glamorizing the drug thing. That was the Beat thing, not me. As for the hard drugs, that's a question of trafficking. It goes on, and it's a bad scene. But you have to realize that junk is not the problem in and of itself. Junk is the symptom, not the problem, as Dr Freud would say." Could he accept the portrait of himself in the film *Don't Look Back*, which had long discomfited him? "Oh, I saw it about a year or so ago. I have more perspective on it now, and I'm less upset about it than I was. I can say that I almost like it now."

All this mellowness from the angriest of angry young men was surprising. In the early years in New York he'd started out charming, then gradually became tenser, warier and more difficult. But here was the moderate man about, finally, to sever his links with his long-time manager, Albert Grossman. "He had me signed up for ten years, for part of my records, for part of my everything. But I'll be out of that next month. I finally had to sue him. I got me a lawyer and was going to sue him, but Albert wanted it quiet and, because of that, he settled out of court. A lot of people would go out of their way to run Albert down, but I wouldn't." (Dylan never used his considerable media power to vent his problems with Grossman, or Columbia Records, or the song publishers who held vital Dylan copyrights until 1965. A sense of dignity, perhaps a remnant of loyalty, then and since, kept Dylan from using his weapon of words here. Perhaps just holding that deterrent weapon enabled him to free himself from the chains and fetters of a contract that had run from obscurity to eternity.) Bob went on to tell me that a lot of deals he'd made with Grossman, such as his first song-publishing contract, had proved better for Grossman than himself. It had all been sticky, a five-year on-and-off divorce that had been painful to both parties. After his exhausting 1965–66 world tour, Grossman had scheduled more than sixty concerts for him.

Dylan was one of the few contemporary artists of the era who had shifted partial control in the music business away from the fat cats to the artists themselves. He had often told me of troubles he'd had with the businessmen, the record company executives, agents, box-office people. He called his own tune as soon as he was strong enough to do so. What sort of a hostile world was this for a *poet* to be working in? He needed a shield. When things were going well with his manager, Bob lauded him to the skies, but even now he held back in attacking Albert, beyond saying: "Albert's got terrible taste—and you can quote that." He was apparently referring to how Albert was citifying Woodstock-Bearsville with a posh restaurant in a farmhouse, and a recording studio. "A country farmhouse!" Bob exclaimed. "It's all unbelievable!" (As early as 1963, he'd written a warning to his fellow *Broadside* singers to be wary of the unseen "buyers and sellers" who play both sides against the other, with the artist in the middle.)

He had his complaints, yet he wasn't vengeful. Even for him, there's a limit to challenging authority before losing some of the power that authority held. The international music business is a colossus, and Dylan had to put a saddle on it to ride it. He knew its rewards, defeats, and hypocrisies. He worked within "the business," but tried to keep some detachment. How successful was he? He had no fan club, he didn't endorse products, he turned his back on several fortunes during his retreats. He'd seen, in the Sixties, the American recording industry grow from an annual gross on pop records of $250,000,000 to more than a billion dollars a year. After that decade, Dylan was ready to characterize the music business to me as "a toy, a game."

We both knew he'd been rudely ignored by Folkways, Vanguard and Elektra before he was signed to Columbia Records by a producer who hadn't even heard him sing! It's an old story, how Presley and the Beatles and Dylan were all shunned or laughed at within the record industry until they tamed the beast. The cruelty of show business is a platitude, but when people of the stature of Dylan and the Beatles wrangled with the businessmen, it was hard for the man-in-the-street to sympathize with them.

Could the music fan sympathize better with the hundreds, or thousands, of those who've been broken on the wheel of show business? One industry leader, who asked not to be named, defended to me the way the business operated. He cited the great competition, the high elements of risk. With Dylan, I share some angers at the way the business works. It is a litany of harsh facts. We can understand Dylan best if we watch how he dueled with that world, to his gain, and to his pain.

Bob and I talked on for hours. If I probed too close to the bone, he stood up, looked out the window, as if leaving. If I released the pressure of questions, he sat down again. Sometimes he spoke in aphorisms: "There's no place to go. There are guys in prison that just can't afford to get out." We joked about how he was never the most organized person in retaining his own mementoes. "I used to write songs on napkins, just like Woody did, and then I used the napkins to wipe my mouth with," he recalled, smiling.

"I was doing new things in 1959. I was pretty raggy then, but I was doing things that haven't been heard since. Listen to my records before 1965, and you won't hear anything that sounds like that." Did songs still flow out as quickly? "A few years ago, when I was in the very heart of it all, I would write a song in two hours, or maybe two days, at the most. Now, it can be two weeks, maybe longer." (A few weeks later, I saw one of those stories about Dylan at a studio session in which he reportedly wrote a song in 25 minutes!)

I tried to sound him out about social action but, at that point, the angry fires seemed banked. We agreed that America was in trouble again, that the masters of war were still in power. Bob made no comment then about how, or if, he might get back on the barricades again. Yet, when he said to me "they're not going to get away with it," there was much steely resolve in his voice. I knew it was only matter of time until he picked up his cudgels against "them."

Bob was keen to look at the basement swimming pool. We drifted downstairs and stood beside the pool a few minutes and his eyes opened wide and glowed an iridescent blue. "Are there a lot of pools like this in town?" he asked, as if I were some authority on Manhattan swimming. "I'll have to find me something like that." We chatted our way out to his new lime-green station wagon. We passed a few people along West 57th Street, but no one took any notice of him.

Dylan and his wife were to fly to Israel in two days. I was to stay on in New York to refresh memories of Greenwich Village and Woodstock. I was living in the past then, turning the time back to those great days of the early Sixties. "Folk City is just a parking lot now," Bob had told me, and there at the corner it was, just torn down and paved over. Mike Porco had moved the club to Third Street. I walked past Dylan's old apartment on West Fourth Street, across the street from the Hip Bagel, then inched my way along to his new place down the road. Sara Dylan, behind sunglasses, was just coming out the doorway, furtively looking both ways, wrapped in a raincoat, taking her little white dog for a walk. New York wasn't even fit for dogs, I thought. There wasn't any room to breathe. Bleecker Street was slummier than ever—tired, dirty, sad cafés. Pizza shops and espresso joints still thrived, but it had all slid downhill. Bob wasn't really going to try to infuse the village with that old spirit until the summer of 1975. For the moment, I was looking back to 1960. The New York in which Dylan had arrived late that year was the concrete jungle of vitality and struggle it'd always been—a lure to all the young men and women of the provinces who'd used up the sparse resources of their home towns.

1960: that's another point where the story begins.

There had seemed so much hope back in 1960. John F Kennedy had won the Presidency by a hair's-breadth from Nixon. Floyd Patterson was the boxing champion of the world. The daytime soap opera, *The Romance of Helen Trent*, went down the drain, after twenty-seven sudsy years. In the South, 1960 was the start of the integration sit-ins in Greensboro, North Carolina. The pilot of an American U-2 reconnaissance plane was shot down by the Russians. Castro was consolidating the Cuban revolution. The Cold War, which looked as if it might start thawing, froze over again.

Americans were reading *To Kill a Mockingbird*, *Born Free*, and *The Rise and Fall of the Third Reich*. Many were getting ready to celebrate the Civil War centennial. Broadway hits included *A Taste of Honey* and

Bye Bye Birdie. Elvis made another dreary film, *GI Blues*, while Paul Newman was emerging as a new screen cult figure. Hitchcock scared the hell out of us with *Psycho*, while a benign Frank Sinatra starred in *Can-Can*. Oscar Hammerstein II, lyricist of *Oklahoma!* and *South Pacific*, died at 65. Emily Post died at 86, and American manners never quite survived the shock. *Never on Sunday* was an international film and song hit. Hank Ballard's "The Twist" was about to be turned into a dance craze by Chubby Checker. The biggest excitement in popular music was coming from folk music, a revival that was to set the tempo for the early Sixties.

In 1960, America stood poised with a young man in the White House we hoped was an idealist. We tried to believe "the New Frontier" was more than a slogan. Before the Cuban Missile Crisis and before assassins' bullets and Vietnam turned all that promise into sorrow, it was a great time to be young and starting out. Before Martin Luther King's passive resistance ran into a stone wall, it was even a time to be black and young and hopeful.

1960 was: after Joe McCarthy, before Eugene McCarthy. After the Beats, before the hippies. After the Old Left, before the New Left. After Campbell's Soup, before Andy Warhol. After dada, before camp. After Batman, before the return of Batman. After the *Village Voice*, before the *East Village Other*. After Marshall Field, before Marshall McLuhan. After Trotsky, before Yippie.

1960 was: post-Thomas Wolfe, ante-Tom Wolfe. Post-Presley, ante-Beatles. After Bill Mauldin, before Jules Feiffer. After tea, before pot. After the Lindy, before the Twist. After apathy, before cool. After the Angry Young Men, before the protest singers. After the Red Cross, before the Red Guard. After Billy Graham, before Bill Graham. After momism, before popism. After the Establishment, before street people.

1960 was a time of promise. For a garland of reasons, world youth was beginning to breathe and stir after the silence and apathy of the Fifties. Pope John XXIII was budging the Church into the twentieth century. Castro and Guevara were trying to bring color back to a revolution that had turned bureaucratic and stifling. The Kennedy "Camelot" was bringing some youth, culture and style to a Babbitized Washington.

1960 was before Bob Dylan got to New York town.

Editor's note: *Originally written in 1977 as Chapter 1, this Prelude was revised in 1980, as Shelton was working on what he hoped would be the final pre-publication edit. At that point, it was repurposed as Chapter 2, following what remains the opening chapter of the book, about growing up in Hibbing. The plan then was to follow it with the 1966 interview undertaken as Shelton and Dylan flew from Lincoln, Nebraska, to Denver, Colorado—a cinematic opening of flashbacks and flash-forwards, as the author suggests in the foregoing text. Shelton was then persuaded that such an approach risked confusing the reader of what was already a complicated book, and it was agreed that the text worked best as a Prelude. In the end, faced with an already over-long book, his then publishers insisted it was cut. Hence the much briefer Prelude, "Lifelessness, the Enemy," to the 1986 edition. It is restored to its rightful place here, Shelton's final intentions respected.*

Opposite: The photograph that accompanied Robert Shelton's *New York Times* review of Dylan at Gerde's Folk City, 1961—that started it all—headlined "Bob Dylan: A Distinctive Stylist."

where i live now, the only thing that keeps the area going is tradition — it doesn't count very much — everything around me rots … if it keeps up, soon i will be an old man — & i am only 15 — the only job around here is mining — but jesus, who wants to be a miner … i refuse to be part of such a shallow death — everybody talks about the middle ages as if it was actually in the middle ages — i'll do anything to leave here — my mind is running down the river — i'd sell my soul to the elephant — i'd cheat the sphinx — i'd lie to the conqueror … tho you might not take this the right way, i would even sign a chain with the devil … please dont send me anymore grandfather clocks — no more books or care packages … if youre going to send me something, send me a key — i shall find the door to where it fits, if it takes me the rest of my life.

DYLAN, 1966[1]

He not busy being born is busy dying.

DYLAN, 1965[2]

Above: Howard Street, Hibbing, 1941.
Right: Dylan in the opening scene of *Don't Look Back*, London, 1965. Many consider this to be the first rock video.

It's a long way home from the movies. The marquee of the Lybba Theater was dark as the plump, sandy-haired boy walked into the merciless cold. First Avenue was even colder by contrast with the heat of the Texas plains he'd felt from the screen inside. Even James Byron Dean couldn't have been a hero on First Avenue. He would have frozen in his tracks. Texas was rugged, but Minnesota was impossible.

Across the street was the sign of the *Hibbing Tribune*—stately Olde Englishe in flaming red neon. Out First Avenue were fainter neon signs, in Moderne American, offering quick credit to the miners and quick drinks to help them forget their instant debt. The boy glanced toward the pool hall, hesitated, then decided against the small talk that would have accompanied a game. The film *Giant* was still in his head, with the stinging disbelief that James Dean was really dead, more than a year now.

The boy turned onto Howard Street. He stood "at one end of Hibbing on the main drag and saw clear past the city limits on the other end."[3] There were red iron-ore mining dumps at nearly every fringe of town. "The richest village in the world" wasn't so rich anymore. They'd cut down the trees and dug the good ore out of the earth. He walked by storefronts, well stocked and confident, and others that had run empty when confidence and money gave out.

Main drag, Minnesota. Sinclair Lewis would have taken notes and James Dean would have built monuments. They'd have known about Howard Street, and would have left it as fast as they could. They were both dead now, just like this town. Hibbing had dug its own grave with sixty years of mining shovels, now only good for burying miners. "Desolation Row," Take One.

The stores of Hibbing, 1956, and those of Lewis's Gopher Prairie, 1926, must have all come from some factory assembly line. Montgomery Ward, J C Penney, and Woolworth patterned small-town America. Would there be the same shop fronts down in Macon, Georgia, where Little Richard was born? At least Georgia didn't have skin temperatures of twenty below zero. The boy stepped into the doorway of Chet Crippa's Music Store. He scanned the record display. No Little Richard, no Hank Williams, no Buddy Holly. Bing Crosby was still dreaming about a white Christmas. So was Little Richard.

In front of the New Haven Lounge, he could hear the sputtering little band wheezing its way through "Moja Decla," the Slovenian national anthem. Or was it a lively polka of "Whoopee John," or the "CIO Polka" for the union men? Some band! The wind from Lake Superior and the Canadian plains knew more songs, but who else listened, as the boy did, "when I first heard the ore train sing," as he wrote in the liner notes to *Joan Baez in Concert, Part 2*.

No songs that night, as he approached Fifth and Howard, where the brick solidity of the Androy Hotel exuded permanence and prosperity for traveling salesmen and local Rotarians. A few hundred yards away, the Zimmerman Furniture and Appliance Company reposed in chrome and Formica. ("A kitchen range for the Iron Range." "Absolutely no part ordered without a deposit.") I would rather be a miner than an appliance salesman, but Jesus, who wants to be a miner or an appliance salesman? As Howard Street tapered off toward the bush, the boy turned right onto Seventh Avenue. The darkness of the side street created a vacuum, which he filled with wide-screen Technicolor.

"James Dean, who was killed in a sportcar crash two weeks after his last scene was shot, clearly shows ... a streak of genius," wrote *Time* magazine in October 1956. "He has caught the Texas accent to nasal perfection, and has mastered the lock-hipped, high-heeled stagger of the wrangler, and the wry little jerks and smirks, tics and twitches, grunts and giggles that make up most of the language of a man who talks to himself a good deal more than he does to anyone else."

The 15-year-old moviegoer, who talked to himself a good deal more than he did to anyone else, filled Seventh Avenue with his own Actors Studio. He pursed his lips, tried a line of dialogue, locked his hips, shambled like a wrangler, contorted his face to erase the North Country twang in his voice, slowing the words into an oozing drawl. As young Bob Dylan passed the looming expanse of Hibbing High School, he halted his monologue-pantomime. The sprawling four-story pseudo-North Italian turreted castle brought one of its students back abruptly from Texas. The last few blocks, to 2425 East Seventh Avenue, were so familiar that in the dark Bob's feet led him past memorized breaks in the sidewalk. The corner house was ablaze with lights. Back to family life in a dying town.

He tiptoed through the back door into the kitchen, wishing he could get to his room without being seen, but the house wasn't built that way. "Bobby, is that you?" His mother's voice was taut with tension. He reported to the parlor. "I've told you a hundred times, if I've told you once," his mother began her litany. "How do you expect to grow up strong and healthy if you don't get your rest? What are the people in this neighborhood going to think of any boy of mine who is always out roaming the streets at night?" Why was she always so worried? Why did she talk so fast, leaving no room for answers?

"Your mother is absolutely right, Robert," his father broke in, his low and controlled voice somehow menacing beneath its even surface. The living room was so clean and orderly. Everything was in its place. Maybe that is what they expected of him, to be just another home appliance, to turn on and off. Bob tried to explain that it was a special James Dean movie that ran late. His voice began to rise with anger. "Robert, stop that shouting," his father said. "You know we don't tolerate shouting in this house."

The argument spilled out of bounds and out of the room. It wasn't just this lateness, his father told me in 1968. It was Bob's "attitude." One night he was late. The next night he neglected his schoolwork. He didn't show up at the store when they expected him. And soon it was going to be smashed-up cars and motorbikes, "that girl," and those "friends" of his. "Robert, you come back here," his father said. But he was gone, through the kitchen, down the stairs to the basement. His father followed, hurling recriminations: "We've given you a good home. We buy you the best of everything. What more do you want? I never had it so soft when I was your age."

In the basement den, Bob tried to explain that he had stayed to see part of the movie over again. He talked about James Dean and waved his hand toward the walls covered with pasted-up photographs of the dead actor. "James Dean, James Dean," his father repeated. He pulled a photograph off the wall. "Don't do that," Bob yelled. His father tore the picture in half and threw the pieces to the floor. "Don't raise your voice around here," he said with finality, stamping upstairs. Bob picked up the pieces, hoping he might be able to paste them together. No, he wouldn't raise his voice around *there*.

> *Hibbing's a good ol' town*
> *I ran away from it when I was 10, 12, 13, 15, 15½, 17 an' 18*
> *I been caught an' brought back all but once…*[4]

Stolen Moment.   Dylan didn't actually run away from "good ol' Hibbing" at all, except in his mind, and there he kept running for years. He spoke about Hibbing rarely and wrote about it only fragmentarily. He had trouble coming to grips with his growing-up days, vacillating between nostalgia and repulsion. Hibbing was small-town Minnesota, his incubus and touchstone. This was Babbitt country, home of provincialism, isolation, backwater conservatism. Dylan could say "Hibbing's got nothing to do with what I am, what I became" and yet sometimes reveal that his flight from small-town Philistinism had shaped him to a degree he was usually unwilling to admit.

"You've been there, you've seen it," he told me in 1971. "That big hole in the ground, where they dug up all that ore? They're actually proud of that, up there. Now they're digging up the whole country. I went back for a graduation party in 1969. I didn't have to look at Hibbing. I'll never forget it. I don't need to be reminded of what it was like. When I was 15, I said to myself: 'They treat me pretty lowdown now, but I'm going to come back here and they're going to look up to me. I said I'll be back one day and they'll run up to shake my hand.' It's true. I made that deal with myself. It actually came true, in 1969. I sat and signed autographs for an hour."

That Faustian "deal" had given him motive, energy, ferocious drive, and will. "North Country Blues," written in 1963, is an understated folk-epic encapsulating the history of Hibbing. His notes to *Joan Baez in Concert, Part 2* dwell upon his early attitudes toward beauty in life and nature. On his third album, the second of his "11 Outlined Epitaphs" paints a dark portrait of his hometown's hollow death and decay, a town which had uprooted itself as it dug beneath for more precious ore. That all had set him running, made him a refugee. Finally, in that "Epitaph," he dreams of accepting Hibbing (and his family and his childhood) without expecting what they could not offer him.

A more figurative retelling of his adolescence was his autobiographical "My Life in a Stolen Moment," written in spring 1963 as a program note for the tradition-hungry folk-music community that demanded roots, sources, and influences. Ringing with Woody Guthrie cadences, "Stolen Moment" was fine early page writing—rhythmic, sardonic, self-revealing. Dylan took years to accept it, denying its veracity and worth, claiming others had "made" him write it. Ultimately, he decided to include it in *Writings and Drawings*. One problem was that his reference to running away pained his family. Perhaps the most revealing omission was his refusal to examine the source of his creativity: "I never ever did take the time to find out why I took the time to do those things."

If he wouldn't, or couldn't, take the time, I felt I had to try to find the clues, setting off like that reporter in *Citizen Kane*, looking for the elusive "Rosebud." Prior to my two visits to Hibbing, in 1966 and 1968, Dylan told me: "I didn't leave home because of my curiosity to see what was going on elsewhere. I just wanted to get away. Yeah, get away. Hibbing was a vacuum. I just kept going because I was bored. I've always been very bored, only I've never settled and accepted boredom. I can lay on my bed for three hours and look at the ceiling, but, you know, that doesn't mean boredom. You see, I don't come from what you would call a 'Great Society middle-class family in the suburbs.' Where I lived, there aren't any suburbs. There's no poor section and there's no rich section. There's no wrong side of the tracks and right side of the tracks." Waving his hands, Dylan continued: "There's no lines where I come from. There never was. As far as I knew, where I lived, nobody had anything that anybody else didn't have, really. All the people I knew had the same things. I've thought about it some, but Hibbing really has nothing to do with what I am today, with that I became. Really nothing!"

He meant it when he said it. For Dylan, reality is a prism, not a plate-glass window. Through that prism he would look back on Hibbing and his formative years there, sometimes with anger, frequently with remorse, but sometimes with love, and warmth. "My family?" Dylan repeated while he chose his response. "I never really had that much contact with them." That's not quite the way his family remembered it.

Home on the Range. History has left no record of what Franz Dietrich Von Ahlen's family thought about his decision to leave Hanover, Germany. Von Ahlen was a restless individualist, who decided, eighteen years after his birth in 1856, that Hanover was not where the action was. He packed his bags for the New World. He left behind his name and took instead an all-American moniker, Frank Hibbing. After farming in Wisconsin, losing three fingers in a shingle mill, and reading law, he became a timber cruiser, a prospector, and a woodsman. In 1885, hearing that the forest and mineral riches of northern Minnesota exceeded those of northern Michigan, he moved to Duluth as a land broker. He made and lost a fortune. When iron ore was discovered in 1890 on the Eastern Mesabi Range, largest of three iron ranges in Minnesota, Hibbing decided to prospect, and led some thirty men westward from Duluth to the area that would soon bear his adopted name. Near what was to become the town center, Hibbing is reported to have stuck his head out of his tent one morning in January 1893. It was forty degrees below zero. Three feet of snow mantled a frozen pine forest. Hibbing, a lean and determined man with a handlebar moustache, high-top boots and a pickax, supposedly said: "I believe there is iron under me. My bones feel rusty and chilly." His men began to dig, and soon found ore. Hibbing helped form the Lake Superior Iron Company, leasing lands and mineral rights. Soon he was the town's first millionaire.

Before big money rolled in early in the 1900s, lumbering provided capital for mining, timber for local buildings. Most of the first 326 residents were lumberjacks earning forty dollars a month and all the salt pork, baked beans, and splinters they could take. Pine Street, the first main drag, had nearly sixty saloons to combat central-heating problems. A frontier town then, right in the Midwest: mud streets, wooden sidewalks, saloon brawls, lumbering and mining accidents, Typhoid fever. A two-square-mile town site was laid out in 1893, first called Superior then changed to Hibbing. The German refugee advanced money to build a sawmill, a water plant, an electric generating station, roads, the first hotel, and a bank. He died at 41 in 1897. For the next ten years, logging was the chief industry. While mining development continued, a slump, which may have been engineered by the big finance men, made the entire Mesabi Range available dirt cheap. John D Rockefeller loaned a million dollars for the purchase of Iron Range land, and made a tidy $50 million on the transaction. Rockefeller connections enabled the US Steel Company to gain a foothold in the Mesabi.

Hungry mechanical mouths were invented to wolf out the ore from above, wood-burning power shovels that snorted and gulped like dinosaurs, and fed the cars of the Duluth, Missabe, and Northern Railway. The big hole in the ground that haunts Dylan's memory was a "stripper," or open-pit mine. By 1964, the Hull-Rust pit covered 1,600 acres, measuring three and three-quarter miles by one mile and a depth of 535 feet. From this running sore was extracted a billion gross tons of earth—more than was dug for the Panama Canal—which yielded 500 million tons of iron ore. Great claims are made for Hibbing's mine—America might not have won both World Wars without this high-grade ore, which supplied nearly a quarter of all the ore used in the nation. The shovels devoured the choice lode under the original township, so the village of North Hibbing was moved a few miles south. "The razzle-dazzle village," "the iron ore capital of the world," "the center of the melting pot," and "the richest village in the world" became "the town that moved."

The transplanting took forty years, beginning in 1918. Some 200 miners' homes and twenty business buildings were slid onto timbers, mounted onto steel wheels, tied to steam crawlers, and shunted to new resting places in Alice, first called South Hibbing. Countless more buildings were wrecked. The journey to Alice took a few days for smaller homes, but nearly a month for the Colonia Hotel. The old Sellers Hotel never made it, ending up as debris. Property owners began complicated litigation with the mining interests, who still calculated that their cache of iron ore was worth it. The courts generally sided with the mines, and the relocation of Hibbing continued piecemeal until the late 1950s.

Dylan witnessed this curious social upheaval, and it left a strong impression on him. In his second "Epitaph," he reflected on that move, on the decaying old courthouse and his mother's school, left rotting like the shattered wreckage of a wartime bomb.

Poor Immigrants. Hibbing was built mainly by Europeans. While urban bankers and financiers made big money, immigrant hands did hard labor. The Iron Range was Louis Adamic country, a melting pot as diverse as any city. The loggers were mostly Scandinavian, Finns primarily. Others arrived to dig the pits: Yugoslavs, Poles, Bohemians, Czechs, Italians. There was even a handful of Eastern European Jews. While Hibbing was digging itself into a golden hole, a pair of local drillers tapped another source of wealth. Andrew G Anderson, a former blacksmith who came to be known as Bus Andy, and Carl Eric Wickham, a young Swedish immigrant, decided to use Andy's unsalable old Hupmobile car to transport passengers between Alice and Hibbing. In spring 1914, regular runs began; a two-mile trip cost fifteen cents. During the mine boom of World War I, the bus service expanded, and by 1916, the Mesabi Transportation Company had five buses, some off to Duluth and Minneapolis. In the 1920s, following more mergers and purchases that added links to small companies as far away as California, the Greyhound Bus Company was formed. All because, in 1914, Bus Andy couldn't sell that brassy Hupmobile to anyone. Fatter with war profits, Hibbing boomed in the 1920s. Residential additions were tacked on, schools built, and Howard Street constructed. During that decade, the village reached an assessed valuation of $90 million, the richest in the world.

While Dylan was later taunted for "having invented his own Depression" out of Woody Guthrie, he had only to listen to a few town elders to know what the slump was like. During the 1930s, mining dropped off and the village fathers issued scrip money for local transactions. Thanks to the Works Projects Administration and World War II, prosperity returned; the Korean War gave the local mines another short-term boost. By 1953, the boomlet was over—the best iron ore had been eaten out of the canyon. The taconite process, in which huge magnets and sifters separate out commercially usable ore, had been developed. But it did not bring economic stability to the Range until the 1960s. By the mid-Fifties, the local Depression couldn't be ignored by anyone in Hibbing. Dylan mined that vein for "North Country Blues," which tells of the erosion of hope in a miner's family. The Iron Age along the Mesabi was over, and only the chamber of commerce held out hope for the taconite process. Miners' children began to drift away—"for there ain't nothing here now to hold them."[5]

The Refugees. Much as veterans rarely speak of combat, Dylan's family rarely spoke of its refugee past. Feelings of separateness, persecution, and landless insecurity do not disappear quickly. The strengths and fears of those who escaped the czars' tyrannies persisted. The link to a young American-born musician becomes clearer if we consider that the life of Russian Empire Jews was not much better than that of black American slaves. Both societies were oppressive, both cultures forced underground. Dylan's natural affinity with the descendants of black slaves was an extension of his background.

With the pogroms, flight to America became as encompassing a dream as did deliverance to black slaves. To flee the czars, money was crucial. Pity the poor Jewish immigrant who had to arrive in America with about fifteen dollars, less than most other immigrants. This was the life that Dylan's maternal forebears left in Lithuania and Latvia, and that his paternal grandparents fled from in Odessa in the Ukraine.

The flood of immigrants, who went by way of Bialystok to Dutch or German ports, usually stayed around New York, but many moved on if a friend, a cousin, or even a rumor said that life elsewhere held promise. After hearing about Iron Range prosperity, Dylan's maternal grandfather, Ben D Stone, made the trip to Hibbing from Superior, Wisconsin. In 1913, he opened a general store at Stevenson Location, a village twelve miles west of South Hibbing. There, some 500 Finns, Italians, and Slovenians worked the mine, in clothes bought from friendly, outgoing Ben Stone. From the handful of Jewish families in the area, he chose a wife, Florence Edelstein, whose family operated a chain of Iron Range movie houses.

Movies came to Hibbing in 1906: twenty-minute, two-reel silents, followed by equally brief, silent westerns. Less than a decade later, the Hollywood dream factory produced five-reel features. By the 1920s, Julius Edelstein, Bob's great-grandfather's brother, was part owner of the Lyric Theater. Julius and B H Edelstein, Bob's great-grandfather, prospered and took over the Garden Theater in 1925. They renamed it the Gopher and in 1928 sold out to a larger chain. In 1947, the brothers built the Lybba Theater, named after Bob's great-grandmother. This family film link engendered Bob's early awareness of show business, a connection—however tenuous—to Hollywood and the glamour of the performing world.

Ben Stone attended Range grade schools. Intelligent, with a keen business sense, he knew his market. Friendly, a bit of a back-slapper, he earned a decent living and the respect of Hibbing. When times were hard, Stone's Clothing tried to help. If a pair of work pants cost $2.00 and a miner had only $1.10, Stone would settle for that. When the Stevenson Location mine dried up, he moved his family nine miles closer to Hibbing and re-established his store at First Avenue and Howard Street in a former bank, keeping stock in an empty vault.

Ben and Florence had four children—Lewis, Vernon, Beatrice, and Irene. Beatrice, born in 1915, was Dylan's mother, a bubbly woman, blonde, headstrong, nervous, volatile, and warm. She felt locked in the small Hibbing Jewish community and longed to get away. Some of Beatty Stone's restlessness was assuaged by her father's magnificent four-door Essex. When she was fourteen, her father offered her driving lessons. "I'll teach you," he said, moving the gearshift slowly. "You don't have to," Beatty replied. She had watched him drive often enough. To her father's astonishment, she got behind the wheel and drove off. "Bobby is very much like I am," she said years later. "You either do or you don't."

For Beatty, the original "rolling Stone," the car meant access to Duluth and its more sophisticated social life. She could drive down to clubs like the Covenant, to see and be seen. She sought status, solidity, and the right marriage to a nice Jewish boy. To that end, she dressed impeccably in Iron Range high fashion, and kept the Essex highly polished. What others thought of her was important; material success meant security. Beatty's dream of getting away from home began to be realized at a New Year's Eve party in Duluth at the start of 1932, a dark winter of the Depression. She was a popular girl, but one man she met that New Year's Eve had something beyond a sense of humor, quiet intelligence, and good looks. Abram Zimmerman had a job.

Swinging Duluth. Born in Duluth in 1911, Abe Zimmerman had, in fact, had some sort of a job since he was seven. His father, Zigman, had run a substantial shoe factory in Odessa, but in 1907 he traded it for a peddler's cart in Duluth. He then sent for his wife, Anna, along with Abe's older brother and sister. Every member of what became a family of eight pitched in. Abe shined shoes and sold papers, and also became a semi-professional ballplayer. Although Duluth had its Jewish ghetto "up on the hill," the Zimmermans grew up in a neighborhood with many Scandinavians. Abe took long walks to play ball with his fellow Jewish boys. He spoke Yiddish to his family, but English otherwise.

The Zimmermans lived in a six-room house on Lake Avenue. Abe's father had finally parked his peddler's horse and buggy, having learned enough English selling fabric to farmers to sell shoes in the Fair Department Store. With everyone working, there was enough money to install a telephone. But whom could they call? They didn't know anyone else who had one! Abe's childhood was apparently uneventful, except for the great forest fire of 1918. Hundreds perished, but the fire was halted three miles outside Duluth.

By the time Abe was 16, the Zimmermans had moved to a nine-room house, and he was hired as a Standard Oil messenger boy for sixty dollars a month. He saved part, and contributed the rest to the family. "You wanted to do something for your parents *then*. You don't see parents working and suffering as hard as they did in those days. " Abe also wanted to do some things for himself. When he sighted the bright and vivacious Beatty Stone at that party, he made a mental note to see her again. She was snowed in in Hibbing for most of that winter. When did they start to get serious? "Weather permitting," replied Abe with characteristic sly humor. They were married two years later, in 1934, and Beatty escaped Hibbing for Duluth. By then, Abe was earning $100 a month. Abe and Beatty feathered their first nest at 519 Third Avenue East, living on the top floor of the two-family Overman frame house. Abe knew that Standard Oil was no place for him to make a fortune, but it was secure. He rose through the seventy-five-employee office to junior supervisor.

One evening in mid-May 1941, Abe and Beatty were listening to the radio. Abe scanned the newspapers. The Nazis were on the rampage throughout Europe. Jews were being hunted again. The Battle of Britain had been won, but elsewhere Axis armies were triumphing. Roosevelt was in the White House. The radio and jukeboxes of 1941 incessantly played "The Hut Sut Song," a bit of nonsense in an unintelligible pseudo-Swedish dialect. (It was remarkably similar to a 1914 folk song, called "Hot Shot Dawson," sung by a blind Negro minstrel.) Minneapolis's own Andrews Sisters had sold their eight-millionth record, and their manager forbade them from taking music lessons for fear of spoiling their success. The radio broadcast family serials like *One Man's Family*, *The Goldbergs*, and *Fibber McGee and Molly*. *The Lone Ranger* was a favorite with kids.

Although it may not have been widely noted in Duluth, the literary world of 1941 mourned three of its giants. James Joyce died in Switzerland. F Scott Fitzgerald and Sherwood Anderson, two of the writers whom critic Maxwell Geismar later numbered among "the last of the provincials," also died early in the year. Meanwhile, Beatty had a news bulletin of literary and musical significance. "Abe," she exclaimed. "Abe, I feel it! I think the baby is coming."

Labor Day. Beatty's bulletin was premature, but by 9 p.m. on Saturday, May 24, she went into forced labor at St Mary's Hospital, and delivered her first child, a hefty ten-pound boy. It was not an easy birth, because the baby had a very large head. The condition of her spine dictated that the obstetrician should operate. Beatty believed it nearly cost the life of the baby, if not her own. Abe bought cigars for the boys at Standard Oil. He was proud to announce that he had a son, Robert Allen, and that mother and baby were doing fine! After a week, Beatty and her baby made the trip home. A nurse and a domestic were there to help with the early difficult weeks.

Even the neighbors had to admit that Bobby Allen was a beautiful child. He had a golden head of hair, and Beatty would say to him: "You should have been a girl, you're so beautiful." She put colored ribbons in his hair and posed him for the camera. "He was always clean. He didn't get dirty," she recalled. A picture at fifteen months showed, indeed, a cherubic child, apple-cheeked and smiling, with that burst of golden blond hair. His father continued at Standard Oil, an essential job that exempted him from military service.

In the late 1930s, when the powerful John L Lewis was organizing, Standard Oil had formed the Tri-State Petroleum Union, a company union to head off the demands of the militant Congress of Industrial Organisations. With around 300 members signed up at a dollar a head, all the new union needed was a leader. They elected honest Abe. "Our personnel man felt that Standard Oil would fold up if Lewis came in with his demands," Abe explained. The company union was soon banned by the Wagner Act and the Duluth drivers entered the tough-talking Teamsters Union. Standard Oil survived, and so did Abe.

When he brought his two-year-old son into the office, secretaries and clerks crowded around. When he was three years old, Bobby Allen gave his first public performances, perched atop his father's desk, talking and singing into a Dictaphone. The boy marveled at the recorded sound of his own voice. Sometimes Abe recorded him alone and would tease secretaries by slipping in a brief performance by Bobby between invoice numbers.

In 1946, there was a Mother's Day celebration in Duluth, where Bobby was taken with his grandmother Anna. "It was the talk of Duluth. In fact, they still talk about it," Bob's mother recalled. "Everyone was getting up to perform, but nobody else but Bobby was listening to what was going on. They talked. Bobby just sat there and watched and listened. Then they called on him. This little four-year-old codger gets up with his tousled, curly hair and goes to the stage. He stamped his foot and commanded attention. Bobby said: 'If everybody in this room will keep quiet, I will sing for my grandmother. I'm going to sing "Some Sunday Morning."' Well, he sang it, and they tore the place apart. They clapped so hard that he sang his other big number, 'Accentuate the Positive.' He didn't know much more than those two songs. Our phone never stopped ringing with people congratulating me. My mother and mother-in-law had lots of other grandchildren, but Bobby was the special apple of their eyes. He was the one they doted on, but he wasn't spoiled. How he remained unspoiled, I'll never know."

Within two weeks, Bob had another gig. Beatty's sister, Irene, had a lavish wedding reception at the Covenant Club. Bob's mother decked him out in a white Palm Beach suit. (In 1968, she still kept the collarless, three-button outfit handy in a front closet.) A fan club of relatives sponsored Bob's first paid performance. Proffering a handful of bills, an uncle said "Bobby, you've got to sing." He refused. The pleading increased, although the fee remained the same. Bob turned to his father. "I told him," his father said, "that he should sing, because all those people had come to hear him. I told him that if he would sing we wouldn't pester him to sing publicly anymore."

"So he sang," his mother recalled, "but not until he had announced: 'If it's quiet, I will sing.'" It was not what you would call a boy soprano, but it was a thin, beguiling voice, and everyone was quiet as Bob's two-song repertoire was delivered. Again the audience cheered, and Bobby walked over to his uncle and took the twenty-five dollars. He approached his mother with his first gate receipts. "Mummy," he told her, "I'm going to give the money back." He returned to his uncle and handed him the money. He was the hero of the day and nearly upstaged the bride and groom.

His father remembered: "People would laugh with delight at hearing him sing. He was, I would say, a very lovable, a very unusual child. People would go out of their way to handle him, to talk with him. I think we were the only ones who would *not* agree that he was going to be a very famous person some day. Everybody would say: 'This boy is going to be a genius, or he was going to be this or that.' Everyone said that, not just the family. When he sang 'Accentuate the Positive' the way other children his age sang 'Mary Had a Little Lamb,' people said he was brilliant. I didn't pay too much attention to this, frankly. I figured any kid could learn a song like that from the radio—if he heard it often enough."

Return to Hibbing. The end of World War II triggered a great migration. Troops returned from around the world. City people moved to the suburbs, country folks to the cities. Everybody who could afford it moved house. The economy moved from swords to ploughshares. Abe and Beatty considered moving to Hibbing. He had lost his job at Standard Oil, which, by 1945, was a post equivalent to office manager, in charge of the stock and auditing division. Abe and Beatty had another son, David, in February 1946. Bobby was then attending kindergarten at Duluth's Nettleton School. On the first day, Bob simply refused to take the big step without his father. Abe escorted him, somewhat embarrassed to be the only father in a sea of mothers. Bobby seemed to fit in well at kindergarten.

Then Abe was stricken in the 1946 polio epidemic. Always one to keep tight rein on his emotions, he took the illness with Spartan toughness, remaining in hospital for only a week because it was short of help and equipment. The doctor was annoyed at his leaving too soon. "I'll never forget coming home—I had to crawl up the front steps like an ape." He remained home for six months, while Beatty was carrying or nursing David. Gradually he recovered, although the ordeal left him with one limp leg and weak muscles in the other. Bobby was left to his own devices, stringing beads together and creating building-block cities.

The parents needed to be closer to their family while Abe recovered. The Zimmermans moved in with Beatty's parents, on Third Avenue in Hibbing and Abe joined his brothers Paul and Maurice in a furniture and appliance business. They had prospects: consumer goods were rolling off assembly lines and everyone who could afford it was getting their home applianced. For Bob, the first two years in Hibbing was a period of bustling confusion. He started first grade at the Alice School right next door to the Stones' apartment. When the bell rang for recess, Bobby thought it meant the end of the day and returned home. After a few dropouts, he began to realize how long the school day was. Ben Stone took Bobby on deliveries and other store business. It was Ben, they say, who was the first to perceive Bob's intelligence.

Before Ben's death in 1952, Beatty and Abe had already found their own home, a spacious corner house on Seventh Avenue in the Fairview Addition. Three floors and nine rooms gave the boys plenty of space to explore and play, even after their widowed grandmother came to live with them.

Their neighborhood was an uncrowded middle-class section of some six houses, containing fifteen children. The families were friendly. Beatty: "I went to all their weddings, confirmations, and graduations. The neighbors were of all different faiths—Catholic and Lutheran and other Protestants—and we were the only Jewish family. But we absolutely respected each other. We have been better friends with our immediate neighbors than we have with some relatives. And our boys? No one ever called me to tell me they were touching their dogs or throwing rocks in the yard. They never stole anything. There was never anything but high regard in the whole neighborhood for my boys. They didn't go out of their way to be a nuisance."

The Case of the Purloined Crab Apple.
"Bobby and I used to steal crab apples from the neighbors' trees all the time. Or we would steal carrots and onions. We just did the normal things that growing boys do," Larry Furlong told me in 1966. "We used to build backyard playhouses that looked just like outhouses. We used to go up to 'Pill Hill,' a few blocks away. Then it was just an old ore dump, long before it was the Lebanon Addition. They call it 'Pill Hill' now because so many doctors live there. But for Bob and me, and Luke Davich, and my brother Pat, and Bob Pedler, it was just a grand wilderness. We constructed forts and campsites and discovered little streams. The kids used to tease Bob, sometimes. They would call him Bobby Zennerman because it was so difficult to pronounce Zimmerman. He didn't like that. Usually, he was fun to be with. He wasn't spoiled. He seemed no different than any of the kids in the neighborhood. But I do remember that his feelings could be hurt easily. He often went home pouting. Later, in high school, he wasn't so well liked, mostly because he stayed to himself so much. We're all very proud of Bob now."

"No artist can accept reality," Nietzsche said, and the same could be said of "no Zimmerman." Middle-class, small-town propriety impelled Beatty not only to say, but also to believe, her own version of reality. Abe freely admitted, with appropriate rising gestures of his hands, "I've got pride up to here and ego up to there." For the parents, their home life and their son's early years were a placid paradise of parental permissiveness and sagacity. For Bob, the Hibbing years were so limiting that he came to accept no limits.

As their son's career developed, the parents occasionally made light of his self-images, but their own image-making was nearly as prodigious. Abe wanted to impress the town Rotarians, and Beatty wanted to impress the "old lady judges," as Bob would call them, of her family and community. Bob wanted to impress the world with a romantic flight to somewhere else. None of them was a liar. All of them were compelled, like Pirandello, to find their own realities.

Dylan's personal mythology was both shield and armor while smashing and desecrating countless other myths around him. Knowing the value of myth, he also knew its potential danger, which he may have discovered the day his mother was told that her pride and joy had stolen the forbidden crab apple.

The Poet before the Electric Age.
Abe was a short man with an appealing smile that revealed irregular teeth. Behind his strong glasses, his eyes were a soft boyish blue, until they hardened. His wavy black hair was flecked with gray. He dressed in sport shirts, slacks, and sweaters that suggested California more than Minnesota. He frequently sported a fine, thick cigar. Abe's speech was slow and deliberate, in contrast to Beatty's torrential flow. He peppered his talk with double negatives, yet he didn't sound unschooled. On his home turf, he was a big man in commercial and community circles, and he wanted to be in charge. When Abe said I *had* to see someone in town, it was less an invitation than an imperative. If I said I wanted to go somewhere on my own, he'd say: "Well you're pulling the strings."

Abe and Beatty were clean and orderly, their house always ready for visitors. The social pivots of their large family, they were very proud to have retained many Duluth friends. They lavished attention on the boys, especially their oldest. Bob learned at his mother's knee to expect and receive a great deal of attention from women. Beatty was warm, effusive, and outgoing. The other neighborhood kids called her Beatty, without concern for formalities. She ran a house "on love, warmth and laughter." Abe enjoyed a good laugh himself. He wanted only what any man wanted—respect, especially from his sons. There were rules, of course, and Bob followed them where he could, for years, before he escaped them and tore up the rulebook with a rip heard around the world. But as Beatty put it: "We were more like friends. We would tell the boys that they could have children of their own one day and they would want to be friends with them."

Abe was an organization man. He had belonged to the Golden Circle at Standard Oil, an executive group whose members "could do no wrong." He was active in various lodges of B'Nai, B'Rith, a Jewish fraternal order, and designed basketball suits for one lodge's team. A loyal member of the Hibbing Rotary, Abe was delighted to have edged Bob into the Boy Scouts. Bob's membership was brief. "He got the uniform and I was glad he joined," his father said. "But I didn't ask him if he liked it or not."

David's earliest recollection of his brother was the day Bob guided him, hand-in-hand, into their new Hibbing home. The place was dark. Carpets were rolled up mysteriously on bare floors as Bob took his brother into their new playground. Bob remained the leader, although not always hand-in-hand. Bob was scrappy, and occasionally the parents returned home to find big brother firmly seated on little brother's stomach, pinning his shoulders to the floor. "This kid was so strong, he could lift a refrigerator," his mother claimed. Beatty tried to show no favoritism, carrying equal-time provision so far as to put two soup bowls on the table at the same moment. The brothers generally got along well, trading *Illustrated Classics* comic books, rough-housing, going to Dad's store to play with a portable disk-recording machine.

Around the early 1950s, Bob began to spend an increasing amount of time in his upstairs room. Beatty will never forget her rapture when on one Mother's Day she saw his first poem. Written on notebook paper, it was carefully rhymed in twelve balanced stanzas of four or five lines each. The sentimental words told how his mother's face shone in the light, and described his fears that without her love he would be "six feet under." It concluded:

My dear mother, I hope that you
Will never grow old and gray,
So that all the people in the world will say:
"Hello, young lady, Happy Mother's Day."

Love, Bobby

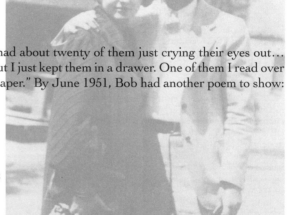

Beatty: "I had to read it to the women. I must have had about twenty of them just crying their eyes out… We were going to frame some of those other poems, but I just kept them in a drawer. One of them I read over so often that the wording was nearly rubbed off the paper." By June 1951, Bob had another poem to show:

For Father's Day

This present is for my dad alone
To use when playing golf or sitting home.
He can use them after supper, or when riding in the car,
He can use them when relaxing or taking a trip far,
I know my dad is the best in the world.
Worth more to me than every diamond and peril [sic]
Though it's hard for him to believe
That I try each day to please him in every little way,
When sometimes he gets real mad at me
I think it best to keep quiet
So that he doesn't get more angry.
I keep his picture on my desk,
And also his handball medal above all the rest.
I'm very lucky to have a Dad this good
And if all the other kids only could,
You just can't beat him at any cost.
And without my dad, I'd be very lost.

Abe and Beatty Zimmerman, 1939.

Happy Father's Day… Love, Bobby.

The poems Bob wrote at ten or eleven were a chance to "make something"; he was not especially interested in crafts or model building. He wrote a great deal. "We thought he would get it out of his system, but he never did," his mother told me. For a time, the writing was eclipsed by an exciting diversion. In 1952, the family acquired the first TV set in Hibbing.

The new gadget delighted the boys and, after several moves, it reposed upstairs, in the room the brothers shared. Bob and David were pioneer TV children, glued to the set for hours, watching everything from Milton Berle to *Kukla, Fran and Ollie*. Bob's superior muscles meant he generally chose the show. He liked music and variety shows, and western adventure series. He loved the bravado and individuality of badman and lawman alike, and the names of the TV frontiersmen rang with earthy American directness. He could imagine himself as Wyatt Earp. Or, even more heroically, as the greatest frontiersman since Daniel Boone, that lean, laconic, fearless man of justice from Dodge City named Matt Dillon.

Words and Music — Traditional.

The emotional tethers of Judaism are as long and strong as the umbilicus. First- and second-generation offspring of Jewish immigrants found many powerful reasons for assimilating into the American grain. In the New World, the biblical-cum-medieval Jewish traditions had no apparent appeals and many obvious drawbacks.

"In Hibbing, the Finns hated the Bohemians and the Bohemians hated the Finns. Nearly everyone hated the Jews," a teacher at Hibbing High told me. "A lot has been done to break down the barriers, but it wouldn't be true to say they have all broken down." The boy called Bobby Zennerman and Zimbo by his playmates before he called himself Bob Dillon sought assimilation. But before he drew his own maps, he followed by rote his parents' traditions, which reached a culmination when Bob turned 13.

Bar Mitzvah means "of an age to observe the commandments." The formal ceremony is rooted in antiquity but became a ritual during the Middle Ages. German Jews refined the formalities to celebrate a boy's attaining legal majority by allowing him to join the public reading of the Torah, the Law of Moses. The festival that Abe and Beatty arranged for their eldest son was lavishly American. Beatty was delighted that out of the 500 invited, 400 attended. "This is only a small town," she noted with pride.

To prepare, Bob studied Hebrew. With the nascent ear of the musician, he mimicked the exotic sounds. His teacher, Rabbi Reuben Maier, of the only synagogue on the Iron Range, Hibbing's Agudath Achim Synagogue, was pleased at Bob's progress. At Friday night meetings, he showed off the prodigy, wishing all his students were as bright and as dutiful. Confirmation day arrived, and Bob stood on the synagogue rostrum with his rabbi, his prayer book, and five thousand years of prophets and pogroms behind him. He was dressed in white, with a raised silken hat on his head and an ornate fringed shawl around his shoulders. He delivered the Hebrew scripture in a form of chanting known as cantillation. The elders told Bob he did a "tremendous" job at the crowded, ostentatious gathering afterward. Having attained manhood, having confirmed his belief in the God of his fathers, Bobby was ready to start living by no commandments but his own.

Strings of Freedom.

Although Abe never called himself a great music-lover, music was important to him. He trooped Beatty off to a lodge dance at the drop of an invitation. A Gulbransen spinet piano arrived at much the same time as the television, and was set in the front room for all to admire. Abe couldn't read a note, but he loved to fake a few chords. He brought home dance records and he particularly liked Billy Daniels's songs and Freddy Gardner's saxophone. When Bob was around ten, curiosity drew him to the piano, and he started to peck out a tune. A cousin, Harriet Rutstein, gave piano lessons. David followed instructions, but Bob endured only one lesson. "I'm going to play the piano the way I want to," he declared impatiently. For a while he simply ignored the piano. But when he was about 14, music surged into his life, though he never learned to read it.

At Hibbing Junior High School, everyone who counted was playing in the school band. Bob started frequent visits to a Howard Street music store, which offered instruments on $10 three-month rental/purchase plans. Bob first took home a trumpet, announcing he would master it soon. For two days, the air around the house ached—he couldn't seem to produce a single succession of clear notes. To general relief, the trumpet was returned in favor of a saxophone. Two days later, he returned in defeat. He tried another brass instrument, then another reed. Neither responded the way he wanted. Finally, amid fears that he had worn out his welcome, Bob rented a cheap guitar, which he caressed like a Spanish heirloom. Following the instruction sheet, he moved his hand gently across the six strings, cramping his fingers against the frets. It almost sounded like music. For hours he sat with the guitar cradled in his hands, experimenting and exploring. His fingers stung and ached. Manoloff's *Basic Spanish Guitar Manual* gave him some clues. But his own ears and fingers soon took the lead. He mastered one position after the other. He found the scale and he found the key.

send me a key — I shall find the door to where it
fits, if it takes me the rest of my life.

The Guitar Picker. The guitar became his cane, weapon, status symbol, security blanket, and swagger stick. Around Hibbing, some remember him walking up and down the streets with his guitar slung over his shoulder on a leather strap. Chet Crippa recalls Bob having his guitar ready even in the coldest weather. As Dylan grew up, he grew inward, communicating less with family friends and schoolmates. He lavished attention on the friend he could fully trust without reservation, his guitar. Like a Delta bluesman, he treated the instrument as confidant and sidekick. "I didn't go hunting, I didn't go fishing, I didn't play on the basketball team," Dylan said later. "I just played the guitar and sang my songs. That was enough for me. My friends were like me—people who couldn't make it as the football halfback, the Junior Chamber of Commerce leader, the fraternity booster, the truck driver working his way through college. I couldn't do any of those things either. All I did was write and sing, paint little pictures on paper, dissolve myself into situations where I was invisible."

Dylan's "invisibility" was partly that of the alien assimilating. Even in "the land of the free," the thirty or forty Jewish families of Hibbing still had to huddle together against the cold. Abe, who loved to play golf, couldn't belong to the Mesabi Country Club. He and David played instead at the public course and continued to do so after the Mesabi lifted its restrictions. Bob tried golf only once: unable to play well quickly, he lost interest.[6]

Bob started to want both personal privacy and public approval. A true Gemini, the introvert grappled with the extrovert, the shy boy turned brash, the kind lad became hostile, the studious boy went bad. There was a duality in his speech. From Abe he inherited a slow and considered pattern of dealing out words, like an Indian, while from Beatty he inherited a constant flow of volatile emotions, a tongue that sometimes could not move as fast as the feelings he wanted to articulate. From adolescence onward, Dylan's swings of attitude and demeanor were always extreme. "I hate to do the predictable," he told me, and he began to be unpredictable in his mid-teens. There he was, the introvert setting his high school on its ear with wild rock 'n' roll; the homebody turned motorcycle cowboy; the courteous youngster acting as truculent as he could; the anti-sentimentalist falling in and out of love; the son of the middle class spending most of his time with poor folk; the white boy studying black jargon.

"Where I lived," later Dylan told me, "was really hillbilly country. The radio stations I used to listen to weren't local, but those on a direct route from Louisiana, right up the Mississippi River." Hibbing's station, WMFG, was square before and after Bob's cousin, Les Rutstein, became its general manager in 1958. Bob often chided Les for not programming rock 'n' roll or rhythm 'n' blues. In 1968, Les still held that "old standards" were what his housewives wanted. "We don't program for the youth," he told me. "Let Duluth do that!" In the early 1950s, WMFG played pop songs like "Too Young" by Frankie Laine, "The Song from Moulin Rouge" by Percy Faith, "Love Is a Many-Splendored Thing" by the Four Lads, and middle-of-the-road Guy Mitchell, Doris Day, and Perry Como. Bill Haley and His Comets? Not on Hibbing radio!

Until eclipsed by Elvis Presley, Haley was the most successful white rock 'n' roll musician. As early as 1953, he had recorded black rhythm 'n' blues hits. Haley's first rock hit was the cover version of Ivory Joe Hunter's "Shake, Rattle and Roll." He borrowed black R&B's choreography and visual games, country music's accent and stagemanship. Haley wanted his lyrical messages bright, cheerful, and escapist. He once said: "I personally have objected to protest … and crying songs. My idea in creating rock 'n' roll was to make kids happy… Kids … have to face problems… when they get older, and I think it's wrong to make them face problems so young."

Haley's work, especially "Rock Around the Clock," became known around the world through the soundtrack of the 1955 film *Blackboard Jungle*, about a problematic city high school. The rock tide had been rising since 1951, when Alan Freed, the late disc jockey, had begun to push the new music on Cleveland radio. By 1954, rock 'n' roll had spread to major Coast stations, but WMFG ignored it. Dylan had to turn his radio on to a thin line that linked him with the farmers of Louisiana and the truck drivers of Tennessee. "'Henrietta' was the first rock 'n' roll record I heard," Dylan said. He also calls Johnnie Ray "the first singer whose voice and style I totally fell in love with."[7]

Bob took most of his journeys down the Mississippi late at night, when the air was clearer. He often placed his radio under the covers to keep from waking anyone with sounds he caught from Shreveport or Little Rock. Gatemouth Page, a voluble southern DJ, alternated country music with R&B. While Bill Haley was syncretizing the two musics, Dylan's radio fed him both. In 1954, *McCall's Magazine* editorialized about togetherness, an idyllic portrait of American family life updating *Saturday Evening Post* covers by Norman Rockwell, Andy Hardy films, *One Man's Family*. For Bob Dylan, who felt increasing separation from his family after he entered high school, togetherness was a midnight radio show from the South that said white and black music got along very well. The *Joan Baez* liner notes again:

> *I learned t' choose my idols well*
> *T' be my voice an' tell my tale*
> *An' my first idol was Hank Williams ...*

Hiram "Hank" Williams was "the hillbilly Shakespeare" to millions of farmers, truck drivers, and factory workers. Born in an Alabama log cabin, he took his only musical instruction from Tee-tot, a black street singer. Williams wrote 125 songs, dozens of which wring pathos out of the simplest lyrics. "I'm So Lonesome I Could Cry," "Your Cheatin' Heart," "Cold, Cold Heart," and "Alone and Forsaken" embody a world of loss and loneliness. Hank Williams, making his sad songs sadder, died on New Year's Day, 1953, at the age of 29. Officially, he died of a heart attack. Unofficially, he died of too much living, alcohol, and drugs.[8]

If Hank Williams was the poet, Little Richard was the pulse, a rhythm 'n' blues John Henry. Richard Penniman, born in 1935 in Georgia, started to sing at the age of 10 in churches and on street corners before going professional with Sugarfoot Sam from Alabam and Dr Hudson's Medicine Show. His music, and life, swung from sacred to secular, from tabernacles to juke joints. Seemingly possessed, he shouted and pranced with demonic emotion that led John Lennon to describe him as the first primal screamer. He was a bridge between black gospel and modern soul. Presley recorded his songs, the Rolling Stones and the Yardbirds identified his style, Paul McCartney was his devotee. In the mid-Fifties, Dylan enrolled as a student of Little Richard in the radio university, heeding his raunchy sermon: "My music is the healing music that makes the dumb and deaf hear and talk." Little Richard briefly retired to become a theology student, then returned to show business in 1962. He worked with the Beatles at the Cavern in Liverpool, instructing them in the high falsetto wail, the "yeah, yeah, yeah" line. Dylan, who had not met Little Richard, assimilated his style seven years before the Beatles did. In his 1959 high-school yearbook, Bob listed his ambition: "To join the band of Little Richard."

Grateful for these early musical influences, but impatient with himself for not having understood more, Dylan once told me: "It was just like an adolescent, you know. When you need somebody to latch on to, you find somebody to latch onto. I did it with so many people, that's why I went through so many changes. I wrote a lot of stuff like Hank Williams, but I never grasped why his songs were so catchy or so classic. As for Presley, I don't know anybody my age that did not sing like him, at one time or another. Or Buddy Holly." Even as he was amassing musical idols, he shed them to rely on himself. As he later wrote on *Joan Baez*:

> *In later times my idols fell*
> *For I learned that they were only men ...*
> *But what I learned from each forgotten god*
> *Was that the battlefield was mine alone ...*

As time passed, however, the forgotten gods were remembered again. During his world tour of 1978, Dylan told me of his reaction to Elvis's death: "It was so sad. I had a breakdown! I broke down ... one of the very few times. I went over my whole life, my whole childhood. I didn't talk to anyone for a week. If it wasn't for Elvis and Hank Williams, I couldn't be doing what I do today."

Soon after Dylan had learned his way around his first guitar, he wanted a bigger, flashier instrument. He saw it in a Sears, Roebuck catalog: turquoise with a little white wing by the strings. He saved toward the twenty-dollar down payment, and nineteen dollars more to pay it off. Fearing his father's annoyance, Bob hid the new guitar until he had paid for it. Abe had to admire Bob's resourcefulness. Bob bought as many records as he could afford without a weekly allowance. His first collection was of Hank Williams 78s. He went on to the new 45s by Little Richard, Buddy Holly and Hank Thompson. Bob gyrated from record player to guitar to the family piano, where he aped Little Richard, who danced from microphone to a standing slam at the piano keyboard. Now, all Bob needed was a band.

In 1968, Le Roy Hoikkala, a shy, slight electronics technician, told me: "I met Bob downtown one day and we got to talking about music. We were in eighth grade, and I was very much involved in playing drums. Monte Edwardson was guitar player, and the three of us got together, around 1955, in Bob's garage for some sessions. Monte played lead, Bob played rhythm and sang. We figured we had the makings of a band, and we decided to call ourselves the Golden Chords. Nobody was the leader. Bob really idolized Little Richard then. He could chord quite well on the piano. Rock was just starting then. Haley and Presley were just beginning to make it big.

"We started to get some jobs, playing at some Moose Lodge meetings and a few PTA meetings. Whenever there was a talent contest, we would show up. I'll never forget the community talent contest at the Hibbing Memorial Building. The judges were chamber of commerce members, so you couldn't expect them to know too much about music. The Golden Chords won on audience applause, but the judges gave first prize to a girl who played classical piano. The kids booed the decision, because we only came in second."[9]

The Golden Chords played some country songs, like Johnnie and Jack's "I'll Be Home," but Bob soon led the trio toward Little Richard's extroversion. Le Roy was impressed by Bob's speed in putting together a song as early as 1955. "He would write a song right at the piano. Just chord it, and improvise on it. I remember that he sang one song about a train in R&B style. He could make sense with a song in an instant." Sunday afternoons, Bob slipped out to jam sessions at Van Feldt's little snack bar and barbecue, at Fourth Avenue and 19th Street. For months, kids filled the place, making it "the scene" in Hibbing. The Golden Chords held public rehearsals, which the young people treated as a show. Dylan's other Hibbing bands were called the Shadow Blasters, Elston Gunn and the Rock Boppers. Because it was Sunday afternoon, no parents objected. After all, the boys would soon outgrow this nonsense.

Be It Ever So Square. Bob's parents did not overtly discourage his music making, but they certainly couldn't share his passion. He occasionally brought Le Roy and Monte home for rehearsals, generally when his parents were away. Only in hindsight did Abe and Beatty realize that, from 14 on, Bob was inexorably drifting away from all they held dear. Dylan touched on his flight from Hibbing with a metaphoric question to me: "Did you ever smell birth? That's why I always had to move when something new has happened." He was talking specifically about leaving one Woodstock home for another after completing an album, but he indicated it was a long-entrenched attitude of his, the flight from a form of death and the escape from the scene of birth. Another time he said: "There were a lot of people who were just plain straight and kind to me, when I was really nothing. You understand, I never was a kid who could go home. I never had a home, which I could just take a bus to. I'm not proud of it. I would not recite it. I made my way all by myself. The only way I could do it was because I did not care. But here I am... I've got to accept what I've done and where I've gone and what I've become."

His parents would have been appalled to know their son felt he didn't have a home with them. Abe still thought that, inevitably, Bob would complete his schooling and join the family business. Whenever he could, Abe found a chore to bring Bob into the shop. It was a losing battle. Bob would "run away" into his music, his writing, his reading behind his closed bedroom door. "Are you there, Bobby?" his mother often called up the stairwell. "It's all right, ma, I'm only reading," he could have replied.

"He was never detached from family or friends, but he dreamt a lot," his mother told me in 1966. "He would go upstairs and dream that he would be very famous. He was going to do something very different. How often that boy told his grandmother: 'Grandma, someday I'm going to be very famous. You are never going to have to worry about anything.' He told her he would make a lot of money and that she would never have to want for anything."

On both visits to Hibbing, I repeatedly pressed Dylan's parents on the genesis of his writings. Mother: "Bob was upstairs quietly becoming a writer for twelve years. He read every book there was. He bought only comics that had some meaning, like *Illustrated Classics*. He was in the library a lot. I don't know what authors he liked, we hardly ever discussed writers. We would just be laughing and talking." Father: "I used to tell Robert that if he needed any help with his studies to let me know. I used to help him with math ... history was always a problem with him. He just refused to get a good mark in history. I used to argue that history only required you to remember what you read. He said there was nothing to figure out in history. I asked him why it was so hard, and he would just say: 'I don't like it.'" Mother: "I remember he said: 'I am not going to take physics, I don't like it.' I offered to get him a tutor. He said: 'I don't like physics. Please, please, let me drop it.'

"Bobby could write and he could draw. He was an artist. He was always drawing or painting the pictures that you put the colors in. I tried to push architecture. I figured at least he could make a living. From these poems, you are going to die and *then* be discovered. I said: 'Please go to school and make yourself a living. These poems aren't going to make you a living.' This was in the ninth and tenth grade. Those poems he wrote in high school, he wouldn't show to anybody, just to me and his dad. I said to Bobby that you can't go on and on and on and sit and dream and write poems. I was afraid he would end up being a poet! Do you know the kind of poet I mean? One that had no ambition and wrote only for himself. In my day, a poet was unemployed and had no ambition. Here we would be at the back of him with a pitchfork. 'Bobby, you have to eat.' He still doesn't eat enough. He eats to live."

I asked if he ever called himself a poet: "No!" they chorused emphatically. Mother: "I never called him a poet. Sometimes, when he was planning to go to college, I would say: 'Bobby, why don't you take something useful?' He said: 'I'll take something in science, literature, and art for a year and then I will see what I want to do.' I told him: 'Don't keep writing poetry, please don't. Go to school and do something constructive. Get a degree.'"

Only minutes after revealing their obliviousness to the import of his early passion for writing and music, Beatty and Abe turned to a painful subject. They couldn't understand why they had not then shared his success, even though he often sent them money. They were mystified at his saying that he ran away from their happy home. For a while they blamed his manager, Albert Grossman, for keeping them out of the picture. Beatty: "Did Albert really think that people all over the world thought Bob was an orphan?" Abe: "I told Albert: 'This can't go on forever, our hiding from the world.' I told Albert we have something to be proud of. We gave Robert his start, the encouragement he needed from the beginning."

The Talent Contest. The Golden Chords fell into disharmony as Bob became increasingly interested in black R&B while the other two drifted toward more popular white rock 'n' roll. Bob soon was the key figure in another nameless band featuring Chuck Nara on drums, Bill Marinec on bass, and Larry Fabbro on electric guitar, with Bob on piano, guitar, and lead vocals. In autumn 1955, the four jammed often, exchanged recordings, and listened to Bob's plans for a life in music. To the others, music was just a hobby.

After about a year, Bob and his no-name band appeared at Hibbing High's Jacket Jamboree Talent Festival. There were reciters and warblers and piano players—all with more gall than technique. Bob said so little in class, was such a quiet loner, that no one was prepared for the sonic onslaught, though the mountain of equipment might have prepared them. Bob had also heightened the shock by insisting that his sidemen tell no one what they were going to do. Even then his rule was: "Don't say what you are going to do, just do it."

Bob wore his hair in mounds above his forehead, Little Richard-style. The band worked with amplifiers at full roar, and when Bob began to sing, in a hoarse, insistent, screaming wail, "it brought as much laughter as it did applause," Fabbro told me. "The songs were drawn from the repertoire of Little Richard and Big Elvis, and the one title that sticks out in everyone's memory was 'Rock 'n' Roll Is Here to Stay.'"

Not at Hibbing High, it wasn't! K L Pedersen, the principal, was guiding around some touring education officials. The combined force of the house mikes with the band's amplification was too much, and he ran backstage and cut the microphones. Seeing that he couldn't raise his voice around there either, Bob seethed, but kept pounding his piano. Some say he broke the pedal off and may have bruised a few strings. "African shrieking," remarked a startled teacher. One student, Jerry Erickson, who had a quiet little trio of his own before he became a banker, had a typical reaction: "Bobby was just ahead of things. We might have thought that day that he was kind of nuts, even though we always thought he was a nice kid." Even Fabbro admitted that their performance was shocking: "Bob's style of singing was quite unique for that time, for that town."

Another student eyewitness: "My first impression was embarrassment. Our little community was unaccustomed to such a performance. I think a lot of people were embarrassed too. I realize now, of course [in 1969], that there was the young Bob Dylan in his very early form. He was a little bit ahead of everyone, but he didn't seem to mind. Because he had such a fantastic confidence in his talent, he didn't care. He just said: 'Here I am. Either you like it or you don't. I know that what I've got is great.'"

The eyewitness was John Bucklen, one year younger than Bob, who became a smooth-voiced pop disk jockey in Fond du Lac, Wisconsin. He was soon to become Bob's best friend, shadow to his light, Sancho Panza to his Quixote. "If a musical opportunity came along, Bob wouldn't hesitate to go to the right person and say what he wanted. He had an unusual way of winning people over." Bucklen, and his mother and sister, were convinced that Bob had learned something from his father. "We thought," said Bucklen, "that Bob would make a very good salesman. As a matter of fact, he ended up being a very good salesman—of himself."[10]

Tales of the talent contest rocked the school. Teachers laughed, students sniggered, parents alarmed. One teacher, Bonn Rolfsen, was upset about the show, but struck by the difference between Bob onstage and in class. Ten years later, he told me that one key to understanding Dylan was geographical: "If you go a few minutes from here in Hibbing into the desolate bush, you'll know why we are so independent here." In class, Bonn remembered, Bob was "very quiet, very introverted, but very bright. I remember him as very much a gentleman, pleasantly mild-mannered. I frankly can't remember what his writing was like. David has since told me that Bob was writing all along, but apparently I wasn't aware of it." Another teacher, Charlie Miller, who taught Bob social studies, remembered him as "different, from the viewpoint that he had a mind. He certainly showed he had talent. When I later heard 'Blowin' in the Wind', I was reminded of the social compassion he had shown in our classes."

After the Jacket Jamboree, Bob slid back into his class chair quietly as usual, although some recall that there was a difference. He seemed to be smiling to himself. Bucklen thought he saw emerging "black humor," not like Lenny Bruce's mordant satire, but rather "the sort of put-on humor of a black person toward a threatening white." Bucklen saw a jokester protecting himself while taunting a differently colored world around him.

Actors Studio Midwest.   Before Elvis donned black leather, the idols of many young Americans had nothing to do with music. A few idolized the genial general who moved into the White House in 1953 but a small circle of Iron Range youths found their models in the Actors Studio, by way of the movies. Brando's *The Wild One* and Dean's *East of Eden*, *Giant*, and, especially, *Rebel Without a Cause* stunned these isolated provincials.

Brando and Dean forged characters who eclipsed the western hero. The new folk hero didn't ride a horse; he drove a motorcycle through the stoplight of acceptable behavior. In a decade of soft American affluence with no visible frontier to challenge, nothing was better than a bike—unless it was a guitar—to symbolize the young man's dream of sexual potency, to defy his father in his "safe" car. Harley and Davidson were the Lewis and Clark of the 1950s.

The best biker in town was Dale Boutang, a cowboy on wheels and a seasoned weight-lifter. He drove a Harley 74. Bob bought a Harley 45, the next smallest model. Le Roy quickly taught Bob how to drive it, out on the West Side. "You can't be *bad*, man, really *bad*, unless you have a motorcycle and a leather jacket," Bob used to tell his friends. One day, the gang drove out to a suburb called Brooklyn, divided from Hibbing by a level rail crossing. The four waited impatiently for a train to pass. Bob gunned his engine, ready to zoom off the instant the train went by. He started to move before he saw another train coming from the other direction on the track beyond. As he saw his error, he swerved sharply left, throwing himself off the bike. The other freight passed by only inches from him. Bob got up, heart pounding, hands trembling, and walked his bike back across the tracks. He could scarcely speak for two minutes. He drove the motorcycle home slowly, never telling his folks he had "come so close to death." For a few days he thought about selling his bike, but he was soon out riding again with his old confidence, perhaps now "immune to death."

Bob wasn't content to ride, posture, and think like Dean-Brando-Presley; he wanted to be photographed like them. He enlisted his brother, David, with the family Polaroid. In their room upstairs, between the ages of 15 and 17, Bob learned how to pose, practicing the art of concealing art. Years later, when I discussed this with Suze Rotolo, his Greenwich Village girlfriend, she registered amazement. "I never knew he had been in front of any camera until he got to New York." David recalled that one of their favorite posing sessions used the long heavy drapes of their bedroom window as a stage curtain from which Bob peeked out, grinning or squaring his jaw. For action shots, Bob roared around the street corner on his Harley, bearing down hard toward his brother on the curb. As Bob swerved past, he yelled:

"Did you get it?" Writing in March 1966 in *Atlantic* of Brando as an American prototype, critic Pauline Kael drew a portrait that sounds like the one young Dylan was filling in with his own colors:

Protagonists are always loners … Brando represented a reaction against the post-war mania for security … Brando had no code, only his instincts … He was anti-social because he knew society was crap; he was a hero … because he was strong enough not to take the crap … Perhaps his special appeal was … the conceit of tough kids: There was humor in it … swagger and arrogance that were vain and childish … He was explosively dangerous without being "serious" in the sense of having ideas. There was no theory, no cant in his leadership …

Because he had no code, except an esthetic one—a commitment to a style of life—he was easily betrayed by those he trusted. There he was, the new primitive, a Byronic Dead End Kid, with his quality of vulnerability … We in the audience felt protective; we knew how lonely he must be in his assertiveness. Who even in hell wants to be an outsider? He was no intellectual who could rationalize it … He could only feel it, act it out, be "The Wild One—" and God knows how many kids felt, "That's the story of my life."

When Dylan was gunning his bike, posing in his own curbstone theater, James Dean was dead, and so was Hank Williams, but Brando was alive in Hollywood, and in Hibbing.

Don Quixote and Sancho Panza.
At 16, Bob used to tell John Bucklen, "You are my main man"—high praise in 1950s patois. Bucklen's family was working-class, mainstream American, probably of English descent. John also had that sense of being "*bad*, man, *bad*." Even with those nice, middle-class boys from the Twin Cities whom Bob met at the Theodor Herzl summer camp near Webster, Wisconsin, he could find some "bad" guys to befriend. Beginning in 1954, Bob attended the Zionist camp run by a Hadassah Club for a few weeks each of four summers. He loved the swimming and didn't seem to mind speaking Hebrew. But by his sixteenth birthday, things were getting too tame. He had begun some singing around campfires there. To perk things up, Bob and a half-dozen other campers climbed to the roof of the shower house, pulling their ladders up after them. They sang, yelled, and taunted their counselors until the rabbi read them a sermon below the mount that got them back on the ground. "Bobby just about took over the whole camp that year," Abe recalled. "I thought they were going to send him home."

The more relaxed atmosphere around Bucklen's home appealed. Beatty insisted on a 9.30 p.m. curfew on school nights. John's family seemed grittier. John and his mother, a seamstress, had known privation. His father, a railway man, had lost a leg in a rail accident, and was a semi-invalid until he died when John was 15. Bucklen told me that he was a born follower, while Bob was increasingly brash and aggressive. Music bound their friendship together with guitar strings and spools of tape. John often taped Bob at the piano: "Those tapes don't have any esthetic value at all," Bucklen told me in 1969, "but they do have nostalgic value." They loved to ad-lib on tape. "We'd get a guitar and sing verses we made up as we went along. It came out strange and weird. We thought we'd send them in somewhere, but we never did." John loved Bob's fanciful tales. On a trip to Highland Park, a suburb of St Paul, Bob told, his main man: "We're going to tell everyone here that we came to cut a record. I will tell everybody that you are my bass man."

They had some fine times with John's sister Ruth at her house out on Highway 165. John hears echoes in Dylan's "115th Dream" of their happy times of music, jokes, and games. Once, near a lover's lane, Bob donned a Frankenstein monster mask and scared several couples. Bob's put-ons extended to his music as well. "Come on over, I want you to hear something I just wrote." John: "I would say: 'No, you didn't write that!' Because it seemed too great. I could never quite understand why he did it. He had the talent, and didn't have to fake it one bit. There really wasn't anything else like music for Bob to express in Hibbing what he felt. When he did express himself, even in music, people didn't really understand him." Another passion of Bob's, from his sophomore year on, was girls. He ran through a lot, reportedly plump and large-breasted. One of the first was Barbara Hewitt, a voluptuous girl he met in 1957. Bob was quite infatuated. But her family drifted off to Minneapolis, and the first of several student flirtations cooled.

Everyone talked of getting out of Hibbing, but Bob's hungers were insatiable. A restless quest for new people and ideas led Bob and John to Jim Dandy, a black disc jockey in his mid-twenties who lived in Virginia, a neighboring town. With so much cheap European immigrant labor, there were few blacks along the Iron Range. Bucklen: "We visited Jim Dandy so often because he was a refreshing change. He was a Negro, involved with the blues. He had a lot of records we liked." Jim Dandy and his wife and kids were the only blacks among Virginia's 12,000 residents. Bob heard him broadcast on station WHLB in the summer of 1957, and searched for the man behind the voice. He and John were startled, but pleased, to discover that the DJ was black. Seeing he was with simpatico lads, Jim dropped his radio "white voice" for hip black slang. They spent hours playing old blues and R&B disks. The meetings went on sporadically for months. Through Dandy, Bob discovered a new Iron Range that his family scarcely knew.

Echo and Pan: The Girl on the Swing.
"One thing that always surprised me was that Bobby ever had anything to do with me, because I was from the other side of the tracks. He was a nice Hibbing boy and I was from out of town. He was rich folk and we were poor folk. He was Jewish and we were German, Swedish, Russian, and Irish, all mixed together."

Echo Helstrom Shivers smoothed down a cascade of whitish blond hair with one well-manicured hand, took a long, calming puff of her cigarette, and settled into the sofa of her Minneapolis apartment. It was spring of 1968, eleven years after she had met Dylan, but to her it remained a vibrant reality from the most exciting, most tortured year of her life. "What harm will it do to get my name in a book?" she asked, rhetorically. "Perhaps I can help you understand what he was like then."

The day before, in a shack near Hibbing, Echo's mother, Martha Helstrom, a genial, matronly woman who resembled Ma Joad, had said to me: "Well, it's about time someone gave my Echo a little credit for what she did for Bob. She was hurt by the whole thing, but she loved Bob well enough to let him go. We always gave Bob the feeling he was welcome here and that Echo and I believed in him. He was restless and impatient. He didn't have enough time to get everything done. He was like a man in a hurry." When Echo and Bob were high-school juniors, Echo was sure that they would marry one day. Their plan was that whoever made it to the top first would help the other up the ladder. Bob was to be a pop hero and Echo a movie star.

David referred to Echo as a nameless girl with whom Bob had been quite involved, but whom his parents did their best to persuade Bob to drop. "She was not Jewish and she wasn't from the right side of the tracks," he said, adding: "Bobby always went with the daughters of miners, farmers, and workers in Hibbing. He just found them a lot more interesting." In 1961, Bob said: "I dedicated my first song to Brigitte Bardot." Echo looked like a Minnesota Bardot, with a touch of Pat Neal. She had full lips, pouting round cheeks. The Helstroms named her Echo because she was born exactly 14 years after her brother. Echo and her mother and older sister were all interested in mythology. But they were not aware that the nymph Echo had been one of the more celebrated conquests of the Greco-Roman wood-spirit, Pan, the musical, mischievous trickster god with a gift of prophecy.

She had thought about acting but, in 1968, Echo was working in Minneapolis as a film company secretary. She needed it to support a child from her brief marriage. The more she talked about the year when she was close to Bob, the more I thought that, although she had left Hibbing, Hibbing had never quite left her.[11] "It was really funny how we met. I was in the L&B Café on Howard Street. Bob had been playing upstairs at the Moose Lodge and he and John Bucklen came downstairs. Bob started to talk to me. Right there in the street, he began to play his guitar and sing for me." In late winter of 1957, she was 16, he 17. Bob wanted to show her what he could do on piano, but the lodge was locked. "Bob slid a knife in the door and broke right in to play the piano. I was probably the only girl in Hibbing who could have known what Bob was talking about. I had always been very interested in music. I took some accordion lessons and sang in the school choir. We had a harmonium in the parlor. I had a record player at home, but my father wouldn't let me play it. I always listened to radio. I will never forget the first time I heard Chuck Berry's 'Maybellene' on the car radio. I got all excited, but my father turned the radio off. I had to go into one of the other little shacks behind our house to listen to the radio. Sometimes I stayed up to five o'clock in the morning listening to announcers like Gatemouth Page from Shreveport. In 1957, who had ever heard of rhythm 'n' blues in Hibbing? They were still playing *waltzes*! So when Bob started talking about rhythm 'n' blues, I knew what he was talking about. I was very happy when Bob said to me: 'Why don't you come over to my house and listen to some records?'"

The friendship blossomed. "I thought at first maybe he just liked me as a friend. This was the way it was—even if we were sweethearts, we were still friends. The first time I met him I asked if he was

Jewish. He just changed the subject." The Zimmermans were courteous to Echo, but kept telling Bob she wasn't good enough for him. Bob's romanticism led him to dramatize their liaison: after a few open, after-school visits, he always sneaked Echo in and out of his home. "He didn't want me talking with his mother very much. The few times I met his father, he was nice to me, but my mother sensed she was disliked in his store, and stopped going there." Once, when Bob thought the house was empty, his grandmother came in suddenly. He hid Echo in a closet and rushed to greet his granny, telling her he was going to the library. Echo followed his instructions by crawling through an upstairs door to a porch over the garage. "With my skirt up to my neck, I hung from the railing until Bobby ran round the back of the garage to help me down. He really loved playing those little games."

Echo's mother was warm toward Bob, but her father, Matt Helstrom, an ailing, embittered painter and welder, a keen hunter and woodsman, didn't approve. One evening, Echo was tending her nephew while John and Bob put on a cowboy and Indian show. "All of a sudden, my father's car drove up. John and Bob leapt out of the front door just as my dad walked in the back. You could hear them crunching on the gravel, and my father went chasing after the sound. 'Someone was here!' my father shouted. I said no one had been there. Bob could never be over when my father was around. Long after Bob had made a million dollars, my dad felt maybe he'd been a nice guy after all. My father had three guitars, one of them with an amplifier. Sometimes Bob would sneak over to play that one. One time, Bob told me that he had a test to prove if I would make a good wife. I had to bake something, so I made him a pizza. And I sewed a tear in a pair of his slacks. I don't remember if there were any other requirements."

The Helstrom house was a box-like, tar-paper shanty on Highway 73, three miles southwest of Hibbing. Often, Bob hitchhiked out there from school. When he had his little blue Ford, they could ride south to the top of Maple Hill. There they looked out for thirty miles across the Iron Range. They drove or hiked along Fire Tower Road, a rutted lane, to the summit, dotted with white birch. At night, the air was crisp and heady, and stars lighted the sky. Mrs Helstrom said later: "They had their dreams to get married and live on Maple Hill. They planned to call their child Bob, whether it was a boy or a girl. You know how teenagers are. They were so young, though. Girls are always ready to marry younger than boys are."

In the afternoon, if Matt Helstrom was away, Echo and Bob would laze in front of the shack. Bob crouched on the wooden stairs with a guitar in his lap, while his golden-haired girl sat in a little wooden swing, gently keeping time with a pendulum motion. Bob improvised verses. "The songs he sang to me," recalled Echo, "were mostly rhythm 'n' blues or talking blues. He didn't repeat the lyrics the way most singers did. His phrases were always different and they almost always told a story." By 1968, the swing was heavily rusted and weather-beaten, but it still swayed in the breeze from Maple Hill. I felt the swing was "Rosebud," the reporter's long-sought clue to lost childhood in *Citizen Kane*.

"John and Bob used to do a lot of talking blues. Sometimes they did a hillbilly take-off of a song like 'Somewhere Over the Rainbow.' They were always trying to teach and learn from each other. I believed in him when nobody else did. When he was singing to me alone, you could see the talent, but whenever he would go out to perform, the amplifiers would be up so high that you couldn't hear him." Echo followed him from one performance to another. The Sunday jams at Van Feldt's moved to Collier's Barbecue. Other audiences were less enthusiastic. "One time they really booed Bob was at the St Louis County Fair in Hibbing in the summer of 1958. There was a combination of laughing and booing." Did he tell her that he would spend his life in music? "That was the whole plan. He didn't tell that to anybody else because he didn't have anyone but John and me to talk to. He had casual friends, but he was always secretive like that. I remember when he decided what his name was going to be. It was 1958, and he was just a junior. He came over with John Bucklen one day and said: 'I know what I'm going to call myself. I've got this great name—Bob Dillon.'"

He didn't change his name legally until 1962, and didn't even begin to use it regularly until 1959. Ethel Merman, also saddled with the rather ungainly luggage of "Zimmerman," simply lopped off the first syllable, remarking: "Can you imagine the name Zimmerman in bright lights? It would burn you to death!" Bob's new name probably had two sources. Although Matt Dillon is thought to be a real frontier hero, he was the fictional invention of television writer John Meaton and producer Norman Macdonnel for the adventure series *Gunsmoke*. The show began in 1952 on Columbia Broadcasting System radio, and premiered as a CBS-TV series on September 10, 1955. Closer to Dylan's home frontier was a pioneer Hibbing family named Dillion. A James Dillion was the town's first drayman. Four families named Dillon were listed in the 1968 Hibbing phone book. Bob parried about the Dillions with a reporter from the *Chicago Daily News* in November 1965:

CDN: *What about the story that you changed your name from Bob Zimmerman to Bob Dylan because you admired the poetry of Dylan Thomas?*
Dylan: *No, God, no. I took Dylan because I have an uncle named Dillion. I changed the spelling, but only because it looked better. I've read some of Dylan Thomas's stuff, and it's not the same as mine.*

Dylan reiterated this popular misconception to me: "Straighten out in your book that I did not take my name from Dylan Thomas. Dylan Thomas's poetry is for people that aren't really satisfied in their bed, for people who dig masculine romance." Although he registered at the University of Minnesota as Robert Zimmerman, students and friends there knew him as Dillon. He told a few friends that Dillon was his mother's maiden name. Others heard that Dillon was a town in Oklahoma. Only after he had achieved some early recognition in New York did Minneapolis friends learn that Bob was spelling his name Dylan. In the interim, he had become acquainted with the life and work of Dylan Thomas.

Echo saw why Bob distanced himself from his family: "His family was trying too hard to form him and he wasn't about to be formed in any manner. I remember how much Bob hated having to sweep up in his dad's shop. I know Bob was afraid of his father, although he never said he hit him. His parents couldn't understand his making a pile of dough with his poetry. I don't think his father gave him all that much money. I think I had more money than he had. Sure, he had all the necessities, but no spending money. That is why I had to buy him all those hot dogs."

Echo and John doted on Bob's humor, on his sense of the ludicrous. Echo: "He was always thinking of something to laugh about." John: "He had a fantastic ability to put people on. You never knew exactly when to believe him." One of the boys' favorite games was hitchhiking. They parked Bob's car near Echo's place and hitchhiked along Highway 73 to see how far they could get. Echo patiently waited for them to return by a car or truck coming from the opposite direction. Bob played a word game he christened Glissendorf. They played it for Echo's cousin, a simple country girl, who nearly cried because she couldn't understand it. Another game was "telephone mental telepathy." Bob would call Echo, tell her he had his mind fixed on some object in his house. If she guessed correctly what it was, he would say this confirmed his belief in telepathy and his ability to put ideas into others' minds.

Bob often pretended to be musically precocious. "He called me and told me he was going to play something he had recorded. He played Bobby Freeman's 'Do You Want to Dance.' He said: 'That was us.' I know now that it couldn't have been one of Bob's bands. He was always making up fantasies and telling little fibs." One of Bob's games always ended seriously. He'd joke with some itinerant musician, then start firing questions about work, life on the road, arrangements, band discipline, pop trends, and get the musician to tell him all he knew.

Echo had no more affection for Hibbing than Bob did: "I couldn't wait to get away. There is a terrible unfriendliness in Hibbing you don't find in other small towns. I think other Iron Range towns are like that because of similar economic problems. After we graduated, the mines almost closed down. So we nearly all got out of town."

The three friends sympathized with working-class people. Mrs Helstrom remembered: "Bob seemed much more humble than his family. Both Echo and Bob seemed so sorry for the working people." She and Echo recalled how interested Bob was in John Steinbeck. In 1968, Echo kept his books on a shelf. "We used to talk a lot about Steinbeck. Bob was always reading something by him—*Grapes of Wrath*, *Cannery Row*. *Grapes of Wrath* gave him his strong feelings for the Depression Okies.

"I was also surprised that Bob had anything to do with me because I had originally thought that Jewish people had *nothing* to do with other people. Bob never talked about being Jewish. I really sensed that the Jewish people in Hibbing felt they were different from others, but I know that Bob didn't want to be separated from anyone. He really loved Negro people like Jim Dandy, even though there were so few around. Bob always used to come back from Minneapolis impressed by the way the colored people danced and made music."

For the junior prom at Hibbing High, Echo bought a pale-blue floor length gown. She kept the corsage Bob brought her until the flowers turned dry and crumbling. In the 1958 Hibbing High yearbook, Bob declared: "Let me tell you that your beauty is second to none, but I think I told you that before. Love to the most beautiful girl in school." They went to the prom, outsiders passing through the mainstream. Echo: "We were so different, we shouldn't have even been there. We really couldn't dance. Bob was a poor leader, and I am a poor follower. He would take little teeny steps and kept saying to me: 'What's wrong with you? What's the matter?' And I said: 'I can't dance with you.' It was just horrible. But we were just there together, with each other. Bob wasn't skinny then. He was more cheeky and had a little bit of a tummy. I thought he was really cute. He was really the clean-cut kid, well scrubbed with rosy cheeks. After the prom we didn't go to any of the parties. We just sat in Bob's car and fell asleep. We weren't like the other people at school in any way. I just couldn't stand being like other girls. I had to be different."

By summer 1958, they had moved in opposite directions emotionally. Echo wanted to marry; Bob wanted to travel and pursue his music, to date other girls. Echo became increasingly possessive; Bob was restless. When he wanted to go to the movies, he entered first, insisting Echo join him inside later. He spent as much time as he could in Duluth or the Twin Cities. By the time he inscribed her 1958 school yearbook, he was already alluding to "St Paul girls."

John, a secret admirer of Echo, suffered divided loyalties. Echo pressed John to tell her if Bob was seeing other girls. John: "I told her it was probably true." Echo decided the situation was too painful and returned Bob's bracelet in a school corridor. "I can still see his eyes—they got so big. 'What are you doing?' he asked. I said: 'Goodbye.' He said: 'Don't do this here in the hall.'" Later, at her house, she demanded to know if Bob was dating others. He said no, but Echo chose to believe John. "Bob needs an awful lot of attention from females."

She spent the summer of 1958 reliving their moments together. She walked up to Maple Hill, but the view didn't look the same alone. She sat on that swing, remembering his voice, singing. "He always said later that he couldn't marry because he had his career to think of. If he hadn't had that determination to make something big of himself, he probably would have married me. He would have ended up doing what his father wanted—working in the furniture store." A decade later, Mrs Helstrom said: "When Echo plays Bob's records, she feels she is still talking with him." John Sebastian, formerly of the Lovin' Spoonful, once told me: "You can't get too close to Dylan. He burns with such a bright flame you can get burned." Echo Helstrom was the first of many people who got too close.

She saw Bob briefly in Minneapolis in autumn 1959, hoping they might revive their romance. When the Hibbing High School class of 1959 held its tenth reunion, two unexpected classmates appeared separately—Echo, and Dylan, who was there with his wife. Five years earlier, Bob had told Chris Welles of *Life*: "The teachers in school taught me everything was fine. That was the accepted thing to think. It was in all the books. But it ain't fine, man. There are so many lies that have been told, so many things that are kept back. Kids have a feeling like me, but they ain't hearing it no place. They're scared to step out. But I ain't scared to do it, man."

So Dylan returned for a moment of quiet triumph, the school's most notable graduate since Francis Bellamy, who wrote the Pledge of Allegiance to the American flag. Bob was besieged by old friends demanding autographs. He signed one for Echo, too.

A Wreath for Buddy Holly. Bob was keen to begin his last year of school because he was keen to get out. "It won't be long now," he told John Bucklen. He slid off the honor roll three times. When Beatty chided him, he snapped: "The honor roll isn't everything." He experimented with drinking and smoking. One time, Bucklen recalled, Bob had been off drinking somewhere on his own and telephoned: "John, I'm going to come over there and kick the hell out of you." John replied: "OK, let's go. I'll wait outside for you." His would-be assailant hove into sight, weaving back and forth. "He swung and hit me in the jaw, but he was in such bad shape that the punch didn't hurt at all. I finally got him home safely. All of a sudden Bob had discovered what it was like to get drunk often."

By the time he went to Minneapolis, Bob preferred wine. In October 1964, he still thought wine was best for Joan Baez, Gregory Corso, Allen Ginsberg, Ornette Coleman, and the other guests at the party he gave after his Philharmonic Hall concert. Our genial host offered us row upon bottled row of Beaujolais. In his first years around the Village, Bob often gave the impression of being high on wine. Suze Rotolo told me: "I don't think I ever saw him sober for quite a while after our first meeting. But half of that was put on. He could watch and listen better to what was going on if people thought he was high."

Even cold sober, young Bob was prone to car accidents. Although his father could later make light of the car problem, it deeply wrenched their relationship. "Bob always had a standard answer for any damage he did to a car. He would call and say: 'I broke the fan belt.'" After one accident, Abe had to settle a claim out of court for $4,000. The worst accident occurred in 1958. Bob had decided to sell his motorcycle, but wanted to take one final ride. As he slowly turned toward home, a three-year-old boy holding an orange ran into the street from between two parked cars and collided with the side of the motorcycle. Hibbing Hospital said the child needed further care, and Abe arranged for an ambulance to Duluth. The child recovered, but Abe regarded Bob and the motorcycle as a deadly mixture. The evening of the accident, Bob met Echo downtown and vowed he'd never ride a bike again. He told Echo several times: "I can still see that orange rolling across the street."

During his senior year, Bob's career plans were crystallizing. He joined a cousin's little band, the Satin Tones, a rough-edged group that played one number on a TV station in Superior, Wisconsin, one dance at Hibbing Armory, and one tape on Hibbing radio. Bucklen: "He was always getting together groups like the Golden Chords and the Satin Tones. He had an uncanny talent for finding an opportunity and taking advantage of it." Bob began to admire Muddy Waters and Jimmy Reed, two Chicago bluesmen up from the South, and white country stars who went into "rockabilly." A new and lasting musical model emerged—Buddy Holly. Bob began to imitate Holly's sweet, naive, almost childlike voice. The vocal quality of many Dylan recordings shows his debt to Holly.

Holly could sing in a belting style like Presley's, or in the sinuous, yearning, "little-boy-lost" voice that turned on 1950s teens, enunciating the yearning quality of youth music. Charles Hardin Holley was born in Lubbock, Texas, in 1936, and by the age of 15, as Buddy Holly, was playing the West Texas club circuit. After a contract at Decca, where nothing happened, Holly and his band, the Crickets, signed on with Norman Petty, who ran a studio in Clovis, New Mexico. With Petty's expertise, they converted an earlier flop into a million-selling hit, "That'll Be the Day." By 1958, Holly's hits—"Peggy Sue," "Rave On," "Early in the Morning"—were sprinkled all over the American and British charts. Holly's influence on the Beatles was probably close to that of Little Richard and the Everly Brothers. Dylan and his mates could identify easily with Holly—another small-town boy; young, slight, vulnerable. Imagine the excitement on January 31, 1959, when Holly and musician Link Wray appeared at the Duluth Armory. (Dylan visited Wray in 1975 and told him: "Link, I was sitting in the front row when you and Buddy Holly were at Duluth, and you're as great now as you were then.") Onstage, Buddy Holly could have passed for Bob's older brother. Hank Williams and Dean were dead, Little Richard and Brando never came anywhere near Hibbing, but here was Buddy Holly right up in the North Country![12]

Only three days after Dylan had seen him, Buddy Holly was dead. The shock was brutal. Bob and his friends studied details of the tragedy. At 1 a.m. on February 3, 1959, a Beechcraft Bonanza, chartered in Mason City, Iowa, took off in light snow for Fargo, North Dakota. Trouble developed in minutes, probably because the 21-year-old pilot couldn't cope with the weather and instruments. The left wing hit the ground first. Killed instantly were the pilot and three musicians, Holly, 22; Ritchie Valens, 17, a Mexican-American whose biggest hit was "La Bamba"; and J P Richardson, 24, who was called the Big Bopper. The deaths had a traumatic effect on Bob. He was no longer a boy brimming with life as much as a young man haunted by death. He acted liked his time was limited. All the car and motorcycle accidents pointed to it. "I was burned with death around me," Dylan said in 1965. Gretel Whitaker, a friend from the University of Minnesota, said: "We never really expected Bobby to live past twenty-one." By the time Bob was 19, he had written a mournful blues, "One Eyed Jacks," passed on to me by Minneapolis friends:

The queen of his diamonds
And the jack his knave
Won't you dig my grave
With a silver spade?
And forget my name.
I'm twenty years old.
That's twenty years gone.

Can't you see my crying,
Can't you see my dying,
I'll never reach twenty-one …

There was a curious footnote to Buddy Holly's death. The Fargo concert manager desperately searched for a fill-in act for Holly. He found two brothers, Sidney and Bill Velline, in nearby Moorhead, Minnesota. The 2,500 kids who turned out to hear Buddy Holly heard the Velline brothers' band. The Vellines let their kid brother, Bobby, sit in. Bobby Velline told the concert manager the band was called the Shadows—a name the high-school sophomore had just invented. Bobby Velline, his name shortened to Bobby Vee, soon became the bandleader. With $500 saved up from a few dances, the Shadows cut four sides for the Soma label in Minneapolis. One of those sides, "Suzy Baby," featured Bobby Vee, singing like Holly. The Shadows later searched around Fargo for a piano player. Someone suggested a kid who had spent the early summer of 1959 as a busboy at the Red Apple Cafe in Fargo. "There were very few rock piano players around," Vee told me in London in 1969. "We gave Bob Zimmerman a chance to work with us, and he played great—in the key of C. His style was sort of like Jerry Lee Lewis. Bob worked two dances with us in Fargo. But we decided that we weren't really making enough money to cut in another member."

Bobby Vee's "Suzy Baby" went on to be a hit in the Midwest. Bobby Dylan came home one night in the rain on a bus from Fargo, but told no one but his family that his first professional chance had failed. He told Bucklen and others that he was the star of the "Suzy Baby" record, and repeated the story in Minneapolis. No one took it too seriously, but no one could challenge it.

The Graduate. Abe and Beatty were radiant at their son's graduation. By early 1959, it had been agreed that Bob would go to the University of Minnesota, the only "acceptable" way to get out of town. Beatty reluctantly admitted there was really nothing much to keep him and gave the biggest graduation party in town. Arrangements moved along with only one hitch—the guest of honor wasn't coming. He was going out with the boys. His mother thought he should come round for fifteen minutes, at least, because she wouldn't call off the party. "To make a long story short, he came home with us."

There is a striking similarity between this party and the one that opened the Mike Nichols-Dustin Hoffman film, *The Graduate*: both were more for the parents than for the sons. Abe: "Robert just couldn't understand a party like this was customary. I told him: 'This is a milestone. You only graduate high school once, you only graduate college once.' He said: 'If I do come, I won't be here very long.' But he stayed, and he felt good that all these people had come." Were any of Bob's friends or fellow musicians invited? "No," Abe replied. "We had neighbors and family. During graduation, the kids have their own parties. All you expect the children to do is to make an appearance. Bob stayed around much longer than we expected. He didn't know half of the people who came to celebrate his graduation, but they knew him."

At midnight, Bob went out—supposedly to see some friends. In fact, he just walked the streets of Hibbing. At 2 a.m. he returned, as Beatty and a cleaning woman were straightening the house. "Wasn't it a nice party?" his mother asked. He admitted it had been. His mother's crowning recollection of her son, the graduate, was: "He was always a gentleman at all times. He might have been a little contrary sometimes, but he was always nice to people. We really loved that party, and we were so proud to have such a courteous boy." The dining room table was heaped with gifts from strangers. Among them was a set of 78s of Leadbelly, who had died in 1949. The recordings of the forceful Louisiana singer, discovered in a southern jail by folk collectors John and Alan Lomax, were a revelation. With only his voice and his twelve-string guitar, Leadbelly filled Bob's head with "Rock Island Line," "Take This Hammer," "Green Corn," and "Midnight Special." The words meant more than most pop lyrics. Bob reveled in the musical storytelling.

Bucklen: "Bob almost shouted over the phone: 'I've discovered something great! You got to come over here!'" They listened, and Bob was flabbergasted. "'This is the thing, this is the thing,' he repeated. Leadbelly was too simple for me in 1959. There was another example of Bob's being way ahead of us all. That afternoon with Bob and Leadbelly was my first real indication that Bobby Zimmerman was turning into Bob Dylan." Leadbelly was a bad man too. He was a black Paul Bunyan who had served time for murder. A father-figure of American folk song, blues and work songs, he led Bob to the roots of the first folk-song revival of the late 1950s. The attraction to Leadbelly was brief, just long enough to open the door to folk music and whatever lay beyond.

After graduation, Bob headed down to Minneapolis to play university student. He returned perhaps a half-dozen times, on school holidays, or on trips from New York with some new triumph to report. In spring 1964, Bob made a brief appearance when David graduated from Hibbing High. Bonn Rolfsen was struck then by Bob's reserve in the same auditorium where he had outraged everyone with his music. Bonn: "He was so popular then that if he'd wanted, he could have torn the town apart. He sought no special attention. He appeared to be under a terrific amount of strain, smoking continuously and very nervous. He was wound up like a tight clock, because he had been doing nothing but driving himself."

The trips became more infrequent and, after 1964, he returned only twice, to my knowledge. There'd been postcards, and telephone calls at all hours from stray places on the road, but Bob had nearly washed Hibbing out of his mind. In 1963, Walter Eldot, Sunday features editor of the *Duluth News-Tribune*, quoted Abe:

"My son is a corporation and his public image is strictly an act," says his father… Playing around Minneapolis, usually without pay, he began to develop his present stage character—with the folk-style attire and accent that go with it. "That is," says his father, "what we found so disturbing and still do. But it's all part of the act."

… About that time, his father came to a definite understanding about Bobby's future. "He wanted to have free rein," says Zimmerman. "He wanted to be a folk singer, an entertainer. We couldn't see it, but we felt he was entitled to the chance. It's his life, after all, and we didn't want to stand in the way. So we made an agreement that he could have one year to do as he pleased, and if at the end of that year we were not satisfied with his progress, he'd go back to school."

Later in 1963, Eldot was legman for a *Newsweek* piece that drove Bob farther from his family. He raged over the telephone to his parents about the two articles. He warned them not to speak to anyone without his approval. This was too difficult for Abe. As late as spring 1968, he still had to tell his version. To Jules Siegel, for the *Saturday Evening Post*, Abe said:

"I used to make him go out to the poor sections to make repossessions… knowing he couldn't collect any money from those people. I just wanted to show him another side of life. He'd come back and say: 'Dad, those people haven't got any money.' And I'd say, 'Some of those people out there make as much money as I do, Bobby. They just don't know how to manage it.'"

The Helstroms, John Bucklen's mother, and Jim Dandy, taught Bob more about poor people than Abe did. Abe, a likable fellow, couldn't help resembling George Babbitt.

The Rotary: Will the Circle Be Unbroken? By spring 1968, Abe was in much better spirits about Bob, but he still felt compelled to tell friends and neighbors that no one saw Bob because he flew his private jet into Hibbing late at night and took off early the next morning. The story saved the father's face and added to the son's mystique. Despite the fact that Bob hadn't been home in four years, the story of the night flights so took hold around Hibbing that some swore they knew someone who had seen the plane.

In the fall of 1967, Abe and Beatty visited Bob and his family in Woodstock, New York. Their famous son was no longer playing orphan. The fact that Bob had married and had a growing family was, by their standards, as much a success story as anything that had happened in the intervening years. Abe took me to dinner in New York a few days later, keen to let me know that there had been a rapprochement in Woodstock. He had already begun to rewrite his own history when I first met him in 1966. No longer was he the square father who thought pop music was nonsense. Behind his shop counter, awaiting the next customer, he would study the latest copy of *Billboard*, the music-trade weekly. "By all means, let's have dinner together tonight. And there's a Rotary luncheon tomorrow at the Androy. If you want to see the best of Hibbing, you have to see the Rotary in action." The manner was soft, but I knew it was an offer I couldn't refuse.

Abe conducted me through a dozen introductions to pillars of the community. He had an easy conviviality, a few personal words to everyone, first-name regards to each wife. After lunch, Paul Harris, a leading lawyer in town, had a few thousand words to say about Rotary's objectives: "One: Service above self. You really should get to know your friends and neighbors. Two: High ethical standards in business. Be proud of what you do. Three: Involvement. Make time for as many community projects as you can." There was a unison rendering of "America" (Clyde Hill, the chapter's choir director wanted "just a little more spirit"), followed by "Rotary," the order's theme song and, finally, "The Battle Hymn of the Republic." Cigar smoke swirled about the room, fanned by forty voices singing full blast. "The Rotary in Woodstock," Abe told me, as he walked out uplifted, "meets Monday nights, so I couldn't get there last time we visited Bobby."

Perhaps Hibbing looked a little different to you if you didn't belong to Rotary or Kiwanis. Perhaps the town was a vacuum if you didn't join the Moose Club, Odd Fellows, Veterans of World War I Auxiliary No 2039, Tenger Lodge of the Vasa Order of America, Bethel No 4 Order of Job's Daughters, the Tuesday Musicale, the First Settlers of Hibbing, the Izaak Walton League, the Hibbing Figure Skating Club, the Wells-Woodland Garden Club, the Mesaba Rosarians, the Guglielmo Marconi Lodge No 1164 of the Sons of Italy, the Hibbing St Francis Court No 610 of the National Catholic Society of Foresters, or the Bunker Willing Workers 4-H Club, B'Nai B'Rith, or the Chamber of Commerce.

Jim Hitchcock was chairman of the Chamber of Commerce in 1966 and publisher of the *Hibbing Tribune*. He admitted the town had seen hard times, but "we're on the comeback trail now. Yes," he said, sadly, "the loss of our youth has been a major problem." According to Hitchcock, Hibbing had three prominent products besides iron ore: Jeno Paulucci, whose Chun King Corporation, packagers of pizza and Chinese food, had recently been sold for millions; Roger Maris, the ballplayer; and Bobby Dylan.

"I know that the town is a little mystified by Dylan. Roger Maris always says he is from Fargo, North Dakota, and gets mad when people say he's from Hibbing. People here are happy that Bob is from Hibbing, even if he is offbeat." Had the town fathers ever invited Bob to do a concert? "No formal invitation ever went out to Bobby, as far as I know. If we knew when he was coming, we'd ask him to perform." Had the *Hibbing Tribune* ever done a feature story about Bob Dylan? "No, I don't think so." In its ambitious seventy-fifth anniversary issue of August 10, 1968, the *Tribune* ran scores of articles about the virtues of Hibbing. Dylan's name never came up.

When Bob was growing up, there was Rotary talk, Chamber of Commerce talk, and sanctimonious "God Bless Our Home" talk at home. In retrospect, did Beatty and Abe know why Bob became the most renowned youth rebel of the 1960s? Dad: "He didn't really rebel. He convinced himself that he had something different to sell." Mom: "Yes, he convinced himself. We didn't. We certainly didn't. You cannot make it anywhere, except in New York." Did they think he left in anger? "Oh, no, he didn't leave in anger," they replied.

In the context of late 1950s parent-child relationships in a thousand Hibbings, Abe and Beatty were not exceptionally square, but their son's heightened sensibilities made them seem so. By the spring of 1968, Abe and Beatty were trying to put it all in context. When asked how they thought their "nice, courteous, mannerly boy" had developed into the most outspoken symbol of youth rebellion in a generation, they could only say: "This is what disturbed us." Abe: "At the time, he was influencing some of the kids in a way he should not have been doing. I think he was a rebel with a cause. He wanted to do things for people, but in a speedy way. He could not seem to understand why these things, why these changes, take time." Beatty: "Even when he was at home he was concerned about the under-privileged. He wanted to give a helping hand to people all the time." Bob had watched *Rebel Without a Cause* a dozen times. What was their reaction to the film? Abe: "I thought it was overdone. I didn't think kids were like this, to tell the truth. Either they were worse than that, or they were much better." Doesn't every kid rebel—didn't you rebel? Beatty: "We didn't rebel, we went along. We knew that our parents were doing the very best that they could for us." Abe: "We were sometimes disappointed by what our parents made us do. We complained or cried a little bit, but eventually we did what we were told."

Abe took me around the house. In the basement recreation room, where Bob's James Dean collection once lined the walls, the parents now had a gallery of their own young rebel: posters, album covers, and publicity and magazine photographs of Dylan. His parents played me old practice tapes of his various high-school bands. Bob's young, harsh voice belted out "Rock 'n' Roll Is Here to Stay." Piles of moldering 78s and 45s stood in a corner, a cross-section of the 1950s. Here was "Dearest" and "There Ought to Be a Law" by Mickey and Sylvia, "Baby Blue" by Gene Vincent and the Hot Rods, Hank Snow, and Nat "King" Cole. Then a flood of Hank Williams' lonesome blues, Bill Haley, Pat

Boone, Bobby Vee, Johnny Ace, Webb Pierce, and, inevitably, Buddy Holly's "Slippin' and Slidin'," Little Richard's "Tutti Frutti," and Presley's "Heartbreak Hotel" and "Blue Suede Shoes."

Abe steered me up to Bob's room, passing on the stairway wall a picture of puffy-cheeked Bob with a neat tie—his graduation picture. Abe: "Both boys shared this room. We had twin beds in here. You would never know where either of them was sleeping. At first, we had a western motif on the walls, horses and saddles, but it's been painted over several times." Abe drew out several albums of family pictures. Almost startled at their number, he remarked: "I wonder if there is any money in these things."

He leafed through: "Here's a picture of Bobby playing bullfighter, holding a bathroom towel as a cape. He was about twelve here. These are priceless now. Here he is playing the bongo. Here is the medicine he used to take for his asthma. He doesn't have too much trouble with that now. Here's the room when it had the cowboy wallpaper. Bobby was fifteen when he posed with a cowboy hat on and a cigarette dangling out of his mouth. I sent the picture to him a while ago with his photo from the ad for *Don't Look Back*. It had exactly the same expression. Here we are at the Paul Bunyan site at the headwaters of the Mississippi. Yes, he liked those tall tales of Paul Bunyan."

What about Bob's fascination with badmen and outlaws? "Oh, yes, he was fascinated. That's true. Everyone was interested in those badmen. I was myself … Here are all those *Illustrated Classics*—*Cyrano*, *The Hunchback of Notre Dame*, *The Corsican Brothers*, *The Pathfinder*." Did he know Bob had done a series of drawings for Victor Hugo's *Les Misérables* when he was a boy? "No, I didn't know that. Wonder where they might be now?" Abe leafed through the memorabilia with a mixture of pride and sadness. So much time had passed and so much had happened since Bob left home.

Did Abe think that Bob would ever come back to Hibbing? There was a long pause, then: "Here's a picture of Bobby as a Boy Scout." "Do you think he will come back to Hibbing one day, or don't you know, Abe?" He went on leafing through the photographs. Three weeks later, Dylan went back to Hibbing for the first time in four years. Abe's son had returned to attend his father's funeral.

Kaddish. Abe suffered his first heart attack in summer 1966, shortly after Bob's motorcycle accident. It was a mild attack, but it forced him to cut down. However, no doctor could cure Abe of worry over his boys, of his public image as a father. In spring 1968, he had a new family problem: David's impending marriage to a Catholic. "When my boys make mistakes, they make big ones," Abe told me a few weeks before he died. The wedding, scheduled for the last week in May, was postponed.

On the morning of June 5, Abe awoke feeling weak and "strange." He stayed home, taking it easy. He was not feeling any better by the time Beatty returned from work. A little after 5 p.m., Abe suffered a fatal heart attack, collapsing on the living room sofa as Beatty summoned their neighboring doctor. At first, Bob was reluctant to appear, lest it charge the funeral's atmosphere. He flew in alone the next day on a commercial flight. David met him at the Hibbing-Chisholm airport in drizzling rain. Bob had on the round black hat he wore on the cover of *John Wesley Harding*. He and David found the house filled with relatives and neighbors. Within minutes, Bob steered his mother and brother into a corner: "This isn't a garden party. Let's get these people out of here." Beatty explained that this was the mourning tradition. Bob insisted the family should be by themselves.

David was struck by Bob's demeanor. His older brother seemed to have quietude, firmness, and serenity befitting "a fifty-year-old man." When the two discussed the funeral, David was startled by Bob's familiarity with Jewish ritual, especially Kaddish, the Hebrew prayer through which the parent's soul benefits from a surviving son's piety. Early on Friday morning, David and Bob went to the Dougherty Funeral Home on First Avenue. Upon seeing his father's body, Bob, previously restrained, was deeply upset. He took the death harder than either Beatty or David, as if he were caught up by all the things he and his father had never been able to say. ("I never knew my father," Bob later told Woody Guthrie's former agent.) By the time the funeral home opened to the lines of mourners, Bob, again his controlled self, stood in one corner, taking it all in like a camera.

Two years before Abe died, Bob spewed out to me in choppy guillotine cuts his thoughts on death and suicide: "I just know that I've been at it too long. I've been at it longer than a fifty-year-old man. Hey, death to me is nothing, as long as I can die fast. Many times I've known I could have died fast. There was a time when I was afraid of dying. I'll admit to having this suicidal thing. I've been living under a suicidal hex now for the last six months.

"I was actually most afraid of death in those first years around New York. When I started writing all those songs and everyone started calling me a genius—genius this and genius that. I knew it was bull, because I still hadn't written what I wanted to. I had written 'Blowin' in the Wind,' but I wasn't satisfied with that. I was never satisfied with 'Blowin' in the Wind.' I wrote that in ten minutes. 'Blowin' in the Wind' was a lucky classic song. No more, no less than 'Your Cheatin' Heart.' But it was one-dimensional.

"I've really got a sickness, man. I don't write when I'm feeling groovy, you understand. I play when I'm feeling groovy. I write when I'm sick. I'm not going to push that on anybody. Man, nobody knows what is the matter with me, and I'm not about to go tell anybody. If I had ever been like Woody Guthrie in his situation, I don't know what I would do. A living decay. I can't decay. I would not let myself decay. I'm against decay. That's nature's will—decay. I am against nature. I don't dig nature at all. I think nature is very unnatural. I think the truly natural things are dreams, which nature can't touch with decay.

"I was so frightened of death when I was in New York. I wasn't turning out anything. Everything I turned out could be done better tomorrow. I did not want to die. I would ride on airplanes not wanting to die, because I just had to get something said. Because I knew people were going to listen. I don't want to see myself die. I don't want to hear myself dying, or taste myself or smell myself dying. All this talk about equality. The only thing people really have in common is that they are all going to die."

At the synagogue service, Bob wore a gray double-breasted suit with jade cuff links, a white tie, and the traditional skullcap, a final concession to his mother. He had wanted to wear his *John Wesley Harding* hat, which could have passed for the black hat worn by some pious Jewish sects. The rabbi concluded the service and most of the mourners prepared for the long ride to the cemetery in Duluth. Beatty, David, and Bob were silent most of the trip.

That afternoon, David took Bob for a drive around Hibbing in the rain. Bob let the town pass before his eyes like a long, silent movie flashback. He passed the hill where some boys had once put up a small sign: HIBBING, MINNESOTA—HOMETOWN OF BOB DYLAN. It was Thomas Wolfe's Asheville and Sinclair Lewis's Sauk Centre. Bob told David the town looked like a giant funeral parlor to him. Again, David was struck by his brother's serenity, "So calm, so reserved, so clean … almost so saintly!" That night, Bob asked to see a few of his old friends. Bonn Rolfsen and Father Michael Hayes of the Catholic Church up Seventh Avenue came by. The priest had been teaching Bob's songs, and their meaning, to his students. The childhood friends had disappeared. Echo, John Bucklen, and Monte Edwardson were gone. And so was Bobby Zimmerman. A stranger in his own house, who, he said, "no longer felt himself the same person he had been in Hibbing," spoke to his visitors gently, courteously.

Beatty was pleased that Bob could stay on until the following Tuesday. He urged her to sell the house and think about doing something different to readjust. They talked about the early years, and Bob assured her that she and Abe had been good parents. To the outsider, Beatty and Abe *had* been good parents. Had they acted differently, had they not resisted him at crucial points, could they have been the diving board from which he sprang? Didn't they give him the impetus to run, the cause to rebel, the materials from which to build his own special personality? The "saintly" son who came home to bury Abe was proof that he and Beatty had not failed as parents. Beatty told Bob that all the family money was frozen until the estate was settled. Bob took out his checkbook and wrote her a five-figure check. Beatty and David were staggered. She insisted: "Bobby, I don't want to deny your children anything." "I can always do a couple of concerts."

Over the weekend, Bob slept in his father's old bedroom, and spent hours poring over his childhood memorabilia—the comics, *Illustrated Classics*, the photographs, the old recordings, the home tapes. Some people around Hibbing now found him amazingly like his father: he was somewhat stern with his children, careful then with his money, reserved and conservative in manner. Could he have become what he had so long opposed?

His wife was expecting another baby, and Bob had to be on hand. On his way to the airport, he took one final swing down Howard Street, passing the window of a drugstore, where, weeks earlier, a visitor to Hibbing had been startled by the juxtaposition of two paperback books. *Don't Look Back*, drawn from the film starring Dylan, was right next to a novel called *The Runaway*.

Top: Greetings from Hibbing, 1940s.
Above and right: High-school photos of Robert Allen Zimmerman before he left
Minnesota for New York.

The old saw around Minneapolis was that Dylan was a pathological liar.
I don't think this was true. Dylan was just a romantic. He remembered
what should have been. He walked around here like a young Shelley.

HARRY WEBER, 1966

Dylan was his own guru.
After learning what he could from others, he taught himself.

DAVE MORTON, 1966

His old self, from Minneapolis,
and what he became in the East, are two different people.

PAUL NELSON, 1968

"How does it feel
To be on your own
With no direction home
Like a complete unknown
Like a rolling stone?"

DYLAN, 1965[1]

Left: Dylan in the studio, August 1963.
Right: Dylan, no longer "a complete unknown," soon after he arrived in New York, 1962.

The highway was a key Dylan used to unlock one of the doors to his future. He arrived at the University of Minnesota on Highway 61, took byways, blind alleys, and detours, and left the University of Dinkytown on Highway 12.

By summer 1959, he was traveling so fast that maps, itinerary and chronology flew out the window. Sometime after his abortive encounter with Bobby Vee in Fargo, Dylan ended up in a reconstructed nineteenth-century gold-mining boom town high in the Rockies, singing in a sleazy striptease joint a thousand miles from home and college. Bob and his family told me he went to Denver and Central City, Colorado, before enrolling at Minnesota, Others have placed him in Colorado in summer 1960. Maybe he was there twice. I *know* he returned in early 1964, and I was with him there in March 1966 (*see Chapter 10*), when he went back to Central City, a museum-without-walls of the American frontier.

In 1959, Bob heard from one of the Golden Chords, Monte Edwardson, that there was a lively folk-music scene around Denver. He decided to try his luck there. He plunged into the coffeehouse folk scene on his own. The Exodus Gallery Bar at 1999 Lincoln Street was the focal point for local beats, artists, and poets, and a sprinkling of button-down college kids. Denver's trendies gravitated to the Exodus for art shows, poetry readings, and folk sessions. Dylan tiptoed around for a few weeks. It seemed like the big time. There was a Kingston Trio offshoot, the Harlin Trio—three crew-cut undergraduates— consistently dull and unoriginal. Other local talent included George Downing, a math teacher who sang drowsy cowboy songs. Dave Wood, a graduate student at Boulder, imitated Mexican singing and talking. One Exodus singer offered to share his flat with Bob for a few weeks. Walt Conley, a large, gentle, black man from Nebraska, had learned folk songs in the late 1940s from Pete Seeger and composer Earl Robinson. From Walt, Bob reportedly picked up a topical anti-KKK song called "The Klan." Dylan and Walt fell out over a girl they both were after, and over the sudden disappearance of a bunch of Walt's favorite recordings. "I was kicked out of Denver," Dylan told me without remorse. "Yeah, I was run out of Denver for robbing a cat's house."

Two Denver performers influenced Dylan. The sweetheart of the Exodus was 19-year-old Denverite Judy Collins, a classically trained musician beginning what was to be a long career in 1959–60. Two songs Judy was singing then ended up on Dylan's first album: "House of the Rising Sun" and "Maid of Constant Sorrow." Judy became one of the first and best interpreters of Dylan songs.[2] Bob also met a rollicking old gamester, the late Jesse Fuller, who often played the Exodus. Born in Jonesboro, Georgia, in 1896, Fuller fused traditional songs, blues, his own writing, rural ragtime, and just plain "good-time" sounds. He was a one-man band, working his twelve-string guitar, cymbals, harmonica, and his own curious invention, the "fotdella," a foot-operated percussion machine that struck a drum and plucked an improvised bass simultaneously. "The Lone Cat," as he called himself, came on with vitality and wit. Dylan watched the way Fuller held his harmonica and kazoo in front of his mouth in a metal neck-brace that allowed him to alternate between singing and running riffs on his mouth harp. Dylan quizzed Fuller, who died in 1976, and learned how to play the harmonica in its distinctive holder.

Bob concedes his few performances at the Exodus and other Colorado clubs were nothing memorable. Yet he was getting some experience and credits, if little money. Colorado also gave him anonymity and a chance to romanticize his background. He told his family that in Denver he had been wildly appreciated and accepted. His parents still thought, as they drove him to Minneapolis, that college would wash away this music compulsion.

Highway 61 Revisited. In 1959, some 25,000 students were attending the University of Minnesota, a Midwestern Big Ten school with a football team, a school of animal husbandry, heavy endowments, and high academic ratings, especially in medicine and technology. The large campus, nestled in a gentle bend of the Mississippi, had spread across from the east bank. By the 1960s, the main campus became the largest single college center in America, with students and faculty accounting for ten percent of the city population. Scott Fitzgerald once lived at the wrong end of Summit Street, across the river in St Paul, and Hubert Humphrey was once Mayor of Minneapolis. *Venture* called Minneapolis "a city as American as Scotch tape and Wheaties, as invigorating as a morning swim in Hiawatha Lake, as wholesome as a Pillsbury Bake-Off … It is not a place … for exotic new excitements, but one where you feel back home among the comfortable, cherished national virtues—friendliness, decency, optimism, humor, enthusiasm, diligence, sanity, pride—virtues that make Minneapolis, with its Indian-Greek name, its Nordic background, its Jewish mayor, so thoroughly and reassuringly American."

Minneapolis had 150 parks and more than twenty lakes, a city of grain elevators. They say that St Paul is the end of the East; the West begins at Minneapolis. Dylan, a small-town boy, was somewhat overwhelmed at the impersonality of his new world.

A cousin, a law student, belonged to Sigma Alpha Mu, and Bob lived briefly at the fraternity house. Bob's first reaction to the group, called—not so benevolently—"Sammies" because it was a Jewish fraternity, was negative. His father recalled: "Bob didn't think much of the college crowd. He considered most of them phonies, just spoiled kids with whom he didn't have much in common. Bobby quit Sigma Alpha Mu even before he was pledged." He wrote, in "My Life in a Stolen Moment":

Later I sat in college… on a phony scholarship that I never had
I sat in science class an' flunked out for refusin' to watch a rabbit die
I got expelled from English class for using four-letter words in a paper describing the English teacher
I also failed out of communication class for callin' up every day and sayin' I couldn't come
I did OK in Spanish though but I knew it beforehand
I's kept around for kicks at a fraternity house
They let me live there an' I did until they wanted me to join
I moved in with two girls from South Dakota in a two-room apartment for two nights
I crossed the bridge to 14th Street an' moved in above a bookstore that also sold bad hamburgers basketball sweatshirts an' bulldog statues
I fell hard for an actress girl who kneed me in the guts an' I ended up on the East Side a the Mississippi River with about ten friends in a condemned house underneath the Washington Avenue Bridge just south a Seven Corners
That's pretty well my college life[3]

Dylan's sardonic summary doesn't do justice to what he learned outside classrooms. Bob left the fraternity house amid bad feeling. A counselor recalled that Bob was "hard to know, kept very odd hours, and moped a lot." The people Bob liked were the few folk-oriented intellectuals who lived around Dinkytown, the University business district, and Bohemia. One of these beatniks, thinkers, rebels, artists, dropouts, and dreamers was "Spider John" Koerner, a middle-class Huck Finn intensely involved in music.[4]

"I first met Bob in the Ten O'Clock Scholar, a Dinkytown coffeehouse that later burned down," Koerner told me. "Bob just drifted in. With us was Len Durasow. The three of us went on to a bar, but Bob wasn't old enough to be served. He was a little heavier then, looked like a little cherub. We bought something to drink and then went out behind the chemistry building. There was a big loading-dock platform there, and we had a little open-air party. Bob and I were playing, and Len was dancing. It was early in the morning and we were both goofing around. Some university guard thought it was pretty funny, so he didn't bother us. Bob and I both played the same sort of guitar things. He was writing some songs, but they were those folky spirituals that were popular, like 'Sinner Man.' He got very interested in those easy-rocking things of Odetta's. Dylan had a very sweet, pretty voice, much different from what it became. I don't remember Bob's talking about making it in show business. We were more interested in immediate things, in making up songs. One thing that struck me hard was the great change in how Dylan speaks. It's almost impossible to recognize the same person. None of us was talking very hip then, except possibly Dave Morton, who was older. We weren't really into the hippie sort of thing then, it was mostly just singing and playing and drinking and going to parties and chasing women."

Campus people thought Spider John would be a star and that Dylan was definitely the lesser talent. One of Koerner's roommates was Harry Weber, a PhD candidate in Latin literature and a ballad scholar. "When I arrived in Minneapolis in 1955 with a guitar," Weber told me in 1966, "folk music was very much underground. The older people came from the Old Left. Their idea of folk music was a union song—Seeger and *The People's Song Book*, Gene Bluestein [who made a Folkways album, *Songs of the North Star State*, in 1958] was the big folk wheel on campus. The early Minnesota Folk Music Society was about eighty percent Jewish, mostly university people. There was a remarkable lack of taste, and it finally split into two camps.

"I became friends with Koerner and later roomed with him," Weber continued. "The first songwriter I ever heard around here was Dylan. Old Dave Morton was the earliest to write songs, but I never heard them. The first song of Dylan's I heard was 'Every Time I Hear the Spirit.' Bob didn't make much of a fuss about it. It was like the Negro spiritual he based it on, except it had a rockabilly beat. A good adolescent lament. When Bob came down here in 1959, he looked pretty, fair-haired, absolutely beardless. His eyes were vaguely popping, and his cheeks were a little bit too full. Dr Dan Pugh, a psychiatrist, was fascinated by Dylan's looks. 'A very interesting endocrine system,' Dr Pugh said.

"When Dylan arrived he looked awfully small-town. He dressed in an almost finicky way. He looked like Peck's Bad Boy suddenly grown five years. He acted very high-schoolish, very brash. He posed a lot, with his hand in his belt, his legs straddling the room. He wasn't big, of course, but he was heavy. I think he weighed at least twenty-five or thirty pounds more than after he made it. Almost from the start, there used to be inconsistencies in Bob's stories, but I don't think he's a liar—just a romantic. He didn't really stay in school very long, maybe six or nine months. The last few months, he wasn't at school at all. He was living on and with different people, and had some little jobs, like bussing dishes.

"After he dropped out, I found him impossible. He could be very pretentious, very annoying. Maybe this was a bid for attention. I think that, like everybody, he wanted to be liked. He could be awfully rude and he certainly was vain. Koerner and Dylan were competing quite a bit. I was afraid Dylan wasn't going to have any voice left. He obviously knew what he was doing, but he was abusing his voice, shouting out raucous, loud songs.

"I met Dylan only about a month after he got here. He would come over to visit Koerner, but he would get interested in some song or technique I knew. We were living at 42 Seventh Street Southeast, a horrible place, sort of a three-man slum. There always seemed to be a lot of music going on. I did not find it easy to communicate with Bob. I don't think anybody else did either. Even the girls he liked had a hard time talking to him, and he had a hard time talking to them. But it was *different* when it got to music!

"If you couldn't explain what was the matter with his way of singing, you could show him. He would pick it up just like that," continued Weber. "I don't think Bob read much, although he borrowed books a lot. He didn't talk about books at all, except of course Woody Guthrie's *Bound for Glory*. I did loan Bob a set of Randolph's *Folk Songs of Arkansas*. I wonder if he still has them. Dylan never cared much about the battle here over tradition. Maybe he became as good as he did because that sort of thing doesn't bother him. He uses what he wants to use. In 1959, Dylan met Cynthia Gooding. After her concert we had a party, and Bob sang to her for half an hour. Cynthia was amazed. It was quite a sight, because she was somebody then." Later, when Cynthia saw Dylan in New York at Folk City, she wrote Harry: "People listen… he talks and he laughs and just when they are about to catch him in a lie, he takes out his harmonica and blows them down."[5]

Weber said he had "trouble with Dylan the person. It relieves my conscience to talk about Dylan the artist. He is a *great* artist. Dylan is a genius, that's all, that's all there is to it. He is irksome and irritating, very much the Chekhov genius. He is not more complex than most people; he is simpler. I was aware when I met him that he was very talented. I was not awed by him then. I am now. Awed with his ability. I don't think he was aware of his talent when he came to Minneapolis. But, wait a minute. I take that back. He walked around like a young Shelley. He was very self-confident. Dylan used to carry a book of French symbolist poetry, but I have the impression of his being a very great listener. When he wasn't singing, he was very quiet. When he got nervous, he would sing. He wasn't a talker. He doesn't chat.

"The attitude of the folk purists toward Dylan when he started with an electric band was like saying that Verdi sold out when he composed *Otello* because he was influenced by Wagner. The purists say art must be static. The people at *Sing Out!* magazine let down Josh White with a great wallop too, hurting him very much. You can forgive such doctrinaire attitudes once in a while, but not very often. Pete Seeger never let himself be caught up in that. What the purists did to Dylan is unbelievable. He is a great artist, and that's all there is to it."

The University of Dinkytown. Although Dylan enrolled at the liberal arts college of the University of Minnesota in September 1959, within a few months he was really at the University of Dinkytown. He was majoring in music with advanced seminars in coffeehouses, minoring in radical life-styles, doing seminars in scene-making, preparing for graduate work in Woody Guthrie. Bob's Minneapolis friends and foes formed a circle of exceptionally intelligent, colorful, talented, and perceptive characters. It mattered little what they did or where they stood on the social ladder. Take a student radical and folk-song enthusiast named Harvey Abrams, whom I interviewed in spring 1966.

"I met Bob in summer 1960. He had already written a couple of beautiful songs, like 'The Klan.' Bob never really went to school, and he carried a notebook that never contained schoolwork. He was playing weekends at the Scholar, earning five dollars a night. Then, Bob Beull and I opened up a coffeehouse. We leased an old house near Oak and Washington Avenue and rebuilt it, and named it the Bastille.

"Dylan and I were pretty good friends by then. I lived in Melvin McCosh's boarding house, above his bookstore. Dave and Gretel Whitaker were also living there. Bob began to play at the Bastille weekends. I thought he was fantastic! He always went as Bob Dillon, not Dylan. The only time we saw it with the Dylan Thomas spelling was in your *New York Times* article [September, 1961]. At school, he was registered as Bob Zimmerman, but all of his music billings here were spelled Bob Dillon. Everyone nearly flipped when he came out spelling it the way Dylan Thomas spelled his name.

"In fall and early winter 1960, he played at the Bastille. Bob Beull, who died in January 1966, was paying him ten dollars a night. Dylan somehow traded his Gibson for a huge Gretsch Ranger, with a sound box of about four cubic feet! Dylan listened to flamenco played by Hugh Brown and by Steve Olson, who had studied with Carlos Montoya. But Dylan wouldn't do any flamenco. His music kept getting better and better. His poetry then was very simple stuff. Rock 'n' roll? Definitely not! If anyone had played him a Beatles or a Rolling Stones record, he would probably have broken it. Dylan was the purest of the pure. He had to get the oldest record and, if possible, the Library of Congress record, or go find the original people who knew the original song."

When Harvey, Morton, and Bob were living at 714 Fifteenth Avenue Southeast, Dylan "would rush home to be there when the mailman arrived. We were rather young then, and perhaps cruel, but Hugh Brown and I had heard so much about Bob's Oklahoma poverty scene, we were really startled when we saw a card from his folks at the Royal Hawaiian Hotel. We finally figured out that his folks must have been sending him money."

Abrams reminisced: "Bob wore Levi's, loafers or boots, and a blue denim shirt. In the winter, an old tweed sports jacket and a thick scarf. Always some kind of eccentric hat or cap. Long before it was fashionable, Bob was saying that school wasn't relevant to life. I know he was writing night and day. A lot of it was pretty infantile. A lot showed complete identification with and copying of Guthrie's material. Somewhere along the line, Dylan got a tremendous burst of originality."

"Whitaker and I probably told Bob as much about politics as anyone. Dylan didn't read about politics; he really didn't seem to read at all. You see, Dylan can *hear*. Musicians have different kinds of ears, a different kind of hearing, than other people do. If Bob were in a foreign country, he'd pick up the language very quickly. When he came here, Dylan didn't really know anything about politics and he wasn't at all interested. There were about fifty of us seriously interested in politics and in the Cuban Revolution. Let's say that Bob got a lot of exuberance about it from us. Bob probably doesn't function with politics, or, let us say, dogma. Probably with him, it's just an identification with the underdog, with the people. It's all on an emotional, intuitive level. Look at 'Hollis Brown.' He feels these things on a very intuitive, emotional level, the way a primitive person might. If there were ever a great strike movement in America, Dylan could be another Mother Jones."

Weber knew the anthropology and genealogy of folk music inside out, but Dylan didn't care a hoot. He related to it on a different level, but that didn't keep them from becoming friends. There were a lot of parties where Harry and Koerner lived. "For a while, people mostly went to parties to hear Dylan play. Later, nobody wanted to give a party because Dylan would come and play. Then he became the first guy to put the guitar and harmonica together, with that frame-holder around his neck. Nobody had ever seen this before. As far as I know, he was the first white performer to combine the Sonny Terry harmonica with the Woody Guthrie guitar."

When money was short, Abrams recalled, "I pawned Morton's and Dylan's guitars several times—Brown's guitar also." Then money would come in from somewhere and Abrams would reclaim the instruments. "We were all living a pretty irregular life, but Dylan especially. For Bob to knock on somebody's door at five-thirty in the morning was not unusual. When he was looking for some sort of action, he assumed everybody else was up. To Bob, Hibbing was just an awfully sad memory that he didn't want to talk about. He didn't want us to know anything about Hibbing. He would hide letters from there. Sometimes he'd been born in Duluth, and sometimes in Oklahoma. We knew that he used to play rock 'n' roll, but he had totally disowned it by the time he was getting known here."

"When the Student Is Ready, the Teacher Will Appear." Weber and Abrams emerged from the Bohemian-beat-hippie scene as straight characters. Others were uncompromising, like the reigning Dinkytown guru Dave Morton, who moved to the West Coast around 1961. Morton, a rigorously avant-garde experimenter in alternative cultures, and Dinkytown's link between the mystic 1950s beats and the emerging 1960s hipsters, had considerable influence on Dylan. A gaunt six-foot-six, Morton looked like Abe Lincoln strung out in the East Village. Hair flowed from every pore; he had forelocks, a beard and moustache, and a mop cascading nearly two feet down his back. He radiated gentle, distilled wisdom, had a reservoir of Eastern aphorisms, and was one of the best professors at Dylan's peripheral university. Morton, who had the distinction of having heard Leadbelly live in 1948, was probably the first to play folk music at the old Ten O'Clock Scholar, although he knew only four or five chords when he began. Similarly, he started writing songs before anyone else — not very good songs, admittedly—about the Bomb and President Eisenhower. Dylan recalled: "There was a lot of unrest, frustration—like a calm before a hurricane. There were always a lot of poems recited—Kerouac, Ginsberg, Corso, and Ferlinghetti. I got in at the tail end and it was magic. Every day was like Sunday."

I caught up with Morton in Los Angeles in 1966. He had become a senior West Coast hipster, painting, editing *Regent*, an avant-garde literary magazine, studying the *I Ching*, and leading a folk-rock band, the New Improved Jukes Savages. As chief Savage, Morton played guitar, piano, and kazoo. "Back at Minneapolis, I studied mathematics, but I didn't get far. Mostly, I was connected with the new All-American Gallery, at the Dinkytown firehouse building. I first met Bobby Dylan at a party there in the fall of 1959. Bob was pretty lively, funny, and nervous. His leg always bounced when he sat down. He never talked much about Hibbing, although he went up there for a day or two. The Iron Range is an international community with a funny kind of isolation. It's a strange place to grow up in."

Morton was deep into Asian and American Indian philosophy and myth, and psychedelic experiences. I asked him to reconstruct talks with Dylan in the old days. He seemed to fall into a trance: "According to Indian belief, there are three steps toward salvation. The first is love. The second is enjoyment of the senses. And the third is the dharma game, which is duty, such as to family and children, to a job, or even to society. Yes, we used to talk of that then. I had a fine experience on acid reading *Paterson* by William Carlos Williams. Acid simply opens up the museums of the mind. On acid, you go through funny places of history and myth. The entire Garden of Eden can be re-created in your mind. One experience I had was the feeling that my voice was not directly linked to myself. The words seemed to come from somewhere else, my memory or my unconscious mind." Morton paused. We realized he had accurately described a phase of Dylan's songwriting. "Some artists could always have been described as psychedelic. Seurat broke up colors into little points. On acid, I've seen colors the way Van Gogh painted them, flowing together like early Persian tapestries. Picasso's surrealism is realistic to me, and has always been, ever since I perceived it on this new level."

Dylan's response? "He always listened, well, intently. Although he didn't talk much to many people, we always managed to communicate. I'm not surprised Bob went on to achieve what he did. He seemed to be working on something none of us fully shared with him. Dylan was his own guru. When the student is ready, the old saying goes, the teacher will appear."

Hugh Brown had been Morton's chum from high school in Portland, Oregon. Soft-spoken and humble, Hugh studied classics, wrote poetry, and later became a highway engineer. Brown: "I always liked Bob. At the time, I think I played guitar better than he did. We ended up living together, along with Dave and Max Uhler and several others. Living arrangements changed week to week. When we were living on Fifteenth Avenue Southeast, three blocks from Dinkytown, I would try to wake him when he had a special test, and it was always a struggle. One time he threatened to throw me down the stairs.

Mostly, he played his guitar. Bob talked about taking off for New York, about going to see Guthrie. He also said he wanted to go to New York to strike it rich. At the Scholar most people liked him, even though he wasn't really very good then. He was on an Odetta kick, singing other people's songs.[6] I don't know why Harvey Abrams says he spelled his name Dillon then, because as I recall, he spelled it Dylan here. Of course, he said a lot of things that proved to be untrue. He was trying to overcome being from Hibbing.

"When I got married, Bob gave us a wedding present of a toaster and an iron. Both the iron and toaster had been mine, but Bob wasn't concerned. He still regarded them as gifts. He was popular around Minneapolis. Most of the people who now dislike him took a dislike to him *after* he became famous. There was a hate rash toward him around Minneapolis for a while. I don't really understand it. He was elated about signing a record contract, but he wasn't particularly egotistical. It is difficult to be passive about someone as outrageous as Bob. He says some pretty outrageous things, in his music and in person. We all thought it was pretty funny he was going to New York to make his fame and fortune. He left owing people a lot of money, but we *all* owed a lot of people money. We all got it back eventually, anyway.

"When Bob was here, the first stirrings of a radical movement were beginning to affect the American college campus," continued Hugh. "Among those trying to get a radical club off the ground here were Harvey, Whitaker, and Herschel Kaminsky, who was quite active down in Mississippi. We organized a Fair Play for Cuba Committee. Bob didn't come to any meetings, but he was around. Bob may have become interested in politics through Guthrie, rather than through the political people on campus. He certainly didn't appear to be politically sophisticated."

There was an anonymous adage around Dinkytown: "Dylan missed out on an extra bowl of chicken soup when he was a boy and spent the rest of his life wondering what and why he had missed." Hugh Brown's reaction was: "If you try to figure out anyone like Bob you will only discover that there is more and more that you simply can't figure out. We had all liked Ginsberg's poetry. I don't know how much of an influence he was on Bob at that time. There was not much use of drugs then. A few people had tried marijuana and peyote, but none of us had even heard about LSD. I had read Aldous Huxley's *The Doors of Perception* when I was eighteen. McCosh's Bookstore carried a few small literary reviews, but not very many. Nobody paid any attention to the *Village Voice* then. When the Dinkytown circle left here, most of them headed west, mainly to Los Angeles. Not many went to New York. Except Bob."

Dave and Gretel. Dylan's Dinkytown circle were dissenters who couldn't accept "the System." Harvey Abrams: "The problem became not just a question of selling out on our student ideals, but a question of who would buy." Among the most committed outsiders were Dave Whitaker and the former Gretel Hoffman, then his wife. By the time I caught up with Dave, he was a San Francisco dropout living hand to mouth. A gentle, somewhat defeated man in his late twenties, Dave seemed prematurely old. Whitaker: "Dylan's association with the Left had been almost totally instinctive. There was nothing in his background that led him toward the Jewish Left. Coincidentally, our university Bohemian circle also included the political Left."

Gretel had sharp memories of Bob: "Between January and March 1960, we used to get together at the Scholar every day. He was living in a horrible green room that had a bed, a chair, a desk, a refrigerator with moldy food in it, some beer. By early 1960, Bob had just about quit school. He was still very bitter about the fraternity house. I was struck by his being just a sweet guy. There was something very gentle about him, something a little bit sad too. He used to say frequently that he would be dead before he was twenty-one. It was clear that *he* wouldn't do it, that he wasn't suicidal, but he just felt that that was the way his life was mapped out. I was never quite sure who he was or where he was from. He was quite good at telling stories about himself, such as having been a rock 'n' roll singer. Bobby was just a kid learning how to sing. I remember Bob's enjoyment when a group of Israeli musicians showed up at the Scholar. The freedom and ease of it all seemed to make him very happy. He seemed to be open to all sorts of experience.

"The key word in those days that describes Bob," Gretel continued, "was *enthusiasm*—about the whole, wonderful world of songs. He was very proficient then, even though still hit or miss technically. He would sit for hours working on new songs, but not until about six months later [autumn 1960] did he really begin to distinguish between what was good and what was new. By a year later, the picture of someone just trying things on for size had changed. Minneapolis was a very good place for someone to develop in music. Bob played at the Purple Onion in St Paul, a Calypso sort of place that was just like every other restaurant in St Paul. Toward the end of 1960, Bob was maturing, beginning to choose his material with much more care. He used to tell stories about playing piano with Bobby Vee. I really don't think anyone ever believed him and I don't think he believed people didn't believe him."

The Record Collector. Two aficionados who helped put Minneapolis on the folk map back then were Paul Nelson and Jon Pankake. With vast listening experience and strong opinions about style, the pair started a lively, mimeographed shoestring publication, *Little Sandy Review*. Cantankerous *Little Sandy* soon made an impression. While not anti-Left, it put musical ahead of social values. Sharp personal and critical arguments among Nelson, Pankake, and Dylan continued for years. *Little Sandy* was the first publication to reveal that Bob had "invented" his new personality and name.

Paul Nelson, who went on to become an editor of *Sing Out!* and a freelance writer-critic, could document changes in his own perspectives through phases of Dylan's growth: "In 1959, Bob and Koerner were playing the standard repertoire, out of Josh White, Odetta and [Harry] Belafonte. There was no promise that Dylan or Koerner were at all exceptional—adequate guitarists and singers, but plenty of other kids were as good. Dylan seemed to learn so incredibly fast. If you didn't see him for two weeks, it would seem as if he'd made three years' progress. He heard Jack Elliott first on a Topic recording from England. Dylan went in two weeks from songs like 'Jerry' and 'Timber' to interpreting Guthrie. He got all the accents and a lot of the guitar and harmonica playing. It would have taken a normal singer two years to accomplish what Dylan did in two weeks! He always seemed to have an unerring instinct for a great song, like 'Constant Sorrow' and learn it from a recording. His old self, from Minneapolis, and what he became in the East, are two different people—he talks differently, acts differently. The old Dylan self is completely gone. When he got east, he came out with some very strange quotes, such as 'I never knew what a folk song was until I got to New York.' That is a hundred percent untrue. He was never particularly likeable at Minnesota, but he has gotten to be a whole lot better since then. None of us were aware Dylan had this *conquering* ability. I don't think Dylan knew he had it himself. Most of us were bowled over when he came out East and made it himself, and did a Columbia record. What impressed us all most was how fast Bob changed. Every few weeks, Bob would become a different person with a different style."[7]

Jon Pankake: "My first impression of Bob was that he was just beginning, still thinking about all his chord changes. I was not especially interested in Bob as a musician or as a person. Bob was very interested in learning what he could about music from me. I played a Texas chain-gang song from an Alan Lomax album for him. He said he was more interested in learning and hearing directly from people rather than from records. He didn't seem to want to make records, just to be a big guy on the coffeehouse circuit, attracting girls and attention."

Pankake was away from his flat for a weekend; following campus custom, he left his door unlocked. Returning, he discovered around twenty of his records missing. "My first suspect was Dylan," Jon told me, "because he had been expressing interest in my records. Tony Glover said he had been surprised to see certain records at Bob's, including some English recordings by Jack Elliott. He took other records—by Elizabeth Cotten [a black songster], *Mountain Music—Bluegrass Style*, and so on. There was also some Woody Guthrie stuff. He had very good taste. When I found out that Bob had them, Tony, Paul, and I burst in on Dylan, unannounced. I got him up against the wall, and slapped him a couple of times and let him know that I wasn't going to take this lightly. I was a pretty good actor playing a tough guy. I even had a cigar that I didn't take out of my teeth. He offered some of them to me immediately, and said he would bring the rest over the next day. Bob insisted I keep his guitar for security. He told a whole bunch of stone-cold lies about some of the kids dropping the records over there. The next morning, Dylan brought the missing records back and exchanged them for his guitar. I think he apologized, but I'm not sure. He didn't come around to see me anymore after that. The funny thing is that I didn't feel that there was anything malicious about his stealing the records. I think he believed that he needed them more than I did. But it expressed a certain amount of contempt for me personally, because you don't steal from people you respect."

"I don't think Bob had ever begrudged me what happened," Paul added. "Apparently he was being chased by quite a few people. He had gone through a string of apartments pretty fast. If it hadn't been for that episode, I think Jon would have liked Dylan very much, but it just colored his whole attitude. We figured that about a hundred dollars-worth of records was involved. He had taken the very best of the lot. He had an unerring sense of what to take."

The Teacher Appears. Dylan also had an unerring sense of what to take when he found his own idol, spiritual father, and musical model in Woody Guthrie. Bob would describe him in his "Epitaphs":

> he was the last idol
> because he was the first idol
> I'd ever met
> that taught me
> face t' face
> that men are men
> shatterin' even himself as an idol …
> Woody never made me fear
> and he didn't trample any hopes
> for he just carried a book of Man
> an' gave it t' me t' read awhile
> an' from it I learned my greatest lesson[8]

Guthrie was an Okie Walt Whitman, carrying his song of the open road down a modern highway, a farm-boy Carl Sandburg, a genuine hobo/tramp/wandering minstrel with dirt on his hands. When Dylan started to study Guthrie's book of man, he really didn't need much more of Dinkytown. Dylan's conversion was a dramatic, explosive turning point. He swallowed Woody's early autobiography, *Bound for Glory*, as if he'd discovered the Bible. An amazing number of people are sure they told him "Bobby, you've got to read Woody." Whitaker was probably the first. Gretel recalls: "After David turned Bob on to *Bound for Glory*, there was an awful lot of talk about Guthrie—what Woody was up to, what he was all about. Bob almost fell in love with Woody Guthrie. When he learned Guthrie was in hospital in New Jersey, he decided he had to go out and see him. Before Bob left, his attitude was 'I gotta get out of here. I gotta go see Woody Guthrie.'"

A few first editions of *Bound for Glory*, published by Dutton in 1943, were floating around Minneapolis: Bob borrowed Weber's copy. The last 200 pages hadn't been cut. Bob took the book to the Scholar and proceeded to devour it like that bowl of chicken soup he'd missed. Some say he read the book at one sitting, cutting the pages with a kitchen knife. Few had seen Dylan read *anything* before.

Harvey Abrams: "The book came as a real shock. For the next two years he patterned his life after what he'd read. Bob started doing everything the way Guthrie did. For many months thereafter, everything Bob sang sounded like Guthrie. He became very good at singing just like Woody. He would sit and listen to a record, then repeat it. It was phenomenal. Even his speech patterns began to change. That Oklahoma twang, which became much more extreme after he left here, came into his voice. That incredibly harsh gravel sound in his voice became more and more a part of him. It really became much more than identification. He *was* the people he identified with, especially Guthrie. I don't know how, but he memorized the whole of Woody's 'Tom Joad' in just one day or two. He could really sing that ballad beautifully. People who didn't know Bob very well were repelled or angered by the change in him, because they thought he was phony or he was making a dollar. Sometimes, we just thought that the Guthrie character and the Dylan character were really very much the same, anyway. We believed Bob was born with this nature, only it had been covered up for eighteen years by living in Hibbing in a fairly bourgeois setup. We really felt that Bob's real self was coming out from underneath."

The role-playing began around summer 1960. To a few close friends, Dylan admitted that the changes grew out of a genuine need for a new identity. He simply wasn't pleased with his former bland, directionless self. Gretel: "He was very open about it. He explained that he was building a character. Tony Glover added: "He said it was an act, but only for about two days. He said: 'After that, it was *me*.'" Bob wanted to contact Woody, slowly dying of Huntington's chorea at Greystone Hospital in New Jersey. Morton: "There were a lot of drinking parties at Whitaker's that fall. Bob would get drunk and call Guthrie on the phone. Some of us would get on the phone to say hello. Bob told Guthrie that he was coming out to see him." Inevitably, there was teasing, and once a cruel practical joke. Someone in Dinkytown phoned Dylan to say Woody had just showed up at a party. Dylan ran over, panting, flushed, and asked: "Where's Woody? Where is he?"

Who was this "hero with a thousand faces"? Woody Guthrie was the archetypal American troubadour, a singer, tale-teller, poet, prophet-singer, roustabout, organizer, union man, traveler, journalist, peach-picker, hitchhiker, rambler, migrant worker, refugee. He was a footloose rebel, an early dropout. He became the voice of the disinherited Okies and Arkies, blown off their land by the droughts and dust storms of the 1930s. He was the bard of the Depression, a walking, singing, cussing, drinking, father of the beats of the 1950s, the hippies of the 1960s, and some of the political activists of the 1970s. Woody was compounded of equal parts of Whitman, Sandburg, Will Rogers, and Jimmie Rodgers. Whatever influences and traditions he embodied, Guthrie was his own man, an uncompromising individualist who may have used his art to serve himself, but who also served music and literature and his own people.

The Guthrie of *Bound for Glory* and on recordings was a vibrantly healthy young man. Woody was really too short to be a giant, too lean and delicate-faced to pose for heroic statues, too ungrammatical to be a poet. His voice was too flat and shaky to be a great singer. Yet, he was all of those things: a giant humanist, a heroic American culture figure, a major poet, still largely undiscovered, and a singer and composer of some of our greatest songs. Woody symbolized the strongest fibers in American folk culture — empathy with the downtrodden, dislike for sham, joy in music, the independence of a man who can't be bought, and a sense of justice that forced him to speak up or sing out when he saw people being pushed around. This wispy hobo and self-educated ballad-maker sang, like Whitman, of himself, but his self was a type, a cross-section, a multitude. His intoxicating vision was of an America of breadth and variety, promise and character, and he was angered when that promise "got busted" by the banks and the cranks and the phonies, by those who would rob you "with a fountain pen," as he wrote in "Pretty Boy Floyd."

Dylan identified passionately with Guthrie's rugged independence, the richness of his language, the soulful and playful ballad-making, the flood of personal creativity, the harmonica, guitar and scratchy voice. At last, he had a model after which to shape himself. At last he could say goodbye to the Hibbing middle-class. At last, he had the big brother and spiritual father he'd longed for. Woody was Dylan's first Tambourine Man and even after he outgrew his specific image, Guthrie remained an indelible stamp upon Dylan's personality. Guthrie provided a way of looking at the world. Most of Guthrie's one thousand or so songs radiate an embracing love of people, the joys of kids' laughter, the dignity of cooperative work:

I hate a song that makes you think that you're not any good. I hate a song that makes you think that you are just born to lose. Bound to lose. No good to nobody. No good for nothing. Because you are either too old or too young or too fat or too slim or too ugly or too this or too that. Songs that run you down or songs that poke fun at you on account of your bad luck or your hard traveling. I am out to fight those kinds of songs to my very last breath of air and my last drop of blood. I am out to sing songs that will prove to you that this is your world and that if it has hit you pretty hard and knocked you for a dozen loops, no matter how hard it's run you down and rolled over you, no matter what color, what size you are, how you are built, I am out to sing the songs that make you take pride in yourself and in your work. And the songs I sing are made up for the most part by all sorts of people just about like you.[9]

Woody hit the road at 17, and the road kept hitting him back. He accumulated wives and ex-wives, a host of children, bills, and bad debts. He used to tell his second wife, Marjorie (Arlo's mother), that he was going downstairs for a pack of cigarettes, and three weeks later would drop her a postcard from the West Coast. When Dylan said he was anything but a poet or a folk singer, he was taking a leaf from *Bound for Glory*:

Guess I'm what you'd call a migrant worker. Guess you had to think up some kind of name for me. I travel, yes, if that's what you mean in your red-tape and your scary offices ... You just set and call me off the whole book full of names, but let me be out on my job while you're doing the calling. That a way, we can save time and money and get more work turned out ... I travel, Hell, yes, I travel ... If I was to stop, you'd have to up and leave your job and start traveling, because there's a hell of a lot of traveling that's got to be done.[10]

Woodrow Wilson Guthrie was born in 1912 in Okemah, Oklahoma, oil-boom country. A few days after his father, a once-affluent hog rancher and land speculator, had built a six-room house, the place burned down. A little later, Woody's 14-year-old sister was burned to death in a kerosene fire explosion. His mother died from Huntington's chorea. Then his father died in a fire, perhaps a suicide. Woody was farmed out to foster families. By 17, he was off for Galveston and the Gulf of Mexico. He joined the westward migrations of rural Okies, Arkies, and Texans. In California, some fruit ranchers paid these "Dust Bowl refugees" a dollar a ton for picking peaches. Woody was soon singing for them and doing a daily radio show for a dollar a day on Los Angeles's WKVD. Like Steinbeck's Tom Joad, hero of *Grapes of Wrath*, Guthrie was of the uprooted, disenfranchised, impoverished migrants.

Woody was part country, part folk singer. From his mother, he learned old ballads and traditional songs. From the radio, the people on his road, he heard country music. Woody's cousin, Jack Guthrie, was a country singer. Woody's guitar playing, and the scores of the songs he adapted with new lyrics, were taken from recordings of the famous Carter family, who reigned over country music from 1927 until World War II. (The "new" Carter family, the late Mother Maybelle and her three daughters, and relations and colleagues of Johnny Cash, rose again to the counry-music pantheon in the late 1960s.)

Two men in Los Angeles stimulated Woody's political education—Will Geer, the actor, and Mike Quin, a poet and columnist for *The People's World*, the West Coast Communist paper. Quin is generally believed to have "discovered" Guthrie. Just like Dylan, Woody had a way of accumulating friends, acquaintances, influences, helpers, and cooperators. Cisco Houston, the rambling singer and hobo, became Woody's traveling companion. When Woody came east in 1939, he met and traveled with Pete Seeger. Pete, a Harvard dropout, was hell-bent on experience in music and in building unions. In 1940, Woody, 28, went down to the Library of Congress's Archive of Folk Culture to record his songs and life story for Alan Lomax. (Three hours of these recordings were later issued on Elektra.) Woody also made commercial recordings, on Victor, then on Decca and Stinson, and finally with folk music entrepreneur Moses Asch on his various labels, mostly Folkways.[11] By the time Woody hit New York, he was the darling of the Left. Twenty years later, Dylan nearly duplicated Woody's embrace by the New York folk-Left.

In 1940, Woody went west to rejoin his first wife and their three children. Seeger, Lee Hays, and the writer Millard Lampell formed the seminal folk group the Almanac Singers, and Woody joined them in June 1941. The Almanacs maintained an early commune on 10th Street in Greenwich Village. Pete Seeger: "We got bookings for five dollars here and occasionally ten dollars there, and by working hard just managed to keep body and soul together. On Sunday afternoons, we held open house. Thirty-five cents was charged at the door, and we and friends would sing all afternoon. We called 'em hootenannies."

In 1939, Woody was making a lavish $200 a week on the *Model Tobacco* radio series. Later, an agent booked the Almanacs into the glamorous Rainbow Room atop Rockefeller Center. In *Bound for Glory*, Woody savors how the group walked out, resisting an attempt to put them in corny hillbilly costumes. He just wouldn't compromise, and he set the matrix for a folk performer's lifestyle that was to have a great effect on Dylan.

Woody could sniff out the hypocrites in progressive or Leftist circles as well. He hated to pander to anyone, and despised show business for "giving the public what it wants." He disdained the term *folk music* because it might possibly group him with the "silk-stocking balladeers." Guthrie's stance helps explain Dylan's frequent refusal to call himself a folk or protest singer. Similarly, Dylan's denial that he was a poet echoed Woody's claim that "I ain't a writer. I want that understood. I'm just a little one-cylinder guitar picker."

It was Seeger who encouraged Woody to start *Bound for Glory*. At Harvard, Pete had known Charles Olson, later a critic and poet who, in 1942, asked Woody to write for the little magazine *Common Ground*. Woody did a brilliant essay, "Ear Music." Suggestions poured in that Woody write about himself. He plunged into *Bound for Glory*, published at the height of World War II and rapturously received— Steinbeck commented: "Woody is just Woody. Thousands of people do not know he has any other name. He is just a voice and a guitar." After time in the Merchant Marines with Cisco Houston, Woody settled briefly in Coney Island, Brooklyn. In 1942, he married the former Marjorie Mazia Greenblatt. Through the late 1940s, he continued to write a flood of songs and poems, to draw, and record. Like Dylan, Woody alternated between periods of intense talk and creativity and periods of silence and reflection. At his fancy publishing party at Amy Vanderbilt's, Woody didn't say a word all evening.

The late Cisco Houston told me in 1959: "Woody is the greatest folk poet we've had. He is like the biblical prophets who sang the news. Woody never cared about material things, except a good car, a fountain pen or typewriter, and a good guitar. Those of us who traveled by the side-door Pullman and the sunburned thumb always wanted cars. Anyone who knew a hard way of life would feel that Woody spoke for them. They identified with him."

Woody wrote at least one thousand songs, from the folk national anthem, "This Land is Your Land," to the classic farewell, "So Long, It's Been Good to Know You"; from his children's songs, like "Car Car," to national paeans, like "Pastures of Plenty." He wrote very few original melodies, but built on folk and country tunes, remaking the songs completely with his own verses. He loved anti-hero outlaws who were really just against the evils of society.[12]

By the end of the 1940s, Woody's health began to fail and his great voice and pen were stilled. Beginning in 1954, Huntington's chorea gave him thirteen years of hospital misery. His writings and sketches were collected by the Woody Guthrie Children's Trust Society, set up by his agent Harold Leventhal, Seeger, and Lou Gordon, another friend. I edited an anthology, *Born to Win*, published in 1965. Bob Dylan's work finally brought Woody to a large contemporary audience, and the success of his son, Arlo Guthrie, reminded a new generation of what Woody had done. In "People I Owe," from *Born to Win*, Woody tried to pay back the human sources of his art. He felt he was only a reporter, taking down the people's poetry: "I borrowed my life from the works of your life. I have felt your energy in me and seen mine move in you. You may have been taught to call me by the name of a poet, but I am no more of a poet than you are. I am no more of a writer of songs than you are, no better singer."

Girl from the North Country. When journalists stumbled on Echo Helstrom, they were convinced they'd found Dylan's "Girl from the North Country." A much likelier candidate was Bonny Jean Beecher. Dylan almost said in "My Life in a Stolen Moment": "I fell hard for an actress girl who kneed me in the guts." Bonny knew she'd made an impact, yet she wasn't about to sell (or to give away) pieces of soul. By the time I caught up with her in 1966, Bonny was leading a West Coast beat actress's life in Los Angeles. Then, the only person this lost, gentle, self-effacing young woman could have been kneeing in the guts was herself. A delicate-featured blonde, Bonny had pellucid diction without drama-school affectation.[13]

It's speculation on my part, but the clear impression I gained from my contact with Dinkytown people suggested Bonny, to at least *some* degree, inspired Bob to succeed in the east. He returned several times to Minneapolis. Although the love affair with Bonny was over, the friendship was not. A sophisticate from a well-to-do family in Edina, a comfortable Twin Cities suburb, Bonny was a rebel before she met Bob at a party in early 1960, as anxious to adventure from her WASP background as Bob was to assimilate into the mainstream. Bonny was worldly; she read the right things, knew the right people and was aware as no girl from Hibbing could ever be.

Bonny often bought records from the shop where Paul Nelson worked. She never thought seriously about using her good voice as a vocalist; she was content to play small university-theater roles. There was instant rapport between Bob and Bonny. Bonny was getting her hands dirty as a short-order cook at an all-night hamburger joint, which suited Bob. If they weren't sandwiching in hamburger meetings, they were going to parties at the Alamo Apartments, known as the Anthill. She was a dedicated encourager, a sympathetic audience for him for a good part of 1960. As friends tell it, Bob fell deeply in love, but for her the relationship wasn't as important. They drifted apart. When there was some triumph in New York, he'd call or write her. When I saw Bonny, she was involved with a Village hipster comic-monologuist, Hugh Romney, also known as Wavy Gravy. Romney, Tiny Tim, and Severn Darden made up the cast of Los Angeles's Phantom Theater, with Bonny hovering around as the troupe's spiritual overseer.

A one-time sorority sister of Bonny's was Cynthia Fincher, with whom Bob spent time in late 1960. They were intellectual soulmates. Cynthia was a banjo player and painter, intelligent and articulate. They played shows together at the Purple Onion. Gretel Hoffman was a special friend, before and after her marriage to Whitaker. By the time Bob saw Echo a few times in Minneapolis, she was part of the past. He was moving faster than any of his friends. The passions that long outlasted Dinkytown were his love of performing and of Woody Guthrie.

Prophet with Honor. One Dinkytown friendship, with Dave (Tony) Glover, outlasted others.[14] In 1963, Bob described Glover as "a friend to everything I am. Dave Glover, who I really love. Dave Glover, who feels and thinks and walks and talks just like I do." Glover helped me reconstruct Dylan's early days in Dinkytown. Glover also saw Bob at Newport, visited him at Woodstock, and attended some of his New York recording sessions. Tony was tough and taciturn, yet gentle, cool as a bluesman, and passionate about his music and friends. Glover had chosen the nickname "Tony" to avoid confusion when he sang with Dave Ray as Koerner, Ray and Glover. Morton used to satirize Tony's frequent dark moods by singing "You Are My Sunshine" every time Glover appeared. His dark, laconic, James Dean-like manner made Bob feel Tony could be trusted.

Glover started cautiously, emphasizing that "Bob is not an ordinary kind of human being. There are two people, the cat I know and knew here and the one who's 'on' in public. Both of us were on the edges of the scene here, accepted, but outside because of some need or difference of our own. I guess that's the real basis of our friendship then, a feeling that there was more, something else, somewhere else. He's changed. Now [1966] he's almost an old man in many ways, patiently accepting that life *is* and nothing much can be done about it. I don't know if he's happy or unhappy. Perhaps he just *is*, period."

Glover was partly fascinated, mostly protective, wanting to be sure that Bob would be treated sympathetically. He kept a full file of tapes, clippings, and memorabilia. Tony was one of the first to *know* that Bob was going somewhere. He liked Bob as much when he was a prophet without honor in Minneapolis as when he triumphed. Tony met Bob in May 1960, at a party for Gretel. Tony: "I found Bob sitting in a corner with a guitar and we started to talk. He was wearing a crew cut and sneakers. He seemed to be out of place and uncomfortable. Lynn Castner was singing Woody's songs. Some people were not listening to Bob's singing and he got very abusive and said he wouldn't sing anymore. Some people there asked who he thought he was."

Glover, who became a music journalist and novelist, was perhaps the first musician friend who dared to criticize and advise Bob. Because it was constructive, Bob apparently took it well. For at least two and a half years, Bob maintained a running debate with Glover, Nelson, and Pankake about topical-political songs. By August 1962, when Bob returned to Minneapolis for his third visit, he was beginning to show signs of questioning topical-protest songs. Bob was pleased to put on a little show in 1962 for his Dinkytown friends. Speaking in his most nasal Guthriesque inflection, Bob said: "I'm gonna sing you a song that isn't done—it isn't done at all." [He tunes his guitar.] "Hello. This is Bob Dylan from Paris. This is a song I wrote for CORE. CORE is a white organization for Negro people. I am sick of writing songs for everybody. You might as well get this on your tape-recording machine and you can play it for all your friends at *Little Sandy Review*. I've got a lot of respect for *Little Sandy Review*. Jon Pankake is a bigger man than I am, I will say that. I'm gonna make up a few verses here, but the last verse is the one I wrote the whole song about. I wrote it because this here thing came into my mind. My girl, she's in Europe right now. She sailed on a boat over there. She'll be back September first, and till she's back, I'll never go home. It gets kind of bad sometimes. Sometimes it gets bad, but sometimes it doesn't. This isn't really my style. This is the Pete Seeger style. You know, he's Mike Seeger's older brother."

Bob sang "Black Cross," then jumped to part of what became "Tomorrow Is a Long Time." Then he did a talking blues, which asked: "What kind of hippo is a hypocrite?" Next, a song he adapted from a traditional tune, "A Long Time Coming." "Do you like that song? I just sort of made up half the words to it. I wrote that for myself. I figure I've been writing too many songs for other people. I finally got to the point where I said to myself: 'Jesus, Dylan, you ain't written no songs about you,' and I said: 'You've got to get somebody to write a song about you.' Then I said to myself: 'You write songs. I can write songs about me as well as anybody else can.' So, I wrote about ten songs in a week about me." Bob was about to sing "Bob Dylan's Blues," but he suddenly found that he couldn't remember it. Then he sang "Corrina, Corrina" and "Deep Down Blues." The party soon degenerated with Dylan being pestered for one song after another. He finally left, saying, "everybody is dumb in Minneapolis."

In summer 1962, Bob was already restive about "songs for other people," yet was far from finished with his first "commitment" period. In 1963, the strongly radicalized Dylan paid another visit to Tony Glover, Paul Nelson, and others, and a hot debate raged. Tony recalled: "Paul was saying that Bob 'had to get more of a balance between his traditional style and his individual style.' Bob sang one of his latest songs, like 'Only a Pawn in Their Game,' and tried to show us that it was about what was happening today, even though it wasn't traditional. Paul was arguing that folk music wasn't good just because the cause was good. Dylan was basically agreeing, but he countered that you can't put something down just because a song is *about* something. He was maintaining social things were more important than music."

Dylan supplied a soundtrack to the debate by singing his new songs, mostly social commentary. Not happy with the reaction, Dylan started to swear. After a long stream of vituperation, he said: "Folk music has nothing to do with it! It's not music when you walk out on the street. You can play it on your phonograph, but it's not there when you walk out on the street." His voice trembled with impatience and frustration with the friends he had left behind.

Of all the trips back to Dinkytown, perhaps the most poignant was the one in July 1963, when he was about to break out nationally as a major folk star. He told the old crowd about his travels to London, called his manager, Albert Grossman, "a beautiful guy, a genius." Then he became unabashedly sentimental about how far he had traveled: "I left this town on the highway, I think it was Highway 12. I wasn't even thinking—it was the first of my non-thinking. I never cared in the three and a half or four years since I left this town about anything. Time and chance. Man, that's why I'm there now. There are a million me's, all over the United States. They are all hung up, but they can't split from where they are." He was being self-deprecating, speaking as a figurehead for song, poetry, and leadership. Whitman's "A Song of Myself," Guthrie's "The Great Historical Bum." Their creed had become Dylan's—all the best ballad-makers were only reporters, taking down the poetry of the people.

As early as 1961, Tony had taped Bob doing R&B-type Chuck Berry songs. Tony often taped Dylan. On Bob's first return to Dinkytown, in May 1961, he was still very much influenced by Guthrie. At a summit meeting of Twin Cities musicians, Tony first heard Bob do an original song, his "Song to Woody." Bob told Tony that Joan Baez wanted to record it. Tony: "I don't know how much effect I had, but I said to Bob: 'Keep it for yourself. You can do a much better job on it than she could.'"

Bob returned to Minneapolis in December 1961, after cutting his first album. Gretel: "The first thing Bob did was show us the *New York Times* clipping. He talked with great velocity. He got out his guitar and said: 'Listen to what I have done. Listen to what's happened to me!' But then, when other people came over, he got almost shy. He had suddenly turned into a really good storyteller. He and David would sit and tell stories and elaborate on jokes for hours. He was delightful. I don't know just how much of Lenny Bruce Bob had seen, but Bruce was very much a household name around here. A lot of people here invented Lenny Bruce riffs."[15] The Lenny Bruce influence was probably indirect, by way of Hugh Romney. Romney and Bruce, both disciples of the late Lord Buckley, the satirist-monologuist, had played in Minneapolis at a downtown club, Minor Key, when Dylan was still in town.[16] Both parlayed the late-1950s impudence, black humor, verbal fictions, parables, and tales that would strongly influence Dylan.

In December 1961, "the change was enormous," Gretel said. "He was just beginning to experiment with poetry and to realize that it would be poetry." One younger chum, Bill Golfus: "Everyone was amazed that anyone from Dinkytown had actually made a record. The only person that had an inkling of what was happening was Dave Morton. We were all kids, just playing beatnik."

Prophet without Honor. Dylan still hadn't gotten his due from many in Minneapolis. In 1966, the big poets on campus, John Berryman and Allen Tate, scarcely took any notice of him. By 1972, Berryman had killed himself, but Tate ignored Dylan until his own death. In May 1964, the student literary magazine, *Ivory Tower*, took cognizance. Roland Flint, an editor of the *Minnesota Review*:

The only things of Dylan I have read were on the record jackets, which included some so-called poems. He is a good popular entertainer. I enjoy his stuff. I like his performances and I enjoy his songs. No, I don't think he is a poet and I don't think he writes poetry. His works lacks any kind of metaphorical complexity. It is simple and simple-minded for the most part … The Minnesota Review is not there to publish popular-song lyrics. That's what Dylan writes, and he is good at it. John Berryman would probably agree with me, and might even be more contemptuous. I would really like to see some things of his that you think have literary merit.

In 1961, Harry Weber, who preceded Flint, was, at 33, the youngest editor of the *Minnesota Review*. Weber told me: "I don't think much of the poems on the back of Bob's albums, but his songs are fine poems. If I were still editor, I would have printed 'Tambourine Man' like a shot, printed his '115th Dream' very quickly. I would have printed 'Maggie's Farm' with great happiness, with all the repeats. Flint was a protégé and friend of Allen Tate. Tate made a special point of putting down Dylan as a poet, but I simply disagree with them. 'Hard Rain' is very much a young man's poem, but I would say that 'Rolling Stone' is a very good poem."

If most of the Minneapolis literary people dismissed Dylan as a serious writer, local journalists were even more hostile. P M Clepper of the (St Paul) *Pioneer Press* made himself a specialist in Dylan history. In 1965, Clepper did a sour piece, which appeared in *This Week*, the Sunday supplement, on March 27, 1966:

Dylan is a millionaire beatnik … piling in money like Irving Berlin. Dylan is not a hillbilly, nor ill-educated … he made himself up … Dylan, in fact, has never in his 24 years had to go to work, not even as a minor … Hibbing gave him no experience with racial class oppression that he could later exploit in songs … Dylan had no Negro friends in Minnesota, so it came as a surprise when he showed up in the heart of the March on Washington in August, 1963. But there was obviously a hunger for such sentiments out there in the great young land … It was an irony … that Dylan was being paid fantastically well by the very society he castigated.

Another who wrote sardonically about Bob was Walter Eldot of the *Duluth News-Tribune*. Eldot told me that a lot of strange characters have come off the Iron Range, like Dylan and Gus Hall, the Communist leader. Eldot cited as prime evidence of Dylan's distortions his song "Walls of Red Wing," about the state training school for young delinquents. "There are no walls there," the Duluth arts specialist insisted.

Little Sandy Review revealed Dylan's Minneapolis background in late autumn 1962. Nelson did a highly complimentary analysis of the first Dylan album, but Pankake tempered his praise in an unsigned review:

We recall Bob as a soft-spoken, rather unprepossessing youngster; he … was well-groomed and neat in the standard campus costume of slacks, sweater, white oxford sneakers, poplin raincoat, and dark glasses, and sang the standard coffeehouse songs … in a skilful, but not noteworthy manner … Dylan left the university … that autumn, hitting the road for New Jersey and a fateful rendezvous with Woody Guthrie. That was the last we saw of Bob until May of 1961, when he returned for a brief but extremely telling appearance at a university hootenanny. The change in Bob was, to say the least, incredible … Dylan's performance … of a selection of Guthrie and Gary Davis songs was hectic and shaky, but it contained all the elements of the now-perfected performing style that has made him the most original newcomer to folk music. Yes, folks, a star was born that night.

Little Sandy admonished Dylan to "steer clear of the protesty people," and demolished the *Sing Out!* story: "Dylan's quotes and his Guthriesque pose on the cover seemed to us to be quite ridiculous; both seemed phony, all-too-hard tries to be Woody himself." Bob first read this in my New York apartment. Rather than focusing on either the praise for his work or the revelation about his name change, he seemed most upset about the description of how he dressed and looked in his freshman year. "I *never* combed my hair, I *never* wore a tie," he told me emphatically.

Bad press in the Twin Cities continued through 1965. After a one-night stand in summer 1965, at the 8,000-seat Minneapolis Auditorium, the amusements columnist of the *St Paul Evening Dispatch* pounced on Dylan for his "reprehensible" conduct:

He refused contact with anyone, horsed around during his show and generally left a sour taste in his wake … Dylan is either very bitter or extremely conceited … he said: "Why should I see these people [including members of his own family living in the area]? They had no time for me when I was nothing. Why should I see them now?" … When the audience finally started to whistle between the long-delayed selections, Dylan said: "I'm just as anxious to go home as you are. Don't you have any newspapers to read?" Headlines the next day read: "Bob Dylan, Go Home!" and "The Fall of an Idol." The show had been a sellout, but since the performance (or lack of one), sales of The Great One's records have nose-dived.

Dylan again filled the auditorium on November 5, 1965, grossing a tidy $26,000 for the evening. The *Minneapolis Star Tribune* reviewer said:

The real show was in the audience. Gum-chewing teenagers in costumes straight out of circus sideshows sat hypnotized… Dylan looks like a scarecrow with ratted hair … 'Desolation Road' [sic] showed real signs of humor and insight and it was the high point of the evening to sit and listen to his political barbs go over the heads of his disciples … it was not his kind of setting … Nevertheless, the crowd loved it. Let the psychologists explain it.

A writer, who called himself only "Mann," wrote in the underground paper, *Twin City a Go-Go*, that Dylan's return visit "only confirmed his popularity and incomprehensibility." Ed Freeman was quoted in the *Go-Go*: "Dylan used to sound like a lung cancer victim singing Woody Guthrie. Now he sounds like a Rolling Stone singing Immanuel Kant." After this concert, Bob rambled around Dinkytown with associates and a local couple they picked up on the streets. They peeked into the Scholar, a few other bars, and doubled back to McCosh's Bookstore. Bob told how things used to look.

Dylan had left Minneapolis five years earlier, but his actual leave-taking is difficult to document. He had been sharing a flat with Brown and Max Uhler, then moved again into his own bleak little room. Dylan often made Guthriesque exits, setting out to hitchhike, but then someone would see him a few hours later at the bus terminal. Whitaker told me that right after one of those phone calls to Guthrie's hospital, Bob took off. Bob's final lines to Whitaker: "I'm leaving for New York! I'm going to see Woody!" Whitaker: "He just up and left. There was a driving blizzard in Minneapolis, but he set off for Chicago." Jerry Connors, one of the local scene-makers, distinctly recalls sitting in the Scholar at a table adjoining Dylan's and hearing Bob say: "I'm going to New York and I'm going to be somebody!" Connors says Bob left that very day. Whether he traveled along Highway 61, as he celebrated in song, doesn't much matter; Highway 61 is as much a metaphor as a highway, for it links Duluth to Minneapolis, then runs right down into blues country at the *right* end of the Mississippi.[17]

Dinkytown chums had some warning that Dylan was going. Landlords and his parents certainly didn't. Abe and Beatty went to look for Bob at his last known address. In a stark, little-furnished room, they found only a few scraps of paper. They pulled open bureau drawers and searched empty closets. He was gone, really gone, this time. They knew then that their son was beyond their command. Dylan said: "I stood on the highway during a blizzard snowstorm believing in the mercy of the world and headed east, didn't have nothing but my guitar and suitcase."

According to a Village street person, Keven Krown, Dylan showed up in Chicago just before Christmas, 1960. Krown places Dylan in Chicago for a couple of weeks, while others maintain he spent several days in Madison, Wisconsin, before heading east. Krown wasn't very believable around New York, so his chronology doesn't impress me, but the Madison interlude seems likely. Bob wanted to revise his story about his arrival in New York, to me at least, to allow for some mad weeks around Times Square before hitting the Village. Here, in "My Life in a Stolen Moment," is one of several times in Dylan's career where metaphor is the message, not the documentation:

That's pretty well my college life
After that I thumbed my way to Galveston, Texas in
four days tryin' to find an ol' friend
whose ma met me at the screen door and said he's in the Army—
By the time the kitchen door closed
I was passin' California—almost in Oregon—
I met a waitress in the woods who picked me up
an' dropped me off in Washington someplace
I danced my way from the Indian festivals in Gallup, New Mexico
To the Mardi Gras in New Orleans, Louisiana
With my thumb out, my eyes asleep, my hat turned up an' my head turned on
I's driftin' an' learnin' new lessons
I was making my own depression
I rode freight trains for kicks
An' got beat up for laughs
Cut grass for quarters an' sang for dimes
Hitchhiked on 61—51—75—169—37—66—22
Gopher Road—Route 40 an' Howard Johnson Turnpike
Got jailed for suspicion of armed robbery
Got held four hours on a murder rap
Got busted for looking like I do
An' I never done none a them things[18]

Know thyself.

DELPHIC ORACLE, 6TH CENTURY BC

Dig yuhself.

DYLAN, AD 1961

The only way is up, at Gerde's Folk City, December 1961.

Dylan pulled himself out of college and, with his own hands, got a tenuous grasp on show business. Actually, he used mostly his thumbs. He thumbed his nose at formal education, thumbed through *Bound for Glory*, his personal bible, thumbed his way (metaphorically at least) to New York to see Guthrie, and thumbed through a roster of important and influential people in folk music and proceeded to get to know them.

Intoxicated with the unbridled romanticism of Guthrie's hard traveling, he made a precipitate exit from university and from Dinkytown. Some saw him heading for the open road out of Minneapolis, others say they saw him a few hours later at the bus depot, buying his ticket east. In any event, Dylan arrived in New York in December 1960 on a cold, inhospitable day. Slush filled the streets but the heat of his mission kept him aglow. He has told of his first attack on New York in several ways. The most entertaining version is in "Talking New York," written in May 1961 at a truck stop west of New York. It pictures a lonesome highway person lurching into town, struggling until attaining "success" at a dollar a day.

No community better represented personal and artistic freedom than Greenwich Village. Within the Village, no scenes were livelier than off-Broadway theater and the new upsurge of folk music, a revival that was part-circus and part-morality play. The folk boom arrived just as the first thrust of rock 'n' roll had run its course. From 1954 to 1958, rock, rhythm 'n' blues, and rockabilly singers had a heyday, then appeared to lose inspiration and direction. Along with this temporary waning of early rock power, came a wave of payola scandals, with DJs found to be accepting bribes to play certain records. For a few years, folk seemed the pure alternative to tainted rock. Steeped in the traditions of musical dissent, of anti-commercialism, or, at least, non-commercialism, folk songs then seemed the sane, musical corrective.

Almost anyone with a few dollars could set up a coffeehouse; almost anyone with a guitar and a few songs could entertain. The music business was jolted by such widespread decentralization of talent and audiences. For a time, the folk movement ran on greased wheels of anti-show business idealism. More commercially-oriented folk singers had to present themselves as idealistic; they had to dress simply and appear indifferent toward money. Some thought they could be idealistic and uncompromising, and still make a good living. "Why not be good *and* commercial?" asked the late Lee Hays, an original member of the Weavers. Many who came after him believed it possible to be idealistic and uncompromising, both musically and philosophically, and still make money. Others abhorred financial success.

Albert B Grossman, who would become Dylan's manager, once remarked ruefully that some "pure" folk singers "act as if money were heroin." Grossman, who denied that there was anything addictive about the acquisition of wealth, did a lot to convince others that they could get rich with integrity. "The American public," he told me in 1959, at the first Newport Folk Festival, which he and George Wein co-produced, "is like Sleeping Beauty waiting to be kissed awake by the prince of folk music." Grossman was one of the first businessmen not only to kiss Sleeping Beauty but also to climb right into bed with her.[1]

Dylan had come east to meet Guthrie but he was also determined to carve his own niche. His ambition was tempered by the style of the folk revival around him, a movement where the individual contributed to the whole, where "making it" also meant making a contribution. Dylan recaptured those early years of folk togetherness in a prose-poem written for the album jacket of Peter, Paul and Mary's *In the Wind* in 1963:

> *Snow was piled up the stairs an onto the street*
> *that first winter when I laid around New York City*
> *It was a different street then—*
> *It was a different village—*
> *Nobody had nothin—*
> *There was nothin t get—*
> *Instead a bein drawn for money you were drawn*
> *for other people—*
> *Everybody used t hang around a heat pipe poundin*

subterranean coffeehouse called the Gaslight—
It was at that time buried beneath the middle a
MacDougal Street …

Everybody that hung out at the Gaslight was close
Yuh had t be—
In order t keep from going insane an in order t
survive—
An it can't be denied—
It was a hangout—
But not like the street corner—
Down there we weren't standin lookin out at the world
watchin girls —an findin out how they walk—
We was lookin at each other … and findin out about
ourselves—
It is 'f these times that I remember most sadly—
For they're gone—
And they'll not never come again—
It is 'f these times I think about now— …
There was not such a thing as an audience—
There was not such a thing as performers—
Everybody did somethin—
An had somethin t say about somethin—
I remember Hugh who wore different kinda
clothes then but still shouted an tongue
twisted flowin lines a poetry that anybody who
could be struck by the sounds 'f a rock
hittin a brick wall could understand—
I remember Luke playin his banjo an singin "East
Virginia" with a tone as soft as the snow outside
an "Mr. Garfield" with a bitin touch as hard as the
stovepipe on the inside—
An Dave singin "House a the Risin Sun" with his
back leaned against the bricks an words runnin
out in a lonesome hungry growlin whisper that
any girl with her face hid in the dark could
understand—
Paul then was a guitar player singer comedian—
But not the funny ha ha kind—
His funnyness could only be defined an described
by the word "hip" or "hyp"—
A combination a Charlie Chaplin Jonathan Winters
an Peter Lorre— …
Anyway it was one a these nites when Paul said
"Yuh gotta now hear me an Peter an Mary sing"
Mary's hair was down almost t her waist then—
An Peter's beard was only about half grown—
An the Gaslight stage was smaller
An the song they sung was younger—
But the walls shook
An everybody smiled—
An everybody felt good— …
An that's where the beginnin was at—

Dylan recording at Columbia Studios, New York, August 1963.

Inside them walls 'f a subterranean world—
But it's a concrete kind a beginnin'
It's concrete cause it's close—
An it's close cause it's gotta be close—
An that feeling aint t be forgotten—
Yuh carry it with yuh—
It's a feelin that's born an not bought
An it can't be taught—
An by livin with it yuh learn t see and know it
in other people
T sing an speak as one yuh gotta think as one—
An yuh gotta believe as one—
An yuh gotta feel as one—
An Peter an Paul an Mary're now carryin the feelin
that was inside them walls up the steps t the
whole outside world—
The rooster never crowed on MacDougal Street—
There was no dew on the grass an the sun never came
shinin over the mountain—
There was nothin t tell yuh it was mornin cept
the pins and needles feelin in yer arms an legs
from stayin up all nite—
But all 'f us find our way a knowin when it's
mornin—
And once yuh know the feelin it don't change—
It can only grow—
For Peter's grown—
An Paul's grown—
An Mary's grown—
An the times've grown[2]

"And Mary's grown." Dylan and Mary Travers, Newport Folk Festival, 1963.

11 p.m. Cowboy. That was the young Dylan we saw around the Village in 1960, and how he saw himself a couple of years later. By 1966, however, he asked me to amend the story. Then, he was trying to portray himself as an urban cowboy, hustling and rustling around Times Square: "I shucked everybody when I came to New York," Dylan said. "I played cute. I did not go down to the Village when I first got to New York. I have a friend … he's a junkie now. We came to New York together. He wrote plays. We hung out on 43rd Street, and hustled for two months, and did everything. I got the ride here in December 1960. I came down to the Village in February. But I was here, in New York, in December. Hustling, with this cat. I'm not scared of people, you dig? You name it, we did it. Sometimes we would make one hundred a night, really, from four in the afternoon until three or four in the morning. We would make one hundred-fifty or two hundred-fifty a night between us, and hang around in bars. Cats would pick us up and chicks would pick us up. And we would do anything you wanted, as long as it paid. It was very cut-throat. You gotta shell out a lotta money just to hang around, so we weren't making anything. We ended up in the Village. And I had the guitar. I didn't have any place to stay, but it was easy for me. People took me in."

Was it a dangerous life around Times Square? "That's where I almost got killed," Dylan replied, "before I came down to the Village. I didn't plan to stay in New York. I left, anyway, in the spring, and didn't plan to come back. I came back because I really missed it. There was no other place that I really could go to. The first places I played in were on 44th and 43rd Streets, between Broadway and Eighth Avenue, in any of those bars. I didn't come down to the Village until two months later. Nobody knew that I had been hustling uptown."

Whatever the realities of those two months around Times Square, Dylan got off the subway in the Village in early February 1961 in a furiously ambitious mood. He looked much as he did when he left Minneapolis, slight and spare in denim, sheepskin, and suede. Village people virtually adopted him. He looked so much in need of love and attention that he brought out the brother, sister, lover, or parent in everyone he met. Dylan was already up to his earlobes in folk music, and soon his boots were deep into beat poetry. Hugh Romney, the poet-comic-fantasist, was big then on MacDougal Street. Dylan arrived with little beat vocabulary. Six months later he was talking, japing, digging everything like Romney. "Dig yuhself" became Dylan's shibboleth as it had been Romney's. The beat poets were working alongside the folk-guitar pickers. Both were cheap labor. Dylan was artistically reborn to dual parentage. Where the romanticism of Whitman, Sandburg, Guthrie, Kerouac, and Ginsberg left off, the new romanticism of the city folk singers took over.

In the mid-1950s, the marriage of modern poetry and jazz had a brief honeymoon in San Francisco. The union of poetry and folk music in Greenwich Village during 1961–63 held, thanks in part to Dylan. By the time he wrote the "11 Outlined Epitaphs" for his third album, Dylan had coupled folk and beat poetry. The Epitaph about Guthrie superimposes Dylan's early days in New York on Woody's arrival from the west. The poem echoes François Villon, "ah where are those forces of yesteryear?"[3] and Seeger's "The Bells of Rhymney"—"the underground's gone deeper/says the old chimney sweeper."[4] By the conclusion, Dylan is far from echoes, leading his own parade:

> an' so I step back t' the street
> an' then turn further down the road
> poundin' on doors …
> without ghosts by my side
> t' betray my childishness
> t' leadeth me down false trails
> an' maketh me drink from muddy waters
> yet it is I
> who is poundin' at your door if it is you inside[5]

Dylan pounded his way through endless doors in 1961: the Commons, the Gaslight, the Café Wha? and the Folklore Center all had doors facing MacDougal, a dark, bustling new main drag that made Dinkytown look provincial. MacDougal Street smelled of creation, romance, art, independence, cappuccino, and sausage sandwiches. Dylan was the sort of hungry immigrant who would walk into a MacDougal sandwich shop and ask for an antihero sandwich, though he'd rather *you* paid. He acquired people with stunning speed. No one seemed to challenge his stories of travel and friendship with obscure black singers like Big Joe Williams or Mance Lipscomb.

Dylan's trademark was a strange little black corduroy hat that he wore everywhere. It was a prop, a badge, and, incidentally, a piece of clothing. With its slightly peaked top, short visor, and cut, it resembled a Dutch boy's cap, or the caps Eastern European immigrants had worn as they stood on deck, gazing in awe at the Manhattan skyline. Dylan wore his hat onstage and off until well into 1962, when he gave it to singer Dave Van Ronk as a keepsake. Tripler, the elegant Madison Avenue men's shop, later sold a version. Arthur's, the Manhattan discotheque, kept a copy in a glass case, with a sign: YES, WE HAVE THE HAT ON SALE HERE. It inspired at least one song, by Tony Herbert. I asked Bob where and why he got it. "I got it someplace. I got it, man, to keep my head warm," he said, grinning.

Among the first to adopt Dylan was a middle-aged couple, Eve and Mac MacKenzie, of East 28th Street, near Bellevue Hospital. The MacKenzies were earthy, generous people, who found another son in Bob. On and off for several months, Dylan called their home his. Mac MacKenzie was a hard-drinking, storytelling longshoreman. Bob recalled: "I really feel bad that I have never seen them again. I used to stay out till all hours but then I came in and slept on the couch. Hey, I'll tell you somebody [else]. Let me put their name on you, right now! Mel and Lillian Bailey, I love those people. Every time I think of them, it hurts, because I never get to see them. Mel is a physician. Lillian, I have no idea. They are two of the loveliest. They took me in, and they let me come over to their house, man, and sleep there, when they had nothing but a room. They gave me everything, man. I could never repay them. I've tried, lotta times. Every time I come across the name of someone like that…" He grew dark and quiet.

The first performance in the Village that anyone recalls was at the Commons coffeehouse. He wrote to Tony Glover about this milestone, sending a postcard of Woody Guthrie and rhapsodizing about having met Woody ("The greatest, holiest, Godliest one in the world") and Jack Elliott. The Commons was a sprawling basement club on the west side of MacDougal, near Minetta Lane. The club has also been known as the Fat Black Pussycat and the Feenjon. When Dylan entered the coffeehouse circuit, an army of folk musicians were struggling for recognition. Folk music was tracking its country boots through Manhattan's night life, from the grimiest Village espresso joint up to midtown's Waldorf-Astoria Hotel. Concert audiences, meanwhile, were paying attention to a moody, sensitive young folk singer named Joan Baez. After her well-staged debut at the 1959 Newport Folk Festival, her recording company, Vanguard, was grooming her for bigger audiences. Joan, Pete Seeger, and the Kingston Trio were really uptown folk singers then—professionals with recordings, managers, and concert circuits. The Village crew that Dylan joined were unknowns trying to break through. At the Thirdside, a Third Street coffeehouse, "passing the basket" was the only way to get a night's wages.

Some performers were dedicated artists, others simply used folk songs as a show-biz vehicle. At Trude Heller's Versailles, a honey-voiced starlet named Beverly Wright, decked out in gold lamé, told listeners she was "booked to sing folk in Vegas." In the Phase 2, Jimmy Gavin, a clean-shaven actor-singer, had a slick, unfolkish manner. At the Café Wha?, Len Chandler, an articulate and charming black performer, told me he had thrown over his classical background to rediscover his people's music. On Bleecker Street, a cheerless bistro called the Cock 'n' Bull floundered financially despite such performing talent as Bob Gibson. Later, a former ad huckster and future film producer, Fred Weintraub, converted the club into the successful Bitter End. Guitarist Dick Rosmini remarked: "The coffeehouses are the cruelest school you'll ever see. But, it's a beautiful way to keep working." At the Café Raffio, probably the dingiest in the Village, singer Tom Paslé commented cynically: "I don't *have* to do this for a living. I *could* starve."

The Village Vanguard, under Max Gordon and Herbert Jacoby, had long fostered talent, as did Jacoby's Blue Angel uptown. The Weavers began at the Vanguard in 1948; the club gave Harry Belafonte his major launch. Another night spot dating back to the earliest days of folk's arrival in New York was One Sheridan Square. This basement club, situated where Washington Place and West Fourth Street come together like the legs of a man, had been Café Society Downtown. During World War II, under Barney Josephson, it had been the hangout of folk-lovers. Josh White was a regular then. By 1960, White was reappearing in the club, revamped and renamed by Kelsey Marechal and Martin Lorin. Other regulars included Carolyn Hester and a group of Irish folkniks, the Clancy Brothers and Tommy Makem.[6] Since its 1958 opening, the Village Gate, run by Art D'Lugoff and his brother, Dr Burt D'Lugoff, had been heavily identified with folk music. Among those who had New York debuts there were Leon Bibb, Theodore Bikel, the Limeliters, and Odetta. A more esoteric music setting was Page Three on Seventh Avenue South, a long, narrow room where many lesbians gathered. Page Three provided the chief forum for that curious campy performer, Tiny Tim.[7]

For a time, the hottest scene was in the Cafe Wha?, a basement *boîte* where manager Manny Roth was always offering jobs to young musicians who drifted in. There, one night in early 1961, Dylan took his harmonica onstage to accompany the gifted white blues singer-songwriter Fred Neil. Neil didn't attain recognition until 1969, when his song "Everybody's Talkin'" was the theme for the film *Midnight Cowboy*. Ironically, with that song Neil beat out his former harmonica player. Dylan told *Rolling Stone* in 1969: "There's a movie out now called *Midnight Cowboy*. You know the song… 'Lay, Lady, Lay'? Well, I wrote it for that movie. These producers wanted some music for the movie last summer. By the time I came up with it, though, it was too late."

Dylan has said that any of several MacDougal Street coffeehouses could qualify for the dubious distinction of saying he sounded like a hillbilly. The Commons and the Cafe Wha? seem the likeliest candidates. (Some collectors maintain that Dylan's first recorded onstage words in New York were at the Wha?: "Just got here from the west. Name's Bob Dylan. I'd like to do a few songs. Can I?") The two folk clubs that gave Dylan his real start in New York were the Gaslight and Gerde's Folk City.

A-Folk a-City. At 11 West Fourth Street, a few blocks east of MacDougal, just a verse or two between the old Bohemia of the West Village and the emerging hippie East Village, stood a dingy six-story brownstone built in 1889, once a spray-gun factory. On the ground floor was a neighborhood saloon where locals and strays off Lower Broadway could escape their loneliness with a beer and a Sinatra song on the juke box. The place was named Gerde's, after its prosperous nineteenth-century owner. Since 1958, the saloon had been run by Mike Porco, a gentle Calabrian with a thin moustache, thick glasses, and a thicker accent. The saloon-keeper and his brother John had emigrated from the impoverished toe of the Italian boot in 1933. Mike had landed in the Village in 1952, and was just about making ends meet at Gerde's. He had experimented a few times with some bongo players and avant-garde jazzman Cecil Taylor.[8]

Late in 1959, two men approached Porco with a proposal that, for four years, converted the sleepy saloon into a thriving cabaret. Tom Prendergast, a New England businessman, and Israel G Young, proprietor of the Folklore Center, a music shop, meeting place, and gossip mill at 110 MacDougal, had been looking for somewhere to stage folk music. They agreed to run the show at Gerde's for a cut of the admissions. Tom and Izzy decided to call the club the Fifth Peg, after the drone device on a folk banjo and, in January 1960, opened as "New York's center of folk music."[9] For several months after the first-night bill of Ed McCurdy and Molly Scott, ballad singers and instrumentalists trouped to the cramped stage. Musicians and fans congregated, but Izzy, an astigmatic visionary, didn't seem to know how to sell at a profit. He kept journals of folk minutiae and loved his role of Village mentor to young folk enthusiasts. Young's and Prendergast's inexperience as producers forced them to quit the Fifth Peg after three months. They had brought in quality performers, such as the Clancys, the Tarriers, Brownie McGhee and Sonny Terry, but the pair lost money while Mike Porco, who barely knew a ballad from a bologna sausage, raked in profits on drinks.

In February 1960, Mike moved in on the Fifth Peg's closed Mondays with what he first called an "amateur night." Eager young performers put on a free show to a packed house. I suggested he call the amateur free-for-all "hootenanny," a word he could scarcely pronounce. When Prendergast and Young pulled out, Porco assumed management and renamed the club Gerde's Folk City, hiring Charlie Rothschild, an aspiring young manager, later associated with Grossman, as the talent coordinator. After a distinguished start with Cisco Houston and the Reverend Gary Davis, a famous blind "holy blues" man, Gerde's continued a policy of booking serious folk talent.

Izzy Young never recovered from his Fifth Peg defeat. One day Charlie dropped into the Folklore Center for a chat. Without warning, Izzy punched him in the face. The brotherhood of the New York City folk revival was beginning to show sibling rivalry. Despite tiffs and acrimony, Folk City prospered. Though musicians earned only union scale, they pushed to perform there. Rothschild left after a clash with Porco, and soon Mike was hiring talent himself, polling customers to determine their likes.

Mike used his "hoots" as public auditions, often listening not to the music, only to the applause. One female folk singer auditioned while he was cutting sandwiches in the kitchen. "You didn't even hear me sing," she complained. "I heard the clapping," Mike said. "We can put you in for a couple of weeks." Not the least of Porco's charms was the fact that he never mastered English. He called his new club "a-Folk a-City," and once telephoned an ad to the *Village Voice* that ran for two weeks billing Anita Sheer as a "flamingo singer" rather than a flamenco singer. Another performer, who sang in several languages, was advertised as "a linguistical folk singer."

If Mike always watered down his English, occasionally his whiskey, and frequently his payments to musicians, he was usually receptive to new talent. "Give them a chance" was his working motto, while "the newer the cheaper" was his fiscal policy. When, in March 1961, one of his regular customers, Mel Bailey, urged him to give Bobby Dylan a chance, Mike showed interest. He liked Bobby, but was afraid he was too young. A Dylan "concert" for the NYU folk club on April 5 made a persuasive "credit." Mel, and his wife Lillian, a dress designer, kept up their campaign, joined by the MacKenzies. If Mike booked Bobby, Eve MacKenzie promised to telephone everyone she knew in order to whip up business. Finally, Mike had a two-week opening for Bob beginning April 11 on a bill with John Lee Hooker, a Mississippi bluesman who had been working in Detroit for years. It was Dylan's first real job in New York, and he was ecstatic.

"When Bobby came in to work the first time," Mike told me years later, "I didn't know if he had enough clothes. I got some of my children's old clothes and I gave them to this woman Camilla [Adams], because I knew she was very fond of Bobby, like a mother. I think he wanted the image then of the dungarees, but my kids didn't have any, so I think Camilla gave those dungarees to Bobby. Then I took him to the union [American Federation of Musicians, Local 802] because he had to join to play. The secretary, Max Aarons, gave Bobby an application, and I put up the money for his initiation. Max said to Bobby: 'Mike tells me a whole lotta things about you. He told me he wants to put you in the union and thinks that you are going to be a star. What do you think?' So Bob says: 'Well, I'll try my best.' So Max says, with a smile: 'Well, if I do put you in the union and you become a star, what'll you do for me?' Bob said: 'Well, if I ever get there, I will do anything that it is possible for me to do.' Now, Max is president of the union," said Mike, as if Dylan had actually helped. Mike continued: "They asked how old he was and at the time he was only 19, I think. The union man says if you are not 21 you should bring your father in to sign the papers. Bob said his father and mother were not around. So the union man looks at me and asks: 'Well, what are we going to do?' I understood that his mother and father were in a different state, and also I had the feeling that he had run away. So I signed the papers as Bobby's guardian, the first contract he had. Bobby held on to that book with the membership like it was the Bible. On the way out, I said to him: Bobby, now you have to go for the cabaret permit. He had to have some pictures taken. We went into one of those Sixth Avenue subway photo machines. His hair was kinda messy, so I asked him if he wanted to comb his hair. Bob said: 'I don't ever comb it.' So, I gave him my comb, but he looked in the mirror and hesitated. He thought he would look better with more messy hair."

Dylan had a theory then: "The more hair you have outside your head, the less there is cluttering up the inside of your head. Crew cuts are bad, with all that hair cluttering around your brain. I let my hair grow long so's I can be wise and free to think." Mike continued: "I think that even then he was thinking about his image. He combed it a little bit, anyhow, for the picture, and I gave him two dollars to get the cabaret card. He came back to the place and he was as happy as if he had won the sweepstakes. 'Mike,' he said, 'I've got the card!' Was he happy! He was a good-natured kid. This is the place they all started. Peter Yarrow once told me: 'Mike, this is the luck place.' The people who started at my place went on to make a fortune—Bobby, Peter, Paul and Mary, José Feliciano, Simon and Garfunkel. I wish I would make one tenth of what they make."

Mike said he paid Bobby a little more than the union scale of $90 a week, plus the old clothes, sandwiches and drinks. Bob thought only about having his name on a New York bill with John Lee Hooker, one of the great bluesmen. His elation soon soured as he sang for apathetic or noisy drunks and heard the carping of jealous musicians. But his coterie of friends and fans kept growing. Bob sensed how much more he had to learn about performing, how much harder he would have to develop his songs. Not a single recording official surfaced. He was stung that I, then the *New York Times* reviewer, had been so busy listening to Hooker and interviewing him that I never heard his own sets.

After he finished at Gerde's, Bob tried to get recorded. "I went up to Folkways," Dylan later reported. "I says: 'Howdy. I've written some songs.' They wouldn't even look at them. I had always heard that Folkways was a good place. Irwin Silber didn't even talk to me and I never got to see Moe Asch. They just about said 'Go.' And I had heard that *Sing Out!* was supposed to be helpful and friendly, big-hearted and charitable. I thought it was the place. It must have been the wrong place, even though *Sing Out!* was written on the door."

Dylan couldn't understand why he seemed to interest only a handful. After another stop to see Guthrie, and a visit to a folk festival in Branford, Connecticut, in May, he visited Minnesota. Before he left, one other New York job added to his temporary despair. A young promoter who had met Bob in Chicago got him a curious job at a hotel on lower Fifth Avenue, playing for a Kiwanis Club. As Dylan described the gig later, it was "Desolation Row" Take 115: "A lot of different acts were on that night— dressed like clowns. When someone sang the clowns would perform. The clowns were paid, but not the performers. I couldn't even hear myself. A clown rolled up to pinch my cheek. I kicked him in the nuts and no one saw me—the rest of the clowns left me alone then."

The trip west to Dinkytown and Madison, Wisconsin, was decisive. Bob realized that New York was still the hurdle that had to be jumped. On his return in June, he began six months of his most intensive work, most purposeful accumulation of contacts. The latter half of 1961 changed Dylan from a provincial folknik into a music professional.

"He Was a Friend of Mine." For most of the summer of 1961, Dylan was everywhere in the Village, impatient to be seen, to impress important people, to learn. He moved through New York and Boston folk circles absorbing everything he heard and saw, spying for his ambitious master plan. While Folk City didn't immediately lead to jobs or a recording contract, he could more easily step on to Village stages to accompany featured singers. He became a sought-after backing harmonica player and guitarist. In mid-1961, he was a fixture at the Folk City hoots, developing amusing stage tricks. One hoot regular was Brother John Sellers, a gospel and blues singer who could always whip up an audience with his exuberant shouting and tambourine banging. Brother John clucked like a mother hen over newly hatched folk performers around him, lavishing praise on his accompanists with a star's beneficence. At a typical hoot, he would hammer out a lively number, like "Big Boat up the River," and two musicians in dungarees, Mark Spoelstra and Dylan, backed him up with guitars and harmonicas. Brother John and the Dungarees were often the event of the evening. People got excited by the Spoelstra and Dylan sound. Bob used to jiggle up and down from the stage to the bar, then, laughing and scratching, cadging a rum and Coke from Mike. When other performers wanted to do a guest set, they'd get Bob behind them. Not many musicians played mouth harp then.

The two musicians who most attracted Bob were Dave Van Ronk and Jack Elliott, arguably the best Village folk singers. Elliott was the living, breathing reincarnation of Woody, a citybilly of whom Guthrie once remarked: "Jack Elliott sounds more like me than I do." Van Ronk was a white urban intellectual who masterfully interpreted black songs and blues. Their impact on Dylan was enormous, a bridge to the past.

Dave Van Ronk was the musical mayor of MacDougal Street, a tall, garrulous, hairy man of three-quarters, or, more accurately, three-fifths Irish descent. Topped by a cascade of light-brownish hair and a leonine beard, which he smoothed down several times a minute, he resembled an unmade bed strewn with books, record jackets, pipes, empty whiskey bottles, lines from obscure poets, finger picks, and broken guitar strings. He was Bob's first New York guru. Van Ronk was a walking museum of the blues. Through an early interest in jazz, he had gravitated toward black music—its jazz pole, its jug-band and ragtime center, its blues bedrock.

Van Ronk was born in Brooklyn in 1936. He dropped out of high school at 15, but never stopped studying or teaching. In 1949, he sang in a barbershop quartet, escaped unshaven, did jazz and scat singing, and became a professional performer around 1956. His manner was gruff and testy, disguising a warm, sensitive core. He sang in a plaintive, gravel voice that helped translate often unintelligible black blues for white city audiences. (Rolf Cahn and artist Ric Von Schmidt in Boston, and Alexis Korner in London were also bringing folk blues to white sophisticates.) Presley had done the same years before, on a splashy, extroverted level. Van Ronk retold the blues intimately. Presley won the world, while Van Ronk (and John Hammond, Jr, Von Schmidt, Cahn, and Korner) won over only coteries. For a time, the most dedicated follower was Dylan.

Later, Dylan outgrew the friendship with Dave and his wife, Terri Thal, but still returned to see them. At times Van Ronk was cynical, because Dylan had taken so much of what he had taught him and made a fortune with it. But he was more often philosophical: "The part of Dylan that was the sponge could function on all eight cylinders. He gets what he can and then discards it. This is why Terri and I are not Bob's best friends anymore. He got whatever he could absorb here, and he moved on. He did the same thing with Joanie [Baez], but there was an element of professional opportunism there too. People from the early 1960s are very bitter about him. Although Bobby did treat most of them rather cavalierly, their reactions are largely their own fault," Dave said. "They just wanted to bask in the light of an obvious talent, to reflect a little glory on them. 'I gave him five bucks when he needed five bucks. I fed him when he was hungry, and the least I expect is to see him now and then and to tell everyone that he still loves me.' Dylan just doesn't give a damn."

Van Ronk was less jarred than most watching Dylan catapult to fame. The Van Ronks had their own lives. Dylan could be relatively free with them. Dave and Terri spent a lot of time with Bob when they lived on 15th Street and after their move to Waverly Place, across the street from me. Terri became his first business manager, arranging most of his bookings for about eight months. "Do you know he is a very good chess player?" Van Ronk asked me. "You know how nervous Dylan is. His knees bounce up against the table so much you think you are at a séance. The pieces keep jumping around the board. But he beats me every time. I agree that Dylan's way of secreting so much makes you want to find out more. But I am quite sure that he is secretive for personal, not commercial, reasons. I think it's because he is neurotic. We would spend hours with him and still find it difficult to communicate with him. For some reason, he has a very, very short attention span."

Van Ronk coined the saying "the folk community is acting toward Dylan like a Jewish mother" when Dylan became a star. Did he miss seeing Dylan? "Not terribly much. When I see him, it's always a pleasure. I listen to his stuff every now and then. The best of Dylan isn't in the drawing room, it's on the stage." Did he think Dylan had a right to use music as a vehicle for personal hostility? "Read *The Divine Comedy*," Dave suggested. "I think that 'Positively Fourth Street' is a great song. It was high time Bobby turned around and said something to Irwin Silber and all those Jewish mothers. It's Dylan's farewell address."

On topical songs, Dave continued: "He was always a very good barometer, very sensitive to mood. But when it comes to analyzing the content of moods, he simply never had the patience. He doesn't care." How can so intellectual a writer as Dylan be so anti-intellectual? "Bobby is very much a product of the beat generation," Van Ronk replied. "Dylan really does belong in a rack with Kerouac. You are not going to see any more like him. Bobby came into beat poetry just at the very tail end. He towers above all of them, except perhaps Ginsberg. But Bob was a latecomer and will have no successors, just as his namesake had no successors."

Did Dylan ever say he admired Dylan Thomas? "He assiduously avoided it. I think the reasons are obvious. I did come on to Bob about François Villon. I also told him about Rimbaud and Apollinaire. I once asked Bobby: 'Have you ever heard about Rimbaud?' He said: 'Who?' I repeated: 'Rimbaud— R-I-M-B-A-U-D. He's a French poet. You really ought to read him.' Bobby kind of twitched a little; he seemed to be thinking about it. He just said: 'Yeah, yeah.' I raised Rimbaud with him a couple of times after that. Much later, I was up at his place. I always look at people's books. On his shelf I discovered a book of translations of French symbolist poets that had obviously been thumbed through over a period of years! I think he probably knew Rimbaud backward and forward before I even mentioned him. I didn't mention Rimbaud to him again until I heard his 'A Hard Rain's a-Gonna Fall,' his first symbolist venture. I said to Bob: 'You know that song of yours is heavy in symbolism, don't you?' He said: 'Huh?'"

Although a stubbornly individualistic Leftist, Van Ronk didn't sing political-topical material: "I don't think anyone was ever converted with a song. I just can't see one of Phil Ochs's songs keeping a movement moving, keeping a picket line picketing, or boosting morale for strikers or civil rights people. His songs are sort of an act of personal conscience, like burning your draft card, or burning yourself. It doesn't do a damn thing, except disassociate you and your audience from all the evils of the world. I can't be disassociated from the evils of the world." Did he regard protest songs as romantic anarchism? "No. It's populism. There is this social patriotism running through all of them, but really less in Dylan. It makes me sick, because I'm an internationalist myself. I don't think the American people are any special repository of goodness and duty, nor are they a special repository of evil. I can't stand songs that pat Negroes on the back. I'd rather hear a song that says: 'Man, if you don't do something, you're going to be no better off than your father was.'"

Van Ronk's influence on Dylan was manifold. He was a colorful but stable guy with an apartment, books, an active, informed mind. He riffed with words, making conversational music, even if you did lose the melody line in the evening. He was self-taught, not a posturing college intellectual. His major influence on Dylan was, of course, musical, though there were only four songs in Dave's repertoire that Dylan performed regularly: "Dink's Song,"[10] "House of the Rising Sun," "Poor Lazarus,"[11] and "See That My Grave is Kept Clean." Bob's debt to Dave was in style, perception, and interpretation. Van Ronk could scat, growl, or keen in rural south idioms. Dylan picked up some of Dave's guitar ideas, but a lot more of his special showmanship, the ability to space sound and silences into a whole that compelled attention. Within six months, Van Ronk was no longer a guru, just a seasoned colleague walking the same endless highway.[12] Dylan had only one lasting idol.

Meeting Woody. One Sunday, probably in early February 1961, Bob came face to face with Woody Guthrie, then deeply ravaged by Huntington's chorea. Woody had written eloquently in *Born to Win* of the way the illness had affected his mother. By November 1954, Guthrie was writing from Brooklyn State Hospital about his own ailment:

Huntington's Chorea
Means there's no help known
In the science of medicine
For me
And all of you Choreanites like me ...
Maybe Jesus can think up a cure of some kind.[13]

By May 1956, Guthrie had been moved to the New Jersey state hospital in Greystone Park for better treatment. His condition deteriorated, but he could still have outings to the Village. On Sunday, July 26,

1959, folk musicians, headed by Ralph Rinzler, John Cohen, and Lionel Milberg, gathered some two dozen friends and fans to greet Woody at Washington Square Park. Surrounded by young singers, Woody stretched out on a balding patch of grass fifty yards from the fountain and called out for some of his own songs and others he loved. The musicians obliged with "Reuben James" and "John Hardy" and "Pastures of Plenty." Woody—gaunt-cheeked, gray circlets of hair tumbling over his creased forehead—indicated how much he enjoyed hearing his own music from young musicians. To me and others there, he was already sick beyond hope.

In summer 1960, folksingers Logan English, the Clancy Brothers and Tommy Makem, Molly Scott, and Martin Lorin held a special day for Woody at One Sheridan Square. On October 23, 1960, when his son Arlo Davy was marking his thirteenth birthday, Woody was brought to a Second Avenue dance studio. I tried to talk to Woody, but could not get through to him. At each outing we could see Woody failing. Soon he could no longer travel even into Manhattan. A pair of middle-aged folk enthusiasts, Robert and Sidsel Gleason, who lived in East Orange, not far from Greystone Park, started Sunday gatherings for Woody. At one, Dylan, who frequently stayed with the Gleasons, finally met his first and last idol. He found the writer who was once "bound for glory" now a suffering shell. Guthrie's hands quivered, his shoulders shook involuntarily, and he spoke only in thin, unintelligible rasps. He could show appreciation, summon a tentative smile, indicate slightly that he had heard what was being said to him.

There was another dying man in the room. Cisco Houston, Guthrie's longtime sidekick, was making his final visit to Woody. For nearly two years, Cisco had been living with inoperable cancer and, by early 1961, he had to stop working. Cisco had been a fixture at Folk City and Mike Porco had done his best to make him feel he could always get a free drink to ease his pain. In early 1961, he went into the office of his manager, Harold Leventhal, and told him, with a chilling calm: "You're gonna lose a good client. The doctor said I have three to six months to live." Cisco completed final recordings for Vanguard and taped his hobo's autobiography. (About a month after the farewell in East Orange, having just recorded the album *I Ain't Got No Home*, Houston went to his sister's home in California, where he died on April 28 at forty-two.)

That day, Woody sat propped up with pillows on the sofa as Cisco tried to tell him that they had both neared the end of their hard traveling. Jack Elliott tried to keep sadness from overcoming everyone. It was a living wake, but even Irish mourners couldn't jest in front of the dying, so Elliott and the Gleasons focused on the youngest person in the room, "that nice kid," Dylan. Whether awed by the company or depressed by the "smell of death," Dylan held back, the modest spy looking at those busy dying and those busy being born. As Elliott described it to me: "Whenever I was around Woody in those days, Bob was there. Funny, Bobby sort of hung back in the shadows, just watching everything, just listening. Bob was shy then, you know. He still is. But, right off, I could see that Bob was very much influenced by everything about Woody. Bob probably felt he could get through more than I could, but I knew Woody so well that we would talk to each other without words. But it was the same with Bob. He told me he had the 'feeling' of talking with Woody that went beyond words. I knew then what he meant. Those were the days, when Bob was sort of commuting between East Orange and various New York sofas."

Jack played and sang for Woody, and Bob played a tune or two. He wrote "Song to Woody" right after that first Sunday visit. Dylan claimed he had met Woody a long time before East Orange. According to a log Izzy Young kept, Bob said he first heard Guthrie's recordings, the *Dust Bowl* album in particular, in South Dakota. "I used to see Woody," Dylan told Izzy on October 23, 1961, "whenever I had enough money. Met him once in California before I was really playing. I think Jack Elliott was with him. [Elliott, who was in Europe from 1955 to 1959, was traveling with Guthrie when Dylan was 13.] I was in Carmel, doing nothing. When I wrote 'Song to Woody' in February, I gave Woody the paper I wrote the song on. Woody liked my song." By February 1, 1962, Dylan was putting still another version into Izzy's chronicle: "I've been seeing Woody steady for a year now. I met him when I was 13. He likes my songs."

Elliott liked Bob's songs too. Jack was always a little unsure of himself, easily hurt behind his Stetson-topped, Marlboro-country cool, so he studied all the masters, young and old. Elliott spent so much of his youth aping Woody that only in his thirties did he become himself. As anthropologist John Greenway wrote on the album *Ramblin' Jack Elliott*: "It is a regrettable characteristic of newly successful folk singers to presume too much upon the limits of originality … Jack's own borrowing has been so extensive that he became in himself a representative cross-section of American folk song."

The quotation pertains as well to Dylan in his most derivative period. Van Ronk helped Bob explore books and city streets, while Elliott helped Bob explore the country. Elliott smelled of horses, leather, and saddle soap. He was also a link between the 1930s hobos and the 1950s beats. Jack could translate the cowboy-western-hobo tradition so well for the city listener because he was a city boy himself.

The son of a Jewish physician, Ramblin' Jack Elliott was born Elliott Charles Adnopoz ten years before Dylan on what he described as "a fifteen-thousand-acre ranch in the middle of Flatbush," Brooklyn. At nine he became captivated by the singing cowboy films. Somewhere between the Flatbush corral and the west, he decided that a singing cowboy from Brooklyn needed a more American name. He called himself Buck Elliott first, then settled on Jack Elliott. Around 1947, Jack met a dude-ranch cowboy, named Todd Fletcher, who taught him some guitar. When he was about 18, Jack met Woody in Coney Island, and for a good five years thereafter, he was Woody's shadow.[14]

Eight years before I met Dylan, I met Elliott when he was trying to study at Adelphi University. In the classroom he was a displaced person. Besides being hung up on horses, Jack was crazy about cars and trucks. A typical entrance for Elliott was a monologue that ran: "I'm sorry I'm late, folks, but my old Mack truck burned out about two miles away. Tried like the devil to get it started, but the plugs are shot and the battery isn't too healthy, and I figured the walk would do me some good anyway." Jack was as good a yarn spinner as a singer. His pacing, bumbling, and Will Rogers homespun cadences could make almost anything seem funny.

After he had spent from 1955 to 1959 becoming the voice of American folk song in Britain, Jack decided to come home. Izzy Young put him in a concert at the Carnegie Chapter Hall on February 18, 1961. Although Elliott was erratic and often lacked discipline, his singing was gritty, plaintive, and supple. Guthrie songs remained his bedrock. He could sing "The Ballad of Tom Joad"—Woody's retelling of *The Grapes of Wrath* which, really, was Steinbeck's retelling of the lives of Woody and other dispossessed Okies—with an immediacy that swirled dust around the coffeehouse. He would do Woody's children's jape, "Car Car," with endless variations. He mulled over phrases as if chewing tobacco. "Here is a song I sung in every bar along Route 40," Elliott would say while tuning up for the hobo's national anthem, Woody's "Hard Travelin'."

After a decade as Woody's disciple, Jack added blues and Hank Williams songs and was strongly influenced by Jesse Fuller's harmonica style, which had also excited Dylan. Jack virtually made Fuller's "San Francisco Bay Blues" his theme song. Like Dylan, Jack played rambler until it was no longer a pose: he had so good an ear for the speech, song, and wit of the American plains that he wasn't a citybilly anymore. At the end of the 1960s, Elliott looked back: "Although I am reputedly a close friend of Bob's, I never quite felt like I was really in touch with him. It was like he always had something on his mind, even when we were spending a lot of time together. Because I'm very romantic about it, I like to think that I am a close friend of his. When I see him, I'm very thrilled to talk with him, just as if I were one of his fans and as if I had never really met him before. There were times later when we did horse around together a bit.

"I know how sensitive Bobby always was, despite that wall he built around himself. I remember meeting him that day after his first record was out but it wasn't really selling. He had on baggy Levis and he looked rather down: 'I gotta get out of this folk-song game and paint.'" Elliott mimicked Dylan. "I always get the same constant message out of Dylan. To me, he's always sort of saying: 'Let's all just dig the world as artists. Let's not measure it in pounds or ounces or money. Let's just be artists, huh!'"

Did Jack resent Bob's success? Elliott munched on that awhile. "He had a tremendous energetic drive for success that I've never had. If he was tramping on anyone's toes to get where he was going, he could have tramped on mine, but he didn't. I suppose I could have made it," said Jack, looking over my shoulder. "It doesn't make me jealous, it just makes me hate myself. It's funny, you know, but for a while Bob Dylan was often known as 'the son of Jack Elliott.' Sometimes I would introduce 'Don't Think Twice' or some other song to the crowd: 'Here's a song by my son, Bob Dylan.' I suppose I taught Bobby a few of my songs. Those old VD songs by Woody that nobody wanted the young kids to know—he picked them up from me. But I also remember when Bob sang some of the grooviest hobo songs in the style of Jimmie Rodgers, like 'The Baggage Coach Ahead.' There was some of that sad spirit in Bob's song about Hibbing, you know, 'North Country Blues.' He hummed it to me once in a taxi. I just thought it was about a deserted mining town; I didn't realize till later that it was about Hibbing."

Jack sipped a Bourbon and tried to focus on the past. His memory was all jumbled, because "today seems like yesterday and tomorrow all thrown together." The first time he'd dropped into Woodstock to see Bob, "it was two in the morning and I just happened to be in the neighborhood. But Sara [Dylan] and Sally [Grossman] and Bobby were very warm to me. He gave me a great big hug. Bobby's funny that way. He loved to kid people. But you have to be careful how you come on to him or you'll knock him right back into his shell again."

Elliott consoled himself that he could remain his own man. "Bob was always a little more uptight when Albert was around. When Bob is having a good time though, his eyes just light up. But mostly he's on guard toward everyone and everything. It was that way from the start. Everything Bob says, he seems to have read over before he says it. When he's letting go a bit, everything is said with a giggle and a gaggle."

Jack was still proud that Dylan had sat in on Elliott's first recording on Vanguard, adding a touch of bronchial harp on the old gospel tune "Will the Circle Be Unbroken?"; Bob used one of his recording pseudonyms, Tedham Porterhouse. One of the ironies of their relationship was that Bob didn't immediately realize that Jack was a citybilly. Around March 1961, Dylan was in the Figaro with musician-publisher Barry Kornfeld and Van Ronk. When they referred to Elliott's being a Jewish cowboy from Brooklyn, Van Ronk said, "Bobby nearly fell off his chair laughing. It seemed to strike him much funnier than it did us, because we never assumed anything else about Jack but that he'd been a self-styled cowboy. It was then, two years before *Newsweek* revealed Bob's own background, that I knew that Bobby too was an actor. He never said anything—he just laughed till I thought he would burst."

Jack also gave Bob a model of the easygoing drifter. While Dylan knew too much slackness wasted time, he also knew that an impression of aimless drifting made people relaxed and communicative. So Bob learned to conceal his ambitions. Elliott had once meandered into a Hollywood parking lot and played his guitar there for James Dean. Dylan, who was wide-eyed at that story, would never have let such a valuable contact rest unexploited. Jack had ached for years to play the film role of Woody. He told *Newsweek*: "No one else can really do it. I know—I've been playing it for ten years now." Ironically, the role Elliott had mastered off-screen was offered to Dylan in January 1968, and again in early 1975. Dylan turned it down, and the part went to David Carradine.

The novelist André Gide once remarked of another French writer, Charles Peguy, that "Peguy threw friendships into the fire to keep the oven going." Dylan's fire reached its peak along MacDougal Street. Woody and Cisco were happy to supply some heat, as were Dave and Jack. The two younger survivors may have been scorched a bit, but they were not unhappy around Dylan's bonfire.

Ramblin' and Tumblin'. Van Ronk, Guthrie, and Elliott were only three strong faces from a crowd. By autumn 1961, Dylan knew so many people you'd think he'd been on the East Coast five years. When the loner turned gregarious he excelled at it, but he turned his sociability on and off. After his first album turned him into something of a public figure, he often showed signs of agoraphobia, walking far out of his way to avoid people along Sixth Avenue. In the beginning, though, he needed to rally large numbers to his side. He was the loner politician, more at home with dreams of what he would do in office than with the necessities of shaking hands and kissing babies. Everything about him disdained Rotarian fellowship and backslapping, yet he knew how to play a variation of it to get himself established. It was tiresome and contrary to his nature, but 1961 was his year for being especially outgoing.

Having lined up the New York electorate, Dylan attacked the vital precinct of Boston and neighboring Cambridge, the hub of northeastern college life. This was Newport Folk Festival turf, where Baez had started. Music dominated the less frenetic scene along the Charles River. In June 1961, Dylan got a three-day job at Cambridge's Club 47, and acquired fans and friends. Betsy Siggins, the 47's hard-driving talent coordinator, was the den mother of the Boston folk clan, and she readily adopted Dylan. He befriended the bearded, uncommonly warm Eric Von Schmidt. Ric, a commercial artist, was as passionately interested in folk song as were the careerists, as smitten with the blues as Van Ronk, and almost as gravelly voiced but considerably less didactic. Another new Boston chum was Jim Kweskin, a bright, rakish singer who later formed his own popular jug band; Kweskin dressed like a 1890s Mississippi riverboat gambler, wore broad-rimmed black hats, and performed with wit and flair. Dylan took to this "hippie dude" at first meeting, while Kweskin dug Dylan's music and personality. Geno Foreman, a zany motorcycle maverick, was another Bostonian whose wildness and irresponsibility appealed to Dylan, and carrot-topped Fritz Richmond, whose wit was as outlandish as his music-making, also found rapport.

One Boston couple helped Bob land his first recording contract. Carolyn Hester and her then husband, Richard Fariña, had moved to Boston because they found it less rancorous than New York. I had introduced Fariña to Carolyn at the White Horse Tavern in the Village and, after a whirlwind thirteen-day courtship, they married, getting to know each other afterward around Boston, and in Europe and North Africa. Later, when Dylan was involved with Joan Baez, he and Fariña met again after Fariña married Joan's sister, Mimi. Carolyn and Richard loved Bob's harmonica playing. In September, when Carolyn cut her first recording for Columbia, she asked Bob to join her sessions. Because Dylan showed up in the right moment, he too won a recording contract.[15]

With Boston on side, Dylan returned to New York for more intensive electioneering. He oscillated between the Gaslight, Folk City, the Commons, the Folklore Center, the bar of the Mills Hotel, the Kettle of Fish, and the White Horse. Sometimes he joined me at McGowan's after the Horse closed. He always carved out hours for practicing, listening to records, and writing songs, but mostly he was a street person, hanging out. His New York friendships multiplied. John Herald, lead singer of bluegrass group the Greenbriar Boys, nearly inarticulate until his music transformed him into a whopping extrovert, found Bob easy to be with. John Hammond, Jr, a gifted young white blues re-creator, also became a pal. A handsome leather-jacketed boy, Hammond occasionally briefed his producer-father on promising talent.

Len Chandler and Dylan became close around this time. Len was not one bit reticent or repressed. Even when things were tough for him, as a black musician, and they were for years, Len had dash and bravado, and he loved a put-on as much as Dylan did. He and Len walked around a cityful of blocks for many a smoke. If Dylan's first Village cronies could be divided into the self-assured and the shy, the singer Mark Spoelstra fell into the latter group, drawn—like John Bucklen before him—to his opposite.

I first encountered Dylan at a Monday night hoot at Folk City in June 1961. Because my reaction to his performing then was so strong, I know that I either never saw him at Folk City the previous April, or that I had looked right through him. Whatever the case, this encounter was unforgettable. At the hoot, Bob was doing his musical shaggy-dog story, "Bear Mountain," inspired by routines that Noel (Paul) Stookey, later of Peter, Paul and Mary, was doing at the Gaslight. It was a tall tale hinged on an episode of overcrowding on a Hudson River pleasure boat and, years later, Arlo Guthrie would triumph with a similar vehicle, "Alice's Restaurant Massacree."

Bob looked like a European street singer or tumbler. He bobbed and swayed, played with his black corduroy Huck Finn cap, made faces, winced, and joked his way through the ridiculous narrative. I walked over to Pat Clancy, the Irish folk singer, and said: "Hey, Pat, you have to catch this kid!" Pat turned from his Jameson's to watch Bob. "Well, what have we here?" he exclaimed, half-curious and half joyful. When the enthusiastic audience released Bob from the stage, I told him how much I liked his work. He appreciated my appreciation. "Yeah, great! I'm glad you liked it. I've done better sets than that. Glad you liked it," he said. I told him when he had his next job to call me and I'd try to review him in the *Times*. "I sure will, I sure will," he replied. "I think you missed me when I was here last April," Dylan said, and I admitted that I sure did, I sure did.

A week or two later, my phone rang and a thin, nasal voice said: "Hi, I'm Bob Dylan. You said I should call you if I got a job. Well, I got a job. I'm at the Gaslight for a week." Several days later, I arrived at the Gaslight to see the regulars listening to Van Ronk and Dylan. At his usual table in the rear was Albert B Grossman, who appeared to be getting a great deal of satisfaction from a cup of coffee. In the early days, Albert often held court in coffeehouses. He usually smoked a king-size cigarette the way an oil sheik would hold a hookah, making a circle of his thumb and forefinger, slightly crooking his little finger, and blowing the smoke out slowly through his hand. I told Dylan the gig was too short to write up, but I introduced him to Albert, saying I thought this kid was going to be the next sensation. Grossman, as usual, said nothing. After Dylan left our table, Grossman asked what I thought of Van Ronk. I was enthusiastic but I predicted that Dylan would go further. Grossman smiled, a Cheshire cat in untouched acres of field mice.

The Gaslight was then owned by a wild-looking Bohemian, John Mitchell, who had fought many legal battles against police and fire authorities who had cracked down on the MacDougal Street coffeehouses. Mitchell found Dylan especially droll. Although Dylan was frequently nostalgic about the Gaslight, he also made fun of his first job there. He once told me the Gaslight was "the Broadway of folk song, where all the stars were—Dave Van Ronk, [banjoist] Billy Faier, [balladeer] Hal Waters." His Gaslight stint ended inconclusively. Grossman said nothing. I hadn't written a word about him. Bob kept working at his music, at his western speech. Sometimes his mangled dialect made words virtually indistinguishable. He started to mumble about "ramblin' and tumblin' with his coat collar turned up high." Soon, a few of us were calling him "the rambler" and "the tumbler."

Dylan rambled and tumbled into his first New York concert appearance and radio broadcast on Saturday, July 29, 1961. The marathon was run by a new FM station, WRVR, operated by the Riverside Church. To inaugurate the station's live-music project, Izzy Young and Bob Yellin mobilized folk musicians. In those days, at a call for folk talent, youngsters like Tom Paxton and Molly Scott, and old-timers like the Reverend Gary Davis and blues singer Victoria Spivey, would rush to perform, even without pay. WRVR's twelve-hour folk parade had enough lapses of broadcasting techniques to gray an FCC commissioner's head. On the hour every hour, eager performers hit their mikes with swinging banjo necks, voices faded in and out, cues were missed. The studio audience was as restless and partisan as a high-school assembly.

There were workshops on the blues, an Eastern Mediterranean segment organized by Jack Goddard of the *Village Voice*, and showcases for various banjo styles. No big-name stars, but the show was an impressive display of available folk-song and instrumental talent around town. Midway through the afternoon, a slight musician who sang, looked, and twanged like Woody Guthrie made his way to the microphone. Introduced as hailing from Gallup, New Mexico, Dylan, with his harmonica in a holder improvised from a metal coat hanger, was on for five quick songs, joined on some by Elliott and bluesman Danny Kalb. In the *Times*, I briefly described Dylan's style as a "curiously arresting, mumbling, country-steeped manner." Dylan's little stint received warm applause, his circle making enough noise to simulate a crowd.

After he left the stage, he was introduced to a 17-year-old, wide-eyed, long-haired beauty named Suze Rotolo, and began two years of an ecstatic, erratic romance. Dylan's reputation was growing as another Jack Elliott or Woody Guthrie, yet recording seemed the only doorway to national recognition. In late summer, a bright pair of Village girls, Sybil Weinberger, who worked in TV production, and Suze's older sister, Carla Rotolo, then personal assistant to Alan Lomax, came up with an idea to help record Dylan and some other unknowns. They suggested a demonstration tape of a half-dozen of the best Village folk singers, including Van Ronk and Elliott.

Describing the project and raving about Dylan in particular, Sybil wrote to producer John Hammond at Columbia Records. "Sybil's letter called attention to a whole group that had tremendous talent," Carla recalled. "By putting in people who had some recognition, we thought we might get some recognition for the unrecognized, like Bobby and John Wynn. But the original idea was to get Bobby something." There was no reply: Carla maintains Hammond just let the letter sit on his desk and may not even have read it. She thinks Hammond did not associate the Bobby Dylan in Sybil's letter and the boy he signed weeks later to a five-year Columbia contract.

Because of the urgings of the Dylan coterie in general, Carla in particular, and my all but guaranteeing that I would review the show, Mike Porco booked Bob into Folk City again for two weeks: SEPTEMBER 25 THRU OCTOBER 8: GREENBRIAR BOYS, PICKING & SINGING THRU BLUEGRASS WITH THE SENSATIONAL BOB DYLAN. The Greenbriar Boys (Ralph Rinzler, Herald, and Yellin) were city bluegrass wizards. Yellin's banjo lines hopped around like confetti in the wind, and Herald's vocal acrobatics keened and soared while Rinzler's delicate mandolin figures coursed like nervous birds nesting. All three sang and whooped it up with wit and musicianship. They were not an easy act to follow, but Dylan followed superbly.

During those two weeks, he alternated between three costumes, each seedier than the next. One outfit was a faded blue shirt, khaki trousers, a dark sleeveless pullover, an incongruous foulard tie, all topped with his famous hat. Other times he wore a chamois jacket or a tieless wool shirt. His Gibson guitar had a song-sequence sheet pasted on its upper curve, and his harmonica holder hung around his neck. He looked studiously unkempt and very slight and frail—until he began to sing. His pinched, constricted voice seemed to be fighting its way out of his throat like a captive breaking jail. It was a rusty voice, suggesting Guthrie's old recordings. It was etched in gravel, like Van Ronk's. It sometimes crooned a bit, like Elliott's. Yet it was also a voice quite unlike anyone else's. You didn't think of it as something beautiful or sinuous, but as something that roiled up from the heart. He didn't sound a bit citified, but more like an old farmhand folk singer. Most of the audience liked Dylan those two weeks, regarding him as a masterly ethnic singer, but many thought he was just a bad joke.

Bob started a typical set with "I'm Gonna Get You, Sally Gal," in a lively tempo. He set up a three-way conversation between his voice, guitar, and mouth harp. Suddenly you saw how he could share the stage with as brilliant a trio as the Greenbriars. "Here's a song suitable to this occasion," Dylan said, as he retuned his guitar and changed his mouth harp. He sailed into a traditional blues dirge, "This Life is Killing Me." His technique was everywhere, the covert technique of the folk idiom. It was anti-technique, anti-polish, anti-conscious of surface form, yet all those elements lay below. He gave the impression that he had started in music yesterday, not five years earlier. But one couldn't be sure.

Between songs, Dylan droned a soliloquy, formless yet very funny. He started to tell a story about a toad. It was an open-ended shaggy-toad story that didn't start anywhere and didn't go anywhere, but it gave him a bit of fill-in patter while he tuned. His face was pouting and boyish. His slow delivery made him sound half-awake to optimists and half-asleep to pessimists. Next, he growled his way through "a train song," "900 Miles." To punctuate certain guitar breaks, he raised the body of his guitar to the microphone, an old country-music gambit that enhanced the stringed sound.

In the background were the usual Folk City distractions. Bartenders clinked and poured as if starring in TV commercials. The cash register rang during soft passages. At the bar a few drunks were gabbing while others tried to silence them. Dylan was all concentration. "Here's a song outta my own head," he said, tuning his guitar for "Talking New York," a very old style of talking blues, in which three sparse chords support wry lyrics more spoken than sung. Dylan delivered his first protest song with a comic's timing.

Bob turned to other songs out of other people's heads. He moaned his way through "Dink's Song," long favored by Josh White and Cynthia Gooding; Dylan said he had picked it up on the Brazos River when he was down in Texas. Actually, the ballad hunter John A Lomax had heard it in 1904 from a gin-drinking black woman who sang it as she wearily scrubbed her man's laundry. It is one of the most pathetic women's laments in American folk song. Bob did a variation on Van Ronk, with vamping guitar figures keeping the underlying pattern moving. At times his voice sounded like gravel being shoveled, at other times like a sob. He caught the original's tension and plaintiveness. "I was never a motherless child," folk singer Ed McCurdy used to say, "but I know what it feels like." Dylan was never a black laundress, but he knew what it felt like. Occasionally, Dylan threw his head back full as if he were scanning the ceiling for his next words.

From Texas, the 20-year-old world traveler took his audience to a famous Chicago bar, Muddy Waters' Place, where he said he had picked up another blues song. He shuffled to the junk-heap upright piano and played primitive chords. Then he hit Woody's road again, with "Hard Travelin'," a lurching, careening road song, sticky with hot asphalt, aching with calloused feet. Then he did another couple of songs out of his own head, including "Bear Mountain" and "Talkin' Hava Negeilah Blues," his little jape at international "stylists" like Harry Belafonte and Theo Bikel.

The audience responded more to Dylan's wit than to his slow, serious, intense material. Audience reaction led him to play Chaplinesque clown. He closed with his own "Song to Woody," suspensefully built to keep attention focused on each new line.

After his set, we went back to the Folk City kitchen for his first press interview. The answers came fast, but I had a feeling that he was improvising and concealing. It went like this: "I'm twenty years old, don't turn twenty-one until May. I've been singing all my life, since I was ten. I was born in Duluth, Minnesota, or maybe it was Superior, Wisconsin, right across the line. I started traveling with a carnival at the age of thirteen. I did odd jobs and sang with the carnival. I cleaned up ponies and ran steam shovels, in Minnesota, North Dakota, and then on south. I graduated from high school. For a while, Sioux Falls, South Dakota, was a home, and so was Gallup, New Mexico. I also lived in Fargo, North Dakota, and in a place called Hibbing, Minnesota. I went to the University of Minnesota for about eight months, but I didn't like it too much. I used to play piano with Bobby Vee and the Shadows, a country rockabilly band. I came east in February 1961, and it's just as hard as any town I've seen."

I asked him about guitar technique. When he sang "Poor Girl," he had pulled out a kitchen table knife and used the back of the blade to fret his guitar. Where did he learn that old blues device, called bottleneck guitar? "I learned to use a butcher knife," Bob replied, "from an old guy named Wigglefoot in Gallup, New Mexico. He was a beaten-down old bluesman who wore a patch on his eye. I do a lot of material I learned from Mance Lipscomb, but not in public. Mance was a big influence. I met him in Navasota, Texas, five years ago. I've been a farmhand too. I learned 'House of the Rising Sun' from Dave Van Ronk and 'See That My Grave Is Kept Clean' from Blind Lemon Jefferson. I like the recordings of Rabbit Brown a lot too.

"Jack Elliott and Dave Van Ronk are the two best folk singers in New York. I can only sing one way, in the way I like to hear it. I don't have a pretty voice. I can't sing pretty, and I don't want to sing pretty." Bob dropped the names of a lot of admired musicians, a mélange of those he had heard on recordings only and those he said he'd met and worked with. He appeared to have known them all. "Yes, I like Ray Charles very much. I picked up the harmonica after hearing Walter Jacobs—you know, Little Walter—of the Muddy Waters band. But I play my own style of harmonica. I played piano for dancers in the carnival."

Had he made any recordings? "The recordings I've made haven't been released. I played with Gene Vincent in Nashville, but I don't know if they have been released. As to that bottleneck guitar, when I played a coffeehouse in Detroit I used a switchblade knife to get that sound. But when I pulled out the switchblade, six people in the audience walked out. They looked afraid. Now, I just use a kitchen knife so no one will walk out." Any other musical influences? "A lot, quite a lot. Woody Guthrie, of course. I have seen quite a lot of Woody since last winter. We can talk; even though he is sick. He likes my songs a lot. I met Jesse Fuller two years ago in Denver and studied with him."

Bob went on for another set. I told Carla that it had been a good interview and that I really loved his work and manner. But, I told her, I had the strange feeling he was putting me on. He seemed to have traveled so far and known so many famous and obscure musicians. He was evasive about his past. I told Carla to tell Bob there was a difference between kidding around with a Village guy and talking for publication. Minutes after Dylan's set Carla huddled with Bobby, and then we continued the interview at a table in between songs by the Greenbriar Boys. "Listen," Bob told me, "I'm giving it to you straight. I wouldn't tell you anything that isn't true." Did he want me to call him Bobby Dylan or Bob Dylan? He thought that one out, as if he were about to sign a contract. Half aloud, he repeated the two names to himself: "Bob Dylan, Bobby Dylan, Bob Dylan, Bobby Dylan… Make it Bob Dylan! That's what I'm really known as," he declared confidently. I wrote the review, which appeared in the *Times* on Friday, September 29, 1961:

A bright new face in folk music is appearing at Gerde's Folk City. Although only 20 years old, Bob Dylan is one of the most distinctive stylists to play in a Manhattan cabaret in months.

Resembling a cross between a choir boy and a beatnik, Mr Dylan has a cherubic look and a mop of tousled hair he partly covers with a Huck Finn black corduroy cap. His clothes may need a bit of tailoring, but when he works his guitar, harmonica or piano and composes new songs faster than he can remember them, there is no doubt that he is bursting at the seams with talent. Mr Dylan's voice is anything but pretty. He is consciously trying to recapture the rude beauty of a southern field hand musing in melody on his back porch. All the "husk and bark" are left on his notes, and a searing intensity pervades his songs.

Mr Dylan is both comedian and tragedian. Like a vaudeville actor on the rural circuit, he offers a variety of droll musical monologues. "Talking Bear Mountain" lampoons the overcrowding of an excursion boat. "Talking New York" satirizes his troubles in gaining recognition and "Talkin' Hava Negilah" burlesques the folk-music craze and the singer himself. In his serious vein, Mr Dylan seems to be performing in a slow-motion film. Elasticized, phrases are drawn out until you think they may snap. He rocks his head and body. He closes his eyes in reverie, seems to be groping for a word or a mood, then resolves the tension benevolently by finding the word and the mood. He may mumble the text of "House of the Rising Sun" in a scarcely understandable growl, or sob, or clearly enunciate the poetic poignancy of a Blind Lemon Jefferson blues, "One kind favor I ask of you—See that my grave is kept clean."

Mr Dylan's highly personalized approach toward folk song is still evolving. He has been sopping up influences like a sponge. At times, the drama he aims at is off-target melodrama and his stylization threatens to topple over as a mannered excess. But if not for every taste, his music-making has the mark of originality and inspiration, all the more noteworthy for his youth. Mr Dylan is vague about his antecedents and birthplace, but it matters less where he has been than where he is going, and that would seem to be straight up.

This was followed by four laudatory paragraphs about the Greenbriar Boys. As good as they were, Dylan seemed to be the news. By chance, the entertainment section had a canyon at the top of one review page. Across three columns ran the headline: BOB DYLAN: A DISTINCTIVE STYLIST. A rough photo of Dylan with his hat, his tie, and his big guitar got three inches of space. The layout, the picture, and the headline, trumpeted Dylan even louder than my story.

Reactions couldn't have varied more. A very few musicians were pleased. Elliott read the notice aloud in his best Dylanesque voice to a few drinkers at the Dugout on Bleecker Street. Van Ronk, cool but gulping hard, told me I had done "a very, very fine thing." Pat Clancy and his brother, Tom, said, "Bobby has a lot of talent. He deserves to go places." Izzy Young said he had discovered Dylan months earlier than anyone. And much of the Village music coterie reacted with jealousy, contempt, and ridicule. Eric Weissberg and Marshall Brickman, two of the ablest instrumentalists about, told me I needed a hearing aid. Logan English, a singer who had suffered inordinate difficulties getting his own career moving, was sarcastic and rueful. To a man, the Greenbriar Boys were hurt that this "kid" had eclipsed them. Bob Yellin didn't talk to me for weeks. Fred Hellerman, a songwriter and arranger, formerly of the Weavers, was openly derisive: "How on earth can you say that he is such a great this-and-that?" he asked me on a street corner. "He can't sing, and he can barely play, and he doesn't know much about music at all. I think you've gone off the deep end!" Manny Greenhill, Baez's kindly manager, said my review was "talking about Bobby in a year or two, not now." Charlie Rothschild said he saw some potential in Dylan "but he's got a long way to go." Most enthusiastic, however, were Carolyn and Richard Fariña. They liked Bob, personally and musically, and he was scheduled to play on Carolyn's upcoming recording. The non-musician fans—the MacKenzies, the Gleasons, Carla, Sybil, Suze—were all delighted.

Dylan showed up at Folk City that Friday night stunned and shaken. There was a very big turnout. As he walked in, patrons turned to each other and said: "There he is! That's the guy!" Bob looked uncertain that he could deliver, now that the order had been placed. He thanked me warmly and began his long years of telling me "you're a very good writer, not just music, but a very good writer." Through twenty years of reviewing, I can recall no other performer who seemed more concerned about a reviewer's feelings. When he was spinning out of orbit, Dylan lashed out at me for things I wrote, but those moments were exceptions. From the start, he knew that writers are as hungry for applause as musicians.

That fourth night of his gig, Bob had an even more engrossed audience. One stranger at the bar puzzled us. He was fiftyish, moon-faced, well dressed, smiled a great deal, and offered drinks to some of the kids who knew Dylan. Bob passed the word quickly: "Fuzz!" Much later he described the man as one of the many police who "followed" him. "He was a cop," Bob said later. "I told you about that at the time. Why, cops have been following me all my life. Cops haven't been following me much after 1964, but until then they used to come from all over." No one ever found out who the wicked messenger was that night.

Later in the evening, Dylan steered me to a quiet corner and said: "I don't want you to tell anybody about this, but I saw John Hammond, Sr this afternoon and he offered me a five-year contract with Columbia! But, please, man, keep it quiet because it won't be definite until Monday. I met him at Carolyn's session today. I shook his hand with my right hand and I gave him your review with my left hand. He offered to sign me without even hearing me sing! But don't tell anyone, not one single soul! It could get messed up by someone at the top of Columbia, but I think it is really going to happen. Five years on Columbia! How do you like that?"

Each participant in Dylan's meeting with Hammond told it differently. A synthesis indicates that Hammond acted on instinct and reputation more than any objective proof of Dylan's talent. Yet Hammond had the experience to trust his instincts. Carolyn Hester's first recording for Columbia was a step forward for the attractive young Texan singer, but proved an even bigger break for Dylan, who was just a walk-on with a mouth harp. Carolyn had arrived in New York in the late 1950s with a gorgeous voice and cascading brown hair. She had first recorded for Coral Records, then for Tradition. Her voice's range and power were astounding. Dylan was also impressed because Carolyn had briefly known and deeply admired Buddy Holly.

At one point, Grossman had considered Carolyn for the trio he eventually named Peter, Paul and Mary. Soon after the Kingston Trio's enormous success in 1959, Grossman set out to form a pop-folk trio that would incorporate aspects of the Kingstons with one cardinal difference, a pretty girl. He openly searched for his "components" for two years. He had briefly considered Molly Scott and Logan English. Next, having long admired Bob Gibson, he thought he would use the former Chicagoan as a keystone. For some months, Grossman worked informally with Gibson, Carolyn, and Ray Boguslav, a commercial artist and highly schooled musician. But this group didn't jell either. Gibson had periodic losses of voice and was befouled with problems. Boguslav was a serious musician, but he wasn't about to chuck his art career unless there were ample guarantees. Carolyn was ready, willing, and able to be the pretty girl. But by March 1960, she began to despair. "I really have grave doubts the trio will work out," she wrote me. "We made some tapes, I wasn't terribly good, but we could do something if we worked at it. Boguslav's range is so much different than mine. We ended up with little semblance of a 'blend' or 'sound.'" The trio also lacked the dedicated toughness Albert ultimately found with Peter, Mary, and Paul.

Dylan's version was simply that he handed Hammond the *Times* review and went around the room doing his harmonica business. By the end of the session, at which Bob had not sung one note, Hammond said that he had heard a great many good things about Dylan from his son and others and wanted to sign him to Columbia for a "standard" contract—one album—with options to do four more LPs for the next four years. Dylan was immediately willing, not even asking contract terms. Fariña generally substantiated this account, although he told me that he had huddled with Hammond during the session to say that Dylan was a first-rate singer and songwriter.

Hammond was one of the great jazz producers, the man who discovered Billie Holiday and was a close associate of Benny Goodman in the 1930s. Hammond had also been closely identified with Count Basie, Teddy Wilson, Benny Carter and the kings of boogie-woogie piano, Meade "Lux" Lewis, Albert Ammons, and Pete Johnson. A wealthy Ivy Leaguer whose devotion to jazz and black musicians was great, he'd organized the "Spirituals to Swing" at Carnegie Hall in 1938 and 1939; they were a preview, by 30 years, of all the elements that would cross-fertilize rock. Big John Hammond, as he was called, to distinguish him from his son, was a tall man of almost military dignity, with a long head and a pleasant demeanor. His mother was a Vanderbilt and his father was a banker, so he pursued the jazz he fell in love with at Yale without any great financial strain, even during the Depression. In 1933, during a fling as a journalist, he had covered the famous Scottsboro case, in which nine southern blacks were accused of rape, for the *Nation* and later for the *New Republic*. He wrote jazz and blues commentaries in *Downbeat*, *Metronome*, *Melody Maker*, the *Brooklyn Eagle*, and the *New York Compass*. In the mid-1930s, he wrote for the left-wing *New Masses*, under his own name and under the pseudonym of Henry Johnson.

Hammond had discovered the gifted, self-destructive Holiday when she was only 17. He had gone up to Monette Moore's speakeasy on West 133rd Street in Harlem to hear Monette, but was more impressed by Billie, and worked with her, in and out of the studio, throughout the 1930s. In a parallel episode, Hammond came away from a fine recording by Hester having, in the course of it, found Dylan.

Hammond has always been uneasy about Dylan's assertion that he offered to sign him without first hearing him sing. After nine frustrating months of being snubbed by the leading folk-music labels— Elektra, Folkways, and Vanguard—Dylan was ironically handed his big chance on a major label without even an audition! Hammond met him at a rehearsal at a West 10th Street apartment that the Fariñas were borrowing. Hammond's recollection is fuzzy: "He had on his cap and he had just come to New York. This was before he opened at Folk City the first time. I liked what I heard of him there so much, I asked him to come up to the studio. I didn't know that he did much singing, but I knew that he wrote. I heard some of the things that he did and I signed him on the spot. He said he didn't have a manager or parents—he was under-age at the time. We made our first album almost immediately. This was when Bob was writing three or four songs a day and was unused to mike techniques. His guitar playing, let us say charitably, was rudimentary, and his harmonica was barely passable, but he had a sound and a point of view and an idea. He was very disenchanted with our social system. I encouraged him to put all his hostility on tape because I figured this was the way, really, to get to the true Bob Dylan.

"So, for about the first eight months I had an absolute ball working with Bob. I had no direction on him at all because I felt Bob was a poet, somebody who could communicate with his generation. Now, Columbia was not known for doing that at the time. I thought the less a record producer interferes, the better results we'd get from Bob. I remember the first album cost something like $402 because he was the only guy on it, no arranging costs, no musicians to pay. While he was doing his second album for us, he came up to me and asked me about Albert Grossman, who wanted to sign him. I said we'd been on the board of the Newport Festival together and I thought I could work with him. I found out later I couldn't."

Hammond was equally fuzzy about his son's role in Dylan's discovery: "My son knew Dylan before he came to New York. My son, who was playing in some coffeehouse in Minneapolis, told me right after I signed Dylan in '61: 'Dad, I've just been out in Minneapolis. Did you know that Bobby's real name is Zimmerman and that he went to the University of Minnesota?' And I said: 'No, that's news to me.' But,

I said, 'It doesn't matter, that's his business.'" John Junior had gotten to know Bob quite well around the Village, and was one of the most fervent touters of his talents. Somewhere in his father's memory was the recollection of his son's enthusiastic praise of Dylan.

Carolyn's record, *Carolyn Hester*, is a pleasant folk album, made as Columbia was beginning to take the folk boom seriously. Dylan can be heard on three tracks. On "I'll Fly Away," a bright, spiritual-type song, his mouth harp comes on strongly staccato and rhythmic, takes a brief break, alternately lyrical and scuffling, and ends with a bluesy little swallowing riff. On "Swing and Turn Jubilee," Carolyn sings with square-dance hoedown joy. Bruce Langhorne, who could play florid Spanish guitar lacings one minute and barnyard fiddle the next, gives the song its dancing propulsion. Dylan's mouth harp blows hot and hard, goading the bouncy tune along. Still another side of Dylan's flavorful harmonica playing comes through on "Come Back, Baby." Bluesy and mournful, Dylan's harp work serves the accompanist's proper function—to give nearly invisible support. Hammond was pleased with Carolyn's sessions and anxious to get Dylan in the following week to sign. It was a dreadful contract, as Dylan was to discover, but it meant a chance to record, and that was all that mattered then. At first, he liked Hammond's enthusiasm, warmth, and encouragement, and was flattered to work with the man associated with so many jazz greats.

"A five-year contract with Columbia Records!" clucked Brother John Sellers at Folk City. "That boy is really something!" As the news filtered around, Dylan felt the sting of professional jealousy. He began to lose friends as fast as he had made them. The folk world tended to knock anyone who was "making it." Harry Belafonte was considered the epitome of the sell-out because he had an organization, an orchestra, a huge cast to accompany him.[16] Burl Ives, who had become a well-known actor, was a pariah.[17] Even when as natural a group of traditional singers as the Clancy Brothers and Tommy Makem got a job at the chic uptown Blue Angel, the Village rumbled that "they had sold out, weren't as good as they used to be." The rueful disdain of mass-media, show business, and recognition continued well into the mid-1960s. Dylan was always caught in the middle. Each time he changed his style, folk purists thought sinister commercial forces were at work.

Once he began to do well, Dylan the performer was the object of an exceptional amount of instant love and instant aversion. With each new success, both his followers and detractors grew in number. There were converts, of course; some who had laughed at him went on to idolize him. Envy even reverberated back from Minneapolis, where folk circles were aghast at both his *Times* review and his Columbia contract. "We couldn't quite understand why Dylan made it and John Koerner, who was really better in those days, didn't," Susan Gardner of Minneapolis told me in 1968. By then, she and the early doubters had long since seen why. Envy and incredulity dogged Dylan's steps from hereon. If he sneezed in Manhattan, some in Harvard Square would praise it, while others in Berkeley were ready to criticize the sound; from coast to coast, interpretations varied.

The pressures that later nearly destroyed him began that last week in September 1961. Could he live up to public praise? Could he ride out jealousy? The doubts rambled and tumbled in his mind as he prepared each Folk City set. There the only thing he could be sure about was that people liked his antics. The laughter, the ringing cash register, the clinking glasses, the verbal snipers, and the curiosity seekers were all easier to handle if he played it mostly for laughs. He moved about the stage more. He used his hat as a prop, pulling it low, tipping it, replacing it on his head, wiping his brow with it, swatting flies with it, dusting his guitar with it. His monologues between songs became more ludicrous, their timing more calculated. He developed so quickly that by the end of his two-week stand he was a stronger, more secure performer. Even those who hadn't liked him took him more seriously by the end of the gig. Very few people felt lukewarm about Dylan; they either loved or hated him.

The First Album. After a brief run-through, Bob and Hammond were ready to move into Columbia Studio A on Seventh Avenue. After all the elaborate big-band sessions, after all the old and limited recording equipment he had known during the 1930s, this was almost effortless. All Hammond needed was his singer-instrumentalist, an engineer, and himself. Dylan brought his talent and the girl with the long brown hair, Suze. He remained outwardly cool, putting down most of his songs in less than five takes. A few songs came off in a remarkable two takes; even Sinatra would do a dozen just to warm up. Hammond was delighted to be working with a kid who knew so much about the blues. He cautioned Bob repeatedly to step back from the microphone to avoid the plosive sound of p's. After the first twenty minutes, Dylan's confidence grew. At one point, Hammond left the control booth and brought back a long-time friend, Goddard Lieberson, a former studio woodwind player, then president of Columbia Records. Hammond had helped Lieberson get his first job at Columbia Records. Lieberson beamed at Dylan in the studio, and both older men voiced appreciation over the studio intercom.

Nothing impressed Dylan more, he told me the next day, than that while he was taping "Fixing to Die," an old black janitor who was cleaning up the hall stepped into the studio to listen. Bob knew then that he could get a lot more people to listen. The tragic old lament froze him in his tracks, and the janitor leant on his broom, watching and listening. Bob never forgot it, for it impressed him more than anything Hammond or Lieberson said.

The first album, simply entitled *Bob Dylan*, was recorded at three sessions in November 1961, but not released until March 19, 1962. A gap between recording and release is customary, but this long delay, caused by bureaucracy, annoyed Dylan very much. He felt he was moving with such momentum in late 1961 that to have the record in limbo for five months was a cruel anti-climax. By the time the album was released, he was embarrassed, regarding it as early work left in a bottom desk drawer. Dylan's let-down had set in as early as December, after the engineering and editing were complete. Few recording artists are entirely pleased with their first work but, within days of completing the album, Bob said that the liner notes were better than the contents, and that he wished he could have done this or that over again. Alternatively, he said how much he liked this or that song as he had done it. His perfectionism surfaced before the ink was dry on the contract.

Over the years, Dylan's negative reaction became typical. After putting enormous energy into writing, singing, recording, and performing, he would have a brief period of elation, followed by despair. Right after he finished each recording he thought it was the best he had done, and then the album became "just something I did." (The 1968 *John Wesley Harding* album was, he thought for a while, his finest work ever, and then, publicly at least, it was "just the sort of album that the people seemed to want at the time.")

The first album was the last will and testament of one Dylan and the birth of a new Dylan. Don Hunstein's cover photograph of the callow boy barely matches the performance by the old man within. A picture of that elderly Columbia janitor leaning on his broom might have better caught the mood. Dylan's picture looks almost delicate and tentative, yet the singing and playing are packed with bold assertion. Even at this time, when he was deeply in love with Suze, Dylan was preoccupied with songs about death and sadness. Death and Love were ineluctably twinned in the eye of the young Romantic. Suze dedicatedly sat at the sessions in quiet admiration, yet their relationship was tempestuous, clouded by her mother's efforts to split them up. Many of the songs were clearly for her, and the changes he made in traditional lyrics showed how strongly he wished to express himself to and about her.

If the cover photograph didn't mirror the album's contents, it did show Dylan much as he looked in those days, the hat making him appear even younger than he was. The unsmiling, pudgy face reflected a mixture of shyness and aloofness. His pseudo-western gear was standard 1961 hippie dress. The absence of a smile was also characteristic, for by then Dylan wasn't finding too much to smile about.

In spite of what Hammond said in late 1969 about the limits of Bob's guitar, harmonica, or mike technique, at the time he was openly rapturous about the album. Dylan's guitar work was strong for a 20-year-old's debut album. His harmonica work may not have been virtuoso, but it gave the album some of its flavor and texture. The mouth harp weaves the fabric of voice and guitar together, and it helped stimulate the resurgence of interest in blues harmonica in the early 1960s. Dylan's understanding of black blues remains the dominant impression of the album, but songs concerned with death and sadness alternate with wit and games. (Later, when Tony Glover, John Koerner, and Dave Ray were recording their excellent white blues albums for Elektra, they asked, by way of writer Paul Nelson: "Who says we can't sing good blues just because we're on the wrong end of the Mississippi?") The album in detail:

"You're No Good": A sprightly jape out of Jesse Fuller's song bag. A one-man band who could get up to six instruments going simultaneously as he sang, Fuller's good-time rural ragtime made people happy. "You're No Good" is typical Fuller gamesmanship and becomes, in Dylan's hands, a nonsense song of the beleaguered male running down the offending female in his life. "You're No Good" was inaccurately listed on the label of some American pressings and the original British release as "She's No Good." Programmed because of its brightness and tempo, the song scarcely proclaims a new singer of stature.

Yet the voice's spirit, drive, timbre, bite and propulsion win attention, as does the instrumental work. At the break, Dylan builds his own one-man band. His galloping mouth harp talks to the guitar, which answers right back. Then the voice soars again, and the colloquy continues. Soon, we have a rollicking tumble of witty nonsense. The guitar work is quite clean here. As Dylan gets into the song, the broadness of his put-on comes forward, culminating in a couple of vocal riffs that suggest Jack Elliott at his slyest. "You're No Good" is one of the album's brightest moments. This old man is a comic.

"Talking New York": Vintage Dylan, this proclaims his own writing talent, his sardonic view of the music business, and his control of humor and timing. One Woody Guthrie song served as a model from which Dylan drew his own; another gave flavor; and still a third supplied a bit of philosophy on which Dylan embroidered his message. The framework Guthrie song was "Talkin' Subway," which went, in part:

> *I struck out for old New York*
> *Thought I'd find me a job of work*
> *One leg up and the other leg down*
> *I come in through a hole in the ground*
> *Holland Tunnel. Three mile tube*
> *Skipping through the Hudson River dew.*

> *I blowed into New York town,*
> *I looked up and I looked down.*
> *Everybody I seen on the streets,*
> *Was all a-running down in a hole in the ground.*
> *I followed 'em. See where they's a-going.*
> *Newsboy said they're tryin' to smoke a rat out of a hole*[18]

The second influential Guthrie song was "New York Town" although, as with the blues above, the Dylan work is a decided improvement in structure and control. In his seventh verse, Dylan cites Woody indirectly, then makes his own summary from Guthrie's "Pretty Boy Floyd":

> *Now as through this world I ramble*
> *I see lots of funny men,*
> *Some will rob you with a six-gun*
> *And some with a fountain pen*[19]

Talking blues is a very old form, speech delivered against simple guitar background. The narrative tells a wry story in near deadpan, each verse ending with sardonic asides. Most talking blues since Guthrie were vehicles for folk humor. The exact origin of the form is unknown, but it can be found in the "preaching" introductions to black gospel songs. The congregation leader flows from verbal sermonizing into song with rhythm building up. And many blues are done in a nearly spoken vocal line. Leadbelly often talked his way into a song.

The "father of talking blues" was a South Carolina singer named Chris Bouchillon, who recorded "Original Talking Blues" in the 1920s. Robert Lunn, a more commercial country singer of the 1930s and 1940s, also called himself "the original talking-blues man." Bouchillon was recorded by Frank Walker, a pioneer field recording official, who hated Bouchillon's singing "but loved the way he talked." A musical genre was born because a man sang so poorly! Guthrie and Dylan generally used Carter family guitar style, with either a flat pick or thumb and forefinger. A bass note is hit, followed by a downward brush across the first three or four strings, and then an upward brush. Dylan's "Talking New York" is in G with just three chords.

This critique of the music business, New York aloofness, the coffeehouse circuit, and music impresarios, was written, Bob said, "in May 1961, [when] I was hitchhiking from the Holland Tunnel, but got a bum steer and started heading toward Florida, instead of toward California, where I wanted to go. I left at 7 a.m., but it was a false start. Then I left at 5 p.m. I started to write out the words at a truck stop on the highway. I just wrote it out on paper. I got as far as St Louis, Minneapolis, and Madison, Wisconsin." Dylan freely cursed the coffeehouse scene: "They wanted satin shirts and gut strings, while I played all steel strings, and you know I don't wear satin shirts," he told me. Dylan's suspicions of the music business, as early as his first recording, is another glimpse of the old man's spirit and insight.

"In My Time of Dyin'": This old spiritual is perhaps the album's most compelling track. Dylan said that he didn't know where he first heard it and that this was the first time he ever performed it. Josh White sang it on *Josh at Midnight* in the late 1950s, but had also recorded it in 1933 under the pseudonym of the Singing Christian. White used the title "Jesus Gonna Make Up My Dyin' Bed" on a considerably sweeter version than Dylan's. Another recording, by Dock Reed on a 1950 Folkways album, was a disconsolate, unaccompanied version. Dylan's is deeper and better structured than White's, as Josh conceded when I played Dylan for him in 1963. He smiled approvingly when he heard the track: "That boy really knows what he is doing!"

Dylan's excellent guitar work reflects his study of Robert Johnson and Rabbit Brown, highly inventive technically. By using open D tuning, he establishes a new texture. The low E-string is tuned down a tone to D, an octave below the fourth string, and the top E to D an octave *above* the fourth string— three Ds in successive octaves. The effect is less bright than the standard tuning. The capo is on the fourth fret, and Dylan used the metal cap of Suze's lipstick as his bottleneck on the little finger of his left hand. With the metal tube, the strings yielded inner resonances and a slightly ringing sound—which many old Delta bluesmen achieved using whiskey bottlenecks. The voice is an urgent vehicle for emotional autobiography. The identification with the spiritual's death-haunted figure is amazing for so young a singer. Dylan didn't sing the song in public, but it stands as one of his finest recorded performances.

"Man of Constant Sorrow": A traditional southern white mountain song permeated with trouble, this folk singer's standard was probably first recorded in the late 1920s by Emry Arthur, a Kentuckian who moved to Port Washington, Wisconsin, where he worked in a chair factory. He claims composition. In the 1930s, a Kentucky miner's wife, Sarah Gunning, wrote her own version, "I Am a Girl of Constant Sorrow." Dylan has rewritten the version that was being sung in the early 1960s by the New Lost City Ramblers, Baez, and others. The place of origin becomes Colorado. Reflecting problems with Suze's mother, he has changed "Your friends may think I'm a stranger" to "Your mother says I'm a stranger." He returns to flat-picking style that is highly understated, in traditional mountain manner. It emerges as a shiveringly lonesome personal statement and one of which Dylan was very fond.[20]

"Fixin' to Die": Dylan learned this other face of death from an old Okeh recording by Booker T Washington (Bukka) White, a bluesman who served time in the Mississippi State Prison Farm at Parchman. Bukka White sang it almost as a hymn, while Dylan brightens the tempo. "Fixin' to Die" opens with the sort of slide or smear that rock guitarists later used frequently, and Dylan's flat-picked guitar is again in open D. Many of the Bukka White images are similar in mood and vein to those of the older spiritual, "In My Time of Dyin'." The title was picked up in 1965 by Joe McDonald of Country Joe and the Fish, whose "I-Feel-Like-I'm-Fixin'-to-Die Rag" was a snorting rant against the Vietnam War.

"Pretty Peggy-O": A rollicking broad satire. Dylan takes a Baez standard and plays a dozen games with it. During World War I, an English folk-song collector, Cecil Sharp, collected several versions in the Southern Appalachians. In Scotland, the song is known as "Bonnie Lass O'Fyvie-O," and in England as "Pretty Peggy of Derby." The Baez version is called "Fennario," which Dylan pictures as some strange locale. Most do it as a rather light, lissome tale, while Dylan clatters into it as burlesque. He aimed, I think, to mock the preciousness of revived tradition with "long gone lieutenant"[21] and rhyming "rodeo" with the archaic "fairest maid in the areo."[22]

"Highway 51": In his first year around the Village, Dylan insisted he was a country or rockabilly singer, or just a singer—but not a folk singer. "Highway 51" may be the first folk-rock recording, even without electric instruments or rhythm. The late Tom Wilson, one of Dylan's producers, believed folk-rock began when the Animals recorded their 1964 electric "House of the Rising Sun." Another starting point was the four electric arrangements Dylan made for his second Columbia album in 1962. Still another departure was the Byrds' 1965 recording of Dylan's "Mr Tambourine Man." Yet here are all the elements of folk-rock *without* electrification.

Travel images permeate American folk song and blues, signifying freedom and change. To the southern black, the train whistle sounded escape, for new life at the end of the tracks, or nostalgia for the old life. Big Joe Williams sang of Highway 49. Robert Johnson keened about "Crossroads Blues" and "Terraplane Blues." Even Nat King Cole sang of "Highway 66." Guthrie and Pete Seeger collaborated on a "66 Highway Blues," about dead ends and fresh beginnings.

"Highway 51," which foreshadows one of his great songs, "Highway 61 Revisited," is credited to Curtis Jones, a Texas bluesman born in 1906. Jones's song, recorded in the 1930s on Vocalion and Conqueror, tells about one of the routes favored by migrant southern blacks. Highway 51 runs from New Orleans up to Madison, Wisconsin. The Curtis Jones song was also recorded in 1940 by that savage, raucous Chicago bluesman, Tommy McClennan. The Everly Brothers did it as rockabilly. Dylan's text and melody differ widely from Jones's. Curiously, Dylan has dropped nearly all of Jones's references to buses and McClennan's specific references to Greyhound buses.

The simple guitar work supplies the equivalent of a full rhythm section, with interweaving stresses that suggest jazz drumming—a precursor of some of the exciting guitar work of Richie Havens, who used the flat-picking brushstroke so inventively. The recurring opening figure is that used on the Everlys' "Wake Up Little Susie." Against this chugging guitar, Dylan delivers a vocally strong blues-rockabilly song. The pulse, tempo, and motion build up into several strong climaxes within two minutes, forty-nine seconds. Death is in the lyrics, but overabundant life is in the voice and guitar.

"Gospel Plow": An old spiritual converted into a modern pop-folk song, done up-tempo in a major key. "Keeping the hand on the plow" was a folk saying from farmland America. The phrase often expresses strong resolve, but Dylan, in his near-yelping voice, stresses motion and drive riding over swarming guitar figures. This is the album's least successful interpretation, because he can't seem to keep his hand steady on the mood. Both sides begin with songs in which the singing is not Dylan's best. "Gospel Plow" foreshadows his later involvement with Christianity.

"Baby, Let Me Follow You Down": After some delicate guitar work reminiscent of Rabbit Brown, Dylan shoulders his way into this song. The spoken introduction satirizes folk-music prefaces of the day, Dylan giving tongue-in-cheek credit for the song to Ric Von Schmidt of Cambridge. In the notes, Dylan said he believed that Ric had gotten some elements from an old recording by Horace Sprott, an Alabama sharecropper whom Frederick Ramsey, Jr had recorded in the field for Folkways. Dylan's three-finger picking supplies gentle harplike backing. A fine colloquy between harmonica, voice, and guitar is established. The singing has a striking sensuousness. "Baby" was clearly for Suze, who regarded it for a time as "her song." Dylan later linked the song to the Reverend Gary Davis's "Baby, Let Me Lay It on You."

"House of the Risin' Sun": Alan Lomax first recorded what he called a "modern southern white song" in 1937 in Middlesborough, Kentucky. Lomax traced it to some older bawdy English songs, the melody with the classic "Little Musgrave and Lady Barnard" (Child Ballad 81) and its American variant, "Little Mathy Groves." This lament of a woman dragged into prostitution has been recorded by Josh White, Cynthia Gooding, Guthrie, Seeger, and others. At this time, Carolyn Hester was singing a highly dramatic version, while Van Ronk had a rough-hewn, laconic interpretation. Dylan said: "I always knew this song, but never really knew it until Dave Van Ronk sang it."

The younger singer made it his own, attenuating the phrases almost to an emotional breaking point, using space and silence with as much effect as sound. Like thin pieces of Giacometti sculpture, the words are surrounded by space drawn toward the work itself. When a male folk musician sings a woman's song, he usually changes the gender, but Dylan let the lyrics stand. Picked up by the Animals, the old woman's song became Dylan's entrée into the English rock scene.

"Freight Train Blues": A relieving light moment here. Bob ascribed it to a recording by "the king of country music," Roy Acuff, though he probably learned it from Elliott. Harmonica slides and swoops set a jolly hillbilly mood, as Dylan yodels and chants. The vocal lines play against a steady, metrical guitar. In the Acuff vein, Dylan sustains one note, simulating a lonesome train whistle, typical country panache. Unfortunately, Bob didn't hit the train whistle on the head, and the note wavers in a few seconds. Hammond chose not to edit out the flaw.

"Song to Woody": Dylan wrote this elegy in February 1961, reportedly at the Mills Hotel bar after the sad encounter at the Gleasons'. The folkish melody, in graceful three-quarter time, sways delicately and is a variant on a traditional tune Guthrie used in "1913 Massacre." It has an intimate atmosphere and a sedative lullaby tone, so that we visualize him only a reach away from Woody. Bob's shock at his idol's decay may have prompted the album's preoccupation with death. The song, however, dwells on the young Guthrie's rambling days. The sensuous vocalizing is set against transparently simple guitar work which, like a line drawing, makes its impact through understatement.

In early autumn 1961, Dylan had performed his "Song to Woody" at a Folk City hootenanny. Joan Baez was there and asked Maynard Solomon of Vanguard to get her the song. I asked Maynard then if he wanted to record Dylan. He said he didn't, but that Joan wanted to sing his "Woody Song." Joan never got a tape or a copy, and forgot the episode until spring 1963, when she met Dylan on the West Coast.

A sad footnote to "Song to Woody" appeared in the April/May 1966 issue of *Sing Out!* Robert Ferris of Youngstown, Ohio, used Dylan's melody and structure for "Song to Woody" to write his own song about his disillusionment with Dylan, who had "gone electric." Ferris wrote: "I have written this song which can be used by anyone to show disgust for their particular fallen idol."

"See that My Grave is Kept Clean": A traditional spiritual that Blind Lemon Jefferson made classic, recording it for Paramount in October 1927. Released in February 1928, it became one of the best-known "race" recordings. When Blind Lemon learned the song, it was a folk spiritual called "Two White Horses in a Line," also known as "One Kind Favor." (Another "Two White Horses," a spiritual with different text and melody, appeared in Carl Sandburg's 1927 collection, *The American Songbag*.) Blind Lemon's and Dylan's versions are rich in traditional Anglo-American ballad imagery—digging of a grave with a silver spade, lowering of a coffin, two white horses bearing the coffin, and so on. Bob reflects tradition while impressing his own stamp. Blind Lemon's recording is sprightly, sweet, and benevolent, Dylan's stark and morose. Bob's sense of timing sustains the drama.

Between September and these recording sessions, he was able to rein in some of his melodramatic excesses. Of the entire album, perhaps only "Gospel Plow" spins out of interpretative control. On such songs as "Grave," his involvement never gets beyond temperate bounds: The coffin is lowered, the epitaph decreed. Mature artists often want to live down their first work. But after five years of preparation, Dylan had made a strong start.

Dylan taped four additional songs not included on the album: "The House Carpenter," a traditional southern mountain ballad, popularized by Baez and Bob Gibson; "He Was a Friend of Mine," which Dylan adapted from a song he learned from a Chicago street singer, Blind Arvella Gray, and which the Byrds later recorded in tribute to President John F Kennedy; Guthrie's cheerful, "Ramblin' Blues," also known as "Ramblin' Round" and "Ramblin' Around;" and "Man On the Street," an original based on an episode on West Fourth Street in the Village—Bob had seen a policeman jab a dead man with his club to stir him.[23]

Hammond sent me the test pressings so that I could write the liner notes under the pseudonym of Stacey Williams, a name I pulled out of a hat. There was an unwritten rule, constantly broken, that members of the *Times'* music department should have nothing to do with the production of recordings they might review. But nearly every member earned supplementary income by writing liner notes, anonymously or pseudonymously. When I told Dylan about the ruse he was delighted, but continued his far larger game of concealing his Hibbing background. We agreed that if anyone should ask who Stacey Williams was, Bob would "just mumble something about some old jazz and blues guy who wrote things for Columbia Records."

To prepare his official story, Dylan came to my pad one afternoon in December 1961 and spoke volubly and quickly, never giving any indication of manipulation of facts. He was keen to praise his sources and influences. "No one could phrase and use timing like those old blues singers," Bob said, singling out Robert Johnson and Big Joe Williams. He emphasized that although he didn't record "See That My Grave is Kept Clean" with one of his own variants, he generally sang: "Dig my grave/With a bloody spade/And see that my digger gets well paid."

Turning to his official biography, Dylan was still not prepared to go far in discussing his early days. He said he had graduated from high school in Hibbing, "way up by the Canadian border." For a spell before graduating, he went on, he lived in Sioux Falls, South Dakota, and Gallup, New Mexico. "I went to the University of Minnesota on a scholarship, but I left after six months. I didn't agree with school. I flunked out. I read a lot, but not the required readings. I read a lot of humanities, economics, Adam Smith's *Wealth of Nations*, I read Zola and Rousseau, 'cause people would recommend 'em. I stayed up all night reading the philosophy of Kant instead of *Living With the Birds* for a science course. I took a Spanish course to get an easy good mark. But the teacher started tearing me apart, even though I could talk with people in Spanish. I lived on the banks of the Mississippi River under the Washington Avenue Bridge with four other guys." Of his pilgrimage east, Bob said: "I headed for Greystone Hospital to see Woody. I talked with Woody, and it was an experience I'll never forget. Now, when I get depressed, I visit Woody in Brooklyn and then I get to feel better. I've visited Woody many, many times, but I would never want to be another Woody Guthrie."

Did he anticipate stardom? Dylan looked as modest as a hobo with a nickel in his pocket. "I never thought I would shoot lightning through the sky in the entertainment field." He sketched his influences: "I started to sing and play the guitar at the age of ten. Hank Williams had just died and I first liked country music—people like Jimmie Rodgers. Then I got interested in old blues, and people like Jelly Roll Morton. I remember Leadbelly and 'See See (C C) Rider,' but I also liked the country songs of Jack Guthrie. I really couldn't decide which I liked best, country or blues. So I suppose I ended by becoming a mixture of Hank Williams and Woody Guthrie."

What about his fascination with Charlie Chaplin? "He influences me, even in the way I sing. His films really sank in. I like to see the humor in the world. There is so little of it around. I guess I'm always conscious of the Chaplin tramp." Then what about death songs? "Well, I feel a closeness to songs like 'See That My Grave is Kept Clean.' I'm representing myself and a whole lot of people who sing in that manner." He was anxious to be in the very best company, song-swapping with Van Ronk and Elliott. He was a great fan of old rock 'n' roll—Presley, Little Richard, and rockabilly singer Carl Perkins.

He linked his harmonica work to Jesse Fuller, "Little Walter" Jacobs, and Sonny Terry. "Now I am 'blowing out' more in my own style." What did the future look like? "I would just like to keep on singing like I am. I just want to get along. I don't think about making a million dollars." If he had money, what would he do with it? Bob smiled: "If I had money, I would buy a couple of motorcycles, a few air-conditioners, and four or five couches." We joked about the folk-record companies, Folkways, Vanguard, and Elektra, who had either ignored or rejected him. "I was around and all the folk-record people heard me. Now, I'm grateful that they didn't sign me."

He summarized his approach to songwriting: "Either the song comes fast, or it won't come at all." (He later said that deadline pressure made him "prolific.") Some songs marinate for a long time. "I just jot down little phrases and things I overhear." He mentioned films that were inspiring his songs. Right after seeing *The Ox-Bow Incident*, about a western lynching, he wrote "Ballad of the Ox-Bow Incident." He had just seen the poignant Soviet anti-war film *Ballad of a Soldier*, and said "I just know I'll write a song based on that." When I tried to probe his fascination with death, Dylan became nearly inarticulate. He said he had been seriously ill three years earlier (presumably with asthma) and had begun then to think a lot about death.

The recording, which came out in March 1962, received several very fine reviews but, as they say in the record business, "nothing happened." Not until two years later did this creditable first recording begin to sell in quantity. Around Columbia, they began to call Bob Dylan "John Hammond's folly." Only a handful of people thought Dylan had much promise. Suze did, but almost from the beginning she feared Bob's death-hauntedness. By November 1961, love was a four-letter word to Dylan, and so was Suze. Bob felt the romance was doomed—enough to make any 20-year-old sing an old man's song and think that life might be over.

Dylan in Studio A at Columbia Records for his first album (top left), November 1961, and at right with producer John Hammond, who signed him to the label.

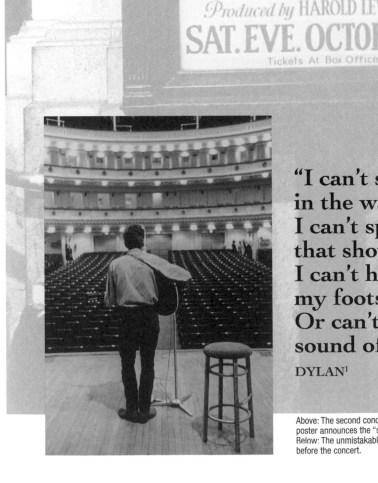

Chapter 4:

Bobby didn't change, he just growed.
BIG JOE WILLIAMS

Bob Dylan

SOLD OUT

Produced by HAROLD LEVENTHAL

SAT. EVE. OCTOBER

Tickets At Box Office

"I can't see my reflection
in the waters,
I can't speak the sounds
that show no pain,
I can't hear the echo of
my footsteps,
Or can't remember the
sound of my own name."

DYLAN[1]

Above: The second concert at Carnegie Hall, October 1963, and this time the
poster announces the "sold out" performance.
Below: The unmistakable form, even from the rear, of Dylan sound-checking
before the concert.

In the old joke, a stranger in New York asks, "how do you get to Carnegie Hall?" A musician replies, "practice." Within two weeks of taping his first album, Dylan found his way to Carnegie Hall—not the main Carnegie, but its neighboring debut room, Carnegie Chapter Hall. For his first important solo concert, on Saturday, November 4, 1961, fifty-three people turned out, mostly the Village gang. Dylan performed with assurance and pointed professionalism. As much as his sad songs could touch, it was still the comic routines, the talking blues, to which the audience responded most warmly.

The concert was sponsored by Izzy Young of the Folklore Center. Charging two dollars a ticket, Izzy, the sweat-shirted Sol Hurok, had pulled off another of his aesthetic coups and financial flops. That Izzy later became the folkniks' noisiest Dylan detractor should not obscure his early encouragement. He kept a chronicle of interviews with Dylan and other musicians who drifted into his shop, talking with Dylan on October 20 and 23, 1961, and February 1, 7, 22, and March 14, 1962. Dylan offered Izzy a few insights, ample wit, and as tall a stack of tales as he had given anyone.

"My songs aren't easy to listen to. My favorite singers are Van Ronk, Elliott, Peter Stampfel, Kweskin, and Von Schmidt. Joan Baez? Her voice goes through me. She's OK. Played piano with Bobby Vee—would have been a millionaire if I'd stayed with him. Have no religion. Tried a bunch of different religions. Churches are divided. Can't make up their minds, neither can I. Never saw a God; can't say till I saw one. Sort of like New York. I like to walk around. Like to ride motorcycles—was a racer in North and South Dakota and Minnesota. Before I met Jesse Fuller in Denver, there was a farmhand in Sioux Falls, South Dakota, who played the autoharp. Picked up Wilbur's way of singing—never remember his last name. Cowboy styles I learned from real cowboys. Can't remember their names. Met some in Cheyenne. Cowboys nowadays go to cowboy movies and sit there and criticize, wear their hat this way or that, pick up their way of walking from the movies. Used to see girls from the Bronx at Chicago, Antioch, with their gut-string guitars singing 'Pastures of Plenty.' No lipstick, brotherhood songs. Struck me funny, not clowns, opened up a whole new world of people. I like the New York kind of girl now, can't remember what the old kind was like. Don't care for classical music. Don't go for any foreign music. I really like Irish music and Scottish music too. Colleges are the best audiences, much better than nightclubs."

Around Christmas, Dylan did a small concert at Rutgers University in New Jersey. He went over very well, but again the comic eclipsed the musician. Throughout, he gibed at a picture of an elderly university trustee on the wall behind him: "Howdy, Mr Rutgers, nice of you to ask me down here."

In February 1962, he went upstate to a small coffeehouse, the Caffé Lena, in Saratoga Springs. Dylan had become a good chess player by then and was also adept at pool and, arriving at a revived spa centre, he headed for the pool hall, like one of the cowboys in his later songs. A local shark challenged him, and Bob obligingly lost the first two games, while the stranger kept raising the stakes. In the third game, Dylan cleaned the stranger out. He had less luck in the Caffé Lena gig, arranged by Terri Van Ronk. Lena and Bill Spencer hadn't been easily persuaded. Lena: "You know I don't book unknowns." Terri: "I've done all sorts of favors for you. Now you do me a favor and take this guy, because he's really good. You won't regret it." Lena regretted it.

Virtually none of the Skidmore College girls were tuned in to Dylan. At one point, when the audience persisted in talking over Bob's singing, Spencer grabbed the microphone: "Maybe you don't understand what this kid is doing. Maybe you are too stupid to understand what he is saying. If you would only shut up and listen, maybe you would understand!" Bob started one of his comic monologues, putting down the audience and the owners as well. If there was anything he disdained, it was fraternities, sororities, and rude audiences. He did very little other stage work during 1962. He had played at a Toronto coffeehouse and a benefit concert at City College in Manhattan for the Congress of Racial Equality (CORE). From April 24 to May 6, he returned to Folk City, where he could always be sure of a warm reception. Right after the Columbia taping, Harry Belafonte was looking for an "ethnic" harmonica player. Why Belafonte did not think of any of a dozen black harp players is a mystery, but somehow Dylan was asked to play on Belafonte's RCA sessions for the album *Midnight Special*. In those days, folkniks used to run Belafonte into the ground, though Dylan wasn't always demeaning. "It's easy to criticize the big money-makers like Belafonte and the Kingston Trio," Dylan reportedly told Izzy in 1961. "The stuff Belafonte does is really like popular singing. I won't criticize him until he sings one of my songs. But then he'll make a lot of money for me."

He developed the story of the session into an offstage talking blues. "You see, this Harry Belafonte is quite a big man," Dylan told me immediately afterward. "He has a small army that fights for him. Why, his arranger just goes crazy trying to think up great new ideas. When I got there, the studio men were working out something special. The first guitar man did this, the second guitar man did that. Another guy scraped two drumsticks together, and another guy shuffled his feet. It wasn't bad. They went over and over it till they had it just right. Then, in walks Belafonte himself. He was nice and friendly, and everyone greeted him like he was God himself. Then Belafonte walked over to where these studio men had been working so hard on this little riff. 'Harry,' the arranger said, 'we've whipped up something really great for that arrangement.' 'That's nice,' Harry says, 'let's hear it.' So then," Dylan continued, giggling, "the first guitar man did this, the second guitar man did that. Another guy scraped two drumsticks together, and another guy shuffled his feet. They finished, and all eyes turned toward Belafonte. 'I don't think so,' said Harry, walking away, and the smiles on those poor guys just froze, they just froze!"

After the release of the Belafonte album, some radio jocks, like Bob Fass of WBAI, played the track, not saying: "That was Harry Belafonte singing 'Midnight Special'," but: "That was Bob Dylan playing the harmonica." (Belafonte and others at the sessions had some laughs at Dylan's expense: To keep rhythm, he tapped out the time with his booted right foot, but the vibrations kept registering on the tape. An engineer slipped a pillow under Bob's thudding foot.)

Dylan's diary as an artist, from late 1961 through most of 1962, was dominated by his seeking out established performers, his songwriting, his contact with *Broadside* and the civil rights movement, and his managerial affiliations. Above all, his long, stormy love affair with Suze Rotolo affected much of what he did throughout 1962.

"The True Fortuneteller of My Soul."

Returning from Minneapolis in early summer 1961, convinced that Bonny and he had no future, Dylan pinned his expansive hopes on Suze Rotolo. Suze (pronounced *Suzy*) had a magic, even to those not in love with her. Her light brown hair flowed below her shoulders, and her pumpkin smile could warm a room. Her manner was shy, tentative, gentle. Her eyes and ears caught everything, although she was often curiously inarticulate. She was creative, whether sketching and drawing, planning a stage production, or helping to run the little magazine, *Streets*.

From mid-1961 through the spring of 1964, whether living with Dylan or running away from him, whether in Greenwich Village, Woodstock, or Italy, whether trying to come to emotional terms with Bob or battling with him, whether trying to get closer than he would allow or farther than he wanted, Suze was a central figure in one of Dylan's most quickening periods, personally and professionally. He probably wrote more than a dozen songs for or about her, and she inspired countless more. She was only 17 when they met. She was a New Yorker from an urbane Italian-American family of readers, political activists, cultured and socially concerned people. Suze looked, acted, and thought just like a woman, not a little girl. Bob wrote most directly of her in an "Outlined Epitaph":

> *I think of Sue most times*
> *beautiful Sue*
> *with the lines of a swan*
> *frightened easy*
> *as a fawn in the forest ...*
> *I think love poems*
> *as a poor lonesome invalid*
> *knowin' of my power*
> *t' destroy*
> *the good souls of the road*
> *that know no sickness*

except that of kindness …
ah but Sue
she knows me well
perhaps too well
an' is above all
the true fortuneteller of my soul
I think perhaps the only one[2]

The "frightened fawn" remained elusive. Although I spent dozens of evenings with Suze and Bob, I had difficulty grasping her spirit. She tended to be overshadowed by Dylan when she was with him. Although I sensed her keen artistic perception, she was generally unassertive in those early years. I tended to take Bob's part, saw through his eyes rather than hers. Dylan must have been a handful to live with, a challenge to an experienced woman, let alone one of 18. I knew only that she had a power over Bob, and, in those pre-feminist days, to her chagrin, I often urged her to put his needs above hers. I couldn't see then that she was right from her side too, grasping for her own identity in the whirlpool of his urgent needs. Before the end of 1961, he was talking about marriage, sometimes flippantly, sometimes in dead earnest, planning the ceremony in detail. One winter night in the White Horse, he told Suze and me how it would go: "We'll get Reverend Gary Davis [the blind street singer-preacher] to perform the ceremony. Naw, he can just sing the ceremony. And we'll have all the singers there." He started to list both probable and improbable guests. Suze smiled, eyes flashing flattery, but she didn't say yes and she didn't say no.[3]

Suze's mother had other ideas. Mary Rotolo was a volatile, strong-headed, intelligent woman in her early forties, whose factory-worker husband had recently died. She was a translator for a medical journal and was planning to marry a New Jersey teacher. Suze was too young to become involved with anyone, let alone that scruffy beatnik, she felt. Mrs Rotolo didn't approve of Bobby at all, although both her daughters, Suze and twenty-year-old Carla, thought so highly of him. "My mother was the only one at that point who disliked Dylan heartily," said Carla (whom Dylan often called "Carla-in-law"). "Yet, when Bob was sick, she put him up at her flat." Suze knew little of Bob's background. Some friends maintained that she thought he was an Italian orphan until *Newsweek* broke the story of his parents and Hibbing in 1963. Carla: "My mother somehow found out that his name was Zimmerman—perhaps he told her. I don't know how, but my mother had a way of finding out things. In fall 1961, my mother knew who he was. She felt he was taking advantage of everyone around to get ahead. She called him a sponge to his face. Dylan could fight anybody's mother, but the fact that she saw through him, which no one else did, scared him. He respected our mother as a person, but he always hated her. He paid court to her, he did everything he could over the years to win her over, and it never worked. The ultimate thing was that 'Ballad in Plain D.'"

Years later, Bob still was protective toward Suze, still had faith in her good sense. She was his witness: "The thing Suze could tell you," Dylan told me, "is that Suze knows, more than anybody else, she knows that I played, back in 1961 and 1962, when nobody was around, all those old Elvis Presley records. She'll tell you that. Actually, I told her not to talk to anybody at all. I told her to shuck off anybody that calls. If anybody ever gives her any trouble, man, I'll fix them good. But if you want to talk to her, fine. But don't come on with her, OK? Everybody comes on with her. Don't come on with her about how I was, ask her what I did. She'll tell you. She'll tell you how many nights I stayed up and wrote songs and showed them to her and asked her: 'Is this right?' Because her father and her mother were associated with unions and she was into this equality-freedom thing long before I was. I checked the songs out with her. She would like all the songs. Suze is a very talented girl, man. But she is very frightened."

At 17, Suze was tortured by her mother's dislike of Dylan. Carla became increasingly negative toward the relationship. Dylan's intensity, restlessness, and darkness also frightened Suze. It was all happening too soon and too fast. Although she tried repeatedly to break away, she was ineluctably drawn to him. Especially in their early days, Bob and Suze seemed to us magic lovers closely bound in a hostile world. I, for one, was surprised at their first split-up—but I was seeing through Bob's eyes, not hers.

In summer 1961, Mary Rotolo was living in the penthouse of One Sheridan Square, atop the old Café Society Downtown, which was in the basement. On the fourth floor lived a folk den mother, Miki Isaacson, who ran a kibbutz for strays. Miki didn't like to be alone and she only felt useful if surrounded. At first, the contingent in her large, triangular living room consisted of Jack Elliott, Greg Levasseur, John

Herald, and, soon, Dylan. Toward the end of the summer, Jean Redpath, a Scottish singer, joined the family-style commune, sloppy but not hippie. Nearly everyone picked or sang until three in the morning, then dropped off to sleep on the sofa. Redpath recalled, "I nearly blew a gasket blowing up so many of those rubber mattresses." Dylan glided into this permissive family, pleased to be sleeping under the same roof as Suze.

Suze graduated from Bryant High School in Queens, spent part of 1961 at the New School, and held part-time office jobs. She was interested in drawing, theater, design, and poetry, and worked as an usher in off-Broadway theaters, like One Sheridan Square. When she first met Dylan at the Riverside Radio all-day hoot, she thought he was a joke, she told me in 1966, through her sunburst smile. "A nice joke, but a joke … I don't think I ever saw him sober for a while. Half of that was put-on drinking, though … I guess I was always aware that he would be big one day. Especially after you wrote that he was a sponge that absorbs everything. Once I got to know him, I knew that quality. I soon discovered that he wasn't a joke at all. When you got to know him separately you knew just how frighteningly sharp he was. Even way back in 1961. He could be sitting in a room filled with people and be absorbing rays from everyone, from everywhere."

Was it difficult to live with a genius? "I guess it was hard," Suze replied. "Their heads are going all the time. But you can't treat them as being so extraordinary. You can't treat geniuses like they are precious china objects all the time. They are just human beings." Did he communicate well to her? "Yes, definitely. But he certainly can express himself better in what he writes than in what he says. Those first few months at Gerde's and at the first recording session, I was very awed. I wasn't fully aware of what was happening. I didn't realize this was such a big phenomenon, and I still don't. When I see his pictures everywhere and see him quoted, I still think it's a joke. You see, to me, it's still old Bobby."

Suze was in Italy from May until December, 1962. "When I came back, it was to the stardom of Dylan. That's when he was really getting big. A lot of things were going on, and I became more aware of his public image. Even though he wrote me often and called me all the time in Italy, he would only talk about us, and would never talk about what he was doing." Dylan was in England in late 1962 when Suze returned and she was greeted not by the man but by his songs sung by Janet Reynolds and others. Hearing "letters" written to her on a jukebox was "very strange. I was torn. It became very flattering to sit back and hear a song like 'Don't Think Twice' or 'Tomorrow Is a Long Time' on the radio. It was especially strange to hear them being sung by other people."

Suze recalled Bob at work in early 1962: "He would just say to me: 'I'm going to do some writing tonight,' and would sit down at the typewriter, or would play with his guitar. I never minded that all that much. The apartment on Fourth Street was a very small place to have someone constantly playing chords over and over again. He was very fast about his writing. He also liked to go out to write. He would sit at a table in some cheesy little luncheonette and write. He would write in his little spiral notebook while drinking coffee. He used to take that notebook with him to places like the Fat Black Pussy Cat." Dylan was as much "the eye of Greenwich Village" as Henry Miller's Brassaï was "the eye of Paris." But while Romney, Stookey, Elliott and other floaters were often brilliant talkers, Dylan, "the spy," was present though almost invisible. He would hang back, rather than hang out, and listen. He'd laugh at their jokes, but more often than not he would make a note in his ten-cent notebook.

Suze and I talked of how mystified people have been about Dylan. Was Suze asked what he was really like? "Yes, often. He *is* mystifying. Most of it he created, and then added to it by just being himself. I think he must have enjoyed it. You get afraid to ask him things because he has a whole cloud around him. People have said that they get afraid of him. A lot of people that know him best don't ask him anything, because they don't know on what ground they will have to defend themselves if he answers." ("Outlaw Blues": "Don't ask me nothin' about nothin'/I just might tell you the truth.")[4]

"That was why," Suze went on, "there was such a horror over what his real name was. He was always very paranoid. I remember that just thinking of going out for a walk, his knee would start to twitch. He would wonder: Who was he going to run into? It used to get to me because I thought there was something weird going on. I just couldn't figure out what made him so frightened of crowds, of strangers." Close as she had been to Dylan for three years, Suze maintained that he was as elusive to her as she had been to him. She told me: "You probably know as much about him in New York as anyone."

In spring 1962, before she left for Italy, "he was especially close-mouthed. The funny thing about our relationship was that it started small but kept getting bigger and bigger all the time. The thing that struck me about Bobby was his despair, that deathlike quality about him. I sensed, long after we had gone our separate ways, a lack of excitement to him. People live with hope for green trees and beautiful flowers as far as I'm concerned, but Dylan seems to lack that sort of simple hope, at least he did from 1964 to 1966 ... It's a philosophy of despair, so to speak." I told Suze how Bob had once talked to me at length about suicide, and the next day had said that if I thought he was pessimistic, then I didn't understand him at all. "He just won't accept anybody's point of view about himself. That's his way. There is something I see in him that I just don't like. Maybe he doesn't like that quality in himself either. It's somehow all too negative, too pessimistic. But on another level he is so alive, so very much alive, it's frightening. And then there is something in him that is so very funny. That's what made me run away in the past. In Italy at eighteen, I was just beginning to wake up to certain things and these are what kept me away from him. Things were just beginning to take shape for me. I'm twenty-two now, and perhaps not all that much older or wiser. There was always that frightening quality to Bobby. It started very small and seemed to get bigger and bigger. It's funny, but it was hard to be around, hard to live with constantly. All I can say of it is that there was something death-like about it."

Suze's sister grew more hostile to the relationship. Carla was fantastically enthusiastic about Dylan and yet often jealous and competitive of her sister. As "big sister," she always seemed to know what was best, and that didn't always mean Dylan. At first, Carla big-sistered him as well. When she was living at 129 Perry Street in autumn 1961, Bob stayed. Carla: "Bobby was still in his dirty period then. But he was very fussy about his clothes. His concern about his image started then. He would always ask if he looked right, jiggling with his dungarees: 'Are they tight enough? Is the shirt OK?' I would go to work in the morning and Bobby would be asleep on my living room couch. He spent most of his time listening to my records, days and nights." He studied the Folkways *Anthology of American Folk Music*, the singing of Ewan MacColl and A L Lloyd, Rabbit Brown's guitar, Guthrie, of course, and blues. He read voraciously. "My library was quite eclectic," Carla recalled, "and he read whatever he found. He started with our poetry books. I think he met François Villon through us. He was borrowing from anyone who had a large book collection." While still giving the public impression of being neither reader nor student, Dylan jumped headlong into the best folk-music collections, by the Lomaxes, Sharp, Child, and as much poetry as he could absorb. Bob read Suze's European and American poetry books, and bought her more, which they read together. All the time he scribbled notes. Whatever dormant energy remained from university was unleashed in the Village.

Carla sensed that the kid she was mothering needed very little protection. "Bobby was still at my flat, and his record was in the planning stages. I'm not sure just when I asked him to move out. What had started as a two-week stay stretched from September into November. We were all concerned about what songs Dylan was going to do. I clearly remember talking about it. Suddenly, I realized Bobby *knew* what he was going to do and how he was going to go about it. He knew exactly where he was going and how big he was going to be. This is a very important point. Up to then he had just been a bumbling kid, and everybody was helping him with money, clothes and everything. Then, suddenly, I remember feeling *this isn't a kid!* Although we were the same age, I always thought of him as being much younger than me, in the sense of emotional maturity.

"Bobby certainly is a classic Gemini," Carla continued. "I've known other Geminis in Italy, just like him—schizy. The classic Gemini definition really fits Bobby—split, flashes of brilliance, contradictions, and the inability to stay in one place. I was Pisces and Suze was a Scorpio. Geminis and Pisces think alike, but can't get along. Geminis are supposed to devour Scorpios, just eat them up, and that's just what happened with Bobby and Suze. I'll never forget that day when I got that feeling that he didn't need me or *anyone*. None of us had seen it, because he was so good at masking it, with the kid stuff, with the indifferent, lost attitude. Even musically, he knew every step he was taking. He used to sing 'Highway 51' very slow, drawling it like Rabbit Brown, yet when he got to the studio, he cut it fast. He had absolutely never done it with such drive and tempo before. Here was a man who instinctively knew which way to go. The only mistake he made was being caught up in the vortex of being 'the messiah.'"

Did Carla feel she had been wasting concern on him? "Not so much that as the feeling of *what a stupid fool I've been. He's probably been laughing at me all the time*. All of us were buzzing about him like mother hens. He put us in this position. We were all used, not necessarily as a sounding board. We were all quite necessary to Bobby, but how foolish we were all in that time, when he was laughing through his teeth at us, and yet he needed us just the same. He may still have been the shambling, bumbling, angelic one with the cap on, on the surface, but he wasn't that underneath, to me. It was a time to pull off the masks. The bumbling child covered over the ambition and the carefully thought-out plan. He didn't need anyone's help or advice. From then on, I made no reference about his recording or how he should do it. My mother was the only one who disliked Dylan. I still liked him very much, and may have even admired him more after I saw how smart he was."

After having slept on so many sofas around the Village, Bob decided to get a sofa of his own. Early in 1962, he found a two-room apartment at 161 West Fourth Street. The building rose four flights over Bruno's Spaghetti Parlor, and Dylan rented the first floor rear for around $60 a month. There was a tiny bedroom and a kitchenette/dining/living area. He had bought a small, secondhand Motorola TV, which he soon discovered didn't work, and he proceeded to rebuild it, covering it with a blond-wood cabinet. He built a table with space for meals, the TV in the middle, and a niche for his typewriter. The portable nearly always stood ready with a piece of yellow copy paper in it, a few lines of a song-in-progress peeking out. The apartment was decorated with dust, a hard wooden chair, instruments of all sorts, a few Mexican belts, guitar straps, and a ceramic bull. There was barely room for one person. When Suze moved in, there was scarcely room for anyone.

Within months, Suze fell under heavy pressures to go to Italy. Her mother and stepfather wanted her to study, and she wanted perspective. She decided to take a summer course at the University of Perugia, then study art at the Accademia. Through the spring, Dylan was miserable and Suze was ambivalent, wanting to stay and wanting to be on her own. She seriously considered marrying him. "Maybe you should marry him," Carla told Suze, equivocating that if the relationship were good it would be just as good after six months. At the end of May, Suze prepared to leave from Hoboken. At the boat, both Bob and Suze were distraught. During nine months of separation, Bob spun chaotically in a great whirlpool of personal loss but artistic gain. Acutely lonely, he turned to his New York friends—the MacDougal Street hippies— me, Sybil Weinberger, Gil Turner, and, increasingly, to various southern civil rights activists.

After Suze left, Dylan suffered many anxieties about his health. He told one friend that he feared he was going blind, that a doctor had once told him he *was* going blind. Still, he was determined to "get myself a motorcycle and to go to Italy." Frequent phone calls to Suze, often costing $100 each, didn't bring her back any earlier. Bob turned to other Village girls, who listened to him talk about Suze. Said one: "I remember ironing his shirt and thinking that I was being such a Jewish mama. Yet, I was frightened by him. There was no real communication."

Sybil Weinberger: "He was a dirty, sloppy, way-out young man; immature, irresponsible. He had a great compassion, always for things outside of himself, like the Negro situation. Bobby was not the least caught up in the pettiness, jealousies, and professional competition around at the time. I respected him for that. But, I resented him for it, because everybody was a critic then, and everybody was busy judging and categorizing everyone trying to make it. Bobby was above and beyond all that. When we walked down the street, it was as if he saw things that absolutely nobody else saw. He was so aware of his surroundings in every situation it was almost like he couldn't write fast enough. He would get thoughts and reactions and he would stop on a street corner and write things down. That was frightening to me too. His reactions to things amazed me—to weather, people, cars, buildings, shapes. I always felt his comments had a great deal of objectivity. He would reach for that little spiral notebook and write about animals on the street or a newspaper headline."

Another Rotolo friend was a drawling Louisianian actor, Quinton Raines, who had been working on *Brecht on Brecht*, a musical. Suze wanted to bring Bob into her theater world; Quinton seemed the ideal bridge. An experimental meeting with Quinton, at Jack Delaney's restaurant, lasted five hours. Carla said they "tried to get Bob to see the Brecht show." (Quinton says Bob claimed he had never seen a stage play before, a dubious contention considering Bonny Beecher appeared regularly in University of Minnesota productions.) *Brecht on Brecht* opened new doors of perception for Dylan. Brecht was the prolific playwright, poet, lyricist-librettist (notably with Kurt Weill in *The Threepenny Opera* and *Mahagonny*), and Marxist theoretician. A refugee from the Nazis, he lived in America during the war years, returned to East Germany, and led the Berliner Ensemble until his death in 1956. Brechtian ideas, language, and style coursed through Dylan's politicized period of 1962–63. Brecht's theme that Hitler's Germany was caused by sheepish belief in leaders was echoed in one of Dylan's cardinal tenets: "Don't follow leaders."[5] "Pirate Jenny" may have influenced "When the Ship Comes In." In the 1970s, a gifted Yugoslav-born London-based singer, Bettina

Jonic, performed and recorded twenty-two works by Brecht and Dylan.[6] Jonic saw the two writers reflecting Germany of the 1920s and America of the 1960s: "To relate Brecht with Dylan was natural. Their simplicity of style and use of language were so alike; yet they were two unique voices speaking with enormous force and directness. A black boy killed out of bigotry [Dylan] or a girl killed for sleeping with a Jew [Brecht] becomes that timeless voice speaking out against atrocity. Following this pattern leaves one with a sense of the poet's rage, despair, his need to speak and hold up to life a bitter mirror."

Quinton says he tried to talk Dylan into writing a play. "Over a period of three or four months, we talked about the songs he would do for the play. Sometimes, after a long drinking session, he would get up, saying 'I feel like I'm gonna go home and write me a whole lot of songs. I feel a lot of songs coming.' And sure enough, three or four days later, he would come up with those songs he had felt coming on. But he never did produce any songs specifically for that play." Quinton noticed that Dylan "seemed to structure personal tempests to give himself the inspiration to write. He was least productive in his songwriting when things got more settled. Strange, isn't it?"

The Ballad of Broadside. One tempest that inspired Dylan was America in 1962, a time when protest started to become a mass movement, a movement so all-embracing that it would even stir a lethargic campus like Kent State. The first American soldier was killed in Vietnam in December 1961, a date scarcely without significance, but the roots of Sixties protest run into the loam of the Fifties, when conservatism and self-interest dominated American youth.

Criticizing the American way of life then was not only unfashionable, but downright dangerous. Eisenhower was in the White House and a paler shade of pale blanched the American temperament. Censorship was rampant, orthodoxy ascendant. Senator Joseph R McCarthy, despite his outlandish sightings of a Communist under every bed, dominated national politics. The John Birch Society used its propaganda to heighten anti-Leftism. The arch-Rightist Minutemen trained at secret rifle ranges to become an armed militia against "the inevitable Communist takeover of Washington." In the 1950s, those who dissented too vociferously, or at all, could reasonably expect to be hauled before either the House of Representatives Committee on Un-American Activities (HUAC), as Pete Seeger was, or the Senate Internal Security Sub-Committee, as I was.

The cold war against Leftists, dissenters, or even independent liberals in the arts had been slowly putting a glacial crust over the landscape. The fifteen gray years that followed World War II, instead of being a liberated era in which the defeat of tyranny was savored, became instead a witch-hunt. Every radical American was perceived as a Soviet agent. Systematically, the steamroller of repression crushed hundreds of careers. The investigators turned to Hollywood in the late 1940s, managing to get nearly every Left-winger in the studios either blacklisted or otherwise barred from work. A group of noted screenwriters, the Hollywood Ten, served a year in jail for refusing to cooperate with the HUAC.

In folk music, there were successive smears against the organizations People's Artists and People's Songs, outgrowths of the war-time radical folk-song movement. For a time, the witch-hunt managed to silence the Weavers, who enjoyed hits in the early 1950s. Being a dissenter, with or without a guitar, was a risky business. Increasingly, sociological pulse-takers found post-war Americans more interested in security than sanity; more anxious to hail the status quo than to expose the status woe. Artists have a way of being independent, no matter the tenor of the times. One freshet of protest art started in the 1950s with the English "angry young men." Playwright John Osborne looked back in anger and wondered what victory the war had achieved, other than a chilling, purposeless conformity. In the States, dissent came from new comics like Lenny Bruce, Lord Buckley, Mort Sahl, and Dick Gregory, who found the repressive 1950s grimly laughable. Sahl suggested that voters would re-elect Eisenhower "to keep the White House empty for another four years." After all, "we've got to do *something* to keep the red barbarians from the East from swooping down and taking our supermarkets away from us."

Another form of dissent came from the beat poets and writers—Allen Ginsberg, Lawrence Ferlinghetti, Jack Kerouac, Gregory Corso, and others—who had different visions of America. The beats retreated from mainstream American life, making dropping out hip. They venerated other gods. How Dylan put the beats and Woody Guthrie on his own highway is one of the themes of this book. During Madison Avenue's 1950s heyday, a precious few began hiking Kerouac's open road. Keeping the flickering light of protest glowing in that decade were Seeger, People's Artists and People's Songs, mostly through

Sing Out! magazine. Nothing that could be said or done against Seeger stopped him using his lanky, country-booted personality to talk and sing of a better world. Pete inspired a new generation, cast his influence on the 1960s. Guy Carawan adopted Seeger's style of being the Johnny Appleseed of folk song and helped spur the "freedom song" movement among Southern integrationists. Two other Seeger devotees where Peter Yarrow and Mary Travers.

Another tireless protégé was Gil Turner from Bridgeport, Connecticut. Portly, open-faced and wholesome-looking, Gil—son of a former opera singer—had been a Baptist preacher who left the church when he discovered Seeger's wider pastorate. His attachment to Pete was like Dylan's and Elliott's to Guthrie. He had a large, warm baritone, played guitar and banjo, and was a wizard chorus master. In autumn 1961, he became Folk City's MC, and met all the singer-songwriters passing through. None struck him more forcefully than Dylan.

Several times a week, after Gerde's closed around midnight, Gil, Bob, and I walked over to the West Village to the White Horse near the docks, or to Jim and Bertha McGowan's Off-Broadway bar on Greenwich Avenue. The Horse was a storied English-style pub, a hangout of Dylan Thomas's during his declining days. Richard Burton used to come by and, in the late 1950s, the Clancy Brothers were regulars. Both Dylans loved the constant party atmosphere. Writer-habitués (like Mike Harrington and Jimmy Baldwin), salty longshoremen, painters, talkers, drunkards, and midnight genies kept the Horse galloping. McGowan's was quieter, but it stayed open until 4 a.m. It was decorated with theater playbills and stage pictures. A framed letter from Sean O'Casey hung on the wall. The McGowans loved Dylan and often subsidized his sandwiches and drinks. One night there, Gil told Bob about a new concept for a magazine, recruiting him into the *Broadside* experiment.

After Seeger had toured Britain in 1961, he returned excited about the burgeoning of topical songwriting there. He wanted something comparable in the States. Seeger longed to develop younger writers to carry on the work that he, Malvina Reynolds, Vern Partlow, Ernie Marrs, and others had done. Pete was joined by his old friend Sis Cunningham, long in the Southern labor movement, a friend of Woody's from Oklahoma, and a member of the Almanac Singers. Her husband, Gordon Friesen, described their idea in Volume 1 of *Broadside Songs*, published by Oak:

How do we know that young people all over America may not be writing topical songs right now? It's just that we're not hearing about it. The big commercial music publishers and recording companies aren't interested in this sort of material. We may just be assuming that songs like this aren't being written and sung. God knows, there isn't much of an outlet for them.

At their first meeting, Pete, Sis, and Gordon launched a little mimeographed bulletin of topical songs called *Broadside*, after Elizabethan song or news sheets, printed for rapid dissemination. Pete retained strong links with *Sing Out!*, but that magazine took a couple of months to publish and stressed traditional folk song. *Broadside* aimed to be small and easy to publish. Pete and Sis needed a spark plug and found one in Gil Turner. Besides recruiting Dylan, Gil brought the liveliest young songwriters to the monthly meetings. Two young music journalists, Josh Dunson and Julius Lester, cut their teeth there. Much later, self-styled Dylanologist A J Weberman honed his analytical ax there.[7]

Dylan was keen on *Broadside* from the start. It printed his new songs and made him part of a movement. He listened to song tapes from around the country, and even tried to improve some himself. He heeded Seeger and what Sis and Gordon could, with authority, interpret as "what Woody would think." *Broadside* clearly stimulated Dylan's writing in 1962 and 1963. Josh Dunson described a typical, lighthearted meeting in *Broadside* 20: "*Broadside*'s home is a small little room ... Gil Turner took out his twelve-stringer, borrowed a flat-pick. Sis took out the mike for the tape-recorder, and out came a talking blues Gil just wrote about the newspaper strike that had us all quietly laughing." Turner's song, "The Great New York Newspaper Strike," went, in part:

So here I am sittin' in the news hungry city ...
The publishers don't care, they ain't got no pity ...
Can't find me a job or a place to stay; this lockout's
took the classified away ... Spent my last cash

*money, a two dollar bill. Went to a folk music
concert at Carnegie Hall … There was old-timey
singers, some blues pickers, too, a cowboy and
Pete Seeger sung a song or two. It mighta been
good, it mighta been swell, but I'll be darned if
I can tell … Got no* New York Times, *Got no Bob
Shelton review … got no Opinion.*

*… So I'm goin' out for coffee with my friend Bob
Dylan, the only major newspaper in New York that's
not on strike.*[8]

"Then," Dunson continued, "Gil took out his six-string Gibson, handed it over to Bob Dylan, saying how Bob's new song, 'Masters of War,' was one of the best Bob had ever written. I kept on thinking he had written … some that had real lyric poetry, like 'Blowin' in the Wind' and 'Hard Rain's Gonna Fall' which makes you think right away of [Federico Garcia] Lorca, and I waited for the images of rain, and thunder, and lightning to come out in great spectacles. But no, this time there was a different kind of poetry, one of great anger, accusation, just saying who the masters of war are, without compromising one inch in its short sharp direct intensity … right after that, not waiting … to get two breaths, Bob came along with 'Playboys and Playgirls,' a group song Pete said 'is going to be sung by a million people in the next year.' Its tune catches whole crowds easy, and the words come right along from the feeling."

In came Phil Ochs, and Happy Traum, another member of Turner's group, the New World Singers. Pete said: "You know, in the past five months I haven't heard as many good songs and as much good music as I've heard here tonight." Dylan was one of a half-dozen regulars at *Broadside* meetings in 1962 but Pete knew, and nearly all of the others came to know, that Bob was turning out topical songs of a quality unheard since Guthrie. Along with Paul Krassner's the *Realist*, and the *Village Voice*, *Broadside* probably pioneered the 1960s underground press.

In 1970, Friesen said of those 1962 meetings: "There was no pressure from the need for commercial success. We recognized that this was unlikely in any event, with *Broadside* strong on protest songs, for which the Establishment would have no liking. I was willing to bet everything I had that Columbia Records would never record Dylan's 'Masters of War' and 'With God on Our Side.'" In fact, Columbia became the first major record label to recognize the topical-song upheaval. Through John Hammond, Columbia signed Pete, and social-comment music began to reach a wider audience.

Seeger was the first established performer Dylan influenced. By the end of 1962, Seeger was performing Dylan songs and singling him out as the most important new songwriter of the time. Dylan had his first song printed in *Broadside*, the lyrics to "Talkin' John Birch Paranoid Blues," in the first issue, February 1962. "Blowin' in the Wind" was on the cover of *Broadside* 6 in May 1962. For eighteen months, the first place one saw Dylan's songs, even before performance, was in *Broadside*, where Bob was listed as a contributing editor and was active in commenting on songs by others.

Among the first of the young singer-songwriters to show up was Len Chandler. Peter La Farge, Ochs, and Paxton, Canadian singer Bonnie Dobson, and Spoelstra surfaced later. When she was in town, Malvina Reynolds, who wrote "Little Boxes," always came in. Said Gordon: "We tried to treat them all alike, looking upon them as a school of new topical songwriters, rather than as individual stars. Bob seemed a little special, but not enough to set him above Phil or Len or the others. (Otherwise, we would have made a lot more tapes of Dylan, and got him to sing more than he did on our first album.) Bob just seemed a kid, somehow, quite nervous when he wasn't singing and playing, doing a perpetual little dance with his boot toes, even seated. He struck me as rather inarticulate while trying to talk, his sentences fading away. But there was a tremendous transformation when he started playing and singing. One was astonished to hear that kind of driving playing on guitar and powerful singing voice coming from a kid who hadn't even started growing a beard. I frankly was baffled by the discrepancy, and harbored the impression for a while that he was somehow putting us on, taking us in. I thought some of his songs were deliberate take-offs on folk songs, hoaxes. One song especially struck me as such—'I Will Not Go Down Under the Ground.' I thought: *who is he trying to kid?* But he had a poker face when he performed and he didn't look at you while he sang, but kept his eyes on his guitar and hands. Another song I thought was contrived to make a joke of folk song in general was the one about 'Playboys and Playgirls.' I forgot these suspicions when he wrote 'Masters of War' and 'God on Our Side,' which seemed deeply profound statements, superior, I thought, to anything Woody had ever done."

Sis and Gordon and those gathering at their apartment in Manhattan's West 90s were strongly political, but not the stolid sort of *Sing Out!* Left-politicos. The two publications regarded each other as siblings. *Broadside* was intimate and human, a good setting for Dylanesque jokes. Because he was under contract to Columbia, Dylan did his tracks on the first *Broadside* album under the pseudonym "Blind Boy Grunt." Friesen: "As you may surmise, Bob looked upon his appearance on that record as a joyful little prank. After all, there was no money in it, the whole thing being a benefit for *Broadside*." The record was out in spring 1963, Turner herding talent into a Folkways studio. Moe Asch advanced $100 for the first of four *Broadside* albums (a subsidiary of his main Folkways label). By the time *Broadside* was a year old, issue twenty of February 1963, "Masters of War" was on page one with illustrations by Suze, "Playboys and Playgirls" was on page two, and the issue included an early version of "Don't Think Twice." (The last, neither political nor topical, indicated *Broadside* 's flexibility.) Nearly every other 1963 issue contained either a new Dylan song or some Dylanology. This continued throughout the 1960s, although Dylan had drifted away from the magazine by 1964.

Later, Dylan paid tribute to *Broadside*, but he also minimized his experiences, reflecting his perennial ambivalence toward sources of help and inspiration, which were always pitted against his disdain of "moral debts." The *Broadside* experiment was seminal. By stressing songs relevant to the real world, by underscoring "songs that said something," by encouraging young songwriters to build a new style of socially conscious musical expression, *Broadside* succeeded, out of all proportion to its modest format, its readership of a few hundred. With *Broadside* 's encouragement, Dylan flowered before he was accepted by the public, and sharpened his craft. The roots of the revolution in popular music that Dylan led lie partly in those monthly meetings and the crudely mimeographed pages of *Broadside*.

Enter the Bear. Albert B Grossman, known as "the bear," had a body and manner to match the sobriquet, and a face suggesting an owl forced into the light. A portly, prematurely gray man, he had large eyes slightly hidden by glasses that suggest Ben Franklin before *he* went electric. After Dylan went electric, the third time, in 1965, Albert knotted his long hair behind his neck, like an Indian brave. "When I first met Albert, I thought he was just a street bear," Dylan told me once of the man who was his personal manager from 1962 until the relationship was legally dissolved in June 1971. After Dylan's accident, dealings between Dylan and his "Dear Landlord" were never quite the same. Grossman, who actually lived in Bearsville, just outside Woodstock, was a teddy or a grizzly, depending on your point of view.

When Dylan met Albert, he was wary. Bob knew how pivotal the right manager would be, and how many would wave pens at him once he had a recording contract. Working informally with Terri Van Ronk, Bob was still in charge, and did not have to deal with the uptown business world, to which he was antipathetic. Albert, however, was always around the Village, chatting with musicians, sitting like Buddha contemplating (they hoped) their futures. Bob's and Albert's strange, often stormy, relationship was in some ways a true marriage of minds and temperaments, each man quickly adopting the worst traits of the other. The striking difference was that Bob had appeared to be a relatively open person with considerable human compassion, while Albert had always been the chess player. At his worst, Grossman was contemptuous; at his best, a tasteful talent manager who worked with a minimum of commercial vocabulary and tawdriness. At his worst, his dominant interest was money; at his best, he made money only with artists of quality and style.

As soon as Dylan had his Columbia contract, music-business sharks smelled blood. Bob played a waiting game. Hammond suggested Harold Leventhal, who represented Seeger, Judy Collins, the Weavers, and, best of all, Guthrie. Dylan's relationship with Leventhal never jelled. Bob started to pal around with Roy Silver, who, with Bob Gibson, an influential musician, had launched a college talent booking group, Campus Concepts. Silver—who later managed comedian Bill Cosby—was such an early Dylan freak that he later told me it cost him his first marriage: "Instead of going home at night, I was haunting Village places where I could listen to Bobby, or just hang out with him." At the end of 1961, Silver and Gibson booked Dylan in Canada at $250 a week. "When we got him a weekend in Syracuse for a hundred and fifty dollars, I screamed we'd hit the big-time." Silver was then working with Grossman, but he sold out to him in 1962, parting with his interest in Dylan and others for $10,000.

Paul Stookey believes he was the first to tout Dylan to Albert. One night at the Gaslight in 1961, he either gave Bob a news clipping about a riot on a Hudson excursion boat, or just mentioned the incident. The next night, Dylan walked into the Gaslight and sang Paul his "Talking Bear Mountain Picnic Massacre Blues." Stookey, dumbfounded, told Grossman that Dylan was a talent to watch. Albert watched. Around the time of Bob's LP release, after months of cultivating Dylan's trust, Grossman made direct overtures. Bob told me then that Albert said he was not interested in working with any artist who couldn't make at least $50,000 a year, a figure which staggered Bob. Dylan said Albert saw him as not just a coffeehouse performer but as a concert and recording artist. Albert had built his reputation representing Odetta, whom Bob had admired since Dinkytown. The growing stature of Peter, Paul and Mary also impressed Dylan. I advised Bob to consider Grossman's bid seriously. I recalled that he had discovered Baez and staged her Newport debut in 1959, though Joan had chosen to work with a gentler sort, Manny Greenhill of Boston.[9] To many, Grossman was a sinister, relentlessly nay-saying figure. "He just thinks he's God," said Tom Clancy. To others, he was a "beautiful cat," dedicated to the highest standards of performing integrity, not a hawker of talent, but a creative force. Even those whom Grossman represented vary in their opinions. And from 1960 onward, Albert changed a good deal.

When he first shuffled into the Village, he often sang sea chanteys and Bulgarian folk music in a booming bass. When he chose to be, he was a convivial talker but Grossman tended to be a sphinx. He was born on Chicago's West Side to a family that valued education and security. After graduating from Lane Technical High School, he took a Master's in economic theory from the University of Chicago. He was interested in acting, politics, and music. One of his professors was Bruno Bettelheim, the child psychologist, so Albert became a trained economic theorist and a semi-trained child psychologist, qualifications that helped him become one of the most powerful managers in 1960s show business.

He preferred to work in the shadows, seeking neither credit nor limelight, but he appreciated his growing reputation as a kingmaker. Enduring his charges' idiosyncrasies, he was confessor and psychiatrist to them all, including Janis Joplin. His chief reward was money—tons of it, bags of it. His subsidiary reward was power, which he used judiciously at first, until he gradually became possessed by it. The performer-clients who most admire Albert describe him as a protector against the machinations of the music business. Peter Yarrow told me in 1970: "Albert is totally involved creatively. His ears are good. There would have been no Baez, no Dylan, and no Peter, Paul and Mary without Albert. He kept us insulated from the flesh-peddling aspect of show business. Next to Albert, Dylan was an amateur at cutting people down. Albert is an expert at destroying other people's sense of self. He readily admits it. Albert only attacks when others are playing a role. Albert basically doesn't trust the press. He is very shy, and cynical, because he has seen friends corrupted. He is also an idealist. Bobby was imitating everyone at one stage, and he naturally began to imitate and learn a lot of Albert's tricks. I think that Albert stimulated Bobby a great deal."

Paul Stookey answered me with a question: "If a plumber comes to your house and unplugs your drains, would you say he was helping your life, creatively? Albert was like that plumber. He would point out superfluous things we were doing or saying. When Albert says to do something, he's always right. When he says he thinks you shouldn't do something, he may not be right." Paul thought Albert was so widely misunderstood "because Albert is brutally honest and has an early-warning bullshit-detecting device that shows personal annoyance very openly." Like Dylan, Mary Travers is a former admirer. In 1970–71, when I was seeing quite a bit of Mary in London, she clearly felt Grossman had taken advantage of her. When she discovered he had been earning more than she or Peter or Paul, she switched to Leventhal. Feeling she had been used, Mary described her once-respected manager in vituperative terms.

Managers are professional villains, doomed to represent their clients' negative sides. When Dylan wanted to say no to someone impolitic to refuse, he would often say: "I have to check that out with Albert." Albert emerged as the sourpuss saying no, and Bob appeared the amiable youngster in the older manipulator's hands. Even as saintly a star as Seeger, who would say "I hate to say no," left Leventhal to say: "Oh, no, not another benefit concert!" Albert expertly finessed management's dirty work. He seemed to enjoy saying no, just as some lawyers enjoy threatening action. Grossman the bulwark, the buffer, took the blame for everything. In 1964, when Dylan left a Tufts University audience waiting all evening for a concert, Grossman's aide, Charlie Rothschild, explained: "Someone in the office made a scheduling error." Whether Dylan was stoned or whether it had been a mistake, Grossman's office took the onus. Some suggested Grossman had engineered Dylan's going electric to make more money but Albert was probably one of the last to know about the change.

Leventhal managed to seem approachable and personable. Brian Epstein, the Beatles' manager, was impeccably polite, making me, and many another journalist, welcome at his Belgravia home. Mort Lewis, who represented Simon and Garfunkel, often hid behind the shield of "the needs and interests of the boys." Greenhill would feign ignorance of decisions. Herbie Cohen, who managed the Modern Folk Quartet, Judy Henske, and Frank Zappa, would evade questions with jokes about a tough business. Grossman said *nothing*. He preferred, like Dylan, to "make myself invisible."

Having known Grossman for years, I see a man not blessed with the infallibility he projected. He had been rapturous over an Israeli duo, the Dudaim, who were talented but never got off the ground. Rejected by Baez, Grossman found and promoted a dark-haired soprano, Lynn Gold, who disappeared into obscurity. In the early days, Grossman was considerably more open, dropping remarks about his stars. He became increasingly tough, distant, and thick-skinned. His stars became "his people," and no one, certainly not a writer, would be welcome to ask questions about them. When I asked Grossman in 1965 what he thought Dylan had meant by something, Albert said, with a smile, "I'm just a Jewish businessman."

That Dylan and Grossman found each other was no surprise. For a while, they were amazingly similar in temperament. Although Grossman was a good dozen years older, no other performer so influenced him. Dylan's taste prompted Grossman's signing of Paul Butterfield, John Lee Hooker, the Kweskin Jug Band, and the Band. Peter Yarrow maintained that Dylan found in Grossman the father he was looking for, and that, as their relationship deteriorated in 1965–71, Bob was symbolically destroying the father, the authority figure, to whom he was indebted. Grossman may have found a rebellious son in Dylan. Bob rarely flaunted the cracks in the family crockery, while Albert pretended there were none.

Grossman's clients tended to like his methods because they knew that the enemies Albert fought were just as cruel. He made demands that few other managers dared, put up with abuse from his artists that few others would take. From 1964 to 1966, he put up with a great deal from Dylan. Grossman feigned modesty when I told him that some people maintained Dylan would never have made it without him: "That's ridiculous! He would have made it without anyone," Albert replied.

Working closely with Grossman was a former Tommy Dorsey Band road manager, a bright, aggressive executive, Artie Mogull, who was with the publishing house of M Witmark & Sons, of Music Publishers Holding Corporation, later Warner Bros Music. In early summer 1962, Grossman and Silver brought Dylan to Mogull. Bob sang him nearly all his songs. Mogull wanted to sign him for Witmark, but discovered that Hammond had already arranged for Dylan to be published by Leeds/Duchess music. In a move vaguely reminiscent of the Russian sale of Alaska, Mogull got Dylan released for nothing; he then signed a three-year publishing contract with Witmark on July 13, 1962. "I offered Dylan one thousand dollars to sign with Witmark," Mogull told me. "I had to fight to get that one thousand dollars, and now the songs have easily earned a million dollars and will continue to earn for years to come." Artie said he had made the advance on his own personal note and had it deducted from his salary for ten weeks. "In his three years with Witmark, Dylan gave them two hundred thirty-seven copyrights. That was unheard of! He is amazingly prolific. Ordinarily, it would have been something to get twenty-five songs out of a writer in three years." (In his autobiography, *John Hammond on Record*, the producer said that Dylan used $500 of Artie's $1,000 to buy his way out of the Leeds/Duchess publishing contract.)

Mogull, the self-described "world's greatest talent scout," may have been instrumental in getting Grossman into the financial big time. For signing Peter, Paul and Mary, Warner Bros advanced $30,000, which Grossman parlayed into millions. Although not under Grossman's roof, Mogull was one of his key people. When MGM Records considered signing Dylan in 1967, Mogull negotiated. Although that deal never came off, luck, timing, and expertise enabled him and Grossman to do an extraordinary job of plugging Dylan's songs. Through Milt Okun, music director of Peter, Paul and Mary, they got Dylan songs recorded by three groups. Izzy Young once told me Mogull had offered him $10,000 to tout Dylan songs within the folk community, an offer Izzy turned down. After autumn 1963, Dylan's songs scarcely needed pushing. Judy Collins, Manfred Mann, and singer-actor Hamilton

Camp—not to mention Grossman's own people, Odetta and Peter, Paul and Mary—were clamoring to record new Dylan songs. Mogull and Grossman guided these song fortunes along until 1965, when the Witmark contract ran out and Dylan and Grossman formed their own music-publishing company. Hired as its manager: Artie Mogull.

My relationship with Grossman reached its low note in late 1965 when, one night at the Limelight in the Village, I told him that some publishers had approached me about writing a Dylan book. "If you do that, I'll sue you, before the book comes out, or after it comes out, or both," Albert exploded. Mary Travers and Canadian singers Ian and Sylvia, who were also at our table, looked astonished. "Albert," I said, "someday we ought to have a talk about power and its abuse." He settled down, and when I saw him in his office a week later, he was not quite so litigious, but still huffy: "It's opportunism, it's premature. You can't report anything that hasn't been specifically stated for publication." How opportunistic was it for him, I asked, to use the press for publicity but not for documentation of what really goes on in show business? "You're being Italianate," he said. "Well," I concluded our chilly confrontation, "let's see what Bob says when he gets back from the Coast." Dylan showed immediate interest in my project, and told Albert to lay off.

As time passed, Grossman mellowed. At one point, in January 1968, he told me: "I would help if I could, but sometimes I feel I don't know *anything* about Bob Dylan." By May 1971, Grossman had his final line: "There's a girl in this office [Myra Friedman] doing a serious book about Janis Joplin, but even though Janis is dead, I had to tell Myra that I couldn't help her. What's public is public, what's private is private." That week, Dylan had told me: "Albert would never help you." Grossman is not interested in facts, only secrecy. When a reporter misinterprets him, he rages, even though a civil interview could have prevented misinterpretation. Perhaps Grossman had more to conceal about his business dealings than one suspected—not even super-hip Tom Wolfe could get him to sit for an interview. "I don't really think he's got the right feel for it," Albert told me.

Hammond's Folly. Whatever differences Bob subsequently had with his record producer, in the early months John Hammond gave Dylan keen encouragement. Even though the first royalty for his initial album gave Bob barely enough to pay his electric bill, Hammond remained convinced that Dylan was a major talent. Columbia cynics continued to call him "Hammond's Folly." Hammond arranged for Dylan to meet the head of the Music Corporation of America talent agency. Talk ensued about his starring as Holden Caulfield in a film of J D Salinger's *Catcher in the Rye*. That project evaporated.

Dylan's other chief advocate at Columbia was an uncommonly bright publicist named Billy James. Even though he was handling publicity for dozens of performers, Billy only once went out of his way to call my attention to a Columbia group, the Byrds. Journalists tended to trust Billy's taste and integrity. He recalled: "Hammond called me and said: 'Billy, I have a marvelous boy in the studio right now. Do you have a moment to come up?' I knew that it was happening—right there! He had such an incredible blend of influences, and presented them with such conviction that my first exposure was very moving. Bobby came up and we spent about three hours talking about everything, but he was reluctant to talk about his past. I had encountered that often before. I was really startled to hear of all the places he had been to. He spoke with knowledge of all those places, not like the traveling salesman who only knows the inside of his hotel room." Dylan asked Billy if he wanted to be his manager. "I told him no, it isn't my line of business."

Hammond suggested Bob get his songs published by Leeds affiliate, the Duchess Music Corporation. Dylan told Billy later: "There were all these little rooms and when they opened up the doors, there were these songwriters sitting there writing!" The regimentation astounded Dylan. He told Billy he felt many around Columbia were not reacting genuinely, and feared that if he met them on the street, they might not be so nice to him. But Billy was different. It was Billy who set up Dylan's first magazine interview, in 1962, with Edwin Miller of *Seventeen*:

There was a violent, angry emotion running through me then; I don't know why ... [Hammond] asked me if I wanted to sing any of them over again but I said no. I can't see myself singing the same song twice in a row ... I don't work regularly. I don't want to make a lot of money, really. I wander around the city a lot, I take the ferry to Staten Island or I walk down by the river. Or maybe I'll sit around all day with a painter I know ... I can't go out after people. If they want what I've got, they always have to come to me with their hands out and take from me. That's the way I am.

Even at 21, Dylan was eminently quotable. He told *16* magazine that "people should develop their own thoughts and feelings and not follow the herd. Everyone has a gift and they should be proud of it— whether it's cleaning the street, sewing a dress or singing a song." Rachel Price of *FM-Stereo Guide* did a thoughtful piece in autumn 1962:

Some people consider me a poet, but I can't think about it. There are too many poets. ... I just returned from a trip to the West and I had forgotten how quiet and pleasant life was there. You don't have to plan things, they just happen. Right now I'm waiting ... waiting for my girl to come home from a trip ... I want to give, but on my terms. Nightclubs are not my terms. People go there to see gladiators fight, and I don't want to be part of the spectacle ... Teenagers have so much stuff shot at them because they buy so much and are such easy prey. I don't want to be one more bullet in the gun aimed at them.

James claims no credit for having coached Bob in how to face the press. Dylan had instinctive canny toward interviews, a publicist's dream. Soon, Billy simply handled arrangements, or even fought off requests for interviews.

Portrait of the Artist. Throughout 1962, while Suze was in Italy, Dylan continued making friends in New York. With Suze away, he needed to fill a large vacuum. Jimmy Richmond, who ran the Music Inn record store a few doors west along Fourth Street, knew Dylan as a regular. He didn't buy but popped in several times a week to hear new tracks. Up the street was the little grocery run by the Brignole sisters, two walk-ons from a De Sica film. Bobby was their favorite, even though he seemed to eat very little. They could always count on him for a few packs of cigarettes a day, for coffee and milk. When Bob was short of money, which was often, he would get credit, because they knew "such a nice boy" would certainly pay them back.

Then there was Harry Jackson, the rambunctious, bearded painter who adulated cowboy life. Harry, another citybilly from Chicago, had hit the road in search of a romantic life. He spent his adolescence in Wyoming, and had a genuine feel for the vanishing West. He kept that horsey ethos alive in his songs and housed his huge paintings in his cavernous loft on Houston Street. Harry, an explosive maverick who did nothing by halves, was captivated by Dylan on stage: "He reminds me of some of those street musicians I see near my studio in Italy, just street waifs with a magic ability to hold your attention, to wring a few lire out of you, despite yourself." Harry told me, and everyone: "Dylan's so goddamned *real*—it's unbelievable." Harry asked Bob to sit for a portrait; maybe it could be an album cover one day. Dylan went down for three sessions, but had trouble sitting still, and while painting Harry told a Stetson-full of stories about the Wyoming range. Bob was interested in painting as well as in being painted. In spring 1962, he told Jack Elliott he was going to quit music and become an artist, and he said it again right after the *Newsweek* story of 1963. In 1966, after his accident, he finally devoted more time to drawing. The portrait, eventually finished without its subject present, wasn't one of Jackson's greatest, yet it gave a strong impression of Dylan's creativity.[10]

Dylan's passion for films continued in New York, often at the Waverly Theater on Sixth Avenue, minutes from his pad. Two films impressed him during the year, he told me. *Lonely Are the Brave* starred Kirk Douglas as an individualist in a modern West that was being eroded by supermarkets and superhighways. The hero failed, pursuing ideals being blotted out by "progress." The other film was *A Face in the Crowd*, from a Budd Schulberg story. It starred Andy Griffith as a guitar-picking "country boy" who became a celebrity, affecting advertising, TV, and, ultimately, national politics. Lonesome Rhodes was a Guthrie without a conscience, a Will Rogers with a power lust. *A Face in the Crowd* rivals *Citizen Kane* as a blistering portrait of an American parvenu undone by power and Dylan was more shaken by *A Face in the Crowd* than any film since *Rebel Without a Cause* or *The Wild One*. He could see here a country con man who used provincial charm and naiveté as a cover for manipulation. Lonesome Rhodes showed how to get to the top, but also what to avoid *en route*.

Dylan consolidated his friendships with musicians, learning and teaching, absorbing and sharing, influencing and being influenced. The music scene was a campus without walls. One of Dylan's favorite new friends was Paul Clayton, a gentle, lost, earnest folk singer, whose knowledge of balladry was wide.[11] John Herald of the Greenbriar Boys became Bob's frequent companion. Herald contributed a wide grasp of folk-based country music, extrovert joy onstage, and meticulous attention to technique. Through "Gentleman Jim" Kweskin, Bob was in touch with an ease and flash, onstage and off, that was rare among Village folkniks. Long before I had really tuned in to Clayton or Kweskin, Dylan was prodding me to write them up. "It's just not fair that they're unknown," he said.

In 1962, Dylan befriended some of the leaders of the "freedom song" civil rights movement. In the summer, on a survey for the *Times*, I had made my own discovery of the breadth of freedom songs in the organizing movements of the South. In Atlanta, I met the articulate, militant James Forman, a leader in the Student Non-Violent Coordinating Committee. Although SNICK, as it was called, was then close to the Southern Christian Leadership Council of the Reverend Martin Luther King, Jr, the student group found its own directions. Music was a prime vehicle. Two young activists, Bernice Johnson and Cordell Reagon, were leading the long desegregation campaign in Albany, Georgia. They and Forman had spent time in jail and made their way north, where folkniks became working allies and friends.[12] Dylan took warmly to the Snick activists, and they to him. He began to think their topical songs were more relevant than *Broadside*. "It's all right there in their back yards. They aren't singing about tomorrow or yesterday. They are singing about themselves and the kind of lives they're leading," Dylan remarked. The New Yorkers embraced Johnson as a young Odetta. At 18, she had a gentle demeanor, yet could uncork a huge, beautiful voice. Bernice was introduced to Dylan by Lena of Saratoga and the first time she heard him, he was singing "Hollis Brown" and "Hard Rain." Bernice, in tribute, mastered the complex "Hard Rain" lyrics and soon began to sing the song. In late 1962, she had her purse stolen and, with few friends in New York, called Dylan. He invited her to stay in his apartment, played her Robert Johnson records and talked with her about the music and rights struggle. Bob told her about his "special girl" in Europe.

"I guess he was embarrassed at his voice then," Bernice later told me. "He seemed to think then that it was really bad. When he came up with a new song he always said that I should sing it, or Gil Turner, because we had better voices. We all thought, those of us in the movement and those of us in the Freedom Singers, that Dylan was fantastic as a songwriter and as a person." Bernice (who later married Cordell) had considerable professional contact with Dylan over the next few years. As a militant, she could assess Dylan's changes. By 1964, he was going his own way, and many activists wrote him off as having "sold out" to show business. Bernice took issue: "I felt he was going through some fantastic emotional things and I didn't want to make any judgment. I knew he was displeased with his Columbia contract and he wasn't too keen to go to Europe in December 1962. I learned that his manager had the power of attorney and sent him there even though he didn't want to go. For a while, I feared that he was possibly just destroying himself. Still, I felt if he stayed alive he would be all right. Some whites moved with us out of some special sort of love of blacks, while others were just loaded with guilt. Dylan wasn't the same. When he simply drifted away from the movement, it was the whites in Snick who were resentful. The blacks in Snick didn't think that, or say that. We only heard the phrase 'sellout' from the whites, not from the blacks. I've always just regarded Bob as a friend. He's never been a star to me, just a friend."

Dylan was also drawn closely to a sixty-year-old bluesman, Big Joe Williams. This Joe, not to be confused with Count Basie's singer of the same name, was born in 1903 in Oktibbeha County, Mississippi. His family had been too poor to own a radio or phonograph, but he heard music around the house. His grandfather was a hymn-singing accordion player, one brother was a gospel singer, and three cousins sang spirituals and played guitar or washboard. According to Bob Koester of Delmark Records, Joe decided early on he "didn't want to plow, didn't want to chop cotton," so he made himself a primitive guitar. When Ethel Waters's minstrel show visited Joe's county, he left with the troupe. He recorded in the 1930s in Memphis for Vocalion. For a decade after 1935, he recorded prolifically for Bluebird, Columbia, and other labels.

When Mike Porco considered booking Big Joe at Folk City in early 1962, Dylan hyped him: "He's the greatest old bluesman. You gotta put him in here." Mike did, for three weeks in February. Dylan showed up nearly every night, jammed with Big Joe onstage several times. For Joe, who had worked the streets, this first job in New York was exciting. It helped stimulate a revival in early blues, and Joe subsequently did LPs on several labels. The chemistry between Big Joe and Little Bob was so good that Joe invited him on his session for an LP he was scheduled to cut with Victoria Spivey, a blues doyenne, on her own Spivey label, on March 2, 1962. Bob was sure Columbia wouldn't give him permission, so he cut the session under the nom de blues of "Big Joe's Buddy." The album, *Three Kings and a Queen*, released in October 1964, had two tracks with Dylan, "Sitting on Top of the World" and "Wichita," both by Big Joe. On "Sitting," Dylan played guitar and harmonica and did some alto-range harmonizing behind Joe's lead.

Years later, Big Joe gave me an interview laced with fatherly nostalgia, maintaining he met Dylan in Chicago when Bob was only six! (Bob probably met Joe in Chicago in 1960 on his way east.) The matter is further obfuscated by Dylan's saying in 1962 that he had run off to Chicago when he was ten: "I saw a Negro musician playing his guitar on the street and I went up to him and began accompanying him on the spoons. I used to play the spoons when I was little." As if to complement Dylan's story, Big Joe reconstructed the trip: "I first met Bob about 1946 or 1947, in Chicago. I disremember the exact year, but he was very very young, probably no more than six. He looked the same that he looks now. I think he was just born with that talent. He used to get up on his tiptoes and was cracking wise just the way he do now. Well, I was just working on the streets of Chicago then, the way I had done since 1927. Somehow or other he knew songs I had made on records, like 'Baby, Please Don't Go' and 'Highway 49.' He met me on the North Side, around State and Grand, and we just walked down to State and 35th Street. I was working, singing, all the way along. If we came up to some cabaret where he couldn't get in because he was too young, I would just leave him waiting outside on the curbstone. It must have taken us about three hours to make that trip. Bob was asking me all sorts of questions. He said that he was going to do this sort of thing one of these days, and I said that he would, because he had a lot of talent.

"We finally got down to that club at 35th and State and Tampa Red was staying there with me. Well, we had one fine time back there in our room. Bob really enjoyed himself singing and playing. About six or seven years later, I saw him in Minneapolis, when he was playing with Tony Glover up there. Same Mississippi River I used to know, only the other end of it," said Joe. "Then, another time, Bob tried to look me up in Chicago, but I was working in Oakland. Bob found out my address there, and wrote me thanking me for the advice I had given him about music. What he earned, what he done, he got it honest. They ask me: 'Is he real?' And I tell them that they should let him live his own life."

In 1962, when I covered a gospel show at Randall's Island, Dylan joined me. I introduced him backstage to one of the warmest, most talented families in American music, the Staple Singers. Daughter Mavis was especially attracted to Bob and made some overtures, but the whole family took to Bob and was delighted, within a year, when they were all booked on a Westinghouse TV special together. Roebuck "Pop" Staples said later that Bob wrote "John Brown" for him in 1962. The featured star was Mahalia Jackson, the gospel queen. Dylan admired her music, but he was astounded that she arrived in a limousine, with aides holding up her long skirts as if she were royalty. The ostentatious show of wealth made out of people's piety rubbed Dylan up the wrong way. He always saw blacks as people — good, bad, indifferent, successful or struggling, beautiful or venal. One lesson he learned from Mahalia was that stars should never display their wealth openly, should never turn *nouveau riche*, no matter how humble their origins.

Despite his depression while Suze was in Italy, Dylan kept himself prodigiously busy, but not as much as Grossman wanted. One night in the summer of 1962, Theodore Bikel, the actor-singer, threw a party at his Washington Square Village apartment. Dylan, our friend Sue Smith, and I went. Bob was more than a bit stoned. Somewhere along the way he had picked up a shiny, gray silk top hat, which ludicrously crowned his denim, suede, and boots. As he careened around the room, many were appalled at this oddball. Lou Gottlieb of the Limeliters, with a background as a musicologist, was puzzled by the Dylan phenomenon and by his antics that night. Theo was gently bemused by this uninvited guest. Six months later, he was singing Dylan songs with passion.

Another guest at Bikel's was John Henry Faulk, the Texas-born broadcaster, a charming anecdotalist, one of the notable victims of the radio-TV blacklist. Faulk had challenged the McCarthyite faction in the performers union, AFTRA, and thereby incurred the wrath of the anti-Left vigilante blacklisting group, AWARE, Inc. Faulk was fired by CBS in 1956 and became unemployable. After years of scuffling, Faulk decided to strike back at the blacklisters. Retaining the lawyer Louis Nizer, Faulk sued AWARE for libeling him as pro-Communist. (The commentator Edward R Murrow put up the initial $7,000 for legal fees.) Faulk won his case against the blacklisters and was awarded damages of $3.5 million, although he collected only a fraction of that amount. He was just writing his book *Fear on Trial* when Dylan met him. Dylan was fascinated by this latter-day Texas hero, friend of Alan Lomax, the folklorist.

Two important concerts in autumn 1962 advanced Dylan. On Saturday, September 22, *Sing Out!* presented its annual Hootenanny at Carnegie Hall. On the bill were Seeger, the Lilly Brothers, the New World Singers, and Bernice Johnson. Dylan was not in good form. Seeger introduced him as an especially important writer. Bob did only three songs, then wandered offstage disappointed with his performance. The audience, however, was not. Two weeks later, on October 5, Dylan was top-billed in a Town Hall concert with Ian and Sylvia, John Lee Hooker, Judy Collins, Lynn Gold, and Sandy Bull. Sponsored by the Folklore Center, the concert presented almost all Grossman clients or choices. The show was an experiment, professionals coupled with amateur volunteers from the audience. "Bring your guitars and banjos," read the program for the show, scheduled to go on to various campuses. Dylan, in much better form, was among the most enthusiastically received. He did his "Talking New York," "John Birch," "Hollis Brown," and finished with "Hard Rain." Those who doubted Dylan's poetic gifts began to see what all the fuss was about.

By this time, the *Sing Out!* issue featuring Dylan was out. The cover showed him dragging on a cigarette, eyes half-closed, *à la* Guthrie. Gil Turner's story called him "the most prolific young songwriter in America today" and had him "rambling" when he was only a few months old. "Part of Dylan's magnetism is he is not the slightest bit afraid of falling flat on his face. If he gets an idea for a song or a story, he does it on the spot without worrying about whether it will come out exactly polished or right … Reality and truth are words Dylan will use often … They are his criteria for evaluating the world around him." Turner quoted him: "The songs are there. They exist all by themselves just waiting for someone to write them down. I just put them down on paper. If I didn't do it, somebody else would."

Sing Out! voiced astonishment at Dylan's output: "Putting down songs fast as they come into his head. The present record is five songs in one night. The latest is a song about blacklisting, inspired by the case of John Henry Faulk." The article included two other photographs of Dylan, the music and lyrics of "Blowin' in the Wind," "Letter to Woody," and "Ballad of Donald White," along with excerpts from other songs.[13] *Sing Out!* never pushed a new songwriter so strongly. By 1962, Grossman had moves ready on his mental chessboard.

Freewheelin' Broadside. Only three new tracks were released during 1962: his bit behind Belafonte, and a single issued at Christmas: "Mixed Up Confusion" backed with "Corrina, Corrina." To evaluate his development, the second Columbia album, *Freewheelin'*, and the first *Broadside* album have to be considered, even though not released until 1963. By the time *Bob Dylan* was released, in March 1962, the singer was miles ahead of it. There were good reviews from the *Village Voice*, *Sing Out!*, and *Little Sandy Review*, but it sold fewer than 5,000 copies in the first few months, a disappointment for a giant like Columbia, and for someone who had garnered as much good press. Bob thought of quitting music. But *Broadside*, Hammond, Grossman, and the Village clique gave him the support that record buyers didn't.

The Belafonte album, which also came out in May 1962, caused only a ripple. Dylan started to tape more tracks for Columbia. The final version of *The Freewheelin' Bob Dylan* was not released until July 1963, a month after the first version "escaped." It followed almost a year of uncongenial dealings among Hammond, Dylan, and Grossman, as well as Grossman's then partner, John Court, a former manager of the Chicago Playboy Club and one-time jazz drummer.

Almost the first management step Grossman took was to try to get Bob out of his Columbia contract. He saw all its flaws, from percentages to its "special publishing rate," under which Dylan's compositions earned more if recorded by others than if he recorded them. Hammond's version of the hassle: "By this time, Bob had written 'Blowin' in the Wind' and Peter, Paul and Mary were convinced this was a masterpiece, as I was. He'd gone over to Warner Brothers [Witmark, later acquired by Warners]. Grossman tried to take Dylan away from Columbia because his parents hadn't signed his contract also. Bobby had told me he didn't have any parents. The letter from the lawyer didn't mean anything, because Bobby by that time was twenty-one, and had been in the studio four times since he was twenty-one. I got Bobby to repudiate the letter, which got Grossman very uptight. We then decided that since Tom Wilson loved Bobby, this would be a very good marriage."

Wilson, a tall, handsome, affable man, was Columbia's first black producer. Although Hammond is listed as producer of Bob's second album, Wilson was the *de facto* producer of "Girl from the North Country," "Talkin' World War III Blues," "Bob Dylan's Dream," and "Masters of War." After Dylan's first single, "Mixed Up Confusion" and "Corrina," was released on December 24, 1962, it soon went out of print, but "Confusion" is historic. Had it been more widely known, "Confusion" could have stemmed confusion that Dylan was only an acoustic-guitar folk-topical performer. "Mixed Up Confusion" was recorded on November 14, 1962. When Dylan endured audience ferocity by switching to electric music in 1965, he was anxious to call attention to his first single and the deleted tracks from *Freewheelin'*. They prove how early he had been into an electric sound. Here was folk-rock long before the Beatles, long before anyone would be able to charge him with selling out to commercialism. "Nobody told me to go electric. I didn't ask anybody. I asked not a soul, believe me, I didn't ask anybody," Dylan stressed later. According to Bob, *Freewheelin'*'s electric songs, including "Rocks and Gravel," were taken out to make room for his "Blowin' in the Wind," "Masters of War," and "Girl from the North Country."

The line from "Mixed Up Confusion," "there's too many people/And they're all too hard to please,"[14] was an aside on the hassles around him. Still another hassle was the exclusion of "John Birch." Just after the Columbia Broadcasting System censor had refused to allow the song on *The Ed Sullivan Show*, Columbia Records panicked. Hammond: "The CBS lawyers, not Columbia Records, decided that the reference to Hitler involved every single member of the John Birch Society, therefore it was libelous, or some crap like that. I get away with much worse material with Seeger than was ever on a Dylan album." Fewer than 300 copies of the album went out with "John Birch" and three other deleted songs on it. These collectors' items went mostly to the Coast.[15] The final *Freewheelin'* album appeared without "John Birch," "Rocks and Gravel," "Rambling Gambling Willie," and "Let Me Die in My Footsteps."

Released just after the tremendous success of Peter, Paul and Mary, *Freewheelin'* did amazingly well, despite all the problems. Its cover shows Suze and Bobby shivering but reunited in a slushy Village street, Dylan in suede and denim, a smiling Suze holding his arm. By the Newport Festival of 1963, scores of young girls were adopting Suze's long hair and boots. Bob asked me to do the liner notes again, but I said that Nat Hentoff could do him more good. The album, track by track:

"Blowin' in the Wind": By release time, a major hit for Peter, Paul and Mary. The civil rights movement was cresting and this understated song summed up the passions and questions of the time. Some Leftists found it weak, asking questions but not answering them. Dylan's reply: "The first way to answer these questions is by asking them. But lots of people have to first find the wind." Gordon Friesen suggested elliptical reference to the American flag, citing Emerson's "an old rag of bunting blowing in the wind," the national flag symbolizing unquestioning patriotism. The song, which became a civil rights anthem, also sparked unjust allegations of plagiarism, charges not fully refuted until the mid-1970s. It's also possible to link the song's central metaphor to a line in the nuclear-holocaust film *On the Beach*. Dylan says: "I wrote it in a café across the street from the Gaslight."

"Girl from the North Country": Tender love song of yearning nostalgia. In the songbook, and subsequently, "from" was changed to "of." Many have pointed out the connection to the English folk song "Scarborough Fair," which singers Paul Simon and Art Garfunkel directly co-opted for a hit. Simon and Dylan probably learned the version from Martin Carthy. Dylan said he'd had this song in his mind for years before writing it down in late 1962. When Echo Helstrom came to light, some used the title to describe her, but there is great reason to believe it is inspired by Bonny Beecher. The song scarcely fitted Echo. Dylan re-recorded it in 1969 in duet with Johnny Cash. (A very affecting version is "La Fille Du Nord" by Hugues Aufray on *Aufray Chante Dylan*.)

"Masters of War": A blistering indictment of war profiteers, it points fingers, in the vein of 1930s plays like *Idiot's Delight* or *Bury the Dead*. Later inquiries into the military-industrial complex confirm the justice of Dylan's charges. When Judy Collins recorded "War," she dropped the final vengeful lines, but Bob said her version blunted his intent. In another powerful recording, taped by Seeger on tour, each line was interpolated by a Japanese translation, setting up an arresting antiphony. The eerie melody of this old modal song, believed to be an old magic song from an English mummers' play, has been handed down via Jean Ritchie's singing of "Nottamun Town." Ritchie affixed the copyright of her Geordie Music Publishing Company on "Nottamun" in 1964. Geordie made claims against Dylan for use of the melody, but he successfully maintained that his variant and his original words made a new song.

"Down the Highway" and "Bob Dylan's Dream": Two faces of the blues—one deep, one superficial. "Down the Highway" has a distinctive modal lay, unified by a stunning guitar figure exuding shivering mournfulness. "Highway" demonstrates Dylan's remark that he saw classic blues as a form of catharsis. Suze's flight is a recurring theme. "Blues" is a sprightly Elliottesque nonsense song that pokes at Tin Pan Alley in the spoken intro, then sets up crisp dialogues between singer and mouth harp. The two blues juxtapose the tragic and the ludicrous. They say to me: Despair is all around, so let's laugh our way through it.

"A Hard Rain's a-Gonna Fall": An apocalyptic vision in a series of grotesqueries foreshadowed by the Cuban missile crisis of 1962. It opens with a paraphrase of the classic ballad "Lord Randall," but the son's reply has become as modern as push-button warfare. Lines etched in acid paint the ruins of war. A panorama of Spanish battle scenes comes to my mind, out of Garcia Lorca's poetry, Picasso's tortured "Guernica," the penetrating anti-war sketches of Goya. Although the title is in modern argot, the diction of the text has a thrust of imagery that owes a debt to Lorca and Rimbaud, who was perhaps the first poet to create, in his late teens, a poetic cosmos whose extremes of horror and lost tenderness somehow match the hells and heavens of modern reality. Dylan said the imagery came so fast that "every line in it is actually the start of a whole song. I thought I wouldn't have enough time alive to write all those songs so I put all I could into this one." "Hard Rain" inspired Canadian poet Leonard Cohen to write songs. A landmark in topical, folk-based songwriting, here blooms the promised fruit of the 1950s poetry-jazz fusion of Ginsberg, Ferlinghetti, and Rexroth.

"Don't Think Twice, It's All Right": Introduces essentially the same studio band that accompanied Dylan on the "Confusion"/"Corrina" single, with the notable addition of Bruce Langhorne, Odetta's guitarist. An early commercial hit, recorded widely, it was clearly about Suze. Dylan's sardonicism contrasts with most recordings by others, who stressed the sweet and ignored the bitter. Only a few days before he finished this song, I had been talking to Bob about Suze's flight to Europe. Trying to support him, I remarked that she was still a child, a line he worked in. The melody was adapted from Paul Clayton's adaptation of a folk tune, "Scarlet Ribbons for Her Hair." Clayton and Dylan had an amicable legal tiff, settling without rancor out of court. Johnny Cash wrote his own version, "Understand Your Man."

"Bob Dylan's Dream": A major work, not widely enough known. I submit there is a touch of vanity in the inclusion of two songs bearing his name. For the melody, he credited his English friend, Martin Carthy, with the traditional singing of "Lord Franklin." The song is imbued with nostalgia, world-weariness at 21, a feeling of lost innocence. As his life grew increasingly complex, Dylan reflects during a return to Minnesota, how simple the answers seemed during adolescence. John Bucklen believed the song directly related to times he and Bob spent in Hibbing with Echo and John's sister. It could as easily refer to days at Minneapolis with Tony Glover or Bonny.

"Oxford Town": The sort of topical statement that heated the *Broadside* mimeograph. James Meredith was the first black to risk enrollment at the University of Mississippi in Oxford. Melody and tempo are jaunty, the lyrics are not.

"Talking World War III Blues": A Guthrie-style, dry-witted fantasy, half of which Dylan composed in the studio. Satire with a capital S, slashing out at everything from doctors to Abraham Lincoln to war to the author himself. The wit is acerbic, the musical line pungent.

"Corinna, Corinna": Lilts beautifully with the back-up band, although the folk-rock beat was muted. A slightly different track from the single. Blind Lemon had his variant of the "C C Rider" tradition in the song "Corrina Blues," the last verse of which resembles this one. Between Blind Lemon and Dylan stood a fine old "Corrina" recorded by Joe Turner and credited to Jay M Williams, Bo Chatman, and Mitchell Parish. Dylan shaped it to be both tender and ruefully jealous. He cited the strong influence of bluesman Lonnie Johnson.

"Honey, Just Allow Me One More Chance": Light-hearted, almost inconsequential. Although Bob claimed to have learned it from a nameless Texas blues recording, his performance owes influence to Jesse Fuller, who often burlesqued sadness.

"I Shall Be Free": A decided anticlimax. Although the album has at least a half-dozen blockbusters, two of the weakest songs are tucked in at the end, like shirttails, presumably a result of all the hassles between Hammond and Grossman, all the decisions about programming.

The other LP that portrayed Dylan appeared in 1962: *Broadside Ballads, Vol 1* was a modest effort, one of those one-take specials for which low-budget Folkways was known. The album illustrated what *Broadside* had been publishing in its first year. Since spring 1963, *Broadside, Vol 1* probably has not sold ten-thousand copies, yet it stands as an important documentary of the topical song movement. In an introduction, Gordon Friesen sketched the trail of topical songs, from prehistory through the English broadsides to contemporary America. The Dylan student will find the album fascinating because it makes clear that Dylan was becoming *Broadside*'s darling. It opens with "Blowin' in the Wind" by the New World Singers, in a small-scale but obviously affectionate version. Quoted in the notes are Dylan's remarks from the October–November 1962 issue of *Sing Out!*, an "explanation" in which he was still affecting Guthriesque language, with double negatives and throwaway rhythms of words that merely teased:

There ain't too much I can say about this song except that the answer is blowing in the wind. It ain't in no book or movie or TV show or discussion group. Man, it's in the wind—and it's blowing in the wind. Too many of these hip people are telling me where the answer is, but oh, I won't believe that. I still say it's in the wind and just like a restless piece of paper, it's got to come down some time ... But the only trouble is that no one picks up the answer when it comes down so not too many people get to see and know it ... and then it flies away again ... I still say that some of the biggest criminals are those that turn their heads away when they see wrong and know it's wrong. I'm only twenty-one years old and I know that there's been too many wars ... You people over twenty-one should know better ... 'cause after all, you're older and smarter.

"John Brown," the debut of Blind Boy Grunt, is a free adaptation of the traditional melody of "900 Miles."[16] An attack on the concept of war heroes, the song tells of a modern-day John Brown, fighting on a foreign shore for some unknown cause. The parents were proud when he left, prouder still of the medals he earned, but distraught when he returned a blinded cripple. Although the ironies of battlefield heroism are timeworn, the story is effective. The song has been rarely performed, but Bettina Jonic does it well beside a Brechtian anti-war polemic.

"I Will Not Go Down Under the Ground"[17] is sung by Happy Traum, then of the New World Singers, later the editor of *Sing Out!* and a renewed friend of Dylan in Woodstock from 1967. From the 1950s on, through the Cuban missile crisis, sales of bomb and fall-out shelters were brisk. A refusal to join the parade to the shelters, this song preaches the pride of standing above ground to fight the threats of war. Dylan is hitting back against the hope of escape, saying we're learning to die, not learning to live. Widely misinterpreted as resignation to the war-makers, the song actually affirms that war itself must be stopped because protection against it is illusory. The last two verses, which Friesen suspected were put-ons, were, in fact, Guthriesque evocations of the American landscape.

"Only a Hobo" and "Talkin' Devil": A Dylan song and a fragment, respectively, also sung by Blind Boy Grunt. "Hobo" continues Dylan's recurring fascination with the misfit outsider squeezed out of the mainstream. The two verses of "Talkin' Devil," a work-in-progress, present a germinal idea about the hidden devils of the earth.[18]

There are ten other songs on the *Broadside* album, sung by others. But five of the fifteen tracks are Dylan compositions. In 1965, the public, the press, and his own impatience pushed Dylan into apparent refutation of his *Broadside* period. DYLAN DISOWNS HIS PROTEST SONGS was the headline in the *Long Island Press* of October 17, 1965. In an inept interview, Dylan called "Wind" and "God on Our Side" "ghosts," and insisted that "Desolation Row" was more important than all his earlier political-topical songs. Later, he did not need to downgrade one past approach in order to elevate a current interest. In the 1970s, his writing and performing still carried echoes of *Broadside* days. His ears could still hear "music in the cafes at night/And revolution in the air."[19]

A walk through the Village for the *Freewheelin'* album photo shoot, with Suze Rotolo, 1963.

Above: "We Shall Overcome"— finale of Newport Folk Festival, 1963.
Inset: With Joan Baez at the March on Washington August 28, 1963.

Dylan is the most important song-writer in the country today … He has his finger on the pulse of America's youth.
PETER, PAUL AND MARY, 1963

I feel it, but Dylan can say it. He's phenomenal. His songs are powerful as poetry and music. Bob is expressing what all these kids want to say. He speaks for me.
JOAN BAEZ, 1963

He is the voice of the oppressed … the champion of the little man.
NEWPORT DAILY NEWS, 1963

It makes me think that I'm not being heard yet above all the mumble jumble and rave praises … there is no guidance at all except from one's own natural senses.
DYLAN, 1963[1]

"Enter the bear," Dylan with his manager Albert Grossman backstage at Newport Folk Festival, 1965.

Timing is almost as crucial to star-making as talent is. Grossman gave the impression of an unhurried, unscheduled man, yet he had a fine Swiss movement ticking in his mind. His timetable for launching Dylan was worked out in strategic, logistic detail. Dylan was not always aware of Grossman's moves, just as Grossman was not always aware of Dylan's. But in 1963, their schedules merged, like a Southern Pacific engine switching on to Sante Fe tracks. Albert's master plan required a hit recording, strong word-of-mouth from stars, and, most of all, a major publicity break, like the Newport Folk Festival. If Newport '59 could launch Baez, he reasoned, then Newport '63 could launch Dylan.

One of Albert's deals had to proceed without Bob's knowledge, for nothing is so fragile as a young performer's ego. Applying economic theory, Grossman bought out Roy Silver's share of their partnership using OPM—Other People's Money. Not that Grossman wasn't enjoying a bumper year in 1962: Odetta was prospering and Peter, Paul and Mary's first album topped the charts. However, the OPM principle minimizes risks and keeps one's own capital free. So, of the $10,000 that Albert paid to buy out Silver and to get Dylan into his fold, half was put up by Peter, Paul and Mary. The deal was kept quiet mostly to give Dylan the feeling that he was achieving everything on his own. The alleys of show business are strewn with the wrecks of young talent who lacked the right support at the right time. Even in 1970, Peter and Paul remained evasive, while Mary, who had fallen out with Grossman, was candid but cautious.

From 1962 on, there were rumors that Peter, Paul and Mary had a part interest in Dylan's future, but the trio's constant denials tended to make the arrangement seem sinister. All it meant was that the trio was backing privately what they said publicly: they believed Dylan had strong potential. Dylan did not learn that they had put a little bit of their money where their beliefs were until sometime after "Blowin' in the Wind" became a Peter, Paul and Mary hit. After he knew, and after the events of 1963, Bob's recurring litany, for a while, was: "Albert's a genius, a real genius."

After signing Dylan to Witmark, Grossman and Mogull got to work spreading Dylan's songs. Bob had already done a prodigious job, but now the powerhouse stepped in. Artie, a hard-sell expert, got tapes, demo acetates, and lead sheets to key people. Albert, the soft-sell specialist, concentrated on Yarrow and Milt Okun, music director not only for Peter, Paul and Mary but also for the Chad Mitchell Trio, and the Brothers Four. Okun had been with Belafonte, and later became John Denver's publisher and producer.

"Albert brought me a Dylan tape of 'Blowin' in the Wind' and 'Tomorrow Is a Long Time,'" Okun told me. "He was flipping out and got me interested." Grossman may have created Peter, Paul and Mary, but Okun's role in giving musical unity to their disparate voices cannot be overestimated. "Albert didn't specifically say that he was thinking of 'Blowin' in the Wind' for Peter, Paul and Mary. My first thought was that the Mitchell Trio would like it," Okun continued. He believed songs should not just be pretty tunes, but should *say* something. Okun brought the tape to the Mitchells, who were performing in Washington, DC. A day later, it went into their show. Two weeks later they wanted to release "Wind" as a single. The Mitchells were then working under the corporate flag of Belafonte, and their records were being produced by the late Bob Bollard. "Wind" started a series of battles between the Mitchells and Bollard, who said: "You just can't talk of such weighty, controversial subjects in a popular single." Bollard didn't always reflect Belafonte's thinking, yet his fiat enraged the Mitchells, who were already annoyed by Bollard's stiffness toward their then controversial number, "The Twelve Days of Christmas." The Mitchells continued to perform "Wind" as their encore to "Christmas" to consistently strong audience response and recorded the song on their album, *In Action*, in late 1962. It was well received, but no hit.

Meanwhile, in late 1962, at the Gate of Horn in Chicago, Grossman played Peter, Paul and Mary another Dylan tape of "Wind." Peter was enraptured; neither Paul nor Mary was quite that ecstatic. "I thought it was an OK tune," Paul recalled, "but I was something of an ostrich in those days." Soon, they worked out their own arrangement, changing some harmonies; Peter was convinced that "Wind" was the ideal sequel to their hit single of the Seeger-Lee Hays "If I Had a Hammer." On June 18, 1963, Warner Bros released the single. Within eight business days, "Wind" sold 320,000 copies. Mogull described it as Warner's fastest-moving single ever. Two key radio taste-makers, Bill Randle and Bill Gavin, began to call it "the record of the year." Some Cleveland, Washington, and Philadelphia stations were playing it hourly. Airplay and sales in the Deep South were surprisingly strong, probably because Peter, Paul and Mary were no strangers to the charts. "Hammer" and "Puff (The Magic Dragon)" had each sold about 700,000. As "Blowin' in the Wind" went over a million, popular hit material in American music was being redefined.

"Wind" inspired a wave of northern freedom songs. By 1962, songs had become a key element in the integration movement. Now "integration" was becoming a hot topic for folk and pop singers. *Variety* did a lead story on message songs, stressing "Wind" as the trendsetter. The Chad Mitchells were then scoring, even on southern campuses, with a satiric college-segregation tune called "Alma Mater" (or "Ole Miss"). Tom Paxton sang his "Dogs of Alabama" in nightclubs. The rage for integrationist songs was so prevalent by mid-1963 that in a coffeehouse in Ogunquit, Maine, I heard a girl call out: "Sing something about segregation!"

One of the wind's strangest undercurrents was the rumor that Dylan had stolen the song. The day after my survey of northern freedom songs appeared in the *Times*, I got a call from a Rutgers economics instructor, Henry Levin. He insisted Dylan had bought "Wind" from a boy in Millburn, New Jersey, named Lorre Wyatt who, he alleged, had written the song at 15; Dylan had heard it around the Village and offered to "buy" the lyrics. What was the price for this unusual deal? "Dylan made a one-thousand-dollar contribution to CARE in exchange for the lyrics," said the Rutgers sleuth. For that charitable act, Levin claimed, Wyatt gave the lyrics to Witmark, the publisher, for Dylan's use. The Rutgers man told me Wyatt's father had a lawyer seeking some of the song's profits.

Mogull dismissed Levin's story as nonsense. That night, Dylan said angrily that if I believed that, I would believe anything. He categorically denied the whole matter, said he had never heard of Wyatt, but guessed the rumor was motivated by jealousy over "some girl" in New Jersey. Gil Turner maintained openly that the melody was vaguely based on the folk spiritual "No More Auction Block for Me," but that the lyrics were Dylan's.[2] The rumor continued to circulate, surfacing in *Newsweek*'s infamous Dylan piece that fall. Meanwhile, Wyatt wrote to *Broadside* on June 5, 1963, disavowing Levin's charge:

Last year, I wrote a song called "Freedom is Blowing in the Wind," long before I'd ever heard Dylan's "Blowin' in the Wind." The lyrics are nothing whatsoever like Bob's, and the tune also is completely different. But the titles were similar ... some kids confused it with his, and were very indignant when they heard that Dylan "stole" my song, which I hadn't bothered to copyright ... I patiently ... explained to them that only the titles were similar—and that was all. I've finally decided to change the title to eliminate the confusion ... to either "Freedom is in the Air," or "Freedom is Everywhere." I've helped convert many indignant people into Dylan fans ... All's well now, I hope.

Not quite. In February 1974, Wyatt wrote "The Story Behind the 'Blowin' in the Wind' Story" for *New Times*, confessing that he had lied in maintaining that he had written anything even vaguely like Dylan's "Wind": "Dylan held the copyright months before I'd 'written' the song." In the article, Wyatt admitted he had fabricated the *Broadside* letter:

The coat of fakelore I stitched years ago is threadbare now—it never fit me very well ... Now is the time to pay the piper. With many people angry at what they view as Dylan's recent metamorphosis from Poet-Prophet to Profit-Poet, the dust of rumors is flying again. It is important that the insidious footnote to Dylan's words which still remains in the minds of many be erased. The only responsible way to delete that footnote is to make the whole story in my words available ... I'm just sorry it's taken me 11 years to say "I'm sorry."

Because Dylan frequently developed songs out of folk tradition, he was often branded a song thief. Seemingly unable to explain himself, he was his own worst defender. Critics sniped that his song, "Farewell," which Judy Collins recorded, was "only" a new set of words to the traditional Anglo-Irish "The Leaving of Liverpool." There were likenesses of his melodies to "I Pity the Poor Immigrant" and "Ballad of Donald White" in two traditional songs, "Come All Ye Tramps and Hawkers" and "Peter Amberley." They could trace Dylan's "Maggie's Farm" to a traditional song on Seeger's first solo album, "Penny's Farm." We've seen that "Song to Woody" derived melodically from Guthrie's "1913 Massacre," for which Woody himself had used a folk tune. Later, a publicity release from Mercury Records said that "Quinn, the Eskimo" was "inspired" by an Irish folk song. "Restless Farewell" resembled "The Parting Glass" and "Willie the Gambler"[3] was influenced by the Clancy Brothers' singing of "Brennan on the Moor."

By the end of 1963, the folk scene was bitterly divided over whether Dylan was a song cribber or a composer working in the accepted tradition of building new songs on the skeletal remains of old folk songs. Ian Tyson of Ian and Sylvia, though a client of Grossman, was one of Dylan's severest critics, as was Bob Yellin of the Greenbriar Boys. Better established performers were less critical of Dylan but a lot of the people who weren't making it took this opportunity to denigrate the man who was. By late autumn 1963, when a claim was made on the melody of "Don't Think Twice," even Grossman began to worry. I suggested to Grossman that Dylan indicate on his albums and in his folios some of his songs' folk sources. I hinted that there must be instances where Dylan wasn't certain where he got a phrase or melodic idea. "He knows, all right," Grossman replied dryly.

"What did I steal?" Bob asked me. "Did I steal the word *the*, the word *a*, the word *so*? Everybody has to get their words from somewhere. Woody didn't write ten original melodies, but nobody ever called him a thief." *Newsweek* was bad enough, but then *Little Sandy Review* got nasty:

The big question in folk music circles these days: who wrote "Blowin' in the Wind," Bob Dylan or some … student? Dylan has neither confirmed nor denied the charges … We don't know the facts … If he has been dishonest, he should be criticized for it; responsible folk music commentators should not close their eyes and mumble "a new Yevtushenko."

With friends like *Little Sandy Review*, Dylan scarcely needed enemies. Yet there were plenty of them. Tony Herbert, a Village folk singer, composed his own verses to "Times Changing," denouncing Dylan's style, philosophy, and success. One of Dylan's "11 Outlined Epitaphs" was a rebuttal to the whirlpool of rumor:

Yes, I am a thief of thoughts
not, I pray, a stealer of souls
I have built an' rebuilt
upon what is waitin'
for the sand on the beaches
carves many castles
on what has been opened
before my time
a word, a tune, a story, a line
keys in the wind t' unlock my mind
an' t' grant my closet thoughts backyard air[4]

Many folk-based songwriters were building on tradition as Dylan was, yet *they* weren't considered musical kleptomaniacs. Paul Simon's "Scarborough Fair" is an adaptation of the traditional English song, his "Bridge Over Troubled Water" echoes the black gospel tune "Don't Trouble the Water," which both Aretha Franklin and Roberta Flack sang as schoolgirls. I once told Tom Paxton that his "Daily News" had a melody just like an old Johnny Horton country tune. Paxton said he didn't know that. John Sebastian helped himself freely to a garland of traditional jug-band tunes to stir his Lovin' Spoonful, a group named after a line by Mississippi John Hurt. Jimmy Webb's "Wichita Lineman" derives from an Irish air. Even "Yankee Doodle" was cribbed by American colonists from an English drinking song. Shakespeare, Stravinsky and Picasso were master borrowers. Adaptation of old material is as old as music and poetry themselves. The folk tunes in Mozart, Bach, even Mahler, would amaze many classical snobs. Charles Seeger, Pete's ethnomusicologist father, explained the folk process: "Conscious and unconscious appropriation, borrowing, adapting, plagiarizing and plain stealing … always have been part and parcel of the process of artistic creation. The attempt to make sense out of copyright law reaches its limit in folk song. For here is the illustration par excellence of the Law of Plagiarism. The folk song is, by definition, and, as far as we can tell, by reality, entirely a product of plagiarism."

"Blowin' in the Wind" had a dual life as a pop standard and a civil rights anthem. Within a year of the Peter, Paul and Mary hit, nearly sixty other versions were recorded by the likes of Duke Ellington,[5]

Lena Horne, Marlene Dietrich, Spike Jones, Percy Faith, Trini Lopez, Glen Campbell, and Bobby Bare. Many more sang the song than recorded it, and as late as 1968, Stevie Wonder had a hit. The clouds of rumor and the dust of suspicion settled a gray patina over Dylan's triumphs for another year. As he wrote hit after hit, the carping diminished. Some thought he might have done a better job of scotching the suspicions, but his metaphorical riposte in the "Epitaph" helped to bury gossip. As Peter, Paul and Mary toured, Peter stressed repeatedly his belief that Dylan was *sui generis*: "Bob Dylan is the most important songwriter in the country today. He has his finger on the pulse of America's youth." The trio was laying down a carpet for Dylan's own grand entrance.

His return to Town Hall in a solo show on Friday, April 13, 1963, was a turning point. Leventhal, who produced it, had terms with Grossman that the concert producer could scarcely lose. Forgetting the late 1961 program, Leventhal and Grossman billed Town Hall as Dylan's first solo concert, and claimed 12,000 tickets were sold. The audience, which predated the widespread practice of "papering" an audience with free tickets to fill unsold seats, actually numbered around 900. Bob was understandably tense and a squabble with Suze just before he left for Town Hall didn't help. Once onstage, he delivered a very strong program. Now he had the material and experience to be a serious performer, as well as a witty one. In the balcony, Seeger and his wife, Toshi, glowed benevolently. Two rave reviews, mine in the *Times* and Barry Kittleson in *Billboard* gave Grossman fuel. A paper dependent on record company advertising rarely offered quotable criticism, but Kittleson was an uncommon trade paper reviewer. Under the heading "A Legend Under Construction: Folk Poet Dylan Weaves a Spell," he wrote that Dylan was "the stuff of which legends are made … an absolute original … profound … poetry born of a painful awareness of the tragedy that underlies the contemporary human condition … It is his primary purpose to speak, not to entertain … The prediction here is that his talent will be around for a long, long time."

Town Hall that evening may have been the last Dylan concert that reminded listeners of his influences. From then on he could be compared only to himself. That night his hobo look evoked memories of Guthrie. With his jeans and a head of hair that shouted unfamiliarity with barbers, Dylan resembled Holden Caulfield lost in the Dust Bowl. His vulnerability, his identification with his material, suggested a young Sinatra. However, Dylan broke all songwriting and performing rules—except those of having something to say and saying it well. Not every line seemed finished and polished, yet there was a sense of structure. Dylan's assurance grew with each wave of applause. "Hollis Brown" was vivid as a film clip. "Hard Rain" bit and churned with its nightmare visions. Then, comic relief. Dylan did his various ironic talking blues, but he was not playing for laughs now, though he did introduce "a 1930 ragtime tune I wrote last week." He read his poem to Guthrie, which won an ovation.[6]

Afterward, there was an impromptu party for Bob. Yarrow volunteered his mother's Upper West Side apartment. Grossman's partner, John Court, gently shooed away the well-wishers and escorted Bob into a waiting taxi. About 25 people showed up. Mrs Yarrow, a warm, volatile woman, didn't even realize that Dylan was the guest of honor. "Would you get some ice cubes for our guests, dear?" she asked him, assuming he was just another admirer of her son, the folk singer. Bob wasn't put off. After a few drinks, he asked her: "How'd yuh like to marry me? I mean it, you're a real groovy chick." The long-divorced Mrs Yarrow was, for a rare moment, speechless.

Through Yarrow, Dylan first visited Woodstock, in early summer 1963. The gracious upstate New York art colony had long been Peter's retreat. His uncle owned a forty-year-old cabin, which Peter subsequently bought, three minutes from the village center, set on a couple of acres. The first summer, Bob and Suze shared the cabin. Suze was painting, Bob was writing, and the three shared household responsibilities. Since Bob's cooking was primitive, Peter and Suze prepared most meals. "Bob was never more at peace with himself than that first summer in Woodstock," Yarrow recalled. In the afternoons, they swam in the Big Deep or at a motel pool.

In 1970, Yarrow reminisced: "We spent a lot of time together, Bobby and I, but we seldom talked. I wasn't really surprised that he wasn't all that articulate then. I just liked him. He was a little scared and within himself. He was a grubber; but we all copped from each other. That summer was a little like his song 'Bob Dylan's Dream,' even though the song didn't actually pertain … Our lives were not that simple. Our stars were beginning to rise, and we just couldn't ignore that. When Bobby and Suze went back to the Village, they were down. When they returned to Woodstock, their spirits inevitably rose. Albert wasn't anywhere near Woodstock then. Milt Glazer [designer of *New York* magazine] brought him up, I didn't. Now, Albert's building an empire up there—a recording studio, a restaurant, and has a hundred-twenty acres of land. Actually, I stopped going up there around 1965, when the place began to be rediscovered. Now everybody goes up there. It's not the same as it was when I was a kid, or not the same as when Bobby and Suze were there with me."

During summer 1963, I saw Dylan when he bounced back to the Village from Woodstock, refreshed. New York summers made him furtive. He told me I should come up where "we stop the clouds, turn time back and inside out, make the sun turn on and off. It's the greatest, man, the greatest place."

Into the Vast Wasteland. Grossman booked Dylan on TV's prestigious *Ed Sullivan Show* on Sunday night, May 12, 1963. The show may have seemed an unscalable Everest for a singer identified with protest, but Sullivan based his format on popular taste. Besides, the ABC-TV *Hootenanny* show had just allowed the Chad Mitchell Trio to sing their anti-Birch satire. The Sullivan booking became an ironic coup for Dylan. Because he was forced to walk off it, Dylan made national news.

For the dress rehearsal, he arrived typically dressed down. Earlier in the week, Dylan had sung his "Talkin' John Birch Society Blues" to Sullivan and his producer, Bob Precht, who liked both the singer and the song. But immediately after the dress rehearsal, Stowe Phelps, editor of CBS-TV program practices—a fancy title for a censor—said the song could not be used. He feared possible libel action because Birchites were compared to Hitler. Sullivan and Precht were annoyed, Grossman irate, Dylan furious. Sullivan asked Dylan if he wanted to substitute another song. Without hesitating, Dylan whirled around and said: "If I can't sing that song, I won't sing *any* song." He stomped out of the studio and crashed around the Village that night in a blazing, raging temper cursing "those bastards!" "What a story that would make," I told him. It did.

Val Adams, the *Times* radio-TV reporter, went after the higher echelons of CBS. Did they stand behind their censor? "No comment." On Tuesday, May 14, Bob Williams of the *New York Post* gave Sullivan's views: "We told CBS: 'It's your network, but … the decision is wrong and the policy behind it is wrong.'" Sullivan said that President Kennedy and Governor Rockefeller were always kidded by TV comedians. "But the John Birch Society—I said I couldn't understand why they were being given such protection." Harriet Van Horne raked the network in her national column: "higher-echelon thinking at CBS continues rigid, narrow, and indifferent to the grave moral issues of our time … The censored song, which was to have been sung by … Dylan, was neither salacious nor libelous. It simply poked fun at a society of political know-nothings whose malicious mischief has already menaced the spirit of free inquiry in our schools, slandered our clergymen and subverted—in the most evil fashion—the minds of many youngsters."

Dylan, in a formal letter, asked the Federal Communications Commission for a public investigation. No hearing was held, but Dylan often retold the story at subsequent concerts. Dylan did appear on a TV show taped before the Sullivan fiasco but not broadcast until late May. The host of this Westinghouse Broadcasting Company special, the second of two hour-long shows tracing American history through folk songs, was John Henry Faulk, making his comeback. Also performing were the Brothers Four, Carolyn Hester, Barbara Dane, and the Staple Singers. Dylan had made his first TV experience on BBC the previous December. With total cool he stood up and sang "Wind," "Paths of Victory" and "Hollis Brown" with no mannerisms and few smiles. During the last song, the cameras crept in from a distance and shot him from below, making him look very tall.

Dylan next appeared on a freedom songs show on WNEW-TV, New York. The producer, Arthur Barron, later did documentaries for CBS and the Johnny Cash biography, in which Dylan had a bit part. Barron hired me as a consultant, and I called Bob and described the civil rights content of the show. He agreed at once to do it and to "tell Albert," no matter what the money was. Odetta and the Freedom Singers rounded out the bill. Barron was shaken by Dylan's rusty voice: "I just don't know if that kind of singing will make it." By the time he heard the finished tapes, Barron was converted. Grossman groused during the taping, in July 1963, because he wasn't sure Dylan and Odetta were getting the treatment they deserved. Another annoyance was that Dylan had called Joan Baez to the studio. Joan's surprising availability for TV, which she generally ignored, unsettled the producer, who had already worked out his timing. He huddled with his director. "It would be a coup to have her on, but my show sense says that it would be wrong to start shifting everything around at the last moment," the producer told me. Grossman, defending Odetta as "star" of a show that should have negated the star system, grudgingly said Joan could appear. The show went on with Joan in the audience.

While cameras and lights were being prepared, Bob and Joan huddled in a corner. Bob played her a ragtimey dance tune, while Joan did an improvised clog dance. They were having their own party, despite audience and technicians milling around. Grossman, whose peripheral vision often matched his foresight, took in the scene. "Can you imagine the offspring of a union of those two?" he asked me. The freedom-songs show was weak aesthetically, but two months after the Sullivan show censorship, Dylan was delighted to sing out on racial issues with "Wind" and "Only a Pawn."

Afterward, his TV work dropped off, despite many offers. He wanted only the right shows under optimum conditions. In early 1964, Dylan appeared on *The Steve Allen Show* from the West Coast. Allen wrote me in 1970: "I had not heard Dylan until he walked on our stage. I confess Dylan's genius escaped my observation at the time. It struck me then that he is somehow not ideally suited to television and that his audience will always be limited to the young. He sang so very softly and his attitude was so off-hand and unprofessional that he seemed rather more a mystery to our studio audience than as a blazing new talent. Dylan's uninhibited manner, monotonous voice and monotonous songs are, I suppose, a separate art-form unto themselves."

If Allen was underwhelmed, Les Crane, who ran a provocative show on ABC-TV, was hooked. When Dylan appeared on Crane's show on February 17, 1965, he dominated the hour. His musical peak was "It's Alright, Ma," done with extensive close-ups. He ragged Crane at every point, about how he dressed, or what he was planning next, or the movie in which Dylan said he was going "to play the part of his mother," or in other byplay with another guest, Allen Ginsberg. Crane's show was Dylan's most sophisticated TV appearance to date. He was outrageously uncooperative, yet effective, leaving the viewer wondering: "What makes this man tick?"

The Hootenanny Craze.

When Mike Porco started his Monday night hootenanny, he had no idea that by 1963 it would become a household word. The hootenanny craze sprang from a TV series on ABC. Dylan never appeared on it, yet the show's influence on mass taste ultimately benefited him and other performers who shunned the show.

Hootenanny is a nonsense word, like *thingamajig* or *whatsit*. In July 1940, according to Peter Tamony, a West Coast word detective, some Seattle Democrats launched fund-raising parties with folk songs. Someone suggested calling them hootenannies, a word remembered from youth in Indiana, and the title stuck. Two young singers at those Seattle hoots were Seeger and Guthrie, who brought word and concept east. *Sing Out!* and the Old Left kept the word alive. Then an ABC producer, Richard Lewine, and his talent coordinator, Fred Weintraub, tacked it on to a TV show set amid lively collegiate audiences. Their cardinal mistake was to blacklist Seeger and the Weavers. Reaction ultimately made the show perhaps the most controversial series on American TV.

A weekly audience of up to eleven million watched *Hootenanny*, and soon the word described or promoted sweat shirts, pinball machines, brogans, and vacations. ("Wonderful things happen at the Balmoral, including a twelve-day hootenanny holiday.") Ford dealers held hootenanny sales. A chain of shoe dealers pushed hootenanny boots. New Jersey's Palisades Amusement Park had a Miss Hootenanny contest. The music business's reflexes were predictable: hootenanny troupes blanketed the provinces, there was a *Hootenanny Hoot* film feature, a dance step called the hoot, and albums titled *Hootenanny for Orchestra*, *Hot-Rod Hootenanny*, and *Surfing Hootenanny*. There were two dreadful magazines called *Hootenanny*, including the late, unlamented monster I edited.

The TV series and fad were anathema to old-guard folk fans who believed folk music was a bastion against commercialism. Because the show barred Seeger, folk singers, led initially by Carolyn Hester and Judy Collins, began a performers' boycott. An embarrassed Seeger decided on a world tour. The folk scene was cut in half, the pure opposed to appearing, and others, needing the work, maintaining that a boycott would betray the audience, leaving the show to those of limited talents. Some of the series' bitterest opponents had never been invited. Others, like Peter, Paul and Mary, *were* genuinely opposed politically, but Grossman turned down a $25,000 offer anyway because he knew TV exposure was bad for college concerts. *Hootenanny* gave a few fine rural performers, like Mother Maybelle Carter and Doc Watson, greater exposure. The Chad Mitchells performed their biting songs, but most quality performers shunned the show.

In 1963, America was greening almost overnight, but there was still crabgrass in the lawn. Andy Warhol said later that as the 1970s were too empty, the 1960s had been too full. The over-exploited hoot craze wore itself out. Dylan and Baez, among others, spoofed it at their concerts. Some listeners got the distorted idea that folk song meant wildly clapping sing-alongs. While the hootenanny fad strengthened the folk elitists' argument that mass culture was a snare and a dilution, some good performances did sneak through; some obscure musicians won recognition. The TV series probably led millions of its viewers toward quality song. At least some of them began to wonder why performers like Seeger, Dylan, and Baez had not been on their home screens.

Festival Fever. Before the Newport Folk Festival of July 1963, when folk-song fever ran to the top of the thermometer, Dylan had four festival-like settings with different audiences—eastern collegiate, West Coast public, Mississippi political, and Puerto Rican commercial. Still only a rising star, his uphill effort demanded as much self-possession as Bob could muster. Spring and summer 1963 inaugurated three merciless years of pressured performing. His increasing popularity could only impress Suze, even while each tour meant another separation. Ready to go almost anywhere, neither he nor Albert was saying no to any reasonable invitation.

On May 10, there was a folk festival at Brandeis University, outside Boston. Grossman made sure Dylan had the two best spots—before intermission and the finale. Brandeis hailed Dylan. (Grossman roared at the festival producer for "the worst sound setup I've heard at five hundred college concerts.") Afterward, Ric Von Schmidt took Dylan, Suze, and me to a very quiet party attended by Boston's hippest—the Kweskins, Geoff and Maria Muldaur, Betsy and Bob Siggins, the staff of *Boston Broadside*, the gang from the Club 47. Bob was solemnly introduced to the Charles River cognoscenti. Albert was disappointed by Bostonian cool, though he reconsidered when I told him that one guest had said they had been so awed by Dylan's presence they just didn't know what to say.

Brandeis secured the North-East precincts for Dylan. Tomorrow: the West Coast. Through agent Ben Shapiro, Dylan was booked for the first Monterey Folk Festival, on May 18; the program included the Weavers and roots folk singer Mance Lipscomb. Dylan was delighted to work in Steinbeck country. "I virtually had to force Dylan down the throats of the Monterey Festival producers," Ben told me later. He got Dylan $1,500 for Saturday night.

Audience reaction at Monterey was quizzically appreciative. Ralph Gleason of the *San Francisco Chronicle* reacted negatively. "It was an old Dylan concert," he remarked later, after he had become a passionate advocate, "and I didn't dig it. The talking blues stuff was poor imitation Guthrie. He looked wrong to me and I didn't like his voice. Although I didn't like 'Hard Rain,' I became haunted by it. Jesus, it was disturbing." Gleason clobbered Dylan, but Seeger leaped to the defense, framing a complaint, co-signed by actor-singer Theodore Bikel and others. Gleason reconsidered and graciously changed his mind in print. "I was deaf," Ralph wrote later. Monterey was Dylan's first real encounter with Joan Baez, who lived in nearby Carmel. Bob had met Joan briefly at a party in Boston in 1962 and she had heard his "Song to Woody" that winter. Monterey was their first intensive encounter and she began to tune in to what he was writing and saying. Monterey affected her life and Dylan's, artistically and personally.

In early July 1963, the Student Non-violent Coordinating Committee (SNCC) had planned a voter-registration rally in Greenwood, Mississippi, a cotton center on the Yazoo River, where Highway 82 curls its way toward the Delta. Local activists had been trying to persuade blacks to register to vote. Since August 1962, the campaign had grown; SNCC was coping with jailings, threats, murders, and disappearances. There were signs that the terror was being overcome. SNCC sent word north that singers were needed. Seeger, Bikel, and Dylan flew down, at some personal risk, to play for a few hundred black farmers. The singers' presence helped win national publicity for the local movement. (Guy Carawan, who'd been spreading songs in the South for years, was startled that Dylan could get TV and *New York Times* coverage with just one quick visit south.) Dylan was now emerging as spokesman and star, and Bikel, who told me he had paid Dylan's plane fare, treated him with deference: "I felt Bob should get a first-hand impression of the struggle in the South. We flew all night, changing planes in Atlanta, waiting there two hours, then changing again. Most of the way down, Bob was writing little notes and lines on envelopes; he didn't really talk too much. I didn't want to pry or shake him, because I felt there was something quite tremulous and sensitive there. I suppose I felt slightly in awe of him. There was something churning inside him all the time, something quite deep. His political attitudes were less strongly formed than many of ours. It seemed a more personal thing with him to be going down into the Deep South. He moved from the universal to the personal, while most artists and writers tend to move from the personal to the universal." Arriving at the Jackson, Mississippi, airport, Dylan saw water fountains and toilets marked WHITE and COLORED. He asked Theo what he thought would happen if he decided to drink from the COLORED ONLY fountain. They arrived, still thirsty, at Greenwood, to be greeted by Jim Forman, Bernice, Cordell, and the Freedom Singers, Julian Bond, Seeger, and Chandler. For two and a half days they worked in the thick of the new abolition movement with dirt farmers and northern college students.

On July 6, two miles outside Greenwood, Pete, Bob, and Theo sang on the edge of a cotton patch. Around 300 people attended, mostly local blacks, with a score of young white supporters, newsmen, and four TV men from New York.[7] The loudest response from the locals was for "We Shall Overcome," the "Marseillaise" of civil rights. Dylan's "Only a Pawn in Their Game," written just weeks earlier, about the murder of Medgar Evers, head of the National Association for the Advancement of Colored People in Mississippi, hit home base. "Wind" had greater impact on the SNICK and northern activists than on the farmers. To the locals, the song's abstractions did not relate closely enough to the concrete realities of their own plight. "I saw Bob observing everything down there," recalled Bikel. "He was also watching the reaction to himself. He was very humble to the farmers, admitting that there wasn't such a problem where he came from. Bob said he hadn't met a colored person until he was nine years old, and he apologized that he had so little to offer." Bernice said she never felt quite so close to Bob. "'Pawn' was the very first song that showed the poor white was as victimized by discrimination as the poor black. The Greenwood people didn't know that Pete, Theo, and Bobby were well known. They were just happy to be getting support. But they really liked Dylan down there in the cotton country."

By summer 1963, even Columbia Records began to realize Dylan's potential. In July, at the annual Columbia sales convention in Puerto Rico, Dylan was an honored guest, along with Aretha Franklin and Tony Bennett. Dylan flew to the Hotel Americana in San Juan with Albert, Suze, and Carla. Albert was busy managing; Bob and the Rotolos, who were introduced jokingly as Dylan's wife and sister-in-law, sopped up sun, swimming, food, and drink. Dylan performed only once, at a dinner, but he was expected to shake hands and banter with faceless regional distributors, sales managers, and field representatives. Except for a few private moments on the beach, he felt ill at ease.

Singing at the salesmen's dinner, Dylan was roundly applauded. Privately, promotion men, especially those from the South, rumbled about Dylan's material. "With God on Our Side" was going to be rough to sell in their market, they murmured. Still, the corporate smile beamed on Dylan. Toward the end of the week, Goddard Lieberson, president of Columbia, invited Dylan and the Rotolos to his suite. At Dylan's first recording session in 1962, sensing his interest in blues and folk roots, Lieberson had spoken to Bob about his recording field trips to the South in the 1930s. Now, aware of his guest's interest in off-Broadway, he chatted urbanely about Brecht and Lotte Lenya, and played a new Columbia set, *The Badmen*, that he expected would appeal to Bob. Dylan kept eyeing the diving boards below, muttering: "I just have to do it, just have to dive off that high board." Lieberson released them with a copy of *The Badmen*.

That evening, Lieberson invited the three to dinner. Dylan wasn't enthusiastic, but he met the magnate in the lobby at eight, dressed in dungarees, work shirt, boots, and tousled hair. Lieberson and Carla suggested Bob compromise and wear a tie to get into the restaurant for the sake of a good meal. "I will never compromise," Dylan snapped at them. "If you can't find a place to eat where I don't have to wear a tie, I'm not interested in going. It's your tough luck." Albert discreetly blended into the drapes. The recording official took Carla out to dinner alone. Later, Carla told me, Dylan decided to play blackjack at a San Juan casino. Discovering that they wouldn't let him in tieless, he went to Albert's room to borrow a tie to get in. Dylan then had his first of many quarrels with Carla, unleashing a "truth attack" at her for telling him how to act. When Lieberson left Puerto Rico, he sent the three some liquor and records, with a note: "Dear Bobby, Suze and Carla—To be drunk only while wearing a necktie. Have a great vacation. Love from Big Daddy."

Newport—The First Woodstock.
Dylan arrived at the Newport Folk Festival of July 26–28 an underground conversation piece, and left a national star. Newport '63 was a dress rehearsal for Woodstock Nation. The weekend's total attendance was only 47,000, less than ten percent of those who turned out, and on, at Woodstock '69. But Newport '63 was the cocoon of an alternative culture. The seventy performers and their audience were high on the music, high on "their" civil rights revolution. Musicians and listeners felt they were saying something to the rest of the country about another way of

living and thinking. The hootenanny craze and the music business only provided the vehicle for a mass expression of social purpose.

Newport '63 was a turning point for folk song as a new popular music, and for Dylan. With his raggedy clothes, biting songs, anti-show-business posture, identification with Negro rights and peace, and shaking off of the outworn myths of history in "God on Our Side," Dylan became the Festival's emblem. His picture was everywhere—lean, gaunt face, frail shoulders covered in a faded khaki army shirt with wilted epaulets, blanched blue jeans. Most of the weekend he walked around with a long leather bullwhip wrapped tightly around one shoulder. Reporters dogged his steps. It all looked as spontaneous as the group spirit of Newport itself. Yet Albert and Dylan had done considerable planning. Albert had insisted on the honored closing spot for Dylan at the first major concert. The pair also had timing on their side: Newport Nation was hungry for a new leader and Dylan was elected by acclamation.

The Newport Folk Festivals had begun back in 1959 as an offshoot of the parent Jazz Festivals. George Wein, the portly, amiable promoter, manager, and piano player, had fostered the jazz events during the 1950s. In 1959, Wein had started working with Grossman on a companion folk fête, which initially ran into opposition from the city fathers. During the 1960 Jazz Festival, riots broke out, causing two years' hiatus for all Newport festivals. Late in 1962, Wein, Seeger, and Bikel, whose idea it was, formed the non-profit Festival Foundation, a seven-man board of musician-directors to choose talent and help Wein direct the festival.

The star system was soft-pedaled, native folk singers billed alongside established names. Everyone got the same fee—$50 plus food, lodging, and expenses. As first-day ticket sales began to soar, I walked around crowded Freebody Park with Grossman. He was no longer in the leadership of the festival, and had also split up his management partnership with Wein. "Isn't this turnout amazing?" I asked. Albert agreed: "It will mean more leisure for me. Naturally, I'm pleased. Although it's too bad that Wein had to do this the way he did, with all this board of directors' stuff." Wein remained technically the producer of the Folk Festival and he and his gracious wife, Joyce, became, along with the Seegers, den parents to the thousands of kids who streamed into Newport. Old-time performers were arriving from the South, white and black Southerners were sharing the stage.

Despite the board's disavowal of the star system, Seeger and other big names still dominated. The first step out of the incubator on Friday afternoon at the Newport Casino Tennis Club was quiet enough. About a hundred youngsters sat, barefoot or in sneakers, as Bikel told a panel discussion that the swelling interest in folk music was more than a fad: it represented a rebellion against canned recreation and a return to do-it-yourself culture. Seeger said TV and its power had to be watched so that it "makes a place in the mass media for minority tastes. We all know folk music has mushroomed, and now we're beginning to worry about the fallout."

A few singers commented melodically. Baez was among the first. Her silken voice was joined by Bob's raspy, raw-edged voice. As the pair went through "With God on Our Side," listeners craned to see the stranger singing with Joan. In the weeks since Monterey, Joan had learned many Dylan songs. Around this time she spoke to Nat Hentoff in *HiFi/Stereo Review*:

The majority of those "protest" songs are stupid. They're without beauty. By contrast, Bob Dylan's songs ... are powerful as poetry and ... as music ... Bob is expressing what all these kids want to say. And I love his singing! Oh, my God, the boy can sing! He can be so terribly moving. I've never heard anyone like him. When he starts singing ... "Hard Rain," I cry and have to leave the room.

That workshop duet was the first time Joan and Bob sang together publicly. For the next two years, and intermittently until 1984, they appeared dozens of times on each other's programs. According to Ralph Gleason: "Much as I dig Joanie, she never sang as well by herself as she did with Dylan. And she never sang as well with him as she did in the dressing room with him. She can't swing, and he can. He can make her swing as much as she can swing. When he has her locked eye to eye with him, those performances are celestial. Whatever they might say, they both had acts, and they both are hams. Onstage, they both had to look at the audience instead of each other." In later years, Joan learned to swing on her own.

For the major opening concert at Newport that Friday night, July 26, more than 13,000 people turned out, as many as at the entire 1959 Festival. Newport police rated it the city's biggest single crowd. The folk stepchild had outgrown its jazz parent. According to the *Newport Daily News*, Peter, Paul and Mary did best on "Wind," after Yarrow's standard homily to Dylan. The audience didn't want to let the trio off the stage.

Of Dylan's solo set in the second half, the *Newport News* described him as "the voice of the oppressed in America and the champion of the little man." Dylan sang "Dream," "God on Our Side," "John Birch," and "Hard Rain." The audience was hushed and reverential, then applauded generously. After his set, Dylan, for once without the leather bullwhip, relaxed backstage on the grass with me and my girlfriend Shelden Ogilvy. He signed a few autographs, fenced with some reporters about interviews, snapped at another newsman: "I don't have time to give you my time, man. Can't you see I'm talking to my friends?" Generally, he was amiable. "We've got a little surprise for you at the end of the show," Dylan teased me. Peter, Paul and Mary returned and sang "Wind" again, then brought on Dylan, Joan, the Freedom Singers, Seeger, and Bikel for a grand finale of "We Shall Overcome." Dylan stood between Joan and Bernice, his guitar and harmonica hanging from his neck. The eleven singers clasped hands, a chorus for Negro freedom. It was the movement singing together as a movement, and the movement nominating Dylan as its spokesman.

Dylan made two more stage appearances during the weekend. A workshop hosted by Seeger, on topical songs and new songwriters, drew the largest crowd, around 500, of the eight workshops. The *Providence Journal*: "It was obvious that many had been waiting to hear the short, slight young man's bitter songs. He did not disappoint them." The audience joined him on "Playboys and Playgirls."[8] Sunday night, at Baez's main appearance, she announced: "Here's another Bobby song," as she returned. "This is a song about a love affair that has lasted too long," she said before singing "Don't Think Twice." In the audience, Suze Rotolo turned pale and got up to walk out. Ric Von Schmidt went with her, trying to comfort her after this public gibe.

Joan then brought Dylan, unscheduled, on to the stage, to join her in "God on Our Side." Grossman was all smiles. The program ended with a mass grouping onstage for "This Land Is Your Land," which was stirring but lacked the impact of Friday night's finale. The concept of a festival run by musicians had worked, and the civil rights commitment gave the event purpose and drive. Everyone seemed to agree that Dylan was the "find" of the festival. The weekly news magazines duly noted that Baez, the reigning queen of folk music, had named Dylan the crown prince. Dylan's apprenticeship was over. He left Newport a star.

Diamonds and Rust.   Right after Newport, Baez had ten solo concerts in the east, her most rigorous schedule to date. In the past, Flatt and Scruggs or the Greenbriars had shared her stages. Everything pointed to Dylan as her next tour guest. Albert worked out details with Joan's manager, Manny Greenhill: Bob would do about a half-dozen songs at each gig, and would earn slightly more than Joan, who wasn't pleased but didn't make an issue about the pie slicing. She was always keen on some cause or other, some musician, some new style or songwriter, and all that enthusiasm converged now on Dylan. There was some *noblesse oblige* on her part. This waif, she seemed to feel, needed looking after. For his part, Bob promised to bring Joan on his future shows.

The East Coast tour blossomed into a close personal relationship, an erratic friendship, a stormy on-again, off-again love affair. Bob's and Joan's fans were fascinated and mystified by their motivations. Rasped Dave Van Ronk: "I think the relationship was purely opportunistic on both sides. Certainly, Dylan the sponge was functioning on all eight cylinders. In 1963, he really needed Joanie and really wanted to make it. He wanted to be a rich man." Couldn't it have been opportune for Joan to want a new toy, a new enthusiasm? Didn't she drop him when she got tired of him? "No," Van Ronk snapped back with oracular certainty. "Joan was burned and Dylan wasn't. She was expecting a new bright light to save the pacifist movement, and Bobby wasn't having any of that crap either."

I had met Joan two years before I met Bob, and remember her changing from a shy young thing at a post-Newport '59 party at my Village apartment to someone with confidence, then into an Amazonian standard-bearer. I cannot ignore her talent, but drawing conclusions about her interaction with Dylan I look from what I assume is Bob's point of view. However difficult he was, at times, as a friend, I feel I can be partisan without losing objectivity. All of which leads me to the certainty that Bob and Joan's attraction and need for each other was not mere professional opportunism. Both tended to worship heroes and heroines. Before focusing on Dylan, Baez had idolized Odetta and Seeger. Dylan, to Joan, could be both idol and protégé, and she could, she thought, teach him the ropes. For Bob, at first, it was flattering to bask in her light, but it also meant a chance to reach many more listeners. Somewhere along the line, they fell in love. In later years, Joan mellowed considerably, and was able to look back on Dylan with genuine, open love, even as she teased, mocked, and mimicked him.

Right after Newport, Joan visited Woodstock. Dylan came back to the Village happier than I'd seen him in months. Now, instead of the endless wrangles with Suze and her family, he'd found a girl whose own identity was established. He was clearly infatuated. Although Suze was still smarting from that introduction to "Don't Think Twice," she may not have realized how serious a rival she now had, and by this point may not have cared much. "I knew what was happening all along," Suze told me later. That summer, Dylan somehow managed to juggle two women.

One night in early August, Van Ronk's new band, the Ragtime Stompers, was making its debut at the Village Vanguard. I asked Dylan if he wanted to go. "Sure, man, I'll call Joan and we'll meet you down there." Joan arrived early and sat chatting with me and my girlfriend while we waited for Bob. Later, either very stoned or very in love, he came downstairs, saying he had been waiting for her upstairs. Joan and Bob gave each other looks that, to borrow Ring Lardner's phrase, you could have poured on a waffle. After the band's first set, Bob hustled Joan out—crowds bugged him and he wanted to be alone with Joan. On the way, they ran into Maynard Solomon, the co-director of Vanguard Records, for whom Joan had enormous respect. Bob may have remembered him as someone who had ignored his talent, and anyway Albert was always falling out with him. Whatever the reason, Dylan launched into a "truth attack," excoriating the gentle Solomon in front of his leading artist.

On August 17, the Baez-Dylan tour was due at the Forest Hills Stadium in Queens, their sixth concert since Newport. The morning of the concert, Dylan called me to join him for breakfast at the Gallery Delicatessen ("Give us this day our deli bread") on Christopher Street. Bob was no longer playing it cool. "She promised to set up a special room in her house in Carmel with a piano for me. Imagine me having my own piano out on the Coast!" He sounded like a struggling painter who had just found a beautiful patroness to buy him oils. Dylan had periodically come up to my apartment to listen to records, talk, and play the piano, despite the sound of my primitive old upright. Now he had the prospect of a piano of his own, and the well-tempered attentions of Baez along with it.

At Forest Hills, Joan introduced Dylan as an unbilled "surprise" guest. Nearly half her program was songs by or with Dylan. "Bobby Dylan says what a lot of people my age feel but cannot say," Joan told nearly 15,000. She taunted the TV *Hootenanny*: "I will appear if they will let Pete Seeger on that program." Dylan's presence seemed to relax Joan, who was obviously getting a lot from having Dylan on her side. At the previous five concerts, audiences reportedly had been restrained toward Dylan; there'd even been complaints. By the time the pair arrived in Queens, he won as much applause as Joan.

After the concert, Bob and Joan were returning to the Riverside Drive apartment of Clark Foreman, whom Joan called her "deputy father in New York." Clark, then chief of the Emergency Civil Liberties Committee, was a former official in Roosevelt's New Deal administration, a leader in civil liberties battles of the McCarthy era. He had also invited other guests—John Henry Faulk, photographer Dick Rohan, me, and Shelden Ogilvy. When Joan and Bob were late, we became concerned. There had been such a crush of admirers around their dressing room and later their car that they had been locked in for nearly an hour. This had never happened to Dylan before, although Joan was used to it. When they finally arrived, Bob looked pale and shaken, despite the evening's success. People clucked and fussed, mothered and fathered him. He listened to it all, but it was clear that he really didn't want all the advice. Joan was hugging and kissing him, but whenever the photographer tried to capture an intimate shot, she shooed him off. "Remember our agreement," Joan chided him, and he meekly lowered his camera.

Foreman and Faulk were Dutch uncles, telling Dylan to stand up to all audiences and crowds, whether sympathetic, smothering, or hostile. The two civil liberties veterans hurled advice and directions. They played Dylan a recording of a speech by Nedrick Young, the late screenwriter, about the social responsibility of writers. If this had been down in the Village, Bob probably would have gone storming out on to the streets, into the coffeehouses, down to where the sound of music, the taste of wine, or the scent of grass would spell freedom. That night, he couldn't escape.

In mid-1963, everybody was fussing again over "Bobby," almost like two years earlier. He didn't want to be treated like a *kid* anymore. Joan probably made her major mistake here: she had three years' headstart; she thought she knew the answers. Then, she was also an unformed, frightened young woman. The simplest way to build herself up was to take the role of the more experienced performer. Although he seemed to encourage her looking after him, Bob eventually resented it. This contradiction constantly put him at loggerheads with others, except for those rare few who could deal with him on totally equal grounds. Yet for all he resented Joan's mothering, he seemed to need her, for a while. That night, Dylan was nearly swallowed by the Old Left. He had not yet defined where he was himself. Seeger was leaving that month for his year-long world trip and Bob had duly paid his respects at a Carnegie Hall reception after Pete's farewell concert.

Dylan's own natural senses told him to accept Joan's invitation to stay with her in Carmel that autumn. He probably still loved Suze, but she had decided to move out of West Fourth Street that summer. It was a break, but not yet the end. Bob still thought he could balance things. I had visited Joan, her sister Mimi, her brother-in-law Dick Fariña, and her mother Joan in Carmel only a few weeks before Dylan arrived. We had watched a report on the August 28 March on Washington. That day, Martin Luther King, Jr enunciated his eloquent dream. Dylan, Joan, Odetta, Peter, Paul and Mary, Belafonte, Mahalia, and 200,000 peaceful marchers had lifted their voices in support.

Joan was waiting for her new home to be built in Carmel Valley, and was living in a modest, modern, wood-beamed cottage, nestled in a secluded brush-covered ravine less than a mile from the Pacific. Glass walls brought the countryside right into the spacious living room, dotted with modern sculpture, benches, and casual chairs. I had a preview of the serenity that Dylan was to find there, a repose that put New York tensions a million miles behind. Carmel and the Big Sur was a land of craggy coastlines and wind-twisted cypresses—Robinson Jeffers country. There, that hermit poet had found his setting, the detached hills like those where ancient Chinese poets wrote. At Joan's place, in autumn 1963, as Dylan had his first sojourn in peaceful country, he wrote, his first withdrawal song, "Lay Down Your Weary Tune," inspired by a recording of a Scottish ballad. "What good are fans?" Dylan asked me just before he headed west. "You can't eat applause for breakfast. You can't sleep with it," he said, after three months of stardom, ready for the simpler country life.

Carmel was the Bakersfield he had dreamed of. Not far north was Steinbeck's Cannery Row in Monterey, and the lettuce fields of Salinas. The district became Dylan's "East of Eden," perhaps even beyond his "Gates of Eden." Under Joan's attentive eyes, he put himself into a disciplined schedule. In the past, chaos and urgency where his stimuli to creativity. Now it was serenity. He could turn day into day again and night into night. Down from Joan's cottage was a deserted beach cove, which they could reach in ten minutes in her sports car or in half an hour's walk. There he loved to swim and ponder the Pacific. He could set up his typewriter in her house and work in the morning while Joan, fearful of intruding, left him to himself. He had the first intimations of the peace he would find again four years later with another dark-haired woman in the countryside.

"I tried to get Bobby to look after his health," Joan told me later. "I tried to get him to cut down on his smoking and to brush his teeth and all of that," she said. When pressed in 1966 as to what Dylan really meant to her, she grew dark and thoughtful. Maybe she still wasn't ready to evaluate what had happened. Choosing words carefully, she said, with a touch of tartness: "He is a complicated, problematic, difficult person. I see Bobby with a slightly damaged diamond in his head. More fragile than the average person. When I was sitting and watching him play, how easily he could be blown apart by a comment or by something passing. But you never know that he feels these things, because he's very good at covering all that up. For some reason, in my opinion, he wants to relieve himself of all responsibility. Any responsibility, about anybody, it seems to me. To barely get by with what people have to offer. If you don't really care about yourself, then you don't have to care about anybody else. He is terribly, terribly bright, with a funny magnet inside him that makes you drawn to him. I mean, I love Bobby, and I would do anything for him, ever. Whatever went wrong between us, I really don't know. I don't know how Bobby feels about me. It obviously can't matter."

I reported that Bob had said little about her aside from matters professional. Joan replied: "Wow, he really keeps it in there, doesn't he? Well, actions scream, and so do his songs. It's just fantastic that he won't admit it. I'm not pompous enough to say that anything was written because of me. But it sure is hard to think otherwise when I hear some of the lyrics, and then I wonder." I looked down at Joan's Egyptian ring. "Is that a little gift from a pharaoh in Cairo?" Joan laughed: "Yes, it's the funniest thing. The fact of the matter is that … Well, that's supposed to be a secret. Anyway, it's in the song. I have only the feeling that I wish that Bobby would be all right. I feel he is killing himself. I feel Bobby could have tremendous power for social good, but he could also have tremendous power to take a lot of people down in the hole that he's in, to coin a phrase. I've already asked him too many things. Even questions about his songs seemed to be imposing on something that he just didn't want to be bothered with. The split between us came on a professional level, but it made things clear in my head about what I wanted to do. At one point in our little scene," Joan continued, "when we were still doing concerts together … although I was enjoying those concerts, I froze up and said to him: 'Bobby, you'd be doing it as rock 'n' roll king, but I'd be doing it as peace queen.' And he was not even rock 'n' roll king then yet, but I just had the feeling he would be soon."

Joan's path was so clearly one of social commitment that nothing would swerve her. Dylan and his songs had helped her find that path, but she wouldn't follow him on any detour. She had to criticize him for leaving the one true way: "There is nothing wrong with social criticism," she said, "except that he criticizes society and I criticize it, but he ends up saying there is not a goddamned thing you can do about it, so screw it. And I say just the opposite. I am afraid the message that comes through from Dylan in 1965 and 1966 is: let's all go home and smoke pot, because there's nothing else to do. We might as well go down smoking. That's where our ways part."

Even though we were discussing Dylan and his world view when he was not actively committed politically, Joan thought that, beneath it all, Dylan was still concerned: "I do think he was really as involved with civil rights, peace, and all the things he appeared to be involved with much more than he would ever like to say." Why, then, did he change in 1964? Was he forced into changing? "No. I don't think he wants the responsibility for anybody, including himself. I just think that Bobby would prefer to be exempt. Period. Exempt from everything that matters. I think he is often trying to say that *nothing* matters. Bobby and I are just direct opposites. It took me a long time to figure it out. I feel that everything has to matter, however difficult it may be. I don't think you can kid yourself into thinking that nothing does matter. Bobby is very, very bright. He can put up a good argument about that."

Joan was often self-righteously critical about Bob's life-style, or death-style, of 1965–66: "Life is what you make it. The way he lives is enough of a bad show. I love the way I live, which is not that bad." Didn't all poets tend to destroy themselves? "I can't answer that," Joan said, but her guru, pacifist educator Ira Sandperl, jumped in: "There are a lot of real poets who have not destroyed themselves. There is Wallace Stevens and e e cummings. I don't think that the poet is always self-destructive." Joan believed pop stars needn't be gobbled up by the pressures of fame. Because she had made her own peace then, spiritually and psychoanalytically, she felt that any star could do the same. "I am giving up concerts for the rest of 1966," she continued. "As to what you call 'the tyranny of the mob,' I have a theory that you can be mobbed if you want to be, if you act a certain way, and you have a press agent. I find I can hide out at the Earle Hotel in the Village and not be bothered all that much." Baez talked about the dangers of "the rat-race, of having to make more money each year, keeping up a public image." She also recalled that somebody had once told her "you sing well when you're in love."

The long, uneven, public and private affair between Bob and Joan was uncommonly complex. Not even they knew what was happening to them. Dylan seemed flattered by her interest and "protection." He had found so little order or calm with Suze that Joan offered the promise of at least a brief escape from the chaos that "accepted" him. Whatever prior experience Joan had as a performer, Bob knew a lot more about music than she did. In an article for *Mademoiselle*, Richard Fariña recalled that in January 1963, before knowing her, Dylan had criticized Joan for lack of contemporary substance in her song choice. "It ain't nothin' just to walk around an' sing," Dylan told Fariña when they were in London. "Take Joanie, man, she's still singin' about Mary Hamilton. I mean, where's that at? She's walked around on picket lines, she's got all kinds of feeling, so why ain't she steppin' out?"

By the end of 1967, Joan had served two terms in jail for "steppin' out" on anti-war protests and was soon to marry a draft-resistance leader. By then, Dylan was looking at things both more mundane and more transcendental. Turning the tables, Joan was then condemning him for lack of social commitment, although she came to understand that his commitment was expressing itself along other lines.

Dylan's attitude toward Joan changed sharply by the end of 1963. She had a short attention span, but so did he. I doubt that, as Baez has said, it was ever a question of his thinking about marriage and her rejecting the idea. Perhaps there was just too much self-doubt, ego, and narcissism under one roof in Carmel. When passionate love ended, professional admiration survived. At times, that too became strained. Years later, Dylan sounded a bit patronizing: "I feel bad for her because she has, nobody to ask, she has nobody to turn to that's going to be straight with her. Ira Sandperl may be straight with her about her school [the Institute for the Study of Non-Violence] but when she is going to make a record, I mean, how can he be straight with her? She has nobody. Hey, you know, I'll tell you who I dig in her family—Joan's mother. Man, Joan's mother is just groovy. She really is a very knowing person. She sees everything. Her sister Pauline is groovy. You know, Bob, about Joan, I could never really *talk* to Joan. I clammed up. Like we made the concert tours, but I wouldn't talk to her.

"Now, me and Joan had this thing. It wasn't a thing at first. It was just that she was getting a kick outta having me come up on stage—baggy elephant me—and sing my songs, which nobody had ever heard before. And her audiences, which are just like pieces of wheat, anyway, when they heard my songs, they were just flabbergasted. Joan brought me up, man. She recorded my songs and she was as important on that level as Peter, Paul and Mary. They are the only ones in the folk-song field I would give my songs to." He undoubtedly learned from Baez. He made some of his most candid comments in the long prose-poem on *Joan Baez in Concert, Part 2*, released in March 1964. In a fine piece of page writing, he mixed childhood memories with Joan's, showing how he learned a new concept of beauty from her. Previously, he had been able to say what Joan meant to him in songs only, a dozen classic songs.

At one point, Dylan said that he didn't feel Baez merited much mention in any book about him. As unbelievable as that is, when Joan's book *Daybreak* was submitted, there was no reference to Dylan. I asked her editor, Ed Doctorow of Dial Press, who later wrote *Ragtime*, about that. In early 1968, he told her that she just couldn't write a whole book about herself leaving Dylan out completely. Joan added a brief passage, entitled "The Dada King," which was a put-down, lovingly talking of his charm, although she never mentioned his name. "A bizarre liar screaming into the electric microphones under the bright bright lights … He was a huge transparent bubble of ego." The passage ended with loving benevolence: "Listen, God, look closely after him. He's more fragile than most people and, besides, I love him. I 'also keep the cards that read 'Have Mercy on his soul.'"[9]

Of course, Joan had a lot more to say about Dylan than that, and she said it down the years in many eloquent ways. In a stunning, two-disk album, *Any Day Now*, which she recorded in Nashville with musicians Dylan had used a year earlier on *John Wesley Harding*, her interpretations were deep and affecting; her involvement with the songs and their composer was obvious. As early as 1963, she had told Bob she wanted to record and album of his songs and when *Any Day Now* was released in January 1969, she told a *New York Times* reporter:

Whether or not he decides to join forces with the human race, he's a genius. Something of Bobby will survive in history … When someone is that much of a mystic and genius, you have to get an insight from listening to anything he's written … I just can't sing his nasty, hateful, ugly songs; I can appreciate the honesty of them, and melodically they're good, but I can't sing them … I was also spoiled by Dylan. When we were closest, I loved all the songs he was turning out … I took all his songs—about a hundred of them—spread them out on the floor, put the ones I thought I'd like on the music stand, and just started singing.

At that time, Joan hadn't spoken to Dylan for perhaps two years. Her all-Dylan album was a letter to an old lover, telling him that she still loved him and his writing, even though that love worked better for her at a distance. From neither Dylan nor Baez, and certainly no observer or friend, can there be a *final* word on their relationship. Their most serious rupture came in England in spring 1965, and lasted years, even after *Any Day Now*. Yet they somehow managed to pick up the threads, well into the 1980s. Joan told me at meetings in London in 1980 and 1982 of her contact with Dylan. She told the world about it in her finest song, "Diamonds and Rust," on the 1975 album of that name. Joan seemed to have, if not a love-hate relationship with him, then the very strong ambivalence that would touch the borderlines of love and hate. She went along with the filming of *Renaldo and Clara*, even though she was embarrassed at how she looked in it. Whenever Joan talked to me about him, she would do the full-scale mimicry of his gestures, slang, smoking, phrasing. It was funny, and yet somehow sad, as if it were the only way she could gain mastery over this impossible, elusive man.

More important is how their work and outlooks were affected by each other. Again, it is not easy to sort out, although the songs of Dylan I attach to Joan are discussed often in this book. When Joan said to me in 1966: "He can say it, but I can't write, but I wish I could," she was forecasting a future direction for herself. That "Diamonds and Rust" is her finest song, and that she continues to perform it so widely and so well, speaks more than any random comment she might have made in praise or criticism of him. I felt her 1971 song "To Bobby," was naive and childlike, almost pleading for him to play the savior — a role he had long ago discarded. After the Rolling Thunder tour, Joan's tempo of songwriting quickened. On the *Gulf Winds* album, "Sweeter for Me," "Oh, Brother!" and "Time is Passing Us By" are all clearly, I think, directed to or influenced by Dylan. Joan could also say things in a song she could never bring herself to say about Dylan to friends.

Love relationships are problematic enough, let alone those in the public gaze. Joan changed down the years, admitting even in song how self-righteous she had been back in the 1960s. Finally, she could admit to her mistakes and a posture toward him that was too judgmental too early, too unrelenting for too long. For either of them to pretend that their twenty-year relationship was not important was just window dressing, for the public and for their own pride. They haunted each other down the years much as they haunted their fans.

Originally, way back in 1963–64, they may have grown apart because no roof could contain two such bubbles of ego. Two lead singers can't always harmonize. Back then, they were still too preoccupied with defining themselves as individuals to have found a consistency as a couple. Perhaps it's just too uncomfortable to make love on a pedestal. It's probably easier to love an idol at a distance.

"I Am My Words." Dylan's illusions about stardom, if any, began to dissipate within three months of Newport. His disillusionment showed in his shifting attitude toward the press. Dylan's news-making instincts were both natural and self-taught. He did not get much advice on press relations from Grossman, who did not hire a full-time press aide until 1968, after he had been a manager for nearly a decade. Until then, Grossman's press relations were handled by his partner, John Court, Charlie Rothschild, record companies, or the artists themselves. The Monterey Festival taught Dylan how wounding the printed word could be. First came Gleason's. criticism; then *Time*, on May 31, 1963, was truculent:

who can believe him? ... Hard-lick guitar, whooping harmonica, skinny little voice. Beardless chin ... porcelain pussy-cat eyes ... he looks 14, and his accent belongs to a jive Nebraskan, or maybe a Brooklyn Hillbilly. He is a dime-store philosopher, a drugstore cowboy, a men's room conversationalist ... something faintly ridiculous about such a citybilly, yet Dylan is the newest hero of an art that has made a fetish out of authenticity ... At its very best, his voice sounds as if it were drifting over the walls of a tuberculosis sanitarium — but that's part of the charm ... something unique to say, and he says it in ... the best songs of their style since Woody Guthrie's ... An atmosphere of ersatz surrounds him ...

After Newport, smart-aleck comments subsided; the folk press was uniformly elegiac. New York *Broadside* continued its hosannas, Boston *Broadside* featured Dylan and Joan on one cover, and, within two months, Bob alone on another. Rhapsodic praise came in the October-November *Sing Out!* which hailed the work of "Bob Dylan, touching the nerve centers of our own time with the measureless flights of the poet who speaks for his generation." On September 12, 1963, Sidney Fields of the New York *Mirror* reported Dylan's comment: "But I didn't want to see the atomic bathrooms and electronic bedrooms and souped-up can-openers; I wanted to watch and feel the people and the dust and ditches and the fields and fences." He elaborated: "Because Dickens and Dostoyevsky and Woody Guthrie were telling their stories much better than I ever could," Dylan says, "I decided to stick to my own mind."

Dylan was both more direct and more fanciful in a New York *Daily News* spread on October 20, 1963, headlined MUSIC WITH A MESSAGE: TODAY'S ANGRY YOUNG MEN DON'T MAKE SPEECHES — THEY BUY GUITARS AND BECOME FOLK SINGERS. Wrote Michael Iachetta:

"Why are we in the midst of a folk music boom?" asked Dylan ... "Because the times cry for the truth ... and people want to hear the truth and that's just what they're hearin' in good folk music today ... When I listen to people talk, all I hear is what they're not tellin' me. "There's mystery, magic, truth, and the Bible in great folk music. I can't hope to touch that. But I'm goin' to try."

Still building his rootless runaway character, Dylan let the press magnify the image. He never said he was misquoted by the *National Guardian* on August 22, 1963, but he chafed at this article, which categorized him as a spokesman for the Old Left:

Dylan utilizes the most trenchant weapons at his command—a poetic imagination and contempt for injustice—to denounce those who want to run it for him, whether they hide behind a KKK hood or a stockmarket ticker. "I don't think when I write," he said. "I just react and put it down on paper. I'm serious about everything I write. For instance, I get mad when I see friends of mine sitting in Southern jails, getting their heads beat in. What comes out in my music is to call for action."

The *National Guardian* extracted his capsule comments on major issues:

Capitalism? "Well, I object to somebody riding around in a Cadillac when somebody else is lying in the gutter." Socialism? "I'd like to visit Russia some day; see what it's like, maybe meet a Russian girl." United States? "Ain't nobody can say anything honest in the United States. Every place you look is cluttered with phoneys and lies." Politics? "No, I'm not gonna vote because there's nobody to vote for; nobody that looks like me, the way I feel ... I'd like to see a government made up of people like Bertrand Russell, Jim Forman, Marlon Brando and people like that ..."

In Mississippi, he says, "there's a feeling in the air. More people are willing to say: 'To hell with my security, I want my rights.' I want to help them if I can. They really dig my music down there, too."

The piece marked the beginning of Dylan's exasperation with the press. After his painstaking image-building, publications beyond his command were now tailoring his image. He felt he was being pushed, as Guthrie had been, into being a troubadour of the Old Left, a puppet laureate who would respond on call with a song for each cause. He tried to pull back from the messianic role followers were thrusting at him, asking him to speak not only for the young folkniks but for youth in general. Suze empathized with Bob's struggle for ideological independence. What Baez later oversimplified as Dylan's "retreat from responsibility" was considerably more complex. Dylan did not want his every word carved in stone, even though he sometimes seemed to walk around with a mallet and chisel in his pocket.

I asked Suze why Bob appeared to be souring on the Left: "I don't think he really soured on it, I think he always saw things personally. The Left opened a door to him, but he just saw more little boxes behind the door, factions that wanted something else from him. I remember just how he felt when he read that *National Guardian* story. It all came out as 'Our Spokesman.' Even then, he didn't want that. Everybody does that when they write something—they turn it around to fit for them. Dylan wasn't Joe Hill then, or ever, and he did not want to be Joe Hill, then or ever. That kind of stuff turned him off."

Carla Rotolo: "The Irwin Silbers of *Sing Out!* were smashing him up against the wall. *Sing Out!* had found in Dylan a prophet for its cause. Bobby was twenty-two then. How, in God's name, could he have the answers? But the messiah-makers told him that he 'had' the answers, and soon they began to believe that he really did. That was the turning point for Dylan. He became the hard, all-knowing, bitter kid. During August and September, 1963, he was really frightened, and Suze saw it and understood it. Part frightened, and part laughing at the messiah-makers and at himself."

At summer's end, Suze moved out of West Fourth Street again. She needed to be alone. Meanwhile, Dylan had a major solo concert at Carnegie Hall, and suffered a trauma with the press. Billy James and John Kurland of Columbia publicity had approached *Newsweek* about a cover story. A *Newsweek* researcher, Andrea Svedberg, was impressed with the Baez-Dylan Forest Hills concert. Then Svedberg telephoned Billy in annoyance, saying she was having trouble reaching Dylan or Grossman. Billy: "She said they were very interested in determining certain things about Dylan's past. I tried to tell her that Bobby didn't like to talk about such things. I told her to let it lay."

The story, on November 4, 1963, turned into a hatchet job that threw Dylan into a depression for months; resulted in him breaking off nearly all contact with his parents and brother for years; interrupted his relationship with Billy James; drove Grossman further into his paranoid distrust of the press; embarrassed *Newsweek*, and led to a new era of tortuous relations between the musician and the media. Dylan turned from an accessible subject into a cagey game-player who toyed with interview questions, who developed the outrageous "anti-interview," saying shocking, even deleterious things, things he often didn't believe. He became dubious that even the emerging underground press could understand him.

The *Newsweek* story appeared, under the headline "I AM MY WORDS." The adjectives were abrasive: "unscrubbed face ... bewildered-hair ... skinny frame ... hip talk, punctuated with obscenities.

His singing voice scratches and shouts so jarringly that his success, at first, seems incredible … his knack for stirring audiences is unmistakable." Attributed to the words of his 200 songs: "simple words that pounce upon the obvious." Admitting that "Dylan is practically a religion," the article challenged his believability:

He has suffered; he has been hung up, man, without bread, without a chick, with twisted wires growing inside him … his audiences share his pain, and seem jealous because they grew up in conventional homes and … schools. The ironic thing is that Bob Dylan, too, grew up in a conventional home, and went to conventional schools. He shrouds his past in contradictions, but he is the elder son of a Hibbing, Minn, appliance dealer named Abe Zimmerman …

"Dig it, man": Dylan admits he was born in Duluth and raised in Hibbing, but … he denied that Bob Dylan was ever Bobby Zimmerman. "Dig my draft card, man," he said. "Bob Dylan." (He changed his name legally on August 9, 1962.) His parents? "I don't know my parents," he said. "They don't know me. I've lost contact with them for years." A few blocks away, in one of New York's motor inns, Mr and Mrs Abe Zimmerman … were looking forward to seeing their son sing at Carnegie Hall. Bobby had paid their way east and had sent them tickets, they had told friends in Minnesota. "He was home a few days in August," said David Zimmerman, Bobby's 17-year-old brother. "We were kind of close. We're both kind of ambitious. When we set out to do something, we usually get it done. He set out to become what he is." "My past is so complicated, you wouldn't believe it, man," said Dylan. "Bobby is hard to understand," said David Zimmerman.

The Image: Why Dylan—he picked the name in admiration for Dylan Thomas—should bother to deny his past is a mystery. Perhaps he feels it would spoil the image he works so hard to cultivate … There is even a rumor circulating that Dylan did not write "Blowin' in the Wind" … Dylan says he is writing a book that will explain everything. But, he insists, the explanations are irrelevant. "I am my words," he says.

The article was illustrated with a photo of Dylan recording, above the caption "Bob Dylan: What's in a name?" The "exposure" of his family was bad enough, but the imputation that he had stolen "Blowin' in the Wind" was the *coup de grace*. He lashed out at Billy James for having suggested the piece. He sniped at his parents for talking to Walter Eldot, not only for *Newsweek* but also for the equally irritating piece in the *Duluth News-Tribune* of October 11, 1963. Finally, Dylan blamed Grossman, who had unsuccessfully tried to bargain an interview in exchange for final approval.

Nothing was revealed. Grossman's lawyers indicated that there was a seven-year statute on limitations of libel regarding the rumor about "Wind." Grossman later began to realize the drawbacks in his surly attitude toward the press. In 1968, he invited *Newsweek*'s music editor, Hubert Saal, to Woodstock to interview Dylan. After the death of Janis Joplin, Albert even said a few words to the magazine.

I spoke to Dylan within an hour of his reading the *Newsweek* article. I was doing a story for *Hootenanny*. Bob was nearly screaming: "You want to interview me? All right, you can interview me, but I'm sticking to my friends from here on in. Just wait till you read that piece in *Newsweek*. No, I won't read it to you. Read it for yourself and then you'll know why Joan told me not to even talk to *Time* and *Newsweek*. *Time* [cover story of November 23, 1962] screwed up Joan's head for a year, and now it's my turn. I've got over five thousand pages written of all sorts of things, poems and plays and a novel. I just want to be known for what I do." Dylan exploded with anger. It was clear to me that this was not so much concerned with journalistic integrity as with a feeling that he had been denuded in a sphere that essentially had nothing to do with his performing or songwriting.

I once asked Joan why, if the *Time* story had so disturbed her, she had never tried to rebut it: "Talking about *Time* magazine, the things that upset you are the things they say about you that are true, or partly true. They said that I had bare feet, stringy hair, and rode about in an open car. They put it in a terrible way, but those things are true, so why bother to rebut it?" (Much later, she wrote and recorded "Time Rag," flaying the magazine.)

Dylan decided not to rebut *Newsweek* directly. After a concert in Boston, he went underground for three weeks, spending time with the Van Ronks and Barry Kornfeld. Grossman bought Bob a few books by Martin Buber, the Jewish philosopher, as a peace offering. During his retreat, Dylan read Buber, mused sullenly, wrote like a flood tide. He would face the press again, but his words often formed curious conundrums. Dylan and the *Chicago Daily News* in November 1965:

CDN: *Will you sing any of the so-called folk-rock music?*

Dylan: *No, it's not folk rock, it's just instruments ... I call it the mathematical sound, sort of Indian music. I can't really explain it ... I was playing rock 'n' roll when I was 13 or 14 and 15, but I had to quit when I was 16 or 17 because I just couldn't make it that way ...*

CDN: *Why did you give up the folk sound?*

Dylan*: I've been on too many other streets to just do that ... the real folk never see Forty-second Street; they've never ridden an airplane ...*

CDN: *You talk as if you are terribly separated from people.*

Dylan: *I'm not disconnected from anything because of a force, just habit. It's just the way I am ... I don't know, I have no idea that it's easier to be disconnected than to be connected. I've got a huge hallelujah for all the people who're connected ... I've been connected so many times. Things haven't worked out right, so rather than break myself up, I just don't get connected ...*

CDN: *Do you avoid close relationships with people?*

Dylan: *I have relationships with people. People like me, also disconnected; there are a lot of disconnected people. I don't feel alienated or disconnected or afraid. I don't feel there's any kind of organization of disconnected people. I just can't go along with any kind of organization. Someday I might find myself all alone in a subway car, stranded when the lights go out, with forty people, and I'll have to get to know them. Then I'll just do what has to be.*

Even the hippest reporters had to cope with Dylan's ironies. On March 25, 1965, Jack Goddard of the *Village Voice* wrote from Woodstock:

Dylan ... had consented to answer all those deep, meaningful, searching questions he's been bombarded with ... for years. The following ... took place between Dylan and the large numbers of newsmen on hand:

VV: *Who did you write songs like before [Woody Guthrie]?*

Dylan: *Ever hear of Gene Vincent? Buddy Holly?*

VV: *Then you had a rock and roll band in high school?*

Dylan: *I had a banana band in high school.*

VV: *So then you heard of Guthrie and he changed your life?*

Dylan: *Then I heard of Josh White ...*

VV: *Then you heard of Guthrie ...*

Dylan: *Then I heard about those riots in San Francisco ...*

VV: *The HUAC riots?*

Dylan: *An' I missed out on meeting James Dean so I decided to meet Woody Guthrie.*

VV: *Was he your greatest influence?*

Dylan: *For a spell the idea of him affected me quite much.*

VV: *What about Brecht? Read much of him?*

Dylan: *No. But I've read him.*

VV: *Rimbaud?*

Dylan: *I've read his little tiny book, Evil Flowers.*

VV: *You're thinking of Baudelaire.*

Dylan:: *Yes. I've read his tiny little book, too.*

VV: *How about Hank Williams? Do you consider him an influence?*

Dylan:: *Hey, look, I consider Hank Williams, Captain Marvel, Marlon Brando, the Tennessee Stud, Clark Kent, Walter Cronkite, and J Carroll Naish all influences ...*

VV: *Tell us about your movie.*

Dylan: *It's gonna be in black and white.*

VV: *Will it be in the Andy Warhol style?*

Dylan: *Who's Andy Warhol? Listen, my movie will be ... in the style of the early Puerto Rican films.*

VV: *Who's writing it?*

Dylan: *Allen Ginsberg. I'm going to rewrite it.*

VV: *Who will you play in the film?*

Dylan: *The Hero.*

VV: *Who is that going to be?*
Dylan: *My mother ...*
VV: *Bob, do you have any philosophy about life and death? About death?*
Dylan: *How do I know, I haven't died yet. Hey you're insulting me all to shit ...*
VV: *What goes on between you and Joan Baez that doesn't meet the eye?*
Dylan: *She's my fortune-teller.*
VV: *Bobby, we know you changed your name. Come on now, what's your real name?*
Dylan: *Philip Ochs. I'm gonna change it back again when I see it pays ...*
VV: *Bob, what about the situation of American poets. Kenneth Rexroth has estimated that since 1900 about thirty American poets have committed suicide.*
Dylan: *Thirty poets! What about American housewives, mailmen, street cleaners, miners? Jesus Christ, what's so special about thirty people that are called poets? I've known some very good people that have committed suicide. One didn't do nothing but work in a gas station all his life. Nobody referred to him as a poet, but if you're gonna call people like Robert Frost a poet, then I got to say this gas station boy was a poet, too.*
VV: *Bob, we understand you're writing a book.*
Dylan: *Yeah, it's a funny book. I think it's coming out by spring.*
VV: *What's it about?*
Dylan: *Angels.*
VV: *... don't you have any important philosophy for the world?*
Dylan: *I don't drink hard liquor, if that's what you mean.*
VV: *No. The world in general. You and the world?*
Dylan: *Are you kidding? The world don't need me. Christ, I'm only five feet ten. The world could get along fine without me. Don'tcha know, everybody dies. It don't matter how important you think you are. Look at Shakespeare, Napoleon. Edgar Allan Poe, for that matter. They're all dead, right?*
VV: *Well, Bob, in your opinion, then, is there one man who can save the world?*
Dylan: *Al Aronowitz.*

Each reporter who got a "rare" interview hoped he or she alone would persuade the sphinx to take the sand out of his mouth. Stuart Crump of the *Brown* (University) *Daily Herald*, left an interview saying, "The result can resemble a farce as much as an interview." Wrote Crump:

When I handed him a copy of his third record album and [asked for his] autograph, he drew a beard and mustache on his own picture, and then signed it ... I asked him to define the blues. He said: "The blues is a pair of pants without any pockets. Do you like that? ... The blues is a pair of torn pants without anything in the pockets." He added: "Blues is a color. That's all." "What do you consider is your place in American folk music?" "I'm not a folk singer any more than anybody is." As he climbed into the car he hollered out, much to the delight of some three or four dozen fans: "Folk singers are Communists."

"What do you think will happen to you as you grow older ... and the upcoming generations (our children) find their own leaders?" Dylan replied ... a little more seriously: "I dig the new generation ... Soon the new generation will rebel against me just like I rebelled against the older generation ... There's nothing so stable as change. I think those are the words ... I try to think about my own life. Important things, like my head. I worry about my head. Not the commercialization of folk music! ...

"Folk singers don't eat enough mushrooms. I think that unless they get on the mushrooms, they're all going to go to waste. They're all going to turn into Harry Belafontes." "Anything else?" "Also frog legs!"

Dylan was quite impartial about whose journalistic leg he pulled. When *McCall's* asked him what sort of beauty he revered in women, he replied: "Dirt on women is very attractive. It triggers the animal emotions. I want dirty long hair hanging all over the place. I hate shaven legs or arms. I hate cleaning and astringent lotions, because those antiseptic smells revolt me." Dylan's refuge in sarcasm, irony, and verbal ploys sent coded messages to the initiates. It was diplomats' mumbo jumbo, poets' veils, Aesop's fables, jokes within jokes, revealing while concealing. "I am my words," he told *Newsweek*, but they didn't believe him. "'There is nothing so stable as change,'" he told a college editor. Was anybody listening?

Just a Voice Singing.   Amid all the offstage turmoil of 1963, Dylan gave solo concerts at Carnegie Hall, Philadelphia's Town Hall, and Boston's Jordan Hall. He carried off all three like a pro. In Boston on November 2, after *Newsweek*, he showed some signs of being rattled.

The Carnegie concert was singular in that "teenyboppers" surfaced. Previously, folk audiences dressed and acted differently than pop audiences. The second Beatles single, "Please, Please Me," was a hit in Britain in February 1963. Beatlemania erupted by October, just about the time the first wave of Dylanmania hit America. The Carnegie audience was younger, more exuberant and unruly than Kingston Trio fans had been. This wasn't a folk-campfire crowd. Dylan churned up his listeners. The folk Old Guard was caught off-guard by this entertainer and haranguer. He moved through about twenty songs: "Hattie Carroll," "Oxford Town," "Hero Blues," and, of course, "Talkin' John Birch" ("Here's a song they wouldn't let me sing on TV.") He had arrived as a moralist. Dylan spoke more than he had since Gerde's. He used stage center to lambast Fabian, soap commercials on TV, *Hootenanny*, censorship in general. In a caustic remark, which few could fathom, he hit out at that rumor-mongering Rutgers teacher who, he said, didn't even know what the phrase "blowin' in the wind" meant.

Dylan still had not conquered all critics. In *Variety*, Leonard L Levinson conceded that "Dylan was the voice of the future … But … the future holds nothing but complaints of the past and the present … Nowhere … one word of hope or remedy … Dylan's numbers vied with each other in lugubriousity …" *Variety* was put off by a style of "writing and delivery … deliberately iggerunt [*sic*]. While several of his lyrics are well thought-out and effective, more are filled with sloppy rhymes, lack of basic literary discipline and an apparent willingness to settle for the first idea and form that entered the writer's head."

Not everyone in the audience was stirred either. A 16-year-old from Westport, Connecticut, Anne Lyons, wrote me that she had left after a half-hour. Paraphrasing "Hard Rain," she wrote: "I saw wealthy girls trying to look depraved; I saw boys with ascetic faces and boys with no faces. I saw people who looked like sheep and who acted like sheep. I saw tangles and tangles of hair. I was extremely glad that I was escorted by a boy with a tie and jacket on."

Leventhal gave a party later at his West 96th Street home for Dylan and friends, including a contingent of Suze's chums, then strong Castro supporters, and Ronnie Gilbert, a member of the Weavers since 1948. Ronnie told me: "Such passion! I've never heard such singing or such songs! It's more than just the topical movement, it's that Dylan is absolutely classic. He's in a class all by himself." The star was being toasted all around. Bob came over to me: "Well, man, you didn't think I could do it, did you?" I assured him I *had* thought he could do it, but he pushed right on: "Well, I did it, I did it!"

But with *Newsweek* his triumph soured. Somehow, amid all that intense work and limelight, Dylan began to lose his sense of whimsy, his youthfulness. Within a month, the assassination of President John F Kennedy on November 22 plunged America into a troubled depression. Although some of Dylan's Castroite friends took the assassination with detachment, Dylan was stunned. To criticize a society where bullets could strike down even the mightiest and wealthiest reformers seemed pointless. When the cover of *Esquire's* 1965 college issue showed a composite drawing of four student heroes—Kennedy, Malcolm X, Che Guevara, and Dylan—we thought Bob might one day join the other three in violent death. It squared with his adolescent death-hauntedness. Men of larger vision than Buddy Holly, Hank Williams, and James Dean were dying. It seemed that the God-like men were the ones to be crucified on earth. Meanwhile, the climate of opinion wanted to elevate Dylan to the role of a messiah who could lead American youth to salvation.

The concept of Dylan as messianic figure stretches far. In November 1970, this letter ran in *Melody Maker*, the British pop weekly, under the headline DYLAN IS THE NEW CHRIST, with a picture captioned "Dylan: Messiah": "Bob Dylan (and not, as previously reported, Jesus of Nazareth) is the living Messiah to today's young people … You can learn more about life from Dylan than from 10 Jesuses … Quote from Dylan: 'Being noticed can be a burden. Jesus got himself crucified because he got himself noticed. So I disappear a lot.'"—Ken Payne

Clark Foreman's Emergency Civil Liberties Committee held an annual fund-raising dinner marking Bill of Rights Day, and honored with its Tom Paine Award some public figure who, to them, epitomized the good fight for freedom and equality. In 1962, the ECLC gave the award to Lord Bertrand Russell. In 1968, the recipient was Dr Benjamin Spock. The choice in 1963 was Dylan, who felt it was more than he deserved because he had "only" written a few songs. He didn't want to be Joe Hill or Tom Paine. Nevertheless, he went to the dinner.

On December 13, 1963, Dylan began to drink too early. He saw the other dignitaries on the dais: Corliss Lamont, writer-educator, heir of the Lamont fortune; toastmaster John Henry Faulk; James Baldwin, the author, dressed in neat suit and tie. The politics were different, but this could have been his father's B'nai B'rith Lodge. Bob looked at the faces and gray or balding heads of about 1,500 Old Left burghers in new middle-class security and mellowed radicalism. Presented with the Tom Paine award, Dylan started to speak. He hadn't prepared, and his almost disembodied voice began a Dylan truth attack:

I haven't got any guitar, I can talk though. I want to thank you for the Tom Paine Award on behalf of everybody that went down to Cuba. First of all because they're all young and it's took me a long time to get young and now I consider myself young. And I'm proud of it. I'm proud that I'm young. And I only wish that all you people who are sitting out here today or tonight weren't here and I could see all kinds of faces with hair on their head and everything like that, everything leading to youngness, celebrating the anniversary when we overthrew the House Un-American Activities just yesterday—because you people should be at the beach. You should be ... swimming and ... just relaxing in the time you have to relax. [Laughter] It is not an old people's world. It has nothing to do with old people. Old people, when their hair grows out, they should go out. [Laughter] And I look down to see the people that are governing me and making my rules—and they haven't got any hair on their head—I get very uptight about it. [Laughter] And they talk about Negroes, and they talk about black and white. And they talk about colors of red and blue and yellow. Man, then I just don't see any colors at all when I look out ... I've never seen one history book that tells how anybody feels ... And it don't help me one little bit to look back. I wish sometimes I could have come in here in the 1930s like my first idol—used to have an idol, Woody Guthrie, who came in the 1930s. [Applause] But it has sure changed in the time Woody's been here and the time I've been here. It's not that easy anymore. People seem to have more fears ... There's no black and white, left and right to me anymore; there's only up and down and down is very close to the ground. And I'm trying to go up without thinking of anything trivial such as politics. They have got nothing to do with it. I'm thinking about the general people and when they get hurt. Now I want to accept this ... Tom Paine Award, from the Emergency Civil Liberties Committee. I want to accept it in my name, but I'm not really accepting it in my name and I'm not accepting it in any kind of group's name, any Negro group or any other kind of group. ... I was on the March on Washington up on the platform and I looked around at all the Negroes there and I didn't see any Negroes that looked like none of my friends. My friends don't wear suits. My friends don't have to wear any kind of thing to prove that they're respectable Negroes. My friends are my friends, and they're kind, gentle people if they're my friends. And I'm not going to try to push nothing over. [Applause] So, I accept this award on behalf of Phillip Luce [an ardent New Leftist who later turned on his radical friends], *who led the group to Cuba which all people should go down to Cuba. I don't see why anybody can't go to Cuba. I don't see what's going to hurt by going any place. I don't [see] what's going to hurt anybody's eyes to see anything. On the other hand, Phillip is a friend of mine who went to Cuba. I'll stand up and to get uncompromisable about it, which I have to be to be honest, I just got to be, as I got to admit that the man who shot President Kennedy, Lee Oswald, I don't know exactly where—what he thought he was doing, but I got to admit honestly that I, too—I saw some of myself in him. I don't think it would have gone—I don't think it could go that far. But I got to stand up and say I saw things that he felt in me—not to go that far and shoot. [Boos and hisses] You can boo, but booing's got nothing to do with it. It's a—I just, ah—I've got to tell you, man, it's Bill of Rights is free speech and* [Someone says to Dylan: "Time's about up"] *I just want to admit that I accept this Tom Paine Award in behalf of James Forman of the Students Non-Violent Coordinating Committee and the people on behalf of who went to Cuba. [Boos mixed with applause]*[10]

The audience buzzed. Had this kid really been saying that Oswald deserved sympathy, three weeks after the assassination? Had he called them outdated, bald, old men ready for the junk pile of history? As the fundraising proceeded, Foreman realized the enormity of his gaff. Contributions were grudging and pale. He was crushed. He had been opposed within the organization for putting Dylan in such an honored position and now the words of the nay-sayers were coming back to haunt him. The outraged, bald old men weren't going to dig deep for an organization that would let that kid speak with such disrespect. Geno Foreman, Clark's son, who died three years later in an accident, told me that the collection was $30,000 short of expectations, although his father later told Dylan the sum was $6,000.

As the repercussions broadened, Dylan realized the ECLC hadn't gotten his message at all. Bob had staged his own Bay of Pigs. Like Kennedy going to consult Eisenhower, Bob went to talk with Harold Leventhal, Guthrie's agent and Seeger's manager. Harold, in his fifties, bald and Old Left, told Dylan those old-timers, who now looked so prosperous and well fed, had been fighting most of their lives. Harold recounted the McCarthy era, when many of these people had been blacklisted, had scuffled for a living, yet had remained socially conscious. Dylan listened, then went to his typewriter. He sent the Emergency Civil Liberties Committee an open letter, which made the rounds of the group's leadership in mimeographed form. Dylan described his moodiness and how futile it was for anyone to try to say what he meant, something he couldn't even do himself. He was only a songwriter, not a public speaker.

He probably just should have said "thank you," Dylan wrote, but he felt more was expected. So, as if walking a plank or running in front of a car, he screamed a last song and jumped. He talked of Lee Oswald and that he was so tired of hearing that we all share the blame for every crime. He qualified his remarks about free travel and how he was sick of having everything interpreted for him by the mass media. He wanted to learn about things for himself.

Dylan wrote of his home country and that, despite the rumors, he was proud of his background and the bloodstreams in his roots. And how New York really made him feel reborn. He qualified his spoken remarks about old people and how much what they had done in the Thirties through the Fifties had affected what he was doing in the Sixties. Repeatedly, he underlined the fact that this was clarification, not apology. Dylan offered to return the beautiful award with Tom Paine's smile on it. He said he didn't know much about Tom Paine, but he would like to sing for him. Yes, he was proud of the award, but he'd give it back if he had to. He hadn't known that the purpose of the dinner was donations, and that his speech had cost the organizers money. He felt he owed the committee a moral debt. He offered to pay the bill, and said that, once again, he'd return to the road.

For him, Dylan continued, writing is motivated by a wish to keep from going mad, a thought too alarming for him to think about. Yes, it's a frightening world, he ended. He sent his love to those whom he knew at the committee. It's so hard to hate, so fatiguing and not even worth the trouble. He likened life to an open window, through which he had then to jump back. He called the letter "A Message."

The episode should have been resolved there. But about six months later, Nat Hentoff, profiling Dylan for the *New Yorker*, heard Bob describe the episode yet another way. When I later asked Bob if he felt accurately quoted, Bob said: "Basically that was what I said about the whole Tom Paine business." As Hentoff took notes, Dylan described the episode to an actor acquaintance from the Living Theater:

I'm not part of no Movement. If I was, I wouldn't be able to do anything else but be in "the Movement." I just can't have people sit around and make rules for me. I do a lot of things no Movement would allow ... I just can't make it with any organization. I fell into a trap ... when I agreed to accept the Tom Paine Award ... At the Americana Hotel! In the Grand Ballroom! As soon as I got there, I felt up-tight ... the people with me couldn't get in. They looked even funkier than I did ... I really got uptight. I began to drink. I ... saw a bunch of people who had nothing to do with my kind of politics. I looked down and I got scared. They were supposed to be on my side, but I didn't feel any connection with them. Here were these people who'd been all involved with the left in the Thirties, and now they were supporting civil rights drives. That's groovy, but they also had minks and jewels, and it was like they were giving their money out of guilt. I got up to leave, and they followed me and caught me. They told me I had to accept the award. When I got up to make my speech, I couldn't say anything by that time but what was passing through my mind. They'd been talking about Kennedy being killed, and Bill Moore and Medgar Evers and the Buddhist monks in Vietnam being killed. I had to say something about Lee Oswald. I told them I'd read a lot of his feelings in the papers, and I knew he was up tight. Said I'd been uptight, too, so I'd got a lot of his feelings. I saw a lot of myself in Oswald, I said, and I saw in him a lot of the times we're all living in. And, you know, they started booing. They looked at me like I was an animal. They actually thought I was saying it was a good thing Kennedy had been killed. That's how far out they are. I was talking about Oswald. And then I started talking about friends of mine in Harlem some of them junkies, all of them poor. And I said they need freedom as much as anybody else, and what's anybody doing for them? The chairman was kicking my leg under the table and I told him, "Get out of here." ... I was supposed to be ... a nice cat. I was supposed to say, "I appreciate your award and I'm a great singer and I'm a great believer in liberals, and you buy my records and I'll support your cause!" But I didn't, so I wasn't accepted that night. That's the cause of a lot of those chains I was talking about—people wanting to be alone ... what is it to be alone? I've been alone sometimes in front of three thousand people. I was alone that night ... You know, they were talking about Freedom Fighters that night. I've been in Mississippi, man. I know those people on another level besides civil rights campaigns. I know them as friends. Like Jim Forman, one of the heads of SNCC. I'll stand on his side any time. But those people that night were actually getting me to look at colored people as colored people. I tell you, I'm never going to have anything to do with any political organization again in my life. I might help a friend if he was campaigning for office. But I'm not going to be part of any organization. Those people at that dinner were the same as everybody else. They're doing their time. They're chained to what they're doing. The only thing is, they're trying to put morals and great deeds on their chains, but basically they don't want to jeopardize their positions. They got their jobs to keep. There's nothing there for me, and there's nothing there for the kind of people I hang around with. The only thing I'm sorry about is that I guess I hurt the collection at the dinner. I didn't know they were going to try to collect money after my speech. I guess I lost them a lot of money. Well, I offered to pay them whatever it was they figured they'd lost because of the way I talked. I told them I didn't care how much it was. I hate debts, especially moral debts. They're worse than money debts. [11]

Right after the *New Yorker* piece ran, Clark Foreman went into battle over the "unpaid debt." He wrote to Dylan on November 2, 1964:

Dear Bobby: Your profile in the New Yorker has caused several of our friends … to ask what bill I did send you. My answer has been that I was waiting to see if we couldn't make out without taking you up on your generous offer. Now I see we can't. As far as I can figure it, the damage to our collection resulting from the fact that many of our potential givers felt that you had insulted them, amounts to $6,000. If you are able to help us with that amount I think that any moral or financial debt will be squared.

A week later, Foreman wrote the *New Yorker*:

Your profile of Bob Dylan was very much in error in that part which dealt with … our Bill of Rights Dinner. It is not credible that he said the things which he is quoted as having said. They were so patently false that no amount of Beaujolais would have produced them. Aside from a moment of silent tribute to the recently assassinated President, there was no discussion of the subjects which are alleged to have caused Dylan to speak of Oswald. Neither the remarks of the toastmaster … nor the … only speaker ahead of Dylan, Mrs Cyrus Eaton, could possibly have made him, as the profile alleges, race conscious … it is hardly likely that Dylan would have been more sensitive to any such remarks than the final speaker, James Baldwin.

Hentoff riposted to Foreman:

The fact is that I quoted Mr Dylan exactly. And when I read him that passage on the phone to make sure that I had indeed been accurate, he had no change to suggest.

On November 20, Foreman wrote Hentoff again:

the remarks you attribute to Dylan about the other speakers are equally not credible, as you had the reason to know not only from the issue of Rights, which I sent you, but also from Dylan's own poem of explanation, which you seem to have ignored altogether. It would seem to me that you did it unconscionably, for by so doing you damaged not only Dylan and the New Yorker, but also the Emergency Civil Liberties Committee.

The scuffling between Foreman and Hentoff continued, Foreman wanting the debt Dylan owed the committee paid off. On November 9, 1964, Grossman made a friendly call to Foreman conveying Dylan's wish to give a benefit concert for the ECLC. The date of February 5, 1965, was set, and a contract signed, but soon John Court called to say Grossman was in Mexico and the February 5 date had to be scrapped because Dylan would be in Europe. According to Court, another date would be offered in the early spring. As spring arrived without a concert date, Foreman began to dun Dylan again. Writing Dylan on December 13, 1965, two years after the original brouhaha, Foreman quoted from the Dylan message: "Please send me my bill, etc … for money means very little t me." "Since then," Foreman snapped, "words, words, words — no concert, no cash. … As you can see from the enclosed statement we are trying to save the boys who don't want to fight in Vietnam. Money now is our greatest need."

The file wasn't closed until May 15, 1968, when Edith Tiger of the ECLC wrote Grossman to say that Foreman was leaving civil liberties work and that a farewell party was being planned, "a sort of cultural festival and buffet lunch at Lamont's place in Ossining … I am sure that you would want to inform Bobby Dylan about this occasion. His association with Dr Foreman has been a close and valuable one. Therefore, I feel that he would like to be present to thank this man for his great contribution to society and all of us." Penciled on the carbon copy of this final letter: "Did not receive an answer."

The episode was gradually forgotten, along with the night in August 1963 when Dylan had sat restively in Foreman's apartment, listening to Foreman's and Faulk's homilies. As Joan hovered around lovingly, the two old battlers had told Dylan never to fear to speak his mind; never, never to shrink from telling any audience anywhere just what he thought. Four months after Dylan had had his weapons of truth sharpened by Foreman and Faulk, he inadvertently turned those weapons on those who had helped arm him. Yet his "message" proved that he was incapable of being just an unruly taunter of the old. He had learned what he once advised me: "You don't have to put something down to leave it." He was wrestling with a major dichotomy: although he could communicate with millions through his songs, he found it virtually impossible to communicate in other ways. Despite his gift of words and vision, he had to admit that the only way he could truly communicate was with his typewriter and his guitar.

All Kinds of Me. Late fall and winter of 1963 found Dylan at low ebb. Just when he deserved to be savoring the fruits of his success, he was swallowing the drugs of despair. Partly it was the let-down many stars experience right after they have made it. Until new goals replace old ones, there's an anticlimax. He was also burdened by the general malaise that clouded America after the assassination. Dylan knew that nearly every day in the South, obscure black people were being shot, beaten, intimidated, harassed. His despair was deepened by increasing loneliness: Suze had moved out and their relationship had become miserable. Suze became suicidal. All his "famiousity," as he called it, didn't spell happiness. He sat alone in his dingy West Fourth Street hole, pouring out his songs and his back pages.

Suze first moved in with Carla, on Perry Street; then she found a place at 106 Avenue B. Bob stayed there often, but it wasn't the same. Frictions between Bob and Suze were exacerbated by Carla and Mary Rotolo. Carla suggested that she and Bob shift apartments, but he still wanted to keep his own place. He brought Suze gifts, like expensive art books. Some nights they sat staring at TV, saying virtually nothing. Carla told me that as Dylan grew famous, Suze grew vegetable-like. She was still fighting for her own identity, sampling art schools and various jobs.

Around Christmas, 1963, everyone tried to bury that dying year. On Christmas Eve, there was a dinner at Mrs Rotolo's in New Jersey. Among the guests was Virginia Eggleston, one of the few at the Paine Award dinner who had actually approved of Dylan's unorthodox speech. On Christmas night, twenty people turned out for a party at the Avenue B apartment. Bob was very outgoing and friendly; Carla recalled that "he seemed to be at peace with himself Christmas Day, and I was his 'sister-in-law' again." The guests sang rock 'n' roll and had a cool Yule. Still, Dylan was planning an extended trip to California. The Rotolos were beginning to get a lot of telephone calls for Dylan from young girl fans, some very offensive. Anonymity for anyone close to Dylan was disappearing.

One night after Christmas, Bob dropped in to see me. I was struggling with another issue of the short-lived magazine *Hootenanny*, which I was editing with Lynn Musgrave, former editor of *Boston Broadside*. Dylan had written two article-poems for *Hootenanny*, yet he was wondering more vocally than I what the magazine stood for. "I don't mind handing you a brick, or a tile if you're building something," he said to me. "But what are you building? A wall? A house? I can't just throw bricks into the air and hope that someone will catch them and build something with them. I want to know where the bricks go." Since the Kennedy assassination, the folk movement's idealism was waning. What good did words do?

Dylan looked at an array of Christmas cards on my mantelpiece and TV. He remarked that the majority of the "season's greetings" were not from friends, but from publicity and promotion departments of recording companies. He said he knew I would have liked more cards from friends. Bob's eye caught a strange little portrait of thin-faced Phil Spector, the pop songwriter and producer. Spector's head was surrounded with long hair, and a black gremlin figure sat menacingly on his shoulder. Dylan doubled up with laughter. "Oh, no," he said, "not that for Christmas!" Spector's outrageous image struck Dylan. Within two years, Dylan had befriended Spector, wore shades and hair at least as long as Spector's, and had approved the hawk-like cut-out photograph that Columbia used to promote his folk-rock albums. But at Christmas, 1963, Dylan gave no sign he would drift into the pop world, with all its seeming absurdities.

On New Year's Eve, a ritual that closed 1963 more than it opened 1964, Dylan was at a small party at the Van Ronks'. A year earlier Bob had been at a big, impersonal party at my place. Now, he wanted to be with very few people. Suze looked subdued, Bob haggard. I had been party-hopping, and the Van Ronks' was my final stop. Dylan and a half-dozen friends in their twenties sat as if at a wake. Bob had started 1963 filled with hope and ambition, and had closed a year with fame and achievement, but he seemed a lot less happy. Even Van Ronk's ribald jokes were not producing smiles. I went across the street to bed, and I thought of how very old and tired those kids seemed. If something didn't change, I felt Dylan would be dead before 1964 was out.

In autumn 1963, Bob had written a remarkable open letter to his friends at *Broadside*. It was the last time — for that period—that he was prepared to publish anything so personal. Dylan could speak honestly to Sis and Gordon Friesen, who always thought in human terms, not slogans. The Old Left, Gordon wrote to me in late 1970, "never did understand how to treat artists. I remembered Woody showing me a letter from his section organizer in the Village ordering him to appear to answer charges for 'lack of discipline.' It seems he had failed to show up at a certain corner to sell *Daily Worker*s as he had pledged to do. Shit! They couldn't comprehend that Woody's role was to write songs, not to sell their paper. I could name other artists who were subjected to this short-sightedness. Novelists, like Richard Wright in Chicago after he published *Native Son*, and photographers and essayists. It was the same old tune when they alienated Bob Dylan at the very first encounter." Gordon understood the plight of the artist in America: "Melville spent his last thirty years drudging away in a customs house. Whitman worked away unrecognized, supported meagerly by the largesse of a friend or two. Nobody bought *Walden Pond* until Thoreau was long dead. Poe and Stephen Foster died in the gutter …" That was the compassion of Sis and Gordon, who published Dylan's letter in *Broadside* in January 1964. It was a remnant of the old Dylan, but hinted that the new Dylan was to be an even more solitary and tortured artist than he had been before the world took notice of him.

This was a soul-baring letter to friends. Through it one could see Dylan was the artist overwhelmed by fame, yet terribly lonely. He sensed the conflict over giving his autographs, he liked and hated it. He found himself living a contradiction. Dylan felt that fears had to be faced up to and feelings admitted. He admitted to feeling guilty. How remarkable that everyone needs to be secure and protected. He asked why God must be so fearful. He flailed the managers and agents, the buyers and sellers. He talked of the *Hootenanny* TV show, and of the heroes of the campaign against those who need the work, not the stars who don't. He described his filthy flat and how he must move out of it amid falling plaster and rotting floorboards. But he could find a certain beauty in it, especially hearing Pete Seeger on his record player singing "Guantanamera." He called Pete a saint he loved more than he could show. And love leads to Suze, who had left, and he wished he could love everyone as he did her. He would be Christ-like if he were to love everyone as he loved Suze. He laughed at that idea.

It is here that Dylan made his prayer for the acceptance of his many selves:

> *away away be gone all you demons*
> *an' just let me be me*
> *human me*
> *ruthless me*
> *wild me*
> *gentle me*
> *all kinds of me*[12]

Dylan made a few comments about the progress of *Broadside*, and the writers Paul Wolfe and Phil Ochs. His "novel" *Tarantula* was stalled, without a plot, just fragmented scenes on little scraps of paper. A few words in praise of Brecht and playwriting. He saw that the greatest virtue of drama over songs is that he can only talk about his own feelings in songs but he can talk of the feelings of many in a play.

He bid a restless farewell to *Broadside*. But not without some old angers at *Newsweek* and the jealous gossipmongers. The nightmares he faced and his hates and angers suffused into his own hope for himself: "An I shall wake in the mornin an try t start/lovin again."

Opposite: Rehearsing for the aborted *Ed Sullivan Show*, 1963.
Center: The icon emerges.
Top right: Performing with Pete Seeger at a voter registration rally in Mississippi, July 1963.
Below right: Happier times with Suze Rotolo, 1962.

It is very important to get poetry out of the hands of the professors and ... the squares ... If we can get poetry out into the life of the country, it can be creative ... Homer, or the guy who recited Beowulf, was show business. We simply want to make poetry a part of show business.
KENNETH REXROTH, 1957[1]

The poets today are talking to themselves ... The competition from the mass media is too much ... Poetry used to have an audience ... Gutenberg had a good idea with printing, but it ran away with him and ruined it for the poets!
LAWRENCE FERLINGHETTI, 1957[2]

The jazz and poetry guys of the 1950s ... woke up 10 years later and here is this squirrelly little kid who has done the things they wanted to do ... to get poetry into the streets, to the people and on the juke-boxes.
RALPH J GLEASON, 1966

Great paintings shouldn't be in museums. Museums are cemeteries. Paintings should be on the walls of restaurants, in dime stores, in gas stations, in men's rooms ... Music is the only thing that's in tune with what's happening. It's not in book form, it's not on the stage ... It's not the bomb that has to go, man, it's the museums.
DYLAN, 1965

The poet as icon, the classic images by Barry Feinstein for *The Times They Are a-Changin'*, December 1963.

Much as he was denying it, in 1963 and '64, Dylan was flowering as a poet. By using the mass-media in his special way, he was developing a new genre. The San Francisco beat poets had tried to wed spoken poetry with jazz—an experiment that scarcely got out of the basement. The French *chansonniers*, like Jacques Brel, had long known that song was an ideal vehicle for poetry, as had history's nameless bards, scops, goliards, troubadours, minstrels, jongleurs, broadside balladeers, and buskers. Dylan saw "poets" all around him and was at the heart of the democratic folk tradition so well described by Guthrie: "I have a storm of words in me enough to write several hundred songs and that many books. I know that these words I hear are not my own private property … You may have been taught to call me a poet, but I am no more of a poet than you are … You are the poet and your everyday talk is our best poem by our best poet. All I am is just sort of a clerk and climate-taster, and my workshop is the sidewalk, your street and your field, your highway, and your buildings."[3]

During 1963, I played editor to Dylan because I felt that he could handle any sort of writing job with speed, flair and originality. He knew I'd run things exactly as he'd written them, retain his eccentric orthography, and wouldn't tell him what to say. My first assignment for him was a piece for the 1963 Newport Folk Festival program, which I edited under the pseudonym Stacey Williams. He chose to write an open letter to Dave (Tony) Glover, his old Minneapolis sidekick. Bob handed me the piece typed single-spaced on tired yellow sheets, written in a cross between Guthrie's folk talk and his own invented punk-tuation. Roughly 150 lines of free verse recollected the good old days and the friend "who knew me before I hit or got hit by New York City."[4]

The Minneapolis group stood resolutely for the old music, mostly blues, and were alarmed by Dylan's drift into political slogans and protest and topical writing. Dylan recalled the old songs he and Glover used to sing, which came out of a time when, in Woody's view, there were only two roads to choose—"The American way or the Fascist way"[5] and two sides to every question. Time changed that, he wrote, "An them two simple sides that was so easy to tell apart bashed an boomed an exploded so hard an heavy that t'day all 'ts left and made for us is this one big rockin rollin COMPLICATED CIRCLE—"[6] After describing the blights on society—John Birchers waving flags and carrying shotguns, killer dogs and sprays, instant food and fads—Dylan wrote: "I don know who the people were man that let it get this way but they got what they wanted out a their lives an left me and you facin a scared raped world—"[7] This pre-echo of "Desolation Row" and "Idiot Wind" indicted what "they" had done to America: "They robbed the Constitution of the land an stuck in the censors of the mind—/They bought up everythin at the auction an left us with a garbage market a fools an fears an frustratin phoniness—"[8]

So Dylan couldn't then sing traditional songs anymore, but rather "Masters of War," "Seven Curses," "Hollis Brown," and others. Yet, he emphasized he was not rejecting apolitical folk songs, for they "showed me the way… that songs can say somethin human—"[9] Although he later claimed that he wrote protest songs specifically to please the New York folk-song movement, this letter was obviously sincere. He was then in the bloodstream of the topical-song movement. Some weeks later, I asked Bob if he'd received a reply from Glover. He grinned. "Not yet, man, but I hope he got my message."

In late summer 1963, I assumed the editorship of a folk-song magazine, *Hootenanny*, that slid into merciful oblivion after four issues, along with the craze that spawned it. I asked Dylan to do a bimonthly column, called "Blowin' in the Wind," for which he could choose any form, length, or subject. I offered him the princely sum of $75 a column, which annoyed Grossman but seemed to amuse Dylan. "It's not the bread," Dylan told me, "it's the idea of it I like."

His first column appeared in early autumn 1963. Knowing that I was planning a magazine considerably broader than *Sing Out!*, Dylan appealed to folk fans to avoid hair-splitting debates about the music. "It just ain't healthy t let the music run yer life like that—/Yer life's gotta run the music … Just get up in the mornin and go—/Just open yer eyes an walk—"[10] Then he hailed the natural beauties of the open country from Monterey eastward. New York was stressful and ugly, yet possessed of a curious sense of beauty; Dylan was fascinated with its energy and variety. The neo-Guthrie tone of the piece was obvious, underlining the need to throw oneself into experience, life, and music, and to learn from them. Don't let the categorizers, analyzers, or rule-makers "boundary it all up."[11]

Dylan's second *Hootenanny* column castigated two unnamed pop-folk singers (Ira and Inman). He described their slick, pandering, bowing-and-scraping black music for whites. The singers' patter, which patronized Negroes, appalled Dylan. As he listened, his mind wandered back to black militants and artists he admired: Ivan Donaldson, Jim Forman, John Lewis, Mrs McGee, Bernice Johnson and the Freedom Singers, Miles Davis, Mavis Staples, Paul Robeson, Diana Sands, James Baldwin. Then, Dylan wrote of "the poor petty thief who gets nailed for/robbin' a jewelry store an' all he wanted t do was/pawn a watch so his wife an kids could get better—"[12] The stage lights dimmed again, as the Uncle Tom act proceeded "an I asked the mirror in my mind…/'What's this word, criminal, anyway?'/'Who's the biggest criminal?'/'Who distorts the most about the world?'/'Who covers up the most about the way things really are?'"[13] If he had his way, Dylan would stand the despised singers against the wall, frisk them, handcuff them, "an hang a sign around their/heads so innocent people wouldn't get too near… 'BUSTED.'"[14]

This was a prelude to many songs he wrote challenging false laws. Aside from his individualistic spelling, punctuation, and syntax, this essay was notable for another stylistic experiment. He succeeded in making the singing style of the duo actually resonate on the page. As they sang "Black is the Color of My True Love's Hair," Dylan attenuated the first word, across three lines of type with thirty letter *a*'s and eight *k*'s.

By the end of 1963, Dylan told me that he had so much work he couldn't continue the *Hootenanny* column. I think he was being polite, for he also challenged me with a barrage of questions. What was the use of this magazine? What difference did it make if he wrote a column or not? My replies didn't convince him, or me, either. After one more issue, *Hootenanny* folded, because of bad management and lack of focus—the folk audience was already too fragmented to accept any single magazine. At least, I'd had the opportunity to encourage Dylan to write for the page. Although Dylan seemed to enjoy journalism, he was already working on *Tarantula*, and was feverishly writing songs and a few surprises for his next album. He knew that records had the greatest power to reach people.

Turntable Literature. When the album *The Times They Are a-Changin'* was released in February 1964, Columbia finally recognized that it had a star in Dylan. He virtually had complete control over the album, which Tom Wilson produced. The jacket notes were a bold departure for a pop LP. Continued on a printed insert, "11 Outlined Epitaphs" constituted Dylan's first published poetry. The cover photograph, by Barry Feinstein, then Mary Travers's husband, showed a ferociously intense and tortured Dylan exuding sullen anger. A strong sense of apocalypse dominates the album. Dylan's development of the topical song had far outstripped even his own previous efforts. "Hattie Carroll," "Only a Pawn," and "Hollis Brown" had been triggered by news items, but Dylan, brimming with confidence, was imbuing his more complex "stories" with larger vision and greater universality.

"The Times They Are a-Changin'": A summation of the Sixties mood. No cautious questioning now, but a prophetic voice trumpeting of a changing order. The song was widely recorded and translated into Serbian, French, Hebrew, and other languages. The imagery is primal, homespun: a flood tide, fate's spinning wheel, a blocked doorway, the storm of battle, a changing road. While this could be played over film clips of Prague, Paris, Chicago, and Berkeley, it is also a timeless dialogue between those restrained by old ways and those daring something new. At first the lyrics' biblical roll seems to reflect black gospel song. The title line suggests the warning in Revelation 1:3: "for the time is near." There is an echo from Mark 10:31: "But many that are first will be last, and the last first." In Dylan's lines: "For the loser now/Will be later to win."[15] and "And the first one now/Will later be last."[16] Flood waters rise and Armageddon approaches—"There's a battle outside/And it is ragin'"[17] and we are warned about "future shock"—change will be too rapid to assimilate. Although it became a youth anthem, "Times Changin'" does not criticize the old as much as entrenched, rigid thinking, "to separate aliveness from deadness," as he later said. In the midst of a stern challenge, Dylan offers parents, writers, critics, and even politicians a chance to join the changing tide: "Please heed the call"[18]; "Please get out of the new [road]/If you can't lend your hand."[19] The hortatory performance, seemingly sung through clenched teeth, matches the lyrics' bold cadences and messianic tone. Dylan calls it "definitely a song with a purpose, influenced by Scottish ballads."

"Ballad of Hollis Brown": A neo-folk ballad that draws heavily on traditional elements, with a melody that suggests the modal sadness of such songs as "Pretty Polly," "Poor Boy," or "Poor Man." A strong musical vehicle for a harrowing narrative of rural poverty and disaster. There is a prevailing sense of loneliness—"If there's anyone that knows/Is there anyone that cares?"[20]—and a build-up of domestic hopelessness, chronicled by rats in the flour, a dead horse, blackened grass, a dry well. As in Shakespeare's *Macbeth*, the murder weapon, a shotgun, takes on a power of its own, drawing us toward the lines: "Seven shots ring out/Like the ocean's pounding roar."[21] During the death tableau, seven new people are born in the distance. Is this sign of hope, or a suggestion that seven more may face a similar fate? "Hollis Brown" deserves wider recognition for its persuasive storytelling, high tragedy in eleven verses.

"With God on Our Side": One of Dylan's most cutting myth-breakers. It preceded widespread challenges to education, curriculum, and textbooks. The title line appears in Robert Southey ("The laws are with us and God's on our side") and in Shaw's *Saint Joan*. Ironically, the song led one fan's mother to relent: "At least he believes in God." This track is not Dylan's best performance of the song, which he often sang with Baez. It is very pointedly cast in a folk matrix, with the naïve, humble lad describing his background and schooling, which entrenched the myth of God's approval for ungodly wars. After shifting God's approbation from our side to even Judas Iscariot's side, the final verse hammers home the narrator's new morality: "If God's on our side/He'll stop the next war."[22] Dominic Behan, brother of Brendan, chided Dylan publicly for lifting Dominic's melody to his Irish rebel song, "The Patriot Game." Actually, Dominic himself had borrowed the melody from the once-popular tune "The Merry Month of May." "God on Our Side" can be contrasted startlingly with his later, evangelical songs on *Slow Train Coming*.[23]

"One Too Many Mornings": One of two songs linked to the loss of Suze. As dull Manhattan dawn creeps in, a weary Dylan trudges back to the Village from Suze's. Sedative harmonica suggests a bluesman solacing his "restless hungry feeling."[24] No anger, no judgment on the lovers' troubles: "You're right from your side,/I'm right from mine."[25] Nothing burdened this young romantic more than the fragility of love.

"North Country Blues": Ready to look back at Hibbing, Dylan distanced himself through the persona of a miner's wife to tell this "tale." Even though he calls it a "blues," the song resembles a nineteenth-century western ballad. Dylan's explanation for the Iron Range mine closings is economic realism: "That it's much cheaper down/In the South American towns/Where the miners work almost for nothing."[26]

"Only a Pawn in Their Game": More social realism—how divide and conquer in southern racialism kept the poor white as suppressed as the black: "But the poor white man's used in the hands of them all like a tool."[27] In early summer 1963, the slaying of Medgar Evers, leader of the Mississippi NAACP, shocked the nation. The *Broadside* circle responded quickly with songs from Turner and Ochs, among others. Dylan's was the strongest, using the murder of one black to probe root causes, power alliances, and confusion of victim with victimizer.

"Boots of Spanish Leather": Another lament of love, longing, and loss, in a dialogue between parting lovers. Archaic language and diction conjure up visions of galleons and exotic lands. While probably sparked by Suze's stay in Italy, the song broadened into a universal plaint. Christopher Ricks has called this Dylan's finest love song.

"When the Ship Comes In": One of Dylan's prophecies, optimistic and vengeful, in heralding the day when evil will be purged. The allusions have the powerful roll of gospel, evoking both Old Testament figures, like Pharaoh and Goliath, and the spirit of the Revelation of St John the Divine. The ship is a universal salvation symbol. Gabrielle Goodchild: "Throughout myth and literature, we find water as the symbol of the unconscious, spirituality, and death, and the ship as the tiny ego of man making its lonely or triumphant voyage across dangerous deeps." Carolyn Bliss in her master's thesis compares Revelation 7:1, where "no wind might blow on earth or sea or against any tree," to Dylan's opening: "Oh the time will come up/When the winds will stop/And the breeze will cease to be breathin'."[28] The line "the whole wide world is watchin'"[29] was chanted by protesters during the 1968 Democratic National Convention in Chicago.

"The Lonesome Death of Hattie Carroll": A news item inspired this ballad about racist justice. On February 8, 1963, a Baltimore socialite struck Mrs Carroll with a lightweight cane. A mother of eleven who suffered from arteriosclerosis, she collapsed and died the next day of a massive cerebral hemorrhage. Her attacker, William D Zantzinger, whose father was active in Maryland politics, was convicted of manslaughter and assault, and escaped with a light sentence.[30] Dylan converted this drama into a song with, he told me, a structure from François Villon. Dylan took poetic license with some facts, but not with the theme of class justice. He never specifically states that Hattie Carroll is black, but we sense she is throughout the song. Ricks has lectured widely on this "national song of faith misplaced in the law," praising its fierceness without an angry tone. He cited Dylan's "exact control of each word," the use of feminine endings for Hattie Carroll's lines, the craft behind what at first seems clumsy: "With rich wealthy parents who provide and protect him."[31] Five years later, the episode and song inspired C Lester Franklin's play *A Scaffold for Marionettes*, advertised in Baltimore as "a sensational and shocking exposé of the bigotry and prejudice that runs rampant in our city." (On *Biograph* Dylan drops the Villon reference: "The set pattern to the song, I think, is based on Brecht, 'The Ship, The Black Freighter.'")

"Restless Farewell": Remorse and self-examination dominate the album's final song, based on the melody of "The Parting Glass," an Irish drinking song. Dylan often ended albums with new departures. At this point, he was unnerved by the *Newsweek* exposé and the weary, misunderstood artist says farewell. "Time" is crucial, contrasting with its use in the album title. The singer realizes that his times are also changing: "Oh a false clock tries to tick out my time/To disgrace, distract, and bother me."[32] During a drinking reverie, the narrator reviews the money he's spent, the friends he's squandered, the bottles he's killed, the girls he's touched, the foes he's fought, the thoughts that have tortured him, the gossip that's surrounded him. He concludes confidently that "I'll make my stand/And remain as I am/And bid farewell and not give a damn."[33] He sang me the unfinished version of this song and asked me if I thought it would be understood. I said that I thought so, but that the only person he ever had to please was really himself.

"11 Outlined Epitaphs." Dylan augmented these songs with prose-poems, published on the back of the album and on an insert. In this subjective cycle he spoke more freely of himself. The epitaphs, published in *Lyrics, 1962–1985*, remind me of the Dylan Thomas line: "Poems are statements on the way to the grave." Tom Lask, poetry editor of the *New York Times*, once tore into Dylan-as-poet for these lines from Epitaph 8:

> *(if it rhymes, it rhymes*
> *if it don't, it don't*
> *if it comes, it comes*
> *if it won't it won't)*[34]

The excerpt holds its own beside the jazz-infused section from T S Eliot's "Sweeney Agonistes":

> *I gotta use words when I talk to you*
> *But if you understand or if you don't*
> *That's nothing to me and nothing to you*
> *We all gotta do what we gotta do...*[35]

For all their unevenness and sometimes apparent automatism, there are flashes of brilliance and insight in the Epitaphs, as the writer steps out without his guitar and harmonica. They can be read as autobiographical notes or as poetry. They appear casual, yet fine balance, control, and contour can be discerned. There are recurring references to the road, and of the writer running. The poems move from early evening to deep into the night and on to dawn. The word *epitaph* has dual connotations here: a commemoration of something in Dylan's life that has already died, and, in Epitaphs 8, 10, and 11, the glorification of what he holds most sacred, of what he might one day choose as his own epitaph. Throughout, his identity evolves from adolescent to man as he says his own "restless farewell" to the past. Ever the songwriter, Dylan imbues the Epitaphs with a high sense of color and rhythm, and there are formulations he later developed into songs, notably "Love Minus Zero/No Limit" and "Hurricane."

Epitaph 1: To surrender to the sanctuary of his own imagination, he must "slam the shutters of my eyes."[36] Voices say "'he's a crazy man/he never opens up his eyes.'"[37] The narrator describes his sundown confusions, his loss of direction and ideology. Then, a flash of enlightenment comes: "the shot has shook/me up … for I've never/heard that sound before."[38] Was it the shot that killed Kennedy, or Medgar Evers, or the shot of recognition that to find his own world he must withdraw?

Epitaph 2: A more mature look at his childhood milieu than "Stolen Moment." Duluth "holds no memories,"[39] but Hibbing "has left me with my legacy visions."[40] He describes the death of old north Hibbing and the movement to the new town. The pervasive decay, the cold wind blowing "as though/the rains of wartime had/left the land bombed-out an' shattered."[41] He's still running: "but my road has seen many changes/for I've served my time as a refugee."[42] He envisions he'll return with "changed eyes."[43] There's a Whitmanesque ring to how he'll talk to the old and the young. At this point he can almost see himself coming to terms with his adolescent rebellion, to stop and embrace and even to love the town "—for I learned by now/never t' expect/what it cannot give me."[44]

Epitaph 3: Dylan considers some of the romantic myths that inspired him, like Guthrie's arrival in New York during the Depression. No union movement was there to greet Dylan. He toys with Villon ("ah where are those forces of yesteryear?")[45] then parallels Idris Davies's and Pete Seeger's "Bells of Rhymney," putting the ringing Welsh mining song into an American setting. He's trying to find his own welcome into New York: He's not lost, nor is he a stranger, "but rather someone/who just doesn't live here."[46] His conclusion puns on a legendary bluesman and Psalm 23 as he declares himself free of past guides:

> *never pretendin' t' be knowin'*
> *what's worth seekin'*
> *but at least*
> *without ghosts by my side*
> *t' betray my childishness*
> *t' leadeth me down false trails*
> *an' maketh me drink from muddy waters*
> *yes it is I*
> *who is poundin' at your door*
> *if it is you inside*
> *who hears the noise*[47]

Columbia Records ran full-page ads for the album using the last four lines.

Epitaph 4: A death poem against organized politics; there is no party or movement he sees that can answer his demands. ("Jim" is probably James Forman of SNCC.) This is also an Epitaph for the "brainwashed dream"[48] of both ideology and education. He "ran for my life"[49] to his highway, his open road, "not carin' no more/what people knew about things/but rather how they felt about things."[50]

Epitaph 5: A visit to the home of writer Al Aronowitz and his wife, Anne, turns into an exchange of vexsome questions and elusive answers. Asked how he can be happy singing such depressing songs, he responds:

> *Lenny Bruce says there're no dirty*
> *words ... just dirty minds an' I say there're*
> *no depressed words just depressed minds*[51]

This Epitaph ambiguously describes poetry as "anything that ain't got no end"[52] and his songs onstage as "nothin' but the unwindin' of/my happiness."[53]

Epitaph 6: On idols and the dangers of idolatry. From his first and last idol, Guthrie, he learned "that men are men."[54]

Epitaph 7: Stop fighting foreign demons, Dylan writes, until we can get the rats out of Harlem kitchens: "ain't there no closer villains/than the baby-eatin' Russians/rats eat babies too."[55] This Epitaph also contains a widely quoted gibe at political labels:

> *there is no right wing*
> *or left wing ...*
> *there is only up wing*
> *an' down wing*[56]

Epitaph 8: He defends himself against gossip that he was a plagiarist. He explains the folk process of building on the old to "grant my closet thoughts backyard air."[57] Acknowledging the myriad influences that play on him, he writes:

> *for all songs lead back t' the sea*
> *an' at one time, there was*
> *no singin' tongue t' imitate it*[58]

There is no one free of guilt, and yet "the world is but a courtroom."[59] He warns that the defendants are busy cleaning up that courtroom and the prosecutors will soon be swept away—echoes of the "Hattie Carroll" theme of false justice.

Epitaph 9: There is another courtroom, of trial-by-press: a defiant riposte to *Newsweek*, *Sing Out!* and other publications that have hectored him: "No I shall not cooperate with reporters' whims."[60] He will not participate in such an exposure, he writes, for "I 'expose' myself/every time I step out/ on the stage."[61]

Epitaph 10: The final two poems leave enemies, causes, and politics behind, and celebrate life, love, and song. They follow Dylan's emotional pendulum: expunging anger before expressing love. This Epitaph is a nocturne—Dylan flies from "the dungeons of my constant night"[62] toward the dawn. Admitting his destructiveness, he has only tender thoughts for Suze. Other friends appear: Eric (Ric) Von Schmidt, Geno Foreman, the Van Ronks. Then he hails music, and his own speeding muse:

> *for I am runnin' in a fair race*
> *with no racetrack but the night*
> *an' no competition but the dawn*[63]

Epitaph 11: Elegiac language now as he forecasts constant change in the climate. As desire drives him onward, he names some of those who have inspired him, a long list that leaps from William Blake to Johnny Cash to Seeger. The lyricism reminds me of Joyce's farewell to Ireland in *Portrait of the Artist as* *a Young Man* where Stephen girds himself with silence, cunning, and exile. Dylan places himself in a continuum of lonely singers:

> *an' mine shall be a strong loneliness*
> *dissolvin' deep*
> *t' the depths of my freedom*
> *an' that, then, shall*
> *remain my song*[64]

For all their artistry, *The Times They Are a-Changin'* and the Epitaphs showed critical reaction still divided. *Little Sandy Review*: "45 minutes of gloom… by far his weakest album, musically." The "822 lines of free-association blank verse" were dismissed as "spiritual masochism." *High Fidelity* cautioned that "Dylan will not entertain you. That's not his line. But he will sear your soul." *HiFi/Stereo Review* had reservations about "this tortured hearer of apocalyptic visions." This reviewer rated Dylan as equal to Guthrie, but feared he might "become only a mannered apologist for his own wounded self-esteem." An obscure Village folknik named Tony Herbert wrote a parody of "With God on Our Side," suggesting there was money in protest. But the album and the poems also won praise and broadened Dylan's reputation. The harsh crucible of public opinion be damned, he was growing beyond anyone's command, choosing his own lonely road to travel. For a man who'd just outlined his epitaphs, Dylan had plenty of life left.

Another Side. After an appearance in London in May 1964, Dylan made a lightning trip to Paris and then Greece, where, with his road manager, Victor Maimudes, he visited the small village of Vermilya. After returning in June, he recorded in only two nights a total of eleven songs, and wrote more poems for the sleeve. Columbia had originally scheduled a *Bob Dylan in Concert* album, for release in early summer 1964 which would have been largely based on Dylan's October 26, 1963, Carnegie Hall concert, along with one song and his "Last Thoughts on Woody Guthrie" poem from his April 12, 1963, Town Hall concert. But this album was canceled, and in August 1964, *Another Side of Bob Dylan* was released.

Many critics were cool. The folk-Left saw him drifting into "too much subjectivity." Other critics carped for aesthetic reasons. Probably the snidest review was a parody doggerel in *High Fidelity*: "but bob/he got two problems/small ones/the language he write in/aint english/the measure he beats out/aint song/n this kind of/inverted intellectuality/just bores/the hell/out of me." *Another Side* was indeed taped hastily and the singing was not Dylan's subtlest. But the album does capture weariness, cynicism, and road *ennui*. It enunciates new self-reliant directions. It brings back Dylan's mocking wit, notably absent on *Times Changing*. Dylan reluctantly accepted Tom Wilson's album title.

"All I Really Want to Do": A jape about a "simple" man trying to relate to a complex, defensive and Freudian-oriented woman. Rich in outlandish catalogs, internal and external rhymes, Dylan laughs at his own jokes as he sings, yodels, and plays games. A lampoon of "boy meets girl" in the era of psychoanalysis and shifting values in social-sexual relationships.

"Black Crow Blues": Dylan's grasp of country blues idioms has always been strong. This original blues simmers with the sorrow, fatigue and longing that might emanate from a Delta farm. A gently swinging performance, in which an out-of-tune, honky-tonk piano adds authenticity.

"Spanish Harlem Incident": The parade of women and muse figures in Dylan's love songs is long. Any friend might have served as a model for this song of surrender to a gypsy fortune-teller. Dylan has often disdained the emptiness of the middle-class, collegiate, intellectual women while proclaiming the life-force of the black earth-mothers, the Arethas of *Tarantula*, who put him in touch with deeper realities. Sung with passionate projection, his voice breaks almost in Mexican *ranchero* style, on the word *homeless*.

"Chimes of Freedom": In language, sweep, universality, and compassion, one of his most profound song-poems. This is among my half-dozen favorite Dylan works, a triumph of word-color and metaphor and encompassing humanity. Dylan's affinity with the underdog has rarely attained such noble expression. He hears "the chimes of freedom flashing"[65] for a legion of the abused. This is perhaps Dylan's most political song and his greatest love song, for he is extending his love and identification: "for the aching ones whose wounds cannot be nursed/For the countless confused, accused, misused, strung-out ones an' worse."[66] The song is set in a dramatic storm, a "wild cathedral evening,"[67] developing his favorite metaphor of tempest: "Through the mad mystic hammering of the wild ripping hail/The sky cracked its poems in naked wonder."[68]

Jack McDonough sees this as part of an album that is making a modern excursion into "a Romantic, Blakean childhood … 'Chimes of Freedom' is an emotional protest against emotional deprivation." The song is laden with extravagant and often violent imagery known as synesthesia, the super-vividness found in Poe, Hart Crane, and notably in Rimbaud's "Sonnet of the Vowels," in which colors emerge from common vowels. In her paper "Bob Dylan and French Symbolist Poetry," Belle D Levinson found in "Hard Rain" and "Chimes of Freedom" "a Dylan whose style as well as theme is close to Rimbaud's." I find "Chimes of Freedom" a landmark lyric in which Dylan has progressed from "Hard Rain" toward his full poetic powers.[69]

"I Shall Be Free No 10": An abrupt shift toward whimsy and Dada nonsense. Gabrielle Goodchild: "After the visions that his own suffering, and the world's disorder, brought Lear in the storm, we are grateful for the Fool's apparent nonsense." Comic relief perhaps explains the positioning of this talking blues, in which Dylan pokes fun at himself: "Now they asked me to read a poem/At the sorority sister's home/I got knocked down and my head was swimmin'/I wound up with the Dean of Women/Yippee! I'm a poet, and I know it,/Hope I don't blow it."[70]

"To Ramona": A gentle lecture, mixed with sexual longing, that urges the woman to fight for her own identity. Although the song could be addressed to an amalgam of Dylan's women friends, it may be meant for one active in the southern civil rights movement, pondering her unease in New York: "The flowers of the city/Though breathlike, get deathlike at times."[71] Yet, as in the blues, the narrator addresses a lover while counseling himself to avoid conformity: "From fixtures and forces and friends,/Your sorrow does stem,/That hype you and type you,/Making you feel/That you must be exactly like them."[72] The narrator is humbler as he offers comfort: "Everything passes,/Everything changes."[73] One day he may need the comfort and direction the woman is seeking. In his paper on Blake and Dylan, Eugene Stelzig wrote that Dylan's attempt to define freedom goes beyond mundane "politics" into "the politics of experience." Dylan had already told Nat Hentoff in the *New Yorker*: "What's wrong goes much deeper than the bomb. What's wrong is how few people are free." Bill King pointed out the King James Bible associations of "to pass" in the line "The pangs of your sadness/Shall pass as your senses will rise."[74]

"Motorpsycho Nitemare": Intimations of the folk-rock to come on the next three albums—the rhythm section can almost be imagined. Here's a rat-a-tat of *double-entendre* lyrics that reshape the old bawdy tale of the farmer's daughter and the traveling salesman. Dylan converts a *Psycho*-like scenario into Middle American panic at the thought of Fidel Castro, and his beard. This sly, charming story of a hipster confronting a reactionary, whose first weapon is *Reader's Digest*, is well-sustained satire.

"My Back Pages": A mournful melody reminiscent of "Hattie Carroll," this is a landmark declaration of independence from cant, doctrine, and easy answers. As early as the Newport letter, Dylan realized that he could no longer accept from "corpse evangelists"[75] the message that "life is black and white."[76] He even turns upon himself for becoming his own enemy "In the instant that I preach."[77] There is an internal dialogue between what he once accepted and now doubts, the celebrated refrain suggesting death and rebirth: "Ah, but I was so much older then,/I'm younger than that now."[78] From Blakean "Experience," Dylan has moved back toward "Innocence," which will keep him forever young. According to Jack McDonough: "One of Dylan's most important poetic achievements has been this transposition of the worlds of Wordsworth and Blake into post-war America."

"I Don't Believe You": In *Writings and Drawings*, Dylan offers an alternate title, "She Acts Like We Never Have Met." Usually it's the woman who voices abandonment, not the man, after a "wild blazing nighttime."[79] He contrasts love's illusions with reality: "It's all new t' me,/Like some mystery,/It could even be like a myth."[80] The jaunty melody is a cross-current to the sardonic words. Dylan laughs in verse three, perhaps because he'd reversed the last five lines as published with verse four.

"Ballad in Plain D": One of Dylan's most directly biographical songs, an unvarnished narrative brimming with regret. "Plain D," a key indication, could easily stand for death, desperation, or desolation. In mid-March 1964, there was a harrowing row at Suze and Carla's apartment on Avenue B. As Suze got hysterical, Dylan and Carla scuffled on the floor. Two friends, Paul Clayton and Barry Kornfeld, were dragged in. The crisis effectively ended Bob and Suze's romance. There was no contact between them for some months and they did not re-establish a friendship for several years. Although Suze understood why Bob wrote the song, in 1968 she told me: "That song just went too far. There are some things you just can't do, no matter how much power you have." Carla told me that she was only trying to protect her sister: "I was no parasite. I always worked, I always contributed to the food and rent." She said Dylan ultimately apologized to her for the song. But Dylan stuck to his position, telling me: "I think the song pretty well summarized the situation." Dylan, who generally spouted slang in conversation then, used totally different diction here: "unknown consciousness,"[81] "silhouetted anger to manufactured peace,"[82] "the tombstones of damage."[83] The final verse likens the losing lover to a prisoner who has no wish to be free:

> *Ah, my friends from the prison, they ask unto me,*
> *"How good, how good does it feel to be free?"*
> *And I answer them most mysteriously,*
> *"Are birds free from the chains of the skyway?"*[84]

"It Ain't Me, Babe": A catalog of love's burdens. Stelzig sees this song, and "Don't Think Twice," as reflections of the "Female Will" that Blake attacked in his proverb from "Eternity"—"He who binds to himself a joy/Does the winged life destroy"—although Dylan has just declared that even winged birds aren't free. If, as Bill King maintains, "Dylan used the love song to speak metaphorically about human relationships in general," this song, a rejection of the mythology of true love, could also represent Dylan's rejection of audience demands.

"Some Other Kinds of Songs ... Poems."

The jacket notes for *Another Side* were titled "Some Other Kinds of Songs … Poems by Bob Dylan." As his songs extended page poetry, his page poetry extended his music. Columbia printed five of the poems in a cramped, telephone directory-sized typeface. *Writings and Drawings* offers a more readable text and the cycle of eleven poems, the same number as the Epitaphs. "Some Other Kinds of Songs" further documents Dylan's experimentation with verbal music and his often elusive world view. The style is impressionistic and surreal.

Poem 1: This monometrical, highly rhythmic episode bounces in the jaunty tempo of a skip-rope or hopscotch rhyme. (This form of street poetry has been collected by the Opies, by Tony Schwartz, and sung by Dominic Behan, and by Ewan MacColl on the album *The Singing Streets*.) The central figure of Dylan's first poem is "baby black," apparently a young Harlem girl, who has been forced into a cruel life to survive: "baby black/hits back/robs, pawns/lives by trade."[85] We recognize the hustler of the first *Hootenanny* column. "Baby black" is also related to "Spanish Harlem Incident": "you ask of order/she'd hock/the world/for a dollar an' a quarter … I'm givin' you/myself t' pawn."[86]

Poem 2: Dedicated to the gentle French singer Françoise Hardy, a tender evocation of Dylan's Paris visit in spring 1964. Snapshot visions of Paris in the spring counterpoint a top-level political meeting.

Poem 3: A chess game opens with a dialogue in which a compulsive winner wants to make the loser "crawl." Another section foreshadows the Rolling Stones' 1966 song, "Mother's Little Helper," describing "common housewives strung out/fully on drugstore dope, legally/sold t' help clean the kitchen."[87] The third episode alludes to a ping-pong game Dylan played in California with the late novelist Henry Miller. Dylan gibes at a lady reporter who "wants me/t' say what she wants me t' say. she/wants me t' say what she/can understand."[88] The final section is a dark scene of "eviction. infection gangrene an'/atom bombs.

both ends exist only/because there is someone who wants/profit."[89] After elliptical references to Jesus, the section comes back to the natural world of insects, snakes, ants, turtles, lizards, and eventually to the chess player: "an' everything still crawls."[90]

Poem 4: From chess imagery to a card game, with that serviceable old trump, the jack of diamonds, taken from traditional blues. This poem cries to be read aloud, thumping along rhythmically, bright with rhymes and lightning pictures. Dylan roamed the Paris night streets with an American actor, Ben Carruthers, who adapted some "Poem 4" lines for a song unauthorized by Dylan, "Jack O' Diamonds." In 1965, Carruthers and a British group, the Deep, recorded the song; it was also recorded by Fairport Convention. Odetta's "Jack" had been an early influence.

Poem 5: A highlight of the cycle, fragmentary glimpses of self-examination played out against the black spiritual "Joshua Fit the Battle of Jericho." There is a compelling scene of a man on the Brooklyn Bridge poised to jump to his doom: "i could tell at a glance/he was uselessly lonely."[91] In the watching mob, Dylan feels shame that he *wanted* to see the man jump. He identifies both with the mob and with the jumper. He ponders the hollowness of the modern world's lonely crowd, then shifts to New Orleans mobs at Mardi Gras. A foretaste of *Tarantula*: "intellectual spiders/weave down sixth avenue."[92] He rambles along 14th Street, meeting someone who wants to draw him down to his own level, despair. He knows he must fight self-destructiveness or others' destructiveness. Compassionately, he views the movie-going, escapist mob: "slaves are of no special color/an' the links of chains/fall into no special order."[93] His guitar sets an old Greek woman dancing and laughing. He ruminates on lost love and vows: "for the rest of my life/i will never chase a livin' soul/into the prison grasp/ of my own self-love."[94] So he tells Joshua to go fight his battle while the narrator retreats to Walden-like woods, believing, as an existentialist and romantic, that self-awareness can best be gained in isolation. Dylan slyly tells Joshua he will join him in battle next time, and that Joshua may even have his battling celebrated in song.

Poem 6: A brief declaration of envy and past hate toward a rival for Suze's affections, Enzo. It echoes "My Back Pages" in its effort to fight jealousy.

Poem 7: Six-line enigma about a man called Charlie who slept on a Michelangelo cherub's face.

Poem 8: Saga of a girl hitchhiker who gets a lift and makes small talk with the driver. That Kerouac road feeling carries dangers with its freedoms.

Poem 9: The wistful tale of poor, empty Johnny, whose parents took care of him, no matter what he did. But they couldn't buy him into college, so they said, "here son have a [Cadillac] car good boy"[95] instead. He crashed it.

Poem 10: Could be titled "There Are No Politics." A dialogue between a cynic and a person whose life seems organized and structured, but who is one of the hollow men: "holy hollowness too/yes hollow holiness."[96] A fine section returns to Dylan's fascination with riddles and truth:

> you ask me questions
> an' i say that every question
> if it's a truthful question
> can be answered by askin' it[97]

Poem 11: In the cycle's final poem, "high treachery sails" amid bells and wedding songs that again echo "Bells of Rhymney." Although larkish in tone, it closes with a shivering blast of shattered illusions:

> inside of the altar
> outside of the theater
> mystery fails
> when treachery prevails

the forgotten rosary
nails
itself t' a cross
of sand
an' rich men stare t' their
private own-ed murals
all is lost Cinderella
all is lost[98]

For all their obscurities, these "other kinds of songs" show metaphoric daring, control of nuance, flowing rhythms. Dylan's self-probing concludes that more questions must be raised to find meaning. His seemingly random arrangements make his words into fortune-telling cards that reveal his emerging inner self. These poems were written in a period of personal loss and reorientation. The discovery of the hidden, or gradually emerging, inner self is a hallmark of the Romantic poet. Dylan has arrived at a major insight: the question can be the answer. Ahead lies the frenzied vision of his three great albums of 1965 and 1966, and the larger questions they posed.

Literature Turns Tables.

To put a tombstone over all narrow definitions of literature, can't we now reverse Dylan's definition of his poems as "some other kinds of songs" and call his songs "some other kinds of poems"? After these two albums of 1964, the acceptance of Dylan as a literary voice grew. Still, two decades later, there is a widespread reluctance in the glacier-like literary establishment to accept any sort of song lyric as literature.

Ironically, this attitude fails to acknowledge the roots of poetry and literature as an oral art. In almost every culture, song is the oldest vehicle for poetry. Lying at the roots of poetry and music is the unifying element of rhythm. Since pre-history, oral literature has been a vehicle for tales, legends, myths, epics, and romances; it has accompanied work and worship; it has venerated heroes, heroines, gods, and goddesses; it has taught moral precepts; and it has entertained. Before Gutenberg, poetry was a social art—only gradually did it then become a private art. It was once a popular form, long before it became patrician or elitist. Dylan's central achievement was to help make poetry popular again. A great deal of page poetry benefits from being read aloud. Shakespeare and Blake are filled with song, whether for the speaker's voice or the singer's.

There is certainly nothing unique in fighting for the acceptance of quality song lyrics as oral literature. Folklorists have been waging that battle for a long time. Led by Professor Francis James Child, a group of Shakespeare scholars at Harvard championed the classic Scots-English ballads.[99] Biblical scholars contend that much of the Old Testament was sung before it was written. Blues scholars, like Paul Oliver, Charles Keil, and Samuel Charters, and ballad collectors, like the Lomaxes, have drawn portraits of a people or a community from blues, folk songs, and ballads. The well of folk song and folk poetry has watered the roots of such composers as Mahler, and Bartók, and such poets as Yeats and Sandburg.

For the moment, we have to avoid the measuring of quality. Those who refuse to recognize any trace of oral literature in popular music will always head for the jugular vein of the ephemeral, banal, and vapid. But who among us could deny the poetic gifts of Chuck Berry, Smokey Robinson, Hank Williams, or Robert Johnson? Biblical prophets and psalmists chanted their heirloom wisdom. Hellenic mythology and literature? Homer was a busker, and the mythic Orpheus and Dionysus were fountainheads of music and poetry. Medieval Welsh poets? Robert Graves's *The White Goddess* details the attainments of court poets and bards.[100] The tellers of the great Germanic and Scandinavian epics entered that tradition as they chanted mouth to ear, the oral/aural history of their tribes.

My favorite example of historical literary singers is the goliards, the singer-poets whose heyday was about 1160, just 800 years before Dylan got to his Village. The goliards composed Latin lyrics, using styles and forms drawn, subversively, from Church litany, in order to celebrate pagan joys of the tavern and the flesh. They were rebels who used burlesque and parody to hound corrupt clergy, to satirize errant monks. Most goliards were threadbare drifters, dropouts and runaways who often hit the open road, traveling from university to university, begging, stealing, cadging, singing. Goliard songs passed into classical music when Carl Orff used them in his masterpiece, *Carmina Burana.*

What of the most storied of the mythic Greek singing poets, Orpheus, whose legend has been told repeatedly in opera and drama? His love for Eurydice sent him to Hades on a rescue mission. Losing her on his return ascent, he was a doomed man, refusing to know women thereafter. The women of Thrace tore Orpheus to pieces, as a crowd of rock teenyboppers would a rock star, if they could. Only the head of Orpheus was saved, taken to the Isle of Lesbos where it became a famed oracle, figurehead of the religious cult of Orphics.

I'm not arguing that Dylan is a reborn Orpheus, a neo-goliard, or a resurrected François Villon. Yet, the vagabond-poet-protest-rebel-priest figure inhabits our consciousness. The folk movement knew what it had in Woody Guthrie. When beat poets of the 1950s took their poems into the San Francisco jazz haunt, the Cellar, Lawrence Ferlinghetti, Kenneth Rexroth, and, later, Allen Ginsberg, knew that poetry and music were natural bedfellows. Dylan made himself internationally known and imitated as a neo-troubadour. The mass media accepted Dylan's prototype faster than the academics did. In 1965, John Ciardi, poetry editor of *Saturday Review*, granted that his nephew thought Dylan was a poet: "But like all Dylan fans I have met, he knows nothing about poetry. Neither does Bob Dylan." Four years later, Ciardi still challenged the aesthetics of "rock poetry": "Is it poetry? How would it look written out? Animal sounds could be put to the same beat ... I think the critics have flipped their categories." *Exactly!*

At the other pole stood Rexroth, writer, poet, and translator, who'd often appeared in *Saturday Review*. In 1957, he had been a prime mover in the Cellar jazz-and-poetry scene, and, in the 1930s, had experimented with jazz-poetry fusions in Chicago. Rexroth told me in 1966: "Dylan is the first of his kind in America. There have been singers in that tradition in France and Germany since Charlemagne, but Dylan developed in a vacuum. The importance of Dylan is that he is being imitated right and left. It is a very important phenomenon that in the new-leisure society of barefoot boys and girls, poetry is dissolving into the community. All of this is creating an extremely broad base for poetry. It is diffusing out. In classical China, all civil servants had to write a couplet of poetry to qualify. It led to a heaven built upon the highest poetry." In *Holiday* magazine, March 1966, Rexroth's summation of the prospects for poetry concluded: "Probably the most important event in recent poetry is Bob Dylan... he is the American beginning of a tradition as old as civilization in France, and some of his stuff is surprisingly good read over in hypercritical cold blood. This Dylan breakthrough is another great hope for poetry."

In December 1965, *Books* magazine called Dylan the American Yevtushenko and polled writers on Dylan and poetry. Poet Sandra Hochman: "I think it's wonderful that poets are becoming bards again. Since all poetry has to do with song, he is making a real contribution to our idea of what poetry can be." Novelist John Clellon Holmes: "Dylan reminds me of an American Brecht, the Brecht whose poems were meant to be sung. There is the same cold humor, the same ironic warmth, the same violent and splintered imagery, the same urgent idiomatic involvement in the way things actually are ... Dylan has returned poetry to song." Samuel Bogorad of the University of Vermont told *Books*: "Anyone who calls Dylan 'the greatest poet in the US today' has rocks in his head ... having once heard him on a record, I can testify that he can't even sing! Dylan is for the birds—and the bird-brained!" Hart Leavitt of Phillips Academy: "His poetry sounds like a very self-conscious imitation of Kerouac."

In September 1963, the *New York Times* magazine dismissed my proposal of a serious appraisal of Dylan as poet, philosopher, and moralist. They wanted him portrayed only as an entertainer. By December 1965, the magazine ran a major piece on Dylan, headlined PUBLIC WRITER NO 1? The subtitle ran: "WHO NEEDS SAUL BELLOW? There are those who say that *the* literary voice of our time—and a poet of high degree—is ... Bob Dylan." The writer, Thomas Meehan, said that, since the death of Faulkner and Hemingway, an informal survey of students majoring in English at three leading Ivy League colleges "revealed" that "their favorite contemporary American writer" was Dylan. A Brown University student: "We don't give a damn about Herzog's *angst* or Mailer's private fantasies. We're concerned with things like the threat of the nuclear war, the civil rights movement and the spreading blight of dishonesty, conformism and hypocrisy in the United States ...and Dylan is the only American writer dealing with these subjects in a way that makes any sense to us. As modern poetry, we feel that his songs have a high literary quality ... any one of his songs, like 'Hard Rain,' is more interesting to us ... than an entire volume of ... verse by someone like Robert Lowell." Meehan wrote that some of Dylan's social protest echoed Clifford Odets and Maxwell Anderson of the 1930s, and compared some lines from "It's Alright, Ma" to a "hillbilly W H Auden—specifically the earlier Auden of such poems as 'September 1, 1939.'"

In *Esquire* in May 1972, literary critic Frank Kermode and poet Stephen Spender pondered Dylan's poetics. *Esquire* added: "Finally, we called up Dylan, after months of fruitless trying, and asked the Wordsworth of the microgroove himself. 'Well, how do *you* see me?' he responded. 'Well, as a kind of human metaphor at the end of a corporate funnel,' we answered. 'Well, that ain't bad,' he said, and hung up." Spender found Dylan "highly skilled… It is difficult to judge the lyrics as 'poems' because they don't really have to be poetry. They just have to produce their simple effects of feeling, color and mild wit."

Kermode, much more rhapsodic, had even contemplated a book on Dylan's poetics. He stressed the importance of *hearing* the songs: "He is a virtuoso executant, and since he writes the words with virtuoso performance in mind, they can't, on the page, be more than … reminders, hints or shadows." Much good poetry, such as Greek tragedy and the medieval ballad, began in a similar way, Kermode wrote. "Certainly," he continued, Dylan's "long-established preference for mystery in the verbal texture has been an important factor in his development… This preference for mystery, opacity, a sort of emptiness in his texts, a passivity about meaning, is no doubt a deep temperamental trait." Kermode was intrigued that while Shakespeare and Beethoven are traditionally "allowed four periods," Dylan, by 1972, had already used up three. He found Dylan's rapid stylistic changes a response to "necessary public participation." Kermode concluded that Dylan's strength is "mystery, not just opacity, a geometry of innocence which [the listeners] can flesh out. His poems have to be open, empty, inviting collusion. To write thus is to practice a very modern art, though, as Dylan is well aware, it is an art with a complicated past."

In the *Village Voice* of January 26, 1967, Jack Newfield's front-page piece hailed Dylan as "the Brecht of the jukebox." He complained that "almost nobody over 30 in the literary and intellectual establishments even pays attention to his electronic … nightmare visions of America." Calling Dylan "the clown juggler of fact and fantasy, the bastard child of Chaplin, Céline and Hart Crane," Newfield concluded: "And he is a poet. If Whitman were alive today, he, too, would be playing an electric guitar."

In Britain, as early as April 16, 1965, the *Guardian* had assessed Dylan as "Homer in Denim," finding his "loose framework of assonant and consonant rhyme, using shifting eight to twelve-syllable iambic rhythms, which adjust themselves as naturally to speech as to song put him in a league with the youthfully committed Pound, Auden and MacNeice." The newspaper was astonished at the size of Dylan's audiences for a writer working in "the same tradition, in essentials, as Homer."

I have periodically conducted my own survey about Dylan as a poet. British novelist Anthony Burgess replied: "The trouble is that, though I've heard him, I've never seen any of his lyrics set down on paper. I know that verse being oral/aural, this ought to be a good thing, but I like to look at words, sometimes. I know that his skill as a composer of 'folk' lyrics is considerable, though I'm dubious as to whether folk art exists as more than a pastiche form among the sophisticated. I would say that he has achieved a very high standard in a very limited genre—first-class pop art, some might say. But that he can't compare as a poet with, say, people like Philip Larkin or even Adrian Mitchell. I'm not disparaging, but praising. I'd like him to tackle a volume of verse, separable from song, and then make my judgment."

By August 1968, Rod McKuen, a singer-songwriter, had sold a million copies of his three volumes of slight verse, and had become the best-selling "poet" in America. In trade papers, record companies were pushing songs by Jerry Jeff Walker and Laura Nyro with full-page ads running texts of their lyrics. Columbia University professor F W Dupee saw growing acceptance of pop poetics among academicians. "After all," he told me, "Homer was chanted and so were the Scandinavian epics. I think that in general the movement is great. They can arrive at standards later." During the middle to late Sixties, the pop audience and the pop critics, rather than major literary taste-makers, were discovering this outpouring of new poetics. As Dylan, a poet of the electric age, entered millions of homes, poetry became once again a democratic, social art. The shoe-shop clerk and the PhD candidate—even though they may have had little to say to each other at the record shop—were both buying Dylan, Beatles, Fugs, and Byrds albums. Enthusiasts felt pop had joined film as the first real contemporary "mass art." A sober report on young poets in *Newsweek* (March 3, 1969) saw an incredible flowering, offering not only survival but also success.

One common ground for young poets, white and black, is rock. "My poems are involved with the spoken voice and with melody," insists Tom Clark, 27. "My listening to rock—its spirit and gaiety—is bound to affect what I write." The extraordinary popularity, and talent of the rock poets—Cohen, the Beatles, Jim Morrison and Dylan (sometimes called "the major poet of his generation")—has prompted some word-poets to incorporate rock lyrics in their work.

A bloodless cultural revolution was taking place, led by "rock intellectuals." No longer, we then believed, could the dance hall, the discotheque, or the record collection be dismissed as mindless teenybopper blare. We saw the shows at the East Village's Dom, the Balloon Farm, the Fillmore in San Francisco, at Murray the K's Long Island airplane hangar as our arts festivals. The senses were assaulted with the insistent beat, light play, strobes, film clips, kinetic murals, all against that heavy sound. Through it all, the lyrics were repeated until they became part of us. Perhaps we were naïve, like Richard Neville in *Playpower* and Charles Reich in *The Greening of America*. If it was naïveté, then it was also sheer idealism, the belief that youth culture could change society. Viewed from the cool, cynical 1980s, we need to accept that deep change is not that simple to effect. We didn't necessarily think that the Gutenberg era was over or that books and the theater were dead; we thought their vitality and energy had passed over into popular music.

Pop pacemakers did not disdain books; they wrote them. John Lennon wrote two Edward Lear-like books, *In His Own Write* and *Spaniard in the Works*. Leonard Cohen closed his poetry readings with guitar in hand. Cohen told me that Dylan had inspired him to sing his own poems. "Dylan is not just a great poet, he's a great man," Cohen told me. Paul Simon's work reflected this new wave, and he was soon singing about alienation and vacuums. Jim Morrison of the Doors wrote astonishing lyrics. Allen Ginsberg taught Indian chants to the Byrds. Richard Fariña moved from page writing to singing and composing with his wife, Mimi Baez. Five experimental New York poets, led by Ed Sanders, taught themselves music and formed the Fugs. Phil Ochs adorned one of his album jackets with poems by Mao, and told me: "I want to be the first Left-wing star."

The young person of the Sixties was more adult. In their songs, Randy Newman and James Taylor, like sensitive memoirists, plumbed lonely episodes of their adolescences. The Beatles sang about the hollowness of the lonely crowd, and about tortured existences like Eleanor Rigby's. Pap records still made hits, but we were convinced in the Sixties that a sort of Pop Millennium had arrived. Fariña wrote in 1965: "One could argue … that if verse is never very far from song, that more people are listening to poetry at the moment than have in the history of mankind."

The Greening of the Campus. Such a burst of 1960s rhetoric may now ring hollow. The intervening years have seen growth in the literary and sociological study of popular music. During the period, the scrutiny of popular culture as a multi-disciplinary field has mushroomed. As many as 6,000 courses in popular culture have been offered in American colleges. Dylan's work is stage center in a many of them. As early as 1977, a survey of 150 heads of English departments at major colleges and universities undertaken by Professor Louis Cantor, a historian, of Purdue-Indiana University at Fort Wayne, suggested that more than a hundred courses had by then been taught on Dylan's poetics alone. Cantor reported that "Dylan's roots have, at last, been firmly planted in the groves of academe. It's not unusual to find Dylan being taught in literature survey courses along with Blake and Eliot. Dylan is apparently winning out in the academic controversy over his legitimacy as a poet." I've had a lively interchange with academics regarding their literary analyses of Dylan's lyrics. I've read several dozen dissertations and papers linking aspects of his visionary Romantic song-poetry to that of Yeats, Eliot, the Cabala, Whitman, biblical prophets and apostles, the French symbolists, Blake, Kafka, and the beats.

Perhaps the most prestigious Dylan commentator is Christopher Ricks, whose books include *Milton's Grand Style*, *Tennyson*, and *Keats and Embarrassment*. He has lectured internationally on Dylan's poetics and calls Dylan "a great amuser, a great entertainer, who belongs with the artists who've looked for the widest popular constituency, like Dickens and Shakespeare." Ricks believes that, since the deaths of John Berryman and Robert Lowell, Dylan has become "the best American *user* of words." Although "reluctant to call him a poet," because "he's got more than words to use," Ricks praises his "great, brilliant work as a rhymester." Says the Professor: "I'm not so besotted with Dylan's genius not to know that not all of his work is perfect. He's only as good as Shakespeare, who had a lot wrong, too!"

The first big conclave of Dylan literary scholars occurred in December 1975, at the annual meeting of the Modern Language Association in San Francisco. A popular literature seminar on Dylan was organized by Professor Patrick D Morrow of Auburn University in Alabama. Some faculty folkniks played and sang the songs, and three papers were read: Belle D Levinson's "The Deranged Seer: The Poetry of Rimbaud and Dylan," Emily Toth's "The Women in Bob Dylan," and W T Lhamon's "Dylan and the Cultural Context." Richard Goodall organized the Dylan Revisited conventions in Manchester,

England, at which films, tapes, and videos were used, and serious discussion mixed with trivia, the fevers of collectors with Ricks and Lhamon, and musicologist Wilfrid Mellers. During the 1970s, literature PhDs were granted to Bill King by the University of North Carolina and to Betsy Bowden by the University of California at Berkeley for their Dylan dissertations. Other doctoral work was in progress by the early 1980s in West Germany, Belgium, Britain, as well as in America.

A valuable essay on Dylan and Blake has been written by Eugene Stelzig of the English department at the State University of New York at Geneseo. "Once I started to look at Dylan's songpoetry critically," Stelzig wrote me, "it was obvious that he is one of the major contemporary voices rooted in the whole Romantic tradition of the artist as a seer/prophet." A widely published literature professor, David R Pichaske, of Bradley University, compiled an offbeat anthology, *Beowulf to Beatles: Approaches to Poetry*, in which ten complete Dylan song texts are printed alongside works by Ben Jonson, Auden, Frost, and others. In a seminar at Dartmouth, Louis A Renza had the students "discuss the songs as if they were poems, or treat albums as if they were somehow unitary texts … keeping alive the issue of a strictly 'literary' interpretation. … The students are often surprised at the poetic quality of his lyrics and his insistent meta-poetic turns."

A literature professor at Florida State University at Tallahassee, W T Lhamon, Jr, has written brilliantly about Dylan in *New Republic* and *Bennington Review*. In his trail-blazing essay, "Poplore and Dylan," Lhamon maintains that poplore has succeeded folklore in contemporary America: "Pop helps a few people make money. Poplore helps the rest of us live. Investing pop images with mythic resonance, poplore locates patterns of usefulness in the bewildering panoply of instant images that the electronic media and other distribution nets of consumer culture throw before contemporary audiences … A society that has no available folk—but still needs lore—produces poplore … Dylan's embrace of rock altered the course of American culture. This return to the on-going rhythms of popular culture has always been the hallmark of a new cultural era's beginning. Such a return occurred when literature, via the novel, turned in the eighteenth-century from the life of the aristocracy to the life of the middle class."

The Popular Culture Association of the South has heard several papers on Dylan, from such scholars as Dr Kenneth J Cook and Greg Keeler of Montana State University, and from Tulsa University, Bob Graalman and Lynn DeVore. Professor Suzanne H MacRae of the University of Arkansas has included Dylan's work in several humanities courses, "and I've even compared him to some writers in the medieval satiric tradition." Her essay, "Bob Dylan is the Weatherman," written long before *Slow Train Coming*, is strong on the rebirth theme. At the University of Texas at Arlington, Jerome L Rodnitzky, associate professor of history, encourages graduate students to work with popular music in research courses. His book, *Minstrels of the Dawn: The Folk-Protest Singer As a Cultural Hero*, contains a thirty-five-page chapter on Dylan, entitled "Beyond Left and Right."

Dylan literary studies have even weathered the waters out to Pelican Island, off Galveston, to the Texas A & M University's Moody College of Marine Sciences and Maritime Resources. There, Dr Thomas S Johnson, a lecturer in the humanities, holds that "Dylan's work is certainly hearty enough to bear the close examination of any open-minded humanist." Johnson wrote me of his concern that academic studies of a figure like Dylan run the risk of "didacticism—of overwhelming the reader's or listener's ability to respond directly, personally to the lyric, itself." At North Texas State University, Dr James Baird has taught courses on the lyrics, using the albums and *Tarantula* as study materials. Baird says: "We're trying to broaden the traditional range of English and provide a new frame of reference. Most students don't realize that Dylan has read a lot, and his songs reflect that reading." Steven Tucker, studying for a history doctorate at Tulane, reported to me that "Dylan is alive and well in the academic world." At Rutgers, Kevin Hayes has taught a course on "three revolutionary visionary writers—Blake, Ginsberg and Dylan."

As Dylan studies spread throughout the academic world, as the Sixties accrete an ever-deepening luster of great times past, it's impossible to predict where it will all end. There's always the danger of the academic world's analyzing popular culture artifacts in a fashion inimical to its original vitality and street validity.

Gutenberg Rolls Back. Despite the McLuhanite predictions, the book hasn't died yet. Even in the study of oral/aural literature, the printed word is not completely replaceable by the recording. Ideally, the published song lyric will resonate off the page for those familiar with the recorded song. Dylan's first book, *Tarantula*, also proves, conversely, that some page writing can best be fully appreciated when it is read aloud, reminding us of Gerard Manley Hopkins's suggestion: "Read it with the ear."

Dylan's first collection of song lyrics, aside from the album song folios, emerged in *Writings and Drawings*, published in April 1973 by Alfred A Knopf. Robert Gottlieb, Knopf's president and editor-in-chief, wrote me that it "delighted" him to work on it. "I have a life-long passion for pop music and a great admiration for Dylan in particular. The book had a very smooth passage, once we had found a design or tone that Bob liked; everyone worked well with everyone else." Within two months, Cape published a British edition; across Europe and in Japan, others followed. The work is set out in chronological order, in eleven sections ranging from the first album through *New Morning*. There are a total of 187 song lyrics, seventeen drawings, five pages of manuscript text, and twenty-six poems, including the "11 Outlined Epitaphs" and "Some Other Kinds of Songs." There are the lyrics of songs that have been officially recorded as well as some yet to be heard. Of special interest, two years before their official release, were *The Basement Tapes* lyrics.

Dylan's folkish line drawings remind us of his debt to Guthrie, who also illustrated many of his songs and other writings. A dedicatory note rolls with Woody's open-plains cadences. Guthrie and Robert Johnson, the great Delta bluesman, are lauded for having "sparked it off." Those wanting an insight into Dylan's battle for just the right word and phrase will be drawn to the four endpapers of songs in progress and a full-page reproduction of an early draft of "Subterranean Homesick Blues." Although *Writings and Drawings* has gone through many reprintings and editions and continues to sell well, it was not received by the establishment or literary press as a poetry volume of significance. Ralph Gleason devoted a column to it, citing its value "for anyone who is interested in the cultural history of America, for those interested in the most important contemporary poets … Napoleon in rags cannot be dismissed merely as a fad or as a topical songwriter. He is a poet."

The British edition got ample notice in *The Times* and *Observer*, but the reviews were dismissive on the question: "Is it poetry?" Snorted Robert Nye in *The Times*: "as a poet he is strictly for the birds. He emerges from this book as a canny-hearted, miserable fellow, with an uncontrollable gift for imperfect rhymes and a positive genius for repetition." Clive James, himself a one-time lyricist for songwriter Pete Atkin, wrote in the *Observer*: "The frustration of reading this book lies in the realization that no stanza will ever be as good as its best line and no song will ever be as good as its best stanza."

Tarantula. While Dylan students can grapple with one of his ambiguous phrases in a song lyric, his "novel," *Tarantula*, has curiously not deeply engaged many of them. The literary world barely paid it any credence at all. *Tarantula* is an enigma wrapped in a question mark. Some of it is automatic writing, most of it is highly musical, and all of it offers more when read aloud. Dylan held the book back at the time of the crucial motorcycle accident of 1966, having reservations about how it was being built up and promoted by Macmillan. He also had doubts about how book reviewers would deal with it. With Macmillan already touting him as a "young James Joyce," the publication of the book would put him in that literary coliseum in front of lions he chose not to face.

I asked Gabrielle Goodchild to undertake an analysis and discussion of *Tarantula*. She found the book "a circus of dreams … concerned with night-time truths and half-truths." Linking the bite of the poisonous tarantula to the dancing mania called tarantism, she found "it is as a mad 'dance' and as 'music' that the book succeeds." Although the Left was vexed with Dylan for not having made more overt comments on the Vietnam War, we find a great deal of that war in the book. Goodchild holds it is a surrealist sort of "war" going on "beyond our control and yet poisoning our lives." From Dylan's phrase "combined in a stolen mirror," she reads the book as a two-way mirror "that looks out one way to the actual world of supermarkets and malnutrition" and the other way into the artist's mind. He is searching for order while accepting chaos. Goodchild places *Tarantula* in the *Highway 61 Revisited* frame "in dramatic stance, personae, sound patterns," and rhythm. She finds him using "language of concurrence, coincidence, and contradiction." From the standpoint of revealing Dylan, his veneration of a junkyard angel, Aretha, is important, especially in the light of his later association with many women gospel singers. Aretha is "a symbol of innocent physicality whose 'nakedness is a piercing thing.' She's also spiritual renewal in the hollow desert of modern existence."

Goodchild maintains that *Tarantula* "works best where the combination is funny… where the 'wit' is effective, language is pressurized into producing a new and purposeful energy, a lateral connection, time-warp, a new world: extra-sense. It repeatedly falls flat, becoming only obscure: nonsense." Many reviewers invoked Joyce, one even calling the book "*Finnegans Wake* of the Pepsi generation." Goodchild says it is more useful to place the book in the context of the beat writers, notably William Burroughs, with a debt to Jack Kerouac for spontaneity. "*On The Road*, but ten years on, and light years into inner depths, and into a different sense of guilt and involvement, a greater inner awareness of a greater inner and outer violence. A lot had happened in the ten years between *On the Road* and *Tarantula*."

Goodchild found the influence of Kenneth Patchen's *The Journal of Albion Moonlight* most relevant, even though it dates from 1941. (I was clued in on that one night by George Plimpton, at a Village party after he had received the original galleys of *Tarantula*. Patchen was also a favored writer of Tony Glover.) "The similarity between the two books is more than that of sound, surface, and jokes, for both are dramas in which the writer struggles to get a response from us and is often frustrated. Both are halls of mirrors, where illusion is the only reality," Goodchild writes. With Patchen reaching back to Blake and Dylan reaching back to Rimbaud, Goodchild wonders: "Why is this dream-world so violent? It is because there's a war going on: for Patchen, in 1941, Hitler's war, and for Dylan, in 1965, Vietnam."

The novel, she wrote, reflects Dylan's "hilarious love of the wisdom and idiocy of words … it carries us, in great waves until we are deposited, dizzy, danced out, with only dim memories of the stoned laughter and manic violence … Dylan presents his 'world' in the very process of its being created and discovered, its outlines sometimes only half-formed before the mirror cracks, the image fades, the scene fragments and disperses, its contents all jumbled up and reassembled into another picture." If *Tarantula* has a subject, Goodchild wrote, it is about chaos, and the artistic struggle to find artistic form for expressing it. "After the accident, it became less and less possible for him to rewrite the book. By 1968, he was repudiating the project" to *Newsweek* and *Sing Out!* And in 1969, he was saying he'd thrown it together like a collage of scraps of paper. But Goodchild believes "this was partly smokescreen," for it had been "a serious, deliberate, perhaps desperate endeavour." Citing Stephen Pickering's essay, "The Two Tarantulas: A Textual Comparison," she wrote: "We see how rigorously Dylan had edited the earlier manuscript, *Tarantula Meets Rex Paste*, which ended with an epilogue from Rimbaud's *Les Poétes de Sept Ans*." She believes that "certainly the book wrote him as much as he wrote it … We make better sense of the electric prose, originally to have been called *Off the Record* or *Side One*, if we hear behind it the melodies from *Another Side* to *Blonde on Blonde*. The novel only really works where we can hear it with the emphatic rhythms of Dylan's 1965 voice, the way he sang, in italics."

Of the many characters who appear in *Tarantula*, Goodchild finds only two are dominant: "Aretha, a soulful Mama, Muse and helper … a symbol of innocent physicality who is also spiritual renewal in the hollow desert of modern existence. Her element is Music … The other figure is the narrator, both entirely Dylan … and everything he is not … There is one other main player in this pitchfork drama—the reader. We are challenged and hectored; occasionally, courted … If the book can partly be seen as a Courtly Love Poem, an Adoration by the kneeling yet fearless lover to the unattainable beloved he has created, she of the 'religious thighs,' then we make up the court in which the madman-jester performs and is judged."

But the book is alive with other characters, "crammed together at Desolation Row carnivals, society parties and with funny psychedelic soubriquets, characters from TV and film, nursery rhymes and comics, art and philosophy and literature, the Bible, legend, history, politics, the folk songbook, the book of the blues, jazz, pop music, show business, and the news." Finding some relationship to Kerouac, she also links *Tarantula* to the New Journalist and his celebration of violence, paranoia, and artificial stimulants. Dylan inspired some of the Novel Reporters and shares with them the decision to produce under pressure, using language with a Shakespearean disregard for Latinate grammar, with nouns as adjectives and capitals as exclamation marks, taking from the mud of the immediate moment, garlic or sapphires, hurling it all together inside of the frozen traffic."

For all the effort it demands, Goodchild urges readers not to fear it, and listeners to try it. "Travelling back along Highway 61 in a different Buick is worth the undertaking even if you never actually make it to Edge City… Beware the Spider's Web, the Lady Tarantula, and Beware America. Beware the dream and beware the reality! But, above all, 'live before you board your *Titanic*.' We all know it sails at dawn." *Tarantula* is difficult reading. It is howlingly funny, at times very violent, but it is original, inventive, and challenging. I suggest you give *Tarantula* a go. Try reading it aloud. Play *Highway 61* a few times before you plunge in. Good luck, and have a nice trip. Gutenberg would roll over in his grave!

Opposite: Dylan poses for *Another Side* album photo shoot.
Above: *Tarantula*, written between 1965 and 1966, and eventually published in 1971;
and on the road from Cambridge to Amherst, Massachusetts, April 1964: the Ford station wagon was Dylan and Victor Maimudes' first road car.

I've walked and I've crawled on six crooked highways.
DYLAN, 1963[1]

To be in hell is to drift … to be in heaven is to steer.
GEORGE BERNARD SHAW, *DON JUAN IN HELL*

I accept chaos. I am not sure whether it accepts me.
DYLAN, 1965[2]

You certainly look like an intense young man.

CARL SANDBURG TO DYLAN, 1964

Above: On stage
Newport, 1964.
Right: Victor Maimudes
and Bob Neuwirth with
Dylan on the newly
acquired Triumph.

13 Before we join our anti-hero on a mad, careening, chaotic road show that began on February 3, 1964—and scarcely paused for breath for two and a half years—let's retrace our steps a bit. While all that stage/page/electric poetry we examined in the last chapter was pumping out, the narrative of Dylan's outer life picks up at the end of 1963: Kennedy dead, the romance with Suze dying, the Tom Paine award more pain than gain, Dylan's summary of the dying year in his letter to *Broadside*. In 1964, when he decided to try rediscovering America, he was not yet 23.

The journey that began in February 1964 went from New York to California with a half-dozen detours to see embattled miners in Kentucky, a pilgrimage to visit a father-poet, New Orleans and Mardi Gras, and a linking of arms again with southern civil rights fighters. Only four concerts were scheduled. Dylan carried no compass, just "road-maps of the soul."[3] After years of steering toward goals, Orpheus was descending for several seasons in hell. He rolled like thunder across America's landscape, right through Whitman's "Open Road," Guthrie's *Hard Travelin'*, Kerouac's *On the Road*, Hopper and Fonda's *Easy Rider*, and Kesey's Acid Test. Beyond the restlessness, curiosity and hunger for experience was Dylan's compulsion to keep in physical and spiritual motion.

He chose his companions carefully; the alchemy of four young men in a station wagon was not easy to balance. Later, Dylan told me: "I'm lucky. Not because I make a lot of bread, but because I can be around groovy people. I don't fear anything and nobody around me has to fear anything. That's where it's at: bread, freedom, and no fear." Doing most of the driving and keeping business affairs straight was Victor Maimudes. Tall, taciturn, suggesting Clint Eastwood crossed with Vittorio Gassman, Victor had penetrating dark eyes, turbulent hair, and an uncanny ability to keep his mouth shut. Wanting to be an actor, or work in films, he often seethed in personal frustration but he rarely criticized Dylan, even while his duties were often those of a flunky.

Pete Karman was a longtime friend of the Rotolos, seen by mother Mary as Mr Responsible, with a job and a vast range of neckties. He came along for kicks. He had worked on the *Daily Mirror*, and later became a travel magazine editor. He never wrote about the Dylan trip, just talked of its madness and his disillusionment. The previous year, Karman had visited Cuba. "Dylan is an incredible person, but Che Guevara is probably the most impressive person I've ever seen ... Che Guevara, or Bobby Dylan, would never light a cigarette for you, but Che and Dylan are still the two greatest folk heroes of our time. I used to call Dylan 'the punk.' I used to ask: 'How're you doing, punk?' I was twenty and he was only nineteen.'" By the time of the trip, Pete wasn't calling him the punk anymore. Dylan later told me: "We had to kick Pete out and send him home on a plane."[4]

The final member of the supporting cast was Paul Clayton, an introspective singer and folklorist, with a Jesus' beard and gentleness. A scholar and romantic, Clayton wanted to live his old ballads. With some twenty albums to his credit, he was once called "the most recorded young folk singer in America," yet he was scarcely known. Despite two degrees and encyclopedic knowledge of folklore, Clayton remained unpretentious, self-effacing, and dedicated to his art and his friends, of whom none was greater than Dylan. Karman said that during this trip, Clayton seemed to be traveling under some undefined personal burden. Paul had been going out with Carla, and at times he and Dylan and the sisters had become so involved with each other that the problems of all the relationships were geometrically enlarged. According to Pete, Paul got stoned more often than anyone on the trip. (Succumbing to professional frustrations and a dependency on drugs, Clayton was found dead in his bathtub, of electrocution, on April 6, 1967.)

The trip began unceremoniously. Victor loaded up with several thousand in traveler's checks. Pete showed up at Grossman's at 10 a.m. but with farewells to Suze and the Van Ronks and rounding up clothes for striking miners in Hazard, Kentucky, they didn't leave until dusk. The blue Ford was cluttered with suitcases, instruments, and old clothing. Once the clothes were delivered, Dylan often perched in the rear of that mobile writer's garret to scribble lyrics or a chord progression. Between talk and games, the foursome frequently fell into long silences. The solitude into which Dylan withdrew, a shell that created space around him, was palpable. He wrote at least two important songs on the trip: "Chimes of Freedom" and "Ballad in Plain D."

The first night's goal was Clayton's gracious old university town, Charlottesville, Virginia. Eighteen months earlier, Clayton had taken Bob into Charlottesville's Gaslight, praising him to folkniks like Bill Clifton and Mike Seeger. Clifton recalled "a good, late evening with Bob, just picking and singing." Although Clayton had a rough country cabin outside town, the four stayed with Paul's friend, Steve Wilson. Buying two dozen copies of *Times Changing* to hand out along the way, Dylan was recognized by students and sales people.

They left Charlottesville next morning, for eastern Kentucky. Coal country. Near Abingdon, Virginia, they picked up a young coal miner, Robert Swann, wearing a miner's lighted helmet, his face smudged with coal dust. Dylan gave the miner *Freewheelin'*, and the hitchhiker seemed impressed. Swann was their introduction to Harlan County and the men of the other underground. They crossed Harlan County and looked for the strike leader, Hamish Sinclair, secretary of the National Committee for Miners. Sinclair, who had sung at benefits in New York, linked the pickets and their supporters. He greeted Dylan's group warmly; they unloaded the clothing. Hamish was up to his ears bailing people out of jail, seeing to strikers' welfare, organizing legal moves. Dylan wanted to contribute more than clothes—a benefit concert, perhaps. Sinclair was too preoccupied, and sent them to visit miners and picket leader Jason Combes. Dylan's crew left earlier than expected, I think because the memories of Hibbing were too painful.

They headed south-east. First night, a motel in Pineville, Kentucky; then, Asheville, North Carolina, birthplace of novelist Thomas Wolfe, who wrote *You Can't Go Home Again*. Asheville was still segregated, although during store hours, the white shops welcomed black customers. The group went bowling in a black bowling alley, shot pool, and went to a nudie movie—Dylan recognized a girl who'd been a Gaslight waitress in the Village.

On to Hendersonville, near Flat Rock, North Carolina. They couldn't find the home of Carl Sandburg, the writer, but were directed to the home of a Sandburg who raised goats. Same man. Sandburg was a towering figure to his visitors. There was much that Dylan had in common with the 86-year-old poet, biographer of Lincoln, collector and singer of folk songs. Sandburg was born of immigrants in the Midwest. Much as the young Sandburg had revered Whitman, Dylan now revered Sandburg. The old writer had been, in critic Harvey Breit's words, "milk-wagon driver in Illinois, wheat harvester in Kansas, dish-washer in Colorado, coal-shoveler in Omaha, soldier in Puerto Rico ... hobo, newspaper man, novelist, historian, biographer, balladeer, goat farmer." In 1919, in a letter to French novelist and pacifist Romain Rolland, Sandburg had written words that might have come from Woody: "I am an IWW,[5] but I don't carry a red card. I am an anarchist, but not a member of the organization ... I belong to everything and nothing ... I would say I am with all rebels everywhere all the time as against all people who are satisfied."

When the travelers' station wagon pulled into Sandburg's 240-acre Connemara Farm, on the porch was a buxom grandmother figure out of Norman Rockwell, Mrs Lillian Sandburg. She didn't seem startled by the hairy foursome. According to Pete, Dylan announced: "I am a poet. My name is Robert Dylan, and I would like to see Mr Sandburg." She disappeared into the house while they looked over the serene, sloping pasture, where goats grazed, into a heavy wood backed by Sugarloaf Mountain. To the rear, large pine trees ran thickly from Little and Big Glassy Mountains down to the house, built a hundred years earlier by Christopher Memminger, Confederate Treasury Secretary. The Sandburgs and their daughters lived there from 1945 until his death in July 1967.

The waiting seemed interminable. Finally, the poet appeared, a genial, slow-moving man. His gray hair tumbled over his left ear, his face was stubbled. He obviously didn't care about shaving daily either. He wore an old plaid wool shirt, baggy trousers, and a green eye shade over shell-rimmed glasses. Sandburg's penetrating eyes assessed his visitors carefully in their dungarees, jackets, cowboy boots. Instinctively, his pale blue eyes locked with Dylan's bright blue ones. (Pete later told me: "Sandburg looked at the rest of us, but he just wasn't as interested as he was in Dylan. There was an immediate, unspoken communication between them.") Sandburg: "You look like you are ready for anything. I would like to ask you about forty good questions. Your group looks able to prepare for any emergency." Dylan handed the old writer *Times Changing* and Clayton stepped forward with one of his albums. Sandburg said he didn't know Dylan's work at all, but he was interested in poetry and folk singing and regarded them as kindred arts. The visitors praised Sandburg for his pioneer song-collecting, indicating familiarity with his *American Songbag* (280 songs and ballads first published in 1927).

For around twenty minutes, the five chatted on the porch. Dylan had wanted the great writer to "open up" and take them into his study to see his books, his piles of manuscripts. Sandburg repeated that he'd listen to the two albums, and Dylan reiterated that he too was a poet. Every time the word *poet* was mentioned, Sandburg seemed to prick up his ears. The old poet excused himself, saying that he simply had to work on some manuscripts and letters. Pete recalls: "We had a definite feeling of disappointment, mainly because Sandburg had never heard of Bobby. As I recall, during the rest of the trip Sandburg was never mentioned again. Dylan sank into one of his quiet funks."

From Flat Rock into South Carolina, where fireworks were sold legally. They filled the car with rockets, whizbangs, and cherry bombs. Then, Athens, Georgia—another university center. Dylan, pinball wizard, headed for a pool hall, and they played the tables and machines. Along the streets, students right and left recognized Dylan; some sidled up for an autograph. Another record-shop flurry of recognition soothed the disappointment of Sandburg's detachment. Next day, they looked around progressive Atlanta. That evening, Dylan's concert at nearby Emory University. The student audience knew nearly every song by its opening phrase. Afterward, a party, to which local *éminences grises* of folk music and southern radicalism were invited. Grainy, gritty Ernie Marrs, a chip off Woody's quarry, looked over "this Dylan kid" with curiosity. Fresh from some picket line or sit-in were Bernice Johnson and Cordell Reagon. Next day, Dylan visited them in Atlanta.

Westward through the Deep South black belt toward Mississippi: WHITE ONLY signs, garish billboards. They couldn't believe they were still in the United States. The South hadn't really changed all that much. Dylan scanned the roadside. He scribbled a few notes on small scraps of paper and heard "Chimes of Freedom" ringing in his inner ears. Crossing into Mississippi, a fork on their road. Should they join SNCC at Tougaloo College, as half-promised, or drift southward toward New Orleans and Mardi Gras? Excitement and curiosity pointed them toward New Orleans. They stopped overnight at Meridian, Mississippi, the birthplace of Jimmie Rodgers, the "singing brakeman" who became the father of country music. Did anyone need to remind them what a fabled music city New Orleans was? The lures of colorful Crescent City and its yearly carnival of abandon sent them skittering toward the Gulf.

Many had made the pilgrimage before to the fountainhead of jazz, home of the Creole street cry, focus of the swamp music from the Cajun bayous, a town where the heat of the blues was stoked up in a cauldron of musical cross-currents. There had been a great cavalcade of sounds through New Orleans: brass-band music to and from the cemeteries, pianists toying with the cakewalk and ragtime in Storyville's red-light houses. New Orleans was the town of jazz giants Buddy Bolden, George Lewis, Louis Armstrong. Here Mahalia Jackson learned to sing. In the streets, clogs and buck-and-wings, shufflers and juba dancers, had competed for pennies. Here was the town of street violinists and alley fiddlers, the town that took an old-world folk ballad like "Derby Ram" and turned it into that jazz classic, "Didn't He Ramble." Everything about New Orleans's musical past spelled freedom, a hell-bent stew of styles, where nobody told a jazzman he couldn't play this or that; he played whatever he wanted, borrowed and embellished what he pleased. New Orleans was the Jerusalem of all musical faiths, where the work song mated with the spiritual to give birth to the blues, where the blues moved from country to city, where anything that could be banged, hit, struck, or malleted, blown through or blown at, became an instrument. The chimney sweep and the hawker of wild berries had sung through these streets. All that was vibrant and classic in American popular music was at home in this languorous, easy-talking city. New Orleans was a carnival any time of the year, but especially at Mardi Gras.

Each year, just before the onset of gloomy Lent, New Orleans blows its collective cool in a multi-million-dollar festival that lures world visitors. Mardi Gras (literally, "Fat Tuesday") had passed from pagan to Christian to commercial. Now it was partly a come-on for nightclubs, souvenir shops, and hotels. Still, the most crowded part of the festival took place on the streets, for free. WELCOME TO CRESCENT CITY, SIGN UP FOR THE MARCH OF KING ZULU, or THIS WAY FOR KING REX PARADE read the banners. Masked and costumed marchers, dancing bands, and marching societies lined the pavements. It was *Black Orpheus* and *Easy Rider* on one reel, with Mephisto as stage manager and Dionysus tending bar. The only room they could find cost $50. They started to explore the whirling streets. Pete, out on his own, made a few foolish moves. Somewhere along Bourbon he met a stripper with a New York accent who'd known Hugh Romney. She was looking for grass, and

Pete said he might know where to get some. He gave her the motel number, but supposedly didn't tell her whom he was traveling with. Back at the motel, everyone turned in early. At 3 a.m., the stripper called Pete. Pete tried to explain his indiscretion to his half-awake companions, and was swamped with instant paranoia. They threw him out. When he blearily returned the next morning, he found the others ready to take on Mardi Gras at full tilt and find the stripper who knew Hugh Romney.

By tradition, Mardi Gras street revelry surrounds the parades, and everyone carries his own bottle. Another tradition of segregationist New Orleans soon became apparent. The four positioned themselves at a crowded corner where the view was good. Although the time was just after breakfast, each carried a bottle of wine and took huge gulps. A costumed Negro dancer passed, carrying candlelit flambeaux, aloft. The torchbearer stopped in front of Dylan's group. Having danced for two miles he was exhausted and thirsty. Bob handed him his bottle and the dancer took a generous gulp. The crowd around Dylan became uneasy. A kindly faced little old lady whined: "You mean that you would give a nigger a drink out of your very own bottle?" Dylan didn't reply. Several sailors moved forward menacingly. Pete said: "This is it, boys. We're all going to be murdered!" Dylan told his fellows: "Disappear into the crowd." When they reassembled, Dylan mused: "It's not the same country."

Although Mardi Gras madness made many lasting impressions on Dylan that appear in songs from "Desolation Row" to "Visions of Johanna," he made only passing specific references to it in his writings. On the liner notes of *Another Side*, he mentioned the carnival fleetingly, in the fifth poem, referring obscurely to a "white Southern poet," Joe B Stuart. Although he had misspelled the name, Dylan remembered an instant New Orleans friendship. Joe B Stewart remembered Dylan and set down his recollections in 1967. He was a high-school English teacher from Mobile, with a shining young face, a sharp ear, and warm eyes. Joe took an immediate liking to Dylan and vice versa. By the time he chanced to meet Dylan, Joe and his friends had been up for five days and nights: "It had been sweet and I was open for anything," he wrote. "Standing in the second bar of La Casa, I would not have been surprised if Walt Disney had come through the door. I looked at his little pale face, which was set in a serious scowl with eyes darting back and forth, waiting to see if he would be recognized." Joe simply said: "Hi, Bob." Dylan's response was to keep moving.

In New Orleans too, 1964 was the year of the folk singer. Around the corner from La Casa, a contingent of folkniks sang in a bar in exchange for free beer and tips. Young white folknik pilgrims congregated on the street, strumming, singing, and trying to look like Dylan. At one corner stood an old black woman, large-boned and intense, dressed in white, who preached about hell and salvation and then sang gospel songs and spirituals, keeping time with her tambourine. Stewart: "Back down near La Casa, I again passed Dylan and his 'buddies.' They were moving along, quiet, serious, and not drunk. I said hello once again, but, just as before, he kept right on going." Stewart and a friend, Jim Furhmann, moved on through the chaos. Somewhere, they picked up a young girl from across the river. She was with them when Joe saw Dylan for the third time. Bob ran up and said: "Man, I'm so sorry I didn't speak to you before." Then, looking at their Louisiana girl, Wendy, Dylan said: "Look at those watery blue eyes!" Wendy to Dylan: "You sure do have long hair." He replied: "Yes, and I'm gonna let my hair grow to the streets and write my poems from the top of these buildings."

Jim and Wendy departed, and Dylan opened up to the Alabama teacher. Dylan wanted more wine, so back to the weaving, lurching La Casa, throbbing with Spanish music. Some of Joe's friends were there. Norman Boyles, working on a PhD at Tulane, debated the values of formal education with Dylan. The graduate student defended education as a road map. The music rose and the drunken shouting increased. Dylan produced the address of a private party. As the five stood at the corner of Iberville near Canal and watched, another flambeaux carrier, the Comus Parade, the last and best, was stretching out along the road. The five passed the bottle and jumped for the beads and doubloons that the paraders were throwing. Stewart: "We were all caught up in the magic and there was no holding back on anyone's part."

As the Comus ended, they moved to Wanda's Seven Seas, a bar as noisy as the streets. Dylan tried to get into every conversation, moving from group to group, asking questions and interjecting comments. Exhausted, he and the others tumbled out onto Bourbon, where a kid was standing against a wall, playing his guitar and singing "Don't Think Twice." Dylan: "You sing that very well. Let's hear one more." The boy started to sing and Dylan and others joined in. The folk singer stammered: "You! I mean ... it couldn't be. No, it's impossible!" Dylan repeated: "You sing that real well," and they moved on.

Dylan approached a worn-out black man and invited him to join them for a drink. They headed to Cosimo's. As the five whites and one black approached, the bartender came running to meet them at the door. "Joe, don't come in here," the bartender pleaded. "Get him out. We don't want any trouble." An argument, then a compromise: Joe would buy a beer for their black friend but bring it out for him to drink on the street. Joe suggested another bar where there would be less trouble — Baby Green's, run by blacks. The black man: "If I can't go into one of your places, you can come to one of mine." All six were blasting down Burgundy, and the minute they got to Baby Green's, Dylan got into an argument. "Why, man? Why?" Dylan kept shouting at the black bartender. The bartender: "We don't want any trouble. The cops'll come and put us all in jail. Go on, son. Somewhere your mother is on her knees praying for you." The others persuaded Bob to stop challenging segregation. They headed into the French Quarter and the Seven Seas bar, where Victor and Joe played ping-pong and chess. The others followed Dylan to the Morning Call coffee bar nearby, then joined up again.

Joe had a friend in the *vieux carré*, and as they headed that way, Joe felt an urge to run. Dylan ran after him, a drunken chase leading nowhere, until Dylan tripped on a curb and sprawled out on the pavement. They carried Bob to a friend's apartment. A married woman named Susan had endured drunks dropping in on her all week and was fed up. Joe shouted back that Bob Dylan was with him. Susan opened the door. They delivered a giggling Dylan with a sprained ankle. Sitting in a rocking chair he poured himself a jelly glass of wine and rocked rhythmically back and forth, sometimes hitting a table filled with fragile objects. He and his hostess, Susan, did most of the talking. Dylan described his entire journey as a series of encounters with famous writers. As he watched, Stewart thought: "This guy won't last long, he'll either burn himself out or get himself killed in some stupid accident, the way James Dean did." Joe had seen Dylan running out in front of cars without looking. Victor had told Joe over their chess game that on the highway Dylan wouldn't let him stop the car; he just "wanted to go on and on." The dialogue between Dylan and Susan touched on names of southern writers. Dylan dismissed Tennessee Williams as a "guilty cat, man." Faulkner headed his list of writers to meet.

Dylan wanted to walk the streets again, and they headed for the Gin Mill. As the group walked along toward Canal, Stewart quoted from a poem. "Who wrote that — Hank Williams?" Dylan asked. "Naw," Joe replied, "I did." Dylan said: "Man, I wish I had had some crazy schoolteachers like you." He complained that his formal education had been predictable, dull. Joe asked him when he was due to go into service. Dylan: "I tried to join, but they wouldn't take me." The growing group of wanderers returned to La Casa; they spent a few minutes at each of the saloon's bars in search of some new excitement. Someone suggested a lively Greek bar. By now, they'd picked up yet another teacher. Dylan: "Schoolteachers! Schoolteachers! I'm surrounded by schoolteachers!" He told Joe that he liked college students and was very interested in what they were thinking. As they teetered toward the Greek bar, a bunch of roughnecks screeched up beside them in a car. They jumped out: "All right, Dylan, are you coming with us, or not?" Bob backed off and murmured coolly: "I don't have anything to say. Victor speaks for me." Victor, drawing himself up to his full height, told the hoodish crew to get lost. "Well, all right, man, have it your way," one shouted from the car, and they were gone in the night.

The Athenian Room, nearly 3 a.m.: Upstairs, a drunken sailor was dancing with a drag queen. The transvestite swooped the sailor over half-backward, kissed him, and pinched his bottom. At a nearby table, the drag queen's friends roared. The drinking, walking, and excitement were wearing out everyone except Dylan, who kept pummeling the teachers: "Will you teach my poems to your students? If you do, I'll come to your class." Stewart and his friends bid Dylan goodbye. He tried to delay them: "Why do you have to go, man?" Joe replied that he had to get up at eight. "You're a brave cat," Dylan said, "to teach high school, a brave cat." Dylan said they had to get on the road for Denver. Joe Stewart, just an album-cover note in Dylan's life, left at 3.30 a.m. Mardi Gras was over; penitential Lent was beginning. The last time Joe saw Dylan, he was standing by the jukebox, all wound up, with a lot left unsaid. He seemed a little sad and lonely as he waited for dawn.

Back on the road again. Victor, at the wheel, knew there were only two days before the Denver concert. They had to put in an appearance in Tougaloo, where the big Mississippi summer was being planned. They zoomed in and out, time only to greet civil rights people, like Dorie Larner, Robert Moses, and Tom Hayden, who pulled together an audience. Dylan sang for an hour. After well-wishing, Victor made apologies for Dylan and hustled his group into the station wagon. They stopped to study road maps again. Jackson to Denver in two days! Dylan suggested they go by way of Dallas.

It was only three months after the Kennedy assassination, and the papers had been filled with reconstructions. As the freeway swung near Dallas, everyone was keyed up. They asked several people for the street on which Kennedy was shot, but no one seemed to know it by name. Even asking for the Texas School Book depository failed to bring a response. Finally, they asked: "How do we get to the place where the president was shot?" The first man replied: "Do you mean that son-of-a-bitch Kennedy? Well, you go up two blocks this way, and turn a block right." At Dealey Plaza, they appraised the theory that Oswald acted alone. Then, they took the station wagon along Kennedy's path, everyone but the driver looking back toward the depository from which the shots supposedly came. Pete recalled: "Everybody, including Bobby, started acting like a detective. We looked at that distant row of windows and we all pretty much decided that if someone had shot Kennedy from that window, he would have to have been a fantastic marksman."

On to Denver, via Forth Worth, through the Panhandle, toward Wichita Falls. Somewhere near the Texas–New Mexico border, they stopped at a little chili joint. A waitress, no more than 19, asked, "Where y'all from?" She'd never met anyone from New York. When somebody said Bob was a singer, she flipped. They gave her an album. She kept looking from the picture to Bob's face with total disbelief. A few hours later, another Texan roadside joint, near Claude. Sarcastically, they inquired: "What's been happening here, lately?" "Ain't nothing happened here lately, but about a year ago we had a big fuss when Paul Newman and all them Hollywood people came in to shoot that movie *Hud*, right here." The swaggering, thumb-in-belt arrogance of *Hud* was echoed by Dylan in dozens of pictures taken by Barry Feinstein. They learned what they could about the filming.

In southern Colorado, Dylan spotted Ludlow on the map. Paul gave them some background about the site of a vicious 1914 anti-union massacre that inspired many ballads, notably Guthrie's. John Greenway, labor historian, had called the incident "the most wanton atrocity in the history of American unionism." Some southern Colorado mining areas then were so strongly ruled by coal operators that they constituted a government unto themselves. On September 23, 1913, the impoverished Ludlow miners struck. When the state militia illegally imprisoned a union leader, Mother Jones, a thousand women and children protested. Adjutant General Chase organized a company to meet this demonstration, but *en route* the general toppled off his horse. The demonstrators laughed and he ordered his mounted troops to charge, inflicting saber wounds on four women and a boy. The actual massacre occurred in April 1914, when the strike was in its eighth month. The miners, evicted from their company-owned homes, were living in tent colonies. Chase, although relieved from command of the militia, organized two National Guard companies of roughnecks. On April 20, after an accidental shooting, 200 so-called Guardsmen riddled the tents with bullets from a ring of machine guns. All day long they fired; that night, they set fire to the tents. Many miners survived by hiding in trenches but, after a fourteen-hour battle, more than 100 members of their families were wounded and more than thirty were dead. Dylan and friends stood before a memorial plaque put up by the United Mine Workers of America. The young man who had never paid much attention to history at school was getting his lessons on the road.

Denver: Dylan washed, shaved, and changed from dirty old clothes to clean old clothes. The concert producer, Hal Neustadt, was pleased with the performance at the Denver Civic Auditorium. Later, Bob's group made the rounds of the local coffee shops and folk hangouts, looking for Judy Collins. She was out of town, so Dylan took his companions up into the mountains to see Central City, his first return to the reconstructed boomtown since 1959. It was snow-clogged and ghostlier than ever. They went into the only open shop, a drugstore, to pick up some historical postcards.

Heading to San Francisco, they had to go over the Rockies in one of the winter's worst snowstorms. Loveland Pass: their tire chains broke under the effort. They spent a night in Grand Junction, Colorado, where the temperature was down to zero, yet they could run from the hotel and plunge into a naturally heated spring pool. Victor took the wheel from Pete. Before them was a long funeral procession of thirty cars twisting up a mountain road. Victor passed the funeral at more than seventy miles an hour. A police car led the procession. A chase began. "We panicked," said Pete. They hid all the smoking materials fast. Victor talked to the cop: "We're part of a singing group, have to be in Reno in a couple of hours or we miss out on a job." He showed the car's registration, and the cop, seeing the name of some unknown corporation, Ashes and Sand, decided to relent, and let them go.

The four roared with relief, but Dylan told Paul and Pete to share the driving. They arrived in Reno at 8 a.m. and tried the gambling tables, but lost. Pete quickly ran through his last $32 and was then totally dependent on Dylan, who lost about $100 at blackjack. As they were leaving, Bob stopped in front of a slot machine and put in his remaining quarters. Suddenly the machine lit up like Times Square. Quarters came out in a flood. Pete reflected on winners and losers. Somewhere near Reno, at a desert space—as in the film *Zabriskie Point*—they set up the fireworks from South Carolina. They giggled like kids at the magnificent bursting rockets and flares. When they got to the Sierras, they had one more boyish fling. Sitting in the swaying chairs of a ski lift, they climbed the side of a mountain—another freedom game. This was their farewell to spacious landscape. As they hurtled toward San Francisco, the roads were busier, and there were signs of farming and commerce. The trip was nearly at an end.

Dylan had a concert at Berkeley on February 24, 1964. Anyone with as free-floating a temperament as his would be at home on the West Coast. There was Berkeley's radical tradition, San Francisco's openness to new ideas, and the whole ambience of California, where people put no ties around their necks and few around their thinking. The leading West Coast critic had swung firmly into Dylan's corner. Ralph Gleason gave Dylan's concert at the Berkeley Community Theater a strong advance story and review. Opinion-makers, like Malvina Reynolds, spread the *Broadside* gospel around local territory. Gleason, who reported that no concert in recent memory had stirred so much advance interest, was beginning to see Dylan as a standard-bearer for the developing counterculture. Even to the Bay Area, where beats, bohemians, outsiders, and rebels were no strangers, Dylan's arrival meant something special. Wrote Gleason: "To the generations who were raised on solid Judeo-Christian principles, on the rock of moral values of our fathers, on the idea that cleanliness is next to godliness, the deliberate sloppiness, the disdain for what we have thought of as perfect by Dylan's generation is shocking. But we are wrong. Look where our generation has gotten us … a hard core of reality connects the music of Dylan, the best of jazz, of contemporary poetry, painting, all the arts, in fact, with the social revolution that has resulted in CORE and SNCC, Dick Gregory, James Baldwin and the rest."

Fariña was at the Berkeley concert, taking notes for a *Mademoiselle* story. His report augured his own motorcycle doom and Dylan's deliverance:

There was no sensation of his having performed somewhere the previous night or of a schedule that would take him away once the inevitable post-concert party was over. There was, instead, the familiar comparison with James Dean, at times explicit, at times unspoken, an impulsive awareness of his physical perishability. Catch him now, was the idea. Next week he might be mangled on a motorcycle.[6]

After the Berkeley concert, the station wagon headed toward Joan's place in Carmel. Karman was, by this time, completely on the outs: "I'm not going on with this trip. If I do, I'll be going crazy," he said. The others were happy to see him replaced by Bob Neuwirth, the vagabond madcap artist/moviemaker/country singer who later succeeded Victor as Dylan's road manager. They arrived at Joan's with gifts of nuts and fruit. Joan's mother whipped up a beef stew. "The only overt reference to Dylan's music came," Fariña chronicled, "when Joan said she might want to record an entire album of his songs and he told her 'sure thing.'" The next day, Bob and Joan each headed toward southern California. Joan drove her Jaguar XKE while Dylan and the others continued on in the station wagon. Fariña: "Dylan stayed at the Thunderbird Motel in Hollywood, drifting out to parties and local folk nightclubs between engagements; Joan stayed with family friends in Redlands, lying in the sun, going to bed early. She sang at her old high school one afternoon and was moved to tears by the standing ovation. When she did an encore, her mention of Dylan's name brought cheers. That same night, he returned the compliment to a devoted audience in Riverside."

Dylan was reluctant to return to New York. It meant more turmoil with Suze. The affair finally ended in March 1964. The same month, at Folk City, Dylan had an encounter typical of New York's instant paranoia and rivalries. An unusual duo, Simon and Garfunkel, was making its debut. As Tom and Jerry, the pair had enjoyed an earlier pop life and a chart hit with "Hey Schoolgirl." Looking now to do something different, Simon had floated from London's East End to the Village, reemerging with a style more in keeping with the surge of interest in folk music. One night, Carla introduced Dylan to Simon, assuming they'd have a lot in common, at least their friendship for English singer Martin Carthy. Simon and Dylan chatted, but only guardedly. A few nights later, Dylan and I were at Folk City as Simon and Garfunkel came on. Their ethereal harmonies, which would soon be so popular, sounded out of place at Gerde's, home of weather-beaten ethnic songs. At the bar, Bob and I had been doing quite a bit of drinking and we had an advanced case of giggles over nothing. We weren't laughing at the performance, though Simon perhaps thought we were. Dylan had in fact deprecated the work of other singers, usually to their faces. On their first album, Simon and Garfunkel recorded "Times Changing," but by the second album, Simon, while sharing much of Dylan's sense of alienation, protest, and brotherhood, was also directly parodying Dylan: "Simple Desultory Philippic" was a burlesque. Its harmonica playing and shouts for "Albert" left little doubt about its target.

Bob had little to laugh about through most of 1964. Despite depressions, he kept growing, professionally and artistically. The bust-up with Suze, the confusions with Joan, the anchorless feeling of being alone in front of thousands of people, all colored his life in dark shades. That year, he was often one very stoned rolling stone, apparently out of control, racing at his "own chosen speed."[7] He was kept from spinning right off the road, I believe, by the demands, urgency, and discipline of his writing.

Streets of London. May 1964: Off to England again. Dylan had mixed feelings dating from his first trips there—December 1962 and January 1963, when he had been scheduled to star in a BBC play, *Madhouse on Castle Street*. Very much the bewildered young man from the provinces, he reported to London's Mayfair Hotel: "The Mayfair had these hooded little guards outside looking you over. They looked like George Washington all dressed up. They come and take your baggage into the hotel. Then you get inside the door and somebody else comes to meet you there and you tip the guard from outside for having taken your baggage inside. Then when your baggage goes from inside to the elevator, someone else hits you for a tip to take your baggage to the elevator. Then you tip him and then the elevator chap puts your baggage in and you have to tip him when you get out of the elevator. Then someone else takes the baggage out of the elevator and he opens the door to your room and puts your baggage by the end of the bed. Man, you end up tipping about ten guys." After running this changing of the guard, Dylan looked around his room and decided he really didn't belong. He checked out, went looking for Philip Saville, producer of his play, and asked him if he would find some "groovy" people for him to stay with. Of his aloneness in London, Dylan said: "I knew then what it is like to be a Negro."

He drifted into a well-known London folk club, the Troubadour, and there met Anthea Joseph, who made it her business to look after strays and later became an official in artists' relations for EMI and CBS Records. "I was on the door and these boots came marching down the stairs; large, brown leather boots. I thought to myself: *Oh, my God, here comes another one of those children from Southend*. There are a lot of dreadful children from there, some dressed like Jack Elliott, while some wore Dylanesque gear. As those boots came down the stairs and were connected to legs and a body above them, I said to myself: *I know that young man!* Then I recognized the face at the other end of the boots. It came up to me and said: 'Are you Anthea? I'm Bob Dylan, can I come in?' 'Of course,' I said, 'providing that you sing for me; then you won't have to pay to get in.' I found him completely charming, great fun. Although he didn't talk a lot, he seemed to be enjoying himself enormously inside. He never stopped watching people, never stopped laughing. That was the day he had walked out of The Mayfair and he asked me if I knew where he could stay that night. I was amazed that no one had arranged a room for this waif. He went off with somebody he met at the Troubadour after singing there. Generally, people were terribly impressed by his singing; they thought he was marvelous."[8]

Anthea took Dylan to the Singers' Club at the Prospect of Whitby pub, Gray's Inn Road. "Peggy Seeger *had* to ask him to sing because too many people knew who he was. She really didn't want to. They are funny people, Ewan MacColl and Peggy. After Bob sang 'Hollis Brown,' the audience almost fell apart, because they had never come up against anything so forceful in their lives. Hearing that terrifying chorus going through it every time, I, for one, felt the need for a good, strong drink. Peggy and Ewan just sat there in stony silence. Peggy went up to him and said: 'Thank you, very much,' and that was all. I was shocked. Not one word of praise from her, and Ewan didn't even bother to say anything. We left straightaway. Bob didn't want to stay. And he was the one who would sing for hours if the atmosphere was right."

On his first trip, Bob instantly befriended Martin and Dorothy Carthy. Carthy's catholic approach toward modernized tradition put Bob at ease. Recalled Carthy: "I had read about him in *Sing Out!* Naturally, I asked him to sing. When the King and Queen audience heard his guest set, they fairly went mad. Strange, though, that after he left the club, that same audience started to put him down and said his appearance there 'was all a big mistake.'"

The Carthys had written several times, but Bob only wrote them one long letter, in spring 1963, which showed how strongly he was thinking about the topical-song debate, the demands on his time, and his loving memories of them: "I remember Martin singing 'Lord Franklin' and I still got faith in singer and song to tell the truth and still be what they are … I still remember Martin and Dorothy and getta feeling that no tongue can explain on the printed page, movie-house or record player. There ain't many folks like you."

Dylan went to Britain originally for the BBC play, which had a role for "an anarchic young student who wrote songs." Having signed this unknown for what was then a large fee of £500, Saville discovered he'd also hired a would-be playwright. "We found he had trouble delivering the lines Evan Jones had written for him. Bob wanted to write his own lines," Saville told me in 1971. "At rehearsals, when he did show up, there was no problem with his saying his lines, but he was such an individualist that he wanted to write the play, or at least his part, over completely. Mutually, we realized that he just couldn't play it as written. We decided to make the central character into two people." David Warner, a rising Shakespearean actor, who later starred in the film *Morgan*, took the speaking role originally meant for Dylan. Bob and Warner got on famously. Staying at Saville's Hampstead home a few nights—one way Saville could guarantee his appearance at rehearsals—Dylan began to run through his song repertoire. The producer, quite impressed, decided to have Dylan sing "Blowin' in the Wind" behind the opening and closing credits. (Saville also recalled that Dylan was working on "Tambourine Man.")[9]

Several technical hitches developed in the play, and Saville told Grossman there would be a delay of several weeks. Albert said Bob had a commitment, and wrung another fee and round-trip airline ticket out of the BBC. "This became undoubtedly the most expensive money ever paid for a singer to do the opening and closing music for a play and to deliver only one spoken line," Saville told me. (The line: "Well, I don't know, I'll have to go home and think about it.") Nevertheless, Saville felt proud to introduce Dylan and "Blowin' in the Wind" to Britain. He was charmed with Dylan's "almost Buddhist inner concentration, and his little naïvetés about sophisticated London."

The extra time in London allowed Dylan to meet two old friends from Boston, Ric Von Schmidt and Richard Fariña, who were cutting an album on the Folklore label. They easily persuaded Dylan, as Blind Boy Grunt, to fill in with his traveling mouth harp on "You Can't Always Tell," "Xmas Island," "Cocaine," and "Glory, Glory." The sessions were at Dobell's Jazz Record Shop on Charing Cross Road on January 14 and 15, 1963. Dylan also played at the Establishment Club, where his anti-establishment songs made him a triumph.

England became a rich source of anecdote. He told me about various surreal parties, with fat Americans, an adolescent English girl who looked French, and a crippled old lady who took ten minutes to hobble from the door to the middle of a room. At another party, while the piercing English winter was penetrating his bones, everyone else walked about in short-sleeved shirts. At a party of "England's top hippies," Bob positioned himself so close to the gas fire, his trousers nearly caught fire. They danced to Everly Brothers records. "The English could do the twist by moving only one leg!" He sang for them, but their looks matched the room's chill. When Odetta was ready to go to Rome, he flew there with her for a few days. Suze had already returned to New York. Upon his first return from Britain I asked him how he liked London: "Man," he said, "you gotta see Rome. Rome is wonderful!" In Italy, Bob wrote "It Ain't Me, Babe," "Girl from the North Country," and "maybe" wrote "Boots of Spanish Leather."

Fifteen months later, in May 1964, Dylan returned to England. A booking at the Royal Festival Hall, May 17, 1964, perked him up. Anthea couldn't buy a ticket, so he insisted she come backstage. "You gotta come to this one, because the Rolling Stones are coming," he said. A line several thousand yards long stretched all the way along the Thames to County Hall—the 2,700 seats had long since been sold out. Anthea: "In those days, we all had long hair, wore jeans, and the boys with their long hair were carrying bedrolls, with their chicks walking exactly two steps behind with the guitar. Here the birds always carried the guitar. There were no returned tickets. Bob's first question was: 'Are the Rolling Stones here?' I said: 'If you want to see rolling stones, put your head out the door.' He said: 'My God, I've never seen anything like it!' His admirers had hitchhiked from absolutely everywhere."

The concert was successful. Bob misplaced his capo and asked if his listeners had one. There was a general surge forward: "Have mine," "Please take mine." Dylan smilingly accepted one: "Don't forget that

I have it, or you won't get it back." *The Times* said Dylan's drawing power put him in a class of "sheer personal magnetism," shared only by Callas, Segovia, and Count Basie. The London *Daily Sketch* headline: NO VOICE—BUT SOME SINGER. The singer, who only little more than a year earlier had found England so cool, heard cheers from an audience of intellectuals and beats who thronged around the stage door like pubescent fans. Publicist Kenneth Pitt: "I worried about his safety, because he is such a slight person. I remember almost giving him a bear hug as we worked our way through the crowd to a waiting taxi. The fans started to bang on the side of the car. Finally, we got away, but at one point the kids seemed determined to stop the car and pull Bob out. Dylan kept saying: 'Hey, man, get me out of here.' I realized what a wonderful thing had happened. I think the people in this crowd just wanted to touch him. This was not wild fan hysteria. They seemed to have a genuine love for the man and wanted to express it."

Dylan then taped a half-hour show for BBC-TV's *Tonight* and also recorded for BBC radio's *Saturday Club* and the TV *Hallelujah Club*. He left behind the makings of an articulate audience that, in 1965, would project him to superstardom. The English singer-songwriter, Sydney Carter, told me: "A large part of the young songwriters in Britain are inspired by Dylan. Dylan Thomas had more influence on Bob Dylan than Woody Guthrie did, with an image of the bard who went forth as a kind of romantic prophet, doomed to an early death. One was mistakenly brought up to think that such romantic bards usually are doomed, that they live in garrets or caves. Shakespeare did very well commercially. Tennyson became a lord. But one's image of a poet is someone, preferably under twenty-five, revolutionary, good-looking, and doing something to excess, whether women, or drugs, or wine. It strikes the imagination very powerfully. There are many intimations of death in Dylan's writing, but what attracted me has been, rather, the affirmation of life. It's like the blues, in which one is struck by the hopeful things that push through the gloom. There is plenty of life and guts in Dylan, as there was in Dylan Thomas. Joan Baez reminds me of that classic painting by Delacroix of the "Woman at the Barricades." This is what is happening to folk music, and I am not knocking it. This romantic picture is as much with us in the 1960s as it was in the 1830s. There was trouble in Greece, and Byron the poet had to go right out there, the way your folk singers have had to go to the South. Fight for right and die young doing it. The word poet means different things to different people. Strange, you can talk about a commercial artist, but you can't talk about a commercial poet. A poet has to be something holy as well as to have genius. As difficult a role as this must be for Dylan, he definitely fits into that romantic concept of a poet, the listener to inner voices that are driving him. What the poets have been trying to do for a long time—to get through to a large public—the folk singers have done behind their backs. There is no doubt that in the folk song clubs of Britain they are singing poetry. It is also a matter of image. He's like the footballer or the bullfighter, only his weapons are words and harmonies. It's a new kind of hero-image for youth, and it's also a way to become rich and famous. You can fail your grammar school and still make a million. It's like the bullfighter in Spain or Mexico, like a Negro boxer rising out of the slums with power, grace, and strength."[10]

Sometimes a boxer without grace. Karl Dallas, the folk-song reporter and critic, ran into Dylan during his 1964 visit. Dylan: "Are you for me or against me?" Dallas: "Frankly, I don't know you." After that, Dallas said, "I was given the polite bum's rush." One veteran of the British folk scene, Rory McEwan, recalled the night he asked Bob out to dinner and "about thirty people" showed up with him. He was as repelled by Bob as he was attracted: "I disliked his arrogance. He runs through so much experience because of his pressured existence. He can walk into a room and give the impression that he knows just a little bit more about the world than anyone in that room. He probably does, but it rankles a little that he should act as if he does. Perhaps Dylan is the first of the real twentieth century technocrats. He turns all the knobs. But after his breakout in Britain, he was on the horns of a dilemma, because acceptance can be as great a problem to him as rejection."

Elaine Dundy, writer, well-known hostess and one-time wife of Kenneth Tynan, was smitten, calling him a genius. At another party, he met Robert Graves, who asked Dylan to sing and then talked throughout.

After Festival Hall, Dylan darted off for a few days in Paris, and then traveled with Victor to Greece for a short holiday. In the town of Vernilya, outside Athens, Dylan did a great deal of writing for *Another Side*. He was beginning to feel some calm. He wanted to stay on in Greece, but had too many commitments, so returned to New York and to Woodstock. Each time Dylan left England, he vowed never to return. (This was before his triumph of 1978, when he totally reversed his opinion.) Earlier, though, he found most people cold, the folk community narrow, and the aggressive British press particularly difficult. But each year he returned. His return in 1965 was to change his attitude toward Britain dramatically.

Newport '64 Revisited. Newport '63 had been so Dylan-centered that, not surprisingly, Bob found the 1964 festival an anti-climax. He'd had time to consider the burdens of leadership and to decide that overtly political songs were only part of his work. No longer was he "writing songs for everybody else, but writing songs now for myself." As Dylan had grabbed the spotlight in 1963, he virtually shunned it in 1964. He was prepared, like Seeger before him, to step back from stage-center and feel wonder at the numbers who were working the same vein. Phil Ochs was coming on strongly as the chief political banner-waver. For the Newport program book, Phil wrote that there'd been such an upsurge of topical song "that I wouldn't be surprised to see an album called 'Elvis Presley Sings Songs of the Spanish Civil War' or the Beatles with 'The Best of the Chinese-Indian Border Dispute Songs.'"

In the year between the two festivals, topical songwriting had established itself. Ochs was becoming a campus darling; Tom Paxton, the careful craftsman, was not far behind. Len Chandler was a rising figure; and Buffy Sainte-Marie was emerging as the most adroit woman writer, while Malvina Reynolds was still the doyenne. Seeger remained the leader, although he was still away on a world tour. Other rising topical songwriters included Billy Edd Wheeler, Pat Sky, Fred Hellerman, Peter LaFarge and Tim Hardin, Jim Friedman, Julius Lester, Shel Silverstein, Bob Gibson. Two newer talents had difficulties in establishing their own identities: Eric Andersen and David Cohen (also known as David Blue) began almost as replicas of Dylan. Although both were concerned about human folly and errant institutions, neither trod on Dylan's early political path. Their writing was more subjective and personal. Still in the background was 13-year-old Janis Ian, soon to cause a stir with "Society's Child."

Dylan performed publicly three times at Newport '64. On Friday afternoon at the topical-song workshop, he sang "It Ain't Me, Babe" and "Tambourine Man." No one seemed to mind that Dylan's two new songs were topical only to the singer. At that night's evening concert, which broke all previous Newport attendance records, Baez closed by bringing Dylan on for a duet of "It Ain't Me, Babe." The audience hankered for political inspiration and Joan obliged, leading "We Shall Overcome." Dylan's solo appearance was Sunday night, and he opened with "All I Really Want to Do." Many were glad to hear his wit surface again in a new "anti-love song." The rest of his set was not very well received; the longer he stayed on, the sloppier his performance became. "To Ramona" was so lackluster that I wrote a tentative question in my notebook: "Has the American Yevtushenko turned into the American Edgar Guest?" He sang "Tambourine Man," but so haltingly, between clenched teeth, that the floating imagery sagged. As he tuned between numbers, Dylan sometimes staggered onstage. Being stoned had rarely prevented his giving winning performances, but he was clearly out of control. He finished with "Chimes of Freedom," and then for an encore, called Joan on for a duet of "With God on Our Side."

The desultory performance surprised many, but not two friends backstage. Before he had gone on, Bob had been chatting with Tony Glover and Betsy Siggins of Cambridge. Tony had noticed that Bob was extremely uptight about facing the capacity audience of more than 15,000. Dylan said to Tony: "I don't care. I'll just do my music. I don't care." Tony, teasing, suggested Dylan turn his back on the audience to avoid hostility. For a moment during his performance, he actually did so. Dylan got his round of applause, but there was uneasiness. John Hammond, Sr, scolded: "He ought to be spanked for putting on that sort of a show." "He's too great a talent, Bobby is, to throw away a performance like that," Pat Clancy clucked. As I headed toward the press tent, I conveyed the general disappointment to Charlie Rothschild, who was trying to convince me that I had just seen a great Dylan performance.

The evening emphasized something Bob already knew well: a performer must be always on his mettle. Critical ears won't accept mediocrity from masters. At Newport, perhaps no one felt let down more keenly than those who had earlier heaped praise on Dylan. Friends, old and new, began to give him pep talks in person or in print. In the November 1964 issue of *Sing Out!*, editor Irwin Silber wrote "An Open Letter to Bob Dylan," which summarized past veneration but expressed worry: "I saw at Newport how you had somehow lost contact with people … the paraphernalia of fame were getting in your way … I thought of Jimmy Dean … and I cried a little … for that awful potential of self-destruction … in a sense we are all responsible for what's been happening to you … The American Success Machinery chews up geniuses one a day and still hungers for more."

The letter cheered Dylan as much as a week's holiday in Hibbing would have. Everything he did seemed to displease someone. Minneapolis people hit him for carrying picket signs; then he was stoned for selling out. Now the preachy folksters were sermonizing. Was there no way an artist could listen to himself, could write, perform, act, dress like himself? All kinds of himself? Not when he is public property. Many waited for the November release of *Another Side* to confirm that Dylan was "going apolitical." In December, a *Broadside* writer, Paul Wolfe, who Dylan had praised, treated Newport '64 as the point when Ochs emerged the political-song champion and Dylan "renounced" protest. The "new" Dylan, Wolfe found, has "defected … into higher forms of art." Pitting Dylan vs Ochs, the writer weighed "meaning vs innocuousness, sincerity vs utter disregard for the tastes of the audience, idealistic principle vs selfconscious egotism." Wolfe deemed "Tambourine Man" "a failure," and lambasted "Chimes of Freedom" for raising "bewilderment to the highest degree." The Dylan he sketched was a Lonesome Rhodes—a trickster, hypocrite, and manipulator of his audience. Ochs leaped to Dylan's defense: "It is as if the entire folk community was a huge biology class and Bob was a rare, prize frog. Professor Silber and Student Wolfe appear to be quite annoyed that the frog keeps hopping in all different directions while they're trying to dissect him … Who does Dylan think he is anyway? When I grow used to an artist's style, I damn well expect him not to disappoint me by switching it radically. My time is too precious to waste trying to change a pattern of my thought." Ochs's sarcasm here was followed by straight anger: "To cater to an audience's taste is not to respect them, and if the audience doesn't understand that, they don't deserve respect."

A key word in Silber's letter was "entourage," meaning that Dylan was now surrounded by pay-rolled sycophants. Dylan always had an ability to encircle himself, even though he was constantly centrifugally shedding those at the outer perimeter. Back at the May 1963 Brandeis Folk Festival, Dylan had seemed a maharaja in denim held aloft by an elephant pack of supporters. In spring 1964, *Life* magazine showed Dylan in his surliest mood with Geno Foreman and Albert Maher. Maher, a Harvard Square radical who had visited Cuba in 1963, traveled in 1964 on some Dylan concert tours out of his own romantic radicalism and admiration for the singer. Maher was the son of John F "Big John" Maher, a millionaire Houston industrialist. The son's radicalization began at 15, when he read Castro, then accelerated in 1961 after the Bay of Pigs. In early 1964, Dylan hung out with Maher sporadically. Some months after Bob and Suze split up, she and Maher began a long relationship.

A closer member of the Dylan entourage was Paul Clayton, whom folk moralists found difficult to criticize. Of the Dylan of 1963–64, Paul said: "He gave the appearance of expecting success, but he found himself before a public he wasn't ready to face. Once he had the public, he was frightened to death, mostly of all the questions people asked him. I remember a concert at Brown University. After the concert, Victor, Neuwirth, and I formed a cordon around him. Reporters ran after him with tape recorders, asking if he thought he was a folk singer! That's the sort of confrontation he feared. He may pour forth for half an hour without a stop, but is almost apologetic about his opinions. He never gives concrete evidence, but lets you draw a conclusion. He almost always lets you challenge yourself to make a choice, but he doesn't make you want to reach it. He uses all the hip slang, all the grunts and the *hey, man*s as a shield when he's unsure of himself. But he doesn't do that when he writes. He can always edit his writing, but not his speech, and so he doesn't completely trust himself verbally. He always gets reticent in front of a lot of people. There are about twenty people he feels safe with, and only about five or six of those whom he can spend much time with. Even with people around, he spends a lot of time with himself."

Around the Village, what *Eye* later titled "the Dylan Gang," was a half-dozen folk singers whom he felt to be kindred spirits—Jack Elliott, Eric Andersen, Dave Van Ronk, David Blue, Phil Ochs, Tim Hardin, and a very few others. These Villagers felt compelled to explain and defend Dylan when he did not do so himself. Ochs (describing him as "really Shakespearean in quality") remained the most articulate, even after the many times Dylan put him down. Summarizing Dylan's impact on his Village entourage, Michael Thomas wrote in *Eye*, August 1968:

Dylan made everybody aware of themselves, while he became aware of himself, and because he could hear the tambourine man, he was a prophet. He touched his contemporaries at the core of their ambitions. Some, like Ochs and Paxton and Tim Hardin, felt his energy and were energized; some, like Andersen and Blue, and others, like Richard Fariña, the destructive hero of his own life, and Paul Simon, the last great sophomore, were stricken by Dylan, but he was not to blame.

After Newport '64, there was another round of controversy. If Dylan worked in blues, he was a white man stealing black music. If he developed Woody's talking blues, he was an imitator. If he adapted Anglo-

Irish folk songs, he was a thief. If he wrote topical-protest songs, traditionalists thought he was a traitor, yet if he turned subjective, he was a self-involved existentialist. Watching the melée, Gleason concluded: "The one unforgivable sin in the American money culture is to break through to the top rungs of success while, at the same time spurning the power apparatus. Do that and the demons that lurk beneath the surface come up and attack you."

Dylan's defenders came from all corners. In March 1964, Johnny Cash, the country singer then known only vaguely to the folk crowd, had leaped into *Broadside* with the demand: "SHUT UP!... AND LET HIM SING!" At Newport '64, Cash did a stunning performance. The Festival, in its finest hour, brought in an established Nashville star who also spoke folk. Cash was the real thing—off an Ozarks farm, tough as rawhide, tender as raw flesh. Son of a railroad man, product of a Depression childhood, part Cherokee Indian, Cash was also a sophisticated man who would walk the line in several music worlds. Right after his performance on Friday night, Cash was hustled off to Baez's room at the Viking Motor Inn, where he and Dylan taped some songs for her. Cash, whose craggy, granite-hewn exterior made him look tough all the way through, was deeply touched by his acceptance. He had been a big country star and then his emotions and hard living had nearly done him in. He was beginning that long march toward stardom again, and he was filled with fears, mostly of his own turbulent self-destructiveness. To find Newport so warm made him feel even taller than he was. It touched him to find that the two young stars of the folk world, Baez and Dylan, cared enough about him to spend the whole night taping him. To show his appreciation, he gave Dylan one of his own guitars. The next morning, Baez talked proudly of the evening: her protégé had sustained another victory.

Sensitive ears at Newport may have heard another modest giant, Muddy Waters, from Chicago, who showed that the blues had many faces and foreshadowed Dylan's going electric in 1965. Muddy was a farmhand and sharecropper, much like Cash; only Muddy had been a Mississippi black, which meant he was poorer and just a little more desperate. At 13, Muddy, born McKinley Morganfield, had been blowing his mouth harp at Saturday night fish fries for fifty cents a night and all the fish and liquor he could hold. In 1941, Alan Lomax had recorded Morganfield's country blues for the Library of Congress. Muddy got the idea that his salvation lay in music up north. As Cash had gone to Memphis, Muddy "came up to Chicago on a train. Alone. With a suitcase, one suit of clothes, and a guitar." In the city after the war, his country blues grew tough, projective, and electric. In 1954, Muddy recorded a strong rhythm 'n' blues song, "Rollin' Stone," which provided Mick Jagger with a group name, Jann Wenner with a magazine title, and Dylan with a song title and a name for his cat in Woodstock. "Rollin' Stone" gathered no dust.

The historic moments at Newport '64 tended to pass people by. Only when Dylan later appeared with rock backing and, still later, went to Nashville, did all the pieces fit together. It was all brought back home at Newport '64, when Dylan went beyond topical songs, Cash sang of country troubles, and Muddy Waters brought on his band to show that music, if it is alive, is always in motion.

Hamlet of Woodstock. In summer and fall of 1964, Dylan had more time to spend in Woodstock. The barren pad on West Fourth Street was too empty. He was anxious to move his few possessions. If he had to stay in New York, he could always stay at Albert's big apartment on Gramercy Park West or at the Chelsea Hotel. Woodstock was then an unpressured and uncrowded hamlet, and he had devoted friends there. He had a special room with a private entrance at Albert's large house in nearby Bearsville, and a place to hang out, the Café Espresso at 59 Tinker Street, in Woodstock.

The Espresso was a bit of Greenwich Village in the country. It had a well-worn brown look; the lighting was soft and indirect, the tables far enough apart for conversation. There was a large open fireplace, and tables outdoors with a view of main-street amblers. Chessboards and checkered tablecloths gave a Gallic feel. The place was owned by French-born Bernard Paturel, whose easy manner helped give the Café and Dylan's Woodstock their informality. Bernard had moved to Woodstock in 1961 after serving his time at such lustrous New York restaurants as Le Veau d'Or and Lutece. The old Woodstock reminded him of the French art colony in St Paul-de-Vence, in the hills above the Côte d'Azur. Hearing that the Café Espresso was up for sale, Bernard and his wife, Mary Lou, bought the place on credit. "We pasted it together and kept it going for five years." For live entertainment, folk music seemed right. There had long been a folk colony around Woodstock. Sam Eskin, an early ballad collector, was a veteran resident, and Billy Faier, banjoist-singer, had been a town mascot since the late 1950s. Bernard called on Billy and a French folk singer, Sonia Malkine, to help him get singers. The first group Bernard booked was a duo, Dan and the Deacon. Among others who worked there were Paxton (who performed for three days for $50 and food), John Wynn, Ed McCurdy, the Reverend Gary Davis, and Happy Traum. The first Bernard heard of Dylan, he was causing a storm at Gerde's and making $200 a week, more than Espresso could afford. He first saw Dylan in his Café one Sunday afternoon in summer '63. Bob was at a table with Joan and several others, tinkering with a wind-up phonograph. Establishing himself as a Mr Fixit, Bernard repaired it for them and watched the relic rotating at 78rpm as Bob and Joan played an old spiritual. Those were days when Woodstock was a refuge, not yet a zoo or a "nation." Dylan often practiced on the streets, sitting on a fence here, a bench there. Bernard soon saw Bob back in his club with Joan again. Bob had been drinking a bit and his genial host politely escorted him upstairs to a large white room in the Paturels' apartment, where Bob slept off his binge. Dylan took an immediate liking to the room. It was quiet and secret, and yet so close to the club downstairs that it fought off loneliness. "He kind of moved in with us and held a symbolic key to the room," Bernard told me. "No rent involved, just a mutual understanding that he could stay there whenever he pleased."

After his hectic trips in winter and spring of 1964, Bob returned to Woodstock. He was getting ready to record *Another Side* and the refuge he found with Bernard and Mary Lou was duly acknowledged in "Some Other Kind of Songs." In Bearsville, Albert was always surrounding himself with people: his wife Sally, filmmakers Jones and Howard Alk, Peter Yarrow, John Court, visiting singers like Judy Collins, Odetta, and Ian and Sylvia. Among the amenities at Albert's was a swimming pool that Bob favored. He kept a motorcycle in the garage so that he could roar around the back roads. Sometimes Bob liked the "in-crowd" excitement around Grossman's, but he often needed to be alone. Although Albert's was only three miles from the Espresso, Bob frequently hid away in Bernard's room. He spent hours downstairs playing chess with Victor or Bernard, or drove with Bernard to Kingston, to a musty old poolroom over a Chinese restaurant.

In front of Albert's Bearsville house, a sign warned: IF YOU HAVE NOT TELEPHONED, YOU ARE TRESPASSING. Albert had three listed Woodstock phone numbers; Dylan had none. Dylan's own guest list was highly selective. Clayton used to come often in early 1964, but he was gradually ostracized. After Newport, Johnny Cash visited. Daniel Kramer went to Woodstock in 1964 and began several months' intermittent service as Dylan's court photographer. Later, Kramer was summarily dropped, and Jerry Schatzberg took over until *he* fell out of favor. Kramer found Dylan a restless subject, insistent about poses. He wanted to capture Dylan writing music or playing the guitar, but Dylan objected because he only wrote alone. Kramer did take some wonderful shots of Dylan walking up country roads, sitting in the Espresso, rocking on the porch of Albert's house, standing high in the branches of a tree. When Bob saw the tree picture, he said that he should try singing from a tree branch at his next concert. One of Kramer's best shots was a smiling Bob on a porch swing, like the swing in front of Echo's shack in Hibbing.

During Dylan's time in Woodstock in 1964–65, he turned out many songs. Amid its greenery, gentle hills, and quiet lanes, he worked on the sharp, declarative, tension-filled music of his next albums. If we accept Wordsworth's commonplace about poetry, then Dylan recollected his emotions in Woodstock's tranquillity. Concerts and recording sessions were always beckoning, so that he only could catch his breath in Woodstock. Had he remained in New York, he might have lost his emotional equilibrium entirely. From Woodstock, he traveled to two major concerts in 1964.

On August 8, 1964, Joan sang at the Forest Hills Music Festival to an outdoor audience of 15,000. Her singing was typically smooth and orderly. In the second half, she slipped out of her shoes onstage then brought Dylan on. I have never heard him in such poor shape. Bob seemed to be struggling on one wing, never quite able to leave the ground. His voice was harsh, badly projected. Joan's cool only heightened his disorder. I had to write some stinging words about him. Later, Joan and her manager told me that after Dylan read the *Times* review he went on a rampage, swearing at me, vowing vengeance.

I had another chance to hear Dylan, on October 31, 1964, at New York's Philharmonic Hall, the so-called Halloween Concert. Dylan gave one of his greatest performances. For the first time in nearly six months, he was back at the tiller steering, not drifting. He dusted off "Times Changing," "John Birch," "Hard Rain," "Hattie Carroll," "Davey Moore," "Dream," "God on Our Side." He sang "It Ain't Me, Babe" in well-rehearsed tandem with Joan. The luminous wanderings of "Tambourine Man" began to shine through. "Gates of Eden" was stunning. Dylan did "It's Alright, Ma," and the stinging lines hit hard. I ended my review: "After half a year of detours, Dylan seems to have returned his enormous musical and literary gifts to a forward course. His developing control of those gifts and his ability to shape a meaningful program added up to a frequently spellbinding evening by the brilliant singing poet laureate of young America."[11]

After the concert, Dylan gave a party at a banquet hall off Second Avenue. I arrived with friends. Joan and Bob, linked arm and arm, greeted me warmly; Dylan had apparently forgotten my harsh review in August. He knew he had just triumphed. He made sure that everyone had enough wine—Beaujolais of course. Among those present were poets Allen Ginsberg and Gregory Corso and jazzman Ornette Coleman. It was not a celebrity party so much as a chance to see friends in post-concert relaxation.

He had quite a few things to say to all his detractors via the Philharmonic Hall program book. "Advice for Geraldine on Her Miscellaneous Birthday" included such sardonic rules that tried to bind him:

stay in line. stay in step, people
are afraid of someone who is not
in step with them. it makes them
look foolish t' themselves for
being in step. it might even
cross their mind that they themselves
are in the wrong step. ...
when asked t' define yourself exactly,
say you are an exact mathematician.
do not say or do anything that
he who standing in front of you
watching cannot understand, he will
feel you know something he
doesn't[12]

Typical of many of his "middle-period" finger-pointing songs, like "Positively Fourth Street," "Advice for Geraldine," may have sounded like a paranoid talking blues, but it was an artist's declaration of independence. Dylan hated authority figures, including arbiters of taste who wrote for *Sing Out!*, *Broadside*, *Billboard*, or the *Times*. No one was sure just whom he meant, and many were positive that he meant them. Dylan simply did not want to conform. His "truth attacks" were outbursts he rarely examined to weigh the damage he might inflict. He still felt the message serviceable enough to reprint in the Carnegie Hall program book on October 1, 1965, when he appeared with the Hawks (later the Band).

Dylan preferred to battle his critics obliquely. Face to face, he was as polite as possible. Shortly after his weak performance at Forest Hills, I spent an evening with him in the Village. He made no reference to my negative review. Although slightly reserved, he had a bit of information and another bit of free advice. The information, stated in roundabout terms, was that he was about to gross his first million. He was clearly startled, even though he knew that he would be lucky to see twenty percent of the total, after paying his team and taxes. Turning the conversation to me, he asked what I was writing, and I told him about various projects, some for pleasure, some just for bread. Charlie Rothschild had told him that under the pseudonym of Adam Barnes I had written the liner notes on Linda Mason's mediocre album of Dylan songs. Bitingly, Bob said that if I ever got that hard up for money again I should ask him for some, which I never did. I told him of a book I was writing on country music and some other projects. He suggested I try my best to get beyond the bread-and-butter writing: "Find something that you feel strongly about and just write it," Dylan told me, as we sat in the Gaslight. I didn't realize it then, but he was obliquely leading me toward this book. He was strongly reminding me that my protégé no longer needed protection.

The next day he returned to Woodstock, away from professional judges and old Village friends who reminded him of a past he was quickly outgrowing. In the next few months he made new, influential friends, including several young musicians who called themselves the Byrds and the Beatles.

Bob Dylan
Bringing It All Back Home

Left: *Bringing It All Back Home*, the album cover, March 1965, and at home in Woodstock, July 1964, Dylan expresses the sentiment.
Right: In repose after a press conference in Leicester, England, 1965; and below, on stage with the Byrds, Los Angeles, 1965.

If they can't understand my songs, they're missing something.
If they can't understand pornographic ashtrays, green clocks, wet chairs,
purple lamps, hostile statues, charcoal … then they're missing something,
too… It's all music, no more, no less.
DYLAN, 1965

Dylan was the single most important force in maturing our popular music.
JOHN PEEL, 1970

Can there be no songs as violent as the age? … Maybe Dylan didn't put it
in the best way. Maybe he was rude. But he shook us. And that is why we
have poets and artists.
JIM ROONEY, 1965

THE music scene is alive with talk of the new trendsetters. Internationally, there is nobody getting a hotter reception than Bob Dylan. Some say he is a genius.

Dylan is a 23-year-old American who suddenly become a remarkable "modern" he has been making ads into t Now, wit ing a ng on th m, many usic worl gger succe 65.

The singer guitarist - har s already claim as a conceived e Wind". ngs have mmentaries les like " r Side", "T e A-Chang War" and song about ects. Other Dyla like "House

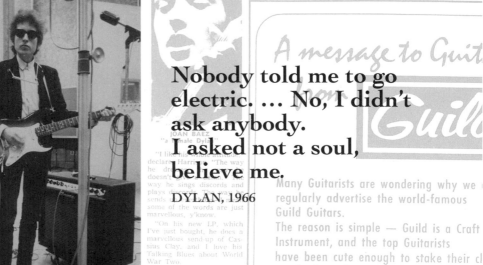

Nobody told me to go
electric. … No, I didn't
ask anybody.
I asked not a soul,
believe me.
DYLAN, 1966

I like his whole attitude declares Harris "The way he dra doesn't way he sings discords and plays a sends some of the words are just marvellous, y'know.

"On his new LP, which I've just bought, he does a marvellous send-up of Cassius Clay, and I love his Talking Blues about World War Two.

"Oh, we met Joan Baez, as well, in Denver. She's good, too—a sort of female Dylan as far as the words of her songs go, but more

Many Guitarists are wondering why we regularly advertise the world-famous Guild Guitars.
The reason is simple — Guild is a Craft Instrument, and the top Guitarists have been cute enough to stake their cl on the limited supplies available.
We sincerely apologise to the many oth Guitarists who wanted a Guild and

Above: "Dylan shows the way," the *Melody Maker* headline, January 1965.
Left: Demonstrating the direction forward in the studio with Fender
Stratocaster and recording *Bringing It All Back Home*, January 1965.

As the "roads scholar" through time and space, Dylan had never really abandoned his high-school rock 'n' roll, his schoolboy radio music. In late 1964, the Beatles were only one of many new rock groups proliferating. The monophony, if not the monotony, of the self-accompanied folk singer yielded to multitracked panoplies of sound. The mock-rock era of Fabian, Frankie Avalon, and Bobby Vee was history. Because Vee hadn't signed Dylan in 1959, he'd been free to find folk songs, where he could draw from areas previously unexplored by rock musicians.

Yet, by 1964, amid Woodstock's stillness, Dylan heard drum rolls, cymbals, thumping Fender basses, and squirming metallic lines sliding from electric guitars. He didn't discard his old solo singing with acoustic guitar and mouth harp. He still knew the flow of his words, gentle or angry, was his greatest influence. He only wanted to put those words into a different context. But public and critical reactions to his 1965 albums, *Bringing It All Back Home* and *Highway 61 Revisited*, couldn't have been more extreme. He was traitor-opportunist to some, genius-messiah to others.

Dylan had not been surreptitiously manipulated. He alone decided to leap back into rock, taking with him folk song's storytelling and comment. The controversy over his adding a beat and subtracting topical sloganeering detracted from a significant development: Dylan was creating a new *kind* of expression, more sophisticated than that of his previous three years. His creation of "folk-rock" was a turning point in popular culture. Before Dylan's new work, most rock musicians, including the Beatles, had been using insipid, frivolous lyrics. While many folk slowpokes took time to assimilate Dylan's new approach, his new pop pastorate tuned in quickly.

Despite widespread reviews, most critics dwelled on obvious points: *Back Home* and *Highway 61* changed pop lyrics by successfully amalgamating oral literature, folk tradition, and rock experimentation. Where was Dylan headed in 1965? I think his road maps pointed toward three aesthetic and philosophical concepts: exploration of the grotesque and the absurd in art; existentialism; dreams and hallucinations as mirrors of consciousness.

The Grotesque: There are plenty of grotesques among Dylan's new *dramatis personae*: "Einstein disguised as Robin Hood,"[1] and "Napoleon in rags"[2] fall into a venerable tradition. Mister Jones, Doctor Filth, Savage Rose, and the Phantom of the Opera are second cousins to the medieval gargoyles on Notre Dame, stepchildren of types in Rimbaud and Apollinaire, neighbors of the vermin in Kafka's *Metamorphosis*. His rogues' gallery is distantly related to tortured figures in the paintings of Goya, Velazquez, Bosch, and Callot, as well as the French surrealists. Dylan had Coleridge's "shaping power of imagination"—the ability to create his own poetic otherworld, into whose dramas we enter half-fearfully. From life's cruel parade, he enlarged, distorted, shaped, and misshaped a host of unsettling demons, spirits, devils, and malignant muses. Rilke saw his angels, Blake met his prophets Isaiah and Ezekiel; Dylan painted freaks and geeks.

We don't have to spend a season in hell to meet grotesques in everyday life. Turn your radio on. Sing a song of Adolf Eichmann and Lieutenant Calley.[3] The black laughter of the grotesque has long echoed in the arts. The grotesque tends to grip humanity when belief in a natural, protective, traditional order of life has broken down. Then people are delivered into the control of demons, caricatures, and spirits, which surge up from the underworld, the chaotic subconscious.

By 1964, Dylan saw that slogans could change nothing. Had "Blowin' in the Wind" improved life for American blacks? Wasn't it like a church hymn—buoying the spirit and affirming the goal? But could it *really* effect change? What happens then to the social prophet who has passionately preached solutions only to find them ignored? Perhaps the prophet-singer fears he is really unheard. Perhaps he turns inward, becomes a seer whose slogans have changed into strange riddles. Darkness and satiric humor fill the vacuum of unresolved crisis, seem the best way to deal with an insane world. The following definition of the grotesque could apply to surrealist painting, the monologues of Lenny Bruce, the howls of Ginsberg and Ferlinghetti, and many of Dylan's song-poems.

In *The Grotesque in Art and Literature*, Wolfgang Kayser wrote that "suddenness and surprise are essential elements of the grotesque":

We are ... terrified because it is our world which ceases to be reliable ... The grotesque instills fear of life rather than fear of death ... the progressive dissolution, which has occurred since the ornamental art of the Renaissance; ...the loss of identity, the disorder of "natural" size and shape, the suspension of the category of objects, the destruction of personality, and the fragmentation of the historical order. Apocalyptic beasts emerge ... demons intrude upon us ... What intrudes remains incomprehensible, inexplicable and impersonal ... We are unable to orient ourselves in the alienated world, because it is absurd ... As an artistic genre, tragedy opens precisely within the sphere of the meaningless and the absurd possibility of a deeper meaning ... the creator of grotesques, however, must not and cannot suggest a meaning ... The grotesque is a play with the absurd. It may begin in a carefree manner ... But it must also carry the player away, deprive him of his freedom, and make him afraid of the ghosts which he so frivolously invoked ... In spite of all the helplessness and horror inspired by the dark forces ... the truly artistic portrayal effects a secret liberation ... The darkness has been sighted, the ominous powers discovered, the incomprehensible forces challenged ... a final interpretation of the grotesque: an attempt to invoke and subdue the demonic aspects of the world.[4]

In finding artistic structures that could contain the absurd chaos he saw, Dylan somehow gained control over his world, his material, and attained a form of liberation.

Existentialism: Dylan now avoided political, social, or moral philosophizing. In his *Broadside* days and nights, he provided shallow social analysis—discrimination is bad, poverty is unjust, war is evil, peace and brotherhood are where it's at, man. In 1964, earlier than most radicals, Dylan found picket-sign philosophy no longer serviceable. Following Sartre, Camus, and others, he traveled to a street existentialism that came less from ordered thinking than from emotional reaction. Dylan didn't discard earlier insights or orientations; he didn't spout Sartre or Heidegger. But if we take existentialism out of the seminar and onto the highway, we can find compass points throughout Dylan's 1965–66 work. Here is *The Reader's Encyclopedia*'s working definition of existentialism:

The point of departure is human consciousness and mental processes ... the concept that a man has an essential self is shown to be an illusion ... A man's self is nothing except what he has become; at any given moment, it is the sum of the life he has shaped until then. The "nothing" he begins with is thus the source of man's freedom ... Man's mind cannot discern any meaning for this existence in the universe; when he abandons his illusions, he finds himself horrified by the absurdity of the human condition ... Thus man must create a human morality in the absence of any known predetermined absolute values. Honesty with oneself is perhaps the major value common to existentialist thinking; all existentialist writings describe the emotional anguish of trying to achieve it ... The man of good faith judges a potential action by estimating the result if everyone, not just himself, were to perform it. Yet despite the difficulty of choice, he does not withdraw from life, but is engagé, actively engaged in the business of living with himself and with other men.[5]

After citing the Jewish mystic Martin Buber as one writer in this tradition, the distinction is then made: Camus's "'man of the absurd' resembles Sartre's 'man of good faith' in that both acknowledge man's lonely condition in the face of the silence of the universe; both reject despair and commit themselves to the anguish and responsibility of loving as best one can; and both consider the exercise of one's own freedom inseparable from the opportunity for all men to exercise theirs, which is contingent on their freedom from poverty, political oppression, and other avoidable external limitations."

Dylan was also engaged in an anguished search for honesty amid an awareness of death and despair, to which one does not succumb. Out on the streets, he was weighing his anguish and his responsibility, pitting his loneliness against that of the lonely crowd, filling his absurd rock life with absurdist inventions of his imagination. To him, they were all "real people."

The Dream-Hallucination as a Mirror of Reality: The priest-seer-artist dreams of a reality that lies outside ordinary time and space yet mirrors the everyday world. The dreams set him apart, make him seem a "difficult" as well as a gifted person. Artists see more intensely and clearly than the rest of us and may also, by giving their vision structure, help us to perceive and understand things we may have only fleetingly glimpsed. For surrealist artists, dreams, imaginings, even hallucinations, natural or chemical, have helped broaden and deepen the scope of art. To these artists, life is sur-real, life is sur-earnest. This is the aesthetic of surrealism. The folk aesthetic maintains that all men and women are potential artists. The artist-in-every-man and the "holy" artist co-exist and overlap. The artist, as dreamer-in-chief, lends structure, shape, and color to the visions he will, at some point, *share* with his audience. The best art is a flame warming our own imaginations, a global campfire that irradiates some universal human experiences.

Especially since the late 1950s, when use of marijuana became more widespread, pot-induced dreams have made many feel they are artists and visionaries. Dope smokers grunting to each other "Beautiful, man!" are scarcely artists. A Blake or Coleridge, a Rimbaud or Baudelaire, is able to communicate back through the doors of perception, able to find the words, sounds, and colors that give existence and substance to that "other world" that cannot otherwise be communicated. Innumerable Dylan followers have assured me it is *impossible* to understand much of Bob's 1965–66 work without dropping acid. "Acid music," the three middle-period albums used to be called. The listener does not have to shop at the same drugstore as the artist. One does not need the same quantities of gin and fizz Fitzgerald required to savor *The Great Gatsby* or *Tender Is the Night*. Dylan certainly asks of his listener intense concentration and an ability to let go and follow him. At first, literal-minded folkniks were simply not prepared to let go. While they were still following heroes of the Spanish Civil War, Dylan had followed his Tambourine Man into decadent, alienated, surrealist, existential sensation and vision.

Bringing It All Back Home, recorded in New York City on January 14 and 15, 1965, is not a series of intentionally "difficult" song-poems. The album title is a fine colloquial phrase which Dylan tattooed on to our language. It reminds Beatles' and Stones' fans, who vaguely thought rock a British invention, that it all started in America. The phrase also means a homecoming for Dylan's own beloved rhythmic music. Trenchant protest returns, not for any sect, but for all of us. The dishonesties Dylan sees leveled at American youth are cataloged to be fought and ridiculed. And the love songs are bringing Dylan back home to consider himself, his search for identity, his comprehension of what constitutes Eden. About this time, he said: "Chaos is a close friend of mine. Truth is chaos. Maybe beauty is chaos." Yet in portraying chaos, of the society or of the soul, he converts his "close friend" into artistic order.

Daniel Kramer's cover photograph is an essay in symbols. Dylan fondles his cat—named Rolling Stone. Behind him, albums by Ric Von Schmidt, Lotte Lenya, Robert Johnson, the Impressions. Far behind him stands his own last album. The attractive brunette is Sally Grossman, Albert's wife. Elsewhere, a fallout shelter sign, a copy of *Time*, a nineteenth-century portrait. Just left of center on the mantelpiece is Dylan's "The Clown," a glass collage he made for Bernard Paturel from fragments of colored glass Bernard was about to discard. On the back of the album, other photographs offer glimpses of the singer's life: Joan goofs with a Dylan mouth harp; Peter Yarrow scratches his head at the gendarmes while Dylan seemingly boards the Orient Express; a sedate Allen Ginsberg appears in top hat and tie; Dylan works at a studio keyboard; filmmaker Barbara Rubin gives the master a head massage; wearing the top hat and a broad grin out of *Alice in Wonderland*, Dylan meets some fans. Many regard *Back Home* as a high point of his recording career. Although several tracks have rock backing, an after-echo of the electric band resonates through the second, mainly acoustic, side.

"Subterranean Homesick Blues": The first indication that Dylan was going electric again was this song, released as a single early in 1965 and rising to number thirty-nine on the charts. It shows heavy musical influence from that impudent rhythm 'n' blues fantasist Chuck Berry, from whom Dylan borrowed the simple blues-chord structure, use of the voice as a prominent instrument, sarcastic lyrics, bright mood, and tripping tempo. "Subterranean" grew out of "Motorpsycho Nitemare" and the "Baby Black" poem of *Another Side*. The lyric structure, with short, punchy phrases, owes much to skip-rope rhymes. Blues and R&B often use this traditional form, known to every kid who ever played on an American street. Guthrie and "Paul Campbell" (a Seeger pseudonym) used the device in "Taking It Easy":

Mom was in the kitchen, preparing to eat,
Sis was in the pantry looking for some yeast,

Pa was in the cellar mixing up the hops,
And Brother's at the window, he's watching for the cops.

Dylan's rapid-fire rhymes seem like sheer fun, but black absurdity shadows this inspired nonsense. The militant Weatherman faction of the Students for Democratic Society took its name from "You don't need a weatherman/To know which way the wind blows."[6] "Don't follow leaders"[7] is a basic anti-authoritarian tenet. Dylan takes another swipe at formal education: "Twenty years of schoolin'/And they put you on the day shift."[8] "Subterranean" lyrics resemble fast-forward images of cops, government men, and district attorneys in a silent-movie slapstick chase, followed by a "Baby Black" life story—a sad, meaningless life, always one jump ahead of failure—told in a few deft strokes.[9]

"She Belongs to Me": Dylan may have invented the anti-love song. In the past, pop had dealt almost exclusively with sophomoric love. Dylan considerably matured the form, without hesitating to hit back at women who hurt, disappointed, or confused his narrators. Irony was always his best weapon. If this song, in quite symmetrical blues form with orderly rhyme scheme and line length, is not partly about Baez, then there must be some unknown woman artist to whom Dylan gave an Egyptian ring. "She never stumbles/She's got no place to fall"[10] is echoed in verse three from a traditional folk blues, "I'm a Stranger Here." Dylan's first verse contains the seed of his later film title *Don't Look Back*, itself the title of a John Lee Hooker blues. The song's bitter words are couched in a gentle, warm melody and the phrasing is relaxed; the loping, swaying tempo has waltz-like grace. Engineering brought Dylan's presence physically closer. Electric guitar and mouth-harp embroidery sweeten this bitter song.

"Maggie's Farm": During 1961, Dylan used to sing "Hard Times in the Country," a rural protest song about the tough life of a tenant farmer with an exploitative landlord. I traced that song to "Penny's Farm," which Seeger recorded in 1950. Seeger's George Penny was as mean a landlord as ever drew breath. After living with "Hard Times" on "Penny's Farm," Dylan gradually remade their words and melody completely into "Maggie's Farm." Dylan learned early that traditional protest material doesn't limit itself to heavy-handed, somber songs, but can wrap social comment in many guises. As in "Subterranean," the laughter is satanic, the social criticism stern. This "anti-work song" contains a strong condemnation of all meaningless labor. Dylan sounds a declaration of independence against conformity. His voice projects with cornet-clarion hardness over a band swinging on a simple R&B structure. We may laugh at the plight of the narrator, until we realize that we're *all* working on somebody's farm. In Britain, the song had a strong revival after 1978 as a gibe at Maggie Thatcher's Conservative government. The title was adapted for a cartoon series in *Time Out* magazine.

"Love Minus Zero/No Limit": Although increasingly sardonic in his anti-love songs, Dylan still dreamed of a faithful woman, wise enough to avoid all the entrapping games of neurotic, competitive love. The title, borrowed from gambling parlance, suggests all love's a wager.

My love she speaks like silence,
Without ideals or violence,
She doesn't have to say she's faithful,
Yet she's true, like ice, like fire.[11]

Here Dylan exercises new poetic sinews. Christopher Ricks has delighted in the linking of ideals with violence. Jack McDonough linked Dylan and Boris Pasternak's fascination with the "two godmothers of silence and mystery." He found another Dylan preoccupation, "self-awareness through isolation, a theme both romantic and existential." The musical flow of "Love Minus Zero" is so sedative that even the ominous images of cloaks and daggers and a bridge trembling at midnight do not mar the tranquility that the love object exudes.

"Outlaw Blues": Lots of primitive R&B beat and a chord structure from the suburbs of Berry's "Memphis." In the traditional R&B context, Dylan satirizes some blues writing. Drawn again to the image of stumbling, he slides over pathos and lands in a goony lagoon. Verse two, badman mythology: Jesse James was shot by his so-called friend, Robert Ford, while hanging a picture. Verse four, another R&B take-off: instead of some mojo-voodoo symbol, Dylan has a black tooth and dark shades. He ends the verse with a couplet that epitomizes his attitude toward the press: "Don't ask me nothin' about nothin',/I just might tell you the truth."[12] The song rocks nicely and allows one vocal break at the end of each verse. (Paul Williams used *Outlaw Blues* as the title for a book about rock; it also became the name of a 1977 film on country music that starred Peter Fonda.)

"On the Road Again": Enter the grotesque, a foretaste of things to come. Daddy in a Napoleon mask, milkman in a derby, contentious mailmen and butlers, frogs inside socks—just a quiet day on a phantasmagoric farm. A bright, simple rock structure against which flash some effective harmonica breaks. But musically, the track, with thrusting beat and opposing riff overriding everything, is as untidy as a lot of early rock.

"Bob Dylan's 115th Dream": Skipping blithely over 113 dreams since his first dream-song, Dylan offers his "115th." In a studio session, there's often a great deal of tension. Tension's brother, laughter, often sits nearby. When the band missed its entrance cue on the first take, the laughter was so natural and contagious that Dylan and producer Tom Wilson decided to leave it in. Dylan loved the tall tale and shaggy-dog story as a vehicle for free-floating satire and odd snippets of instant wit. This time, the grotesque dream concerns the discovery of America. The famed hunter of Moby Dick is disguised as "Captain Arab," and the whale of chaos he found is America. Again, the choppy, comic jump cuts of film: Keystone Kops chased and chasing, and the trotting tempo and fluid meter keep this film galloping along at high velocity, one scene superimposed upon the next. Before Dylan's dreams turned dark, he still found life ludicrous rather than horrific. His ear was always looking for the rhyme that would work, unsettle, and amuse.

The flippant impudence that began *Back Home* scarcely prepares us for the second side's poetic flights. The four songs here rank among Dylan's most durable classics. If given a time limit to illustrate his gifts, I would play the 23 minutes of side two. Even the tracks' lengths set trends; Dylan broke the pop convention that the album track should be limited to the length of a three-minute single. He inaugurated what was known by the late 1960s as the "heavy" album track.

"Mr Tambourine Man": A great lyric poem about the artist's search for transcendence. Dylan's concern again is with feeling—its nature and whether to surrender to it or control it with humor and toughness. Originally better known in Judy Collins's and the Byrds' versions, Dylan brings us closer to the song's elusive core. In 1968, Dylan told *Sing Out!*: "There was one thing I tried to do which wasn't a good idea for me. I tried to write another 'Mr Tambourine Man.' It's the only song I tried to write 'another one.' But after enough going at it, it just began bothering me, so I dropped it. I don't do that anymore."

In the (New York) *Sunday News* of November 11, 1973, Al Aronowitz recounted that Dylan wrote the song at his house in Berkeley Heights, New Jersey:

> *Bob must have stayed up past dawn, rapping away at the keys in his cigarette fog. He had just broken up with ... Suze ... For him, it was a long step farther into loneliness ... I found a wastebasket full of crumpled false starts. I took it out the side door to empty it into the trash can when a whispering emotion caught me ... I took the crumpled sheets, smoothed them out, read the crazy leaping lines, smiled to myself at the leaps that never landed and then put the sheets into a file folder. I still have them somewhere.*

"Tambourine" is bold in definition, yet resonates with ambiguity. Dylan asks what experience, path, new door can bring us to happiness and fulfillment. The most widely accepted decodification is that Dylan was talking about drugs. (Richard Goldstein was planning to title his first book, about drugs on campus, *Mr Tambourine Man*. Grossman's partner, John Court, requested, or demanded, that the publisher change the title.) The drug-metaphor case is easy to build: transcendence, freedom, escape, and direct references, in verse two, to a trip and stripped senses, and in verse four, to "the smoke rings of my mind."[13] Thomas De Quincey's *Confessions of an English Opium-Eater* refers to opium as "the dark idol," a translation from the

Latin, *Mater Tenebrarum*. Is it possible that Dylan, reading De Quincey, could have been sufficiently intrigued by the sound of *Mater Tenebrarum* to have rendered it as Mr Tambourine Man?

Yet the song reaches toward a more universal experience than drugs. Knowing black gospel music, Dylan could certainly identify the Tambourine Man as a bearer of religious salvation, bringing a "joyful noise" into the church. Any Salvation Army curbside troupe worth its faith uses a tambourine to brighten its gospel. The Tambourine Man could easily be some embodiment of the muses of music and poetry, or a sandman for adults, a spirit who draws us out of our daily parade to escape "far from the twisted reach of crazy sorrow"[14] with the hope that we can "forget about today until tomorrow."[15] Gabrielle Goodchild once suggested a comparison with Yeats, for whom dance was also a transcendence image. His Tambourine Man was the Emperor, or a dancing child on the seashore. In Yeats's "Byzantium," the poet follows a superhuman image until he finds himself, at midnight, "Dying into a dance,/An agony of trance,/An agony of flame that cannot singe a sleeve."[16] Dylan's vision becomes "frozen" movement, a dance under a "diamond sky."

Dylan has cited Fellini's film *La Strada* and musician Bruce Langhorne at a session with a giant tambourine as direct inspiration: "Drugs never played a part in that song." Part of the song's magic is that there are legions of Tambourine Men. I find Mr Tambourine Man is Bob himself, playing a song for me, taking me following, casting me under his dancing spell. The very spirit that is seducing his own senses is the effect Dylan has had on so many others. Listening to him, we are indeed ready to go anywhere. He lets me forget about today, and tomorrow he'll have yet another song for me.

"Gates of Eden": The quest for salvation. Ultimately, the promise or dread of heaven and hell faces everyone. In *The Orphic Vision*, Gwendolyn Bays: "A barrier between the realm of sleep and waking was perceived by both Homer and Virgil … both made a distinction between the two kinds of visionary experiences. In the celebrated imagery of the gates of ivory and the gates of horn they represented this fundamental poetic insight … through the portal leading into the realm of the dead, came nothing but truth, whereas through the gate 'of gleaming ivory' false dreams often came to men. Thus, the ancients wisely saw that dreams can be the bearers of both truth and error."[17] Gabrielle Goodchild: "He is not really talking about Eden, but about what is *not* Eden … He is talking about *this* world, a lying illusion of destructiveness, savagery, false promises, prophets and pimps, false security. The only comfort is that 'It doesn't matter inside the Gates of Eden.'[18] It will all end and oblivion will come. If oblivion is the only thing to hope for, what a terrible world this is." The crowning irony of "Eden" is that heaven is both more *and* less than we've been taught to believe. In Dylan's hands, belief in a life after death without worry or care is the ultimate myth because it takes us past the ugliness of life. When we are there, we are dead, and what is more restful than eternal sleep?

In verse two, the metallic, mechanical city covers the cries of babies, the longing for Eden's silence. Verse three, savage soldiers and deaf hunters await their mythic boat ride. In verse four, the magic of Aladdin and the magic of cloistered monks promise a paradise that no one laughs at, until he is in Eden. Verse five portrays the Marxists whispering from the wings, awaiting one king-leader to succeed another, while their audience escapes the political-philosophical struggle, knowing that there are no kings in Eden. Verse six finds the motorcycle hipster and his antonym, the gray-flannel business-man mental midget, equally appalling and equally concerned with sin, which is non-existent in death or in Eden. History, implies cynical verse seven, doesn't teach us all that much, for Blakean "kingdoms of Experience"[19] just rot in the wind. The poor battle for what other paupers have, while nobility talks on; none of it matters, in Eden. More gloom as "friends and other strangers"[20] try futilely to change their fates. No matter, inside the Gates of Eden. Finally, even his lover's dreams should not be scanned for meaning or truth. No truth but in Eden, in sleep, in death.

In 1793, Blake issued a series of pictorial emblems titled *The Gates of Paradise*. In 1818, he reworked many of the plates and added a text called "The Keys of the Gates." The emblems traced man from cradle to grave, through various states of the soul's desire and mortal frustration. To Blake, the grave was not a place of death, but of spiritual mystery, echoing the Bible, Spenser, Shakespeare, Milton, and Swedenborg. Is "Gates of Eden" both a Blakean song of innocence *and* of experience? Coleridge said the best way to know poems is to make them "generally, but not perfectly understood." Compare "the ships with tattooed sails"[21] to the timeless metaphor of a ship as the vehicle to death. The monks sitting sidesaddle on a Golden Calf recall that ancient Hebrews worshiped a Golden Calf until Moses delivered the Ten Commandments.

"It's Alright, Ma (I'm Only Bleeding)": The title's a sly play on "That's All Right, Mama," the Arthur "Big Boy" Crudup song that became Presley's first single. I once mentioned the similarity of titles to Bob, who mordantly replied: "Yeah, they are the same sort of song." "It's Alright, Ma" is the ultimate protest song, demolishing so many myths and social evils.

I find "It's Alright, Ma" more sad than angry. He seems to be talking simultaneously to a generation of parents and would-be parents. In fact, to everyone. Measure the growth of two years' writing since "Times Changing." Try transcribing one verse and you see the plummeting energy, the demonic drive that pushes him along as if he had to get it all said before time runs out. In his dissertation "Bob Dylan: The Artist in the Marketplace," Bill King wrote that this song "is to capitalism what Koestler's *Darkness at Noon* is to communism." The setting is again phantasmagoric and the new crucifixion ("Darkness at the break of noon")[22] eclipses everything. Then, the great attack on lifelessness, on succumbing to despair: "he not busy being born/Is busy dying."[23] Perhaps the biggest ambiguity is the shifting point of view. Is the singer speaking of himself, or describing the plight of his listener? Besides several misspelled or poorly transcribed words, the folio and *The Bob Dylan Song Book* omitted verses four and five, forty-five lines. Note his later changes in *Writings and Drawings*.

"It's Alright, Ma" belies criticism that Dylan was no longer socially conscious. He moved his protest here to a higher level, to polemicize the human condition. In a remarkable verse, Dylan previews a sexual revolution that was still three years away. He lashes out at the "Old lady judges"[24] he knew so well in Hibbing. The fierce defense of security, he knows, is no insurance against death. His targets have widened to include advertising, propaganda, obscenity, false gods, and goals. Despite his anger, he accepts lies and malaise as part of life, tempering an outraged snort into sadness that this is the way things are. Implicitly, he sees that the flaws of life are beyond good and evil. This is almost a spoken poem, like Ginsberg's "Howl." In fact, an excellent melodic, rhythmic base provides hammer strokes for nailing down a steel spike. Repetition of certain phrases heightens dramatic impact, builds tension.

"It's All Over Now, Baby Blue": Farewell on several levels—an *adieu* to any of his women, a farewell to the Left, or to his own youthful illusions. It's also Dylan's conversation with himself; he is the orphan telling himself to "Forget the dead you've left, they will not follow you."[25] This is no epitaph, for one can "Strike another match, go start anew."[26] Consider verse two ("Take what you have gathered from coincidence")[27] in light of the foreword to the *I Ching*,[28] where Jung expounded his theory of synchronicity, which "takes the coincidence of events in space and time as meaning something more than mere chance, namely a peculiar interdependence of objective events among themselves as well as with the subjective (psychic) states of the observer." "Baby Blue" was Dylan's finest song about pain—before *Blood On the Tracks*. The vocalizing captures harsh experience softened into tender resignation. On *Biograph*, Dylan makes an association with Gene Vincent's "Baby Blue."

The liner notes begin with *Tarantula*-like nervous thought-fragments, name lists, and wild juxtapositions. The second section is riddled with aphorisms: a farewell to perfectionism, annoyance at White House Philistinism, acceptance of chaos, a description of fear, and his discovery that "experience teaches that silence terrifies people the most."[29] For all his gnomic games, he was ready now to declare "a poem is a naked person ... some people say that I am a poet."[30] He's almost ready to declare himself a poet, but not quite.

Highway 61 Revisited.

Highway 61 Revisited was released in August 1965. There was no gap in Dylan's momentum, for "Like a Rolling Stone" had been released as a single in June, topping the charts for weeks. Despite that success, Dylan split with his second producer, Tom Wilson. For a time, he found an ideal match in Bob Johnston, a shy, soft-spoken Nashville cat, who had been an independent producer for two years before joining Columbia in early 1965. Two years later, he became director of Columbia's country and western A&R. He also produced Cash, Simon and Garfunkel, Louis Armstrong, the Byrds, Aretha, Patti Page, Flatt and Scruggs, Seeger, and Leonard Cohen. Although he wrote several hits, some of which were recorded by Presley, Johnston thought the record producer should extend help while allowing the maximum amount of freedom. "Dylan's king, and I'll not tell Dylan what I think of his material unless he asks me," Johnston once said.

Dylan, according to Johnston, developed a very good studio atmosphere: "If it gets to the point where it doesn't feel right, we split and come back next afternoon or evening. Dylan has got his songs worked out definitively. No matter who he's working with." Of studio musicians in New York or Nashville: "They know they are playing with one of the greatest artists in the world, so Dylan takes advantage of it. Dylan's not a follower, he's a leader and he's always changed. When Dylan recorded a country song, the rest of the world followed. Change is one of the things that keeps him where he is and what he is. If he just wanted somebody to push a button he'd get himself an engineer," Johnston said. He described a typical session: "Bob will suddenly ring me up and say that he's got a whole new batch of songs together, which he'd like to record. The studios are usually well booked, but it's quite easy for me to get another group, no matter how big, to vacate the studios. Everyone has so much respect for Dylan. The studio session men may be guys Bob has heard and wants to use. With Dylan, almost everything is done live, with a minimum of overdubbing. This way we can get things done in just a couple of takes. Dylan is incredible. You are just proud to work with him. He's a very dear friend and I want things to be right for him. I can work a week on the mixing, and if it's wrong as far as he's concerned, I would do it again. The sequencing lies with him. He's the boss, but we work together. Dylan is a perfectionist. He won't settle for second best. Dylan is so intense, he is quite unlike any other artist I've worked with. I don't really 'produce' his albums, but just do my best to make him smile when he leaves the studio. Bob is a man whose music is in his head."

Highway 61 generally has a cleaner ensemble sound than *Back Home*, giving more definition to individual instruments and the overriding voice. Another Kramer photograph adorns the album. Although Dylan poses indoors, his motorcycle T-shirt and colored silk shirt put him on the road again. On the back, three studio shots catch Dylan in the session.

"Like a Rolling Stone": Often regarded as the greatest rock single of all time, its magnitude and tension develops right through its six minutes. At first, the narrator seems vindictive, as if he enjoys watching an over-protected person forced out into a cruel world. Dylan had little sympathy with those who hadn't fought easy comforts. Yet this and subsequent versions reveal a sad resignation that softens the tone of "I told you so." One night, I got Dylan to talk about the song: "Why does everybody say of something like 'Like a Rolling Stone,' 'that Dylan — is that all he can do, put down people?' I've never put down anybody in a song, man. It's their idea. 'Like a Rolling Stone,' man, was very vomitific in its structure. It seemed like twenty pages, but it was really six. You know how you get sometimes. And I did it on a piano. And when I made the record, I called the people who made the record with me, and I told them how to play on it, and if they didn't want to play it like that, well, they couldn't play with me. When I wrote ['You've gone to the finest school, all right, Miss Lonely,/But you know you only used to get juiced in it'],[31] I wasn't making this song about school. That's *their* idea. Their definition of school is much different than mine. My language is different than theirs. I mean *really totally different!* The finest school, I mean, might just be out in the swamps. 'School' here can be anything. This song is definitely not about school."

He was probably using "school" as a symbol of a way of life. Dylan sees horror enveloping anyone who suddenly makes a break after being closely attached to any form of life. For some, the experience is liberating; to others, it brings panic and helplessness. The "schoolgirl" he seems to be chastising here is probably anyone afraid to step out of his or her cocoon and into life's mainstream without guidance, parents, structure, or crutches. The words seem crueler on the page than they sound in performance. A song that seems to hail the drop-out life for those who can take it segues into compassion for those who have dropped out of bourgeois surroundings. "Rolling Stone" is about the loss of innocence and the harshness of experience. Myths, props, and old beliefs fall away to reveal a taxing reality.

Musically, the song jells beautifully; there is little feeling of pre-studio rehearsal, just of a group that takes off on a splendid progression of chords. Dylan says the song was recorded in one take. The organ work — Al Kooper's strongly cohesive legato tones, the lighter filigree of runs and configurations — is brilliant. Thanks to Mike Bloomfield's guitar, even clichés are flavorful and skillfully timed. The drums swing brightly, while Dylan's voice urgently seems to anticipate the beat. The basic chord sequence is simple, familiar, yet the massive, full sound builds into a complex structure. In *Backstage Passes*, Al Kooper tells how he improvised the now-famous instrumental part to the delight of Dylan and all hands. Twenty years later, Dylan recalled recording it in a single day. Sara [Lowndes, whom he would shortly marry] and he lived in a Woodstock cabin and he wrote it there. "It just came, you know," he said.[32]

"Tombstone Blues": A Chuck Berry-ful thrust in this up-tempo number. The basic chord sequence in the verse is C, C7, F, and back to C, while in the middle eight bars, F and C chords alternate. This is a song of the grotesque, but we're more amused than frightened by the incongruities. The cast is large: children in bed, city fathers, Paul Revere's horse, Belle Starr, Jezebel, Jack the Ripper, John the Baptist, the list goes on. Allusions to Vietnam are apparent throughout, especially in the title and in verses three and four, where I see Lyndon Johnson as King of the Philistines. Another skip-rope-like rhyme in the refrain mixes insouciance with complaint. It's highly episodic; one well-planned absurdity suggests another, whether biblical, historical, or musical. Ma Rainey, the blues singer, and Beethoven are superseded by brass-band tuba players rehearsing a military march. One impudent image reminds us that Dylan's control of language was absolute: "The geometry of innocence flesh on the bone/Causes Galileo's math book to get thrown."[33]

Musically "Tombstone" trots along effortlessly. The slide-guitar breaks are primitive, yet so well-timed as to seem inspired. In one break, the foot pedal changes the texture of an elongated guitar figure. The song goes out on a finger tremor, wobbling on a string for yet another texture. Recorded on July 19, 1965 on the same day as "Positively Fourth Street" and "It Takes a Train to Cry." A cop's talk about death was an influence on his lyrics. Dylan calls "Jet Pilot," released for the first time on *Biograph*, the original version of "Tombstone."

"It Takes a Lot to Laugh, It Takes a Train to Cry": Wry title for a traditional blues form, rooted in an old shuffle sound from Kansas City or St Louis of the 1940s. Bobby Gregg's lazy-slap drumming sets the draggy tempo with an ever-so-slight emphasis on the offbeat. No room here for technical flourishes, which would have robbed the song of its old-timey feeling. The unusual harmonica fabric adds to the rough-hewn texture. The singing is straightforward blues, with sustained holds on *sea* and *boss* that add a little dramatic push to an otherwise low-key blues.

"From a Buick 6": The title reminds us of how Chuck Berry raced automobiles through his lyrics, as a symbol of freedom, status, escape, and sexuality. The feel of this blues in C is quite antique, predating Berry; the principal guitar figure sounds like electrified riffs out of Robert Johnson, Charley Patton, or Big Joe Williams. Aside from some incidental spoofing, the lyrics are traditional couplets. An earthy tribute to another funky earth-mother.

"The Ballad of a Thin Man": "Mister Jones," one of Dylan's greatest archetypes, is a Philistine, an observer who does not see, a person who does not reach for the right questions. He piously pays his social dues through self-serving tax deductions, pays to watch freak shows but doesn't like the entertainment, is superficially educated and well-bred but not very smart about the things that count. I once tried to corner Dylan about Mr Jones: "Mr Jones is like a very weak, ah, well-to-do person. Not well-to-do in the terms of bread or shelter, but well-to-do, knowing he can always go home. Friends will put Mr Jones up, not because they like him, but because they must, out of the mores in which they live. He has his own environment and his own people. His loneliness can easily be covered up to the point where he can't recognize that he is alone. Mr Jones is suddenly locked in a room, he stumbled into a room. God knows, we all do that! It's not so incredibly absurd and it's not so imaginative to have Mr Jones in a room with three walls and a midget, and a geek and a naked man. Plus a voice ... a voice coming in his dream. I am just a voice speaking. Any time I'm singing about people and if the songs are dreamed, it's like my voice is coming out of their dream. Mr Jones is powerful, because it's very concise and very emotional, do you dig?"

We all know many Mr Joneses who just don't seem to be aware of what's happening. Who, specifically, might Mr Jones have been to Dylan? A *Time* reporter named Jeffrey Jones wrote in *Rolling Stone* in 1975 that it must have been him. I would nominate Pete Seeger, thrown for a complete loss by Dylan's electric music; Tom Wilson, not understanding Dylan's concepts about recording; another *Time* reporter, Horace Judson, whom Dylan scourged in *Don't Look Back*; Howard Alk, husband of Jones Alk, both members of the film crew. Mr Jones is undoubtedly a composite. To Dylan's free-flowing accusations, many people pleaded guilty. Other theories bandied about: Mr Jones was LeRoi Jones, militant black writer; Mr Jones is patois for the heroin-user; Jones is a masculinization of Joan; Mr Jones is the farmer in Orwell's *Animal Farm*. When I was slow in getting Dylan's rock message, some people thought I was Mr Jones, but I hadn't been a thin man in years. Musically, the song is almost stately, with fine organ work again lending cohesion. Novelist Joseph Heller reportedly took his title *Something Happened* from this song.

"Queen Jane Approximately": A puckish title, wide open to interpretation. Some believe Dylan is still on an anti-Baez kick here, with *Jane* barely disguising *Joan*. There is a classic early-sixteenth-century English-Scottish ballad (Child Ballad 170) written not long after Jane Seymour gave birth to Prince Edward, and which Baez sang, called "The Death of Queen Jane." How does Mick Jagger's Queen Jane relate to Dylan's? Since "Mary Jane" is Aesopian for marijuana, some think the song alludes to drugs. The lyrics stingingly attack a formalized, dutiful family life, filled with joyless, meaningless, ritualistic proprieties. Musically, a bit lackluster. The band sounds muddy; the electric guitar, if not out of tune, is certainly out of phase. A minor work that says very little to me, other than an undercurrent of rueful feeling.

"Highway 61 Revisited": Because US Highway 61 passes from Duluth through Minneapolis before heading down through Wisconsin toward the blues country of Mississippi, it is a particularly useful highway for Dylan to hitch back on. It links America's most alienated group, southern blacks, with the singer, alienated at his end of the road. This bright blues shuffle is augmented by a police-car whistle. The band trots along, paced by the drumming, flavored with bottleneck guitar and fine piano that is almost too subdued. The verse begins with a takeoff on biblical lore, less "holy blues" than Lord Buckley or Bill Cosby. If God were chatting with Abe close to the northern end of the highway, the son would be Dylan himself. The "killing" would have struck him down just as he was setting off on the road. The song's ludicrousness grows with mention of Georgia Sam, poor Howard (a folk figure), Mack the Finger, Louie the King, and the bluesy mumbo-jumbo of mystical magic about seventh sons. Finally, a jab at a concert promoter who, when asked to promote another world war, says he'll try. There's a disturbing undercurrent of probability.

"Just Like Tom Thumb's Blues": Before arriving at "Desolation Row," the singer visits a border-town skid row. In seamy Juarez, our anti-hero stumbles amid sickness, despair, whores, and saints. "When you're lost in the rain in Juarez/And it's Eastertime too"[34] establishes a smoldering nightmare under Malcolm Lowry's volcano. The mournful exoticism supports the ugly scene, jangly piano adding a honky-tonk edge. A man's "going down slow," pulled by gravity, negativity, drink, illness, remorse, memories, until the surprising final couplet: he has found the means of returning to New York, an intimation that things might go better there. Beautiful scene painting, with edges purposefully scumbled out of focus. Was Rue Morgue an avenue or a nightmare alley where echoes of Poe suggest murder and suicide?

A Halifax academic, David M Monaghan, has written that it all suggests "The Love Song of J Alfred Prufrock," T S Eliot's near-definitive version of modern alienated man. Monaghan finds Dylan "calling on modern man to seek the spiritual values that are to be found by looking in the past."

"Desolation Row": What does your neighborhood look like after that hard rain fell? Dylan describes it here. Both songs are apocalyptic visions thundering with prophecy: unless we renounce materialism, this will be our future. Dylan articulates the rock visions of contemporary apocalypse. "Desolation Row" belongs beside Eliot's "The Waste Land" and Ginsberg's "Howl" as one of the strongest expressions of apocalypse. Eugene Stelzig maintains, however, that "Eliot's disillusionment is resigned; Dylan's is charged with rebellion." The scenery is a dreamed landscape and Dylan's description powerfully combines the grotesque, the existential, and the dream. "Desolation Row" is a grotesque Mardi Gras where heroes and villains of our mytho-history range side by side. They are laughable, but our smiles freeze. The writer who questioned society for two years now sees answers, but doesn't like what he sees. Everything is cockeyed, topsy-turvy; all is lost; all is ludicrous; the only truth lies along Desolation Row. Bizarre as his cast is, they are real people. To maintain their veil of secrecy, the faces have been rearranged and the names changed—shades of Cubism. There is no point in inspecting the traveling papers of Cinderella, the Good Samaritan, Ophelia, Einstein, Doctor Filth. Follow the gargoyles as they head down Desolation Row. Along the way, we encounter Dylan's condemnation of the modern assembly line: mad human robots out of Chaplin's *Modern Times*. Then, almost as an aside, Dylan makes a shambles of simple-minded political commitment. What difference which side you're on if you're sailing on the *Titanic*? Irony and sarcasm are streetlamps along "Desolation Row," keeping away total, despairing darkness. Gallows humor for a mass hanging.

The slow musical matrix heightens the song's biblical roll. Repetition, like Old Testament cantillating, underscores the warning. A masterful, romantic guitar above and behind the vocal line softens the repetition somewhat, but is repeated until it provides only underlining, not relief. This image of the world is far removed from marches toward social progress. One of the curses of poetic vision is seeing too clearly the difference between how things are and how they ought to be.

"I Just Might Tell You the Truth."[35]   Dylan made press interviews a performance. Fans cherished several that were particularly outrageous. If the reporter was knowledgeable and sympathetic, he generally revealed more. If he didn't like the questions, he would give oblique or absurd responses. Bob knew that by limiting interviews he could ultimately guarantee himself more space. He also knew how elusiveness intrigues. Locked eye to eye with an interviewer, he could still parry adroitly. Like his music, statements that appeared unguarded or spontaneous were often thought out in advance. He knew how a line sounded, how it would look in print. In late summer 1965, Nora Ephron and Susan Edmiston of the *New York Post* got a fair amount from him, but also hit stone walls:

NYP: *Some American folk singers—Carolyn Hester, for example—say that what you're now doing, the new sound, "folk-rock," is liberating them.*
Dylan: *Did Carolyn say that? You tell her she can call around and see me anytime now that she's liberated …*
NYP: *Who is "Mister Jones"?*
Dylan: *He's a real person. You know him … I saw him come into the room one night and he looked like a camel. He proceeded to put his eyes in his pocket … It's all there, it's a true story …*
NYP: *Who is Queen Jane?*
Dylan: *Queen Jane is a man …*

When I interviewed Dylan for *Cavalier* in winter 1965, I was struck by his control: "All I do is write songs and sing them. I can't dig a ditch. I can't splice an electric wire. I'm no carpenter. I'm in the show business now. I'm not in the folk-music business. That's where it's at. So is Roscoe Holcomb, Jean Ritchie, Little Orphan Annie, Dick Tracy, all the way up to President Johnson." Dylan was beginning to look wizened, but he remained sharply acute. "Don't tell me anything I say is off the record. A performer is always on the record, all the time." When I asked about Silber's critical "Open Letter" in *Sing Out!*, Dylan sidestepped: "His letter was all right. If it makes him feel better, that's OK. People write me letters all the time." Was he interested in lowering the drinking age or legalizing pot? "You name it, I'll legalize it. I'm not making any rules for anyone," he said, as he finished his salad and started eating mine. Was he looking after his health? "If I died tomorrow, the world would go right on. Kennedy died. Edgar Allan Poe died. The world goes right on. Marx died. Winston Churchill died. Johnson'll die, too. Time doesn't stop."

At press conferences, he was so often misunderstood his annoyance would show. From his December 3, 1965, press conference for San Francisco's KQED-TV:

KQED: *Do you think of yourself primarily as a singer or a poet?*
Dylan: *Oh, I think of myself more as a song-and-dance man.*
KQED: *Josh Dunson implies that you have sold out to commercial interests.*
Dylan: *I sincerely don't feel guilty.*
KQED: *If you were going to sell out to a commercial interest, which one would you choose?*
Dylan: *Ladies garments.*[36]
KQED: *What's your new album about?*
Dylan: *… all kinds of different things—rats, balloons …*
KQED: *How would you define folk music?*
Dylan: *As a constitutional replay of mass production.*
KQED: *Who is "Mister Jones"?*
Dylan: *Mr Jones? I'm not going to tell you his first name. I'd get sued.*

KQED: *What does [Mister Jones] do for a living?*
Dylan: *He's a pinboy. He also wears suspenders.*
KQED: *What are your own personal hopes for the future and what do you hope to change in the world?*
Dylan: *I don't have any hopes for the future and I just hope to have enough boots to be able to change them.*

At a Los Angeles press conference a few weeks later, Dylan was close to overt anger.

Q: *I wonder if you could tell me, among folk singers, how many could be characterized as protest singers today?*
Dylan: *I don't understand. Could you ask the question again?*
Q: *How many people who labor in the same musical vineyards in which you toil, how many are protest singers? That is, how many use their music to protest about the social state in which we are today?*
Dylan: *How many? One hundred thirty-six.* [Laughter] *It's either one hundred thirty-six or one hundred thirty-two.*
Q: *What does the word protest mean to you?*
Dylan: *It means singing when you really don't want to sing. It means singing against your wishes to sing.*
Q: *Do you sing protest songs?*
Dylan: *No.*
Q: *What do you sing?*
Dylan: *I sing all love songs.*
Q: *Is it true that you changed your name? If so, what was your other name?*
Dylan: *Kunezevitch. I changed it to avoid obvious relatives who would come up to me in different parts of the country and want tickets for concerts and stuff like that. Kunezevitch, yeah.*
Q: *Was that your first or last name?*
Dylan: *That was my first name.* [Laughter and applause] *I don't really want to tell you what my last name was.*
Q: *Bob, why is there such a widespread use of drugs among singers today?*
Dylan: *I don't know. Are you a singer?*
Q: *Do you take drugs yourself?*
Dylan: *I don't even know what a drug is. I have never even seen a drug. I would not know what one looked like if I saw one.*
Q: *Bob, what sort of technique do you use when you write a song, or don't you call it any sort of technique?*
Dylan: *Well, I just sit down and the next thing I know, it's there.*
Q: *Why are you putting us, and the rest of the world, on so?*
Dylan: *I'm just trying to answer your questions as good as you can ask them.*
Q: *I am sure you must have been asked a thousand times—what are you trying to say in your music? I don't understand one of the songs.*
Dylan: *Well, you shouldn't feel offended or anything. I am not trying to say anything to you. If you don't get it, you don't have to really think about it, 'cause it's not addressed to you.*
Q: *Are you trying to say something when you write? Or are you just entertaining?*
Dylan: *I'm just an entertainer. That's all.*
Q: *Do you really feel that it's important for you to write and sing?*
Dylan: [Menacingly] *Now, you are gonna make me mad now.*
Q: *Or do you just want to do it because you're successful? Do you really feel the things that you write?*
Dylan: *What is there to feel? Name me some things.*
Q: *We are talking about standard emotions—pain, remorse, love …*
Dylan: *I have none of those feelings.*
Q: *What sort of feelings do you have when you write a song?*
Dylan: *I don't have to explain my feelings! I am not on trial here!*
Q: *You sound and look very tired, very ill. Is this your normal state?*
Dylan: *I take that as an insult. I don't like to hear that kind of thing.*
Q: *What's the reason for your visit to California?*
Dylan: *Oh, I'm here looking for some donkeys. I am making a movie about Jesus.*
Q: *Where are you making it?*
Dylan: *Back East.*
Q: *Did your parents give you any special advice when you last saw them? Did they say "goodbye" or "good luck" or anything like that?*

Dylan: *No, do your parents do that to you?*
Q: *As a little boy, did you want to write songs and be a singer?*
Dylan: *No, I wanted to be a movie usher. It's been my life-long ambition to be a movie usher, and I have failed, as far as I am concerned.*
Q: *Why do you think that kids are listening to you now?*
Dylan: *I really don't know. I just heard something a couple of days ago that amazed me … Outside a concert we played at San José, there was this fifteen-year-old girl … being interviewed as to why she was there … She knew all the poets, like William Blake, and she knew his works and she was hip to all kinds of different things which people are usually not acquainted with at that age. So, maybe, it's just a new kind of person, a new kind of fifteen-year-old. I do know that today there's more freedom in the mind of twenty-two-year-old college students. I know that, that's true.*

In March 1965, Bob was in Woodstock in a jaunty mood; Maura Davis pretended to be from a high-school paper. *Cavalier* ran the interview opposite a photograph of Dylan in a bright yellow and brown plaid wool tie. Some highlights:

Davis: *Mr Dye-lan, I'm from the New Buffalo Consolidated High School, and all the students want to know, what's the most important thing in the world to you?*
Dylan: *Oh, my God! Do they really want to know that? I'd say this tie I'm wearing right now.*
Davis: *Why … that tie?*
Dylan: *Well, President Johnson used to wear a tie like this—before he got to be President. It's a sign of the common man, and I'm a common man. So I wear a tie like this just to, just to get involved.*
Davis: *Do you wear that tie when you're writing your songs?*
Dylan: *When I write? No, I usually wear this after I finish something very good. To make myself feel good, I put on the tie, and then I feel much better about it—and usually I have a hit.*

An intrepid Los Angeles reporter asked Dylan in September 1965 what the most important thing in his life was: "Well, I've got a monkey-wrench collection and I'm very interested in that." Why did he hold such sway with teenagers? "I have no recollection of ever having been a teenager myself. I can't say why they like me. It's a different world." Then Dylan turned irascible: "The protest thing is old. And how valid is it anyway? Is it going to stop anything? Is anybody going to listen? People think this helps. But songs aren't gonna save the world."

That month, Dylan flew to Toronto for rehearsals with the Hawks. Robert Fuller, book columnist of the *Toronto Star*, later wrote that seeing Dylan "is just a little more difficult than arranging a private chat with the Pope." In Toronto a few months later, Margaret Steen interviewed the pop pope and did a substantial story about Dylan's electric music under the headline: NOT YOU, BOB DYLAN! SURELY NOT! IT CAN'T BE THAT THE FOLK-SINGING IDOL OF THE YOUNG HAS GONE COMMERCIAL. THE STAR WHO IS NEVER—WELL, ALMOST NEVER—INTERVIEWED TELLS A *STAR WEEKLY* WRITER HOW IT REALLY IS. Had Dylan really "sold out"? He replied: "It's easy for people to classify it as rock 'n' roll, to put it down. Rock 'n' roll is a straight twelve-bar blues progression. My new songs aren't. I used to play rock 'n' roll a long time ago, before I even started playing old-fashioned folk, ten years ago when I was a kid, for God's sake … the music industry is totally different … Rock 'n' roll singers now … make the old people look sick … Tin Pan Alley! I know that scene. Fat guys chewing cigars and carrying around gold records, and selling songs, selling talent, selling an image. I never hung out there … The singers ten years ago were kids, but the old guys ran things; now the people actually in control are younger—the managers, the record company bosses, kids, in their twenties … Why, man, just with the experiences I've experienced already, I could never step outside this room again and still write songs until the end of time … No. I'm not disillusioned. I'm just not illusioned, either. The civil rights and protest songs, I wrote when nobody else was writing them. Now, everyone is. But I've found out some things. The groups promoting these things, the movement, would try to get me involved with them, be their singing spokesman—and inside these groups, with all their president-vice-president-secretary stuff, it's politics. Inside their own pettinesses they're as bad as the hate groups. I won't even have a fan club because it'd have to have a president, it'd be a group. They think the more people you have behind something the more influence it has. Maybe so, but the more it gets watered down, too. I'm not a believer in doing things by numbers. I believe that the best things get done by individuals."

In an interview with the *Chicago Daily News* on November 27, 1965, Dylan was asked if he had any religion or philosophy: "Philosophy can't give me anything; religion can't give me anything, not anything I don't already have." The only thing that was "amazingly true, period" was the *I Ching*, which "encompasses it all ... besides being a great book to believe in, it's also very fantastic poetry."

In the first draft of Nat Hentoff's famous *Playboy* interview, too much editing angered Dylan and led him, in a second session, to sarcastic heights. He told me: "I read the proofs and I said: 'Where in the fuck did you get these words?' Hentoff told me that the man from *Playboy* wrote in things to make it sound a little better ... And they were downright fucking, silly-ass, you know, geech-like phrases. Peacock phrases. Just dumb bullshit, asinine things that anybody that has ever met me and heard me talk knows I would not say. Everything was out of context. I said: 'You're not getting this article, man.' I called the lawyers right away, and Albert. And the lawyers sent *Playboy* a letter and they got frightened. So they called back and I said: 'Could I have the article rewritten?' I answered the questions. I did it very bad, man. I should have done it much better." Hentoff, and most readers, felt he'd done it brilliantly. Hentoff, in an interview in the fanzine *Zimmerman Blues* (issue 6), told Brian Stibal that he thought *Playboy* editors "put some words in his mouth. They fooled around with it." Hentoff played straight man as Dylan improvised the outlandish interview that eventually ran:

Playboy: *Why have you stopped composing and singing protest songs?*
Dylan: *... message songs, as everybody knows, are a drag ... what I'm going to do is rent Town Hall and put about 30 Western Union boys on the bill. I mean, then there'll really be some messages ...*
Playboy: *You told an interviewer last year, 'I've done everything I've ever wanted to do.' If that's true, what do you have to look forward to?*
Dylan: *Salvation. Just plain salvation.*
Playboy: *Anything else?*
Dylan: *Praying. I'd also like to start a cookbook magazine. And I've always wanted to be a boxing referee.*
Playboy: *Did you ever have the standard boyhood dream of growing up to be President?*
Dylan: *No. When I was a boy, Harry Truman was President; who'd want to be Harry Truman?*
Playboy: *Well, let's suppose that you were the President. What would you accomplish during your first thousand days?*
Dylan: *... the first thing I'd do is probably move the White House ... McGeorge Bundy would definitely have to change his name, and General McNamara would be forced to wear a coonskin cap and shades. I would immediately rewrite "The Star-Spangled Banner," and little schoolchildren, instead of memorizing "America the Beautiful," would have to memorize "Desolation Row." And I would immediately call for a showdown with Mao Tze-Tung; I would fight him personally—and I'd get somebody to film it.*[37]

In an elegiac March 1966 cover story for *Ramparts*, Ralph Gleason got Dylan to discuss his "complex" songs: "These songs aren't complicated to me at all. It's all very clear and simple to me ... There's nothing hard to figure out for me. I wouldn't write anything I can't really see. They're all about real people. I'm sure you've seen all the people in my songs at one time or another." Dylan still respected the complexity and subtlety of folk songs "based on myth and the Bible and plague and famine and all kinds of things like that which are just nuthin' but mystery and you can see it in all the songs—roses growin' right up out of people's hearts and naked cats in bed with, you know, spears growing right out of their back and seven years of this and eight years of that and it's all really something that nobody can really touch." Dylan tried to explain his changes: "I just went through that other thing of writing songs until I couldn't write like it anymore. It was just too easy and it wasn't really right ... But now I just write a song like I *know* that it's just going to be all right and I don't really know exactly what it's all about, but I do know the minute and the layers of what it's all about. 'Rolling Stone' is the best song I wrote. I wrote 'Rolling Stone' after England. I boiled it down, but it's all there. I had to quit after England. I had to stop and when I was writing it I knew I had to sing it with a band. I always sing when I write, even prose, and I heard it like that."

Break-out in Britain. Dylan's trip to England in spring 1965 was a turning point. Although he played to only 50,000 people in eight concerts, the April to June tour changed him from a folk star into an international pop superstar. At this time, most pop excitement emanated from England and Dylan's shock waves flashed back to America. The first clue: In March, 7,000 tickets for his May 10 Albert Hall concert sold out within two hours.

If a single external factor triggered Dylan's British breakthrough, it was the Beatles' public endorsement, which wrought magic. If, as he once said, Dylan was "reborn in New York," then he was certainly reincarnated in England. Before then, in early 1965, he was doing concerts on both coasts. He was writing furiously and recording and, in February, made a brilliant appearance on the Les Crane WABC-TV show. He'd made a star's bed and now tossed fitfully in it. When Dylan had played New Haven and Santa Monica in March 1965, there were local reviews, not the lionization he was to receive in the British national press. In a small country, excitement was like steam in a kettle. The pop and national press had a carnival. Reporters were appalled, bemused, entranced. Dylan made good copy. Dylanmania was probably triggered by Ray Coleman's article in *Melody Maker* on January 9, 1965, headlined: BEATLES SAY—DYLAN SHOWS THE WAY. The story, with photos of Lennon, Harrison, and Dylan, was reproduced on the sleeve of the Columbia single of "Subterranean," backed with "She Belongs to Me." It read, in part: "Two Beatles particularly go for Dylan in a big way. Harrison has all his LPs and plays them regularly and Lennon admires him too." Lennon: "The first time you hear Dylan you think you're the first to discover him. But quite a lot of people have discovered him before us … I think Bob Dylan's music will grow steadily in this country, but I can't see him becoming the new craze." Harrison: "I like his whole attitude. The way he dresses, the way he doesn't give a damn. The way he sings and plays discords. The way he sends up everything."

Coleman, later editor of *Disc* and *Music Echo*, and then of *Melody Maker*,[38] wrote me: "1965 was the year Dylan conquered Britain, the year 'Wind' and 'Times Changing' became favorites of the university students and the pop screamers. Dylan emerged from the relative obscurity of the folk world to the wider, more dangerous world of pop idol. For Dylan, it was fraught with trouble. I was among the hundreds who met Dylan at London Airport. He was bemused by it all. In seven major cities, Dylan faced an uncanny audience. Half was converted, half was the pop cult. Dylan made absolutely no concession to hit-parade status. He commanded utter silence at his concerts. Even the noisy pop fans were stunned into silence by his words, the honesty of his performances. Bob consistently showed an endearing modesty. He wandered on stage with no sign of the 'big star' atmosphere we had come to expect from pop immortals. At Leicester's sensationally successful concert, a cross-section of the audience agreed his performances were more electrifying, more important than his recordings. They clutched copies of *Back Home*. A student said: 'What made it for us was that he sang the words of his songs as if they had meaning. You see so many artists who perform like zombies, as if they're there for the money and that's all.'"

The build-up began long before his arrival on Monday, April 26. The March 19 *London Evening News* and next morning's *Daily Sketch* announced that his Albert Hall tickets were selling "like gold dust." The *Daily Mirror* did an advance story from the States. The pop weeklies ran background stories. Additional blessings from Manfred Mann and the Animals helped build anticipation. As Dylan's plane came into the London airport, 200 fans waited in the rain, some wearing replicas of "the hat." They began to give him Beatles treatment, pulling at his hair and tugging at his clothes, virtually carrying him into the airport conference room. Police helped him through the mob; Dylan, looking somewhat shaken, said: "It's never been like this before! It was OK—they didn't hurt me. They just gave me a haircut. I'm ready to get drunk now." Dylan looked to see how the rest of his party—Baez, the Grossmans, and the film crew of *Don't Look Back*—was faring. Dylan carried an outsize light bulb, a prankish Diogenes lamp. Asked, "What is your message?" Dylan replied: "Keep a good head and always carry a light bulb." Brushing aside questions about Baez, the Beatles and Donovan, he asked the whereabouts of Christine Keeler, who had been at the centre of a political scandal.

Mike Hurst, who taped a ten-minute interview for the BBC, told me later: "He was a living myth before he got here. Many in the press were waiting to break the myth. At first, he was very vague. When I got down to his music, he really started to talk. He was almost interviewing *me* then." Dylan met the press at the Savoy Hotel, individually and in conference. "Hair that would set the teeth of a comb on edge … A loud shirt that would dim the neon lights of Leicester Square," read one description. "He looks like an under-nourished cockatoo" wrote another. "Mr Dylan managed to exasperate practically everybody … He wafted a red rose beneath his nose and could be heard … to say: 'Stiff, cold and mortistic,'" wrote Maureen Cleave of the *Evening Standard*. (Cleave, who was friends with the Beatles, complained: "What do I do with him, how do you make him talk? He just says yes or no and rocks and sways as if he is masturbating himself.")

Dylan had considerably more to say to her than that: 'I don't want to give the impression of being a star, because I don't think of myself as one … I've … seen all these crazes come and go, and I don't think I'm more than a craze. In a coupla years' time, I shall be right back where I started—an unknown … All I'm really interested in is singing to people who want to listen to me … I seem to be more popular here than I am at home … the only difference success has brought is that I now feel I must make my records even better … I am bored with the atom bomb, I am bored with our Government. I do wish somebody in our Government had a beard, just to be different."

A *Daily Mail* reporter was offered Dylan's heavy green glasses. Dylan: "See the world as Bob Dylan sees it … I'm alone up here. I was over here three years back and on the streets. In two years, I'll be gone and you'll be talking to someone else." Why was he staying at the Savoy, a hotel where even minor clerks wear swallow-tailed jackets? Dylan snapped: "I can't live in a shack!'" Grossman hustled the *Daily Mail* man into another room, saying: "We're not here to sell rubber dolls, you know. We're not here to perform for newsmen … Bob is one of the most important figures, not just in pop, you know, but in American life." Baez sat singing "Sally, Go Round the Roses." For the *Mirror*, Bob and Joan posed together on the balcony. One reporter wanted to know why Dylan sounded like a man of 75 who was always cross. Dylan: "I hate injustice, that's why I sing about racial discrimination and freedom, and I preach for people to be able to do the things they want. On some of my earlier records, I sounded cross because I was poor. Lived on less than two cents a day in those times. Now I'm cross because I'm rich … I'm not spreading disillusionment by singing the truth … I guess listening to me is like reading a newspaper. I wanna be entertaining as well as truthful."

Singer Martin Carthy told me: "All the times we went to visit him, only half a minute of the time could we actually contact him. The Savoy rooms were always filled with people. Bob became very, very detached; he had so many people to cope with. The more famous he became, the more he tended just to sit in his hotel." Dorothy Carthy added: "One very high window looked out over a stone balustrade. Pennebaker was in a corner with his camera. Everybody was eating and talking, when Bob suddenly came in through the window from the bathroom next door with an absolutely straight face. He walked along the tops of chairs, settees and whatever other furniture there was. He walked right out of the door and nobody else noticed."

Dylan clashed with Laurie Henshaw of *Disc Weekly* after the tour. *Disc*: "You must obviously make a lot of money nowadays. "I spend it all," Dylan replied. "I have six Cadillacs. I have four houses. I have a plantation in Georgia." Henshaw persisted and Dylan became angry. "Listen, I really couldn't care less what your paper writes about me … The people that listen to me don't need your paper." *New Musical Express* had the temerity to send Dylan one of its "LifeLines" questionnaires: *First important public appearance:* Closet at O'Henry's Square Shop. *Other disc in bestsellers:* "I Lost My Love In San Francisco, But She Appeared Again in Honduras and We Took a Trip to Hong Kong and Stayed Awhile in Reno But Lost Her Again in Oklahoma." *Latest Release:* "The Queens are Coming." *Albums:* Yes. *Personal manager:* Dog Jones. *Musical director:* Big Dog. *Favorite food:* Turkish Marvin (a form of eggplant coming from Nebraska). *Favorite clothes:* Nose-guards. *Favorite bands/instrumentalists:* Corky the Kid (Sombreros). *Favorite composers:* Brown Bumpkin and Sidney Ciggy. *Favorite groups:* The Fab Clocks. *Miscellaneous likes:* Trucks with no wheels. French telephones, anything with a stewed prune in the middle. *Miscellaneous dislikes:* Hairy firemen, toe-nails, glass Mober forks, birds with ears. *Most thrilling experience:* Getting my birthday cake stomped on by Norman Mailer. *Taste in music:* Sort of peanut butter. *Personal ambition:* To be a waitress. *Professional ambition:* To be a stewardess." A reporter for the *Jewish Chronicle* asked him: "Are you Jewish?" He replied: "No, I am not, but some of my best friends are." Dylan assuaged the *Chronicle*: "You'd better interview Tito Burns, the agent for the tour, because I know he is Jewish."

Burns was delighted with the tour. He felt three elements had helped make Dylan in Britain: his initial appeal to the folk audience, the tour, and the fact that CBS Records, Columbia's English affiliate, had begun pushing his records. Dylan's seven concerts sold out in an hour or so. Burns: "We got threatening phone calls and letters from people who had not had a chance to buy tickets. I asked Albert to get me off the hook. I said *I* wouldn't get lynched, but he and Bob would. I got Albert Hall for a second concert, May 9. Those tickets sold out in about an hour and a quarter, and still thousands of people were turned away. I went up to Sheffield. I have never seen Dylan work before and I went in, for a few numbers. I stayed there two hours, because it got to me. I'm not an intellectual, and I only understood about half of it, but the magic still got to me. In 1964, I don't think he took in a lot of money at Festival Hall. In 1965, he took the maximum. In his coming concert tour, in spring 1966, when he could double the price of the tickets, he is refusing to do that. They said to me leave the prices exactly the same, of a one-pound top for tickets.

"The Beatles and the Stones were at Albert Hall and we had to get them boxes way back. They came in just after the show commenced and got out just before it stopped. Everyone was there! Marianne Faithfull rang up for eight tickets. Her mother is a baroness, you know. Just about every star was there. We held back about one-hundred-and-fifty house seats because we knew what would happen. The names that were coming through ... The Earl of Harewood—fantastic!"

The first concert, Sheffield, April 30: "We approached Sheffield in a fleet of Austin Princesses, looking like royalty," Fred Perry, the English road manager, told me. The Sheffield City Hall auditorium was circular; an overflow audience sat onstage. Perry: "I have done thirty English tours, but never saw anything like this! The audience acted as if they were going into a church. In their minds, Dylan was a legend, and you could see the awe on their faces." *New Musical Express* reported such reverent silence in Sheffield Hall that Dylan, peering out into the darkness, said: "It's mighty quiet. Where are you all?" The *Guardian*: "The audience ... radiated a religious fervor ... the second coming of Bob Dylan, their singing Messiah ... The times, they are a-changing ... when a poet and not a pop singer fills a hall. For this ultimately is what Dylan is ... With his voice, the lyrics are astonishing; without it, in print, they are poetry."

Dylan brought it all back home May 1 to Liverpool, the Beatles' hometown. "If there would be any adverse reaction to Dylan, it would be in Liverpool," Perry said. "They just walked in quietly to the Odeon and sat down as if they were in church." The Adelphi Hotel was a Liverpudlian Savoy, requiring ties in its restaurant. In walked Dylan with a black turtleneck sweater, his tie around his waist. "It hung there like a sporran on a Scot's kilt," said Perry. The management was caught off-guard; he had to be served. The next morning, several hundred fans gathered at the hotel.

By Leicester, *Melody Maker* was calling Dylan "the most important folk singer of today," and proclaiming: "Dylan fever is sweeping the country." The *Daily Worker* reported the singer's "magnetism ... power to hold an audience captive, his perfect timing ..." The concert manager called the response "the biggest thing since the Beatles." Around 300 girls from the audience of 3,000 tried to mob Dylan's car—he mockingly brandished a shillelagh at them. After two days rest, Dylan played Birmingham Town Hall. Some paid £5 for a ticket priced at less than a £1. The *Birmingham Post*: "This boy has the poet's power to open our eyes and to make us think of our little world anew."

Before the Newcastle Town Hall concert, May 6, the local High Sheriff's Lady, all fox furs and teenage sons, burst into the dressing room.[39] After starting to give her welcome speech to two roadies, she finally found Dylan and gushed, in cut-glass tones: "And these are my three boys. They think you're so marvelous they've left all their exam papers. They've left everything to come and listen to you. I think the songs are very wonderful and you write them yourself too, don't you, sometimes? I think you're really a good example for the youth." Neuwirth gave her one of Dylan's mouth harps and as she chirped goodbyes, she said to her escort, loud enough for all to hear: "Why, he's *charming*." Robin Hood had conquered a High Sheriff's Lady. Newcastle, despite a microphone that died for six minutes, was another success. May 7, Manchester Free Trade Hall: similar program and response. Perry agonized that they only had forty minutes to catch their plane. He told the troupe: "Don't bring in someone who's hitchhiked from Glasgow who wants a lock of his hair."

The two Albert Hall gigs resembled the provinces. *Melody Maker*'s Max Jones: "Like a mysterious troubadour who'd lost his horse," Dylan had quietly taken over "with his weirdly compelling songs." Maurice Rosenbaum, in the *Daily Telegraph* and *Morning Post*: "There are better singers, better guitarists, better harmonica players and better poets. But there is no other 23-year-old who does all these things with even a semblance of the power, the originality, or the fire ... this haystack-headed young American has achieved in an age of more and more pictures, and less and less text, of emotional noises rather than meanings, an astounding popular victory for the word."

Dylan still had to tape a BBC-TV show, do some recording, continue to star in *Don't Look Back*, meet fellow musicians, and sit for his portrait and for yet another long *Melody Maker* interview:

It's hard for me to accept the silent audiences. I think a lot more about what I'm singing and saying when they're so quiet ... I was kinda inhibited ... People don't grow up the same way, you know? ... in England they are more ready, the young people ... Over there, you could get killed for having long hair, if you're in the wrong part of the country ... You could actually get killed for saying something out of place ... I think England's more open-minded. Don't put me down as a man with a message. My songs are just me talking to myself ... I have no responsibility to anybody except myself. If people like me—fine. If they don't, then maybe I'll do something else. Songs are just pictures of what I'm seeing—glimpses of things—life, maybe ... You know, every one of my songs could be written better. This used to bother me, but it doesn't anymore. There's nothing perfect anywhere, so I should not expect myself to be perfect ...

The tour gave Bob occasion to see old friends and to make new ones, including the Manfred Mann band, notably Paul Jones. During Dylan's tour, Manfred Mann's recording of "God on Our Side" was on the English charts. "Dylan's influence on the English pop scene was absolutely enormous," Jones told me later. "You can even look at the Beatles and see how much they were influenced." Dylan had been on good terms with the Animals, notably Eric Burdon, lead singer, and Alan Price, singer, pianist, and organist. In 1964, the Animals had made Dylan's version of "House of the Rising Sun" a British chart hit. Early in 1965, when the Animals were on an American tour, Dylan had corralled them, along with the Supremes, who were appearing at Harlem's Apollo Theatre, down to the Kettle of Fish, where I was among the surprised Village folkniks. In *The Sound of the City*, a history of pop music, Charlie Gillett said the first Animals record was a version of Dylan's version of "Baby, Let Me Follow You Down."

Lennon visited Dylan late one night at the Savoy. He thought those who criticized Dylan for staying at such a plush hotel were fools. Lennon asked: "What's wrong with staying at the Savoy? Does starving in a garret make his points any more valid? They say that to be ethnic as a *folker* you must also be poor and act the part. Absolute rubbish! Especially when you consider that the people he's sometimes having a go at—politicians especially—are probably twice as well off, anyway. If you've got a lot to say, like Dylan has, and if you want to make it heard, you've just got to elevate yourself and make yourself famous so people will listen. Earning a fortune's nothing to do with that side of it, but if he happens to do that as well, good luck to him." As soon as he discovered Dylan couldn't be served at the Savoy, Lennon invited him to his house in Weybridge, Surrey, for dinner one evening. Lennon: "We played a few records and talked. He's an interesting bloke with some good ideas. We swapped addresses and said we'd exchange ideas for songs, but it never happened. He said he sent me things, but he got the address wrong and it never arrived. Maybe that's why we get on well—we're both pretty disorganized blokes."

Bob told me: "I sent John these pictures—two pictures we had fixed to the roof of my car, but he didn't get them. I got John's address wrong. Now I've got his address, I'm going to send him some things if anything comes into my mind. I dig John. As a writer, a singer and a Beatle. There are very few people I dig every time I meet them, but him I dig. He doesn't take things so seriously as so many guys do. I like that." Lennon was, Bob told me, "a full bold Beatle, a very untalkative cat, but very, very clever."

Between Dylan's visits to Britain in 1965 and 1966, he told me about his visit with Lennon: "I dug his situation where he lived. It was a twenty-two-room house. Do you know what I did when I got back from England, man? I bought me a thirty-one-room house, can you imagine that? Mine! I bought one just as soon as I got back from England. And it turned into a *nightmare*!" (In the *Biograph* notes, Dylan said he and John tried writing a song together on a tape recorder.)[40]

Reporters tried to stoke up a rivalry between Dylan and Donovan, the monomial minstrel from Glasgow, whose first recording, "Catch the Wind," was Dylanesque in style. Once clued in to Donovan, Bob joked about him at several concerts and changed the lyrics of "Talkin' World War III Blues" to "I turned on my record player—it was Donovan." Bob had listened attentively to "Catch the Wind," and reportedly said: "It's a great record. I didn't care for those de-de-de-de parts, but I did like the way he said the word *uncertainty*. You know, there's this guy in the States who sounds exactly like him. He's got an imitator, I'm telling you." When a reporter asked if he had been influenced by Donovan, Bob asked:

"Who is this Donovan? I'd never even heard of him until yesterday! Let's put him on the wall and talk to him." At the Savoy, Donovan played several songs for the master. Donovan's manager barred journalists: "We don't want any stunt, the disciple meeting the messiah."

For CBS Records in Britain, Dylan's tour came at an ideal time. Their first single, "Times Changing," released in March 1965, did very well. "Subterranean," released during the tour, sold even better, thanks to its electric beat and Beatles' endorsement. "Maggie's Farm" came out as a single as the tour ended. CBS Records' manager of merchandising promotion, Stan West, told me later: "During 1965, from March through December, Dylan's recordings sold substantially more than anyone in our entire catalog." West credited pirate offshore radio ships that were flourishing in 1965, carrying advertising and challenging the BBC state-owned radio monopoly. "Subterranean" and "Rolling Stone" were especially strong on pirate radio, which also broke the Byrds' "Tambourine Man."

Encouraged by Dylan's breakout in Britain—four LPs on the Top Twenty with *Back Home* the number one album—Columbia Records began to push "Hammond's Folly" heavily back home. In June, Columbia announced a major American promotion campaign: "The slogan that Dylan is 'Bringing It All Back Home' is the primary theme of the campaign." Columbia cooked up another slogan, "No One Sings Dylan Like Dylan," an eight-inch, die-cut cardboard Dylan doll, a deluxe press kit featuring a line drawing of Dylan by Feliks Topolski, sketched at the BBC studios at Shepherd's Bush, and national advertising.

On May 12, Bob went to Levy's Recording Studios on New Bond Street for a brief session that became a bootleg tape. Tom Wilson[41] greeted James Craig of *Record Mirror*: "We're going to try a little experimental stuff tonight," he said, waving toward a piano and two organs. "Some new material Bobby wants to get on tape. Maybe we'll get an album out of it, maybe not. In walked Albert and Sally, folk singers Nadia Cattouse and Sydney Carter, Eric Clapton, Paul Jones, John McVie, Hughie Flint, bluesman John Mayall, and three female backup singers. Dylan cut "If You Gotta Go," for a promotional message to a CBS sales committee, and, reportedly, "Help." While mikes were tested, Dylan said in a southern accent: "Hello there, folks. Great to be here in Miami and I sure wish I could really be with all you folks now, but I'm kinda tied up. Anyway, God bless y'all and thanks for buyin' ma records."

Baez was "around" but curiously absent from the stage. She was at the airport, the Savoy press conferences, and on several legs of the provincial tour. En route to the Midlands and Liverpool, Joan rode in a separate car. She did not appear on Dylan's TV shows. I later asked Bob why she was along. "She came on with me, man, and I didn't owe her nothing. As far as I'm concerned, I paid her back. I told her while we were in the States that she couldn't sing with me. I told her that before we left. And she came on like a little kitten. She's done everything I've done, man. She liked to watch and see what I do. There is no place for her in my music. She don't fit into my music. Hey, I can fit into her music, but she doesn't fit into my music, my show. It would have been dumb. It wouldn't have added to me, and it would have been misleading to the audience."

After a brief holiday in Portugal (referred to in his song "Sara"), Dylan returned to England in late May for the BBC taping. It was delayed for a couple of weeks because Dylan had a viral infection and spent a few days in St Mary's Hospital in Paddington. According to Richard Fariña, Joan came to visit but Sara was in his room and told her Dylan didn't want to see anyone. Baez had never appeared in Britain, and was keen to establish herself there. It was only natural that she would have expected reciprocity in getting some time on his concert tour. She didn't, and was visibly shaken, and her "farewell kiss" is her exit cue from *Don't Look Back*. Joan later said: "I thought he would do what I had done with him, would introduce me. I was very, very hurt. I was miserable." She should have left after the first concert she admitted, but felt an inner compulsion to stay. On June 8, Dylan showed up at the TV studio looking pale and tired, and finished taping two half-hour segments on June 24.

Despite the breadth of his British triumph, the folk old guard was still ready to pounce. To the purists, led by Ewan MacColl and Peggy Seeger, success spelled compromise. In September 1965, in a *Melody Maker* interview, MacColl predicted: "We're going to get lots of copies of Dylan—one foot in folk and one foot in pop ... Dylan is to me the perfect symbol of the anti-artist in our society. He is against everything—the last resort of someone who doesn't really want to change the world ... I think his poetry is bunk. It's derivative and terribly old hat ... Dylan songs accept the world as it is."[42]

Don't Look Back. During the 1965 English tour, hand-held cameras were focused on Dylan for about 20 hours, as he improvised dialogue and starred in his first feature-length film. Its title, *Don't Look Back*, suggests an arch twist on *Look Back in Anger*, the 1950s play by John Osborne. The title also recalls the biblical story of Lot's wife. Released in 1967, the film earned as many raves as negative reviews. Until 1975, it played in isolated art and college theaters, portraying the urgency and confusion of Dylan on tour, onstage, backstage, at ease and ill at ease, in flight from fans, tilting with reporters. It was re-released in 1982, and got feature treatment at the ICA in London.[43]

Dylan's reactions to the film shifted. After he'd seen the unedited footage, he told me: "It's a documentary kind of thing. It's going to be just a piece of film, no matter what it turns out to be. [Donn] Pennebaker [the filmmaker] is the best." Later, Dylan was at loggerheads with Pennebaker and Grossman about the film's portrait of a man too restless to sit for portraits. After some years during which he was apparently embarrassed by the film, he changed his mind again. By 1971, Dylan told me: "In the last couple of years, I've come to like the film a lot more than I used to." Did he mean the man who said "don't look back" was ready to look back at a portion of his life? "No, I meant don't look back *over your shoulder*," Dylan joked. *Don't Look Back* includes a half-dozen stage performances, a few songs offstage by Dylan, Baez, and Donovan, arguments, interviews and plenty of *cinéma vérité* confusion-cum-realism.

Don't Look Back was produced by Grossman and John Court, and Leacock Pennebaker, Inc, the firm Pennebaker formed with Richard Leacock, another cameraman. "*Don't Look Back* has a peculiar life because Dylan is an extraordinary person," Pennebaker told me in 1971. "A lot of people still can't stand the idea that this 'degenerate long-hair hippie' could be somebody important, but he keeps a peculiar sort of balance. People want to know about him and they're never going to. His whole interest is his charisma, the mystery. With a music film, your first concern is the actual performance. You must use a hand-held camera—that's fundamental. You cannot become part of a piece of music unless you are free to move that camera in any direction at any time. The idea of the film was from his wife, Sara. She worked with me for about one year as liaison between us and Time-Life. One day, February or March, 1965, Albert came in: 'Would you like to do something with Bob?' Of course, I said I would. Albert put up an initial three or four thousand dollars and then we approached Bob Altshuler [vice-president of press and public affairs, CBS Records Group] with the idea of supplying some footage for Columbia. We offered him half the film for only five thousand dollars, but Columbia turned it down. I wanted to make the film without loading any burden onto Bob. I shot about twenty-five thousand feet, at about two and one-half reels a day. I was really hoarding film. I'd shoot a line of a song here, another line there. When we got down to the editing for two or three weeks in the winter of 1965–66, I found that we had wasted very little film.

"There were a lot of big hassles with Albert. He wanted to go into colleges and I wanted to go to the quality art theaters. I felt the film, like Dylan, should be hard to see. Doing it in theaters calls for a lot of money. Some big Hollywood producers Albert brought in didn't know what to make of the film. We got the Art Theater Guild, with forty houses, interested in distributing. At first, we never called it a documentary. We regarded it as an entertainment film. We opened it in San Francisco, [in May 1967] because we were frankly afraid we would be killed in a big New York release. After four months outside New York, at all forty houses of the Guild, we brought the film to the 34th Street East and it was a hit with critics and audience.

"Dylan's great strength is in the questions he leaves unanswered. It never occurred to me to supply *information* in the film. Dylan asked me if I could take out the fight in the hotel room. He didn't want it to indicate that was the way he lived. I understood, but thought there were more important considerations. 'You are what you think you are.' What a marvelous thing to say! It's the fundamental existentialist concept. And Dylan's doing it, not like Norman Mailer, writing about it; that's what the film's about, so it couldn't be left out. When Bob first saw the film, in North Hollywood, he was shocked and said we needed a lot of changes. The second time he saw it, with a writing pad in his hand, he came out saying 'no changes.' These guys [Kennedy, Mailer, Dylan] don't say lines. They would never put up with the ceremony of a written script. The central problem is that the person shooting must do the editing." The film's cost, including editing, music rights, and the blow-up from 16mm to 35mm, came to about $40,000, Pennebaker told me. The film's box-office gross was more than a million dollars, one third of which was the producer's gross. Leacock and Pennebaker were splitting about $100,000 with Dylan.

Critical reaction to *Don't Look Back* centered on Dylan, not the film. Ralph Gleason saw it as "really about the problem of the artist in communicating with his audience and the problem of the Old World in communicating with the New Youth and vice versa. Dylan can be shown snarling, swearing, singing, smiling, shining, and sulking and still be the genius he is, and this honesty in portrayal makes the film very valuable." Joe Morgenstern of *Newsweek*: "Pennebaker's camera is as much an intruder into Dylan's life as any of the other intruders it records ... The honest truth it shows is a singing genius who does not know where his songs come from, and who is brave enough and wise enough not to let it bother him too much." *Life*'s reviewer found the film engrossing, but complained: "the picture is incomplete. What we do not see, or feel, is what is going on inside Dylan. Things happen to, and around him, and he reacts ... Dylan is skilled at guarding his personal life and feelings from the public and he does not let down for the movie." Richard Goldstein, in the *New York Times*, thought it showed Dylan "feeling around the edges of fame, like a chambermaid in a new mink coat." The singer-songwriter was "Shakespeare and Judy Garland to my generation. We trust what he tells us. But his flagrant mysterioso—even if it is sincere—evokes hungry demands for at least a penetrating glimpse of the oracle-star ... Pennebaker's camera is almost too willing to play cinematic straight man. Without a program, you can hardly tell the vaudeville from the *vérité* ... [The film] poses the same problem ... New Journalism presents ... With realism heightened by novelistic technique, how do you tell fact from formula?" Citing Grossman's role as producer, Goldstein called the film "at best a commissioned portrait. It's an artistic job, but still a bit flattering around the edges."

Some ads, and the Ballantine paperback of the film, carried such blasts as: "The worst film I've ever seen. Repetitious, boring, as organized as a small boy's room" (*Kansas City Star*). "Should be buried ... a cheap, in part, a dirty movie, if it is a movie at all ... certainly not for moviegoers who bathe and/or shave. It is 'underground' and should be buried at once. Burn a rag, as was once said of filth. Phew!" (*Cleveland Plain Dealer*). "Boring, off-color home movie of the neighborhood's biggest brat blowing his nose for 90 minutes" (*Atlanta Journal*).[44]

Dylan joined Pennebaker during the 1966 tour for the rarely shown *Eat the Document*, made for ABC-TV.[45] Although he often received scripts, he didn't find one that "seemed right to me," for a film encore, until a part was written in for him in Sam Peckinpah's *Pat Garrett and Billy the Kid*. Two of Dylan's frequent film courtiers were Harold Leventhal, manager of Alan Arkin, and Arlo Guthrie, star of *Alice's Restaurant*, of which Leventhal was associate producer. In 1969, Leventhal arranged an Arkin-Dylan meeting but, according to Leventhal, "Bob didn't communicate." By early 1971, Leventhal said that if Dylan wanted to star in almost any film, Leventhal "could pick up the phone and get two million dollars" to produce it.

For a while, Dylan appeared to be sidling into films through Marlon Brando. After meeting Brando in September 1965, Dylan told me: "I hung out with Marlon Brando so much, in California and also when he came here. We talked here about four or five hours. He came to a concert and he called me in New York. Marlon Brando's a friend of mine, I actually consider him a friend of mine. I love him. Somehow, Brando pulled through all the bullshit he had from the press and the public." As early as 1964, Brando was considering a script, *Fargo*, which had a role for Brando's younger brother. Agent Ben Shapiro thought Brando and Dylan should meet. In September 1965, Ben arranged a party after Dylan's Hollywood Bowl concert, just a modest affair with about 300 guests—like Burgess Meredith, Dennis Hopper, John Barrymore, Jr, Jean-Pierre Aumont, James Coburn—"a cross-section of Hollywood society," but it didn't result in a film.

The year 1967 saw the premiere of *Festival*, a ninety-five-minute documentary produced and directed by Murray Lerner from footage of the 1963–66 Newport Folk Festivals.[46] Dylan, one of fifty performers, sang "Tambourine Man" and "Maggie's Farm." In 1965, there was speculation that "Dylan probably will star on Broadway next season." Not another word of that project, or of Dylan starring in *Catcher in the Rye*. In 1963–64, Dylan was touted as a likely co-star in a Les Pine script, *Duffy*, with Hayley Mills. In June 1965, Allen Ginsberg told the London *Daily Mail* he was writing a film for Dylan: "It will be shot all over the world, including Russia, we hope." Dylan often joked about a film he was either writing with or for Ginsberg. In 1966, Dylan reportedly held talks with Paul Sills, a Chicago writer-comedian, about a Hollywood film. By 1970, reports circulated that Dylan was writing the music for a Broadway version of *A Face in the Crowd*, but he later denied it.

Dylan had long wanted to direct a film biography of Woody Guthrie, but in 1975, Harold Leventhal told Bob he could not be considered because Hal Ashby had just been signed. Bob almost immediately uncorked the Rolling Thunder Revue, his national tour, for which many stars joined him, and assembled his own crew to film it. The result was Dylan's most venturesome, but troubled, film effort, *Renaldo and Clara*. As usual, Dylan wanted to run his own show.

"Bring Back Cousin Emmy!" At the Newport Festival in July 1965, Dylan starred in another kind of drama. All he did was play three songs with a rock backing yet he unleashed a storm. From the start, Newport '65 did not augur well. Baez sported her newest protégé, Donovan, on her arm. At an afternoon workshop, Alan Lomax, folk purist, and Albert Grossman clashed openly, over the way Lomax had introduced Grossman's soon-to-be clients, the Paul Butterfield Blues Band. Hosting the Bluesville Workshop, Lomax, never a skilled diplomat, waxed elegiac over the panel's black bluesman. He challenged the Butterfield Band in words to this effect: "Let's see if these Chicago boys know what the blues are all about." After the Butterfield Band had played to an ovation, Grossman belabored Lomax for his patronizing introduction. Invective began to fly, and shortly the giant of folklore and the titan of folk business were wrestling on the ground. Onlookers separated the two hulks. While the scuffle had been personal, it had some theoretical roots. Lomax's concept of rock as black man's music only permeated deeply in folk circles.

Even before the Sunday night, Dylan seemed under some strange new duress. Typically, he told few people about his plans, relishing the shock, the dramatic departure. He couldn't envision a backfire. Since January, his two electric singles and an album had done fabulously well. At Newport, the Butterfield Band and the Chambers Brothers this year, and Muddy Waters the year before, had shown that electric instrumentation and heavy rhythm were not taboo. It was, to Dylan, "all music, no more, no less."

In the 1965 Newport program book, I had appealed for tolerance toward folk-related popular and country music: "The middle-class collegiate audience of folk music is only a part of the music scene. The tastes, interests and social attitudes of the high-school student or drop-out, the working-class kid, must also be appreciated." I was by no means preaching to the converted, for all too many folk fans, while twisting their radio dials to the Beatles, other English rock groups, and R&B, felt their traditional music embodied the only "healthy" elements, the only "honest" verities.

To compound Dylan's difficulties, Seeger announced that the Sunday night final program was a message from today's folk musicians to a newborn baby about the world we live in. Unfortunately, this theme did not correspond to Dylan's conception of his performance. His Sunday segment was sandwiched between Cousin Emmy and the Sea Island singers, two very traditional acts. Cousin Emmy's high spot was "Turkey in the Straw." Dylan had to fill his appointed slot, without a sound-check for his pick-up band.

There's a lot of folklore about how the band was picked up. Al Kooper's session work had already impressed Dylan. At the Festival, Kooper was strolling about when Albert said Bob was looking for him and gave him some backstage passes (so giving Kooper a title for his 1977 memoir). Dylan told Kooper he wanted to bring the "Rolling Stone" sound onstage. Three members of the Butterfield Band were recruited: guitarist Mike Bloomfield, drummer Sam Lay, and bassist Jerome Arnold. At a party in Newport, Dylan completed his band with pianist Barry Goldberg, and Dylan rehearsed this instant group until dawn at a nearby mansion. They kept their plan secret until they walked onstage, Dylan in a matador-outlaw orange shirt and black leather, carrying an electric guitar. From the moment the group swung into a rocking electric version of "Maggie's Farm," the Newport audience registered shock. What happened next depended on where you were, but I heard enormous vocal hostility all around me. As the group finished "Farm," there was some reserved applause and a flurry of boos. Someone shouted: "Bring back Cousin Emmy!" The microphones and speakers were all out of balance, the sound poor and lopsided. For even the most ardent fan of the new music, the performance was unpersuasive. As Dylan led his band into "Rolling Stone," the audience grew shriller: "Play folk music! Sell out! This is a folk festival! Get rid of that band!" Dylan began "It Takes a Train to Cry," and the applause diminished as the heckling increased. Dylan and the group disappeared offstage, and there was a long, clumsy silence. Peter Yarrow urged Bob to return and gave him his acoustic guitar. As Bob returned to the stage alone, he discovered he didn't have the right harmonica. "What are you doing to me?" Dylan demanded of Yarrow. To shouts for "Tambourine Man," Dylan said: "OK, I'll do that one for you." The older song had a palliative effect and won strong applause. Then Dylan did "It's All Over Now, Baby Blue," the words taking on a new meaning, as if he were singing *adieu* to Newport, goodbye to the folk purists. He left the stage having vanquished the hostility of those who wouldn't accept his electric music.

Backstage, there had been almost as much excitement as out front. At the first sound of the amplified instruments, Pete Seeger had turned a bright purple and begun kicking his feet and flailing his arms. (A Festival official said later: "I had never seen any trace of violence in Pete, except at that moment. He was *furious* with Dylan!") Reportedly, one board member—probably Seeger—was so upset that he threatened to pull out the entire electrical wiring system. Cooler heads cautioned that plunging the audience into darkness might cause a real riot.

At a party later that night, the Chambers Brothers played rock for dancing, and a discotheque ambience descended on Newport. I asked George Wein, the Festival's technical producer, why he didn't like folk-rock. He countered: "You've been brainwashed by the recording industry." Off in a corner, a sullen Dylan sat on the lap of Betsy Siggins, of Cambridge's Club 47. He looked stunned, shaken, and disappointed.

The outbursts at Newport that Sunday night, July 25, 1965, brought to mind another startling event in music history. At the premiere of Stravinsky's *The Rite of Spring* on May 29, 1913, at the Theatre des Champs-Elysees, the Paris audience was torn in two by Stravinsky's pioneering score and Nijinsky's choreography. When the curtains parted on the ballet troupe, a storm broke loose. Stravinsky stomped backstage. Carl Van Vechten wrote later that many outraged listeners thought Stravinsky's work "was a blasphemous attempt to destroy music as an art." There was so much racket, the orchestra played unheard. Catcalls, boos, and hissing interrupted music and dancing. People in the gallery called out for a doctor, two doctors, even a dentist! Backstage, pandemonium. Diaghilev, the celebrated choreographer, thought the only way to curb the noise was to turn off the lights. He kept ordering the electricians to turn the house lights on, then off. On a chair in the wings, Nijinsky stood, with Stravinsky behind him, "beating out the rhythms with his fists and shouting numbers to the dancers like a coxswain." At the end, orchestra, dancers, leaders of the production, and audience, were completely exhausted. Less than a year later, Pierre Monteux conducted the same score in Paris. He and Stravinsky were given standing ovations.

As cast and audience left Newport '65, a definite break in community brotherhood had occurred. Dylan had served another declaration of aesthetic independence. Later, in *Sing Out!*, Jim Rooney, a gentle Boston musician, wrote: "It was disturbing to the Old Guard … Bob is no longer a Neo-Woody Guthrie … The highway he travels now is unfamiliar to those who bummed around … during the Depression. He travels by plane … the mountains and valleys he knows are those of the mind—a mind extremely aware of the violence of the inner and outer world. 'The people' so loved by Pete Seeger are 'the mob' so hated by Dylan … They seemed to understand that night for the first time what Dylan has been trying to say for over a year—that he is not theirs or anyone else's—and they didn't like what they heard and booed … Can there be no songs as violent as the age? Must a folk song be of mountains, valleys, and love between my brother and my sister all over this land? Do we allow for despair only in the blues? … The only one in the entire festival who questioned our position was Bob Dylan. Maybe he didn't put it in the best way. Maybe he was rude. But he shook us. And that is why we have poets and artists."

I saw Dylan twice in New York the week after the Festival. He still seemed stunned and distressed that he had sparked such animosity. He was shaken that people had yelled "Get rid of that electric guitar!" But he refused to enter squabbles. Of his introducing electric music at Newport and the years of controversy that ensued, Dylan said, over and over again: "It was honest. It was honest."

NEWPORT FOLK FESTIVAL

This page: The electric storm breaks—Dylan wired up during an afternoon rehearsal at the Newport Folk Festival, 1965.
Right: In the studio, recording *Bringing It All Back Home*, January 1965, and inset, recording *Highway 61 Revisited*, summer 1965.

God, I'm glad I'm not me.

DYLAN, READING A NEWSPAPER ACCOUNT OF HIMSELF, 1965

If you live under the magnifying glass of public curiosity, just as your every honest act seems heroic to some, so your every weakness seems criminal to others. Even your honest acts come into question ... Readers are too despotic. Once in love with a poet for something, they expect it to appear again and again, forever. They interpret any change in a poet's character, and consequently in his poetry, not as a normal development, but as a retreat from principle.
YEVTUSHENKO[1]

The poet skims off the best of life and puts it in his work. That is why his work is beautiful and his life bad.
TOLSTOY

Above: Reading about himself while on tour in Birmingham, England, 1966.

The booing didn't stop at Newport, but continued sporadically at Dylan's American concerts until October 1965, and resumed during his world tour until late spring 1966. The year beginning July 1965 was, for Dylan, ridden with personal stress. He was lionized now by the pop world as he was being rejected by many folkniks who had once deified him. He was imitated, castigated, emulated, berated, upbraided, and celebrated. All he really wanted to do was write and sing. "Oh, the hours/I've spent inside the Coliseum,/Dodging lions and wastin' time"[2] was surely heartfelt.

Dylan sustained himself with little sleep and food and with what he once called "a lot of medicine." As public pressures devoured him, he was planning to marry. Debate about his going electric raged on internationally. Singer-actor Theodore Bikel said of the Newport debacle: "Dylan made a tactical mistake. He should have started with acoustic music, then gone into electric. He didn't bother to reach out. He didn't talk to the audience. A lesser person would have given up performing after such a reception."

Dylan remained silent about the Newport noise until his August 28, 1965, concert at the Forest Hills Music Festival in Queens. Charlie Rothschild telephoned the *New York Times* to offer an interview. From my notes: "I'm not really bothered by Newport, because I know in my own mind what I'm doing. If anyone has imagination, he'll know what I'm doing. If they can't understand my songs, they're missing something. I'll have some electricity at Forest Hills. At Newport, whoever was in charge of the sound didn't know what was happening. This time I'll have a couple or three or four new songs. Time goes by very fast up there on stage. I have to think of what not to do, rather than what to do. I get very bored. I can't sing 'With God on Our Side' for fifteen years." As to folk music versus rock: "It's all music, no more, no less. I try to be as good as I can, but I'm only me."

That summer, only Dylan, Sinatra, and Streisand had sold out the 15,000 seats at Forest Hills, grossing $75,000 for one evening. At Dylan's concert, after a warm-up group, DJ Murray Kaufman, known as Murray the K, chanted: "It's not rock, it's not folk, it's a new thing called Dylan. Dylan is definitely what's happening." The fans waited. Grossman, backstage, blew his top: "Who let Murray the K up there? I'll sue you all."

Dylan began an acoustic set with "She Belongs to Me," followed by "Ramona," "Gates of Eden," and "Love Minus Zero." The reception was respectful, the applause generous. Dylan was in control. "Desolation Row" had a stunning debut, the audience hanging on every grotesque image. Then, "Baby Blue" and "Tambourine Man." After intermission, Dylan returned with Robbie Robertson on electric guitar, Al Kooper on electric piano and organ, Harvey Brooks on electric bass, and Levon Helm on drums. The band and high-voltage singing raised a crackling intensity. At the end of each number, there were boos and shouts of "We want the old Dylan!" After "Maggie's Farm," someone shouted: "Traitor!" Others yelled: "Where's Ringo?" and "Play folk music!" In a confused jangle of music and audience discord, someone yelled: "Scum bag!" Dylan replied: "Ah, come on now." Some "listeners" threw fruit, and some young rockers were evicted. One prankster got onstage and knocked Al Kooper off his chair. Dylan told the band to keep playing the intro to "Thin Man." After five-minutes, the palliative worked. The muted backing for "It Ain't Me, Babe" elicited very few catcalls. By the time Dylan did "Rolling Stone," already a hit single, the audience mostly sang along. Critics of Newport '65 and the new music were proved wrong. At Forest Hills, the sound was right, the programming intelligent, the presentation persuasive. The problem lay with the audience.

The *Village Voice* gave Forest Hills a front-page headline: MODS, ROCKERS FIGHT OVER NEW THING CALLED "DYLAN." *Variety*: "Dylan has apparently evolved too fast for some of his young followers, who are ready for radical change in practically everything else." My story in the *Times* before the concert (headlined POP SINGERS AND SONG WRITERS RACING DOWN BOB DYLAN'S ROAD) and an enthusiastic review (DYLAN CONQUERS UNRULY AUDIENCE) elicited more letters—pro and con—than anything I had written in seven years.

The booing was virtually over in the East. When Dylan played Carnegie Hall on October 1, he heard cheers for the new music. In the interim, he had spent three weeks buoyed by the freedom of Los Angeles. "I was almost disappointed that there was no trouble at the LA concert," he told me. At sold-out Carnegie, Dylan's backup was Levon and the Hawks. After "Rolling Stone," dozens rushed the stage screaming for more. "I didn't know you felt that way," Dylan said drily. Before an encore, he mumbled: "I didn't think you would like it." One commentator likened the concert to a "Defend Bob Dylan Rally." Jack Newfield, writing in the *Village Voice*, observed "a new cultural tradition is evolving … the opposite of High Culture … Seymour Krim once called it 'the culture of the streets.' Charlie Parker … Allen Ginsberg and Lenny Bruce and William Burroughs contributed to it. And so, too, does Dylan, with his fusion of symbolic poetry and a new kind of folk music."

Folk into Rock. Folk-rock became a runaway music-business trend and a clattering controversy. Another Dylan change that turned into a mass movement, it was a logical outgrowth of his art and revolutionsed pop music. Having rejected political leadership, Dylan had assumed musical leadership. As we've seen, he had potential folk-rock sound on his first album, four electric tracks for his second album, and a single with a band as early as 1962. Even on his bandless fourth album, the beat and drive of folk-rock is implicit. As for protest folk-rock, Dylan also set the style. Sonny and Cher and P F Sloan, who wrote "Eve of Destruction," were following the Dylan of two years earlier. As a craze, folk-rock had run its course by the end of 1965, but dozens of styles that grew out of folk-rock are still flourishing.

Folk-rock roots lay deep in the sociology, messages, protest and social commentary of blues and country music. Jazz had also been an expression of rebellion. In the 1950s, folk-rockery was to be heard in Chuck Berry and the rockabilly stories of Johnny Cash, in Eddie Cochran's "Summertime Blues," in songs by Phil Spector, Leiber and Stoller, Mann and Weil. Trini Lopez rocked "The Hammer Song" and "Lemon Tree" in 1963 and 1964. There had been poetry in pop ballads by the Gershwins, Rodgers and Hart, Cole Porter. Musical theater had long delivered messages.

In 1963, American protest had centered on civil rights; in Britain, it was reflected in Ban the Bomb marches. In autumn 1964, massive student demonstrations at the University of California at Berkeley ushered in the new dissent. The Free Speech Movement foreshadowed student uprisings in Paris and Prague in 1968, Athens and Bangkok in 1973. American collegians were questioning not only the form and substance of their education but also the bias of its teachers and textbooks and the relevance of studies to daily life. Students were also protesting the support the military-industrial complex was giving university research. Some "masters of war" were wearing mortar boards and gowns. Students began to attack what Dylan called "the mongrel dogs who teach." In such a climate, the new music could only thrive.

Off campus, an even greater social malaise was developing in American involvement in the Indo-Chinese war. Lyndon Johnson was leading America deeper into what Pete Seeger's song called "The Big Muddy,"[3] ordering mass troop shipments, stepping up the draft. Without being consulted, American youth was about to be drained of its energy, its talent, its blood, its life. Peace campaigns affected more people than civil rights did. A rage for protest and comment made folk-rock considerably more than a simple merger of styles. In *The Making of a Counter Culture*, Theodore Roszak wrote that "one is apt to find out more about … youth … by paying attention to posters … and dance—and especially to the pop music, which now knits together the whole 13 to 30 age group." Earlier, Dylan had been regarded as the voice of his generation, although he spoke for only a radical fringe. Now, in front of folk-rock's greater audience, he represented his constituency.

The Byrds, who in 1965 cut "Mr Tambourine Man," one of the decade's most successful singles, amplified Dylan's entry into rock, and later into country music. He once said of them: "They're cutting across barriers. They know it all. If they keep their minds open, they'll come up with something pretty fantastic." The Byrds, whose early publicity was handled by Billy James, frequently recorded Dylan songs; as they grew more popular, they took Dylan with them.[4]

The chief Byrd, twelve-string guitarist Jim (later Roger) McGuinn, had played with the Chad Mitchell Trio, the Limeliters, and Bobby Darin. McGuinn saw that in 1964, folk music "was getting very commercial and plastic packaged in Cellophane. I wanted to get into something else." In summer 1964, McGuinn met Gene Clark at the Troubadour in Los Angeles, and they formed a group. David Crosby then joined them, and they rehearsed as Jet Set. Jet Set's debut, *Preflyte*, which included a weak "Mr

Tambourine Man," wasn't a direct hit. Manager Jim Dickson asked Chris Hillman to join. Drummer Mike Clarke rounded out the group. McGuinn: "I saw this gap, with Dylan and the Beatles leaning toward each other in concept. That's where we aimed." And that's where they hit. To avoid sounding effeminate, they eschewed "the Birds." In January 1965, signed to Columbia, the Byrds re-recorded "Tambourine Man." (The producer was Terry Melcher, Doris Day's son.)

How they got hold of the song is unclear. Most likely Dickson obtained a copy before Dylan made an official acetate, probably as an outtake from his fourth album, with Jack Elliott also singing.[5] Hillman claimed Dickson "picked the song; we didn't really like it or even understand it at the time, but he drove it down our throats until we realized what it was." McGuinn saw Dylan in LA "and we showed him our arrangement of 'Tambourine.'" Dylan said: "Wow, man, you can dance to that!" McGuinn described Dylan as "astounded. We sang him some of his other stuff and he didn't even recognize it. We got pretty chummy for a while, but he was the guru and we were the students. He didn't start influencing me until I started singing his material. But then he started doing to his own music what we had done with his earlier stuff—so we couldn't really do any more of his music because he was doing it himself. I got the feeling that he was guilty about making all the bread. He said: 'Man, I don't know how you're ever going to make a million dollars. I'd like to help you somehow.' We got into some beautiful philosophical things about the nature of the universe, deep stuff, then we'd go back to trivia, riffing on words, playing on word games. I sort of miss him."

One of the ironies of the second recording of "Tambourine Man" was that, instrumentally, McGuinn was the only Byrd on the recording. The others couldn't make the session, so the famous bass introduction was by Larry Knechtel, with Hal Blaine on drums and Leon Russell on second guitar. The Byrds added crucial vocal harmonies later. There were three other Dylan songs on their first Columbia album. The "Tambourine" single was released in March 1965, while the Byrds were at Ciro's in Los Angeles. Everyone who was anyone, including Dylan, showed up. SRO at Ciro's marked a new American hip scene. Hollywood danced again! Columbia press releases had the song topping the charts "immediately" but it actually took three months in America, four in Britain, where the Byrds were the first American group to top the charts since the Beatles breakout. In June, they released another single, "All I Really Want to Do," but in the States a Sonny and Cher cover version eclipsed it. McGuinn said what most disappointed him "was Dylan coming up to me and saying, 'They beat you, man'—and he lost faith in me. He was shattered—his material had been bastardized; there we were, the defenders and protectors of his music, and we'd let Sonny and Cher get away with it!"

The Byrds returned to Columbia's studios. They tried "Baby Blue" and "Times Changing," and decided neither was right. Finally, they did Seeger's "Turn! Turn! Turn!," allowing its release after a reported eighty takes. In five weeks, it was number one. McGuinn once described the Byrds as "an electronic magazine." When they moved from folk-rock into acid-rock, raga-rock, and country-rock, they often chose Dylan songs as vehicles. In 1971, McGuinn told Penny Valentine of *Sounds*: "I didn't ever come to idolize Dylan. I always regarded him as a peer ... Dylan's always been a step or two ahead of me ... I think what I did to lose his favor was 'Ballad of Easy Rider.' When I wrote that track for the film he had something to do with it, and so his name came up on the original screen credits. He called me up very angrily and he said: 'Take that off. I told you not to give me any credit. I do things like that for people every day. I just gave you a line—that's all.' Which actually was true, we hadn't really got deeply involved together over that song." By 1973, Crosby and Hillman and others had joined influential 1970s rock bands. McGuinn, the original Byrd, was recording solo sessions on the West Coast when Dylan dropped in to wish him well. To seal the renewed friendship, Dylan played harmonica behind the lead track, "I'm So Restless," on *Roger McGuinn*. By 1975, McGuinn was featuring in Dylan's Rolling Thunder Revue.

Back in 1965, Dylan was soon appropriated by the music business as the trend of the year, "the biggest thing" since the Beatles. *Variety*, September 8, 1965: "Bob Dylan a One-Man Music Biz in Creation of Rock-Folk Genre?" At that point, eight Dylan songs, half of them his own recordings, were in the Top Forty. *Variety* caught the sense of music-business stampeding: "This week, Dino, Desi and Billy are rush-releasing 'Chimes of Freedom,' Sonny and Cher have etched 'Blowin' in the Wind' and Cher is to include three Dylan tunes in her next album ... David Rose will incorporate two Dylan ditties in his next album ... and the Liverpool Five ... was also doing a Dylan tune ... You need a computer to keep track."

A hit of mid-1965 embodying folk-rock protest was "Eve of Destruction," by P F Sloan, recorded by Barry McGuire, formerly of the New Christy Minstrels. "Eve" cataloged social inequities and warned that if change were not imminent, a nuclear holocaust was. Still, "Eve," with its easy beat and puerile discontent, not Dylan's "Subterranean," swam right to the Top Forty radio mainstream. Then the censorship began in earnest. A number of stations, including the ABC radio network, blacklisted "Eve." Sociologist R Serge Denisoff, in *The Journal of Popular Culture*, found the song's march-like qualities similar to "Spanish Civil War songs and, indeed, to Nazi hymns." Perhaps because the indictments of "Eve" were so broad, Denisoff found that only fourteen percent among a sampling of college undergraduates understood the theme, and only forty-five percent understood part of the message. "Eve" was opposed by Right and Left. *Sing Out!* called the popularization of protest a confusing sop. A third-rate group, the Spokesmen, recorded an "answer" song, "Dawn of Correction," which saw nothing but beauty and optimism.

Dozens of Dylan-inspired folk-rock hits came out during summer 1965. "It Ain't Me, Babe" provided a chart entry for the Turtles. Both Sonny and Cher tried to sing like Dylan and aped his general style. Their "I Got You, Babe" was an instant hit. When asked to leave a restaurant because of their wild clothes, they ground out a quasi-protest folk-rock tune, "Laugh at Me," that was soon selling 5,000 a day! Janis Ian, a 15-year-old *Broadside* alumna, wrote "Society's Child," a defense of interracial dating. Shunned by major labels, finally recorded on Verve/Folkways, it was systematically banned from radio.[6] Other folk-protest songs returned in folk-rock garb: Buffy Sainte-Marie's "Universal Soldier," Ochs's "There But for Fortune," and several Donovan tunes. Only when Simon and Garfunkel overdubbed their acoustic "Sounds of Silence" with a rhythmic beat did they emerge from obscurity into their second career.[7] Some pop composers who had been striving to put substance into rock lyrics also surfaced. Barry Mann and Cynthia Weil's "We Gotta Get Out of this Place," which protested black ghetto life, was recorded by Eric Burdon and the Animals.

In September, Dylan told *Newsweek*. "I've never written a political song. Songs can't save the world. I've gone through all that." Pressed about his "enemies," Dylan replied: "They can crush you. They can kill you and lay you out on 42nd Street and put the hoses on you and flush you in the sewers. They can put you on a subway out to Coney Island and bury you on a Ferris Wheel. Who cares?"

Sometimes, Dylan got more "credit" than he wanted for fathering folk-rock. A *Life* survey was headed "The Children of Bobby Dylan"—yet Dylan's desire to have *any* relationship with P F Sloan and Barry McGuire, let alone as father, is doubtful. By 1966, *Look* called Dylan "Folk-Rock's Mr Tambourine Man" and regarded him as "unchallenged as the teen-and-college crowd's Absolute Hipster, their own 'hung-up' idol, and singing annalist of a jingle-jangle reality that makes more sense to them than any secure, whitewashed American Dream." Dylan told *Look*: "I define nothing. Not beauty, not patriotism. I take each thing as it is, without prior rules about what it should be."

Soon, such folk singers as Phil Ochs, Eric Andersen, David Blue, Hamilton Camp, and Judy Collins added electric backing. In Britain, Donovan was exploring contemporary folk-rock permutations. Manfred Mann played "God on Our Side" on a British TV show, *Ready, Steady, Go*. By September 1965, British charts listed McGuire's "Eve" and Donovan's cover of "Universal Soldier." By October, at least a dozen protest songs were on the British charts. The Hollies' "Too Many People" talked of over-population and ended with an H-bomb explosion. Jonathan King's "It's Good News Week," written for the group Hedgehoppers Anonymous, had a ridiculous lyric about bombs dropping. By December, British protest was no longer chic. Paul McCartney told *Melody Maker*: "Well, the songs are getting a bit silly, aren't they? Protest songs make me concentrate too much on the lyric, which I don't like."

Folk-rock has been repeatedly misconstrued as entirely protest. Was "Turn, Turn, Turn," Seeger's musical setting from Ecclesiastes, a "protest" song? Murray the K preferred to call folk-rock "attitude music." Although the folk-rock protest boom waned in early 1966, folk-rock, or attitude music, has persisted. Before 1965, many assumed that pop and rock were *supposed* to be about trivia, to be not only non-intellectual but even *anti*-intellectual. This surface judgment belied a true understanding of popular music as social expression. Folk-rock, after its fad phase cooled, effected a major improvement of popular music. For that, one must credit Dylan.

Heresy Toward What Dogma? What forced Dylan to battle prejudices among listeners who had once worshipped him? From mid-1965, he was treated by many as a heretic, an apostate. A heretic from what orthodoxy, an apostate from what creed? A brief look at folk orthodoxy shows how, in the name of purity, vast numbers held so rigidly to a dogma that they rose in outrage at Dylan's deviations from doctrine. The prime architects of folk doctrine were academic folklorists and collectors who believed that "folklore ain't nothing but history born out of wedlock." The folklorists saw music (and legend, tale, art, and design) passed on orally as a great body of popular knowledge, craft, and art—a richness reared in poverty. These scholars could understandably decry the shallowness of mass culture, and the depredations that resulted whenever mass culture tried to adapt or "refine" folk materials. Most folklorists simply couldn't envision the potential benefits of folk elements in popular, commercial culture. Hard-core folk determinists espoused elitist views. They wanted things kept "small," music unamplified, without ballyhoo, framing, or staging. In their veneration of the real wonders of traditional arts among the unlettered poor, they closed their eyes to the potential benefits of putting some folk elements into popular culture.

These views were most flamboyantly advanced by Alan Lomax, no mean popularizer himself. In notes for a Carnegie Hall program Lomax produced in 1959, he stressed traditional artists, but was keenly aware of new developments in bluegrass and gospel. Although bluegrass modernized old-time string-band music, it won Lomax's approval. Black music, he felt, could withstand *any* permutations. But he drew the line at white rock and urban folk interpreters. By virtue of his forceful personality and his vast knowledge, Lomax spread his views widely.

In Britain, the two leading folk-song theorists were A L (Bert) Lloyd and Ewan MacColl, both creative, articulate singing scholars. To MacColl, popularization meant linking folk music with the proletariat. He scorned middle class, urban singer-songwriters, even though he himself was one. Since 1950, when the folk audience was small, *Sing Out!*, under editor Irwin Silber, had laid down the "correct line" on folk song. Trumpeted by these men, the folk aesthetic denounced show business and mass culture, and advocated that Leftist, humanist views always be reflected in folk song. Deviation from belief in "art as a weapon in the social and class struggle" meant a sell-out to commercial forces. Small wonder that Dylan's freewheeling exploration was apostasy.

Silber's "Open Letter to Bob Dylan," published in *Sing Out!* in November 1964, was particularly sharp: "I saw at Newport how you had somehow lost contact with people … some of the paraphernalia of fame were getting in your way." Dylan was outraged that another "father" was telling him publicly how to write and behave. Why didn't Silber telephone or write a personal letter? Silber was just using him to sell his magazine. Dylan told Grossman that his songs were no longer available for publication in *Sing Out!* Aside from "Advice for Geraldine," he gave no direct reply. In September 1965, singer MacColl scourged Dylan again in *Sing Out!* "Our traditional songs and ballads are the creations of extraordinarily talented artists, working inside disciplines formulated over … time … the present crop of contemporary American songs has been made by writers who are either unaware or incapable of working inside the disciplines, or are at pains to destroy them. 'But what of Bobby Dylan?' scream the outraged teenagers of all ages … a youth of mediocre talent. Only a completely non-critical audience, nourished on the watery pap of pop music, could have fallen for such tenth-rate drivel. 'But the poetry?' What poetry? The cultivated illiteracy of his topical songs or the embarrassing fourth-grade schoolboy attempts at free verse? … Dylan … exemplifies contemporary American song-writing, a movement where journalism is more important than art, where flabby sentimentality and shrill self-pity take the place of passion."

Izzy Young's *Sing Out!* column for November 1965: "Dylan has become a pawn in his own game … has settled for a liaison with the music trade's Top-Forty Hit Parade … the charts require him to write rock-and-roll and he does …" Animosity reached its high-water mark in the *Sing Out!* of January 1966. Tom Paxton lashed out in a column headed "Folk Rot": "it isn't folk, and if Dylan hadn't led, fed and bred it, no one would ever have dreamed of confusing it with folk music." Josh Dunson complained: "There is more protest and, guts in one minute of good 'race music' than in two hours of folk-rock."

Although I had misgivings about performers like Barry McGuire and the Turtles, I took on the doctrinaires. In the *Sunday New York Times* on January 30, 1966, I swung a two-paragraph right hook at *Sing Out!* It unleashed such a personalized and vitriolic storm that some people asked the *Times* to remove me! I was accused of nefarious dealings with big-business music interests. I had accused *Sing Out!* of being "disturbingly narrow-minded," of not encouraging experimentation, of being opposed to the avant-garde. It reminded me "of Soviet cultural organs denouncing Yevtushenko for heresies, prodding him back to the pastures of orthodoxy." Silber riposted testily, and my editors offered fees to Nat Hentoff and Paul Nelson, former managing editor of *Sing Out!*, to enter the debate. Hentoff and Nelson joined me in an affirmative view of folk-rock. It appeared Silber was on the run, but soon there was a fusillade of letters circulating the folk scene, either lining up behind my positive view of folk-rock, or behind Silber-Dunson-Young.

Dylan avoided the scuffle as much as he could, occasionally claiming he gave the matter little thought. But he was hurt, and he seemed curiously unable to "explain himself." His bitterness was tempered by satisfaction over his new audience. In *Broadside*, Gordon Friesen hoped the disputants would not destroy each other with vitriol. Ed Badeaux, the new managing editor of *Sing Out!*, wrote that Silber's views were personal, and that not all the editorial board agreed with him. Seeger somehow managed to stay above the scuffle. The battle lines remained relatively firm for years. After the folk-rock fad waned, and Dylan had surprised everyone with *John Wesley Harding*, the Old Guard ultimately relented. In Britain, in spite of initially rigorous objection to folk-rock, musical developments were even more imaginative. English, Scots and Irish groups like the Incredible String Band, Steeleye Span, Fairport Convention, Albion Country Band, the JSD Band, and Gryphon, infused traditional materials with modern ideas. Eventually, September 28, 1968, Silber rendered an eloquent mea culpa in the American Leftist weekly, the *Guardian*:[8]

Many of us who did not fully understand the dynamics of the political changes … in America … felt deserted by a poet who—we had come to believe—cared. And Dylan did desert—not us, but an outmoded style of values which had become unequal to the task of reclaiming America. "This land is not your land," Dylan told us in 1965. But some of us raised on the songs of Guthrie and Seeger … inheritors of a superficial "Marxism" based on diluted Leninism and rationalized Stalinism were not ready to accept the revolutionary implications of Dylan's statements. Because if we accepted them … we would have to act on them! So long as the diagnosis was chicken pox or mumps, we could think of applying some new medicine for our social ills. But the poets were telling us that it was cancer …

Well, we learned. And for some of us older heads, the learning process was painful, involving, as it did, a reappraisal of so many basic assumptions … Dylan is our poet—not our leader. Poets touch us where we want to be touched … And if he fails to touch, the failure may be ours, not his. Is Dylan political, anti-political, apolitical, unpolitical? The question is sillier than it sounds. If they listen to and play Dylan's songs in Fayerweather Hall during "liberation week" and in Lincoln Park during "free elections week," then someone is communicating where it counts. The question remains: Why has Dylan remained the emotional essentialization of the SDS generation?[9]

Paxton also admitted he'd been too harsh. To my knowledge, Young never recanted. MacColl chose not to write about Dylan again.

The Band. Since Hibbing, Dylan had dreamed of having his own band. As early as the studio-combo sessions for his second album, Dylan was thinking about sidemen. From 1961 to 1964, he loved to jam. Forming the right band took time and work. One night in early 1965, Dylan, Neuwirth and I went to the Village Gate to hear the Paul Butterfield Blues Band. I'd heard them at the Gaslight and suggested Bob check them out, and he watched with fascination as Butterfield, who'd worked with all the great Chicago bluesmen, led the band in some explosive R&B. "He sounds like Sonny Boy Williamson the Third or Little Walter the Second," I said, as we listened to his harmonic sorties. "No," Dylan replied, "he's Paul Butterfield the First." Within a few weeks, Grossman had signed Butterfield. Dylan thought of working with Butterfield and his brilliant guitarist, Mike Bloomfield, but chemistry and career direction kept Dylan from hiring them.

Bob finally found his men in summer 1965, in a Canadian-based group, the Hawks, later briefly known as the Crackers, and, ultimately, the Band. Dylan's involvement with the Band became what *Time* called "the most decisive moment in rock history." It developed into one of the most enduring relationships between a pop star and a supporting group. Their rapport began with musical ideas. Steeped in blues, country, R&B, the old rock 'n' roll, and the new rock, the Hawks provided Dylan with the camaraderie he'd enjoyed only fleetingly with other musicians. The group had been on the road—surviving, if not thriving—even longer than Bob. They had a maturity Dylan sorely needed in a trying year.

The comradeship apparently did not entail great sacrifices. If Dylan waxed outrageous, the Hawks could take it in its stride. When they joined Dylan on his world tour of 1965–66, he continued to perform at least half of his programs solo. But by the tour's end, the Hawks had become a strongly stylistic entity, not just a backing group, as was Dylan's wish. Amazingly, they retained their own identities in a field where stars without their backing groups, or the converse, can be lost. Artistic and commercial success unleashed a creativity they scarcely knew they possessed.

For Robbie Robertson, Levon Helm, Rick Danko, Richard Manuel, and Garth Hudson, the transition from years working out of Toronto with the raunchy Ronnie Hawkins to Dylan was a quantum leap. As the Hawks, they'd endured a grind only young musicians could romanticize: one-night stands, discos, raffish honky-tonks, Saturday nights in stale-smelling gymnasiums, pounding out hard-beat music of minimal subtlety to raucous crowds. When the Hawks left Hawkins in 1965, they were essentially bluesmen. Dylan's world tour promised to be an enviable assignment, but folkniks still roared at Dylan's going electric, and his five wicked messengers were vilified for the electric shrieking and heavy-metal rock thrust.

Not until their first album *Music from Big Pink* (1968), did the public really hear the Band (as they had by then become) as a totally individualistic group. The album ran counter to the voguish, psychedelic acid-rock wave, for their music was played at humane volumes with an understated, almost diffident stagecraft. *Big Pink* took rock into serene pathways, filled with country breezes and a sort of devotional religious timbre. There was something so rooted in our subconscious past as to evoke a church in a peaceful valley. *Big Pink* followed Dylan's *John Wesley Harding*, and the two albums were on nearly every list of the best 1968 albums. Their sedative influence on pop was almost immediate. Dylan found solace, healing, and rebirth in the country. The Band followed him, geographically and aesthetically, into the same curative pastures of plenty.

John Hammond, Jr, reportedly "discovered" the Hawks at a Toronto gig in 1964. Hammond asked three Hawks to back him for his spring 1965 taping of his album *So Many Roads*. Listed as sidemen were Jamie R Robertson on guitar, Mark Levon Helm on drums, and Eric Hudson on Hammond organ, along with C D Musselwhite, Bloomfield, and Jimmy Lewis. Hammond's enthusiasm about the Hawks spread. Mary Martin, Grossman's executive secretary, who later led Leonard Cohen out of Canada as a songwriter, had heard the Hawks on visits home to Toronto and was ecstatic, possibly earlier than Hammond.

"Easy enough" to get together, Dylan once said, not mentioning the hours of jamming and rehearsing, discussions, exploring, and soul-searching to determine if the Hawks spoke Dylanese and if Dylan spoke Hawktalk. Robbie Robertson could only vaguely describe those important early meetings: "Let's just say that he didn't call us and we didn't call him. That's all I can remember. We'd had one of his albums and we all liked it, but it didn't snap us like that, you know. And we had no idea he was as strong as we later found out he was. We were a scrounge road group when we met him. He taught us about flying in airplanes, about meeting important people." Earlier, Robertson had said: "I think we were playing in Atlantic City. I didn't really know who he was or that he was that famous. I didn't think we could play with each other, at all. Then we jammed together and a lot of things happened. We've had a great effect on each other." Helm remembered a phone call to Somers Point, New Jersey, where the Hawks were playing. "You wanna play Hollywood Bowl?" Dylan asked. Helm said they had never heard of Dylan, and proceeded to inquire who else was going to be on the show. "Just us," Dylan said to the astonished Helm.[10]

Dylan became especially close to Robertson as was obvious when the two stood face-to-face on stage, weaving sound patterns like strands of friendship. Dylan's most often quoted paean to Robbie was an absurdist metaphor: "He's the only mathematical guitar genius I've ever run into who does not offend my intestinal nervousness with his rear-guard sound." Meaning, presumably, that Robbie was as strong on technique as he was on a gut sound. Like Dylan, Robertson was from the North Country, from Toronto. Both had fought boyish isolation with radio from the South-East. Both led loner, dream-filled youths, and both were interested in composing and writing. They shared an interest in older musicians. At 15, Robbie joined Ronnie Hawkins as a roadie. The Hawks' Fred Carter schooled Robbie on bass, then on rhythm guitar. Around 1960, Robertson became lead guitarist.

They were shortly joined by Levon Helm, a high-school dropout from West Helena, Arkansas, which Hawkins also called home. Until he was 12, Helm had sweated his summers picking cotton. He formed a high-school band, the Jungle Bush Beaters: "The way to get off that stinking tractor and out of that 105-degree heat was to get on that guitar." He soon turned to the drums and won the top prize in a county fair, accompanied by his sister on washtub bass.

The Hawks' organist was Garth Hudson, son of a World War I pilot turned farm inspector. He studied music at the University of Western Ontario, rebuilt pump organs around his house, then fingered and pedaled his way through Bach, playing organ at an uncle's funeral parlor. At 12, Hudson played accordion in a country band, and later formed his own rock group in Detroit.

Rick Danko, bass-guitarist, came from Canada's tobacco belt. The son of a woodcutter, Rick lived in a house without electricity until he was 10. Before his teens, he played regularly with a local rock 'n' roll band. His worldly musical education came from Grand Ole Opry broadcasts from Nashville. Having learned mandolin at five, Danko was the first Hawk to decide on a music life. As a toddler, he had sat in with his three brothers at weekly home music sessions.

Richard Manuel, pianist from Stratford, Ontario, also relied on Nashville radio for early influences. When Helm opted out of part of the first world tour with Dylan, Sandy Konikoff took over on drums on the American leg. Overseas, Mickey Jones, former drummer with Johnny Rivers, filled in. Bobby Gregg also played drums on some Hawks-Dylan dates during Helm's absence.

Onstage, the Band, a no-nonsense ensemble, kept theatrics to a minimum. Garth would rock like a jolly bear, Danko would puff out his cheeks, or Robbie would stroll about restlessly as if pursuing ideas. Four could alternate lead singing, while Hudson often sang along on ensembles. Between them, they commanded 17 instruments and used their technical skills to play music, not to whip up applause. They sought excitements in subtleties and nuances, curves and circles rather than jagged edges. On guitar, Robertson is a perfectionist technician, while Dylan remains primarily an expressionist who generally uses instrumental technique as a vehicle, not an end. Vocally, Robbie soon joined the legions who felt the strong pull of Dylan's hydra-headed singing—the urgent, pained involvement, the hand-on-shoulder intimacy, the eccentric accentuation, the chilling directness and the raw bones of honesty.

After Robertson and Helm appeared with Dylan at Forest Hills in 1965, Bob signed the group for the world tour. When that ended, the Band followed Dylan's retreat to the country. They took a house called Big Pink, outside Saugerties, near Woodstock, to concentrate on their own new directions. The Band soon aped Dylan's petulance to the press. In 1968, Robbie was delegated to halt the puerile publicity campaign Capitol Records planned to launch for *Music from Big Pink*. Capitol wanted to unleash a clattering "Big Pink Think Campaign," with a contest to name Dylan's album-cover drawing, a watercolor in primitive folk-art style of five musicians at play.

Dylan singled out Robertson to play on *Blonde on Blonde*. The first public indication of later recording collaboration was in 1967, on the bootlegged *Basement Tapes* of Dylan and the Band playing in Woodstock. The Band backed Dylan at the two-performance Tribute to Woody Guthrie on January 20, 1968, at Carnegie Hall. Dylan made a surprise appearance with them on July 14, 1969, at the Mississippi River Festival in Edwardsville, Illinois. Introduced as Elmer Johnson, Dylan sang three numbers, including the old hill tune, "In the Pines." He returned with the Band to do an encore of Buddy Holly's "Slippin' and Slidin.'" A few weeks later, on August 31, 1969, Dylan and the Band appeared at the Isle of Wight, where they suffered from the Festival's vast, impersonal setting and general mismanagement. On New Year's Eve, 1971, Dylan popped up, again unannounced, at an ambitious Band concert at Manhattan's Academy of Music. With supplementary horns, the Band was recording the *Rock of Ages* double album.[11] The most notable, sustained, and prominent evidence of the collaboration between Dylan and the Band was their tour in 1974 and the simultaneous release of *Planet Waves*, the collaborators' first commercially released album. Out of the tour came the double-LP set *Before the Flood*. Dylan appeared November 25, 1976, at the Last Waltz, the Band's farewell public concert at Winterland, San Francisco.

Among the many Dylan songs the Band recorded, the group gave four their official debut to the American public: "I Shall Be Released," "Tears of Rage," "This Wheel's on Fire," from *Big Pink*, and "When I Paint My Masterpiece," from *Cahoots* (1971). "Released" first surfaced on *Big Pink* and was later recorded by Dylan and Happy Traum in October 1971 for *Greatest Hits, Volume II*. It has the religious yearning of the *John Wesley Harding* album. Vague mysticism surrounds a recurring Dylan subject: the physical or spiritual prisoner contemplating imprisonment and deliverance. Lyrics have a biblical flow and serenity that swell toward each verse's line about ultimate release. Dylan may be speaking of his jail of isolation, or his earlier imprisonment in entangling relationships. On *The Basement Tapes*, "Released" links *Blonde* and *John Wesley Harding*. By the time the Band recorded it, they had arrived at a spacey effect in which the keyboards suggest eerie disorientation.

"Tears of Rage" is cut from similar cloth. Music was by Richard Manuel. "Rage," a parent's desperate plea for a child's love, inhabits the same landscape as *King Lear*. Written while Dylan himself was learning about fatherhood, it can also be read as an allusion to Steinbeck's *East of Eden*, a retelling of the biblical Cain and Abel story.

"This Wheel's on Fire," also on *Basement*, surfaced on an English recording by Julie Driscoll and Brian Auger. The Band did it on *Big Pink* and *Rock of Ages*. Danko wrote the music. The title comes from the biblical prophet Ezekiel's vision, recounted in the black spiritual "Ezekiel Saw the Wheel." The image of man's life as a wheel of fortune appears in Chaucer and other medieval literature. Shakespeare described King Lear in decline as "bound/Upon a wheel of fire." Dylan's shadowy narrator is a returning traveler who develops a vague personal tale into a grim portent of the future fire and explosion as the mysterious wheel rolls onward. A motorcycle wheel causing a personal explosion? In *Writings and Drawings*, Dylan's jaunty sketches convert this dark wheel into a play-thing. "Wheel" contains some of Dylan's most opaque writing, yet the song builds firmly in a series of tension-and-release peaks. Sometimes the words' sonorities become more important than their literal sense.

A song that leaves much clearer marks is "When I Paint My Masterpiece," performed often during the Rolling Thunder Revue. The Band recorded it superlatively on *Cahoots*, their fourth album. The accordion effect here is electronic, played on the clavinette. On the page, the words seem somber. This recording (and Dylan's own version in the track produced by Leon Russell) hones the edge of the ironic wit that lies dormant on the page. In "Masterpiece," the narrator relates the monuments of an old culture to himself, product of a young culture. Michael Gray, in his book *Song and Dance Man: The Art of Bob Dylan*, has made a cogent case for the "Masterpiece" narrator as an extension of Dick Diver in F Scott Fitzgerald's *Tender Is the Night*. Gray finds "fragmentary pictures" from the novel, notably the Roman episode when Diver's affair with Rosemary collapses, and he watches Rome and its mystique disintegrate. Gray links the footprints and the Spanish Stairs directly to the novel. While Diver is in Rome, "he comes to admit to himself that he is never actually going to write the masterpiece that he's been aiming at. So Dylan's title line has this fascinating double-edge: 'when' may mean 'never.'"

This song is the last in *Writings and Drawings*, perhaps as a parting preamble. The narrator lets fly an impassive wisecrack, so that we do not mistake this for melodrama. Dylan's visit to Rome in early 1963 brought him back to the Village with renewed hope. One night he told Gil Turner and me that if he made any money he would fly us both over to Italy. "We'll drink red wine, night and day, until we explode," Dylan said. The Coliseum motif is a metaphor for the gladiatorial public arena of the star's life. After the delicious rhyme of "gondola" and "Coca-Cola," the narrator is off to Belgium. "Newspapermen eating candy/Had to be held down by big police"[12] is a finger-pointing couplet in his hostile fashion. The song is memorable for its easy mix of the direct statement and the elusive.

Given the close relationship between Dylan and the Band, it is strange that so much time passed between 1965 and the two albums of 1974. The collaborators may have agreed that detachment allowed air for more ideas to circulate with other musicians behind Dylan at sessions. There was some recording collaboration in 1965: the Band supplied backing on the single "Can You Please Crawl Out Your Window?" Before their work on *The Basement Tapes* and Tour '74, Dylan and the Band enjoyed their best chemistry during the world tour of 1965–66.

Blonde on Blonde.   The pressure was merciless. The world tour of 1965-66 was Dylan's dance of life and death, choreographed for the eyes of thousands and orchestrated for the ears of countless more.

Everything crowded in on him: three, sometimes four concerts a week; listeners hungering for a new album; acolytes awaiting new direction; businessmen demanding more product, more profit. No one stopped to think of the personal cost which, to Dylan, was high. From autumn through spring, as he careened around the States, Dylan continued to write new songs. During a concert break, he scribbled an idea in his dressing room. While the Band slept on the tour's chartered Lockheed Lodestar, Dylan worked past the midnight hours on a new melody. In the back of a car, while others made small talk, Dylan saw visions beyond the passing landscape. In smoky motel rooms, he squeezed out a riff, a phrase from his guitar.

Although *Blonde on Blonde* was not released until May 1966, its material had been evolving for more than a year. Some ideas burst forth in the heat of a session but many had been simmering for months. It was all pressure cooking, but Dylan seemed to thrive artistically under the deadline, giving first-rate performances and assembling the remarkable contents of his first double album. But every day the strain became increasingly obvious. He was chronically tired, boiling with anxiety under a surface he strove to keep cool. When I told John Court I was starting a book about Dylan, Court replied sardonically: "You better hurry."

All of which heightens the achievement of *Blonde*, a hallmark collection that completes his first major rock cycle, which began with *Back Home*. No Dylan recording until then required as much studio time. Preliminary work began before Christmas, 1965, and ran on, intermittently, through the winter. Sessions began in Columbia's New York studios, where one eleven-hour taping yielded nothing. Not until the whole operation moved to Nashville in February 1966 did things jell. Nashville studios, "the Mayo Clinic of pop," have long proved therapeutic. Even Perry Como, Rosemary Clooney, and Burl Ives had restored their jangled nerves by working there. Tennessee's capital is less abrasive, and quality sidemen can be corralled quickly. On the *Blonde* sessions were Wayne Moss, Charlie McCoy, Kenneth Buttrey, Hargus Robbins, Jerry Kennedy, Joe South, Al Kooper, Bill Aikins, Henry Strzelecki, and Robbie Robertson. Dylan went to Nashville for relief, but also because his producer, Bob Johnston, was based there.

Al Kooper said Johnston's faith in Nashville sidemen convinced Dylan to go south. At one point, Johnston wanted to do "Rainy Day Women" in Salvation Army style, but he needed a brass player instantly. At 4.30 a.m., McCoy made a phone call. Half an hour later, Kooper swears, a trombone player marched in, sat through three takes, and went home in an hour with the hit recorded. Although Kooper was nearly beaten up by some local toughs, he reported good vibrations in Nashville. (Emptying studio ashtrays was a young janitor named Kris Kristofferson.) As usual, Dylan did a great deal of writing and rewriting in the studio, developing his songs from roughed-out versions he had brought with him. For "Johanna" and "Sad-Eyed Lady," Dylan hunched over his piano in his hotel room for up to five hours. Occasionally Kooper would come in, strum some chords to Dylan's work in progress, then teach the rest of the crew the changes.

There is a distinctive "sound" to the album, which Dylan later tried to recreate in *Street-Legal*. He described it as "that thin, that wild mercury sound." *Blonde* begins with a joke and ends with a hymn; in between, wit alternates with a dominant theme of entrapment by circumstance, love, society, illusions, and unrealized hopes. "We sit here stranded, though we're all doin' our best to deny it"[13] describes the singer's position. "We see this empty cage now corrode"[14] offers some hope. Dylan is "stuck" inside Mobile, inside roles in a highly personal album. He perhaps best summarizes his effort to remain strong and cool, despite his weariness, in "Pledging My Time":

> *I got a poison headache,*
> *But I feel all right.*
> *I'm pledging my time to you,*
> *Hopin' you'll come through, too.*[15]

More amazing weariness, yet more resolve to keep cool and to pledge time and effort. Lawrence Ferlinghetti's characterization of Dylan's work as "higher than surreal" certainly fits *Blonde*. Through the shadow and smoke we feel his doomsday imprisonment, as he pledges his will to go on living, loving, and singing. Still that battle against lifelessness.

There's a remarkable marriage here of a funky, bluesy, rock expressionism and Rimbaud-like visions of discontinuity, chaos, emptiness, loss, being "stuck": "the room is so stuffy,/ I can hardly breathe,"[16] he sings. Words can be explicit, but also have a musical value beyond cognition. As Wallace Fowlie wrote of Rimbaud, we can think of Dylan here "bent upon subordinating words to their sounds and colors." If, as Fowlie maintains, one breed of modern poet "must be possessed by the night," then *Blonde* is Dylan at the break of midnight. "Ain't it just like the night to play tricks when you're trying to be so quiet?"[17] he asks.

"Rainy Day Women #12 & 35": This song, which charted at number two, satirizes the 1960s generation gap. Dylan at his most truculent—toying with the title, the raggle-taggle ensemble singing, the giggling, the manic instrumentation, and a variety of implied games about liquor or dope. "Rainy Day Women" is an outburst of sheer joy. His drollness triggered a drug-song controversy so feverish that Dylan announced: "I never have and never will write a 'drug song.'" "Rainy Day Women" was banned by

American and British radio stations. *Time*, July 1, 1966: "In the shifting, multi-level jargon of teenagers, to 'get stoned' does not mean to get drunk, but to get high on drugs … a 'rainy-day woman,' as any junkie [*sic*] knows, is a marijuana cigarette."

When former Vice-President Spiro Agnew attacked rock drug songs that were leading American youth toward the heroin needle, he included Valerie Simpson and Nicholas Ashford's "Let's Go Get Stoned," which Ray Charles performed widely. "That's really silly, isn't it," Valerie Simpson said. "It was written so long ago, it was obviously about gin, not dope." Phil Spector was with Dylan in a Los Angeles hang-out, the Fred C Dobbs Coffee Shop, when they heard the Ray Charles "Stoned" on a jukebox. Both of them, Spector told me later, "were surprised to hear a song that free, that explicit." A few months later, Dylan recorded "Rainy Day Women." The sound is comparable to a jazzy old street procession, *à la* Bunk Johnson. The lugubrious slide trombone and oompah drums evoke New Orleans. The shouting and laughter all convey abandon, being high—or stoned—on music, life, chaos, watermelons. There is also a bitter undercurrent: that year, crowds were figuratively stoning Bob.

"Pledging My Time": A slow blues, strong and pulsing, with heavy Chicago influence. Mouth-harp swipes and extended breaks after the third and fifth verses build atmosphere. The lyric resembles improvised blues, with sophistication creeping in. Continuity of mood vanquishes disorder in phrasing. In the light of Dylan's subsequent motorcycle accident, the last verse seems prophetic. How does one get "lucky" with an accident?

"Visions of Johanna": A major work in which five long verses and a coda structure an aura of nightmares, hallucinations, trances. The instrumental introduction draws us into a seven-and-a-half-minute work. The mournful mouth harp plaintively breaks the silence; chugging drums and stealthy organ insinuate themselves. The organ maintains the haunting feeling. The singing is superb, so purposefully phrased, so weary with rhythmic emphases as portentous as heartbeats. Electric guitar fills in, underlining and deepening. The skittering images hurl off like fragmentary chips from a mind floating downstream, neither time nor structure holding forces in check. The non-sequential visions are like a swiveling camera recording a fractured consciousness. The atmosphere is almost unbearably fetid and sad until verse four, where the rapidly piled-up rhymes of "freeze," "sneeze," "Jeeze," and "knees" lighten the mood. We are back again among the grotesques: peddlers, countesses, all-night girls, lost little boy, Mona Lisa.

Bill King's doctoral thesis, "The Artist in the Marketplace," calls "Johanna" Dylan's most haunting and complex love song and his "finest poem." He finds that the writer "constantly seeks to transcend the physical world, to reach the ideal where the visions of Johanna become real. That can never be, and yet life without the quest is worthless: this is the paradox at the heart of 'Visions,' the same paradox that Keats explored in his 'Ode on a Grecian Urn.'" In the final two ambiguous lines of the song, King is tantalized by the Keatsian ambiguity of the skeleton-key image, "suggesting both death and the key which opens every door."

"One of Us Must Know (Sooner or Later)": A startling change, from the shadowiness of "Johanna" to the almost mundane literalness of this colloquy. This brisk rouser ticks away in 4/4 like Big Ben on amphetamines. On one level, it's the story of a man talking to a girl about the difficulties of intimacy. He also may have been talking to the folk world, a lover that turned on him. The music has bite and drive: piano block chords set the pace.

"I Want You": Once rumored as the album title, only Dylan knows why he dropped it. He could quite readily turn out a chart hit; this reached number twenty. A study in contrasts: the hook that ends the four verses sounds nearly inane, with the short, easily remembered cadences that make a hit. They are counterbalanced by the felicitous metaphors that pepper the main verses. The presence of that guilt-ridden undertaker and the boozed-up politician add the implied sense of frustration. (Bill King also found a "rebuttal of the 'true love' myth," a song about "wanting and never getting.")

"Memphis Blues Again": Dylan couldn't quite decide what to do with this "big blues." The song folio called it "Stuck Inside of Mobile With The" (ending abruptly there), while *Writings and Drawings* made it

"Stuck Inside of Mobile With the Memphis Blues Again." In blues and country songs, there is recurring lamentation about places left behind. Whatever flights of mad imagery the song takes, the full title, and its mordant message of disruption, make a jackhammer finish to each of the nine verses. The singing is blues shouting, moaning, drawling. Band support enhances the drive that makes a giant lyric speed. What a cast: the ragman, Shakespeare as a dandy, and a bunch of "neon madmen." If "Desolation Row" has become Main Street, then "Memphis Blues" has become the national condition of a mobile, lonely, and lost society.

"Leopard-Skin Pill-Box Hat": A sustained joke about mindless excess. The hat could mean any trend in fashion or speech, popular or high culture. Bitingly, Dylan shows how tastes are subject to external manipulation.

"Just Like a Woman": Despite this work's enduring melodic appeal, its view of women is controversial. In an article "Does Rock Degrade Women?," Marion Meade wrote in the *New York Times* on March 14, 1971, that "there's no more complete catalogue of sexist slurs" than this song where Dylan "defines women's natural traits as greed, hypocrisy, whining and hysteria." The title is a male platitude that justifiably angers women. I think Dylan is ironically toying with that platitude.

Bill King has called this Dylan's "finest poem on the failure of human relationships because of illusion created by social myth." Dylan may be implicitly criticizing sexist men as much as the woman, or women, who fail them. Roberta Flack has recorded a vastly different version, in which she converts the song into a compassionate lament for women's victimization and depth of feeling. She achieves this through an interpretative shift, but also changes the lyrics' viewpoint. Perhaps she was trying to write an "answer song" based on the original. Re-examine "Woman" in the light of the imagery of *Blood on the Tracks*, where rain, pain, and thirst are also recurring allusions, but in a context of remorseful self-criticism. Were his later, gentler performances of "Woman" an attempt to say it had been misinterpreted? For those who find sexist slurs, I recommend Flack's recording, as either reinterpretation or rejoinder. The song is on the soundtrack of the film *Coming Home*.

"Most Likely You Go Your Way (And I'll Go Mine)": Bright-tempoed blues riff with a walloping forward motion, structured on one insistent pattern above and an almost martial drum figure below. Dylan gave the song fresh life during Tour '74, then as the lead track on *Flood*. "Most Likely" became one of his most infectious stompers. The lyrics, for all their mundaneness, build with economy a dialogue of lovers parting.

"Temporary Like Achilles": This smoky, slow-drag blues is barrelhouse New Orleans, with brothel piano and Tennessee Williams summertime sloth. The singing is classic blues, croaking and rough, with ax-chop emphasis, especially in the last line of each verse. Achilles is standing guard for the woman whom the narrator is losing. Why name her bodyguard after the vulnerable Greek hero? Why is he "temporary"? A whole poem could grow from one throwaway line: "I'm helpless, like a rich man's child."[18]

"Absolutely Sweet Marie": Up-tempo blues shuffle, pure Memphis. Some effective little stage props: a ruined balcony, a yellow railroad,[19] a man beating his trumpet, a riverboat captain. The narrator has done time, but he is also bitter about the time he's done for Marie. Old blues here, even though touches, like the Persian drunkard, are strictly Dylan. The six white horses echo Blind Lemon Jefferson. One phrase, often quoted as a rationale against oppressive class law: "But to live outside the law, you must be honest."[20] The song is catchy and bright, sparked off by a great organ proclamation. The interlude after the first and third choruses extends the hard riffing. The Band's ensemble sound is tight, over insistent drumming. A pungent harmonica break comes after the fourth chorus.

"Fourth Time Around": John Lennon thought this was a take-off on the Beatles' "Norwegian Wood." Dylan had played it for them in London. Lennon, who later admitted he was very paranoid, said he didn't like it. Later, he described it as "great." Dylan's voice is the tired, old bluesman. The guitar figure repeats a rippling, romantic Mexican cadence. I asked about the Latin influence: "I was hip to Tex-Mex music and to *cangacero* music [a Mexican pop-folk sound somewhat deeper than *ranchero* and *mariachi*] all my life. I was in Mexico in my youth. 'Baby Blue' and 'Tom Thumb's Blues' is all back to that." The lyric is runaway fantasy, almost incongruous against the soft musical flow.

"Obviously Five Believers": Perhaps the best R&B song on the album, pure honky-tonk. Riding high is the mouth harp of Charlie McCoy. This rattletrap blues chugs along with vintage R&B *honeys* and *mamas* coming right off the street. More developed images, as in verses three and five, are also traditional. "Black dog," like black snake, is a sexual image, a blues trademark.

"Sad-Eyed Lady of the Lowlands": Jamming on tour and getting ready to record this, Bob told me he regarded this as "the best song I ever wrote." The 3 a.m. jam on which I sat in (*see Chapter 10*) between Dylan and Robbie Robertson in a Denver motel merely hinted at its ultimate effect. In the last side of *Blonde*, folk tradition meets modern poetry. The title line, echoed in the five verses, has an antique flavor, since Scots-English balladry often refers to lowlands. Paul Nelson called this haunting portrait of a woman: "celebration of woman as work of art, religious figure, and object of eternal majesty and wonder."

The other-worldly Lady suffers from the incursions of the material world. She is spiritual, yet corporeal; mystic, yet human; noble, yet pathetic. Her travails seem beyond endurance, yet she radiates an inner strength, an ability to be reborn. This is Dylan at his most romantic. "Bob never wrote a song about any one person," Bob Neuwirth once told me. "They are about a lot of people, and sometimes not about any people at all." One can savor "Sad-Eyed Lady" without knowing its model. Yet this is virtually a wedding song for the former Sara Shirley H Lowndes, who was married to Dylan in a private civil ceremony on November 22, 1965. Only a few close associates, including Grossman and one of Dylan's lawyers, Saul (Pete) Pryor, attended the ceremony, which was generally kept quiet until a *Melody Maker* report on December 25. Nora Ephron broke the story in the *New York Post* on February 9, 1966: HUSH! BOB DYLAN IS WED. (The couple were divorced on June 28, 1977.)

While determined to keep Sara from fans' fishbowl stares, Dylan revealed her through many songs. Dylan zealously guarded the privacy of his wife and their five children, yet Sara was often a prominent image in his work. While Lennon and McCartney made public rituals out of their respective marriages to Yoko Ono and Linda Eastman, Dylan kept his family life and artistic processes covert. Until he wrote "Sara" in 1975, he would talk only in metaphors about the "Madonna-like woman," whose sagacity, calmness, and warmth changed his life. Until "Sara," he never dedicated songs to her, never talked explicitly of her, relying on his songs only to proclaim his love or pain.

There are specifics in "Sad-Eyed Lady" that reveal Sara. She had dark hair, well-sculptured features, a short, graceful body. And she did have sad eyes. Dylan's greatest praise of Sara was that "she is a very private person. She doesn't have to be on the scene, any scene, to be happy." He admired her inner resources, her quietude and philosophic calm, her ability to be herself, with or without him. The song tells us of a woman mystic and mysterious, half-child, half-woman, deep, detached, compassionate, frightened, scarred by her past, but full of life. In Woodstock, Sara was quietly respected. Her manner, while never cold or rude, seemed to say: "No trespassing, please."

Lynn Musgrave, a music journalist who lived in Woodstock, told me: "Johnny Herald and I were walking and Bob came along driving his blue station wagon. Sara was in the front seat with Bob and her little girl. Neuwirth was in back. Sara's little girl turned to me and asked: 'Where do you live?' I said I couldn't show her because we had already passed the house. Then she asked, pointing at Johnny, 'Do you live with him?' I said yes, and Sara turned around with glee in her eye, just rolling glee. I think Sara is very clearly described in the song as 'the junkyard angel.'[21] She is not Mother Earth in the heavy way, but she just rolls with nature. She has a low center of gravity, if not quite indestructible, then something close to it. That is what it must take to sit up there in Woodstock, being married to Dylan and never going out much. I don't think she complains much, either. I got the impression of her being strong. That line, 'she speaks like silence'[22]—that's Sara."

Bob and Sara's first major outing together was an appearance at the Guthrie tribute at Carnegie Hall in January 1968. Sara, mostly on her own, moved about rather shyly, gravitating toward people she knew from Woodstock. She appeared demure, yet slightly ill at ease in a throng fascinated by her husband. I chatted briefly with her, and noted the deep large eyes, the glowing complexion, the air of quiet detachment.

Friends of Sara considered her then as extremely warm and devoted toward a select few. Her ability to suppress her own ego was described as graceful and reassuring to Bob. She had a Romany spirit, seeming to be wise beyond her years, knowledgeable about magic and folklore and traditional wisdom.

Dylan evidently felt he'd still revealed too much about his sad-eyed lady, for when Richard Goldstein cited the lyric in his 1968 book, *The Poetry of Rock*, he was denied permission to quote the third verse. However, the verse, which had appeared in the album folio, was later published in *Writings and Drawings*. Goldstein: "'Sad-Eyed Lady' is one of Dylan's least self-conscious songs … the most moving love song in rock. Even its foibles conspire to convey the paradoxical reality of its heroine; this sad-eyed lady who can be so nonchalantly strong, and so predictably weak; so innocent, yet so corrupted … His sad-eyed lady is everyone's girl, and everyone's girl is what the love song is all about."

The successive similes seem thoroughly successful at draping a subject in a richly brocaded tapestry of language. Dylan has brought high metaphoric development and literary allusion into rock. The sad-eyed lady, like Shakespeare's dark lady, is an elusive source of inspiration and wonder. Sara and Bob for a time built a new life together, perhaps using "skeleton keys" to open another door. Until 1973, they stood as a most solidly loving couple. In Dylan's songs after "Sad-Eyed Lady," a highly romanticized view of an ideal woman recurs. For a while, Sara fleshed that image.

Blonde closed a period that, until 1974, has often been regarded as Dylan's most fluent, poetic, and experimental. He and others were turning rock into a new art form of vast horizons. Dylan's art stimulated a coterie of new commentators. One was Paul Williams, who launched a mimeographed, rough-and-ready bulletin called *Crawdaddy*, and collected some of his best pieces in a book with a Dylan title, *Outlaw Blues*. *Rolling Stone* and pop coverage in the *Village Voice* and other alternative periodicals reflected new acceptance of rock. Some fan magazines turned literary or sociological. Ellen Willis, who in 1968 became the *New Yorker*'s rock critic, wrote about Dylan with great insight. The *East Village Other* quoted the poet Frank O'Hara on "Sad-Eyed Lady": "such sweet Rimbaud lyricism." Dylan also reminded O'Hara of young Auden, "in the sense of being a public poet. Even if the work was in the form of song, it was essentially presented as poem."

Goldstein, then regarded as America's hippest rock critic, wrote in the *Village Voice* in September 1966, that *Blonde* was neither mysterious nor forbidding and was Dylan's "least esoteric work … The songs are all about women." In his folio preface of Blonde, Paul Nelson called the album a "circus-book of styles that would challenge a Picasso."[23] The title suggested to him "both the singularity and the duality we expect from Dylan's music of illusion and delusion—with the tramp as explorer and the clown as happy victim." Jon Landau, in *Crawdaddy*, thought his singing "one of the most brilliant rock performances ever recorded." In his *Saturday Review* cover story (May 30, 1970), Steven Goldberg found Dylan's poetic talents "at their zenith" and saw in "Johanna" and "Memphis Blues" Dylan's "imminent discovery that the mystical experience must give way to a life infused with mysticism and compassion lest even the mystical experience be perverted into an excuse for evasion."

At the time of *Blonde*'s release, the older pop critics were reorienting their sights and the new rock critics were realizing that literature, art, and rock were all converging. Some performers, like Leonard Cohen and Richard Fariña, were flexing their muscles as singing *writers*. A few weeks before his death in April 1966, I interviewed Fariña: "What bugs me most about the contemporary music scene is that people demand change within a four- or five-year period. I suppose we're all expected to move as quickly as he does." Why did people find Dylan so enigmatic? "Paradoxically, because he's the real thing. What he says and what he does are the same thing. His expression is precisely what he is. Probably because he is so blank, so open. Although he has been hit a lot for affectation, he tries a lot of things. It's very human. I find him not ready or willing to talk about a lot most people are willing to talk about. The only thing I know for sure about him is that he is fragile. But I don't believe that I understand what is going through his mind. The particular magic that Dylan has over, say, twenty million people, is the paradox and the inaccessibility of him. In his music, people are struck by something and yet they don't really seem to know what it is. That's always been the case with the most acute and exalted poetry. There are lines of Shakespeare like this, in which you don't have to know who plays what to be struck by the magic of words. Then the insight of the listener is followed by intense perplexity. We hear something that we finally realize is saying something we think ourselves and then we want to know more about the writer who can tell us something about ourselves. Joan [Baez], on the other hand, reinterprets what others have written in a way that makes us listen. Joan is a mother who gives birth to a new meaning in a song for us, and Bobby is the father, the one who does the fertilizing. While Hemingway has brought us the physical hero, whose presence and appearance are so exciting, Dylan has brought us the 'head hero,' whose brain attracts and compels our interest. But he is complicated! Everything he does and writes is complicated. How can you possibly be walking around upright on this earth and possibly be simple?"

Hard Traveling into Future Shock.

Launching a tour after Newport and Forest Hills took nerve, but Dylan wanted to "show the audience what we're doing these days." He described his mood then: "There doesn't seem to be any tomorrow. Every time I wake up, no matter in what position, it's always been today." Many in the heavily politicized audience wanted slogans, not the new beat. The times were indeed changing: On October 15, 1965, 100,000 gathered in Washington to demonstrate against the Vietnam War. Half were students. In Ann Arbor, Michigan, thirty-eight were arrested for a draft-board sit-in. At the University of Wisconsin, fifty students marched on Truax Air Force Base and tried unsuccessfully to arrest the commander as "an accessory to mass murder and genocide." At November 1965 anti-Vietnam War teach-ins, buttons and posters articulated youth outrage: MAKE LOVE, NOT WAR! POWER TO THE PEOPLE! YOU CAN'T TRUST ANYBODY OVER 30. Dylan had spent three years supplying marching songs for the campus protest against war, hypocrisy, and discrimination, but now he was changing the tempo, saying he wasn't "a schoolteacher, a shepherd, a soul-saver." He was looking for "salvation."

A minority of Dylan's audience could accept a salvational message, but only in a folkish vein. Most listeners came to him with empty baskets labeled "political power and direction," "some kind of salvation," "stone me." They were yearning for an experience comparable to pop in the visual arts—the museum, the comic book, TV, fashion. In these areas, *pop* stressed fun, rebellion, silliness, the hip-kicks pleasure principle of a restless, experimental society. Pop art was an offshoot of post-World War I Dadaism. Susan Sontag, in her famous essay "Notes on Camp," found pop the "triumph of the epicine style ... love of the unnatural; of artifice and exaggeration." Trivia was camp; old movies were pop nostalgia. Andy Warhol, who became a Dylan freak, regarded pop as a way "to see beauty in all things." Warhol opened his own Village rock club, the Plastic Inevitable, and sponsored a punk-rock band, the Velvet Underground.

To heavily politicized youth, most rock ("the new numbness," Dave Van Ronk called it) represented escape to a palmier time before Vietnam. Dylan's *Blonde on Blonde* visions were very much in the new pop mood. Although most pop—shoddy Carnaby Street clothes, comic books—was disposable, Warhol's canvases became classics, and Dylan's art endured. But Dylan did not have an easy time setting out on his 1965–66 world tour in this jumbled environment of dope and Batman, teach-ins and screech-ins. Dylan later described it to me: "I was touring for a couple of years. That's a fast pace. We were doing a whole show, no other acts. It's pretty straining to do a show like that. A lot of really unhealthy situations rise up. I was just going out there performing these songs. Everyone else was having a good time. I did it enough to know that there must be something else to do. It wasn't my own choice. I was more or less being pushed into it—pushed in and carried out."

The first concert was at Hollywood Bowl, on Friday, September 3, 1965. An earlier press conference became an hour-long cat-and-mouse game. Charles Champlin of the *Los Angeles Times* found Dylan "as cryptic, elusive, and biting *a capella* and in recitation as he is in full song." To a Mr Jones reporter who asked why he wasn't "as accessible as Frankie Laine," Dylan said: "I should hope not. I'm not a preacher or a traveling salesman. I do what I do. There was a time I cared if anyone understood. Not anymore." Later on, he explained: "I'm hard. I don't have to look to anyone to tell me I'm good. I know I'm honest. When I do something for the wrong reason, I'm embarrassed to be around people." Dylan was so caustic in Los Angeles that Billy James doubted such interviews should continue.

The autumn 1965 itinerary: Austin, September 23; Dallas, 24; Carnegie Hall, October 1; Newark, 2; Atlanta, 9; Worcester, 22; Detroit, 24; Boston, 29 and 31; and Hartford, 30. Concerts resumed November 12 in Cleveland; 14 and 15 in Toronto; 19 in Columbus; 21 in Syracuse. Dylan and company played November 26 and 27 at the Arie Crown Theatre in Chicago, and 28 in Washington, DC. They swooped down on California beginning December 3.

Moving Dylan and the Hawks on the thirteen-seat, twin-engine Lockheed Lodestar took generalship. Bobby Neuwirth and Victor Maimudes alternated as road manager. When Neuwirth was aboard, Victor or Bill Avis served as Hawks roadie. Two movers and truck drivers loaded eight crates of equipment and raced all night to the next stop, where they set up the $30,000 amplification system. Sporadically, *Variety* totted up the tour's receipts, calling Dylan "one of the hottest phenomena of show business today." The sold-out Boston concert grossed $12,000. In Toronto, it reported, he "grossed a whopping $17,278 on November 14 and 15, at Massey Hall. Dylan took away 70% of the gross." The Syracuse report was less than euphoric: On November 21, 3,486 out of 6,600 seats grossed $12,500, and there was a hassle with the local musicians union, which demanded at least fifteen musicians on stage.

In early autumn, trouble began that continued for the remainder of the tour: most of the halls had inadequate sound balances. Sports-arena acoustics were a far cry from those of theaters and concert halls. After each concert, Dylan asked: "How did it sound? I don't mean the songs, but how did it actually sound where you were?" From Newport to Albert Hall, concerts were plagued by distorted amplification. With better acoustics, the audience conversion to folk-rock might have been faster.

The *New York Herald Tribune* ran a major feature on the tour in which William Bender called Dylan "probably the greatest urban professional folk composer this country has ever known." Supplementing his piece was a six-page spread, billed as Daniel Kramer's "photographic portfolio." (Actually, Dylan's pal, Al Aronowitz, wrote the text and Dylan rewrote it.) This piece caught the non-sequential rock madness of the time: musicians maundering in droves, dudes and groupies coming and going. In what sounded like Grossman's Gramercy Park pad, Dylan is playing a Temptations disk while Robertson strums an autoharp. Brian Jones of the Rolling Stones rolls up in a Rolls. All tumble over to a bar, where Dylan says: "You can write on the walls here … and nobody calls you a poet." Enter a muscular woman, sailors, the chauffeur, Neuwirth. A sailor leaps on their table. The merry pranksters go to an underground cinema, with no film "but instead a group of green painted musicians … presenting a spontaneous ritual which had taken them three months to prepare." On to a pinball arcade, a fortune-teller's, a disco, and a cathedral. Finally back to "the borrowed pad," where Dylan muses: "I think … Brando should play W C Fields … Warren Beatty should play … Johnny Weissmuller … I plan to play the life story of Victor Mature."

This episode was not all fantasy. Shortly before Christmas, 1965, I witnessed an evening almost as absurd. Paul and Betty Stookey gave a black-tie party at their lovely old brick house on Bedford Street in the Village. Scruffs were transformed into dudes. Grossman looked like a penguin headwaiter at an iceberg Bar Mitzvah. His lieutenant, Charlie Rothschild, fell asleep in the bathtub, while a chamber trio on the minstrel's gallery sawed away at the greatest hits of Boccherini, Corelli, and Vivaldi.

As the party loped toward finale, in marched a mob of uninvited street people. Heading the invading force was a very stoned Dylan in jeans and suede. Betty Stookey looked aghast as her careful planning evaporated. She stood beside me while Tommy Flanders of the Blues Project systematically assailed the party, the guests, the chamber trio. "Meet your hostess," I said, waving at Betty, and they glowered at each other. Dylan launched a heavy discussion with Albert, circling him so that the manager had to pan 360 degrees to listen to his client.

At almost 3 a.m., Dylan assembled Dave (Blue) Cohen, Phil Ochs, my date, Liz Newman, and me to depart for the next stop. We piled into Bob's rented limousine, chauffeured by a middle-aged uniformed driver named Morris, who looked as relaxed as a charioteer in *Ben Hur*. Dylan directed him to an all-night club, the Clique, at 158 East 49th Street. The hangout fell silent as Dylan led us to a table. Strangers came by with questions, menus to be autographed, regards from some second cousin's brother-in-law in Kansas City who thought *he* was Mister Jones. A former Village friend of Bob's, Kathy Perry, bounced up, but Dylan was so tired he dismissed her as if she were a groupie. Bob said he'd read my letter about my tackling his biography and it sounded like a good idea to him. "As long as it's in context," he repeated, over and over. He asked piercing questions: "What sort of contract do you have? Do you have control over your words? Will they chop it up and change it all around? Will they write in things against the truth?" I reassured him. "I'll help you out on it," Dylan said. He said he'd call me later in the week to go into details. A tired Dylan sat with his "entourage," and told me how much he hated that idea: "I resent it very much when I read in magazines that people say: 'Dylan was here with his hangers-on! I never had, in my whole life, any hangers-on. That's a very ugly word, *entourage*. It puts down everyone who works for me and it puts you down for having *friends*."

Cohen was a comparatively new friend, who later took some acting honors in *Renaldo and Clara*. Just as Dylan was elevating Cohen, he was downgrading Phil Ochs, even though Ochs had revered Dylan for years. Two months earlier, Dylan had played his single "Crawl Out Your Window" for Cohen and Ochs. Dave loved it, but Phil said he didn't think it would be a hit. That night, Dylan stopped his limousine and made Ochs crawl out the door, saying: "You're not a folk singer, you're just a journalist." Undaunted, Ochs was back, risking more abuse. Dave hung back, while Dylan attacked Phil's political-topical songwriting: "It's all wrong, you know. That isn't where it's at anymore. It's way beyond that now." Dylan's familiarity with his works surprised us. Ochs drank in the abuse, and while Dylan was away from the table, I asked him how he could take it all. Ochs said: "After all, man, if Dylan tells you something, you *gotta* listen." Dave split early, perhaps fearing he might be next on the carpet. Dylan returned to the table and continued the ax-chops. "Why don't you just become a stand-up comic?" he asked Phil. Dylan wasn't amusing; he looked ghostly pale, and was reluctant to go home to the Chelsea Hotel. As we hailed a taxi to the Village, Liz said: "My God, he looks like he's dying."

We old friends had only the vaguest idea of what Dylan had been doing on tour during the previous weeks. He'd pass a remark about what a drag Austin was, or how great the Coast was, but only hinted at his daily tensions. Sitting in the Village, we had no idea what Texas had been like to him. Austin had concert ushers from the American Legion, who paraded smartly in their little soldiers' caps. Shades of "Masters of War"! The press conference before the Austin concert attracted some reporters playing district attorney:

Q: *What do you consider yourself? How would you classify yourself?*
Dylan: *Well, I like to think of myself in terms of a trapeze artist.*
Q: *You said before that you sang because you had to. Why do you sing now?*
Dylan: *Because I have to.*
Q: *Your voice ... here is gentle ... in some of your records, there's a harsh twang.*
Dylan: *I just got up.*
Q: *Are you trying to accomplish anything, to change the world or anything? Are you trying to push idealism to the people?*
Dylan: *Well, what do you think my ideas are?*
Q: *I don't exactly know. Are you singing just to be singing?*
Dylan: *No. There's a much deeper reason for it than that.*
Q: *Who are your favorite performers? I don't mean folk. I mean general.*
Dylan: *Rasputin. Charles de Gaulle. The Staple Singers.*
Q: *What is your belief in a God? Are you a Christian?*
Dylan: *Well, first of all, God is a woman, we all know that. Well, you take it from there.*

In the San Francisco KQED-TV interview on December 3, Philistine questions elicited verbal slingshots:

Q: *What poets do you dig?*
Dylan: *Rimbaud. W C Fields. The trapeze family in the circus. Smokey Robinson. Allen Ginsberg, Charlie Rich.*
Q: *What do you think of people who analyze your songs?*
Dylan: *I welcome them, with open arms.*
Q: *For those of us well over 30, could you label yourself and perhaps tell us what your role is?*
Dylan: *I'd sort of label myself a "well under 30." And my role is to just stay here as long as I can.*
Q: *Have you ever played a dance?*
Dylan: *No. It's not that kind of music.*
Q: *It is.*
Dylan: *Well, what can I say? You must know more about the music than I do. How long have you been playing it?*

In the winter of 1965–66, Ralph Gleason agreed that Dylan looked close to death: "I was very worried about him. I figured he was in mortal pain. I wanted to ask him what was killing him. I was astounded he was still working, because I figured he would have had a breakdown. I thought he was having some severe abdominal pains, or a brain tumor." The audience at Dylan's northern California series, sold out by mid-November, had no clue of Dylan's condition. Shows were set for December 3 and 4 at the Berkeley Community Theater, the following Saturday at the San Francisco Masonic Auditorium, and the next night at the San José Civic Auditorium. Another Masonic concert was added on Sunday, December 5.

Agent, Mary Ann Pollar worked with Grossman on these bookings, and also arranged three parties. Gleason ran the KQED-TV press conference and attended all the California events. Gleason told me: "One night we walked up and down Broadway in San Francisco, with Dylan complaining he couldn't go anywhere on the streets. We arranged to meet later. Where did we meet, at his direction? At Mike's Pool Hall, right in the center of the San Francisco night life, on Broadway near Enrico's. In the pool hall! I think it's absolutely beautiful! He insisted on sitting in the window! In full view of the street! In ten minutes there was a crowd there and he had to leave. He looked very tired and very hard."

At the first Berkeley concert, Gleason recalled, "in the front row were Larry Ferlinghetti, Ginsberg, Ken Kesey, and two Hell's Angels. The following week, there must have been a dozen Hell's Angels. Allen is very big with the Angels. In a way, he thinks he invented them." What turned the beat poets on to Dylan? "Larry turned him on to Allen or Allen got a letter from Bob after reading [Ginsberg's poem] 'Kaddish.' Dylan keeps talking about Rimbaud, and not Ginsberg, even though Bob gives the appearance of having memorized everything that Ginsberg ever wrote. Michael McClure [poet/playright, author of *The Beard*] was sitting in Dylan's dressing room at the Masonic. McClure was cross-examining him on how you write a hit song and get to be a millionaire. The San Francisco poets freaked out when they saw this Dylan thing happening. I thought Larry was a tragic figure that weekend, a shaken and embittered man. You know. 'What is that stringy kid doing up there with his electric guitar?' I mean, 'I am a major poet, and this kid has thirty-five hundred kids in this hall.' And Larry has been mumbling to himself ever since. The rest of them just flocked around. This is the first time the poets ever showed up. Allen made Dylan and the Beatles respectable. Dylan and Allen had long talks about 'Desolation Row.' There's Dylan sitting in the corner, and on the floor, like some ancient tribe of hill people about to go on an assaulting raid, is this mob of bearded Hell's Angels with all that leather and medals dripping off them. Obviously, Dylan couldn't talk to them. He just kept repeating: 'Good seats? Got good seats?' When Dylan's cigarette and leg start going, they're a thermometer of his tensions. He is a power figure, surrounded by satellites—Grossman, Neuwirth. The only person he can really believe is Robbie. What we have here is a study in power. His trivial, momentary, superficial reaction is translated in hard, real, life-or-death orders, and this goes for Grossman. No matter what kind of a guy Albert is, Dylan represents a great deal to him. Anything, rather than have Napoleon get mad."

Why did Ralph frequently compare Dylan to Miles Davis? "Both are little bantam roosters, seriously proud. Distrustful, on the surface, of the whole world. Really aching to trust somebody. Sentimental, and filled with all sorts of good instincts, which they won't, for an instant, admit they have. If you ask Miles or Dylan a question, that's certainly not the way to get an answer. The only way I can have a rational relationship with Miles is to leave him alone. It's like winning the confidence of a scared puppy that has been mistreated. Patience is the only thing. You've got to demonstrate that you are not like all those other people that have been bugging him. You are never proven. You are always on trial. You can always blow it. One false move …"

On dope and musicians, Gleason said: "Dylan is the sort of glowing, charismatic character that if you spent six months with a team of doctors spending every waking minute with him and you wrote that he does *not* use heroin, nobody would believe it. I keep running into people all the time who tell me they were with Dylan when he had his first fix. He would have had to have had his first fix over a period of seventeen years to account for all those people."

By the time of the Berkeley concerts, the single of "Positively Fourth Street" had charted at number seven. Gleason could report in the *San Francisco Chronicle*: "Dylan's band went over like the discovery of gold … Dozens of university professors were scattered in the audience, some looking rather shattered by the experience … the audience lingered … They simply didn't want to go home. Something most certainly is happening here." Four paintings by Neuwirth hung above the Berkeley stage, an early attempt to heighten rock visually. Gleason thought each painting was "an abstraction of Dylan's own image, or so it seemed to me after two glasses of milk and a Hershey bar."

If the senior journalist was tripping on milk and chocolate, many in the audiences were into pharmaceuticals. Some of the concerts were conventions of heads, hints of future Woodstocks. The only way to get answers from Dylan about dope was never to ask questions. Usually, he spoke elliptically, or not at all. Although Dylan had been the first person to turn me on with pot, I confessed no knowledge and considerable fear about other chemicals. Dylan conveyed the feeling that he knew what he was doing, that he had everything under control, legally and medically.

During visits to Los Angeles in autumn 1965, Dylan befriended producer and songwriter Phil Spector. Gleason again: "In a certain sense, Dylan appealed directly to Spector for help. There are so many parallels in their careers. The type of help that Bob was looking for was 'tell me how to live.'" Indeed, Bob told me: "When I first got really, really famous, I looked around for who else was like me. And of the people I saw, Phil Spector was one. He's young and made all his bread on his own." Getting to see Spector was no easy matter. He was in the throes of producing "River Deep, Mountain High" and I waited nearly an hour at his Sunset Strip offices, then nudged Spector's secretary for the third time. She disappeared within, and I heard a frantic, high-pitched shout from behind the imperial doors: "Tell the son of a bitch that I'm not here!" The secretary emerged looking pale. I spared her a lie: "I get the idea." I grumbled to Billy James, some phone calls were made, and I was told to show up two days later at the Gold Star Studio. In the studio, Spector was a wizard with a dozen ears, presiding over eighteen musicians. In her booth, with headphones, singer Tina Turner waited for cues. She and the band were into their third week of work on the single. After every phrase, everyone turned to the producer for reaction. Spector was a perfectionist who elicited relaxed performances by joking. Three pianos and three rhythm guitars helped build his "wall of sound." A run-through sounded superb, but Spector stopped and asked one of the acoustic guitarists if his instrument was in tune. The guitarist, to everyone's amazement, found one string slightly off-center.

After the session, the wiry little producer, with a feline grin, puckish eyes, and a hipper-than-thou manner, said: "I could give you one of my put-on interviews, you know, pulling your leg like I usually do, like the Beatles and Dylan are doing these days. But you look straight to me, so why bother?" We drove to a modest Hollywood restaurant. The chauffeur sat, not eating, waiting for his master's voice and, midway through supper, was dismissed. Afterwards, Spector drove me to his home tucked away behind a Hollywood Hills driveway and heavy iron gate. Intermittently, for the next six hours, he talked on about Dylan and the pop life. His opulent mansion evidently housed a tremendously lonely young man. (Dylan had just told a California press conference: "It's always lonely where I am.") Spector told me how hurt he had been when the Righteous Brothers, after years of his careful grooming, had left him. Spector: "Songwriting is poetry, but the only poet around is Bob Dylan. The Beatles should play Dylan's records five hours a day and learn what he's doing. Dylan doesn't compete, he doesn't care. It's very easy to talk a poem, but very difficult to sing a poem. Dylan is a reporter, a philosopher. A unique talent, the most piercing and the most aware insight at work today. His genius lies in his insight into the truth and the phony. If he were only in the hands of someone who really knew how to record him." Would he like to produce Dylan? Spector's eyes gleamed assent. "There are avenues untouched. I knew that he was going to go through periods like this, when everything was getting him down. The whole image of Dylan was created by others. He became a Beatle, but he really wasn't. They gave him a role, he didn't take the role, he just sort of worked inside it.

"Dylan doesn't owe anyone anything. What he was writing three years ago, he was living. They poisoned Socrates. What happened to Jesus the last time he went out in public? Two or three years ago, they said Dylan was a social-protest singer. Now, he becomes a possession. Dylan's going through things I went through a couple of years ago. He is nervous and he is suffering. The most amazing thing, I think, was when Dylan and Baez were doing 'With God on Our Side.' The hardcore American is one of those Midwestern coal miners, the flag-wavers. With that song, he challenged everything they believed in. I am surprised there aren't more outraged pickets outside every one of his concerts. He sang an atheistic song in a country that has 'In God We Trust' on every penny."

During the evening, lush young Hollywood girls showed up, looked around, giggled, watched Spector for a sign. A bust of Wagner glowered on the piano. There was a telephone in every richly furnished room, none bearing numbers. Spector played a master tape at screeching level. He found someone to drive his limousine out to a club out on La Collina Road to watch Ike and Tina Turner. Energy flow! You wondered how Tina could return to Spector's studio the next day. He dropped me off at a friend's apartment. Spector sat in the backseat of his limousine, enveloped in soft luxury and unabated loneliness.[24]

One evening, in December 1965, Dylan, Neuwirth, and Suze Rotolo sat at the back of the Kettle of Fish with filmmaker Barbara Rubin. Suze and Bob were having a pleasant reunion as old friends. Dylan was ranting on about the "literary establishment": "Those cats at the Poetry Center want me to go up on their stage now. Where were they all a few years ago? Now, they are just getting on the bandwagon, but

I couldn't care less." Lurking at the bar was a gentle man in a black leather jacket, Andy Warhol. He shyly waved at Dylan, who waved back but made no effort to draw Warhol to his table. Next in line was Jan Cremer, a Dutch professional hipster, who had dedicated his modest book *I, Jan Cremer*, to Dylan. Cremer approached, but Neuwirth fended off the Dutch intruder.

A black-leather motorcycle type—a Hell's Angel in spirit if not membership—approached Bob with photographs. I assumed he was showing pictures of his girlfriend or baby. Dylan remarked approvingly of each picture, and when I asked to see, Bob handed over a pile of snapshots of the guy's motorcycle. Dylan's conversation was hardly sequential. He raved about Michael McClure: "I gave him an autoharp and told him he ought to sing his poems." Then Dylan sang the praises of Ginsberg. "Read 'Kaddish,' man, if you want to read something really great." He had seen the anthology of Woody Guthrie writings, *Born to Win*, which I had edited. "I like it, all right," Dylan said, "but that was for a particular time and place." I told Bob that Mary Travers thought Dylan was turning into "another Norman Mailer." "I never read Norman Mailer," Dylan snapped. (Mailer had once said: "If Dylan's a poet, I'm a basketball player." Later, in 1975, he told *Rolling Stone*: "Dylan may prove to be our greatest lyric poet of this period. Like many another lyric poet, he can't necessarily read his own lyrics.") Had Dylan liked Judy Collins's single of his "I'll Keep It with Mine"? He did, but when I asked if it referred to Sara and her child, Dylan chafed: "You don't know where it's at!" Neuwirth leaped in to say: "That song was for Nico, man. Just for Nico!" Dylan calmed down. (Nico was the star of the Velvet Underground band. There should be no surmise that Dylan and she had ever been involved.) I told Bob I was heading to England in January and wanted to get started on the English aspects of his biography, so he scribbled out a note to Martin Carthy and his wife, telling them they could speak openly with me: "This man is an old friend here—he is happening right now to be a reporter." Then he said goodbye to Suze and we left for a party at some East Village pad. Dylan had on a stylish belted brown suede topcoat. We found a taxi and, as we got out, no one made a move to pay, so I fished out the fare. "I never carry money," Dylan said. "Never."

Soon he was back on the road again. February 5, at the Westchester County Center, White Plains; 6, Rochester Auditorium. Then, a sweep through Memphis, Richmond, and Norfolk. The Westchester County show, which 5,000 attended, drew typically mixed reactions. The *Eastchester High School Eaglet* said Dylan resembled "a sad marionette … he looked half asleep or half dead." February 10, Memphis. Granville Allison, Jr, of the *Memphis Commercial-Appeal*, reported to me: "The crowd was so young, so well-behaved. There were 2,995 in the Ellis Auditorium Amphitheater, which seats 5,778. A crucial basketball game undoubtedly held down the crowd. There weren't 100 people in the audience who were over 25. Although Memphis, with 600,000 population, is 35% Negro, I saw no Negro kids, and there's no segregation in Memphis public facilities. The sound system was awful. Not one word in ten was intelligible, but it didn't seem to bother the crowd."

Richmond, February 11, Norfolk, 12, New Haven, Ottawa, Montreal on February 20, two concerts at Philadelphia's Academy of Music, then West Hempstead on Long Island, February 26. *Newsday* found Dylan "in a tight form-fitting brown-checked suit inspired by Liverpool out of W C Fields … Before an audience of 5,100, nearly all teenagers, nobody seemed … surprised that the social critic for the disenchanted had run out of things to say … These days, Dylan has little to protest against, except, perhaps his tailor."

I went to the two Philadelphia concerts on February 24 and 25. An usher warned one amateur photographer away from the stage politely: "The artist doesn't like the flashing while he's performing." The man sneered: "What's an artist for?" The performances were absorbing. I polled some listeners. Three students from the Camden Catholic High School said their favorite poets were Dylan Thomas and Ferlinghetti. A Susquehanna University undergraduate praised "Dylan's special weirdness. I believe in his freedom of choice. That is what he says to me, and I don't care whether he says it alone or with electricity." By the arrival at Miami Beach, on March 3, Sam Hood of the Gaslight was arranging the Convention Hall concert. The *Miami Daily Sun* interviewed a girl: "I think Dylan is the Tennessee Williams of song-writing." Another girl: "My sister thinks he is the Messiah. I think he is a great poet." A surprise guest at the Miami concert was Anthony Quinn, the actor who had portrayed an eskimo in a recent film. No one needed to ask what brought "The Mighty Quinn" out of his igloo.

Return to Middle America. I joined Bob on tour in St Louis in March 11, 1966. I checked in to his hotel, the Holiday Inn Downtown, and headed for the Kiel Municipal Auditorium, a fine hall with good acoustics that made for a thrilling concert and a standing ovation. Dylan was wearing his "rabbit suit," a mod black and brown houndstooth check, which he said had been made for him by Robbie's tailor in Toronto. He was impressed by "some of the mail that comes in. It's amazing! I couldn't ever hope to read it all, let alone to answer it all. From people all over, talking about my songs and records. And talking about their problems and their heads and how they're stuck somewhere and want to get out." One St Louis University undergraduate told me: "If I were Dylan, I'd drop out of sight for a few years. Like, to an island in the Pacific. There has been so much stupid criticism of him, he ought to go away and make people appreciate him more."

Back at the Holiday Inn, I asked Bob if I gave him the feeling of being followed. "Glad you could make it, man. How did you get here? I'm not too happy with our plane. I fly it only when I have to. I'm thinking of buying a DC-3 instead." He said he'd see me on it the next night—tonight they were fully loaded.

Lincoln, Nebraska, March 12, 1966. Plumb dead center in the Great Plains, Dylan was on Middle America's home ground. Population 120,000, ninety-eight percent white. Flour mills, creameries, meat packing, insurance companies, grain and cattle markets, brick and tile works. Cultural center: site of Nebraska State University, with about 20,000 students. The big news, aside from basketball: President Johnson said spending on Vietnam was running below estimates. In Laredo, Timothy Leary got a thirty-year sentence for transporting marijuana. No Dylan news, but the manager of the Pershing Memorial Auditorium was still delighted: "It's really amazing, how much press that boy gets. None here in Lincoln, mind you, but a lot nationally."

By now, Dylan had enforced rules: no picture taking, no tape recorders in the hall. I had to park my Marantz in the hall manager's office. Dylan told me later people were beginning to sell tapes of his concerts. What struck me then as over-protectiveness was just the opening phase of bootlegging. The audience filed in for the electric set. Dylan plugged in his black-and-white, solid-body electric guitar, chatted with Robbie, turned his back to the audience. The listeners stared motionless. Dylan turned his toes in like a pigeon. His longish hair fell down to his collar. His trousers bore an impeccable crease. As he led the band behind him into the song, he spread his legs so far apart you feared he'd do the splits. Another standing ovation. Back at the hotel, I found a note from Victor to call Dylan in his room. I was asked down immediately. Two dozen kids were in the corridor outside. Robbie and Dylan were stretched out on twin beds, other Band members lounging about. Dylan: "Bob, you're older, maybe they'll listen to you. Tell those kids I can't see them. Tell them I'm really tired." I tell the kids and half leave; the others hang about. Dylan and Robbie and I chat and Dylan explains the tape recorder ban: "You wouldn't believe what's happening. Tapes are going out of my songs in concerts before I even record them! And people copy the tapes and copy the songs!" Bob talks about my book: "I'll go along, if it's a respectful book. I resent it when they try to treat me like a kid. I resent being placed in some little pigeonhole as some sort of 'rock-star millionaire freak.'" Victor comes to tell Bob there's room on the plane. I race to pack my bag.

Two cars heading for the Lincoln airport waited in front of the hotel. Half of us went down the stairs while Dylan and the rest took the elevator. In the lobby, fifty fans clustered. We rushed for the cars, so quickly the fans said: "There he is. There he goes!" We took off like bank robbers. Victor smiled as wheels screeched from the curb. "That wasn't too bad," Dylan said. "Sometimes you can't even get to the car."

Right: Public curiosity as paparazzi hustle Dylan while in Paris, 1966.

Opposite, above: Dylan and Allen Ginsberg in Woodstock, July 1964—Dylan said: "I know two saintly people … Allen Ginsberg is one."
Opposite, left: Dylan with John Sebastian on the infamous Triumph and about to hit the main street in Woodstock, July 1964.
Above: Album cover for *Blonde on Blonde*, 1966.

I have a death thing. I have a suicidal thing, I know. If the songs are dreamed, it's like my voice is coming out of their dream.

DYLAN, 1966

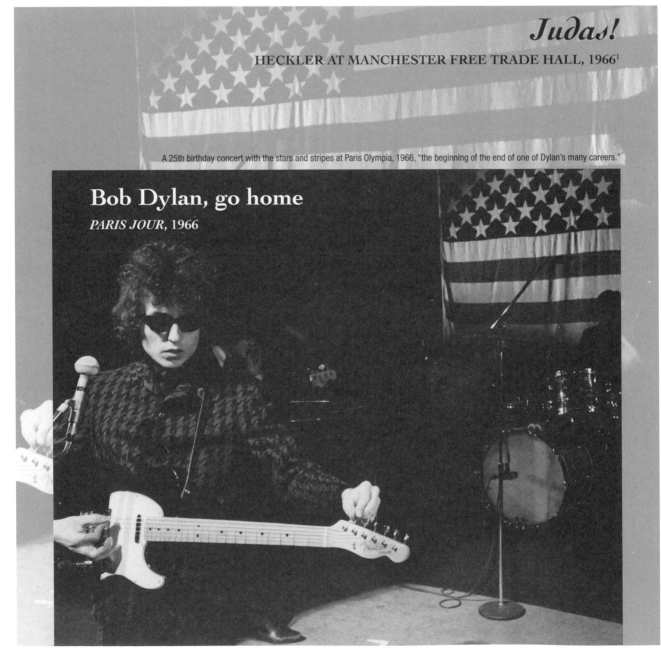

Judas!

HECKLER AT MANCHESTER FREE TRADE HALL, 1966[1]

A 25th birthday concert with the stars and stripes at Paris Olympia, 1966, "the beginning of the end of one of Dylan's many careers."

Bob Dylan, go home

PARIS JOUR, 1966

It was just past the break of midnight, Saturday night, mid-March, 1966. Lincoln Airport, in the dark, blended into the surrounding farmland. Dylan, five members of the Hawks, two roadies and one guest were in two cars speeding toward the airfield. As we arrived, runway lights flashed on, tower controllers stirred and mechanics busied themselves around the twin-engine Lockheed Lodestar, Dylan's private plane. The pilot and co-pilot went through their pre-flight check. Denver was next, then back to New York for some studio work, then up to the Pacific Northwest, Hawaii, Australia, Scandinavia, Ireland, England, and France, and back to the States. This was the beginning of the end of one of Dylan's many careers.

Dylan walked into the dark canteen. He took a plastic cup of muddy coffee from a machine, then stood at the window beside a mechanic in white overalls who was peering into the night. "It must get lonely out here," Dylan said to the mechanic. Both looked at the field, not at each other. "It does," the mechanic replied, "but it's a job. I just take the hours they give me." "I know how that feels, I really do," Dylan said, as they both stared across prairie land. Soon he walked on to the field. He'd just evaded fifty fans at his hotel lobby, but a half-dozen were clustered around the plane. "It was a great concert," one fan said. "We really liked it, Bob," another said. "When are you coming here again?" Dylan said he didn't know, adding: "Thanks a lot, I'm glad you liked the show."

He scribbled his autograph a few times. A shy youth, about 17, approached him. He wore glasses, a neat white shirt and tie. "Mr Dylan," he said, nervously, "I'm interested in poetry, too." "Yeah, is that so?" Dylan replied. "Yes, sir," the boy answered. "I was wondering if you could spare a few minutes, sometime, to read some poems I've written." "Sure," Bob responded. The young man handed Dylan a large envelope stuffed so full it bulged like a football. "Are all these poems?" Dylan asked. Proudly, the boy said: "Yes. I've been writing more since I began to study your songs." "Well," Dylan said, "thank you. I'll try to read some tonight. Is your address on the envelope? I'll let you know what I think of them." The boy glowed: "That's wonderful. I hope you like them."

Inside the plane, the band members were already dozing off, a pile of slumping bodies. Bob probably needed sleep more than anyone, though he had revived now and seemed eager to use the minutes until the plane was ready to depart. Literature: "Rimbaud? I can't read him now. Rather read what I want these days. 'Kaddish' is the best thing yet. Everything else is a shuck. I never dug Pound or Eliot. Shakespeare was commissioned to write. He wasn't a mystic, just one of the arch-queens of all. I dig Shakespeare. A raving queen and a cosmic amphetamine brain." On his new music: "There was never any change. No instrument will change love, death, in any soul. My music is my music. Folk music was such a shuck. I never recorded a folk song. My idea of a folk song is Jeannie Robertson or Dock Boggs. Call it historical-traditional music. I want to write songs now. Until *Bringing It All Back Home*, songwriting was a sideline. I was still a performer. Then I knew I had to write songs. I don't have to look to anyone to tell I'm good. I know, I'm honest. Get some of those literary people, some of those poetry people to sit down with my records, that would be good." On civil rights: "Look at the South. Blacks are taking over the town. But how groovy is it? Power, that's all it is. Rich blacks will take over. The kids are just a start. If I was black, I don't know if I'd want to go to school with whites." The words poured out of him. "It's bullshit. All is death, I'm afraid. I don't want to see myself die. I'd just as soon drive a car off a cliff than do something I don't believe in. Got to beat the pressure … I saw Chuck Berry at St Louis Airport. You can listen to Buddy Holly when you're all alone, but Chuck Berry? You have to be out on the highway."

The road managers, Bill Avis and Victor Maimudes,[2] checked everyone's seatbelt. Dylan and I sat face to face. On one knee, he held a packet of proofs of his book, *Tarantula*, just sent him by his publisher for approval. On the other was the fan's envelope. I knew he probably wouldn't open either that night. I fussed with my tape recorder, cursing the engine noise. I held the mike a foot away from him. His eyes were slits. He was exhausted, but he told me he wouldn't have slept, even if I hadn't been there. He just had too much to do.

"It takes a lot of medicine to keep up this pace," Dylan said. "It's very hard, man. A concert tour like this has almost killed me. It's been like this since October. It really drove me out of my mind. I never had it like this before. It's been a very weird time, and it really had me down. I'm really going to cut down. Next year, the concert tour is only going to last a month … or two. I'm only doing it like this, this year, because I want everyone to know what we're doing." Dylan sipped his tea, sent a cloud of cigarette smoke over his head, tugged his shirt-collar, and continued: "It's just absurd for people to sit around being offended by their own meaninglessness, so that they have to force everything else to come into the hole with them, and die trying. That's the hang-up here. But I'm not involved with that anymore. I've told you that many times. I don't know if you think I'm kidding, or if you think it's a front. I really just don't *care*— honestly just don't *care*—what people say about me. I don't care what people think about me. I don't care what people know about me. It matters nothing to me.

"Playing on the stage is a kick for me now. It wasn't before, because I knew what I was doing then was just too empty. It was just dead ambassadors who would come and see me and clap and say: 'Oh, groovy, I would like to meet him and have a cocktail. Perhaps I'll bring my son, Joseph, with me. Joseph clapped a lot. You liked the program, didn't you, Joseph?' And Joseph, of course, said: 'Oh, yes, father, father. Yes I did—oh, whoopee!' And then they ask: 'Can I bring Isabella?' And the first thing you know you've got about five or six little boys and girls hanging around with Coke bottles and ginger ale bottles and you're confronted by some ambassador who's got his hand in your pocket trying to shake your spine and give you compliments. I won't let *anybody* backstage anymore. Even to give me a compliment. Give me no compliments. I just don't care."

The speech rhythms and the vitality of his thoughts began to rouse Dylan. His eyes cleared as he continued: "You can't ask me about how I sleep. You can't ask me about how I make it, and you cannot ask me what I think I am doing here. Other than that, we'll just get along fine. You just ask me anything and I will shoot right back. Now, we have one thing straight about the book. I'm going to tell Albert we have come to an understanding about the book. I'll give you as much time as I can. I'll come very quickly to the point in all the things that I want done, but you can easily go back on me. You can easily do it anyway that you want. But I won't forgive you for doing that, man. It's not going to be a biography, because I'm not dead yet. It's going to be a timeless thing, right?

"Nobody knows about me. What do people really know? That my father's name is Zimmerman and my mother's family is middle class? I'm not about to go around telling people that this is false. I'm not covering up anything I did before. I'm not going back on anything, any statement or anything I've ever done. I'm not copping out on anything I've ever done since I was born. I've given up trying to tell anybody that they are wrong in their thinking about anything, about the world or me, or whatever it is. I don't care. You can write anything you want to write.

"But you're not going to cut this book, are you? Are they going to edit it? Is that in your contract? Because that is a hang-up if it isn't in your contract. No matter how objective you are at putting your stuff down, no matter what you put down, they can twist it all by adding their own words. Now, you are not going to say 'authorized by Bob Dylan.' I'll write that on the cover. I'll write four sentences on the cover and sign my name, to something like: 'Bob Shelton wrote me up in the *New York Times* five years ago. And he's a nice guy and I like him. And he wrote this book, and for that, it is not'—just to make sure it sells in Nebraska and Wyoming—'it's not chintzy.'" Pleased with such a ludicrous endorsement, Dylan smiled.

"There is nothing that anybody can expose about me. Everybody thinks that there is such an exposé, on millions of little tiny things, like name-change or anything. It doesn't really matter to me. The only time it did matter to me, when people would bring up these things like saying, 'you've got pimples.' Or, 'your underwear's dirty, when you are down on the ground.' You understand? It bothered me, then. I don't mean music things. I mean the people, the people for whom that was written. Obviously, there are people who like to read that shit. And people might say: 'Oh, I don't believe it' or 'that doesn't matter to me.' But it tickled them, you know."

Twisting restlessly, Dylan was getting animated now, angry at the phantoms that haunted him, angry at the hungers of his audience. He seemed to want to *explain* himself. It was so unusual for him to be explaining anything, because no one ever seemed to understand, anyway. He tried a new beginning: "I think of all that I do as my writing. It cheapens it to call it anything else but *writing*. But there is not a person on the earth who takes it less seriously than I do. I know that it's not going to help me into heaven one little bit. It's not going to keep me out of the fiery furnace. It's not going to extend my life any and it's not going to make me happy."

"What do you think will make you happy?" I asked. "I'm happy, you know, I'm happy to just be able to come across things. I don't need to be happy. Happiness is a kind of cheap word. There's some kind of happiness that is very, very snobbish. Let's face it, I'm not the kind of cat that's going to cut off an ear if I can't do something. I would commit suicide. I would shoot myself in the brain if things got bad. I would jump from a window. I sure as hell wouldn't cut off my ear, man, I would shoot myself. You know, I can think about death openly. It's nothing to fear. It's nothing sacred. Death is nothing sacred. I've seen so many people die." I asked: "Is life sacred?" "Life's not sacred either," Dylan replied. "Look at all the spirits that actually control the atmosphere, which are not living and yet which attract you, as ideas, or like games with the solar system. Or look at the farce of politics, economy and war."

It was another variation on an old Dylan theme: his inner despair battling his outer hope. "It's become so easy for me to do everything, you have no idea, man, everything at my command. I can make money now doing absolutely anything. But I don't want that kind of money. I'm not a millionaire now, in terms of everything I have. But it is really close. This time next year, I'm going to be a millionaire, but *that means nothing*. To be a millionaire means that next year you can lose it all. You must realize that I have not copped out on one thing. It is very hard for somebody who does what he does not to have to cop out on some things. I mean, I love what I do. I also make money off it. Hey, I sing honest stuff, man, and it's consistent. It's *all* I do. I don't give a damn what anybody says. Nobody can praise me and have any effect on me and nobody can criticize what I do that's going to have any effect on me. *Nobody*. I'm not going to read anything for me or against me that can possibly have any effect on me. So, therefore, I never really read what people say about me. I'm just not interested.

"When I first really knew that I had money that I couldn't see, I looked around to see what a few of my agents were doing with it. First of all, I like chauffeurs. When I came back from England last time, I didn't buy a chauffeur, but I sure rented one. I make no bones about it. I *need* the money to *employ* people. It all works hand in hand. If I had no money, I could walk invisible. But money now is necessary. It costs me money now to be able to walk *invisible*. That's the *only* reason I need the money. I don't need the money to buy clothes or nothing." Again his anger mounted. "I'm sick of giving creeps money off my soul. When I lose my teeth tomorrow, they are not going to buy me a new pair of teeth. I've got a lot of people I can give money to and the money that is rightfully mine I actually want. I don't like little short people who smoke Tiparillo cigarettes and have their pockets turned inside out all the time and wear glasses and who once wanted to be Groucho Marx making all the money off me. And there are a lot of them. All in the music business.

"Oh, if it's not the promoter cheating you, it's the box office cheating you. Somebody is always giving you a hard time. Even the record company figures won't be right. They are never right. For one reason or another, they are never right. Nobody's going to be straight with you because nobody wants the information out. Do you know that up to a certain point I made more money on a song I wrote if it were on an album by Carolyn Hester or anybody than if I did it myself? That's the contract they gave me. Horrible! Horrible!"

The flashes of despair faded. Dylan could not lose his sense of the ludicrous. "I'm not going to be accepted, but I would like to be accepted, by the Hogtown Dispatch literary crowd, who wear violets in their crotch and make sure that they get on all the movie lists. By those who write record reviews and book reviews and movie reviews and TV reviews and also write about the ladies' auxiliary meetings and the PTA gatherings, you know, all in the same column. I would like to be accepted by them people. There's no reason not to be. But I don't think I'm ever going to be. Whereas the Beatles have been." Did he want the Beatles' sort of acceptance? "No, no, no, I'm not saying that. I'm just saying the Beatles have arrived, right? In all music forms, whether Stravinsky or Leopold Jake the Second, who plays in the Five Spot, the Black Muslim Twins, or whatever. The Beatles are accepted, and you've got to accept them for what they do. They play songs like 'Michelle' and 'Yesterday.' A lot of smoothness there."

When I told him Joan Baez planned to record "Yesterday" on her next album, Bob responded: "Yeah, it's the thing to do, to tell all the teenyboppers 'I dig the Beatles' and you sing a song like 'Yesterday' or

'Michelle.' Hey, God knows, it's such a cop-out, man, both of those songs. If you go into the Library of Congress you can find a lot better than that. There are millions of songs like 'Michelle' and 'Yesterday' written in Tin Pan Alley."

There aren't millions of songs like *his* being written by anyone, I suggested. "I don't know if I fully appreciate that because it's going to get to the point where nobody else is going to be able to sing my songs but me. Like, I'm going to drive myself right out of business. I'll have to put out 10,000 records a year, for God's sake, because nobody will record the songs I write." Did he influence young people because he broke the rules? "It's not a question of breaking the rules, don't you understand? I don't break the rules, because I don't see any rules to break. As far as I'm concerned, there aren't any rules."

He sounded like Lenny Bruce. He was riffing, on a vocal cord, not a guitar chord. The words flowed like music. He was in and out of communication, like a jazzman going in and out of a melody line. It was "all music, no more, no less," word music, chin music, talk and symbol music. He was fully awake now, riffing on a melody. From colors to poetry, Dylan improvised: "My thing is with colors. It's not black and white. It's always been with colors, whether with clothes or anything. Color. Now, with something like that driving you, sometimes it gets very fiery red, you understand? And at times it gets very jet black.

"You just have to make it. When I say 'make it,' I don't mean being a popular folk-rock star. 'Making it' means finding your line. Everybody's line is there, someplace. People think they just have to go through living hell on earth, but I don't really believe that attitude. The only people who believe you have to go through living hell on earth, or that life is a tragedy, are the people who are simple, close-minded people who have to make excuses for themselves. Everybody's line is there. Despite everybody who has been born and has died, the world has just gone on without them, I mean, look at Napoleon — but we went right on. Look at Harpo Marx — the world went around, it didn't stop for a second. It's sad but true. John Kennedy. Right?"

Isn't the difference, I asked, in what people did when they were here on earth? "Don't you see they did *nothing*? Has anybody done anything, really? Look at anybody who you think has done anything. Name anybody you think has done something," Shaw, I said. "George Bernard Shaw," Dylan slowly repeated one name at a time. "Who has he helped?" "He helped a lot of people to use their heads," I replied, adding, "You've helped a lot of people to use their heads and their ears." "Well," Dylan rejoined, "I don't think I have, that's all. It's funny that people think I have. I'm certainly not the one to go around saying that that is what I do. At one time I did read a lot of the stuff that was written about me, maybe three or four years ago. Now, I don't even read anything anymore. So I have no idea what people say about me. I really don't. I do know that a lot of people really like me. I know that."

Eight miles high, flying over the Great Plains, he jiggled his knees, like the trays of a scale, proofs of *Tarantula* on one knee and the Nebraska boy's poems on the other. One went up and the other down, in an unconscious seesaw of literary weighing-in. Did he think *Tarantula* was going to be accepted by the Establishment literary people, by the serious poets? "First of all," he said, animatedly, "you have to realize that if you are going to write for poets and literary people — " He stopped short. "I think a poet is anybody who wouldn't call himself a poet. Anybody who could possibly call himself a poet just cannot be a poet. They have just settled for the romance of their ancestors and their historical knowledge of facts that never were. And they would like to think that they are a little above it all. When people start calling me a poet, I say: 'Oh, groovy, how groovy to be called a poet.' But it didn't do me any good, I'll tell you that. It didn't make me any happier.

"Hey, I would love to say that I am a poet. I would really like to think of myself as a poet, but I just can't because of all the slobs who are called poets." Who was a poet, then? Allen Ginsberg? "He's a poet," Dylan fired back. "To be a poet does not necessarily mean that you have to write words on paper. Do you know what I mean? One of those truck-drivers that walk down the stairway of a motel is a poet. He talks like a poet. I mean, what else does a poet have to do? Poets," his voice trailed off in inchoate formulations, ideas running too fast for his tongue. "Poets, old people, death, decay, people like Robert Frost poetry about trees and branches, but that isn't what I mean. Allen Ginsberg is the only writer I know. The rest of the writers I don't have that much respect for. If they really want to do it, they're going to have to *sing* it. I wouldn't call myself a poet for any more reason than I would call myself a 'protest-singer.' All that would do would put me in a category with a whole lot of people who would just bother me. I don't want to be in their category. I don't want to fool anybody. To tell anybody I'm a poet would just be fooling people. That would put me in a class, man, with people like Carl Sandburg, T S Eliot,

Stephen Spender, and Rupert Brooke. Hey, name them—Edna St Vincent Millay and Robert Louis Stevenson and Edgar Allan Poe and Robert Lowell.

"I know two saintly people," Dylan continued. "I know just two holy people, Allen Ginsberg is one. The other, for lack of a better term, I just want to call 'this person named Sara.' What I mean by 'holy' is crossing all the boundaries of time and usefulness. Hey, I dig a lot of people, I love a lot of people, but I certainly don't consider them poets." Two other writers he admired suddenly occurred to him: "William Burroughs is a poet. I like all his old books, and Jean Genet's old books, but I'm talking about writers of this country. Genet's scholastical lectures are just a waste of time, they are just boring. But if we are talking now in terms of writers I think can be called poets, then Allen must be the best. I mean Allen's 'Kaddish,' not 'Howl.'

"Allen doesn't have to sing 'Kaddish,' man. You understand what I mean? He just has to lay it down. He's the only poet that I know of. I can't really tell you all my feelings of him because they are just too total. He's the only person I respect who writes, that just totally writes. He don't have to do nothing, man. Allen Ginsberg, he's just holy, one of the two people that I know are holy." How is Sara holy? "I don't want to put her in this book. I want to keep her out of this, I don't want to call her 'a girl.' I would rather refer to her, if I refer to her at all, I can't really refer to her by any other name than—I don't mean to come on, I know it's very corny, but the only thing I can think of is, more or less, 'Madonna-like.'"

I was beginning to think that he had forgotten my tape recorder, when he asked me: "Are you getting it all? How much tape do you have left? Is it still running?" I told him we had hours of fresh tape and he plunged on: "Love and sex are things that really hang everybody up. When things aren't going right and you're really nobody, if you don't get laid in one way or another, you get mean, you know. You get cruel. Now, why in the world sex should force this is beyond me. I truthfully can tell you that male and female are not here to have sex, you know, that's not the purpose. I don't believe that that's God's will, that females have been created so that they can be a counterpart of man's urge. I just can't really believe that. I can't believe that it is that way. There are too many other things that people just won't let themselves be involved in. Sex and love have nothing to do with female and male. It is just whatever two souls happen to be. It could be male and female, and it might not be male and female. It might be female and female or it might be male and male. You can't turn your back on it, man. You can try to pretend that it doesn't happen, and you can make fun of it and be snide, but that's not really the rightful thing. I know, I know."

The kaleidoscopic monologue was running at full tilt, his verbal flood stream driven by a submerged pressure built up during years of talking more guardedly for publication. Inevitably, music displaced all other topics, even though he had remarked to me before we got on the plane "music is only twenty per cent of what I am." Still, music was his *métier*, compulsion, work, and play.

"I want you to have explanations of my songs in your book," Dylan said. "Things nobody else will ever have." "Such as," I broke in, "who Mr Jones is to you?" "Well," Bob parried, "I'm not going to tell you that way. I'm going to tell you about the stuff that *I* want to tell you about. I could tell you who Mr Jones is in my life, but, like, everybody has got their Mr Jones, so I can't really say that he is the same for everyone. I can't give Mr Jones a name, you understand. I know he's there—" and he plunged into the subject of "Ballad of a Thin Man" and "Like a Rolling Stone." Nothing struck me so strongly as this passage from the surge of Dylan's two-in-the-morning flood: "Mr Jones's loneliness can easily be covered up to the point where he can't recognize that he is alone, suddenly locked in a room. It's not so incredibly absurd, and it's not so imaginative, to have Mr Jones in a room with three walls with a midget and a geek and a naked man. Plus a voice, a voice coming in his dream. I'm just a voice speaking. Anytime I'm singing about people, and if the songs are dreamed, it's like my voice is coming out of their dream." I marveled at Dylan's "outside insight" to describe how his singing might reach others. He was speeding along now, attacking some false myths about schooling and the professions.

"Why, I don't even want to talk about college. I have no respect for college. It's just an extension of time. I hung around college, but it's a cop-out, you know, from life, a cop-out from experience. A lot of people started out to be lawyers, but I venture to say that a hundred per cent of the really groovy lawyers haven't gotten through school the way they ought to. They've always been freaks in their school, and have always had a hard time making it; so many lawyers just take people for what they're worth. They all make deals and all are very criminal, but doctors, lawyers, all these kind of people—they're just in it for money, and for resentment. They put in their time and they're going to get it back. I agree with them that way. But I'm sure it could be done in other ways, and it's not—I've known people who've been really loaded down with burdens and who have been in the right to collect, and who have been so innocent, that when they got lawyers to get them what they deserve ... Do you follow me? The party's lawyers they are suing make deals with their lawyers. Like, it happens all the time, man. How anybody could have respect for lawyers baffles me! I have lawyers working for me I never see. I don't see my lawyers. Anytime they see the chance, they jump on it."

Did he want to talk about Joan Baez? I wondered if he would shed any light on his attitudes *then* toward one of the most intriguing show business liaisons of the time? Or would he bite my head off? "Me and Joan?" Bob asked. "I'll tell you. I hope you do explain it, if you can do this book straight. She brought me up. I rode on her, but I don't think I owe her anything. I feel sorry for her. I want to explain this. I want you to print that, because I am not joking. I feel sorry for her, knowing that I don't have to feel sorry for her because she would definitely not want me to feel sorry for her, or anybody to feel sorry for her. I feel bad for her because she has nobody to ask, nobody to turn to that's going to be straight with her. She hasn't got that much in common with the street vagabonds who play insane instruments. She's not that kind of person. Her family is a very gentle kind of family. She's very fragile and very sick and I lived with her and I loved the place. Can you write all this in your book? If you can't man, it's a waste of time. I mean, is your book going to be a mature book, or is this all just a waste of time?" I reassured him.

Dylan was in a strangely defiant mood, seeming to stress his most unappealing, anti-heroic side, daring me, it seemed, to take at face value all his negative thinking or self-destructive patterns. In retrospect, I think that he was pleading for understanding that, behind all the applause, there was a lot of pain. He talked of an earlier time, when we had knocked around the Village together. "After Suze moved out of the house, I got very, very strung out for a while. I mean, really, very strung out." But, he told me, he'd survived those emotionally straining periods.

"I can do anything, knowing in front that it's not going to catch me and pull me, 'cause I've been through it once already. I've been through people. A lot of time you get strung out with people. They are just like junk. The same thing, no more, no less. They kill you the same way. They rot you the same way." I didn't press him as to who could rot him and kill him, but I suggested that it reminded me of the line in Sartre's *No Exit*, "Hell is other people." Dylan joked: "Whatever it is, man. I don't know Sartre. He's cross-eyed, that's all I know about him. Anybody cross-eyed can't be all bad." He hit the bottom, saying: "I have a death thing, I know. I have a suicidal thing, I know."

Later, I asked him if he wanted to leave all this despair on the record. He said: "I haven't explained those things I said against myself. I'll explain them, and you better well use them, you can put in what I talked about it, if it's in context. Nobody knows about where I was at. A lot of people *think* that I shoot heroin. But that's *baby talk*; I do a lot of things. Hey, I'm not going to sit here and lie to you, and make you wonder about all the things I do. I do a lot of things, man, which help me. And I'm smart enough to know that I don't depend on them for my existence, you know, and that's all. Man, that's where it lays, like that."

I'd been thinking then of how, one night at the Gaslight, Dylan had once advised me "to just write about something that is really important to you." At that time, I couldn't envision that it would be a book about the man who'd given me the advice. Dylan continued: "I can't be hurt, man, if the book is honest. No kidding, I can't be hurt. I want you to write an honest book, Bob, I don't want you to write a bullshit book. Hey, I'm trusting you. The only reason that I am here with you now is that I know that you are the man who, if there is anybody I want to do it with, is you. I've talked with so many people and I've come to the conclusion that a lot had to be kids, around 22, who also know and who write and who know there is a gap, and that nobody understands and could write it down. But I don't want to do anything with them. That's just a shuck. I'll do it with you."

Our conversation drifted to the folk-song "movement." We were bitter then because the folk world was so hostile toward his electric merging of folk and rock. "Nobody told me to go electric," he said emphatically. "No, I didn't even ask anybody, I asked not a soul, believe me. Hey, I went electric on my second record. Why don't you bring that out in the book?" The *Freewheelin'* album, released in May 1963, Dylan reminded me, had "four electric songs. The only reason they cut out the electric ones was because I didn't write them. Columbia still has them; they are trying to retouch them." Before the Beatles were known in America and before the "folk-rock" craze of 1965, Dylan had tried to show he was not a performer to nest in any pigeonhole. "I hate all the labels people have put on me, because they are labels. It's just that they are ugly, and I know, in my heart, that it's not me. I have not *arrived* at where I am at now, I have just *returned* to where I am at now, knowing that it's the only way. What I am doing now is what I must do before I move on."

Dylan began digging his heels in about the music world and his early attraction toward folk music. I scarcely needed to ask questions, for he was monologuing now. "I hate to say this, because I don't want it to be taken the wrong way, but I latched on, when I got to New York City, because I saw a huge audience was there. People I knew I was not taking advantage of. I knew I wasn't going to stay there. I knew it wasn't my thing. Many times I spoiled it. Many times I went against it. Any time they tried to think I was like them, I knew I wasn't like them. I just told them whatever happened to be in my mind at the time. I didn't have any respect for any of the organizations. In New York City, they are all organizations. I had respect for the people. Woody [Guthrie] turned me on romantically—Woody used his own time, in a way nobody else did. He was just a little bit better, just a little smarter, because he was from the country. I met Woody and I talked with him. I dug him, I would dig him, I imagine, if he were around today." He cited some reservations about Guthrie's style, and I asked if Woody's work then seemed too simple for him. Dylan shot back: "No, not simple at all. The fundamental objection is that I can see *why* he wrote what he wrote. I can see him sitting down and writing what he wrote, in a very calm kind of a way. I am *not* putting him down. You can print all this, man. I'm not copping out on my attraction to him, and his influence on me. His influence on me was never in inflection or in voice. What drew me to him was hearing his voice. I could tell he was very lonesome, very alone and very lost out in his time. That's why I dug him."

Dylan stressed that at the height of his involvement in the folk world, he still loved rock 'n' roll. "Suze Rotolo could tell you, because Suze knows more than anybody else that I played, back in 1961 and 1962, when nobody was around, all those Elvis Presley records. She'll tell you how many nights I stayed up and wrote songs and showed them to her and asked her 'is this right?' Because I knew her father and mother were associated with unions and she was into this equality-freedom thing long before I was. I checked the songs out with her. She would like all the songs. Suze is a very talented girl, man, but she is very frightened."

We talked about *Sing Out!*, the folk-song magazine that had lionized Dylan, then turned against him. In defense of Dylan's changes, I had wrangled with them. He cautioned me against my wasting time with polemics. "Don't you understand? If you're smart, you just gotta keep going, you're just not going to stand still. Everyone else is going to die. I don't mean *die*. I mean, they are going to decay and go crazy. If I could help them, I would love to see them straightened out. But I know in my heart that it is impossible to straighten all these people out, because they are all so nine-to-five, and so involved with that life that it is impossible. I don't want nothing to do with it. *Sing Out!* has a big organization; they know they control a lot. They have a very big hand in a lot of money. They have an Establishment. Believe me, Bob, they make a lot of money. The only person in that organization I respect is Moe Asch, who is old and hip. He's the only one who knows that he's not serious, that he is not a clown, that the whole world is not a circus. He knows. The rest of the people there don't know it. They have power, fake, phoney power. They're dumb, man. They're clods. I never signed their petitions. Hey, dig it, man. They're gonna decay. If you're out of it, groovy! But I'm telling you, man, get out of it. It's not that you have to put them down to leave it."

He eyed the packet of poems from the Nebraska fan, knowing he wouldn't read them that night. I told him how touching it was when he told that airport mechanic how lonely it got out there. "Well, I loved him, man," Dylan replied. "He's a poor cat. What's he doing out there in Nebraska? I just wanted to know. I was just curious. Hey, it's lonesome everyplace. The people that can't live with it, that can't accept it—they are just going to blow up the world, and make things bad for everybody, only because they feel so out of place. Everybody has that in common—they are all going to die.

"Hey, I could be right here right now and anybody could be jealous of me and whatever I've got, the same way that I've been jealous of people before. I know what that's like. But, it's like you've got no faith, like you don't like yourself. I'm not talking any Zen Buddhism bullshit. I don't mean to say that you have to like yourself and everything's groovy. I wouldn't tell *anybody* to follow any formula at all. None at all. I don't want nobody's mind; I would quit. A lot of people know I would've quit. A lot of people know that, man. I quit after England, and it was just done, I could quit again." Already, he told me, he'd withdrawn, for a while, from Woodstock: "I moved out a long time ago. Before the summer [of 1965] ended, I moved into New York City. I couldn't make it up there anymore because it wasn't private anymore. It will *never, ever* happen again. I'm *never* going to tell anybody where I live again. People want to tear me apart, man. Hey, I don't take people up to the country now, because the country is a very alone place. And if you don't dig being alone, if you haven't got something to do, you're just going to take the bus back. You're going to get bored and go back. I can be alone as long as I have to be alone. I don't give a shit about being with people. I don't have anything to say to anybody. But it's hard for other people like that."

Dylan's search for the place to be "alone" has kept a lot of real estate agents and moving men busy. He asked me: "Do you know what I did when I got back from England, man? I bought me a thirty-one-room house. Can you imagine that? It turned into a nightmare, because, first of all, I wrote *Highway 61 Revisited* there and I don't believe in writing some total other thing in the same place twice. It's just a hang-up, a voodoo kind of thing. I just can't do it. When I need someplace to make something new, I can't go back there because—have you ever smelled birth? Well, I just can't stand the smell of birth. It just lingers, so I just lived there and tried to go on, but couldn't. And so the house is up for sale now, and I've moved back into Albert's."

We talked a bit about the Beatles, whom he had first seen at New York's Delmonico Hotel during their 1964 tour. He told me, however, that he felt, at that point, much closer to Marlon Brando than he did to any of the Beatles. "I wish you could meet Brando. There's nobody like Brando. Nobody has treated him right, in the press."

On this tour, I'd seen a lot of cracks developing in Dylan's relationship with his manager. "There are some things that Albert tries to push on me. There are some things Albert and I naturally agree on, and some things that I have to tell him to agree on. He's only come across once on his side. The rest of the time, I don't want him telling me shit." I suggested that people should realize a manager is a star's employee, not his employer, but Dylan flared at that. Like the man who grumbles about his wife but wouldn't let anyone else criticize her, Dylan leapt to Grossman's defense: "It's not that Albert works for me. People who put Albert down ought to be—I mean, critic people. First of all, did you know—Sara told me this, and it's true—that in hell there is a special place for critics? Did you ever know that? That was before Dante's time. Before the *Inferno* and before the Black Plague. And when you think about it, it is very weird. Obviously, now, you see the ragman walking around a couple of thousand years BC did not like to be confronted with a bunch of mouths. That's still where it's at."

Dylan's wide swings in mood were something I'd grown accustomed to long before. Only after the fact could I figure out what was elating him or depressing him. After one encounter on this trip, in which he expressed what I could only view as his deep and pervasive pessimism, I tried to counter his depression. A few days later, he scorned me for misunderstanding his moods. "I am *not* pessimistic," he told me. "I am just trying to get that across in the shortest, most concise way possible. If I am pessimistic, I am not even going to talk. I'm just going to go in the corner. One thing I have never done and will never do is force my moods on other people. Why should I sit around and talk to somebody for hours and then have them think that I am pessimistic? That's an insult!

"I'll tell you what the drag is, what hangs everybody up is that I'm not *stopping*. They call me dead. It is very silly for them to call me dead, and they know it. There was a time, last year, when it just went overboard. Everybody recorded my songs and it would have been very easy for me, at that time, to have written up another huge batch. Everyone would have done them. They would have just lapped them up," he said of the great folk-rock surge of 1965.

Dylan's ambivalence has confounded and confused everyone who's ever been close to him. It sometimes confuses *him*. As late as 1976, he was saying that his Gemini personality "forces me to extremes. I'm never really balanced in the middle. I go from one side to the other without staying in either place very long. I'm happy, sad, up, down, in, out, up in the sky and down in the depths of the earth." At least that was consistent for, ten years earlier, as we rode on this plane, he was swinging widely. When I said I'd like to interview Phil Spector, Dylan said, "Sure, sure, go see him." Then he told me how Spector had annoyed him but "tell him that when I think about him, I really love him." Another area of ambivalence is the press, critics, tastemakers and opinion-molders. Dylan dislikes them and repeatedly taunts them, even as he is ineluctably drawn to them. Dylan went on: "Hey, magazines, critics, *Newsweek*, *Time*, *Look*, *Life*—all of it is very meaningless. It doesn't seem to me to change anybody's mind. When people *like* something, other people go around trying to figure out why people like these things. I mean, when they really like something, they like it. They just get involved in something, that's all. It happens to them. And anything that happens to you, happens to you. 'Like' and 'dislike' are just unreal words."

Sic transit the Fourth Estate, in the estimation of one who has used the press with much artfulness. I sought to move to an area of his enthusiasm, black musicians. "Ask Aretha Franklin about me, man,"

Dylan said, "or talk to the Staple Singers. Why don't you talk to Mavis Staples? I'd be interested in what she says. And to Purvis and Roebuck Staples, too. Remember that night when Mahalia Jackson came out from the dugout in three limousines? Remember, from the dugout [at a 1962 gospel festival at Randall's Island in New York] with her goddamn maids, who lifted up her dresses and opened up her doors? She sure has class.

"A lot of people think that the modern spade musicians are getting a raw deal. A lot of them are, because there are real genius people playing in dives. A lot of them are. But an awful lot of the records you hear are all copies. They, too, are imitating who they think they should think they should imitate. That don't mean you have to give them a million dollars and a house in the suburbs and a golf course. That's what we're talking about here. We're not talking about equality, or enough food to eat."

Why had he become so hopeless about the civil-rights movement, when it had once so engaged his energies and songwriting? "I'm not pessimistic about it. No, no, I don't want to be misunderstood about it! I don't think that anybody who is taught to get his kicks off a superiority feels—man, that's a drag! But the word 'Negro' sounds foolish coming from my mouth. What's a Negro? I don't know what a Negro is. What's a Negro? A black person? How black? What's a Negro? A person living in a two-room shack with twelve kids? A lot of white people live in a two-room shack with twelve kids. Does this make them Negro? What's a Negro? Someone with African blood? A lot of white people have African blood. What's a Negro? An Ethiopian kind of thing? That's not a Negro, that's an ancient religious pajama-riding freak! I've got nothing against Negro rights. I never did."

Dylan immediately reminisced about a string of his black friends from his early days in New York: about Mel and Lillian Bailey, who had treated him like a son and brother; about Jim Forman, the former leader of the Student Non-Violent Coordinating Committee. He spoke nostalgically about some other young blacks from Albany, Georgia, whom he had worked and played with, like Bernice Johnson and Cordell Reagon. "Put their names in the book. I love Cordell. He's a madman. He's the only faithful madman, the only madman—let me put it this way—that really looks bad, that can wipe you out with pure strength, who I could trust to go anywhere with. I never get to see so many people. That's why I would like you to say things about a lot of people that I loved. Say that I said good things about them. Hey, I've turned down everybody, Bob. I'm giving you all this. I'm trusting you to go along with me. Hey, I've never been wrong. I'll tell you something about this book. If I tell you something, I'm not trying to horn in. I don't want any of your bread."

Knowing how mercurial Dylan was, I tentatively began to explore with him how he changes his mind about people, about his own music, his own past work. I said: "You have always been wildly enthusiastic about the recording you have just finished, and then you turn around a few months later and say it was nothing. At least, you always did that in the past." "No, no," Dylan flashed. "I like the last record. Hey, I made *Bringing It All Back Home*, and I love that record. I made *Highway 61 Revisited* and I love that record, I love the *Blonde on Blonde* album. What I was trying to do on my fourth album, on *Another Side of Bob Dylan*—well, I was just too out of it, man, to come across with what I was trying to do. It was all done too fast. All done in one session. I liked the idea of it. No, I don't like the first album. You know, though, I've done some stuff on that first record that still stands up. Like my harmonica playing. Like in 'Man of Constant Sorrow,' the arrangement of that I like. 'In My Time of Dying' still stands up. But as a whole, it doesn't make any kind of sense, you understand? It's not consistent."

Wasn't he really his own worst critic? "Of course I am my own worst critic! Those aren't my words, those are your words. A lot of the stuff I've done, man, as far as I'm concerned, the last three things I've done on records, is beyond criticism. I'm not saying that because I think I'm any kind of god. I'm just saying that because I know, I just know. I've been at it too long. I wanted to call that album *Highway 61 Revisited*. Nobody understood it. I had to go up the fucking ladder until finally the word came down and said: 'Let him call it what he wants to call it.' I have to fight for songs on the album. I put them on there because I know it is right. And sure enough, it turns out to be right."

One thing that repeatedly disturbed Dylan on this tour was the problems of sound amplification, despite the brilliant set-up that engineer Richard Alderson had assembled. Acoustics still had been giving them trouble, especially in sports halls. Dylan continued: "This year, I'm doing the tour because I want everybody to know what we're doing. It turns out that we have wasted a lot of time, because it took me so long to realize that no matter how groovy and good it is, if it can't be heard, then it doesn't do anybody any good. Then, the only people behind you are your loyal fans. Those are the people you just have to react to. But now, and you have heard it yourself, there is nothing in the world like this sound system we are using." He asked me in detail my reactions to the sound at the various concerts I'd heard. He said he wanted, at the end of this tour, to bring the show into Carnegie Hall. I jokingly suggested he try, for really great acoustics, the Metropolitan Opera House. Dylan laughed, then asked, seriously: "How many people does it hold?"

Our talk drifted back to some things he'd written about himself, like the 1962 prose-poem memoir "My Life in a Stolen Moment." Dylan wove a web of ambivalence: "I don't disavow it. Please don't get me wrong. I don't disavow it. It is just not me. Somebody else wrote that. But I am not that person of five years ago. It's almost as if I were him," he said, pointing at one of the sleeping Band members. "That's what it's like in my mind, Bob. I have no question to answer about it. I don't disavow it. I wasn't me, then. You are talking about something that somebody else did, because they had to do it." I asked him: "Can I say that when I quote things you wrote or said in the past, then?" Dylan replied: "Sure. All right, but put it in context. It was done out of—it was bled from my hand and from my arm." "By who?" I asked. "By my brain," Dylan replied. "I remember all of it. I remember the drafts. I remember the words I used to write then, thinking they might someday be novels. I remember why I did them. I remember all the reasons. I remember all the shucks and all the cons. All the cute, funny things. Like, man, I am so lucky now. I wouldn't be lucky if I couldn't produce. That's what I thought the last six months. Oh, I was really down. I mean, in ten recording sessions, man, we didn't get one song," he said, referring to *Blonde on Blonde*. What slowed things down? "It was the band. But you see, I didn't know that. I didn't want to think that. I'm not saying it was a mistake, because I know I'm going to do it all again. If I go back to Nashville, man, and everybody down there can't make it, I'm going to take a plane until something else happens. That's just the way it is. You can't blame anybody else. I don't have the right to blame anybody else. It's not that I blame myself, man, it is just that I was down, I was down."

I chanced a Hollywood star-interview question—just what does he do with his money? I held my breath for his outraged response. "Tell them," Dylan said, making his first and last full financial disclosure, "tell them to check their pockets." We laughed. I asked him what he saw in his future. "I can't talk of the future," Dylan said slowly. "I can only talk a little more about it than I used to be able to talk about it, but, still, I can't talk about it all that much. I know there's a movie. I'm going to make a movie, and it's going to be groovy, you know. Then, there's this book for Macmillan," Dylan said, tapping one of the envelopes still resting on his lap. "It's already been fucking publicized and written about, and everybody's expected it and that kind of stuff," he went on, eyeing the *Tarantula* envelope warily. "Every time I look in the paper, there is something about this book. And I gave away the title, which I shouldn't have done. So, I'm thinking of changing it now. You know, I just don't like the obvious. Obvious things are a step backwards. Nobody should step backwards because nobody knows what's behind them. The only direction you can see is in front of you, not in back of you."

The plane's vibrations had been diminishing, even though it hadn't been descending sharply. We'd forgotten that Denver is so high, the ground comes up to meet a plane from the East. The Hawks stirred themselves, wiping sleep from their eyes. They looked at Dylan, surprised he was still wide awake, still talking. Bob gave directions to Victor and Bill about deplaning. He asked Robbie Robertson if he was up to a few hours' work when they got to the motel, and Robbie nodded. As the plane touched down gently on the runway, Dylan kept talking. He looked at the package of poems from his fan in Nebraska, and said he'd have to read them some other time. His eyes went back and forth between the two envelopes of writing on his lap. "I know how that boy feels. I know what it's like being a boy in a small town, somewhere, trying to become a writer."

The arrival at Stapleton Air Field was almost imperceptible, the ground coming up to meet the plane. At the airport, Dylan called Sara in New York. Luggage assembled, cars rented, the convoy sped off to the Motel de Ville on West Colfax Avenue. The rooms were reserved for Ashes & Sand. Dylan took room 102, Robbie 104, and I was up the corridor at 108. Although there had been a time change, it was nearly 3 a.m. now, and I thought Dylan was finished for the night. "Give us about ten minutes, Bob," Dylan said, "and then come down to the room."

Robbie and Dylan were again sprawled out on twin beds, each holding acoustic guitars, starting an hour's jamming. I drank some coffee and tried to bring myself to life to tape them at work. It was all new material; I couldn't put a title on anything. When Dylan came to "Sad-Eyed Lady," he said: "This is the best song I've ever written. Wait till you hear the whole thing." Robbie's face was gray with fatigue.[3] I had to get to bed and assumed that tomorrow would be a long sleep-in. Dylan said: "Let's go out to Central City tomorrow morning. You'll like it. Meet me here at about eleven."

Next morning Bob was on the phone to Grossman in New York. "I've got five new songs to tape," Dylan told the telephone. "Uh-huh, uh-huh. I don't think they're giving us a fair count. Yeah, yeah. Sinatra wants it? What about Otis Redding? I'd rather he do it." The trip to Central City seemed to relax Dylan but he was quiet on the drive and I thought he was depressed. "I want to save my voice," he explained. "It's hoarse this morning."

Dylan had first made the twenty-five-mile trek from Denver to Central City by bus and thumb. It was the Wild West reincarnate—gold mines, sheriffs, buildings out of a movie set. It was a Sunday afternoon in 1966 when Bob made another sentimental return, with Bill Avis and Victor Maimudes in our car, circling slowly along twisting Highway 58. Once a lifeline to Denver, for supplies going up and gold nuggets going out, this route through scrubby, eroded hilltops was just a tourist road now.

Bob sat in the front of the car, conserving his voice for the Denver concert. Looking like the *Blonde on Blonde* cover, his frizzy electric halo, which Hendrix and others soon affected, surrounded a lean face drawn with fatigue. "I don't know how it will look to me today," Bob said to me, "but when I first went up there, Central City looked like paradise. It seemed so far away from anything I'd seen or done before, it was sort of magic to me. Imagine a kid just out of high school coming up here in the mountains! Feeling like he was discovering the world." We passed a jerry-built shack of corrugated iron, tar-paper and wood scraps. "Look for the TV aerial, just look for it!" Bob commanded. First we saw a bearded recluse puttering with his goats and pigs—and then the aerial. Bob fingered the dial until a DJ's voice poked through the mountain passes. "Here's the latest hot single from Simon and Garfunkel, 'Homeward Bound.'" Dylan listened silently, fingering his collar, then his chin.

Within a few turns, we were back in 1859: worn stone buildings, gingerbread wood houses on hillsides. In May 1859, nine Georgia prospectors, led by one John Gregory, struck gold here. Gregory's Diggings, as it was dubbed, was mobbed with 20,000 people in three months. Cornish miners brought their love of music. The first local hit song was "Paddy Casey's Night Hands," about a legendary Irish miner. Show business was show business, even in 1862, when George Harrison, owner of the Montana Theater, fired thirty-five shots into Charlie Switz, a rival. Old George, more popular than his victim, was acquitted. Some high-culture people began to settle, and an opera house was built in 1878. Boosters called the town "the American Salzburg." By the time Dylan first got there, arts festivals were annual events.

We parked near the old courthouse, ambled down Eureka Street into Main. "Nothing's changed. It's almost exactly the way it was," Bob said. We passed the opera house, like a film crew sizing up a location. Some tourists ogled Dylan. A teenager yelped, "What's *he* doing here?" Up Main Street, a small nameless bar was dark. It had a large, circular window front, like an aquarium. "This was the place," Dylan said, peering into the fishbowl. This was where the Gilded Garter had been, where Dylan had "scuffled" for a few dollars that summer. As he described it to me in 1961: "I was onstage for just a few minutes with my folky songs. Then the strippers would come on. The crowd would yell for more stripping, but they went off and I'd come back on with my folksy songs. As the night got longer, the air got heavier, the audience got drunker and nastier, I got sicker, and finally I got fired."

We edged away from the saloon. "Oh, it only lasted a few weeks," Dylan said, "but I suppose I'll never forget it. They paid me very little, but they threw in sandwiches and drinks, and all the strippers I could watch. All the noisy drunks were thrown in free too." We went in to a little curio shop where Dylan spent fifteen minutes rummaging for mementoes. He bought some postcards with a dollar he'd borrowed from me and, with the change, a tiny cowboy hat. There was an original snapshot of John Dillinger, the public enemy shot down in his prime. The shopkeeper told him it was twenty dollars, "a very rare item." Dylan studied the picture, like a still from *Bonnie and Clyde*: "I'll think about it and let you know." After a quick lunch of eggs and hamburgers, we headed back to Denver. "The time has gone so fast," Dylan mused. "It almost seems like it happened to someone else."

After the outing, we returned to the Motel. I assumed Bob wanted a nap before the concert but he said I should come down in half an hour. When I did, he was puttering around in a faded old shirt and jeans—we were suddenly back four years to simple times in the Village. I turned on the tape recorder and threw questions at him for another two hours. He was less frenetic than he'd been in the airplane, but no less articulate, no less candid. We talked about Hibbing, New York, Dinkytown, Woodstock, Memphis and London. Dylan flicked on the television and, without ever losing the continuity of his thread, became engrossed in a horror film. Some miscreant was brewing an evil potion. "Hey, look at that!" he exclaimed boyishly, "He's going to get his back full of cyanide!"

He shuffled around the room, hanging up some of his clothes, one eye on the TV. We talked about his hat, his first gigs, and the folk scene then. Would he ever write his own autobiography? He snapped: "No, not interested." Mine might save him time, if he liked it: "What I'm hoping from your book—I told Albert about it, that you were with me. His reaction was *'what?'*" We both laughed. Bob continued: "Well, I told him, just 'uh-huhs, uh-huh.' He gave me a few uh-huhs and I assured him." He wants to protect you, I said. "Of course he does, but—" and Dylan stormed about managers in general, the losers, the winners, the manipulators."

"How the hell can you get any work done on a tour like this? How can you write?" I asked. "It's very hard, man. It's killed me, ever since September, and it really drove me out of my mind. I never really had it like that before. It was a very weird time. It really had me down." He would cut down next year, he said. "It embarrasses me to talk about the career thing, because it's very hard to talk about. It's been so dumb. Because in my own mind, I know how lucky I am, and I don't know how long it could go on.

We talked about people who had been important to him along the way. "Suze, I will be kind to her the rest of my life. Suze, any time she wants anything, she could always come to me." But he had no patience with some others: "Just con people—they shouldn't be associated with me, because they are just going to get hung up by idiots that know they have known me." We ranged wide and free, in time and in geography. Dylan recalled his earlier encounter with Robert Graves in 1963: "I met him in England. He talked to somebody while I was singing 'Hollis Brown.' And I didn't even know who Robert Graves was. I was singing for a few people, and he was there. He got up and talked to four young guys who called themselves 'professionals.' They sang in the Blue Angel, or something like that. One played the accordion, one played the string bass and one played the Gretsch rhythm guitar, and the other one sang and played slide trombone. And Robert Graves went over and talked to them, to find out about music, while I was singing 'Hollis Brown.' So I stopped singing and said: 'Who's that guy?'" As to Ewan MacColl: "I thought he was dead. So many people are like him, man, the things that MacColl has said about Tom Paxton and Phil Ochs are downright nasty, just worthless, and obvious—yeah, it's very limited. Traditional folk music in America is great music, and it's so criminal the way people want to stick it in a little bottle, with water in it, and keep it in a swamp."

Time passed quickly and I was afraid I was wearing him out. "Don't worry about it, I'm OK. He played around with a little cowboy hat he had bought for his daughter, then dramatically pulled out his "rabbit suit," brushing it off for another night's performance and saying how unusual it was to be dressing up for a concert. He laughed at himself. I turned off my tape recorder. "I wish you could come down to El Paso next week," Dylan said. I told him I had to see a dozen people on the West Coast first. He said two concerts in Oklahoma had to be cancelled because of further work on *Blonde*. "You couldn't make it to Europe in May, could you?" Dylan asked. I said I doubted it—I had to work. "Well, I've got to go to work. Drop back after the show."

Dylan's reserve of energy to tackle another concert for 3,000 people amazed me. He'd been doing this since autumn. At Denver Municipal Auditorium, where the acoustics were a jangled echo, the audience was unaware that he'd done this seventeen times in less than a month. After the concert, I returned to Dylan's crowded motel room. The air was charged, Dylan obviously quite stoned. He started to describe Lennon and McCartney beating a retreat from his Albert Hall concert a year earlier. Dylan mimicked the Beatles running downstairs, halting for breath at landings, looking to see if they were pursued, then running down another flight. It was good pantomime. The Hawks roared. Some fans began calling up and friends dropped in. Bob was expansive, but couldn't conceal his fatigue. I decided it was time to quit and he saw me to the door.

"Now, Bob, I'm trusting you to be honest with your story." Through all the fatigue and stoned haze, the old graciousness was coming out. "See if you can't make it to El Paso, or to England. It'll be different there. It'll be better there. Say hello to Ralph." Ralph? Oh, yes! I had told him several days ago that *I* was going to see Ralph Gleason in San Francisco.⁴ I couldn't believe that with all he had on his mind he could remember something that I said *I* was going to do. He returned to the room and started telling everyone that it was getting late and he had some things to do. One by one they left. The party was over, for that night.

Then, Middle Australia. Grossman should have guessed that Australia, even more middlebrow and muddled than Middle America, would spell trouble for Dylan. But the Kingston Trio and Peter, Paul and Mary had sold there—why not Dylan? After concerts in Seattle, Tacoma, Vancouver, and Honolulu, Dylan and the Hawks arrived in Sydney on April 12 for a fifteen-day tour. The *Melbourne News Weekly* greeted them: "Manly boys and sweet girls are OUT, now. Young men who look like girls soon begin to think like girls; young girls who look like men eventually try to play the role of men ... whenever this happens, civilization falls apart, and a more primitive virile race takes over."

There was not much advance notice that Australian civilization was about to fall apart. Pre-tour publicity was minimal, and disc jockeys were not spinning Dylan. He flew from city to city, meeting reporters who were mostly hostile, inane, callous, or uninformed. He gave them his best truculence. Newspaper stories seemed more like counterattacks than reports. After each concert and to mixed reviews, the troupe pushed onward. At the arrival of Flight 305 in Sydney, some fifty fans joined the press. He signed a few autographs as "The Phantom," then his ringleted hair and shades provoked this: *Why have you started playing rock 'n' roll?* "Is that what they call it?" *Are you a professional beatnik?* "Well, I was in the Brigade once—we used to get paid, but it didn't pay enough, so I became a singer." *Why don't you see your family?* "I wouldn't know where to find them." *Why do you wear those outlandish clothes?* "I look very normal where I live." *Does it take a lot of trouble to get your hair like that?* "No, you just have to sleep on it for about twenty years." The *Sydney Sun* described the encounter: "pygmy-sized, pallid-faced ... the expression of a man being wheeled out of the operating theater still partly under an anesthetic ... 45 minutes of nonsensical spluttering, ho-hum mumbling and vague gabbing." The *Australian*'s headline was DYLAN'S MANY HATES COME TO TOWN, while the *Sydney Daily Mirror* flailed Dylan's "insincerity." Throughout Dylan's tour, the Australian press indicated he didn't deserve publicity, but they grudgingly gave it to him.

The most balanced and sympathetic reporting was in the *Sydney Morning Herald* by Craig McGregor, whose report to me was later reworked into the Introduction to *Bob Dylan: A Retrospective*. Dylan spent most of his time writing, reading and playing new material, but he made tentative efforts to meet compatible people, holding court in hotel rooms. A road manager invited McGregor to the first Sydney concert and backstage, on April 13, in the 10,000-seat Sydney Stadium, where Dylan was somewhat unnerved by a revolving stage which swept a full ninety degrees after each song. McGregor found him during the intermission, squatting on the floor, chain-smoking, and tried to explain to him that he was "a writer," not a member of "the press," which Dylan was rampaging against.

The *Sun* shone in two directions, the first day headlining SYDNEY'S WACKIEST CONCERT, and the second day calling the concert "a rare blend of integrity, artistry and intellectualism." On April 15, the troupe flew north to Brisbane. The *Telegraph* fanfared: NO FANFARE TO GREET FOLKSINGER, a curious piece of non-news. To the Brisbane press, Dylan conceded that his songs had a message, but couldn't say what it was for fear of offending people. The two-hour Brisbane concert had amplification problems, although some witnesses said the sheer volume of sound was "colossal." No particular animosity during the electric set. The next day, the *Bulletin* carried a cover story with two pages of inaccurate, speculative appraisal. The *Brisbane Courier* headline: ADVICE TO DYLAN: STAY DYLAN. Caption in the *Adelaide Mail*: "Folksy Millionaire." The *Perth News* went to lengths: "10-inch long hair, half-inch long fingernails and a very long bank account. And a long list of Australian fans were shocked when he said ... he was not disturbed about color discrimination nor young people dying in war." No such list could be compiled. Dylan's main Australian support came from Sydney artists and writers, including the founders of the underground magazine *Oz*, Richard Neville and Martin Sharp. Among folk fans, controversy ran high, but the *Australian*'s folk critic, Edgar Waters, wrote sympathetically: "Dylan remains the most effective voice for the feelings of the most intelligent and sensitive people of his generation. The ugly sound and the hysterical tone are essential for what he has to say."

For his final Sydney stadium concert, which was sold out, the sound system was better and the audience more appreciative. Dylan was beginning to feel somewhat more at home. The following morning, Sunday, as the *Sun-Herald* headlined: DYLAN NOT HERE TO WIN HEARTS, the troupe flew to Melbourne for two concerts. They were greeted by around 400 fans and/or curiosity-seekers and the press: *What is your greatest ambition?* "To be a meat-cutter." *Can you enlarge on that?* "Large pieces of meat." *Do you think it's a good thing or a bad thing that youngsters try to copy you?* "It's a thing." *What do you think of Australia?* "Since I was a little boy, I've wanted to come to Australia. I once knew someone who knew somebody whose grandfather was supposed to have heard of Australia. This gave me a tremendous curiosity to find out whether this fellow really did have a grandfather." *You also came for the money, I take it?* "I take it." *How do you present your show?* "With my clothes on. That's the only part of my act that I haven't got under control yet." *Is it true that you don't care about color discrimination or war any longer?* "I'm just a storyteller." *Don't you really care?* "I can't really tell you how I care. I just can't. They never ask me these questions in America. They tried to make a clown of me for three years and now I won't give interviews. I have been writing myself—for fifteen years. I know how reporters have to eat, but I won't let them use me. Sure, I have a feeling about war, about Vietnam. My thoughts lie in the futility of war, not the morality of it."

At the two concerts in Melbourne, audiences were puzzled rather than annoyed by the rock segments. A *Melbourne Age* reporter showed some understanding: "Dylan rocked backwards and forwards as if feeling faint from the onslaught … for a few he wove long answers of fairy-tale fancy— nonsensical but sharply amusing ... if anybody had been tempted to lose his patience, it was Dylan … Dylan tries without conceit to explain that he's a 'watcher,' embroiled in nothing … But the publicity people these days demand non-conformists who are conforming non-conformists" The *Melbourne Sun* thought his writing "shows a deep understanding of human motives … it is ruthless, cutting but not cruel. It simply is."

Early on April 21, Dylan headed to Adelaide, where several hundred people milled about on the tarmac, though it was said that only eight were Dylan's reception committee. "Where are all the cowboys, huh?" he asked, before driving off to another hotel, another press conference. During the show's electric segment a few people walked out. The *Adelaide Advertiser* said he "captivated his audience," but described him as "sounding … like Peter Lorre, looking like … Harpo Marx and walking like a marionette." The next day, he flew two thousand miles westward to Perth. On arrival, a barefoot Dylan said: "I had a choppy flight across your desert." Around a hundred people met him. Another press conference found him in good, bitter form:

When do you write your songs? "I never write on Fridays, or on Tuesday nights. It's an old Mexican tradition." *Why do you write?* "People get thirsty, they drink. People get hungry, they eat. When I get hungry, I write." *What do you think of the Vietnam War?* "Nothing. It's Australia's war." *But Americans are there.* "They're just helping the Australians." *Some people call you a genius—do you agree?* "People who call me a genius don't have any grandparents." *You say you don't want to be thought an oddball. Why do you wear clothes like that, and long hair?* "My clothes are traditional." *Is it true you don't wash your hair or clean your teeth?* "It's a lie. I have four sets of teeth." *How much money have you made out of your songs?* "Seventy-five billion dollars." *How have you found your Australian tour?* "It's the differentest I've done."

After a concert at Perth's Capitol Theater on April 23, Bob went to a party briefly, then returned to his hotel to find a young actress, Rosemary Gerrette. Her mother was the *Canberra Times*'s features editor and, although Rosemary knew virtually nothing about Dylan, she wanted an interview. She befriended him over the next few days. Evidently deeply affected by the encounter, she retold it for years afterward. She contacted me in 1977. When I said she'd already been heard from, albeit as an anonymous actress, in several pages in Anthony Scaduto's book, she replied: "I deserve more than that." Her account, in the *Canberra Times* of May 7, was of a typical all-night songwriting session. Dylan read to her from *Tarantula* and told her: "People don't value their obscurity. They don't know what it's like to have it taken away." She heard a lot of literature talk and observed Baudelaire, Durrell, Australian poetry, and a Norman Mailer work strewn around the room. Dylan and crew left Perth on a twenty-seven-hour flight to Stockholm. Ripples in the Australian press continued for some weeks. "Rainy Day Women" was duly released, and duly banned.

Crusade in Europe.   Heavy with fatigue and jet lag, Dylan and the Hawks arrived in Stockholm for a one-nighter on April 29. Scandinavian audiences were surprised by the presence of "the Group," which some saw as a sell-out. In Stockholm, Dylan did a five-minute radio interview, which has since been bootlegged, and a press conference. Dylan had some questions for the Copenhagen press: "How far is the nearest cow?" and "Where's Hamlet's castle?"

Dylan's May 5 concert in Dublin's Adelphi Theatre was a critical disaster. By now the show was truncated to ninety-five minutes, with fifty minutes for the acoustic set and the last forty-five minutes electric. *Disc and Music Echo* said an "appreciative and orderly" audience erupted during the second half. Shouts of "traitor," "throw out the backing group," "stuffed golliwog," and "lower the mike" broke out. The Anglo-Irish form of derision, the slow handclap, resounded. Even the music press was taken aback. *Melody Maker*: "It was unbelievable to see a hip-swinging Dylan trying to look and sound like Mick Jagger … for most, it was the night of the big let-down." The *Irish Times*: "a minor [poet] were he to publish in slim volumes without … a guitar, harmonica and publicity machine, it is something to sell poetry to a mass-audience at all."

Ray Coleman summarized the reaction: "If the 1965 tour was an unequivocal success, his return must be reckoned as taking the British public back to square one. There was widespread bitterness about his abandonment of the acoustic guitar. The Beatles turned out for his Albert Hall concert and pronounced Bob 'great, just great.' Afterwards, George Harrison defended Dylan's right to use a band: 'The people who walked out must have been idiots and they couldn't have known the real Dylan. It was all still pure Dylan, and he has to find out his own directions. If he felt he wanted electrification, that's the way he had to do it. Who's laying down rules?' When the jeering was going on," Coleman continued, "the Beatles, sitting in a box behind me in Albert Hall, shouted 'Leave him alone—*shut up*!' to the moaners."

By the time Dylan arrived in London, his camera crew—many of whom had worked on *Don't Look Back* the previous year—had taken over. They shot a one-hour, 16-mm color film that was originally scheduled for the ABC-TV series *Stage 67*. The film, *Eat the Document*, has rarely been shown publicly. It was screened twice on February 9, 1971, at the Academy of Music in Manhattan, and from November 30 through December 13, 1972, at the Whitney Museum of American Art. By then the film ran fifty-four minutes, after Dylan's and Howard Alk's editing. The Museum's publicity described it as an "anti-document … an adventuresome … challenge to all the preconceived notions we have of a star and his public image." Jonas Mekas wrote in the *Village Voice*: "About the richest … the best, of all films on rock … we can feel his attitude … a combination of expectation, exuberance, and great joy of living."

Vincent Canby in the *New York Times* (December 1, 1972) was skeptical about this portrait of "the poet of paranoia." He credited Alk for having shot much of the film with Pennebaker, and also for making, with Dylan, the new cut after ABC had rejected the version for not telling "what city are we in, what's happening?" From Alk's program notes: "the editors looked … for … conversations unheld, events untranspired. Some real music, some not. Murder, villainy, travel, slavery and lust. We hope a real movie. Perhaps even a comedy."

During the shooting, Donn Pennebaker was again nominally in charge, but he later told me that *Eat the Document* had "become Dylan's film. He took over. He was quite dragged by the performances, but I thought the songs were extraordinary. The original title was *Dylan By Pennebaker*, but Dylan changed it to *Eat The Document*, from a line by Al Aronowitz. This time, Dylan got much more involved in the actual filmmaking. Some of it was shot at the Olympia in Paris. I think some of the very best footage was at Bob's birthday party. In Scotland, I stayed right on stage shooting—an incredible thing to do. The best was probably in Glasgow. The halation effect from the fast film was incredible. It really caught the psychedelic aura of drugs and rock on stage. Whatever Bob's reservations about the final cut, I think it was a major jump forward from *Don't Look Back*."

A twenty-minute press conference in London brought out some hostility, but the reporter from *Disc and Music Echo* understood his quizzical style: "He is rude … to people … he considers they ask stupid questions. He is uncooperative … but is also a very sympathetic man with a vast sense of humor … this man … was asked … ridiculous questions … no wonder he lost his patience." Another *Disc* writer, Jonathan King, said Dylan treated the press like "a faceless crowd of starving vultures … downright bad manners."

The first English concert was on May 10 in Bristol's Colston Hall. Walkouts among the capacity audience, no encores, and uniformly bad reviews. The *Gloucester Citizen*: "The majority who stuck it out remained icily indifferent to their idol's sacrifice of lyric and melody to the god of big beat." Letters to the *Bristol Evening Post*: "the outstanding poet who had meant so much in my life, has now ruined himself." Another: "I have just attended a funeral … They buried … Dylan … in a grave of guitars … and deafening drums … My only consolation, Woody Guthrie wasn't there to witness it."

The Welsh audience at Cardiff's Capitol Theatre, May 11, showed more respect. While ironing out amplification problems, one of the English roadies evicted all press and even theater staff: "One would not expect to be allowed to see Marlene Dietrich before she was completely ready." *Stage and Television Today* remarked that the Cardiff audience "seems to have accepted the new image ... with remarkably little pain."

In Birmingham on May 12, the show at the Odeon started forty-five minutes late. The pre-Cardiff pattern returned: respect for the acoustic solo section, hostility toward the rock segment. There were huffy walkouts, cries of "Folk phony," "Traitor," "Give us the real Dylan," "Yank, go home," and "We want folk." The *Birmingham Mail and Dispatch*: DYLAN, THE LEGEND, DISAPPOINTS. *Melody Maker*: "Birmingham flatly rejected ... all-electric folk ... Between numbers, he turned his back to the audience for long periods ... giving the hecklers plenty of opportunity." The *Stratford-upon-Avon Herald* saw this as image destruction: "hero of our time, a sort of demi-god we had all gone along to worship ... tried to smash his halo ... I'm with you, Bob, all the way."

Then to the Beatles' turf, the Liverpool Odeon, on May 14.[5] No advance publicity and precious little notice he had been there. When one heckler shouted: "Where's the poet in you?" and "What's happened to your conscience?" Dylan retorted: "There's a guy up there looking for a saint." After a successful first half in Leicester on May 15, jeers of "get them off" greeted the Hawks, along with whistling and walkouts. The *Cambridge Times*: "to say his audience didn't appreciate this 'kick in the teeth' would be ... an understatement." In the *Illustrated Leicester Chronicle*, David Sandison, later press chief for Island, EMI, and CBS Records: "Dylan has a great band to support him ... probably one of the greatest young poets alive ... doing what ... Ginsberg and Corso have been doing in free verse ... Dylan is producing poetry ... Perhaps those who spoiled ... the concert will also mature ... and realise ... their prejudice is almost as great as the prejudices Dylan used to campaign against."

Probably a crank, not a folklore purist, telephoned the Sheffield Gaumont on May 16, warning of "a big bang." The fire brigade and bomb squad searched fruitlessly while 2,000 people remained unaware in the theater. By the Manchester gig, the rude part of the press and audience was a conformist mob with reactionary views and Neanderthal aesthetics. Why they continued to hoot is difficult to fathom. Certainly, they knew by then what to expect, yet they seemed to delight in taking folk-rock as a personal affront. The Manchester Free Trade Hall concert on May 17 was another station of the cross. Dylan apologized that the sound was too loud, but this didn't quell the hostility.

Although there were hecklers and walkouts at the Glasgow Odeon on May 19, those who liked the new music shouted down those who didn't. Someone yelled: "We want Dylan." Bob replied: "Dylan got sick backstage. I'm here to take his place." While the antis were yelling: "Traitor!" and "Belt up!" the pros were shouting: "Get your ears washed!" Edinburgh, Friday, May 20, the ABC Theatre, another divided audience. Dylan found a broken reed in his mouth harp, but Andrew Young of Haystack Cottage handed up his own. Dylan finished the song, got a new harmonica backstage, and returned the borrowed harp along with one of his own. The Scottish *Daily Express*: "booed off the stage again last night ... Some of the audience took out mouth-organs and tried to play down his singing" When Dylan played the Newcastle Odeon on May 21, "One Too Many Mornings" elicited shouts of "Show us what you can do" and "Take some lessons from the Animals!" But when he began "Rolling Stone," listeners greeted it warmly.

Dylan's Paris Olympia concert was on May 24, his twenty-fifth birthday. Two-thousand seats costing up to sixty francs sold out a month in advance. Some tickets went to French performers Johnny Hallyday, Charles Trenet, Françoise Hardy, Hugues Aufray, and Antoine. Nowhere did the press gallivant as in France. The day Dylan arrived, some 10,000 young people were attending a festival at Oullins organized by the French labor unions. Aufray, whose Barclay recording of Dylan songs had made him the leading Gallic interpreter, announced the arrival, "at this moment," at Le Bourget airport, of "my friend" Dylan. Remarked the Lyons paper *Le Progrès*: "The applause doubled in intensity. The star, one sensed, was Dylan, not Aufray." Other references compared Dylan to Rimbaud, Proust, James Dean, François Villon, and Homer. The French "hipoisie" had an especial affinity for Dylan because of their *chansonniers*, poet-singers like Jacques Brel, Gilbert Becaud, and Georges Brassens. Even Hallyday, then the 23-year-old Gallic rock star, felt Dylan was *un ami*. He spent one night taking him around Paris, and gave him a Turkish water pipe for his birthday. Paris has more astrologers than psychotherapists, and the French press relished the coincidence that Hallyday, Antoine, and Dylan were all Geminis.

The French also liked Dylan for his allegiance to peace, for his fondness for Beaujolais and Bardot, and for his poetics. Philippe Labro in *Elle*, May 6: "He ... sings of the America of backstreets, dirty little bars, back-room pool-players ... air filled with smoke, heavy and sweaty ... snatches of speech ... nothing actually happens, but it is from this that the greatest books (Steinbeck, Caldwell, Faulkner) and the greatest films (Rossen, especially) have come ... Dylan is an authentic poet, a writer. He is, in this milieu, the only true writer."

One newspaper inaccurately reported he had sold 18 million recordings and that his annual income was more than a million dollars. Parisian journalists also noted that at the Olympia, Dylan would command as much as Maria Callas—"more," opined *Paris Jour*, "than a worker earns in ten years." The press was also truculent about Dylan's staying at the George V Hotel, where he was ushered into a luxurious suite bedizened with Spanish master paintings and Louis XV furniture. "What's this?" Dylan reportedly said to the *maître d'hotel*. "You should have known I don't dig Louis the Fifteenth. If you don't get me a decent suite in the next five minutes, I'll take the airplane right back to America." *Monsieur* was shown into another luxurious suite, sans Louis XV—but with a carpet whose color *monsieur* didn't like. He relented, "Well, if we have to camp, let's camp." The press conference at the George V on May 23 was a predictable debacle. One reporter asked what Dylan thought about the Allied invasion in World War II! Dylan was offhand and petulant. Some photographs show him holding a large wooden puppet, named Monsieur Finian. Asked what song he would choose to conclude the conference, Dylan said: "Hello, Dolly."

In Paris, an old friend surfaced—Mike Porco of Gerde's Folk City. Returning from his native Calabria, Mike went to considerable lengths to see "Bobby." Heading toward the George V, Mike ran into Grossman, who said, "Dylan isn't seeing anyone. He is tired. I don't think it can be arranged." Mike persisted and got into Bob's suite, where he got a gracious welcome. "Bobby couldn't do enough for me, just the opposite of what Grossman had made me feel. He introduced me to everyone, and said I was like his father, like his uncle, like his pal. It really made me feel good. It was funny, remembering what he'd looked like here, to see him in that hotel in Paris."

The concert was anticlimactic. The audience tended to be unruly, but Dylan wasn't passive to heckling. Someone had draped the stage with a large American flag. Many shouted: "Happy Birthday!" When he took time to tune his guitar (some said fourteen minutes), jeers were silenced by Dylan saying: "I'm doing this for you. I couldn't care less. I wouldn't behave like that if I came to see you." The Paris *Trib*, reporting that Dylan's nervous strain had weakened his performance, concluded that "this strange figure, with his beautiful handling of an unruly audience and his haunting 'Desolation Row' ... leaves an impression that will linger."

The Olympia crowd seemed to like the electric set; the Hawks thawed out a rather tense audience. Still, most reviews were vitriolic. *Le Figaro*, under the headline THE FALL OF AN IDOL, suggested that the audience had heard Dylan's double, an ill-looking puppet "unable to overcome his narcotism." *Arts Paris* lambasted Dylan for abandoning music-hall tradition, and concluded that derision, violence, and mental breakdown were themes too serious for songs. *Le Havre Libre* unequivocally called the concert a failure. *Paris Jour* took umbrage at Dylan's remarks during tuning breaks, such as "Hasn't anyone got a newspaper to read?" and "Don't worry, I'm just as eager to finish and leave as you are."[6]

A few critics were sympathetic. *L'Évenement* said he was misunderstood. *L'Humanité* wrote that "they found his 'Dylano-American' difficult and consequently did not understand what he was singing about." In fact, Dylan had asked his audience if they understood English, and many in the audience had said yes. Rouen's *Liberté Dimanche* acclaimed Dylan because he had "re-established poetry for the masses. He is in some way the Homer of the 20th Century." A Paris paper, the *Detective*, proffered a clue: "The secret of his success is his indifference. He is irritating, and therefore he interests people." *Paris Jour*'s headline writer was most explicit: BOB DYLAN, GO HOME. After returning to London's Albert Hall, he did.

The Victorian pile that is Royal Albert Hall, despite its notorious acoustics, its antediluvian pomp and impersonality, is Britain's Carnegie Hall. There, on May 26 and 27, Dylan's first world tour ended with two contentious concerts that followed the provincial pattern: rapt attention for his solo acoustic work and anger during his electric set. According to Ray Coleman: "Hundreds walked out during his final show. There is no doubt Dylan was angry with the people who walked out. He was visibly hurt and their walkout seemed to inject even more determination into him to carry on with the electrified group. I thought the group was a shame, because on that night it was such a shambles of noise. We just couldn't hear his words. It was tragic."

The *Times* reported that Dylan's voice was "all but drowned out by his accompanists," while the *Sunday Times* critic found himself with "about 9,000 in the audience, agreeing with the heckler who shouted 'turn the drummer off!'" Praising the opening half for its "savage melancholy," he felt the group created "pandemonium out of chaos." The *Morning Star* called the concerts "Dylan's musical disaster ... one of Albert Hall's most bizarre musical occasions ... rare moments of brilliance came wrapped up in slurred phrases and ridiculously accented diction."

Dylan probably talked most to the Albert Hall audiences. To hecklers demanding protest songs, he said: "Oh, come on, these are all protest songs." The *Daily Telegraph* wrote that this remark "checked a dangerous situation, but after that, whole rows sat with scarcely a sign of applause ... He is beginning to show the signs of a man who does not care whether he communicates or not."

Mysteries remain about the sound projection. Dylan students there, including those who appreciated folk-rock, said the sound was dreadful. Yet the famous Albert Hall bootleg has long been regarded as technically brilliant. Rock critic Dave Marsh, in *Creem* and *International Times*, called it: "The most supremely elegant piece of rock 'n' roll music I've ever heard ... royal music." The other startling aspect was his remarkable speech from the stage. Coleman wrote me that Dylan exploded to his listeners: "Aw, it's the same stuff as always—can't you *hear*?" Evidently completely fed up at the heckling and the growing storm over "Rainy Day Women," Dylan stormed back. The "Rainy Day" single was being blacklisted by American radio. Home Secretary Roy Jenkins had received an appeal from one Birmingham city councilor to ban it in Britain along with the Byrds' "Eight Miles High." According to *Melody Maker*, Dylan lashed back during the acoustic set: "I'm not going to play any more concerts in England. So I'd just like to say this next song is what your English musical papers would call a 'drug song.' I never have and never will write a 'drug song.' I don't know how to. It's not a 'drug song,' it's just vulgar. I like all my old songs. It's just that things change all the time. Everybody knows that. I never said they were 'rubbish.' That's not in my vocabulary. I wouldn't use the word 'rubbish' if it was lying on the stage and I could pick it up. This music you are going to hear—if anyone has any suggestions on how it can be played better, or how the words can be improved—we've been playing this music since we were 10 years old. Folk music was just an interruption, which was very useful. If you don't like it, that's fine. This is not English music you are listening to. You really haven't heard American music before. I want now to say what you're hearing is just songs. You're not hearing anything else but words and sounds. You can take it or leave it. If there's something you disagree with, that's great. I'm sick of people asking 'what does it mean?' It means *nothing*."

The *Melody Maker* reporter heard shouts that included "Woody Guthrie would turn over in his grave" and "Rubbish!" But the majority wanted to hear Dylan and shouted down the hecklers. Dylan continued with "Desolation Row," "Baby Blue," and then the final electric set. Finishing with "Rolling Stone," he fairly yelled the line about having to get used to it. Summarized Coleman: "The crowd who stayed, the loyal ones, cheered. He had conquered again, all right, despite the outbursts. But still we were left asking: 'Where is he going? Does anyone know? Does he?'"[7]

A Complicated Twist of Fate. Dylan and the Hawks limped back to America in June, dispirited, exhausted, and angry, only to find that Grossman had scheduled sixty-four concerts in the States for the immediate future. Dylan could say, "don't look forward" as well as "don't look back." Late Friday night, July 29, I received a telephone call from Hibbing. Dylan's father sounded distraught: "They just called me from the radio station here. They said they had a news bulletin that Bob's been badly hurt in a motorcycle accident. Do you know anything about it?" I said this was the first I had heard of it. "The Grossman office won't help me one bit on this," said Abe. "And I can't get through to Sara. Would you please see if you can find out something—anything—and call us back, collect? Bob's mother is very worried—and so am I." Four months earlier, a similar phone call had informed me of Fariña's death in a motorcycle accident. I rang the *New York Times* for more information.

"Don't Look Back," *en route* to Belfast from Dublin, May 1966, where the concert had been "a critical disaster."

That man is very far from being an artist ... who does not know longing for the innocent, the simple ... for a little friendship, devotion, familiar human happiness — the gnawing, surreptitious hankering ... for the bliss of the commonplace.
THOMAS MANN, *TONIO KRÖGER*

The condition of alienation, of being asleep, of being unconscious, of being out of one's mind, is the condition of the normal man.
R D LAING

The poet seeks refuge in muteness.
GEORGE STEINER, *SILENCE AND THE POET*[1]

...by leaving things out, he allows us the grand privilege of creating along with him. His song becomes our song because we live in those spaces. If we listen, if we work at it, we fill up the mystery, we expand and inhabit the work of art. It is the most democratic form of creation.
PETE HAMILL, 1974[2]

By silence, [the artist] frees himself from servile bondage to the world, which appears as patron, client, consumer, antagonist, arbiter, and distorter of his work ... Once he has surpassed his peers ... his pride has only one place left to go ... the craving for silence is to be ... superior to everyone else. It suggests that the artist has had the wit to ask more questions than other people, and that he possesses stronger nerves and higher standards of excellence.
SUSAN SONTAG, *THE AESTHETICS OF SILENCE*

Details about Dylan's motorcycle accident on July 29, 1966, were not easy to ascertain. It was widely reported that Dylan nearly lost his life. To me, it seems more likely that his mishap *saved* his life. The locking of the back wheel of Dylan's Triumph 500 started a chain of redemptive events that allowed him to slow down. Ellen Willis in *Cheetah*: "Gruesome rumors circulated: Dylan was dead … badly disfigured … paralyzed … insane … the new rumor was the accident had been a cover for retreat … Not since Rimbaud said 'I is another' had an artist been so obsessed with escaping identity … Dylan as an identifiable *persona* has been disappearing into his songs, which is what he wants. This terrifies his audiences."

Journalists speculated endlessly about the accident. A Tokyo music journalist even published a hospital-bedside "interview," which Dylan emphatically told me never happened. The *Chicago Tribune* in 1967: "A traditional gesture of the prophet is the retreat and the re-emergence … with a new message. A good deal of what will or won't be in pop music hangs on Dylan's re-emergence and his message." What most confused things was that while Grossman was sending out one set of signals about the accident, Dylan was sending out another.

Grossman, who had set up more than sixty concerts for 1966–67, was shopping around for a good recording contract. Dylan emphasized the serious after-effects of the accident. Albert said that although Bob had broken his neck, he would need only a couple of months before resuming work. Even this got garbled. His brother told me: "Bob never said he broke his neck. Albert broke *his* neck." So, I speculated in print that the accident's effects had been exaggerated. Immediately, David came down from Woodstock insisting: "There *was* an accident. There definitely was an accident." Hubert Saal, music editor of *Newsweek*, interviewed Dylan in early 1968 and concluded: "Dylan's current reluctance to give concerts has nothing to do with the accident, from which he appears fully recovered. 'I have more responsibilities now,' he says."

Dylan told me only: "It happened one morning after I'd been up for three days. I hit an oil slick. The damp weather still affects the wound." To others, he said he was riding along Striebel Road, not far from his Woodstock home, taking the bike into the garage for repairs, when the back wheel locked and he went hurtling over the handlebars. After the fall, he was rushed in a friend's car to Middletown Hospital with reported broken vertebrae of the neck, a possible concussion, and head and facial bruises. A major concert at the Yale Bowl, scheduled for eight days later, was canceled. Dylan only knows just how severely he was hurt and at what point in his convalescence he discovered that he wanted to think, reorganize his life, spend time with his family, and listen to the silence. Even if it was as bad as reported, the accident became a metaphor, a time for change, a possibility of release, the start of seven and a half years of withdrawal to a more tranquil existence.[3]

The music business machine doesn't like "undisciplined" performers who fall off motorbikes. Grossman is reported to have said after the accident: "How could he do this to me?" His aide, Charlie Rothschild, asked me: "Do you know how much work was involved in setting up sixty concerts?" (When I told Bob about Grossman's remark, he laughed: "That shows you where he was at, worrying about those concerts!")

Allen Ginsberg visited Dylan in late September, bringing some Emily Dickinson and Bertolt Brecht books, and said he didn't think Dylan was seriously hurt. By January 1967, Dylan's editor at Macmillan, Robert Markel, was saying: "Dylan is making a slow recovery from a bad accident. He couldn't use his eyes for a period of time and it made it difficult for him to work. But he's alive and well." Donn Pennebaker, the filmmaker, told *Melody Maker*: "I know he wasn't as sick as he made out. This provided the basis of an excuse for delaying delivery of that TV show, which is what he wanted to do. But I know he was at a doctor's. I went to see him a number of times and he was in a brace … I knew he'd been hurt in other ways, so in either event, what he was doing was recovering."

A *World Journal Tribune* reporter got as far as the rambling Cape Cod house behind Albert's, where Sara, presumably, turned him away: "We are afraid of all kinds of nuts coming around and bothering him … It gets very lonely here. Very few friends have come up and we never go into town." In January 1967, a *New York Post* reporter was chased off the property by two watchdogs, and Sara, who said he was trespassing, called the local deputy. The first reporter who did get through was Michael Iachetta of the *New York Daily News*. Dylan told Iachetta, in May 1967, that he'd been "seein' only a few close friends, readin' little 'bout the outside world, porin' over books by people you never heard of, thinkin' about where I'm goin' and why am I runnin' and am I mixed up too much, and what am I knowin' and what am I givin' and what am I takin'. And mainly what I've been doin' is workin' on gettin' better and makin' better music, which is what my life is all about." The *News* story described him as "emotionally and physically scarred." Yet Ralph Gleason quoted Grossman as saying that Dylan was putting on the *News* reporter and "is well, absolutely unscarred, and is planning possible concerts this fall."

During Dylan's retreat in Woodstock and New York City until the end of 1973, his creative work flourished. He immersed himself in the family life so often denied the pop star. Apparently in retreat behind a cloud of mystery, he was continually sending out messages to friends in random interviews and in songs. A handful reveal Dylan's changing world view. "Too Much of Nothing," with its Lear-like stress on nothingness, and its "waters of oblivion" line echoing the English poet Ernest Dowson, indicted the vacuous rock scene from which he was detaching himself. "I Shall Be Released" was clearly a search for personal salvation. "The Drifter's Escape" was a transparent parable about a person, trapped by a role, who awaits a sentence of doom before a hostile crowd, when he is almost magically delivered from the courtroom. The song's "bolt of lightning" could be Dylan's accident. In "Watching the River Flow," a man changes from participant to observer. "Sign on the Window" and "If Dogs Run Free" are the apotheosis of personal contentment in a love relationship. The audience, not aware of what he and the Band had endured around the world, couldn't understand his need for privacy, and felt rejected. Dylan was repeatedly compelled to justify his withdrawal.

To *Newsweek*, he said: "I stared at the ceiling for a few months. But since I've often sat around staring at ceilings, it didn't bother me much. I haven't been in retreat. I'm a country boy myself, and you have to be let alone to really accomplish anything." In the *Chicago Tribune* on April 28, 1968, Dylan already seemed to be thinking about the 1974–75 Rolling Thunder Revue: "If I'm going to be out there it's got to be something that moves, that takes everyone along." The rumors still accreted, including one that Dylan feared he would be assassinated. By 1969, Dylan could tell London's *Evening Standard* that the accident "in many ways … was good for me. It really slowed me down … touring had been such a pace to keep up. And I was getting in a rut."

Robbie Robertson told the *Saturday Evening Post*: "We did it until we couldn't do it anymore … We were so exhausted that everyone said this was a time to rest. We stopped listening to music for a year." As late as spring 1975, Dylan was explaining to Mary Travers on her radio series that "we needed to dry out." Dylan was saying that there must be another way of life for the pop star, in which *he* is in control, not *they*. He had to find ways of working to his own advantage, with the recording industry, his book publisher, the TV network. He had to come to terms with his one-time friend, long-time manager, part-time neighbor, and sometime landlord, Albert Grossman.

Dylan's Columbia recording contract had run out. Grossman had asked the new Columbia chief, Clive Davis, for an enormous guaranty for a long-term contract. When Davis asked why the figure was so high, Grossman reportedly said: "Because it is there." In 1966, when Davis took over, Columbia was in some trouble. Davis, an aggressive young corporate lawyer, had risen as a protégé of Goddard Lieberson. Before Davis left in 1973, he had changed the record division's pretax profits from $5 million a year to $50 million. In 1966, Davis was a master at pressuring his employees and artists. He wanted to keep Dylan under contract, but did not want to get involved in the high-money sweepstakes Grossman was playing with MGM and Capitol, among others. Davis felt he held the trump card because he knew that Dylan's influence then ran considerably ahead of his actual sales.

By Christmas, 1966, MGM was announcing that Dylan had been signed. According to contract provisions, Dylan owed Columbia another fourteen tracks, or one album. In the *New York Post*, Nora Ephron revealed that a flaw in Dylan's contract would allow Columbia to dump an enormous amount of past royalties on him in one year, delivering about ninety percent of his profits for that year to the tax people. In April 1967, Columbia halted all Dylan's sales. This suspension was settled almost immediately, with Dylan committing himself to supplying the songs. Davis told Allen Klein, the controversial manager involved in a proxy fight at MGM, that Dylan's sales were not quite what MGM thought. Although MGM had Dylan's signature, MGM hadn't countersigned.

Meanwhile, Grossman and Dylan were having second thoughts about MGM. Grossman went back to Davis offering Dylan for double his former royalty. Davis wrote in his 1974 autobiography, *Clive: Inside the Record Business*: "I thought it was a perfect solution, and I grabbed it. The royalties were twice anything we'd ever paid before, but it was worth it to keep Dylan." On August 21, 1967, Columbia proudly announced it had re-signed Dylan to an exclusive, long-term contract. Soon Bob was back in the studio, recording *John Wesley Harding*.

Dylan's two previous Columbia contracts had scarcely inspired his confidence. Davis had persuaded Dylan not to challenge his first contract because he had signed as a minor. Davis had also informed Dylan that his John Birch song was potentially libelous. But as Columbia's chief operating officer, Davis got on better with Dylan. Davis maintains that at a meeting between the two Guthrie memorial concerts in January 1968, the pair established a working rapport. Dylan started to send Davis tapes from studio sessions. Davis recalls that just before each album came out, Dylan would surface. As Dylan started to handle his own business and drift away from Grossman, Davis "had the feeling that he needed someone to bring him ideas, goad him a bit, make suggestions, offer help if he needed it. This is not easy to do with Dylan, of course, and I had to tread very softly." Bob told me that there was recurring friction at Columbia: "Whatever I want to do, somebody is against it. I work with whatever A&R man I want and have nothing whatsoever to do with Clive Davis."

After the "Lay, Lady, Lay" hit from *Nashville Skyline*, which became Dylan's best-selling album to date, reaching 1.2 million copies, Davis's litany ran that Dylan could double each album's sales with a hit single. Dylan refused to release a single from *New Morning*, which sold only half of what *Nashville* did. "Sometimes … he was as mercurial and unpredictable as the legends said. He would be gentle, polite, and cooperative — or indecisive, suspicious, and quite impatient … in the studio, he was an efficiency expert's dream … things happened fast … most songs in one take. Simon and Garfunkel might take up to eighteen months to record an album … Dylan came into the studio, played his songs … and that was it. He took an extremely casual, almost lax attitude toward the recording process … To him, the song was the thing and everything else was secondary."[4] After the taping, Dylan would become an absolute hawk about album design, title, timing. Then, the album released, he would drift back into his silence.

When Dylan's Columbia contract expired in 1972, another period of uncertainty began. Bob, wary of any long-term commitment, also had some deep differences of opinion with Columbia. When the film *Pat Garrett and Billy the Kid* was negatively reviewed in the *New York Times*, Davis and others suggested Dylan hold back his soundtrack album. He released it, and film and album ultimately did very well.

Dylan's contract renewal also came at a time when Davis was deeply embattled at Columbia. Still, his was probably the strongest voice in the company for letting Dylan do things his way. Davis said a new contract was drawn up, allowing for the *Pat Garrett* album plus two more, at "a guaranty of about $400,000 per album." After Davis left the company, the agreement was canceled. By this point, Dylan had already planned Tour '74 and was getting close to David Geffen of Elektra/Asylum Records, part of the WEA empire, Columbia's chief rival. But Dylan gave Geffen only one album, *Planet Waves*. In the light of millions of requests for tour tickets, Dylan was disappointed when the album sold only about 700,000 copies.

Meanwhile, Davis remained in touch with Dylan. At the end of 1973, at Columbia's annual sales meeting, Lieberson, back at the helm, announced: "I don't doubt that there were times when record companies exploited artists, but it had come to the point where the artists were exploiting the record companies." Nevertheless, Dylan had Lieberson and Geffen bidding up the royalty for the live double album, *Before the Flood*, until Dylan finally released it with Asylum. Then, Davis maintained, Columbia wanted Dylan back, "seemingly at any cost. They had come to understand their loss … Columbia will spare nothing to bring Dylan back into the fold. They finally understand that they need Dylan and have no choice but to lure him with an outstanding royalty, not only on new albums, but also on his extensive catalogue. It's been an expensive lesson, indeed."[5]

The post-accident period also saw problems between Dylan and ABC-TV over the two-hour special for its *Stage 67* series, the film that later surfaced as *Eat the Document* and which was shot in England during

Dylan's 1966 world tour. In April 1967, an ABC spokesman said the show had been canceled because of a disagreement over the format. For a $100,000 advance, ABC had received footage in November 1966 that the network described as "totally unsatisfactory." ABC was contemplating legal action. In the 1968 *Sing Out!* interview, Dylan told John Cohen: "The film had been cut just to nothing … we were hoping to discover something … we tried to construct a stage and an environment … the program folded and by the time we handed it in, they had already a state-wide search begun to confiscate the film … So we were a little pressured here and there … it's hard to do a tour, and in the after hours to make a movie."[6]

The accident also delayed publication of *Tarantula*. Dylan had been appalled by Macmillan's pre-publication publicity and still had reservations about the book. He told *Sing Out!*: "I learned not to do a book like that … where the contract comes in before the book is written, so you have to fulfill the contract … there was no difficulty in writing it at all, it just wasn't a book, it was just a nuisance. It didn't have that certain quality which now I think a book should have. It didn't have any structure at all, it was just one flow. It flowed for ninety pages … they were short little lines, nothing within a big framework. I couldn't even conceive of doing anything in a big framework at that time."[7]

Dylan's relationship with his manager was in delicate shape. In November 1965, they had organized a music publishing company, Bob Dylan Words and Music, to follow his three-year contract with Witmark/Music Publishers Holding Corporation. Artie Mogull managed this enterprise, for a time. Grossman and Dylan were otherwise tightly linked but, by early 1968, Dylan wanted to be free. During the Guthrie memorial concerts in January 1968, Albert and Bob scarcely spoke to each other.

At the Isle of Wight, Grossman's partner, Bert Block, handled arrangements. By November 1969, Block sold out his interest to Grossman, after a three-year association. (Block joined Jerry Perenchio's Chartwell Artists, and was soon representing Kris Kristofferson.) In late 1970, Woodstock buzzed with reports of the falling-out of its two glamorous residents. Taxi drivers and motel owners talked of an unverified "huge settlement" that ran to more than a million dollars. Bernard Paturel, owner of Woodstock's Café Espresso and friend to both, asked me later: "The poet and the stern businessman—how long could it last?" In spring 1971, Charlie Rothschild told me that Naomi Saltzman, an executive secretary at Grossman's, had played "an important role in Dylan's split with Albert." She denied this to me. Dylan subsequently hired Saltzman as his music publisher. In May 1971, Dylan was expressing relief that his contract with Grossman was finally settled, and that he'd be free by June. Bob told me: "I finally had to sue him. Because Albert wanted it quiet, he settled out of court. He had me signed up for ten years … can you believe that? For part of my records, for part of my everything. He only had me for twenty percent. There were others who had to give him fifty percent." We talked about Albert's Woodstock empire—his recording studio and his restaurant, the Bear. Dylan expressed astonishment that Grossman could drop a sophisticated Continental restaurant into an old farmhouse. Dylan was describing the restaurant, but possibly more, when he said: "Albert's got terrible taste—and you can quote that." Amazed that things had finally reached the impasse I'd seen growing since 1964, I wondered if Dylan was finished with Albert. He was equivocal: "A lot of people would run Albert down, but I wouldn't." Although the three years in Woodstock after the accident may have looked idyllic, Bob told me afterward: "Woodstock was a daily excursion to nothingness." He said he'd moved back to the Village in late 1969 because his Woodstock home "had become a joke. There were tours, people up there were trying to pick up a piece of the earth, a piece of the lawn, or the shrubs." Another paradise lost; still no direction home.

"The Town that Fathered a Nation."

Woodstock, some 130 miles up the Hudson from Manhattan, in New York's Ulster County, at the eastern fringe of the Catskills, numbers 6,000 residents year-round. It swells to perhaps four times that number in the summer. For more than eighty years, Woodstock has been a magnet for those seeking creativity in the clean air. Originally an arts-and-crafts colony and a rural theatrical center, it is inhabited by descendants of Dutch settlers, successive waves of artists, craftspeople, dancers, musicians, urban dropouts and rebels looking for a green alternative to Greenwich Village and executives from IBM and trendy accountants seeking to put a little color in their lives. In the early 1960s, Pete Yarrow seduced several people up the Woodstock Valley, and soon the place had a new pop-music mystique pasted atop its old art frame. Nearly everyone agrees it used to be a lot better.

Dylan's efforts at finding refuge, rest and restoration in Woodstock spread over six years, from 1963 onward. He moved there in 1965, but by 1969 he was ready to regard it as a dream lost. His sanctuary had turned into a zoo. For a recluse who really likes and needs people, the secret of where he lived was difficult to keep. Although famous artists had been migrating to Woodstock since the early 1900s, none drew as many pilgrims. The writers Tagore and Thomas Mann had at one time lived in Woodstock, as had actors Lee Marvin and Edward G Robinson, the painter Kuniyoshi, scholars, and art collectors. Among Dylan's neighbors were composer Aaron Copland, painter Anton Refregier, writer Mason Hoffenberg. Woodstock's center is an alfresco Greenwich Village—book and antique shops, health food stores, boutiques, head shops, galleries, restaurants, real-estate agents. Richard Goldstein called Woodstock Valley "the great green hope for the urban blues"—the beautiful reservoir, the Big Deep swimming hole, Overlook Mountain and Echo Lake, the waterfall at Haines Falls.

In 1902, the heir to a Yorkshire textile fortune, Ralph Radcliffe Whitehead, set up an arts colony in Woodstock to embody a wholesome return to nature, a refuge against the Industrial Revolution. Whitehead had been influenced by English philosopher John Ruskin's alternatives to the industrial society. Whitehead, with Hervey White, a writer and social worker, and Bolton Brown, an art professor, spent years combing America. Brown had climbed Overlook Mountain above Woodstock and saw there "an earthly paradise." Whitehead disliked the Catskills because they were "full of Jews," but his two aides and the scenery persuaded him. Since the 1870s, the Valley had been friendly toward circus and theater folk. Whitehead bought up seven farms, about 1,200 acres, below Mead's Mountain, and began constructing thirty buildings. He dubbed his colony Byrdcliffe, and spent $500,000 to set up workshops, homes, and schools. In June 1903, craftspeople, students, and teachers poured in. Byrdcliffe colonists, in corduroy and denim, romanticized rural life.

The patrician Whitehead was no democrat; he liked to be called the Dictator of Byrdcliffe. The colony could not support itself making furniture and color prints. After the first summer, students recoiling from Whitehead's authoritarianism dropped out; the staff was divided. Brown, fired by the "Master," bought thirty acres in Woodstock's Rock City district. White, infused with Whitmanesque idealism, led a secession from Byrdcliffe in 1904 and founded the Maverick Colony on a farm three miles south-east, in Hurley.

By 1906, the Art Students League Summer School moved to Woodstock, into a former Woodstock livery stable and undertaker's shop. The art students shook up the town. Beards and berets were in, then out. For a time, shaved heads and paint-smirched trousers were student uniforms. These first Woodstock hippies reveled in penury, slept out of doors with whom they chose. The separate colonies began to divide the town three ways. The students called Whitehead's Byrdcliffe "Boredstiffe." The League became a leading landscape school, attracting two hundred students by 1912. The Maverick let its cabins to musicians, writers, and Clarence Darrow and Thorstein Veblen.

Eventually, the Maverick and Byrdcliffe colonies began to join forces. In August 1915, at Woodstock's first festival, all three colonies joined in White's money-raising jamboree—campfire suppers, eccentric costumes, chamber music in a natural quarry amphitheater. After ten years of aloofness, Whitehead began to treat White civilly. The Woodstock art colony matured in the 1920s. Although the Art Students League School closed from 1923 to 1946, several private art schools filled the gap. The Maverick Concerts thrived, as did White's restaurant, the Intelligencia. By 1924, the Maverick Theater was built, and later Woodstock had as many as six rural theater productions at the same time. Edward G Robinson, Eva Le Gallienne, and Maria Ouspenskaya became linked with Woodstock. An art association and a chamber of commerce found much basis for cooperation. The old prejudice against Jews diminished, but not without some Ku Klux Klan activity in the district. With Whitehead's death in 1929 and the Depression, a new phase began. In the 1940s, Leadbelly and Pete Seeger used to visit; Sam Eskin was the local folk song authority. By White's death in 1944, neither the Maverick nor Byrdcliffe dominated; Woodstock was one community.

After the war, industry marched up the Hudson, engineers and administrators from Kingston bought Woodstock homes. Although Whitehead had imported the "simple" life of folk music, dance, and peace— Whitehead's son, Peter, kept Byrdcliffe alive, barely—the town now resisted the influx of young 1960s rebels and seekers. Now, the city fathers rallied to defend moral and land values with anti-hippie harassment. There were arrests for drug possession or trespassing, for skinny-dipping in local swimming holes. The spring before the 1969 Woodstock Festival, locals looted and burned a "Karma meditation center" on the state forest preserve in Woodstock. Finally, the town banned the 1969 Woodstock Festival and tried unsuccessfully to force the happening in Bethel to drop Woodstock's name.

Dylan's friend/chauffeur/bodyguard Bernard Paturel on Woodstock: "There's a magic here, an emanation. Lots of musicians, artisans, and writers. A gifted person would feel these vibrations, and get support from people like that living there. There is something in the air. You can visit someone who might have the same spirit, the same attitude. But all this could be lost with over-saturation. Many people are coming up here who having nothing to *give*, they're only here to *get*. Some are trying to just bring the city up to the country." Public and private Woodstock are different entities. What you see in the restaurants, boutiques, or in music clubs like Sled Hill, are only surface matters. The "scene" in Woodstock is behind shrubbed driveways and closed doors. The pilgrims rarely got that far. At the time of the Woodstock Festival, living in and around Woodstock were Dylan, the Band, Van Morrison, Frank Zappa and the Mothers of Invention, Tim Hardin, and a fluid roster of Grossman's musicians, aides, and roadies.

After staying at Peter Yarrow's rough Woodstock shack in 1963, Dylan used to steal up there often. He started to use Bernard Paturel's upstairs hideaway at the Espresso, even if he was staying at Albert's estate in adjacent Bearsville, where there were often too many people. By 1970, Albert's house, the old stone Striebel place, was said to be worth three times the $45,000 Grossman had paid for it. Albert put in a sauna and a greenhouse. Fariña used to visit: "It's very pretty, very quiet. A nice place to work, sort of like a farm, especially nice during the days because everybody was doing something separate … Albert and the others were very generous, very open." Albert built his Bearsville Studios in Woodstock. For a while, the music business tried to popularize "the Woodstock Sound," but the phrase never caught on.

After using a room at Albert's, Dylan moved into a studio behind Albert's house. By mid-1965, Bob was ensconced in his own house at Byrdcliffe, the seventy-five-year-old Webster place. Ben Webster had been an architect and influential stage director. Some structural work yielded about twenty-one rooms—big and ranchlike, but far from luxurious. His house was of dark brown cedar wood, built on four acres along the hillside. There was a swimming pool formed from a natural quarry.

But too many people knew about Byrdcliffe. In spring 1969, Dylan moved his family to the south side of Woodstock Valley to the old Walter Weyl place. Weyl, a political economist and a founder of the *New Republic*, is believed to have been the first Jew to whom Whitehead had rented a house at Byrdcliffe. Dylan followed Weyl's footsteps from Byrdcliffe to the lonely farm on Ohayo Mountain, up above the Maverick. The Weyl place still had more than one hundred acres of farmland that served as a buffer against the outside world. Here Dylan sat out the excitements of 1968, including the Newport Folk Festival, and, with journalist-friend Al Aronowitz, mulled over his invitation to the 1969 Woodstock Festival.

During three years at Woodstock, Bernard "changed fuses, drove the Cadillac or the baby-blue Mustang, tried to keep Bob's privacy. When I told Bobby, after the accident, that I might work for IBM, he said: 'I'll give you a job.' I named my own salary, but it was always a question of my saying to him: 'Tell me to do something.' My boss didn't, but his wife did. A lot of the people who came up here, the pilgrims, all said they were Bob's friends. One Australian came every day, and finally Bob talked to him. He left happy. Some people on bad trips would show up, strangers—and that was a problem. Then there was some crazy guy who said he was an ex-convict who called up and said he was going to kill Bob. The police stayed there for a while."

Friends drifted up or lived nearby: Ginsberg, in bare feet and white robes, wafted about, and Gregory Corso. Happy Traum, and filmmakers Howard and Jones Alk. Bernard: "Until Sara, I thought it was just a question of time until he died. I was afraid for his life and for his mind. But later, I had never met such a dedicated family man. There's so many sides to Bob Dylan, he's round." In the hospitable Woodstock atmosphere, the family man also pursued his painting. His proud father told me in 1967 that Bob was turning out canvas after canvas. "There's a guitar in every one," Abe said. Bernard left Dylan's employ in spring 1969, working briefly at the Bear restaurant. Then his wife opened a little pizza parlor out on Route 212, near the Swim O'Links, on April 10, 1970. They called it Country Pie, a slice from *Nashville Skyline*.

The Woodstock period was a time of sickness in America but a time of healing for Dylan. Violence was growing, antagonism and suspicion were abroad, while Dylan was exploring the tranquil life. I think his motivation for holing up in Woodstock was philosophical as well as personal. When he left and moved into a house on MacDougal Street, he found for a time in the Village both a certain connectedness and a privacy that Woodstock could no longer give him. He told me: "The Village is depressing. We're just passing through." People passing through Woodstock, before and after Dylan lived there, would be hard-pressed to find the fountain of magic, inspiration and solace they assume he found there. They could find the superficialities of an artsy, green-swaddled town. They could find a shop, bar or restaurant where he'd been, but that didn't mean they'd found the soul of the place, or put their finger on its heart-beat. The "scene" in Woodstock for Dylan was not physical so much as spiritual. It could take place on a hillside, in wooded acres, in farmland. In quiet visits with the guys in the Band, with stray artist, writer, musician friends. The "scene" and "soul" of Dylan's Woodstock couldn't be photographed or filmed. It could, however, be taped in a basement.

The Basement Tapes. Anyone concerned about Dylan's personal or artistic health in 1967 could have looked at the bed chart provided by *The Basement Tapes* and seen a patient who had *not* cracked up, vegetated, abdicated or run out of inspiration. For nearly eight years, all but one of his *Basement* songs circulated illegally, as publishing demo tapes or in bootleg collections. In July 1975, the Dylan tapes, in modified versions, plus six previously unknown songs by the Band, came up out of the basement and were officially released as a two-LP set, *The Basement Tapes*.

Comment ran to superlatives at the songs' variety, vitality, richness, and evergreen pertinence. John Rockwell in the *New York Times*: "The greatest album in the history of American popular music." Robert Christgau in the *Village Voice*: "We don't have to feel ashamed because this is the best album of 1975. It would have been the best album of 1967, too." Charlie McCollum in the *Washington Post*: "He may perplex, irritate and disappoint, but Dylan has to rank as the single greatest artist modern American pop music has produced."

The material was taped on a home recorder in the basement of the Band's house, Big Pink, in West Saugerties, New York, near Woodstock. Their roughness, which pleased many, contrasted starkly with the Beatles studio extravaganza, *Sergeant Pepper*, another 1967 landmark. McCollum likened them to "the first draft of a Doctorow novel or the rough cut of an Altman film." Jon Landau of *Rolling Stone* had just panned *Blood on the Tracks* for the lack of polished studio production. Lo and behold, then Landau backtracked and overdubbed his opinion of Dylan's spontaneous approach to recording.

Dylan's sixteen tracks surfaced initially like snapshots from home, a peek into his Woodstock wilderness. They were originally meant to be demos to interest other artists in recording some new Dylan songs. In his liner notes, Greil Marcus dates the sessions from June to October, 1967. The cellar compositions take a pivotal position between *Blonde* and *John Wesley Harding*. Without the transitional evidence of *The Basement Tapes*, the leap made between the two other albums could be exaggerated. The LP carries an overwhelming impression of the joy of jamming, right along with flawed ensembles, rough-hewn singing, unkempt instrumentalism, disbalances, distortions, the lot. This isn't Sunday parlor neatness, just basement scuffling. Sheer bravura, intimacy and excitement is caught, very much as in jazz sessions. The bizarre cover echoes *Tarantula*—a dwarf, a sword-swallower, a weight lifter, an Eskimo, a gypsy, a clown, a fat lady, a nun, a belly dancer, and a ballet dancer. Song characters Tiny Montgomery, Mrs Henry, and other eccentrics provide another link. Dylan has moved away from the death-heavy atmosphere, the trapped chaos of *Blonde*, into a communal feeling, somewhere between a bar-room rumpus and a gospel choir. (Note how many punchy choruses the six sing.) The meditativeness of *John Wesley Harding* is forecast. The wonderment of these sessions can only increase when we realize that, soon after, the Band recorded *Big Pink* and Dylan twelve other songs for *Harding*. Links forward and backward make this such an important album historically.

Dylan's *Basement* songs fall into two principal categories. The first is songs tinctured with the search for salvation, including: "I Shall Be Released" (from the demo, not on the album), "Too Much of Nothing," "This Wheel's on Fire," "Tears of Rage," "Goin' to Acapulco," "Nothing Was Delivered," and, possibly, "Long-Distance Operator." The second category is songs of joy, signaling some form of deliverance and including most of the remaining titles: "Million Dollar Bash," the single from the album, certainly embodies this feeling. "You Ain't Goin' Nowhere" would easily fit in with the last two gentle love songs on *Harding*. Dylan had his community at last; he was not alone. Yet the continuing lonely quest is underscored by "Tears of Rage," "This Wheel's on Fire," "Nothing Was Delivered," "Too Much of Nothing," and "I Shall Be Released." The germinal seed may well be Shakespeare's *King Lear*. ("Thou art a soul in bliss; but I am bound/Upon a wheel of fire"). Throughout these songs, as throughout *Lear*, "nothing" and "nowhere" perplex and nag. ("Nothing will come of nothing," Act I, Scene 1.) In the 1968

Sing Out! interview, Dylan gave an oblique clue to his interest in *Lear*: "I think it was Benjamin Franklin. He said (I'm not quoting it right) something like 'For a man to be—(something or other)—at ease, he must not tell all he knows, nor say all he sees.' Whoever said that certainly I don't think was trying to cover up anything. " A couplet from King Lear runs: "Have more than thou showest,/Speak less than thou knowest." The "nothing" echoes the artist's dilemma: death versus life, vacuum versus harvest, isolation versus people, silence versus sound, the void versus the life-impulse.

Divide the Dylan songs on *The Basement Tapes* as you will, light or heavy, soul-in-bliss or wheel-of-fire, this album could have been titled "Roots."[8] What a massive catalog of chanteys, old blues, early rock, and truck-driver, hoedown, gospel, and folk songs! Consider how much "Odds and Ends" owes to Fats Domino. Or "Orange Juice Blues" to early 1950s R&B. There is parody and toying with clichés. Put "Lo and Behold" next to a truck-driver song—say, Dave Dudley singing "Six Days on the Road." Put "Clothes Line Saga" out to dry with the old jug-band songs. Note the raggy gospel feel of "Apple Suckling Tree," and envision the old black preacher shaking his tambourine. Beneath the nonsense of "Yea! Heavy and a Bottle of Bread" emerges that very deep American escape mechanism: let's get the hell out of here and try somewhere else. Chuck Berry, the "godfather" of folk-rock, is back in "Long-Distance Operator," which recalls his "Memphis, Tennessee" and the twin technologies of the automobile and the telephone, and teenage sexual liberation.

The old agonies of *Blonde* have not disappeared completely. "Acapulco" proposes a romp in that posh Mexican resort, but the heavy spirit is down in Juarez again. "Open the Door, Homer" derives its title from the Jack McVea/Don Howell 1947 novelty hit of the Dusty Fletcher/John Mason vaudeville routine. Despite its light source, there's still a lot of agony tempering the joy. Such contrast in mood is another indication not only of Dylan's dualities and conflicts, but of the Fitzgerald-Mailer test of the mature artist and the man: the ability to hold opposing ideas and impulses in the mind and spirit but not be neutralized or nullified by their conflicts; still to move ahead, still to grow, contrasting not only Dylan's conflicts but also his ability to grow despite holding opposing ideas and impulses in his mind. The Band rarely sounded brighter, and more spontaneous and involved, than on *The Basement Tapes*. Here, the Band and Dylan were relaxed and joyous, breaking the country silence.

John Wesley Harding.

In January 1968, the release of this major album, which he later called "the first biblical rock album," created several new myths about Dylan and desecrated several music-business myths. In the wake of the frenzied trilogy of 1965–66, the *Harding* album brings to mind one of Blake's "Proverbs of Hell": "The road of excess leads to the palace of wisdom." We've seen Dylan's excess of piled-up images, of wild living, of spontaneous action. Now, in his post-accident period, he was contemplative, compassionate, exuding a sense of musical, physical and spiritual calm. The elliptical tale on the album cover is a contemporary Christ parable in ironic reverse: the Three Kings come to get, not to give. This album ushered in a period in which Dylan's life and work would reject past excesses and embrace moderation in all things.

Although Dylan did not tour to promote the album, it reportedly sold 250,000 copies in its first week. Not until April was it certified as his fifth gold album, which then meant a retail sale of $1 million, at that time about 250,000 albums. (Later, with the rise in cost of albums, platinum certification came to mean the sale of a million units.) Buyers were looking for "the word" and "the way," and many were shocked at how he enunciated them. They were geared for excitement, anger, wit and frenzy and found in *Harding* a startling reversal by a man who'd learned the value of silence, meditation and self-knowledge. Dylan, who once said he accepted chaos, was now saying: "I believe there should be an order to everything."

The surface order belies the songs' underlying complexities. In his Woodstock study, Dylan kept a huge Bible open on a wooden lectern, and the songs of Hank Williams near at hand. He had assembled the cast of Colin Wilson's *The Outsider*—the outlaw, outcast, loser, victim, the oppressed, lonely, and alienated. From these elements he sketched a series of studies in allegory, psalm, parable, symbol, metaphor, and morality. Biblical allusion, style, and syntax mixed with commonplace language and folklore run throughout the album. As Gwendolyn Bays wrote in *The Orphic Vision*: "The true seer must be able to decipher myth, and legend," especially ancient ones, "since early peoples concealed their most profound truths under the guise of a simple story."[9] Dylan's simplest album may be his most complex.

Think only of what Paul Williams called "the claustrophobia" of "All Along the Watchtower" and its haunting line, "There must be some way out of here."[10]

Bill King saw Dylan producing "the new myth of the moderate man, the basis for a new personal and artistic identity. The internal process of this rebirth is the subject." He found the old outlaw-loving, outsider-identifying Dylan locked in debate between his new and old selves. David Pichaske sees the first side "filled with a very Judaic, even Christian sense of guilt and the need for atonement" and the second side focusing on that atonement and achieving, in the final two love songs, "an actual state of grace." Eugene Stelzig saw Dylan reemerging with "an altered, restored and even more potent vision … deeply religious and moral … not only a soul-searching self-portrait and confession … but also a visionary probing of the abiding spiritual realities of salvation and damnation."

Now that he'd caught his breath and balance, Dylan revealed a little about his songs and techniques. On February 26, 1968, *Newsweek*: "I was always with the traditional song. I just used electricity to wrap it up in. Probably I wasn't ready yet to make it simple … A song is moral just by being a song. We're all moralists … I only look at them musically … as things to sing. It's the music that the words are sung to that's important. I write the songs because I need something to sing. It's the difference between the words on paper and the song. The song disappears into the air, the paper stays. They have little in common. A great poet, like Wallace Stevens, doesn't necessarily make a great singer. But a great singer always—like Billie Holiday—makes a great poet. I could have sung each of them better. I'm not exactly dissatisfied but I'm just not about to brag about the performance … I've always tried to get simple. I haven't always succeeded. But here I took more care in the writing … In *Blonde on Blonde* I wrote out a song, we'd do it, they'd go back to their game and I'd write out another song … I used to think that myself and my songs were the same thing. But I don't believe that anymore. There's myself and there's my song, which I hope is everybody's song.'"

John Cohen of *Sing Out!* said he gave Dylan a copy of Kafka's *Parables and Paradoxes* because these stories "really get to the heart of the matter, and yet you can never really decipher them." In the *Sing Out!* of October 1968, Dylan said: "the only parables that I know are the Biblical parables. I've seen others, Khalil Gibran, perhaps … you certainly wouldn't find it in the Bible—this type of soul. Now Mr Kafka comes off a little closer to that. Gibran, the words are all mighty but the strength is turned into that of a contrary direction. There used to be this disk jockey, Rosko … Sometimes … Rosko would be reciting this poetry of Khalil Gibran. It was a radiant feeling, coming across it on the radio. His voice was that of the inner voice in the night … I have always read the Bible, though not necessarily the parables." Cohen: "I don't think you're the kind who goes to the hotel, where the Gideons leave a Bible, and you pick it up." Dylan replied: "Well, you never know."[11] (Rosko, long a disc jockey on WNEW-FM, was a devotee of the Lebanese poet whose most renowned work was *The Prophet*. Gibran, a religious mystic, gained wide popularity among Western collegians. Rosko's album *Music and Gibran* consists of readings backed by Middle Eastern music. The "shadow" of Gibran on Dylan seems less discernible on *Harding* than in some earlier works, such as "Hard Rain.")

There was disagreement over *Harding*'s political content. In the *Saturday Review*, Steven Goldberg said the album "appeared at a time when the indescribable revulsion toward Lyndon Johnson was at its zenith … Dylan's declaration that he was not about to argue or to move contrasted with the student rage that was asserting itself." Jon Landau found political awareness in *Harding*, however veiled. He wrote in *Crawdaddy*: "Dylan manifests a profound awareness of the war and how it is affecting all of us." In the *Village Voice*, Richard Goldstein wrote that *Harding* "not only eludes, but dares interpretation … Dylan's major theme is human vulnerability … Dylan confronts a cliché the way a butcher eyes a chicken. His new songs abound with slaughtered platitudes … Dylan is his own motif. So listen for the outlaw-confessor in *JWH*. Under the suede smile, he is still naked." Stephen Pickering applied his readings in mysticism and Jewish literature, and saw the mystical experience as the core of the album. He found that Dylan's Jewish background "extends and pervades everything he has ever written."

The album's sparse music startled everyone. In a period of wild musical explorations, Dylan had turned to folk-country simplicity of melodic line and laconic backing. It was almost the progression from Symbolism into Imagism—from a rich overload of symbol buildup to unembellished essentials, from "too much of nothing" to just a bit of something else, from a modernist carnival of the elusive and the intuitive to a classic sort of simple line, terse stories meant always to be "listening to the silences," the meanings between the words. His dramatic change of music styles flew in the face of the Beatles'

Sgt Pepper, a daring foray into studio techniques. Dylan's spare, effective background was supplied by only three Nashville session men — Pete Drake, pedal-steel guitarist; Charlie McCoy, bassist, and Kenny Buttrey, drummer. Here was Dylan whispering in a climate of shout and scream. He had pulled the plug on electric music.

The album's cover previews mystification. Pictured with Dylan are a Woodstock workman and two Indian Baul singers of Bengal, traditional singers Grossman recorded for Elektra. Some fans saw "hidden" Beatles pictures in the trees. One *Melody Maker* reader spoofed: If you hold the album cover "right-way-up, then turn it in a clockwise direction, the record falls out." I first heard about *Harding* from Milt Okun, a messenger once associated with Grossman and Mogull, but later with Dylan. Milt was pleased Dylan had gone "full-circle" back to songs that were "fully comprehensible, almost complete folk, sometimes reminding me of Ewan MacColl." He indicated that Grossman and Mogull were not all that pleased with the tapes. Okun was certainly an enthusiastic messenger.

The "Three Kings" liner note is, to some, *Tarantula*-like nonsense. Pichaske read it as "a short story in the Kafka-Böll-Borchert tradition which draws on both the Bible and Brecht." The "Three Kings" can be a Christ parable, or Dylan-as-Frank proclaiming himself, frankly, as the moderate man. Either way, Dylan is dealing again and three kings make a strong hand.

"John Wesley Harding": Gentle irony, with the protagonist holding guns in "every" hand. At the time, the whole youth culture was shaken by the Warren Beatty–Arthur Penn film, *Bonnie and Clyde*. Rather than tell the story of John Wesley Hardin, the song, in Bill King's phrase, "condenses into poetic form the mythic outline of the outlaw hero." Hardin, born in Texas in 1853, started young as a gambler-gunman. In 1877, he got twenty-five years for killing a sheriff. In prison, he studied law until pardoned in 1894, then started to practice in El Paso. A year later he was killed by a local constable. (When Okun asked Dylan to name his "favorite" traditional folk song for the book *Something to Sing About*, Dylan characteristically chose a badman song, "John Hardy.") When the record was released, I twitted Dylan in print about his adding a gratuitous g to Hardin's name, for repaying his orthographic debt after all his singin', ramblin', and walkin'.

"Harding" is a badman ballad about an essentially good man, an unembroidered fable. In a consciously rough, ethnic folk voice, he kept the story brief. The fully armed outlaw-saint, his lady beside him, "He was never known/To make a foolish move."[12] Harding disappears, just as Dylan did at this period. The song has an open-range roll, the feel of caked mud on the boots.

"As I Went Out One Morning": The Anglo-American songbook is heavy with beginnings like this archaic opening line. I see Tom Paine as a dual metaphor for a freethinking Dylan and the revolutionary writer for whom that 1963 civil liberties award was named. Dylan hints that Paine, who once proclaimed that his own mind was his church, would have been appalled to see libertarian ideas enchained by dogma. A traditional form is used here to move the story along, and to comment on the clash of contemporary values. The girl enchained is actually a dual reversal: Traditionally, fair damsels are the enslaved, not the enslaver.

"I Dreamed I Saw St Augustine": The first two lines paraphrase "Joe Hill," the Earl Robinson–Alfred Hayes union hymn to the singing Wobbly organizer who became a martyr. A folk saint is eclipsed by a Catholic saint, but Dylan gently disdains both houses. Preconceptions and ideology are dead; he hungers here for salvation, for answers. His isolation from a comforting faith is deeply felt. Augustine was not martyred, but died a bishop, an honored church father. His *Confessions* and *City of God* are visionary chronicles of his early wastrel life, subsequent conversion, and search for grace. Stelzig sees the narrator "among those who put the Biblical prophet of resurrection out to death. The realization ... of his complicity and guilt is conveyed with a poignancy ... new in Dylan's poetry. He wakes up alone, terrified — he bows his head and cries." Carolyn Bliss — the singer awakes from his vision of himself as a saint and cries "for the futile self-sacrifice of sainthood, which precludes full understanding and insists on service to the unattainable. All that was a dream and Dylan is awake now." Bliss thinks Dylan is saying: "Go with my compassion and companionship, but not with my guidance. Go through your own darkness; go find your own light." Dylan examines martyrdom and why people hunger for martyrs. But there remains much mystery in these three verses. What is "the glass" he touches before crying? A window, a telescope, or a mirror? He seems to identify simultaneously with the sinner-turned-saint and the lost souls beyond redemption by Leftist or Catholic saints.

"All Along the Watchtower": Many believe this twelve-line distillate gem to be the album's high point. After a menacing guitar introduction, intense singing and mood mix colloquial speech with archaic setting and *personae*. Emptiness is peopled with the joker, a wise fool out of *King Lear*. And the dialogue with the thief supports the theory that both are Dylan's contradictory spirits in dialogue. Gabrielle Goodchild: "The watchtower seems related to the fortified city as a recurring image for the moral state of man or the body politic. Here the moral order seems to be threatened by the duality Dylan sees within himself of clown and holy pickpocket."

Are the mysterious pair inside or outside humankind's fortified city, trapped or exiled? "The question is the answer." Is it worse to be locked in or locked out? In "George Jackson," Dylan said that some of us are prisoners and some are guards, but there's little difference. Jack McDonough linked the song to Isaiah, Chapter 21, foretelling the fall of Babylon. Pickering linked Isaiah also to "Messenger" and "Immigrant." At this time, Dylan must have felt that businessmen were drinking his earnings and that critics and listeners were trampling his soil. Dylan had great praise for the Jimi Hendrix recording, and strong memories of the man.

"The Ballad of Frankie Lee and Judas Priest": The gloom, if not the doubt, is relieved by a comic tall tale in frontier-ballad style. Echoes of Mark Twain, Bret Harte, and Robert Service. This fable offers a story as light, or a message as heavy, as the listener chooses. A possible "key" is that Frank on the liner notes and Frankie Lee might both be Dylan. Judas, the tempter with the bankroll, then becomes the music business, or success. Having exhausted himself with the alleged pleasures of the brothel of fame, which the tempter called home, Frankie is dying of thirst in a moral desert. "Nothing is revealed,"[13] except stay where you want, do what you want, and don't let people tempt you with money and false claims of success. Dylan pulls off a dozen jokes here—on frontier balladry, on western types, on Bible story. We search, we hunt, we strive for meaning, for a system, and Dylan taunts us that meaning itself may be an illusion, something we can never grasp.

"Drifter's Escape": Another tale of an outsider, threatened but not defeated by society. Excellent singing with anguished intonation, careful phrasing. The song recalls Hank Williams, a victim of the music life who went by the soubriquet of Luke the Drifter. Some of his lonesome chants have a similarly beseeching tone. Dylan's retreat couldn't blot out the outrage he'd heard the previous three years. The drifter is the Kafkaesque victim, offense unknown. Enter God with a bolt of lightning, making the persecutors cry while the drifter escapes. The lightning could well be that motorcycle. Dylan's hatred of mob behavior was deep. After seeing the film *The Ox-Bow Incident*, he worked on a ballad about a lynching of an innocent. The terror of the world tour underlines "Drifter," which is yet another walk down "Desolation Row." There are prototypes of the scansion, rhythm, and meter of this song in the Old Testament.

"Dear Landlord": One of Dylan's trumps has always been matching a textual phrase with a musical phrase, as in this title. The vocalizing maintains a tone of invocation; a personal plea becomes a prayer. I see this as very personal, Dylan sending a message to Grossman when his manager was agitated by his continuing retreat. Grossman once owned Dylan's Woodstock cottage, and Dylan owed "rent" then to Columbia Records, Macmillan, and ABC-TV. Jack McDonough links the catalog of sins of the hobo and the landlord and the immigrant to Proverbs 6:16.

"I Am a Lonesome Hobo": Another view of an outsider. The last four lines moralize heavily: avoid jealousy, accept no one else's code of behavior, and keep your judgments to yourself. A sort of vagrant Polonius preaching his credo. "Hobo" has a peculiar unity with the earlier "Drifter"—this sounds like the drifter is now a few miles from the courthouse, recalling his "crimes" before walking off alone.

"I Pity the Poor Immigrant": Compassionate and doom-laden, this lyric has always confounded me. Dylan may be having a tortured colloquy with himself, a love-hate debate between his own (everyone's) good side and the acquisitive, opportunist, insatiable element. Alain Rémond has suggested an attempt to balance fate and liberty—he saw us all as immigrants or exiles from "The Gates of Eden." Dylan was now outside New York City, city of immigrants, but sending down messages of how sick the city seemed to him. The singing is outstanding, to one of the most beautiful melodies in Anglo-Scots tradition. He must have remembered Bonnie Dobson's singing of the Canadian "Peter Amberley," which borrows from "Come All Ye Tramps and Hawkers." The immigrant's dreadful deeds are set against such caressing cadences that the harshness of the crimes recede. Perhaps the final line, "When his gladness comes to pass,"[14] with its biblical serenity, offers hope of grace.

"The Wicked Messenger": Biblical allusion enriches this quizzical fable, right down to its archaic diction. Eli is Hebrew for "God is high." The biblical Eli was a high priest and judge of Israel, teacher of young Samuel. The lyric's concept is ancient and often revived. According to Proverbs 13:17: "A wicked messenger falleth into mischief/But a faithful ambassador is health." In Sophocles' *Antigone*, "None love the messenger who brings bad news." Shakespeare, in *King Henry IV, Part II*: "The first bringer of unwelcome news/Hath but a losing office." Dylan may be talking of the poet's duty to tell the truth. The musical line is one of the album's most inventive, a bluesy, harsh, descending contour.

"Down Along the Cove": At first, this and the final song seemed misplaced. Later, I saw emotional, rational, and musical sense of order in their positioning. If this album is about one man's search for salvation or answers, or one man's autobiography of change, then such appealing love songs provide balance and symmetry. Now the messenger brings good news. Salvation through love—of a person, an ideal, or a religious faith—can be complex, or as simple as a woman's smile. This tune really swings, lightly, like a dance.

"I'll Be Your Baby Tonight": Dylan toys again with the clichés of commonplace love. The contrast suggests forget philosophy and ideology and settle for simple pleasures, simple verities of "moon" and "spoon." The album that he begins with a badman cowboy ballad ponders the immutable and the intangible until he decides to savor the comforts of love. Hank Williams used to sing about mockingbirds too, and he was far from the simple man his verses suggested. "Cove" and "Baby Tonight" not only close out one period of Dylan's work and life, but point ahead to new vistas along the Nashville skyline.

A Song for Woody.

Finally, Woody Guthrie's wasting decay, trembling, and pain ended. On October 3, 1967, he died, after fifteen years of illness. Woody's long-time agent, Harold Leventhal, briefed the press on Woody's turbulent career. The obituaries startled many who thought Woody had died in the 1940s. The fragmented folk movement seemed to close ranks at the death of its elder statesman. Leventhal told me: "A lot of people got in touch to say how sorry they were, but only one singer actually suggested that we *do* something—Bob Dylan." A benefit concert seemed the appropriate tribute to a ballad-maker. The proceeds could help fight Huntington's chorea, or start a library in Woody's hometown of Okemah.

With Dylan pledging his time, the concert was easily arranged. Millard Lampell, screenwriter and former Almanac Singer, wrote and directed the production. Two Hollywood actors who had known Woody, the late Will Geer and Robert Ryan, were narrators. Singers? You almost had to fight them off. In December, an unobtrusive notice in New York papers announced twin concerts at Carnegie Hall on January 20, 1968. Listed were Dylan, Judy Collins, Jack Elliott, Arlo Guthrie, Richie Havens, Odetta, Tom Paxton, and Pete Seeger. Nearly 6,000 seats sold out within hours.

Dylan's return threatened to upstage the concerts' purpose. He made some severe proscriptions: no pictures, tape recorders, or mob scenes. Still, audience and press were keyed up not to mourn the death of Guthrie so much as to celebrate the return to life of Dylan. At the first concert, in the afternoon, Dylan sidled on from stage left, and was not immediately recognized. He wore a Jesus beard and moustache, and was dressed in a conservative gray suit with a light-blue dress shirt open at the neck. He looked very serene. As the audience began to recognize him, a series of whoops and shouts began an effusive day.

"Nothing so perpetuates a legend as the disappearance of its subject," Richard Goldstein wrote in *Vogue.* Even though Dylan was at the microphone only briefly, the day was his. The entire company started with an instrumental ensemble, then sailed into "Bound for Glory." Ryan began to read Lampell's script: "He had a little sign pasted on his guitar that said: THIS MACHINE KILLS FASCISTS. He believed in stepping up and speaking out what he was for and what he was against. His whole hard-traveling life was a one-man demonstration. He was against poverty and hunger, bigotry and bargain-basement justice, con artists, jackleg preachers, and crooked politicians … He was for the outsider and the outcast, the radical and the rebel. He was for the drifter and the stray."

The heroic celebration of the Guthrie legend began. Lofty ideas in simple words, angry feelings in cutting phrases. Always the rub of the language, the American language that perhaps no other writer since Mark Twain had caught with such gritty idiom. One by one, or in varying combinations, the singers interpreted Guthrie's songs, taking over where Lampell's narration or Woody's words left off. The transition from singing prose to singing lyrics was easy, for there was melody to both. Some of Marjorie Guthrie's dance students performed to one song, and slides of the Pacific Northwest accompanied the federal bard's scratchy old voice singing "Talking Dust Bowl." In a period of harsh politics, acid music, pop art, and assassinations, Woody's words sounded like scripture: "I'm one walker that's stood way up and looked way down across aplenty of pretty sights in all their veiled and nakedest season. Thumbing it. Hitching it. Walking and talking it. Chalking it. Marking it. Sighting it and hearing it. Seeing and feeling and breathing and smelling it in, sucking down me, rubbing it all in the pores of my skin, and the wind between my eyes knocking honey in my comb."

The lights went out for ten seconds after Ryan finished, and there was some shuffling at stage right. The lights rose and a country jamboree ensued. Dylan and the Band jolted out one of Woody's best dam songs, "Grand Coulee Dam." Real hillbilly, strong, shouting, crackling with tumult, Dylan picking his acoustic guitar one minute, then raising it up high to the mike, or raising his right arm to "conduct" the Band with decisive ax chops. Listeners were either on their feet cheering or were smiling. A *Rolling Stone* reporter beside me was laughing out loud. With the first song still roaring away, the audience settled down. Seeger sat, chin on fist, like "The Thinker." Odetta smiled broadly, like another spotlight onstage. Dylan and the Band sailed into "Mrs Roosevelt." Bob shifted keys like a racing driver shifting gears. The organ and the drums filled out the pattern. Who says folk music can't be done with a beat? Who says Guthrie can't be sung by a rockabilly band?

After the applause subsided, Dylan steered his drifters into "I Ain't Got No Home." It was startling to hear Woody's songs done this way. Seeger, apparently recovered from his electric shock, was drumming the back of his guitar. Dylan's voice soared over the ensemble. How unlike *John Wesley Harding*! Now his singing had become astringent. Vocal harmonies with the Band brought it all back home down in contemporary country. At intermission, everyone was chattering about Dylan. Only thirteen minutes onstage, and he'd upstaged everyone but Woody.

Security was tight. Leventhal threatened disruption of the program if cameras were used. Just before the evening intermission, someone snapped a flashbulb, and out ran Leventhal and a uniformed guard to oust the miscreant. After the concert, Lampell was furious. He asked me, rhetorically: "What has all this policing stuff got to do with Woody?" As I went backstage before the first concert, armed with a "staff badge," David Gahr, the official photographer at the show, whispered heatedly: "He's here!" In one of the dressing rooms, Dylan was sitting near Robbie and Jack Elliott. Everyone looked nervous except Rambling Jack, who was cracking wise. I greeted Bob, and he stood up to shake my hand, a rare concession to manners. We were talking about the weather and the outlook for spring crops when Grossman hove into view and handed Bob a piece of paper, which Dylan read, then laughed at. My first impression on seeing Bob that day was like his brother's in Hibbing later that year—"like a fifty-year-old man, so calm." He'd had a good rest, I thought.

Not everyone had been pleased by Dylan's segment of the Guthrie tribute. Some folkniks thought the show "too Hollywood," overly star-oriented. But more important, many listeners who were drawn by Dylan had been introduced to Guthrie. As the show continued, Dylan was back in perspective as a Guthrie disciple paying homage. Geer and Ryan rolled on with Woody's prose-poems: "I just happen to believe in my soul that the rough people in this world are the best singers, the hard-hit people, the hard-hitting people." More songs about the little people, the union people, the good old American earth. Judy Collins sang "Roll on, Columbia." Seeger and Havens harmonized "Jackhammer John." Paxton told the story of "The Biggest Thing Man Has Ever Done," then Judy joined Pete on "Union Maid." Seeger led a 3,000-voice sing-along on "Reuben James." Arlo had his finest moment with "Jesus Christ," his dad's sardonic song that asked whether Jesus, if preaching today, would be crucified again. Odetta and Havens teamed up on the rarely performed "I've Got to Know."

At both performances, the sing-alongs exuded a revival-meeting spirit. People needed some affirmation, as the war droned on into the Tet offensive, civil rights became embattled, politics remained as shabby as ever. The faithful tried to find some hope in Guthrie's words that we were, against all the evidence, "born to win." Everyone sailed into "Bound for Glory." Dylan took his verse, momentarily forgot the lyric, smiled, recaught the line, and everyone joyfully sang on. Finally, the folk national anthem, "This Land is Your Land." We all tried hard to believe what it said. A few cried; most clapped, stamped, jumped to their feet, or shouted themselves hoarse. Gone for the moment was fractionalized, suspicious, partisan, self-seeking individualism. We were all together around the campfire of brotherhood and sisterhood, turning on to the fantasy of hope for a real democracy. Marjorie was onstage now, and Odetta grabbed her hands and danced around with her. Elliott did some fancy steps in his clunky cowboy boots. Old Will Geer sang loud, if not clear. The standing ovation went on for perhaps ten minutes. Pete finally soothed us out of the hall, saying we ought to take our songs back to our factories, our communities, our homes. Our factories? Oh, well, who's going to quibble over a bit of blue-collar rhetoric?

Between concerts, Dylan and the Band relaxed at the nearby Sheraton-Plaza Hotel. Robbie had told me at the afternoon intermission to "just wait for tonight," and he was right, for the excitement of their segment was even greater. After the second show, a party for about a hundred members of the cast and friends was held at Robert Ryan's spacious apartment in the Dakota, the Central Park West building where John Lennon lived and died. Leventhal was subdued, explaining later that he had finally been hit by Woody's death that day. About midnight, Bob came in with Sara, Happy Traum, and a few friends. Bob was wearing his Ben Franklin glasses, looking relaxed but drawn inward. Conversation almost stopped when he entered. He began to make the rounds of old friends and acquaintances, including Alan Lomax. Allen Ginsberg spent a considerable time slumped in a chair in meditation.

I chatted with Dylan about the concert. He called almost everything "great, just great." Hesitantly, we drifted on to my recent *Times* review of *John Wesley Harding*. I indicated how frequently I'd listened to the album, getting something different each time. "Well, you'd better listen to it another few times," Bob advised. Faced with some of his old pre-accident cut and thrust, I almost felt more at ease. But we'd had that sort of artist-critic parrying before, so we quickly veered off into small talk. I noticed that he wasn't shunning small talk, and had almost become quite good at it.

The *Times* gave me a column in which to rhapsodize, the *New Yorker* devoted nearly a page to a sympathetic report and the *Village Voice* snagged a good photograph of Dylan onstage for page one. The Associated Press stressed the Dylan comeback over the Guthrie tribute. Certainly there was enough in the Guthrie story, writings and songs, to have launched a national touring company. Eventually, another version of the Carnegie Hall tribute was mounted at the Hollywood Bowl, on September 12, 1970. The cast added Baez, Country Joe McDonald, and Earl Robinson. Sharing the narration with Will Geer was actor Peter Fonda. Some 18,000 people turned out to see the Dust Bowl relocated to the Hollywood Bowl. Two recordings of the twin shows, only pale reflections of the events, were released in April 1972, Volume One by Columbia and Volume Two by Warner Bros. Proceeds went to the Huntington's chorea fund and toward a Guthrie library.

Many hoped that the film of *Bound for Glory*, released in autumn 1976, might enhance Guthrie's standing. Leventhal had been trying to launch such a film for at least ten years. Shortly after Woody's death, he commissioned a script from the late Nedrick Young. Four scripts later, a screenplay by Robert Getchell was accepted. Leventhal co-produced for United Artists along with Robert Blumofe. Hal Ashby directed. The search for the "right" star was long and involved. Leventhal told the *Village Voice* on October 13, 1975: "I wanted a short actor. We talked to Dustin Hoffman ... Jack Nicholson ... Robert De Niro ... Arlo wanted to play the part ... Bob Dylan was considered. We sent him a script, although I was sure I didn't want him, and he called up a week later and said he loved the script but he would never want to play the role. Thank God, I thought. Then a week later, he called back and said he wanted to direct the movie. We had to turn him down, of course." Chosen for the role was David Carradine, best known for his part in the *Kung Fu* TV series. A script devoid of Woody's word-magic got lackluster reviews. Poor attendance left the $7 million production in the red. Dylan and Pete Seeger have achieved more than the film did in bringing Guthrie forward into American life and letters.

The Skyline of Nashville. Where would the late 1960s take rock? By 1969, everybody had to get stoned and make it to Woodstock, cut a psychedelic album, prove they were disturbed by Vietnam by freaking out. Then, a quiet young countryman made his way down to Nashville's Music Row, picked up a few sidemen, went into a studio and, in a few days, cut an album of gently crooned country love songs in a voice he'd never used before. While most of his fans were still stalking Desolation Row, Dylan turned the corner into Redemption Street.

Nashville Skyline proclaimed, in April 1969, a man reformed, subdued, and very much in love. The widespread first reaction was: "How can he let us down like this? Pouring out all that syrupy love while we're marching off stoned to his Woodstock? It's a sellout!" One more sudden experiment unsettled and disoriented. Many reviews stressed what was *not* on the album: no protest, no bitterness, no druggy symbolism, no hipness. How could he *do* this to us?

Variety called Dylan's voice "shockingly transformed." *Time*: "Dylan is definitely doing something that can be called singing. Somewhere, somehow, he has managed to add an octave to his range." Geoffrey Cannon in the *Guardian*: "The new country music, inspired always by Dylan's example, will be played more and more this year, in every American city. It will create some space and calm in the murderously fevered streets." Christgau in the *Village Voice*: "After eight years as psychic wanderer, Dylan is transmuted into man-about-the-house, friendly, stable, secure, and promising not to vomit it back in our face next year." Many thought he'd lost his cutting edge because he'd turned soft and plump. Artists create better work when they are suffering, and they should, indeed, suffer for their audiences and their art. Ed Ochs in *Billboard*, July 12, 1969: "Dylan, the satisfied man, speaks in clichés and blushes as if every day were Valentine's day ... So goodbye, Bob Dylan, I'm glad you're happy though you meant more to me when you were ... confused like everybody else ... though you have withdrawn to your family, your genius defused, I have the funny feeling you'll soon return, as Wordsworth said, to recall your experience in the tranquility of afterthought." *Billboard* invoking Wordsworth! Stephen Pickering cited MacLeish and Bertrand Russell, seeing *Skyline* as a "rare glimpse of Dylan's psyche with its defenses down ... illuminating his private fears ... without benefit of outward circles." Dylan, he thought, "has drawn closer to being a brilliant extension of Gnosticism."

The old Gnostic sat for a *Newsweek* interview published on April 14, 1969: "These are the type of songs that I always felt like writing. The songs reflect more of the inner me than the songs of the past. They're more to my base than, say, *John Wesley Harding*. There I felt everyone expected me to be a poet so that's what I tried to be. But the smallest line in this new album means more to me than some of the songs on any of the previous albums I've made."

I had always found Dylan more aware of the country currents than most other city folk singers. In December 1961, when I returned from my first visit to Nashville to begin work on my book, *The Country Music Story*, Bob asked who I'd seen and heard. He often alluded to Hank Snow, Hank Thompson, Bill Anderson, Dolly Parton. In September 1968, he stole in from Woodstock to catch Johnny Cash at Carnegie Hall. He repeatedly told associates that he regarded country music as the coming thing, long before he cut *Skyline* on his fourth set of working visits to Nashville.

Dylan's first Nashville session after *John Wesley Harding* was in Columbia's Studio A on September 24, 1968. *Skyline* was taped from February 13 through 17, 1969. Session men included Charlie Daniels, dobro steel-guitar player, Johnny Cash, and a passel of Nashville sidemen. Six weeks after its release, the album reached number one. Although pure country, it did not score on country charts. I wondered why Glen Campbell and Johnny Cash appeared on pop *and* country charts, Aretha Franklin on as many as five charts, but Dylan on only one. Clive Davis explained: "We do know that *Skyline* sold very well in the country record market. What the trade papers don't know is how to allocate these sales to its acceptance as a country album, a rock album or both." Lee Zhito, editor of *Billboard*, wrote me: "There is no 'silent resistance' within the country field toward Dylan. The answer lies in the repertoire. When non-country artists choose to invade this field they invariably do so well-armed with established country song material. The country fan simply did not feel at home with this repertoire, and bypassed the album." Michael Clare, managing editor of *Record Retailer*, London: "I, too, often wonder how they compile their charts. Unless an artist publicly states he is a country singer nobody else will do so." When I asked Dylan, he simply said: "The only people who get on country charts are those who are out at the crossroads singing every week."

He could have had no more influential "sponsor" in country music than Johnny Cash. On the last evening of the sessions, February 17–18, Big John ambled into the studio and the two jammed. They put down 12 to 15 tracks together, including "I Walk the Line," "Big River," "Careless Love," "One Too Many Mornings," and "Understand Your Man." The only public results were the duet on *Skyline*, a brief segment of Dylan in a theatrical-TV film on Cash, and Dylan's appearance on the premiere of Cash's TV series. Dylan told a reporter "it's a great privilege to sing with Johnny Cash."

The Cash-Dylan friendship actually dated back five years. By the time of the TV taping, Cash was showing some signs of irritation at being upstaged. "We're just friends. I got lots of friends," Cash said then. Reviewing the friendship in 1975, he said: "I became aware of Bob Dylan when the *Freewheelin'* album came out in 1963. I thought he was one of the best country singers I had ever heard. I always felt a lot in common with him. I knew a lot about him before we had ever met. I knew he had heard and listened to country music. I was in Las Vegas in 1963 and wrote him a letter telling him how much I liked his work. We developed a correspondence." Before they had met, Cash was ready to be Dylan's partisan, inside Columbia Records and within the topical-song movement. (In a letter printed in New York *Broadside* Number 41, March 10, 1964, Cash entered the Dylan controversy on Bob's side with a piece in verse that concluded "Shut Up and let him sing!")

At Newport 1965, Cash gave Dylan one of his guitars, a great compliment from one artist to another. In 1968, Cash retold the episode: "I had brought a couple of guitars with me, and he liked that one handmade in Chicago in the early Thirties. So I gave him that old guitar of mine. I've given away a lot of guitars. We first met at Columbia Records. We just became friends like any two songwriters might, you know? Mutual admiration, I think. I was a guest of his in Woodstock four or five years ago. I saw him in England a couple of years back. Then in Nashville about a year ago when he came to record."

In autumn 1968, I interviewed John in New York for a documentary film: "I think the pop and the new breed as they come along, every year, will borrow from country music. I have a great respect for people like the Byrds and the Lovin' Spoonful. They do country that I could dig. But I don't think it can be a consistent thing with anybody except real country artists. You have to have grass roots. If I don't sound like I know what I'm singing about, the people know it. They know whether or not I'm sincere. I don't say you have to live in poverty in the South to be a country singer. But it helps. Every successful country singer I know has a humble background, beginning, and the colored blues have been a part of their musical heritage. Every one of them, bar none. Elvis will tell you himself that where he got his style is from the colored blues singers."

The Dylan-Cash relationship reached its apogee in 1969 with their opening track of *Skyline* and Dylan's appearance on the Cash TV show on Saturday, June 7. Dylan's part was minimal. He appeared restrained and youthful beside his host's towering hulk. Alone, he sang "I Threw It All Away," "Living the Blues," and then joined Cash in "Girl from the North Country." Dylan was introduced only by name, said nothing, shook Cash's hand after the duet, and then gave his first, tentative smile. Red O'Donnell of the *Nashville Banner* wrote me: "He preferred to appear on the bare, austere stage. Dylan said: 'I never want to work in front of scenery that looks better than I do.' I interviewed him during the taping at the Grand Ole Opry House, and he spoke in a whisper. 'I have a difficulty in talking to people. But I'll put something down on paper and perhaps it will tell something about me.' O'Donnell sent me what he called Dylan's "Ten Commandments" or "Credo":

I love children. I love animals. I am loyal to my friends. I have a sense of humor. I have a generally happy outlook. I try to be on time for appointments. I have a good relationship with my wife. I take criticism well. I strive to do good work. I try to find some good in everybody.

Whether O'Donnell knew he was being put on or not, he pressed Dylan: "I wish I could explain why I'm shy. I can't really analyze my emotions to any great extent. As for my appeal, who knows? I'm not the reporter's perfect interviewee. But perhaps my formula for writing will be of interest. I want to help anybody who wants to write a story about me." O'Donnell asked why he had turned down so much television and was doing the Cash show. Dylan: "Because it is a good show. There are so few good TV shows around these days."

Reporters tried to breach the heavy security at the TV taping. A *Look* team was unceremoniously thrown out. June Carter Cash tried to demystify things by saying that John and Bob spent a lot of their time together in silence. Executive producer Bill Carruthers explained to Carol Botwin of *This Week* magazine: "Bob wouldn't do this unless John had asked him to. I can't tell you how uptight he is … some kid got through and forced himself on Bob, and … the police had to throw the kid out … Bob felt badly about it. Bob was the center of attraction, and he hates it, just hates it. I can only tell you that the string is very taut at the moment regarding Dylan even doing the show … But he's sticking it out because of Johnny. He said to me yesterday, 'Please, no photographers, because I look bad.' Well, he doesn't. Bob looks healthy and suntanned and wants to wear a suit and a tie on the show … He's such a deep little guy you can tell the moment he's upset because there's a little twitch in his eye or lip."

Doug Kershaw, the country fiddler, said he had spent the previous evening in a motel writing songs with Dylan: "The man is so very human. You fail to realize that he's afraid. Deathly afraid." Joni Mitchell, another guest on the show: "Sometimes the most frightening thing is when everyone loves you too much. Dylan's such a sensitive guy. He used to be better off when he was younger and an *angry* young man — he would scream at you and diminish you if he thought your questions were stupid or unartistic. Now, he knows he can't be an angry young kid anymore. He can't growl. Instead, he stays silent and explodes inside. Instead of taking it out on you, he takes it out internally."

Cash tended to deny the "magic" of the duet: "That's something everybody else sees, but I don't. We've done it dozens of times just foolin' around. But everybody here said 'North Country' was the most magnetic, powerful thing they ever heard. Just raving about electricity, magnetism. And all I did was sit there hitting G chords." June Cash suggested that Dylan wasn't scared on the show, just shy. "The Dylans are very good friends of ours. John wants Bob to be comfortable. When they are with us, we just try to keep everybody away because we respect his privacy, but never know quite what he's thinking." The *Johnny Cash Show* went out on ABC-TV and reached millions. It was an instant success, guaranteeing a regular run, budgeted at $150,000 per week, starting in January 1970.

The Dylan-Cash rapport went far beyond music. Cash never tried to conceal that, in spite of his success, he virtually went to pieces from 1961 until 1968. Cash's redemptive marriage to June Carter brought him a new mastery over his turbulent personality. He and Dylan were walking a similar comeback line in this period. Each drew quiet security from watching the other find stability. Dylan agreed to a brief appearance in a TV-and-theatrical film documentary, *Johnny Cash, The Man, His World, His Music*, produced by Arthur and Evelyn Barron. Dylan had met Arthur Barron back in July 1963, when he produced a small freedom songs special for WNDT-TV in New York. Dylan taped seven songs, but approved release of only the duet of "One Too Many Mornings." After a TV premiere on National Educational Television, sixteen minutes were added and the film was distributed worldwide in theaters starting in October 1969.

Nashville Skyline publicly reflects the private rapport that then existed between Cash and Dylan. In Cash's verse paean on the album jacket, he was saying, in effect, to his vast country audience: "Here's a good pal who knows what country music's all about. Forget what you've heard about him as a protester, hippie, or freak, and just listen to the man sing about love." For the first time on an official release, Dylan repeated a song, and did his first instrumental, "Nashville Skyline Rag"; this was also his first use of electronic echo. Most startling was his brand-new voice. In the highly sarcastic 1969 *Rolling Stone* interview, Dylan "explained": "When I stopped smoking, my voice changed … so drastically, I couldn't believe it myself. That's true. I tell you, you stop smoking those cigarettes [*laughter*] … and you'll be able to sing like Caruso …"

No Caruso — but there are some Buddy Holly echoes, some of Roy Orbison's purling tones, some of the Elvis of "Loving You." Mostly, there is a lot of open intonation, without nasality, without an angry whine. It was "another key, another door" for Dylan as a pure country singer. This is not Merle Haggard grit, nor Hank Williams pain. Rather, the open-throated, melodic float of Jimmie Rodgers before illness constrained his voice.[15] Bland and serene, optimistic as the "howdy neighbor" picture on the cover. *Skyline* is certainly without pretense. It begins a trend that continued until 1974 — a retreat from "significance."

Except the significance of an old truism: "Love is all there is/It makes the world go 'round."[16] It is a reactive album, saying again that for him, the "moderate man," his happiness in retreat has been the rediscovery of some basics about life and love.

The opening duet with Cash on "Girl from the North Country" is a rare moment. Rough at the edges, with flawed entrances, harmonies, lyrics. Yet it exudes palpable rapport. As they go out trading phrases, they do have that boozy, early-morning camaraderie. Old-timey sounds of instrumental jamming follow on the "Rag," with sidemen Kenny Buttrey, Charles McCoy, Pete Drake, Norman Blake, Charlie Daniels, and Bob Wilson swapping ideas with Dylan as if he were from the Tennessee hills. The "shave and a haircut" ending underscores the country idiom. A spoken line made "To Be Alone with You" memorable. Dylan asked Johnston if the tape had started, and while the song may have been forgotten, his question, "Is it rolling, Bob?" soon entered fans' patois. Dylan has some fun with the clichés of country and country-music whimsy on "Peggy Day." "Lay, Lady, Lay" became the major single hit from this collection, rising to number seven. "One More Night" is reminiscent of Presley's first single, "Blue Moon of Kentucky," an old Bill Monroe tune. Here, the cowboy and frontier ethos is strong, the individual lonely in his physical and emotional environment.

In the instrumental work of "Tell Me That It Isn't True," there are the slightest musical echoes of the breaks on "Desolation Row." Sheer fun and a child's sense of play dominate "Country Pie." Some reviewers focused on "Ain't runnin' any race"[17] as Dylan's new "statement." Little Jack Horner has replaced Tom Thumb. The album closes with "Tonight I'll Be Staying Here with You," a reflection of the same commitment to a love object that marked "You Ain't Goin' Nowhere" and the last two songs on *Harding*.

The influence of *Nashville Skyline* was unimaginable. At the end of the 1960s, pop and rock were looking for new directions, and strong elements of country had always existed in Anglo-American pop. Still, Dylan provided the strap that began to link pop closer to country, with *Skyline* as the buckle. A good part of the pop and rock of the 1970s explored country music. Soon Nashville studios were crowded with performers who had earlier disdained country as corn. Baez started to record there with *Any Day Now*. Ringo Starr followed eighteen months after Dylan, choosing for his mentor/producer Pete Drake, who had worked on two Dylan Nashville albums. In early 1970, Paul Hemphill, author of *The Nashville Sound*, told the *Village Voice* of a massive change: "Folks called the outsiders 'them weirdos with the funny glasses,' but when they found out those boys could really play and … produce, they gave them … respect. One of the more important people was … Dylan … When John began to play with Dylan, folks asked why he did it … Folks forgot about politics and listened to the way he played."

Within months of *Skyline*, a new flock of Byrds were taping *Sweetheart of the Rodeo*. In the next few years came hip country artists and rock musicians gone country—Poco, the Flying Burrito Brothers, the Nitty Gritty Dirt Band, Tracy Nelson, Captain Hook and the Medicine Show, Kris Kristofferson, Chip Taylor, Kinky Friedman, Commander Cody. The country influence was firmly rooted by a major 1970s group, Crosby, Stills, Nash and Young. Dylan himself remained interested in both the recording environment of Nashville and such country performers as Ronee Blakley, featured on Dylan's 1975 tour, and Emmylou Harris, who came forward dramatically on *Desire*. The brilliance and the bias of Robert Altman's film *Nashville* reflected the old and new country music that met in Dylan's *Skyline* sessions.

The influence of *Nashville Skyline* dwarfed the album itself. Dylan had helped trigger a major shift in taste and style, and was privately amazed at the effect the album had on other musicians. As for the audience, by the time they got to Woodstock, its most celebrated resident had become almost an honorary citizen of Nashville.

Woodstock East, the Isle of Wight. Ending a remarkable decade in pop music, 1969 was the year when several giants of rock resurfaced and the international audience showed what an elephantine monster it had become. During the summer of 1969, Elvis Presley, unseen on stage since the 1950s, sang for a live audience in Las Vegas. John Lennon resumed concerts that year, while the Rolling Stones gave a free concert in London's Hyde Park. The sage of Woodstock, who had been pondering a stage return for some time, got an offer he chose not to refuse—one gig in late August at the Isle of Wight Music Festival. During the Woodstock Festival, held partly in Dylan's honor on his own doorstep, he was appearing 3,000 miles eastward at Europe's own Woodstock. Even in absentia, Dylan cast a long shadow. Greil Marcus in *Rolling Stone*, September 20, 1969: "willingly or not, Bob Dylan was the presence hovering over this three-day jamboree ... he is the elder of this urban tribe ... the tribally tom-tommed message of WOODSTOCK, Dylan's refuge, WOODSTOCK, Dylan's turf, WOODSTOCK, Dylan's bringing it all back home, was as much responsible for moving this massive surge of humanity on to a 600-acre farm as any advertisements, promotion, publicity."

If Dylan wouldn't work on Max Yasgur's farm in Bethel, New York, some 450,000 others would. The spontaneous combustion of Woodstock was, in the words of *Time*, "the moment when the special culture of US youth ... displayed its strength ... it may well rank as one of the significant political and sociological events of the age." Woodstock inspired more hyperbole: Ginsberg called it "a major planetary event." Yippie Abbie Hoffman saw it as "the birth of the Woodstock Nation and the death of the American dinosaur." Local police, farmers, and carpenters' wives were astounded at the numbers and their gentleness. A *New York Times* editorial asked of this pilgrimage of "lemmings": "What kind of culture ... can produce so colossal a mess?" The next day, the same editorial page saw it as just "a phenomenon of innocence."

Two weeks later, like a muted European echo, came the antiphonal response from the second Isle of Wight Music Festival. From all over Europe, perhaps as many as 200,000 young flocked. Among them were most of the Beatles and Stones, Jane Fonda and Roger Vadim, the Paris cast of *Hair*, and a huge press corps. There were hints that a mellowed Dylan was going to be quite chatty with the press. At his Woodstock home, he told Ray Connolly of London's *Evening Standard*: "I don't ... live such a secluded life ... I'm just living a normal happy life like any other guy. I'm very anxious to get back on the stage ... I hope to be able to sing just about whatever the people want to hear ... The accident ... still bothers me a bit. My bones ache in the cold weather, or when it gets too humid. But in many ways it was good for me. It really slowed me down. Touring had been such a pace to keep up. And I was getting in a rut." Connolly was surprised: "The apparent bonhomie of the man is indeed a shock."

In another interview, with Don Short of London's *Daily Mirror*, extracts of which made their way into *Melody Maker*, Dylan explained: "Sara and I grew up as kids together in Minnesota. Then some years back we met again in a New York restaurant where Sara was working as a waitress. We fell in love—although it was not love at first sight, and five years ago we were married in New York State. We didn't advertise the fact as we feel our personal lives are what they mean. Otherwise, we would have gone to Hollywood to live and become members of the show-biz set, which we hope we never will be." Dylan spoke of accepting George Harrison's invitation to record at Apple Studios in London, and of planning a major tour with the Band, "although it won't be like the old days when we fell from exhaustion." He said he was looking for a film with a heavy story line. "I wouldn't mind working with someone like Alfred Hitchcock. He wouldn't do anything thin."

Two brothers, Ray and Ron Foulk, then 23 and 24, had lured Dylan to the Isle of Wight. "We realized we couldn't attract him with money, so we decided to sell him the island," Ray said. A third brother, Bill, 22, made a color film of its beauty spots, the festival site, and the house they'd rent for Dylan. With Bert Block negotiating, Dylan accepted a contract that caused pop-press dismay, although he had turned down sums four times larger. The most reliable figures I could obtain were that the Foulks offered him £21,000 and fifty percent of the net, plus £6,000 for expenses. The Band got £8,000, and Richie Havens was paid £3,300.

The Dylan family boarded the *Queen Elizabeth 2* in New York on August 13. During a small farewell party, Jesse, then four, suddenly lost consciousness. The ship's doctor reportedly wouldn't accept responsibility for Jesse's ability to make the voyage, and Bob lifted his son on to his shoulders and rushed him to a New York hospital for observation. The boy soon revived, his condition "not serious." A few days later, the Dylans flew into Heathrow, and were soon ensconced in a sixteenth-century farmhouse, Forelands Farm, near Bembridge. It had a swimming pool, and a barn for rehearsals. Gates and guards kept the public at bay. Chris White of London's *Daily Sketch* got past them long enough to ask Dylan what attracted him to the Isle of Wight. Tennyson had lived there, Bob replied, and he'd always wanted to visit. "Basically, we are just having a holiday." Of his English fans: "They are the most loyal fans I have and that was one of the reasons to ... come to England to make my comeback. It's not the money I'm interested in. I just want to play music."

Bob gave a twenty-minute press conference. Some reporters seemed to want to provoke an old cat-and-mouse session, so they asked him about drugs and his marriage, whether he was becoming square, why he was there. He stuck to Tennyson. His longest comment: "My job is to play music. I'm just going to take it easy. You've got to take it easy if you're going to do your job well." No anger or defiance. Some reporters were annoyed that their bombshells had been defused. They looked to the festival site for more exciting copy. They found plenty there, with an army crossing the Solent by ferry and hovercraft in what one paper called "a second Dunkirk." Headlines also called it D-DAY, THE ISLE OF DYLAN, and, inevitably, playing with the Beatles' title, TICKET TO RYDE, to describe where the boats landed. Every British national paper had a front-page story, many with photos of the crowds.

The festival began Friday, with Nice and the Bonzo Dog Band. Saturday was dominated by the Who and Joe Cocker. American folk influences, and some Dylan songs, surfaced in sets by Julie Felix and Havens. The evening roster included the Edgar Broughton Band, Marsha Hunt, Family, and Blodwyn Pig. Electric programming Sunday included the Liverpool Scene in mixed pop and poetry; the Third Ear Band and the Indo-Jazz Fusions added other colors. Poet Christopher Logue and journalist Anthony Haden-Guest read contemporary poetry, not Tennyson. One surprise was the impact of Tom Paxton. His folk-topical songs had an audience reaction that *Melody Maker* called "amazing." More folk styles followed with Pentangle.

I was backstage chatting with Gloria Emerson and Clive Barnes, both of the *New York Times*. Dylan's convoy arrived and there, smiling, trying to looked relaxed and very mortal, was Dylan. I checked the time: 7:23 p.m. Dylan had been ready to go on at 7:30, which was noteworthy, since later there was widespread anger at his late entrance and brief appearance. I have never been able to determine the cause of the delay. Bob later told me he didn't know what it was about either, but felt the festival was run very poorly. Karl Dallas in his *Acoustic Music* magazine said the delay was conditioned by Bert Block's demand that Dylan and the Band be paid before performing. The press seats had to accommodate perhaps 500 reporters, VIPs, friends of the high and mighty, when probably fewer than half that number of seats was available. I avoided *that* mob scene and went to the back of the crowd. To get a good spot, I had to climb over hillocks of empty beer cans, around piles of rubbish, over prone, stoned bodies. One tent encampment of fans was signposted DESOLATION ROW. From my location, the figures onstage looked like ants. About 9:30, compère Rikki Farr announced that Grossman's party could come forward to their seats. Every few minutes there was a call for an ambulance, for someone on a bad trip or suffering from exhaustion. Intermission started at 8:00, but the Band did not come on until 10:00. It was a terribly restless two hours, during which Farr voiced exasperation over the mike. Only the Stones' record "You Can't Always Get What You Want" sounded like the truth.

The Band suffered from the same problems that vexed Dylan's appearance—bad sound, impersonality, too distant. From my post, perhaps a quarter of a mile away, the Band was very slow to kindle. A bit of their punch came through on "Brazos" and "Don't Ya Tell Henry." By 10:35, while they were playing "I Shall Be Released," many in the audience were shouting for Dylan. By 10:50 and "The Weight," they'd adjusted to their surroundings, but then their set ended. After interminable mike testing, Dylan walked on with the Band. Standing ovation, flashbulbs and flashlights, Roman candles. Dylan was in white, tieless, with a pastel-colored shirt. He slid into "She Belongs to Me" in a soft jazz-crooner voice that sounded unfamiliar, even after *Nashville Skyline*. Dylan's longest comment to a roaring crowd was: "It's, ah, great to be here. It sure is." During "I Threw It All Away" with acoustic guitar, he didn't appear nervous so much as formal. He played "Maggie's Farm" in a bluesy vein, with strong Band harmonies. Especially for English listeners, he played "Will You Go, Lassie, Go" (or "Wild Mountain Thyme"), taking some florid vocal lines unaccompanied. "It Ain't Me, Babe" and "To Ramona" were rather introverted, but the audience seemed to catch his mood and reached toward him. By "Tambourine Man," they were in his hands. He then sang "St Augustine," "Lay, Lady, Lay," and "Highway 61." The audience, more appreciative than ecstatic, seemed to be waiting for fireworks. Then came "One Too Many Mornings," with a nod to the Manfred Mann recording, "Immigrant," the predictable excitement with "Rolling Stone," a country lullaby on "Baby Tonight," and a bit more extroversion on "Quinn" and "Rainy Day Women." Evidently, he remembered the 1966 "Rainy Day" ruckus in England. He split just before midnight, returning for encores, and repeating "Rainy Day" for the final encore. The crowd thought it was only the beginning. Dylan briskly said, "Thank you," and departed. Rikki Farr bleated: "I'm sorry! Dylan has gone! He came and he did what he had to do!"

Ever since Dylan had told Don Short of the *Daily Mirror* that he *might* do three hours, the pop press and the festival organizers had been teasing ticket-buyers into expecting something transcendent. The

August 30 *Melody Maker* front-page headline ran DYLAN, STONES, GEORGE HARRISON, BLIND FAITH-SUPERSESSION AT ISLE OF WIGHT, adding in smaller type below, "If Bob Approves." *Record Mirror* had forecast "The Biggest Jam Session in History." Hype led inevitably to let-down. Everywhere I saw tired, disappointed kids slogging back toward the ferries. "Dylan, RIP," said one Midlands lad. The Associated Press reported: "There was near pandemonium as outraged fans asked: 'Has he gone? Where is he?' Security guards with dogs raced … to prevent any trouble … no incidents and the crowd soon began to filter away." The *Daily Mail* reported bonfires and chants of: "We want Dylan—music, music, music!" The *Daily Mirror*: "100,000 pop fans threatened to riot."

Dylan left England in a very disappointed mood. The *Sketch* quoted him as saying "I don't ever want to perform in England again" but, according to the *Mirror*, said: "The concert was great—and I am coming back again next year." Levon Helm of the Band told the *Sketch*: "Bob tried everything he knew to reach the audience, but it didn't come off." On Tuesday, September 2, Dylan went to Heathrow Airport in a Mercedes driven by George Harrison. The *Express* quoted Dylan: "I was shattered by stories that the kids were angry because I was three hours late. I was there at 5:30 as promised. I don't know why we were so long before going on. Ask the producers … The fans were terrific." The Beatles offered strong support. Harrison: "The concert was marvelous. Bob did not walk off … half-way through his act. He gave a brilliant performance." Lennon: "He gave a reasonable, albeit slightly flat, performance, but everyone was expecting Godot, a Jesus, to appear."

By the time Dylan touched down at Kennedy Airport, he said he had no wish to return to England. "They make too much of singers over there." He called the Isle of Wight a warm-up for future American tours. During Dylan's first major appearance in eighteen months, he found himself in a situation he could not fully control. In retrospect, I think the festival had a great deal to do with his holding off further live appearances until early 1974 (though he did turn out for George Harrison's Concert for Bangladesh at Madison Square Garden, in August 1971). When he did return, he wasn't doing low-key introverted work, but reaching out boldly for an audience that demanded much greater excitement.

The Isle of Wight was the beginning of a low period for Dylan professionally; many were ready to repeat that he was finished. Yet the *Melody Maker* International Pop Poll of September 20, 1969 listed Dylan as the top international male singer and *Nashville Skyline* as the top LP. But other members of the audience virtually turned Dylan into a political prisoner, telling him what and how to perform, how to spend his money, how to write his songs. One "fan" was even telling Dylan where to dump his garbage.

On stage with the Band, Isle of Wight, 1969.

This page: Rehearsing for TV show with Johnny Cash, Nashville, 1969.
Inset: A Song for Woody, a benefit concert at Carnegie Hall, 1968—Rick Danko, left Dylan and Robbie Robertson.
Right: Another iconic image for *Nashville Skyline*, 1969.

Einstein suffered the fate of many other revolutionaries who boldly take the first steps on a new road but shrink from the next steps. Others may come along to pick up the journey because the road seems too sinister to its discoverer.

WERNER HEISENBERG

So, in every individual the two trends, one toward personal happiness and the other toward unity with the rest of humanity, must contend with each other.

FREUD, *CIVILIZATION AND ITS DISCONTENTS*

Pain sure brings out the best in people, doesn't it?

DYLAN, 1971

Recording *Self Portrait*, Nashville, 1969.

"It's the price of fame, I guess," Dylan told me sadly at the height of the Scavenger's campaign against him. "We loaded up our garbage with as much dog shit as we could—mousetraps, everything—but he still keeps going through my garbage!" The Scavenger was, in the words of Jerry Rubin, John Lennon, Yoko Ono, and David Peel, "leading a public campaign of lies and malicious slander against Dylan." They wrote to the *Village Voice* in December 1971: "The press is all over him trying to get information or gossip about Dylan ... he is a self-proclaimed authority on Dylan's music ... [he] is to Dylan as Manson is to the Beatles—and uses what he interprets from Dylan's music to try and kill Dylan and build his own fame."

The Scavenger was a would-be anarchist star, a wheeler-dealer of the freaked-out New Left, a garbage groupie, a not-so-urbane guerilla, a self-promoting, speedy-talking hustler named Alan Jules Weberman. He proclaimed himself "the world's greatest authority on Dylan" and "the father of Dylanology." Actually, he accused Dylan of countless crimes, harassing and vilifying him for three years. For a while, some accepted his accusations that Dylan was "a pig," a junkie, a super-capitalist backing napalm-makers and reactionaries. From 1968 through 1971, during one of the cruelest assaults ever made on the privacy of an artist, Weberman led delegations to Dylan's home in the Village, telephoned him at weird hours, taped conversations with him, then distributed these tapes and transcripts around the world. I talked to the Scavenger twice on the phone. His voice was raspy and agitated, his language abusive. I decided not to interview him and even discussing him presents me with a dilemma. To give him too much space is to suggest importance.[1]

Weberman began by publishing in *Broadside*, sounding like a Dylan student looking for hidden allusions. He found political content in Dylan songs where others couldn't, even seeing attacks on the System in "Sad-Eyed Lady"! *Broadside*'s Gordon Friesen saw A J, as he was familiarly known, as a freakish, benign analyst of Dylan's work. Then, the Scavenger started to read *himself* into Dylan songs. He cloaked himself in Yippie rhetoric, attacking "pig" Dylan for having earned money for his work. The Scavenger may have turned when Dylan refused to let his lyrics be quoted in a book he had written. Weberman then accused Dylan of commercial rip-offs and bad personal habits. In the 1969 *Rolling Stone* interview, Dylan put down the Scavenger hard, suggesting he find other writers to misread. This only made Weberman more virulent. He began to play Dylan's records backward, finding hidden "clues." Increasingly, the Scavenger's fulminations were relayed through the Underground Press Syndicate and published uncritically.

The Scavenger formed the Dylan Liberation Front and then the Rock Liberation Front, of which he was the self-styled Minister of Defense. He researched Dylan's finances, finding royalty-check vouchers from Columbia, unearthing Dylan's alleged real estate investments. Estimating that Dylan had earned more than $12 million, he called him "the singing real estate broker." Weberman cited Dylan's poetry as "proof" that he used drugs. He had FREE BOB DYLAN buttons made up. The day before Dylan's thirtieth birthday, May 24, 1971, the Scavenger organized a "block party" in front of Dylan's home and sounded a call to arms: "If you want to get more info on the Dylan Liberation Front and rock lyrics in general, or if you want to tell me to go fuck myself and let Dylan 'do his thing,' you can write to me, Post Office Box 340, Canal Street Station, New York City, 10013."

By 1971, the Scavenger seemed to feel that Dylan had somewhat redeemed himself with the "George Jackson" single and his appearance at the concert for Bangladesh; thereafter the attacks diminished. Weberman claimed that Dylan's "political acts" were the results of his campaign! By the end of 1971, other Rock Liberation Fronters admonished the Scavenger publicly, dissociating themselves from his hassling. The Scavenger turned to other pursuits, claiming to have made $900 on a magazine story about garbage. I decided not to visit his "Dylan Archives" on Bleecker Street. I told him I was considering giving my own archives to some university library where they would be available to other Dylan students.[2] "Man, man," Weberman rasped, "What I've got is *mine*."

Which Side Is He On? Others, less extreme than Weberman, repeatedly felt betrayed by Dylan after 1966, for his rock-star indulgences. When Dylan dropped out, he relinquished millions of dollars from concerts and their stimulus to record sales. He turned down TV and film offers that would have swelled his income. In retreat, Dylan refused more money than many pop stars made in a career.

One of the Scavenger's charges disturbed the most: "Dylan supports the racist and counterrevolutionary organization, the Jewish Defense League … a militant organization whose aim is to attack anyone they believed to be anti-Jewish." Even Weberman admitted that the JDL stated that Dylan had never given this group any money. Still, the allegation stuck. Many political sophisticates found Dylan's interest in Zionist militancy hard to take. After the 1967 war, leftists of all backgrounds challenged Israel as an imperialist-maintained military government. Many Jews were alarmed by Israeli denial of Palestinian rights. I saw Bob just before his trip to Israel in May 1971, which he went to great pains to keep private. He only hinted at an interest in the JDL. He also talked of Jewish writers he was reading, of attending a Hasidic wedding. He certainly didn't appear to be endorsing Zionism. Because Stephen Pickering is a specialist in Jewish culture and Dylan's work, I asked his opinion in December 1975:

"Dylan visited Israel in the summers of 1969 and 1970, in May 1971, and shortly after the filming of *Pat Garrett*. After the 1970 visit, Israel Eichenstein … contacted Dylan, asking for his attendance at the Israel Birthday Be-In in Central Park. Dylan declined: 'I would attract too many people who have nothing to do with the cause of our people. I know, man, I identify.' Dylan and Eichenstein grew close, and it was Eichenstein who … persuaded Dylan that the JDL lacked an important Jewish ingredient: compassion. In May 1971, the Israeli newspaper *Yediot Achronot* published a brief interview/profile. Dylan mentioned the earlier visits, that he had friends in Israel. On May 22, 1971, Dylan and Sara walked through Old Jerusalem, and visited the Mount Zion Yeshiva, a famous Cabalistic training center. They sat in the ancient courtyard for the day. Several American students were introduced to Dylan by Rabbi Yoso Rosenzweig, who asked Dylan why he shied away from a personal, direct, unmistakable declaration. 'There is no problem,' Dylan replied. 'I'm a Jew. It touches my poetry, my life, in ways I can't describe. Why should I declare something that should be so obvious?' Two days later, a UPI photographer took two photographs at the Wall of a tourist, then realized it was Dylan.

"Dylan's brief relationship with the Jewish Defense League has been blown out of proportion: Rabbi Meir Kahane first met Dylan when Kahane was on a WABC-FM debate with Abbie Hoffman and Paul Krassner. Kahane asked Dylan for a donation to the JDL Soviet Jewry Fund. What happened is a matter of some disagreement. Kahane claims, as of 1974, that Dylan *didn't* give a contribution," Pickering continued.

"In 1972, Dylan *investigated* the possibility of emigrating to Israel. According to kibbutz Neve Eitan member Ari Davidow, 'the kibbutz had been taken aback by two things: Dylan could bring in dope-smoking groupies sponging off kibbutz hospitality,' and Dylan's five children didn't fit into the kibbutz age bracket. The kibbutz secretary procrastinated, then decided Dylan deserved just as much a chance as anyone else. He sent him an application blank in September 1972, 'but we never heard from him again.' Dylan's identification with the idealism of Israel remains unabated, despite profound upheavals in his personal life. My friend, Roberta Richards, who visited Dylan on January 10, 1974, at his Toronto Hotel, told me: 'He noticed my Star of David and he showed me the mezuzah he wears. It's silver, and he got it in Israel.' Rabbi Shlomo Carlebach has tried to get Dylan to consider his obligations as a Jew … Carlebach believes something serious has happened to Dylan since the 1974 tour … Dylan told of plans to purchase an apartment in Jerusalem. Since then he has shown signs of being under a serious strain … Dylan, on January 3, 1974, agreed with me—that his Israel visits have had a profound effect upon him. On the liner notes of *Planet Waves*, the reference to Hebrew letters is an age-old custom for one to bring prayer/petitions to the Wall, with which to pose operable axioms."

In the September 11, 1976, *TV Guide* interview, Dylan said: "There was no great significance to that visit … I'm interested in what and who a Jew is. I'm interested in the fact that Jews are Semites, like Babylonians, Hittites, Arabs, Syrians, Ethiopians. But a Jew is different because a lot of people hate Jews. There's something going on here that's hard to explain."

Jonathan Braun, president of the New York Union of Jewish Students, wrote a piece in the *Jewish Digest* of September 1971, "The Bob Dylan Rumor Machine." Braun found that "by and large, the stories turn out to be fabrications of … clearly overzealous, young Jewish nationalists …" Braun quoted Theo

Bikel: "Dylan has told me that Israel appears to be one of the few places left in this world where life has any meaning," concluding: "The possibility that Dylan may be examining his Jewish heritage is actually quite plausible. Dylan, after all, is Jewish; and at a time when increasing numbers of … young Americans are experiencing an intense rebirth of ethnic consciousness, it is more than likely that he would find himself taking a fresh look at his past."

Despite his desire for privacy, the El Al flight list alerted the Israeli press to Dylan's arrival on a mid-May Sunday. He brushed unwelcome reporters away. CBS Records in Israel advertised in the *Jerusalem Post*, wishing him happy birthday and asking him to get in touch with them! Catherine Rosenheim of the *Jerusalem Post Magazine* tracked him down on Herzliyya Beach. As Dylan surfaced from the waves, the intrepid reporter waited onshore: "It was all remarkably easy … Perhaps he was just in a holiday mood." The swimmer told the *Post* he'd been "all over the place—we've been here a long time." (Actually, eight days.) Dylan said he was collecting material for his journal, to be published "some time" along with some songs. "Actually, that's the main reason why we're here incognito—it's impossible to work with dozens of people milling around you all the time … I didn't think my records were officially released here and so didn't want any publicity." Would he write any songs about Israel? No, but he had written one about Yugoslavia, he said with a smile. How had he spent his thirtieth birthday? "We went to see a Gregory Peck movie—I'm quite a fan of his." The *Post* reported that "rumors about changing his name were, he said, 'pure journalese and not a word of truth.'"

Through the dust of rumor, I pieced together this picture: while Dylan was listening to the silence after his accident, he was trying to plumb his own mysteries and identities. Reading Jewish writers, going to Hasidic weddings, interest in the "toughness" of the Jewish Defense League—all this, I think, didn't signal any change of dramatic intensity, just a *searching*. Many Jews believe that the only way a Jew can avoid alienation in a hostile world is to assert his Jewish identity. To some Jewish nationalists this becomes tantamount to embracing Zionism. But many Jews are not oriented toward Israel. As a young man, Dylan had wanted to be part of the American experience. Jewish friends, from Allen Ginsberg to his music publisher, Naomi Saltzman, and her husband, might have suggested he could find some peace by identifying with Jewish culture. *All else is speculation.* Dylan wanted to take a look at Israel, without being crowded or pledged to public commitment. Although Ginsberg heard Hebrew cantillation on *Desire*, I hear flamenco and soul. So much depends on the beholder.

Watching the River. The controversy over Dylan's politics, apoliticism or even anti-politicism continued for years. If he didn't speak, his songs did. Ironically, the violent Weathermen appropriated a line from "Subterranean Homesick Blues." Conversely, in June 1972, at a Madison Square Garden benefit for Democratic presidential candidate George McGovern, Peter, Paul and Mary sang "When the Ship Comes In," "Times Changing," and "Blowin' in the Wind." From 1969 on, there had been pressure on him to resume writing protest music. When he released "George Jackson" in 1971, *Rolling Stone* remarked that the song immediately "divided speculators into two camps, those who see it as the poet's return to social relevance and those who feel that it's a cheap way for Dylan to get a lot of people off his back." Robert Christgau hit back in the *Village Voice* on December 17, 1971: "This is ugly nonsense, of course, because the song is neither … the protest Dylan and the anti-protest Dylan are both part of the persona now … Dylan has never lacked social relevance … Dylan responded with real human sympathy to a hideous assassination …" In the song about the slaying of the Soledad brother, Dylan spoke on several planes: "Sometimes I think this whole world is one big prison yard/Some of us are prisoners, the rest of us are guards …"[3] CBS Records, which promoted "the rock revolution" in the mid-1960s, chose as its promotional line: "Dylan's New Single Is a Political Act."

Dylan popped up on TV in November 1971, on a *Free Time* WNET-TV show with Ginsberg, Peter Orlovsky, Gerard Malanga, and other poets, playing background guitar and singing along, unbilled, to the poets' strongly political material. But even Dylan's appearance on August 1, 1971, at the concerts for Bangladesh, before 40,000 people, wasn't enough for politicos. At a Carnegie Hall concert in autumn 1971, Joan Baez said she'd written a song for Dylan, whom she hadn't seen in four years. She launched into "To Bobby," which implored him to retrieve all his little lambs who'd lost their shepherd. Baez would remain on the picket line, but Dylan was one of many Sixties radicals who'd move away and into a new life. Jerry Rubin told the *San Francisco Chronicle* on October 31, 1973: "This is a growth period for everyone, including me. I'm working … on myself … Too much happened too fast in the 1960s, and people are repairing themselves."

On September 12, 1974, in the *Village Voice*, Carole Getzoff described "Tripping Out on Torah": "Former blue-jeaned freaks donning blue suits, replacing funky old cowboy hats with … yamulkas … Former throwers of the I Ching diligently studying the Torah and the Talmud." From Berkeley came a report in the *Times* in late 1972 indicating that the campus had politically hibernated. Berkeley student leaders and Yippies could change, but Dylan was consistently berated for "selling out." Ira Mayer defended him in the *Village Voice* on December 2, 1971: "I don't understand why people continue to pester him about 'commitment.' Isn't music itself 'commitment' enough?" After Israel, 1971, Dylan joined Leon Russell and the Tulsa Tops on a single, "Watching the River Flow," an energetic, funky-gospel rocker. The promotional photograph showed Dylan with a camera to his eye. At that point, he wanted to be just an observer:

> *What's the matter with me,*
> *I don't have much to say …*
> *People disagreeing everywhere you look,*
> *Makes you wanna stop and read a book.*
> *Why only yesterday I saw somebody on the street*
> *That was really shook.*
> *But this ol' river keeps on rollin', though,*
> *No matter what gets in the way and which way the wind does blow,*
> *And as long as it does I'll just sit here*
> *And watch the river flow.*[4]

On May 9, 1974, an unbilled Dylan appeared in New York at a Felt Forum benefit for Chilean refugees from the junta that deposed Socialist president Salvador Allende. Hosts for this Friends of Chile concert were Phil Ochs and actor Dennis Hopper. Dylan jammed with Ochs, Dave Van Ronk, Pete Seeger and Arlo Guthrie. He spent time then with Joan Jara, widow of Victor Jara, the Chilean folk singer whose fingers had been smashed with an ax before the junta executed him in Santiago's National Stadium. Reliving her loss at rallies around the world, she was under great strain. In London later, she recalled how Dylan asked if she could ever relax. "'Come down and see some nice pictures,' Dylan said to me. 'Meet me at Fifth Avenue and 54th Street tomorrow afternoon at three, and I'll take you to see some nice pictures.' I never imagined he would be there. But I showed up, and there he was, leaning against a lamppost. And he took me to the Museum of Modern Art and showed me around, said he was with us." Dylan wanted human contact with a woman who had suffered so much—he didn't want to picket the Chilean Embassy.

Gradually, Leftist critics realized Dylan was still on the side of the angels. Significantly, in 1975, although Dylan was the strongest voice speaking out for imprisoned boxer Rubin "Hurricane" Carter, Dylan's name never appeared on the list of Carter's patron-supporters. Still, the Left had its doubts. During Dylan's 1974 tour, rumors circulated that he was going to contribute some proceeds to Israel. Mimi Fariña told the *San Francisco Chronicle* that ticket purchasers should have the right to know that they were contributing to a nation at war. Jeremy Larner, Oscar-winning scriptwriter of *The Candidate* and former speechwriter for Eugene McCarthy, contested Mimi's view. Characteristically, Dylan remained silent. Meanwhile, as late as summer 1975, there were guns on the Right. South Africa's *Transvaal Educational News* ran a story headed: BOB DYLAN, "A VOICE FOR THE REDS," alleging that Dylan had become "the most successful proponent of communism's new class war, youth versus age" and had "become a millionaire while singing lyrics about the poor overthrowing the rich." And in September 1977, *Soviet Literature Gazette* dismissed Dylan as "nothing more than a money-hungry capitalist now." Which side was he on?

Picasso and Sartre became embroiled in battles with the organized Left and the mal-organised Right. The greater an artist's influence, the more various causes try to align him as a spokesman. Dylan turned political questions back to the questioners—do it yourself, don't ask me or anyone else to do it for you. His message was consistently misunderstood and misapplied. Perhaps the reason he chose to go in and out of "political commitment," to pick the causes he chose to support, was that he simply didn't want to be tied to people who might speak for him without his permission.

Dr Dylan Takes His Own Pulse. Which was the greater surprise? That Princeton offered Dylan an honorary doctorate of music, or that the anti-academic college drop-out accepted? Dylan arrived the night before the ceremony of June 9, 1970, with his wife, David Crosby, and Ben Saltzman, his music publisher's husband. Among the nine to be honored at Princeton's 223rd graduation ceremonies was another writer, Walter Lippmann, and another singer, Coretta King, widow of the Reverend Dr Martin Luther King, Jr. At first, like 25 of the 1,200 graduating seniors, Bob refused to wear the traditional black robe, but he later put it on over his dark, pin-striped suit. He wore no tie or mortarboard. Like most of the graduates, he put on a white armband bearing a peace symbol. Dylan's escort was William H Attwood, editor-in-chief of *Look*, a Princeton trustee, and a key man in the Cowles Communications empire.

Princeton's President Robert F Goheen gave Dylan his DMus, writ in Latin on parchment. The more informal citation read: "As one of the most creative popular musicians of the last decade, he has based his techniques in the arts of the common people of our past and torn his appeals for human compassion from the experience of the dispossessed. Paradoxically, though known to millions, he shuns publicity and organizations, preferring the solidarity of his family and isolation from the world. Although he is now approaching the perilous age of 30, his music remains the authentic expression of the disturbed and concerned conscience of young America." Ill at ease through most of the ceremony, Dylan smiled at "perilous age." On many American campuses, students had been prodding administrations for more substance, more relevance. By 1970, honorary degrees were going increasingly to women, unionists, blacks, and the young. Princeton attributed the choice of Dylan directly to two undergraduates on the nominating committee. A few months later, on *New Morning*, surfaced "Day of the Locusts:"

> *I put down my robe, picked up my diploma,*
> *Took hold of my sweetheart and away we did drive …*
> *Sure was glad to get out of there alive*[5]

The song's title brought to mind both the biblical plague on the pharaoh and Nathanael West's Hollywood-based novel, *The Day of the Locust*. In West's climax, a lower-middle-class mob who feel cheated unleash horrible violence.

As he was receiving his DMus, Dylan released *Self Portrait*, which remains his most contentious album. A *Rolling Stone* chorus of twelve writers voiced outrage. "What is this shit?" Greil Marcus challenged Dylan, warning, "Unless he returns to the marketplace, with a sense of vocation and the ambition to keep up with his own gifts," the music of 1965–66 would dominate his career. Charles Perry wrote: "We know Dylan was the Rimbaud of his generation; it seems he's found his Abyssinia." *Time*: "For a man who charged his way through the 1960s like an Orpheus in Hades," this Dylan is "astonishingly contemplative." *Record World*: "The revolution is over. Bob Dylan sings 'Blue Moon' to Mr Jones."

Self Portrait contains twenty-four tracks, fourteen by Dylan. Three of these are primarily instrumentals, so many people felt over-charged for a double album. Four tracks come from the Isle of Wight sessions with the Band; the others were recorded in New York and Nashville. *Self Portrait*, an elaborate production job, had a cast of fifty supporting musicians and singers; strings, brasses, female vocal ensembles. Some called the resulting melange "easy listening" or "middle of the road." Others thought the double album was a joke, a cynical cop-out, or Dylan's test of his power. It sold fabulously well, grossing $3 million by the end of June 1970, jumping up the *Billboard* chart from 200 to seven in one week, and to number one in *Record World* by August.

I told Dylan that *Self Portrait* confused me. Why had he recorded "Blue Moon"? He wouldn't be drawn, although obviously he had been stung by the criticism. "It was an expression," he said. He indicated that if the album had come from Presley or the Everly Brothers, who veered toward the middle of the road, it wouldn't have shocked so many. My initial reaction was negative, because *Self Portrait* sounded like somebody else, a self-portrait drawn from a cracked mirror, suggested by the cover of a hollow-eyed Rouault-Chagallesque clown looking at his reflection. Was Dylan trying to show us that he saw himself as made up of fragments of folk, country, and old pop songs, accompanied by a modern sound? Was the album an experiment that didn't work? Was he pulling our collective legs? My reaction has since mellowed, although I still place *Self Portrait* among my least favorite Dylan albums. It was another step in Dylan's retreat from significance toward being the simple man, the country squire pictured inside the album jacket standing near a barn, talking to a chicken. Perhaps he figured that if *Nashville Skyline* had reached more listeners than any previous album, he should try a middle-of-the-road approach and touch even more people. Now I view *Self Portrait* as an experiment in appealing to Middle America on its own terms. Dylan later said: "A lot of worse stuff was appearing on bootleg records." It was, "so to speak, my own bootleg record." I think *Self Portrait* could have been one moderately good LP instead of a double album padded with material better left in the can. "In Search of Little Sadie" was an eccentric foray into modulation, yet the song works as excellent, cheery country. "Alberta 1" was mediocre, yet "Alberta 2," with its mournful mouth harp, was fine. Some of the material, like "I Forgot More Than You'll Ever Know" and "Take Me as I Am," are not my kind of gritty country songs, and I think "Early Mornin' Rain" and "Let It Be Me" are pap. At least two jokes on the album simply don't work: "Blue Moon" *à la* Bing Crosby, and "The Boxer" by Paul Simon, in which, using overdubbing, Dylan seems to be sending up *both* Simon and Garfunkel. Quality gets rather lost amid such dross. "All the Tired Horses" and "Wigwam" are hard to forget. "Days of 49" is flavorful period Americana. "Woogie Boogie" is a superb instrumental, full of grinding Fats Domino-Johnny Otis echoes. "Living the Blues," "Gotta Travel On," and "It Hurts Me Too" have moments ranging from fine to excellent.

Self Portrait forced Dylan to show doubters that his inspiration still burned. His early return to the studios in autumn 1970 to tape the twelve songs of *New Morning* certainly seemed like a riposte. This album, and title song, recalled lines from his *Broadside* letter of January 1964: "An I shall wake in the mornin and try t start/lovin again." Many regarded *New Morning* as his best album since *Blonde on Blonde*. The new album was unpretentious, and had more cohesion and shape than *Self Portrait*. It contained Dylan's first prayer ("Father of Night"), first jazz song ("If Dogs Run Free"), first Hank Williams-style talking country song ("Three Angels"), and first *waltz* ("Winterlude"). Another innovation was Dylan gospel-style slow block-chording on piano. Altogether, an excellent collection of quiet gems.

Greil Marcus, in the *Sunday New York Times*, called it Dylan's "best album in years … an act of vitality" Ed Ward, in *Rolling Stone*: "One of the best albums of the year … perhaps his best." Ed Ochs, in *Billboard*: "Dylan is dancing, singing to the sun, you can really love him. Dylan's voice of the year runs free with fresh, determined blues rhythms … Dylan lives!" Lucian Truscott, the *Village Voice*: "'New Morning' is similar to the enlightened anachronism that was 'folk music' when Dylan took it to a pinnacle of visionary art." Dylan was once again reflecting a social climate in America, presaging a shift away from "Too Much of Nothing." In *Rolling Stone*, Ralph Gleason could shout: "We've got Bob Dylan back again … the most reassuring thing … this year of the bombings … This is a hopeful album, and, my God, how we need it." On February 22, 1971, a special *Time* section, "The Cooling of America," saw many of the extremes of the war-scarred 1960s starting a return to "a mood approaching quiet … the calm … suggests a complex of rather sober fear … there is a chastened air … such a weariness—and much more—accounts for the profound hibernation of the radical movement in the US."

New Morning began the 1970s with a statement of serenity, even as *Self Portrait* had ended the 1960s with nostalgic pastiche. *Morning* proclaimed Emersonian "self-reliance," a frontier of personal freedom. Dylan asks: "If dogs run free, then why not we?"[6] This wistful contentment, free of smugness, converges in "Sign on the Window":

> *Build me a cabin in Utah,*
> *Marry me a wife, catch rainbow trout*
> *Have a bunch of kids who call me "Pa,"*
> *That must be what it's all about.*[7]

Dylan recorded "New Morning," "Time Passes Slowly," and "Father of Night" for Archibald MacLeish's play *The Devil and Daniel Webster*. When the producer didn't like "Father of Night," Dylan backed out of the production. When he wrote "If Not for You," he was "thinking about my wife."

Dylan's response to public disappointment in *Self Portrait* was an affirmation of life and happiness. Even when he senses the locusts coming along to snatch all Establishment-trained people after their graduation, he doesn't sing of plague. As the drifter of *John Wesley Harding* discovered, there is an escape route from the horror.

Late in 1969, Dylan had escaped back to the Village, to a house on lower MacDougal Street, below Bleecker. For a time, he enjoyed the anonymity that he lost in the country. But not for long could he dissolve into city streets and live quietly behind closed doors. He surfaced in old haunts, seeing what was left of his old Village gang. A decade had changed the Kettle, Folk City, the Gaslight, the Bitter End.

New York's intrusions on Dylan's privacy reached their apogee in spring 1971. Although he was in Israel, the Scavenger organized that "anti-birthday party" on Sunday, May 23, in front of Dylan's house. In Washington Square Park, street singer David Peel recruited a crowd by banging a cowbell with a drumstick. Peel blew his police whistle and proclaimed: "We're going to Dylan's house now. It's the rich house next to the Hip Bagel. You know why it's next to the Hip Bagel? Because Dylan made a pretzel out of you." In front of the house, Weberman, appropriately atop a garbage can, addressed some 300 people, shouting through a megaphone for Dylan to come out. No response. "You see, Dylan doesn't care about people anymore. Dylan doesn't care if you or I drop dead." A heckler: "Dylan does care. He wants *you* to drop dead." The Demosthenes of the garbage pail went into his litany: "Dylan's sold out, he's ripped you off. Right now, I'm trying to approach him as another human being. I have to try to get him interested in life again. But if he doesn't shape up fast I'm going to read the riot act to him." In the crowd, some of Dylan's friends appeared, including Al Aronowitz, who shouted: "Free hot dogs down the block, that way." Four of GI Joe's Frankfurter Service pushcarts were indeed giving away free Franks, though nobody knew who hired them. Unsigned handbills appeared announcing a party at Weberman's house that evening. Weberman was annoyed: "I was told there would be retaliation."

The Scavenger unveiled a special birthday cake with large candles decorated like hypodermic needles. The party began to break up. Two cops chased someone into the microphone car, handcuffed him, and carted him off. The crowd chanted: "Pigs! Pigs!" Weberman led his march, prudently, to the local police station to look after the welfare of the man arrested earlier, singing "Blowin' in the Wind" through his megaphone.

Concert for Bangladesh. Another plague, in the real world. Early in 1971, during the war in Bangladesh, millions of starving refugees flooded from East Pakistan into India. The Indian army was mobilized to fight West Pakistan, and global help for the hapless refugees began. Ravi Shankar, Indian sitar master and raga interpreter, spoke to his pupil, George Harrison, who sprang into action. On August 1, 1971, two concerts at Madison Square Garden raised $250,000 in one day. A film and recording of the concerts raised much more.

Star power attracted 40,000 people. Harrison and Ringo Starr represented the Beatles. Guitar hero Eric Clapton came out of retirement. Along came Badfinger, Klaus Voorman, Billy Preston, Leon Russell, Jim Keltner, and others. Harrison enlisted Dylan with a phone call. Wrote Richard Williams in *The Times* of London: "The real coup, of course, was to persuade Dylan, rock's own Garbo, to leave his self-imposed seclusion and return to the concert stage. Dylan's set turned the concert into an historic event and allowed it to become … a summary of the best things which happened to popular music in the 1960s."

Harrison simply said: "Another friend of mine … someone we all know." Dylan walked on in a denim jacket, as though at a 1960s folk club. His "Hard Rain," which followed film clips of Bangladesh, stung. Ray Coleman, in *Melody Maker*: "Nobody sings Dylan like Dylan … he demonstrated again in that hesitant, piercing voice that he is the ultimate solo artist in contemporary music. Dylan seemed to have come full circle and to have fallen in love again with his old songs." Dylan contributed "Love Minus Zero," "Just Like a Woman," "Train to Cry," "Blowin' in the Wind," and "Tambourine Man." He did "Hard Rain" and "Wind" solo, but on the other songs he was joined by Starr on tambourine and Harrison and Russell on electric guitars. There was also vocal harmony on "Just Like a Woman."

Hassles followed for months between Apple, Capitol, and Columbia Records over the triple album. It was finally released in January 1972 and became a worldwide bestseller, netting UNICEF almost $4 million. The recording and film ultimately were responses to Shankar's declaration: "Through our music we would like you to feel that agony … in Bangladesh." On brief notice, director Saul Swimmer made a ninety-minute documentary from forty hours of footage. Harrison didn't want the mood impaired by swarming cameramen, and no extra lights were used. Harrison and Dylan played a big hand in editing the film, which was shown in thirteen cities on 70mm film with six-track sound and elsewhere in 35mm film with four-track sound. At its New York premiere, on March 23, 1972, critics were sympathetic. Tom Costner, in the *Village Voice*: "Someone has written that audiences are feminine. If that's correct, Shankar embraced it, Harrison made love to it, and Dylan took it by force." George Harrison said: "It's only through India, Hinduism, yogis, and meditation that I learned what Christ really stood for." By spring 1970, Harrison was preparing to break out as a solo performer, and became a solo star after his triple album *All Things Must Pass*, co-produced with Phil Spector. *Time* wrote: "Dylan's influence can be felt everywhere." Dylan had written the lyrics for the first track, "I'd Have You Anytime." Also included, along with 15 originals by Harrison, was "If Not for You."

George told *New Musical Express*, on November 22, 1969, that Dylan was enduring a similar misunderstanding that had plagued the Beatles: "People don't realize that he has changed quietly … So much attention and pressure have been put on him for the wrong reasons … He didn't make himself into a cult—the press did … Now he can't understand why people want to ask him … what to do about Vietnam. He just wants to write and sing songs." As late as December 1974, when George played Toronto's Maple Leaf Gardens, Dylan was present. They jammed backstage, but Dylan stayed offstage. Harrison told Coleman of *Melody Maker* on September 6, 1976: "Bob Dylan is still the most consistent artist there is. Even his stuff which people loathe, I like. There's always something in what he does, to my ears, because every single thing he does represents something that's him."[8]

Man About Town. After nearly three years of listening to the silence, Dylan started listening to old musician friends and new. He made tentative moves toward the folk movement—the Guthrie concerts of 1968, the *Sing Out!* interview later that year, a meeting with Pete Seeger, a visit to a Clancy Brothers concert on March 17, 1969. He revisited Village streets, clubs, and studios. Publicity agents for performers quickly parlayed any contact into accolade. It became a game of tag—Dylan was here, there, everywhere, nowhere. In September 1973, Dylan quietly blew into his mouth harp while John Prine sang at the Bitter End. After some sessions in 1971 with Leon Russell, Russell fostered rumours that Dylan might tour England with him. Dylan dropped in on Roger McGuinn's Columbia sessions for a brief gig, and at Bette Midler's Atlantic sessions, where she cut a remarkable "I Shall Be Released"; he later sang with her on "Buckets of Rain." In February 1973, he was reported to be at a Willie Nelson Atlantic session with Russell and Kris Kristofferson. He went backstage twice at New York's Fillmore East in November 1970, to meet Elton John and Crosby, Stills, Nash and Young. In 1971, he repeatedly visited the Bitter End to hear Tony Joe White, Prine, and Steve Goodman. In October 1972, he went to Max's Kansas City to see a nervous Loudon Wainwright III. August 1972: Dylan surfaced at the Mariposa Folk Festival in Toronto. The same month, the Grateful Dead jammed for five hours at Jersey City's Roosevelt Stadium while Dylan listened from the wings. October 1972: Sly Stone was rumored to be producer of the next Dylan album. October 1969: Dylan visited Dr John at the Fillmore East and chatted backstage with John Mayall at the Café Au Go Go. March 1971: An old sidekick, Bobby Neuwirth, was at the Gaslight, and Bob visited. July 26, 1972: Mick Jagger turned 29 and threw a party at the St Regis, where Dylan was photographed with Zsa Zsa Gabor. May 1971: Tito Burns said he was having British tour talks with Dylan. Bob was reported to be writing a Broadway musical. December 1971: *New Musical Express* carried an exclusive report that Dylan, John Lennon, and Phil Ochs were holding heavy political talks with Bobby Seale and Jerry Rubin. Recurring reports of imminent tours, of great new departures, of "returns," all proved erroneous.

Dylan didn't quite know how to handle it. Just being friendly got exaggerated. Whatever he did, he told me, got blown out of all proportion. Old friends and new were delighted to have it known that they were back in touch with "Bobby." He was just trying to be neighborly. Leon Russell, who produced two tracks on *More Greatest Hits* and taped much Dylan material, tended to exploit Bob's neighborliness. Happy Traum and Emmylou Harris take honors for not using Dylan to enhance their careers. In London, in 1975–76, Emmylou did two major concerts without making any reference to her appearance on *Desire*. She told me: "I was just an eavesdropper at those sessions. Really! Some mutual friends asked me to drop in, and I just did a bit of harmony singing."

Other studio sessions at which Dylan watched or jammed stirred interest. Dylan had started his pseudonym game when he dubbed himself Big Joe's Buddy, Tedham Porterhouse, and Blind Boy Grunt. As early as 1965, rumors began that Dylan was Roosevelt Gook, the piano player on Tom Rush's Elektra album, *Take a Little Walk with Me*. Actually, Dylan had just visited those sessions. He suggested that Al Kooper use that pseudonym, even though Kooper did take credit under his own name as electric guitarist and celesta player. Grunt made another surfacing, taped at the same 1962 session, with the 1972 release of *Broadside Reunion, Volume 6*. His tracks were "Train a-Travelin'," "Emmett Till," "Donald White," and "Dreadful Day." Also in 1972, Dylan said a few words and jammed on a new version of "Nashville Skyline Rag" on *Earl Scruggs: His Family and Friends*, drawn from a late 1970 Channel 13 film.

One of the most elusive sessions took place with Allen Ginsberg on November 14 and 15, 1971.[9] The album's working title was said to be *Holy Roll Jellyroll*. The recording died a-borning. Allen sent out word that he was recording in New York with Dylan, Happy Traum, David Amram, and poets Andrei Voznesensky and Gregory Corso. Allen had evidently put up $10,000 of his own money. Earlier, Ginsberg had been interested in Indian mantras, and, in 1968, had tried to set Blake's "Songs of Innocence" and "Songs of Experience" to a chant. Not until he got some instruction from Dylan could he play three chords. Aside from Indian music, Ginsberg was interested in calypso and blues. One country-rock song concerned Kerouac and other beats. A ten-minute improvised piece, "Jessore Road," compared East Pakistani refugees to the victims of Vietnam. *Guardian* critic Robin Denselow called this "direct, vivid and very angry. Well produced, it could be a remarkably strong song, but the tape I heard was only distinctive for Dylan's rhythmic piano-playing." Apple was interested enough to press disks and print covers. Dylan used the pseudonym Egg O'Schmillson. But Lennon and Apple were having troubles, and Warner Bros supposedly rejected the tapes as "too dirty." Ginsberg quoted a June 1973 letter from Dylan: "Don't worry, the energy has gone, save your songs for friends and go on to do something else."

Conflicting reports described the spring 1971 sessions in New York that Dylan held with Leon Russell, Claudia Lennear, and others. *New Musical Express* heard that Dylan "had no song prepared when the recording began ... Dylan and the band would jam for about thirty minutes. Then he would sit down and start writing a song. After about fifteen minutes, he would have a song to fit the music they had been playing. And all the songs were masterpieces!" Maybe so, but within days of those sessions, Dylan was terribly critical of the fluency of songwriting. He told me: "Until the accident, I was living music twenty-four hours a day ... if I wrote a song, it would take me two hours, or two days, maybe even two weeks. Now, two lines ..." He paused and grimaced to indicate struggle. Near his Village home, Dylan set up a private studio with first-rate equipment, where he could get fresh ideas down on tape and jam with friends.

In November 1972, Dylan held very enjoyable sessions with Doug Sahm, leader of the Sir Douglas Quintet. On *Doug Sahm and Band*, released in late 1973, Dylan played his own waltzy "Wallflower" and "Blues Stay Away from Me" on guitar, and "Me and Paul" on mouth harp. He joined Sahm singing "Is Anybody Going to San Antone" and "Wallflower." Dylan appeared under his own name. Among the sidemen were Dr John, Dave Bromberg, and David "Fathead" Newman. After Dylan had told me of his interest in the Sir Douglas Quintet, I had tracked Doug Sahm down in Monterey, California, in summer 1966. Sahm, a hip cowboy with a long, lean face and a black Stetson, is a Texan who was into the special mix of Tex-Mex music, Chicano funk, Louisiana Cajun, western swing—call it swamp music—from the border country. Sahm told me, in his Southern drawl, he'd "run into Bob along the road, up there around San Francisco a while back [1965] and I sure hope things would get better for him and that one day I sure would like to work in a studio with Bob Dylan." Sahm had a couple of hits, notably "Mendocino" (1969) and "She's About a Mover" (1965), but then he languished until Jerry Wexler got him to Atlantic. Sahm had great influence on Creedence Clearwater Revival, who split up in October 1972 while Sahm was recording with Dylan. Over three weeks, Dylan came in and out, playing some lead guitar, some piano, sitting in on organ, a lot of harp, and singing with Sahm.[10]

In September 1972, just before the Sahm tapings, Dylan and David Bromberg dropped in on a Buddah session for singer-songwriter Steve Goodman, whose "City of New Orleans" had just been a hit for Arlo Guthrie. Goodman asked Bromberg if he could find him a piano player. Bromberg replied that he knew one who played pretty good "but was kinda undependable." The piano player showed up forty minutes late for work on the single, "Election Year Rag." Dylan, listed as Robert Milkwood Thomas, sat in on "Rag" and the title track of Goodman's second Buddah album, *Somebody Else's Troubles*. Dylan saw a good deal of Bromberg, who played lead guitar on nearly half of *Self Portrait* and came back for further work on *New Morning*. Al Aronowitz, later Bromberg's manager, introduced him to Dylan, who soon started to show at clubs when Bromberg was playing.

In October 1971, Dylan recorded three tracks with Happy Traum on bass, banjo, second guitar, and vocal harmony, for the release, on November 17, of *Greatest Hits, Volume II*. Happy had been with the New

World Singers with Gil Turner, while his brother Artie, with Maria d'Amato and Marlena Tyree, was in a trio called the Poolnot Family, a name Dylan had suggested. Happy was the first of the two brothers to move to Woodstock, and as editor of *Sing Out!* eased the magazine away from its doctrinaire past. At their Bitter End gig in December 1970, the Traums brought down music of other Woodstockers: "Movie Man," by John Herald, and "Going Down to See Bessie," by Rick Danko and Robbie Robertson. Dylan tried taping with the Traums, playing organ. An engineer said: "Hey, buddy, would you give me more sound from that organ?" The session was scrapped after a couple of takes. Happy's three tracks for *Greatest Hits* were done in New York on the spur of the moment, mixed down from five choices of Dylan's.

In mid-summer, 1973, Dylan got together with Barry Goldberg, in Muscle Shoals, Alabama, for an album called *Barry Goldberg*. Goldberg had played piano at the famous 1965 Newport electric set. After teaming with Steve Miller in the Goldberg-Miller Blues Band, he joined Mike Bloomfield when he organized the Electric Flag in 1968. Later, Goldberg started writing songs, and began years of failed attempts to record. Even though he'd won the top-organist category in the *Playboy* jazz poll, dubious record companies asked him for a demo. After some songwriting collaboration with Gerry Goffin, Goldberg began to see Dylan again, and for two days running they jammed for hours. Later, Goldberg went to Dylan's place at Woodstock, jamming there with Doug Sahm and the Band. Goldberg got an offer to do a single for RCA, but Dylan told him to hold off. The next day, Dylan rang him and said: "I'm on the phone with Jerry Wexler from Atlantic Records and I think we can work out a deal, but I'm gonna have to produce you; that's cool, isn't it?" There were five days of sessions in Muscle Shoals with Dylan playing percussion on "It's Not the Spotlight" and singing on the chorus of "Stormy Weather Cowboy," "Silver Moon," "Minstrel Show," and "Big City Woman." Dylan also played harmonica for the 1973 *Chronicles* album of Booker T and Priscilla Jones and for *A Story of David Blue* two years later.

From 1967 onward, the so-called recluse cultivated new and old friends. Without flamboyance, he lent encouragement where he could, doing what came naturally to him—making music. Then he got a call from Kris Kristofferson about a movie he was making down in Mexico.

A Man Called Alias. *Pat Garrett and Billy the Kid* seemed an ideal vehicle for Dylan's commercial film debut and it dealt with one of his favorite themes—the embattled antihero. The filming, from late 1972 to early 1973, involved a crew of super-individualists: Sam Peckinpah, the director, a great stylist; actor James Coburn, a senior Hollywood hipster; Kristofferson, singer turning actor; Rudy Wurlitzer, bright young novelist making his mark as a scriptwriter. Dylan quietly upstaged nearly everyone. Reporters buzzed around, asking Mexican extras about Dylan, and Chet Flippo of *Rolling Stone* and Mick Watts of *Melody Maker* managed to witness the filming and a recording session in Mexico City.

Pat Garrett was the violent story of cocky William Bonney, a kid drawn into the frontier life, working with his guns during the range wars. Death hangs over the film's sunset colors. Little happens and little is said, yet *Pat Garrett* is a classic western, fixing on the confrontation between Billy and his friend-turned-lawman, Pat Garrett. Peckinpah implies that on the pair's deep bond of affection balances the need to destroy or be destroyed. Dylan plays a modern Fool, a youngish printer's assistant who follows and helps Billy. In a somber film, Dylan provides wistful humor. "What's your name?" Garrett asks, and he replies: "That's a good question." Later, he says his name is Alias, "Alias anything you want."

Kristofferson had been a Rhodes scholar at Oxford, tackling a dissertation on Blake. He called Dylan in Los Angeles: "There's a lot of heavies down there—you can get paid for learning." Bob was cautious: "If I do it, then they got me, on film." Kris countered: "Hell, they already got you on records. Come on, we'll have a ball." Three months later, few regarded it as a ball. Peckinpah was a perfectionist. Before Dylan decided to go down to Durango, Mexico, with his family, he later told Flippo: "I saw *The Wild Bunch* and *Straw Dogs* and *Cable Hogue* and liked them. The *best* one is *Ride the High Country* ... I want now, to *make* movies. I've never been this close to movies before. I'll make a hell of a movie after this." Later Dylan said: "I was just one of Peckinpah's pawns ... There wasn't any dimension to my part and I was uncomfortable in this non-role." Still, he admired the director and said it was Sam's lack of final artistic control that was "the problem."

On his second day on the set, Dylan picked and sang his title song, "Billy." Peckinpah offered him a part on the spot. Dylan moved his family down the last week in November, and stayed on in Durango working, writing songs, talking very little to anyone. Durango, a city of 150,000 about 600 miles north of Mexico City, has long been used by Glenn Ford and Kirk Douglas. John Wayne had a production company there. The town, with Mexico's highest murder statistics, fringed by the Sierra Madre, was ideal for the last days of Billy the Kid. There wasn't much to do except drink tequila, eat tacos, sample the local weeds, and luxuriate in the storied landscape.

His first day's shooting was challenging, for Bob hadn't done much riding. But the turkey-chase scene came off well. Kristofferson: "I couldn't believe it. He's got a presence on him like Charlie Chaplin ... you see him on screen and all eyes are on him. There's something about him that's magnetic. He doesn't even have to move. He's a natural ... he has to throw a knife. It's real difficult. After ten minutes or so, he could do it perfect ... He does things you never thought was in him. One night he was playing flamenco and his old lady, Sara, had never known him to do it at all before." Michael Watts admitted he was frightened of Dylan. Kris: "*Sheeit*, man. *You're* scared! *I'm* scared, and I'm making a *pitcher* with him!"

Rudy Wurlitzer thought Alias could have been enlarged considerably, but Dylan let it remain a cameo role. Kristofferson said Bob went for days without even talking to his wife. A publicist: "He's really shy and withdrawn, and it's genuine. Reporters follow him around, and, of course, he won't even talk to them, so they end up interviewing everyone else about him." Dylan was upstaging even the director. Wurlitzer: "It's happening, man. Sam knows he's losing to Dylan." Peckinpah arranged a Durango screening of *The Getaway*, but the others decided to join Dylan for a Mexico City taping session.

In a barnlike studio, Dylan started laying down tracks a little after 11 p.m. one Saturday night in January 1973. Trial and error, adding and cutting. Dylan was in charge in the studio, although the film producer, Gordon Carroll, hovered about. Dylan led Kris's band into "Will the Circle Be Unbroken," then more instrumental tracks. Kris, Rita Coolidge, and James Coburn joined in on vocals. At 3 a.m., Bob was still going strong, taping "Holly's Song." He called for his two Mexican trumpeters, cued them on "Pecos Blues." Some obvious tension between Dylan and the producer. Someone noticed that Dylan used Hollywood as a nine-letter swearword. By four in the morning, the co-stars and the scriptwriter had evaporated. Dylan was still energetic, taping other versions of "Billy." The producer seemed to be warming to Bob's ideas, but Dylan twitted him: "I don't think. Usually, I don't think. I hold it all in and then ... act." By seven in the morning, the studio technicians were exhausted, but Dylan was wide awake.

When *Pat Garrett and Billy the Kid* opened in summer 1973, critical opinion was sharply divided. Calling the film "a slow and ritualistic explosion," David Robinson in *The Times* of London said Dylan "appears as a captivating little figure." The film became a cult movie, frequently revived at art houses.[11] Dylan's soundtrack, a model of economy and another new departure, has been highly regarded. At times, engineering supplies a full and echoey sound. Dylan hand selected some ace sidemen, including Roger McGuinn and Bruce Langhorne. His understanding of the folk ethos served him well, for *Pat Garrett* is almost a folk tale, overhung by imminent death. The score comprises ten related works. The main title theme of "Billy" reappears, as "Billy 1," "Billy 4," and "Billy 7." Dylan's vocals are yearning and keening. Some have attacked Peckinpah's Billy as an over-romantic view of a nasty little gunman, but Dylan seems to share the director's view of the central character. Two songs provide notable contrast: "Turkey Chase" is bright and jumpy, spurred by a soaring fiddle. Then comes the album's hit single, "Knockin' on Heaven's Door." Even as the old-time, frontier-period sound of the harmonium in "Heaven's Door" yields to the final theme, a stately, hymn-like quality continues. "Pilgrims toward death" are the protagonists of this frontier epic, and Dylan's music never forgets that the film is a tragedy.

Despite his impact in *Pat Garrett*, naysayers were again chanting that his career was finished. Columbia Records carved another epitaph with the album they rushed out just before Christmas, 1973. *Dylan* must stand as his worst, least-representative album, reflecting base record company cynicism. Since Dylan had let his Columbia contract run out, they scraped together rejects from the *Self Portrait* and *New Morning* period. Columbia probably managed to sell a few hundred-thousand copies on Dylan's name alone. Critics described this album as "corporate dirty pool," an implicit threat to Dylan not to stray too far for fear of more official bootlegs. Clive Davis had left Columbia, and no one wanted to take credit for this album of nine tracks by other writers, not a few of which are almost laughable. In the long run, it probably harmed Columbia more than Dylan. This dreadful album added to a growing feeling that Dylan's career was at ebb tide, like Sinatra's eclipse before his great film comeback in *From Here to Eternity*. Yet Bob already had plans for a dramatic return to live performances. Dylan had often emphasized that some tours had been killers. To Roy Carr in *New Musical Express* on May 13, 1972, Kristofferson said: "Basically, many of these people are not extroverts. For most of us, like Bob Dylan and James Taylor, it's pretty hard to get up and perform before an audience … that's when you're really naked, especially when you're doin' all your own songs." Carr reported that "from experience, Kristofferson is of the opinion that a lot of people expect, nay, demand, that an artist should bleed onstage." Knowing this feeling, Dylan was ready at the end of 1973 to stand naked and let it bleed onstage again.

Tour '74. January 3, 1974: Chicago can be as heartlessly cold as Hibbing. This time Dylan didn't have to face the cold alone. He had five trusted musician friends beside him and almost 20,000 people in the Chicago Stadium saying "Welcome back." Yet, as the moments elapsed before going onstage, he was alone again. Some out there would have been as delighted if he made a fool of himself as if he triumphed. Outside the Stadium, snow clung to the ground and old winos huddled together in doorways. Inside, Dylan was dressed down in the same "poor boy" outfit he wore the first time he hit Chicago. To relieve the stage's impersonality, he had approved a little set, with a bunk bed, a sofa, a Tiffany lamp, a clotheshorse, and a few candles. Balloons floated through the smoke of cigarettes and joints. The audience was tense and expectant. Then a blue spotlight sliced a hole in the dark, and Dylan and the Band, like five picadors and a matador, ambled on: Dylan, unsmiling, tried to looked casual. The *Guardian* reported: "The sounds that broke with the light was like Chicago tearing in half … a vast mush of swelling, cheering, stamping … Dylan was on the road again."

"One foot on the highway, and one foot in the grave,"[12] he sang—"Hero Blues" from 1963, but he'd rewritten it. Then on through some thirty songs, a career spectrum. The star who had generally avoided live audiences for nearly seven and a half years put both feet on the highway. Some 300 reporters were present from around the world and the tour became one of the New Year's big stories. There'd been near-stampedes at post offices to mail in ticket orders, even though Dylan had told the tour's producer, seasoned Bay Area rock impresario Bill Graham, to "keep it low-key." Tour '74 turned into a media festival, a home-coming, a quasi-religious, demi-political rally for new fans and old.

After intermission, Dylan came onstage truly alone and launched into his solo acoustic set, the highlight of that and the thirty-nine shows that followed in twenty-one cities for six weeks. He and his guitar told again how the times were changing and how Hattie Carroll died. Then, in "It's Alright, Ma," he came to the line about the president having to stand naked; the link to Nixon and Watergate ignited the audience. Mick Watts of *Melody Maker* said Dylan "spat out the phrase with a peculiar venom that … made it nigh transcendental." He quit the stage leaving an uproar behind him. All that gossip about his being finished was meaningless. His encore was "Like a Rolling Stone." *Time*: "arms linked together, swaying in unison, chanting in time to the psychic current, a generation's anthem … not finally understood until a period of adult crisis."

Dylan won a hero's reception, a shouting, stamping, and cheering ovation. The audience lit thousands of matches, cigarette lighters, scraps of paper, turning the Stadium into an Impressionist painting. Dylan and the Band finished with "Most Likely You Go Your Way (and I'll Go Mine)," which had so much punch they used it to start the other concerts. Tour '74 caused audiences to review their last thirteen years, their own successes and failures, their direction home, or away from home. Glen Brunman wrote in *Good Times*: "Every time Dylan opens his mouth, he's telling us how badly we blew it in the Sixties … he shows what we might have had, what we let slip away, and maybe, just maybe, what we can still achieve."

David Geffen, of Elektra/Asylum Records, and Bill Graham had some astounding figures to feed the press. Although only around 650,000 seats were available, some five million mail-order applications came in, a total of $93 million. The tour's gross income was about $5 million. *Melody Maker* called it "the biggest financial response for any event in entertainment history." *Time* said: "Never in the history of American rock has a tour aroused so much public interest … it seemed a moment for a legend—and an era—to live again." From the first rush to the post office until the final concert, the tour sparked a bright flame of public interest. National and international press carried tour news and reviews on page one. TV coverage was extensive. One reported offer of a $3 million feature-film advance was turned down. Many book offers were refused, although *Rolling Stone* produced a paperback, *Knockin' on Dylan's Door*, and Stephen Pickering wrote a book, *Bob Dylan Approximately*, as well as a pamphlet. Dylan and the Band still couldn't erase memories of the hooting of 1965–66. Dylan: "Being on tour is like being in limbo. It's like going from nowhere to nowhere. But at least the audiences are different … they have been very warm." He told John Rockwell of the *New York Times*: "The last tour we did, in 1965–66, was like a hurricane. This one is more like a hard rain."

Dylan was determined to be less the *enfant terrible* with the press. He expressed interest in meeting Richard Goldstein of *New York* magazine. Goldstein recalled: "I have never felt so shy in my life, not in front of any doctor, woman, or corpse. Probably I was supposed to squeeze in some devastating question here, but all I really wanted to do was cry." In Boston, Dylan talked to Tom Zito of the *Washington Post* about the contrast between now and then: "Back then it was the scene. Greenwich Village, Gerde's. There wasn't any audience and performer. It was all one. I wasn't a hero. I wasn't giving those young people anything to focus on back then. It was just something I was articulating that a whole bunch of us felt. But now there's a lot of ambiguity out there in the audience … the younger kids, just not sure why they're there. Maybe they're just curious … the lid came off with drugs … Before that, people used to try to find out what they were all about. Drugs nipped a lot of that in the bud … Now a lot of people just accept things the way they are." Zito failed to get Dylan to talk politics: "I guess I just don't really believe in the Democrat/Republican system. I like monarchies. I go in more for kings and queens."

Despite Dylan's apparent bonhomie, he still used interviews to decry interviews. To *Time*, after sitting for a cover story at *Newsweek*: "All this publicity. Sometimes I think they're talking about somebody else. I take it as it comes, but I'm not certain it's beneficial to my life." Everyone, of course, was speculating about why Dylan had returned to the stage at this point. "I just let people know I was ready," he told *Rolling Stone*. Others thought he needed the money, while A J Weberman was convinced the tour was a Zionist plot. The response that seemed closest to the bone was that the current music scene was a desert. Dylan told *Newsweek*: "What I want to hear I can't hear, so I have to make it myself." While insisting that the show was "up-to-date," Dylan could venerate the past: "I just carry that other time around with me … when music was at that root level—that for me is meaningful music. The singers and musicians I grew up with transcend nostalgia." He began to talk about his parents: "My father had to sweat … In this earthly body he didn't transcend the pain. I've transcended … the pain of material things. I'd be doing what I'm doing if I was a millionaire or not, whether I was getting paid for it or not."

He continued: "I'm not standing at an altar, I'm working in the marketplace." Many tour critics referred to his nervousness onstage, but he radiated confidence to *Newsweek*: "I give out a hard dose—like penicillin. People don't have to worry if Dylan's conning them. If it works, it works. If they don't like it, they don't have to try the dose again … a lot of nervousness has gone. I used to feel nervous all the time before I went onstage." Dylan's singing style for the tour revamped melodies, tempos, emphases. This conscious but unsettling change in delivery disorientated some, who ascribed it to concert nerves. There was another reason why critics and audiences held their breath pending Dylan's return. Summing up, Lucian K Truscott's *Village Voice* review of the Wednesday night Madison Square Garden concert: "Dylan was afraid, that was for sure. But 'Tom Thumb's Blues' showed he wasn't afraid of us, the audience. It was himself he feared … going back over those songs which bore the pain of becoming Bob Dylan, the highs, the lows, all of that life which was *living on the edge* … how desperately we want our heroes to be self-destructive, as if only by living recklessly can they show us their essential humanity, their impermanence and mortality."

Rolling Stone pressed Dylan about rumors of his tour proceeds going to assist Israel. "I'm not sure what a Zionist really is," he parried, dismissing the rumors as "just gossip." What about those religious images in his music? "Religion to me is a fleeting thing. Can't nail it down. It's in me and out of me. It does give me, on the surface, some images, but I don't know to what degree." Dylan wasn't going to suggest that "God's will" had sent him back to the road. "I saw daylight … I just took off," he said. He hinted to *Rolling Stone* that his return then was partially astrological, and that Saturn had been an obstacle in his "system. It came into my chart a few years ago, and just flew off again a couple of months ago."

Maybe it was astrology, or restlessness, or the fact that his children were older. It's also what performers *do*—perform. While tour news leaked out in November 1973, prior to the official announcements in early December, talks had begun the previous summer. David Geffen had long hankered to manage Dylan, and had been trying to lure Robbie Robertson. Bill Graham had been making overtures for years. Originally, Dylan had thought of perhaps only a dozen cities and the very best halls. Graham persuaded him that a limited tour did not make economic sense, considering that the performers would need their own airplane, and many technicians.

An appearance the Band had made at Watkins Glen had persuaded them that not everyone wanted to watch Alice Cooper hang himself onstage. Lengthy planning took place in private; full-scale rehearsals began three months before Chicago. In one four-hour session, Dylan and the Band reportedly came up with eighty numbers as a basic tour repertory. Graham booked halls in twenty-one cities anonymously, "to avoid the hysteria." The Kennedys and the Rockefellers wanted tickets, as did unknown fans who queued up at post offices around the country before the deadline hour. The *San Francisco Chronicle* estimated that the tour netted about half the gross of $5 million. Graham and his FM Productions probably took a half-million, while Dylan and the Band, according to John Wasserman, "will net close to $2 million for their eight to 100 hours of work, not, of course, counting rehearsals." Expenses were high. Full-page ads, and a chartered airplane, the Starship I, a forty-seat 707, was refitted with all a rock troupe demanded, at five dollars a mile.

Dylan was determined not to be put through the discomforts of previous tours, determined that his down-time should be free of frenzy. He reminisced: "The last tour, we were going all the time, even when we weren't going. We were looking for Loch Ness monsters, staying up for four days running—and making all those eight o'clock curtains, besides. There won't be any of that on this tour—for me, anyway." Perhaps not, but the itinerary, interviews, and off-stage activities seemed a staggering schedule for someone who'd long been off the road. The final itinerary, which included the cancellation of a Dayton concert to allow for a third concert at Madison Square Garden, added up to a total of forty concerts in six weeks, with two concerts on most days. Dylan also made forays to folk clubs and to a Philadelphia ice-skating rink. He duly noted the presence in his audiences of Marshall McLuhan in Toronto and Mike Porco at Madison Square Garden. Two of his more colorful visitors were Ronnie Hawkins and Jimmy Carter, then Governor of Georgia. Big, blowsy Hawkins was amazingly benign at the reunion, considering Dylan had abducted his Hawks. He was still holding forth in Toronto's Nickelodeon Club when Dylan, most of the Band, and Graham showed up, with bodyguards. Hawkins put on a special show for his thirty-ninth birthday, singing "One Too Many Mornings" and bits of "Hollis Brown."

In the presidential campaign of 1976, Democratic candidate Jimmy Carter repeatedly quoted Dylan, most notably in his nomination acceptance speech: "He not busy being born is busy dying."[13] In December 1973, in a handwritten note, Carter had invited Dylan to his home. After the first of his two 1974 concerts in Atlanta, Dylan and aides arrived at the Gubernatorial mansion. One of Carter's sons, Chip, had gone to Woodstock in late 1968, and the invitation was apparently his idea. Around thirty people gathered for some of the food Dylan had requested—down-home grits, ham and eggs. When Graham greeted Carter at the concert, Graham told him that Bob was "particularly impressed by the fact that you had gone to Israel." But at the party, Carter said: "When I mentioned Israel, Dylan changed the subject and said he and his wife had recently been to Mexico and had enjoyed that country too." Carter called Dylan "painfully timid." In 1976, *TV Guide* asked about Carter's quoting him. Dylan replied: "I don't know what to think about that. People have told me there was a man running for president and quoting me. I don't know if that's good or bad ... but he's just another guy running for president ... I'd like to see Thomas Jefferson, Benjamin Franklin and a few of those other guys come back. If they did, I'd go out and vote. They knew what was happening."

By the time Dylan got to New York for two concerts at the Nassau Coliseum and three at Madison Square Garden, the *Times*'s John Rockwell, who'd been rather cool about the Chicago opening, gauged an audience mood that was "expectant, even exultant." The shock over Dylan's sharp change of delivery was over, and he could see that "it all came together: the husky, growling baritone, the emphatic delivery, and mocking, laughing distortions of the ends of phrases ... totally convincing." The *New York Times* greeted Dylan with a January 28 editorial that paraphrased "Times Changing," concluding: "Every generation has its Dylan. The generation of the '60s was blessed with a singing poet to help fashion that mood. Some things went wrong, and change is always challenged by stagnation. But as long as Dylan sings, the spirit that moved the land a decade ago will be heard." Ellen Willis, in the *New Yorker*, found that the "two evening performances were masterpieces of controlled intensity ... a catharsis I hadn't even known I needed ... a celebration of the past and a going beyond ... Dylan's earliest songs were not only still alive but resonant with new meanings." Some tour-watchers thought the January 30 Garden matinee was the high point. Wednesday night attracted musician friends and Dick Cavett, Shirley MacLaine, and Jack Nicholson. Mike Porco and the Gleasons were given tickets. A party followed at the St Moritz. By February 11, Dylan was back in the Bay Area. Finally, Dylan and the Band wound up back where they'd started their rehearsals, at the Inglewood Forum in Los Angeles.

The final concert ended, after Dylan had called Graham and his aide, Barry Imhoff, onstage for bows, with "Blowin' in the Wind." There was a party at the Forum, then another at the Beverly Wilshire Hotel for just a few who were close to Dylan—David Blue, Bobby Neuwirth, Robbie Robertson, and a Minnesota friend, Lou Kemp. Tour '74 was over, for the performers and the crowds, but the impact continued. Geoffrey Stokes wrote in the *Village Voice* of April 4, 1974: "Dylan is more than memories. The media event is over for now … we are still talking about the concerts, still trying to figure out what they meant to us … This was a quintessential … American event. Confrontation is, after all, the heart of our national myth … we were the lynch mob to Dylan's Marshal … the nervousness apparently faded, and only the tension was left … driving him through a brilliant performance." Dylan made a promise at the finale of his New York concerts: "See ya next year."

Back in the Marketplace. Columbia Records had a litany for pop artists: Cut a record and tour to promote it. Dylan had resisted the formula, but no sooner were plans set for Tour '74 than he and the Band were in West Los Angeles's Village Recorder studios on November 5, 6, and 9 laying down *Planet Waves*. That done, he concentrated on the tour. During six weeks, Dylan and the Band performed fifty-three songs, only three of which came from *Planet Waves*. Before the album's release in January, two alternate titles had been bruited about: *Lovesongs*, and *Ceremonies of the Horseman*, a chess image from "Love Minus Zero/No Limit." *Planet Waves* echoed a 1968 City Lights anthology of Ginsberg poetry entitled *Planet News*.

The album's theme is the many faces of love—for wifely figures, for children, for various female prototypes. Even "Dirge" counter-posed a love of life against death, a quality also reflected in "Going Going Gone." *Planet Waves* marked a return to stinging, aphoristic expression, free-form melodiousness, self-involvement. If considered part of a trilogy with the two subsequent albums, *Blood on the Tracks* and *Desire*, the album marked a new stylistic period. The jacket's stark, black-and-white graphics are reminiscent of early bootleg albums. A Dylan drawing of three faces suggests any or all may be his own. On the back, hand-lettered words, many misspelled, have the rough rub of graffiti. His notes, ringing with beat poetics, evoke memories, from Duluth to the Place des Vosges in Paris. This is almost another draft of "My Life in a Stolen Moment," tough-guy prose-poetry, urgently scribbled. It was the first album without Dylan's name on the front, although in England a covering wrapper used it.

Planet Waves can be seen as Dylan's edging into a new assault on language. There is a hesitancy, even a bit of clumsiness, as in the "age of fiberglass"[14] line, which sounds like he's revving up his engine. The album is strongly autobiographical, especially when he tells us in "Dirge" that he's "paid the price of solitude/But at least I'm out of debt."[15] The apposition of "Dirge" and "Going Going Gone," the cutting and cruel images amid the munificence of "Wedding Song," are examples of Dylan's recurring theme that pain has to be endured along the way to pleasure, and that pleasure is, above all, transitory. Still, love drives the motor—not just the courtly love of angelic women, but a love, or a deep need, of such earth mothers as "Tough Mama" and "Hazel." No album to date since *Blonde* has had such unity, which goes beyond the sense of lyrics, into a musical cohesiveness. The songs "speak to each other," and certain motifs—dreams, sea, waves, mountains, hills, edges, ledges, and lonely, high places—reappear.

"On a Night Like This" opens in bright and neighborly spirit, with commonplaces and clichés of the standard love song—it's cold outside and I'm all the warmer because I'm inside with you. The mood and content flow directly from the idealized life Dylan painted in "Sign on the Window," only now we're behind that cabin door. "Going Going Gone," resembling an auctioneer's chant, is pure blues in spirit. Robbie's shivering electric guitar menaces. Is the leave-taking death or the dangerous return from solitude? "Tough Mama" is a contemporary boogie urban-blues shuffle, dominated by plosive singing and Hudson's omnipresent organ. Though there are some audacious rhymes—"crotch," "watch," and "notch," for example—there is also the fine compression of "I ain't a-haulin'/Any of my lambs to the market place anymore."[16] "Hazel," melodious and appealing, reminds me of Echo, from the wrong side of the Hibbing tracks. The singer is still looking back in "Something There Is About You," which he singled out during Tour '74 as a favorite—an evocation of times past in Duluth, a name he finds of more poetic weight than Hibbing.

As he had hinted on *Self Portrait*, Dylan was developing the painter's fascination with different sketches of one motif. During Tour '74, he startled listeners with a catalog of old songs in new keys or tempos.

Some had new melody lines, some a new lyric or two. By the time he released *Hard Rain* in September 1976, he was proving that reinterpretation had become his compelling interest. He was arriving at the composer's and jazzman's sense of the way improvisation and free-form variation on a theme can expand a repertoire. "Forever Young," in two different tempos and approaches, foreshadows Dylan's reworking of his old songs during Tour '74 and the Rolling Thunder Revue. The first version is invocational with a spirit, like "Father of Night," while the second is playful. Here there are echoes of the fascinating, unsettling rhythmic thrust of Joseph Spence, an underground folk-guitar hero of the 1960s, whom Sam Charters had recorded on a field trip to Andros in the Bahamas.

On "Dirge," Dylan at the piano carries simple, forceful keyboard figures. This is less a love song than an elliptical essay on morbid dependency. Is he talking about the Left, the city, the audience, drugs, a woman—all the things he once felt he needed? This dark lyric counterbalances solitude with wholeness, loneliness with communal completeness. Dylan reportedly wrote this and the album's other heavy track, "Wedding Song," in the studio. In between the two is a bit of confection, "You Angel You." "Never Say Goodbye" has interesting echoes, notably of "Baby Blue." His dreams of iron and steel call attention to the sly subtitle of the album, "Cast Iron Songs and Torch Ballads." "Wedding Song" is a statement of redemption through love. Even as he talks of how love saved his life, weighted images of knives, blood, and killing show a desperation in love's intensity. As the song ends an important transitional album, it foreshadows *Blood on the Tracks*.

Critical reaction varied widely. Loraine Alterman in the *New York Times* faulted *Planet Waves* for its lack of polish, but *Village Voice* music editor Robert Christgau defended Dylan's purposeful roughness. Derek Jewell in the *Sunday Times*, London, of February 3, 1974: "There's vitality, shot through with tenderness, irony and some anger … Dylan's standing today is paradoxical. He rejects, yet is accepted by millions. And isn't he, despite his evolution, still a man of his age? There is an inward-turning mood today … characterized by non-involvement, a search for privacy and a tendency to look backwards. *Planet Waves* mirrors it in a definitive, disturbing and haunting collection of songs." A 1974 poll of twenty-four critics in the *Village Voice* ranked *Planet Waves* as number eighteen, with *Before the Flood* at six. Although most reviews were enthusiastic, Dylan wasn't pleased with sales in America on Asylum or in Britain on Island. Columbia took a renewed interest in their lost star, notwithstanding their recurrent threats to package at least eight Dylan albums from material they had in the can. Dylan negotiated his royalty for *Before the Flood* to new heights, but it was his last work for David Geffen. At the end of the summer of 1974, he returned to the Columbia fold; the two albums for Geffen were later reissued on CBS/Columbia.

For those who wanted a souvenir from Tour '74, *Before the Flood*, a double album full of new Dylan/Band interpretations, was ideal. The title may have been inspired by the first of Rimbaud's *Illuminations* called "After the Flood," but if Rimbaud's work is a parable of the birth trauma, the album is a parable of a performer's *re*birth. The title also could refer to Columbia's threats to flood the market with old Dylan tapes. *Flood* was drawn from ten sessions dating from the middle to the close of the tour—three from Madison Square Garden, two each from Seattle and Oakland, and the final three from Los Angeles. The dominant impression is energy, extroversion, audience excitement, and a novel approach to old songs. The master of surprise was at it again. How many performers and composers have been content to find a style and spend a lifetime developing it? Here was a brash declaration that he was of the here and now. Dylan profited from the Isle of Wight anticlimax of his introversion. His Tour '74 style didn't ask listeners to reach toward him. Songs they'd memorized in other forms could be re-experienced. Here Dylan almost sounds like 1974's heavy-metal rockers, without their theatricality or gimmickry.

Dylan caught his live audiences and listeners off-guard with biting, punching, sometimes snarling interpretations. "Most Likely You Go Your Way" leaps out from an obscure back page of *Blonde*. "Lay, Lady, Lay" acquires a different profile. "It Ain't Me, Babe" becomes jumping soul *à la* Otis Redding. Frequently, Dylan seemed to be using a black soul voice, grainy but with new range and phrasing. "Mr Jones" becomes "*Mr Jo-hones.*" In "Just Like a Woman," "knows" becomes "*no-hose.*" In "Don't Think Twice," the word "right" trails off with a wounded sound. Several of the songs have "wind-up" introductions, as if cranking up an old Ford that takes off like a Lamborghini. This slow smoldering works to optimum effect in "Like a Rolling Stone." There's a palpable frisson in the audience when Dylan demands to know how they "*fee-heel.*"

Before the Flood was supervised by Phil Ramone, a taping wizard who had been a White House consultant (before Nixon) and had worked with the Band on *Rock of Ages*. He taped thirty-five hours live, using a crew that included two chief engineers, one spare mixer, three men in the recording booth, one man onstage, and another backing up. Ramone called it "the peak of my career." Working with him was Rob Fraboni, who had supervised the engineering of *Planet Waves*.

Critical disagreement raged in the *Village Voice*, in three separate reviews. The third, by Greil Marcus, explained Dylan's change from "generational symbol" into "American artist." "Before the Flood," he wrote, "offers not ideas but passions … the triumph of Dylan's new music is that Dylan seems to take the failures [he sees in American life] as his opportunity for freedom." Marcus drew exhilaration from "the feeling that an artist is working over his head, that you are over yours, that limits have been thrashed. Such freedom — when an artist liberates himself from his form, he makes *you* feel free … There's a good bit of Whitman's *yawp* in this music … Once, Dylan cruised the strip with a cool eye, keeping his distance. Now, he's right in the middle, and so are we. That, of course, is the *burden* of joining a bigger, more mysterious America."

The New Dylans. As early as 1963, many in the music business were talking about "a new Bob Dylan," a phrase I dropped casually in print and which A&R men then began using as a calculated concept. An inexact shorthand for an acoustic songwriter with the touch of a poet, it included, at one time or another, Eric Andersen, Janis Ian, Phil Ochs, Donovan, Simon and Garfunkel, Mark Knopfler, Loudon Wainwright III, John Prine, James Taylor, Carly Simon, Don McLean, Bruce Springsteen and Patti Smith. The Modigliani tomboy street urchin who dressed like a junkyard angel had her feet in ballet slippers and her head in the poetic landscape of Rimbaud, Artaud, Jim Morrison, and Dylan, Smith was into page writing before beginning her mesmerizing rock performances, which she called "dreaming onstage." In 1976, she told me: "I was about 16 and saw *Illuminations* with Rimbaud's picture on the cover. He looked like my father and Dylan. My factory supervisor saw it was a bilingual book and suspected I was a Communist. I always carried *Illuminations* around. Sometimes I read the French. Even though I couldn't understand it, I got the music. Then, *A Season in Hell*. It was the same thing with *Prufrock* and even *Highway 61*. I wasn't man or woman enough to understand it, but the music within it was great! The most beautiful thing about rock 'n' roll is it's an open art that allows you to be a megaphone to the universe. There's no place you can't communicate with rock."

Patti was discovered by Tony Glover and *Creem* magazine. A front page *Village Voice* picture of Dylan embracing her on July 7, 1975, bore the heading: TARANTULA MEETS MUSTANG: BOB DYLAN GIVES HIS BLESSING TO PATTI SMITH. Recalled Patti: "It was so intense, like, when you have a crush on a guy in high school and after a year he finally talks to you and you have nothing to say. It was so adolescent, very sexy. Dylan loves Rimbaud too. He talked about being behind bars, like Artaud, and about being a prisoner in his skin. He's a great singer who's trained his vocal chords for twenty years. What I've trained myself to do is to dip into my subconscious, to dip into the sea of possibilities." Smith found that she and Dylan were both working toward Rimbaud's "derangement of the senses," that knowledge that comes from pain, voyaging, searching. She concluded that something may have been escaping him: "He has levels completely untapped. He just needs someone to help him pierce his skin. I'm committed to him and his songs. They can do no wrong for me, but I still feel he can do *righter*. He's a great improviser. He just needs to be sprung loose again. He's got all this stuff just waiting to come gushing out. He's an incredible guy! The electricity coming from his face, his eyes, is real!"

Countless contemporary poets have been influenced by Dylan's electric fusion of poetry and music. Ferlinghetti was shaken, Rexroth impressed; Leonard Cohen learned to sing and write songs; and Michael McClure fondled the autoharp Dylan had given him. Allen Ginsberg became increasingly interested in exploring the musical side of oral poetry and in 1976 published *First Blues — Rags, Ballads & Harmonium Songs 1971–74*, dedicated "To Minstrel Guruji Bob Dylan."[17] Ginsberg's introduction delineates his musical experiences from unsuccessful piano and violin lessons until 1963, when he heard chanting in India and Japan. He kept hearing "fragments of Blake's 'Grey Monk' moaning through my brain … I experimented, improvising music in F-chord to the 'Grey Monk' on a Uher tape machine given me as a Christmas present in 1965 in San Francisco by Bob Dylan, who suggested that I learn an instrument." Dylan attended a 1971 Ginsberg poetry reading at New York University and, impressed with Allen's ability to improvise words, arranged the recording sessions of November 17 and 20, 1971. Soon Ginsberg was turning back to "modeling my first blues on Richard Rabbit Brown's 'James Alley Blues,'" one of Dylan's early models. Ginsberg's conclusion shows the lines converging anew:

I'd sung ragged ditties & tocattas & fugues with Kerouac under Brooklyn Bridge in 1945–49 and listened with him and Neal Cassady to car radio Rhythm and Blues of Louis Jordan & Fats Domino, moans of Slim Gaillard & shrieks of Little Richard, so I had some kind of American Blues in my heart without knowing it—I could sing but didn't reckon it important poetically, until I met Krishna & remembered Ezra Pound's ken that poetry & music, song & chant (and dance) went together before the invention of the printing press and long after—forgotten by the same academies that forgot that the genre of American Black Blues & rags was as great a treasury of poetics as Bishop Percy's Reliques & Scottish Border Ballads & Elizabethan song books & Tom O'Bedlam folk treasuries … The doggerel element in the poetry has to be dealt with—perceptive doggerel inexcusable & inevitable in the process of learning to sing and making up words on the spot. The ideal in Campion & Nashe is a series of swift images. Dylan's 'Chains of Flashing images.'

Blood on the Tracks. Talk of "new Dylans" faded in January 1975 with the appearance of *Blood on the Tracks*, Dylan's third album in a year. Here was renewed Dylan reaching fresh heights. Critical reaction ran to superlatives, calling *Blood* the best Dylan work in seven or nine years, even his best work ever. Dylan got this album just as he wanted it. He replaced some New York tapings from September 1974 with December tapes from Minneapolis.[18] He scrapped an elegiac liner-note essay by Pete Hamill, which later won a Grammy award, in favor of an abstract drawing.

Blood on the Tracks bore out *Planet Waves*'s forecast in "Dirge" and "Wedding Song:" the artist was in torment. The new album was the spiritual autobiography of a wounded sensibility, whether the pronouns were "I," "he," "she," or "you." One of his most listenable albums, musically lustrous and varied, it contains some of Dylan's most direct, rich, emotive, and supple vocalizing. Like the mid-1960s albums, *Blood on the Tracks* shows what Wallace Fowlie called Rimbaud's "persistent theme of abandonment."[19] The album is about the impermanence and fragmentation of remembrance and relationships. Greil Marcus: "At once, the tale of an adventurer's war with a woman and with himself, and a shattering attempt to force memory, fantasy and the terrors of love and death to serve an artistic impulse to redeem disaster by making beauty out of it … the odyssey of a mythical lover possessed by an affair he can never resolve."

These ten songs show high craftsmanship and control. Translucent surfaces reveal many layers beneath; abstract imagery is rendered into colloquialism. Basic elements—blood, pain, storm, rain—assume dozens of patterns. There are images of conflict—blood and barbed wire; life is a battleground and so is memory. "Rain" falls and falls again, coming with waves, flood tides, hail—"hard rain." Jonathan Cott's essay, "Back Inside the Rain," in *Rolling Stone* (March 13, 1975), equates Dylan's rain with memory. Too simple. I see rain as a fluid image, like blood—nature's blood, bringing life to deserts, life that is flood, tears, pain, loneliness, sensation itself. *Blood on the Tracks*, with its tears, insights, and wit, spells an end to complacency and contentment. Dylan finally admitted that although "being settled" may result in personal happiness, the romantic agony of loss and search are goads to greater art, even if he had to turn his own life into discord. The songs:

"Tangled Up in Blue": Although the second album printing reveals a mottle-hued Dylan contemplating a blood-red backdrop, the predominant color is blue. The blues can be sprightly, and the album takes off with a sense of motion. There is a wistful searching, the quest myth again, but perhaps he always looks for the same thing in a lot of people, and always ends up contemplating the mirror of his self. Dylan puns, as the "day the axe just fell"[20] in the woods; a phrase out of common parlance, "keep on keepin' on,"[21] is returned, renewed, to the language. The Dante allusion remains ambiguous. In the New York tape and the folio, the poet dates from the thirteenth century, while the record makes it the fifteenth. (Dante's work spanned the thirteenth and fourteenth centuries.) Wallace Fowlie reportedly thinks Dylan echoes a poet friend of Dante, Guido Cavalcanti. A new sort of road song, in which a dried-out spirit, not dusty boots, recalls his long march. Did he take the right turns? Dylan prefers the *Real Live* version.

"Simple Twist of Fate": In whispered understatement, the narrator's painful memory, in dreams and imagination, is of loneliness. "He woke up, the room was bare"[22] recalls "Baby Blue" and the lover who walked out the door with "all his blankets from the floor."[23] The singer remains in a dreamlike state of mordant remembrance until the third verse, when he chafes under the poet's "sin" of too much vision, too much feeling.

"You're a Big Girl Now": A sequel to "Just Like a Woman." The phrase is ironically patronizing to anyone but a child. Rarely has his singing been more openly emotional. His stresses on the interjection "oh" remind me of the screaming mouth of the sufferer in Edvard Munch's painting. The narrator, "back in the rain,"[24] is singing through tears, and going out of his mind with "a corkscrew to my heart."[25] The irony is that the woman feels liberated while the narrator suffers. In the *Biograph* notes, Dylan rants at the suggestion that this was about his wife. "I'm a mystery only to those who haven't felt the same things I have."

"Idiot Wind": Generally acknowledged as the album's "big song," this has some of the sting of "Rolling Stone" and much of the anguish of Ginsberg's "Howl." It could be a ranting truth attack, an expression of the narrator's personal disorder, ruefulness, and suspicion in an equally disturbed society in which people's spoken words are in apposition to their real emotions. It is also catharsis, a venting of personal anguish as well as a portrayal of a milieu where gossiping and backstabbing have replaced caring and believing. The ultimate horror is that the wheels have stopped; the air is fetid, paralyzing the body, mind, and spirit. A man, or a couple, undergo harassment and collapse while Nixon and his family are under siege, in the denouement of the Watergate scandal.

Dylan insists we listen to a "primal scream," so that we will not be as naïve as he. This song changed tremendously from its New York version, which had a different melody and even more direct personal links, but an almost benign setting and gentler delivery. This version's relentless shout has the impact of Edward Albee's *Who's Afraid of Virginia Woolf?*—too true to bear, too close to the bone to accept. Yet these truths have to be faced before one can go on. Dylan leaves this version as he does some of his pessimistic songs: the wheels will start to roll again, the winds of plague will blow away, the helpless will learn to feed themselves.

"You're Gonna Make Me Lonesome When You Go": A delicate melody transports witty half-threats. The lover pleads that he never be abandoned, despite his fatalistic fear that he will be. "Situations have ended sad,/relationships have all been bad,/Mine've been like Verlaine's and Rimbaud."[26] This is the first time Dylan directly wrote of Rimbaud. Verlaine, the older, established poet, touted Rimbaud when he arrived in Paris. According to Wallace Fowlie: "The story of Verlaine and Rimbaud in London and Brussels is one of the literal epics of our age, in which the myth of the modern artist is related. It is the same story recast fifty years later by James Joyce in the Dublin odyssey of Leopold Bloom and Stephen Dedalus. The two men, one older than the other, are really one man, and the dual search for love and knowledge is one search."[27] The earlier line about shooting in the dark fleshes out the story. Verlaine introduced Rimbaud to a skeptical coterie of Parisian writers, then left his wife to ramble with the 17-year-old newcomer. On July 10, 1873, after various emotional storms, Verlaine shot Rimbaud. One bullet ran wild and the other hit Rimbaud's left wrist. Rimbaud filed no complaint, but Verlaine was charged with attempted manslaughter and spent eighteen months in prison. Fowlie: "Evil is a way of knowledge. Extreme experiences of evil awaken in most men the deepest desire to understand what they are doing and suffering in order to transcend it. Those who practice evil as deliberately and knowingly as Rimbaud and Verlaine did turn themselves into Satanic theologians much more than mere lovers."

"Meet Me in the Morning": Some of the finest blues singing Dylan has ever done. The intensity, the keening voice, the personal involvement are arresting. A classic blues, "Morning" is rich in traditional idioms and images, with a few contemporary touches.

"Lily, Rosemary and the Jack of Hearts": One of Dylan's longest fables, played out like a card game. Lively action, mysterious death, constant ambiguity. Vaguely reminiscent of "Frankie Lee and Judas Priest," it is a narrative ballad in the western tradition, which Dylan has turned into a fifteen-verse playlet (verse twelve in the folio is not sung) filled with whimsy and mystification. There was some Hollywood talk of turning the song into a screenplay, with speculation that Dylan would play the Jack.

"If You See Her Say Hello": This musical high spot has lusciously intimate singing and warm, massed, Mexican-style acoustic guitars. The narrator, a man trying to be cool about a wrenching separation from a woman, cannot keep his feelings from bursting out: "Either I'm too sensitive/Or else I'm gettin' soft."[28] This attempt to be casual in the face of emotional turmoil gives the text line a sea-wave rhythm.

Dylan's phrasing recalls the voice of Tour '74 when he turns "chill" into "*chi-i-u-ill*," "stay" into "*stay-hay-ay*." Michael Gray considers this a rewrite of "Girl from the North Country."

"Shelter from the Storm": Dylan again uses natural elements to describe his tempest-tossed mood. The caressing melody explores a Yeatsian search for salvation through love. The poet found shelter, but the roof leaked and the rain came in. There are many rich lines, such as "In a world of steel-eyed death and men—who are fighting to be warm,"[29] and "nothing really matters much, it's doom alone that counts./And the one-eyed undertaker,/He blows a futile horn."[30]

"Buckets of Rain": Concludes the album's theme of lost and found, of a fruitless search that uncovers only impermanence. I hear echoes of Mississippi John Hurt's sing-songy blues here, mournful one moment and playful the next, laughing to keep from crying. This is an album of echoes, of the singer's past work, of the poet's images, of intense love for a woman, many women, old friends, all distanced to avoid painful confrontation. The new stirrings in *Planet Waves* have turned into a tidal wave. There are echoes of *Les Illuminations*, particularly "Historic Evening." The idiot wind blows a hard rain down Desolation Row.

Taping for *Blood* began on September 10, 1974, at Columbia's Studio A in New York. Dylan summoned some familiar talents of the 1960s—Eric Weissberg and his band, Deliverance; Buddy Cage, the pedal-steel guitarist; Tony Braun, and Paul Griffin. Mick Jagger dropped in, and at one point considered sitting in on drums and doing background vocals. The chief Rolling Stone danced about, and helped quaff some bubbly. On the eve of release, Dylan raced off to Minneapolis, and on Friday, December 27, and Monday, December 30, got together with some new session men rounded up by his brother, David—Bill Peterson, bassist; Ken Odegard, guitarist; Bill Berg, drummer; Greg Inhoffer, keyboards; and Chris Weber, twelve-string guitar. They recut all but three of the original versions. Four of the final tracks seem to be from the New York sessions and six from Minneapolis. The absence of any musician credits on the revised jacket leaves a discographical muddle.

There was no muddle in reviewers' reactions, however. One English Dylan freak greeted the personal background to these sessions—Dylan's turbulent home life, following Tour '74—with a perverse sort of joy: "Well, now that Dylan and Sara are having problems, maybe he'll start writing some better songs." Dylan was hoist by his own petard—you can't write love songs for a woman for years and then write about a troubled period without inviting gossip, which appears in nearly every review of *Blood*. During a noticeably reticent radio interview with Dylan in spring 1975, Mary Travers told him how much she enjoyed the album. He snapped back, astounded that people could "enjoy" what was obviously so painful for him. In *Rolling Stone*, Jon Landau appealed to Dylan to take greater care with recording production. Landau later backtracked somewhat about Dylan's spontaneity:

He has transcended his limitations more successfully than anyone else in rock ... Dylan hasn't handled every role with equal skill. He was unconvincing as the happy homeowner. People ... reacted to the fact that he couldn't make that experience as real as he could the emotions of anger, pain, hurt, fear, loneliness, aloneness and strength. Like James Dean and Marlon Brando, he was better at playing the rebel than the citizen, the outsider than the insider and the outlaw than the sheriff ... in returning to his role as disturber of the peace, Dylan hasn't revived any specific phase from the past, only a style that lets his emotions speak more freely and the state of mind in which he no longer denies the fires that are still raging within him and us.

On *Biograph* Dylan scoffs: "How many roles can I play? Fools, they limit you to their own unimaginative mentality."

Robert Christgau in the *Village Voice*, January 27, 1975, gave the album an "A": "Dylan's new stance is as disconcerting as all the previous ones, but the quickest and deepest surprise is in the music ... On the whole, this is the leader's most mature and assured record." In the same paper, Paul Cowan's influential review of February 3, 1975, was kind to the artist, but not to the man:

The message is a bleak one. At 34, with his marriage on the rocks, he is an isolate, lonely drifter once again ... Dylan, trapped in the prison of himself, is Tiresias in his dugs ... America is his wasteland ... as in all Dylan's great albums, pain is the flip side of his legendary cruelty … Sometime, probably as his marriage began to shatter, his selfishness must have curdled into self-hatred … Dylan bears a very special kind of curse. He seems unable to establish warm, lasting relationships, but he's too eager for love to make the cold decision to sacrifice his private life to his art, as Joyce or even Mailer can. Blood is a great album because he's writing into the headwinds of that curse … The entire record is the excruciating cry of a man who is tormented by his own freedom. But it is also filled with religious imagery, with hints that the wounded, weary Dylan seeks "shelter," not as a woman's warm home, but as the peace of God … For him, perhaps the faith he is seeking is the only escape from his swirling emotions, the only alternative to madness or suicide.

Cowan's psycho-critique misunderstood Dylan's role-playing. Would he say Shakespeare was guilt-ridden because Lady Macbeth washed her hands, or that the Bard was indecisive because Hamlet was conflicted? Even if *Blood on the Tracks* was literally confessional, Cowan is a less-than-humane witness to a catalog of remorse, self-doubt, and chagrin. Dylan has been a cruel, self-centered loner. After the accident, he tried to change his ways. After his move back to the Village in 1969, he was also trying to rekindle old friendships. From the summer of 1975 onward, he made an even more concentrated effort to forge a community of singers. Dylan has wanted to be liked, but he tried to balance that need with trying to be true to his many embattled artistic selves. Years before Rolling Thunder, Dylan was pondering how to revive his old music community of the early 1960s. The opportunity presented itself after he had purged his feelings, and those of many others, with the brilliant catharsis of *Blood on the Tracks*.

Auld Acquaintance. In early 1975, Bill Graham found a rallying point. With a touch of social conscience, a dash of his own organization, and warm responses from stars, he soon had things rolling. San Francisco's beleaguered school system faced a $3 million budget shortage, which would end all sorts of extracurricular activities. Graham formed SNACK (Students Need Athletics, Culture, and Kicks), reasoning: "We make our living from the youth of San Francisco. This is one way we hope to thank them." On February 4, only two weeks after his brainstorm, Graham announced that he'd signed Jefferson Starship, the Doobie Brothers, the Grateful Dead, Santana, Joan Baez, Graham Central Station, and Tower of Power. Rumored to appear: Dylan and Brando (each had five children), Neil Young, and the Band. On March 23, 1975, some 60,000 people, mostly teenagers, besieged Golden Gate Park's Kezar Stadium. Football and baseball stars, notably Gene Washington and Willie Mays, joined the rock constellation. Radio station K-101 broadcast that "a surprise guest, the man from the Fairmont" was expected momentarily.

When Brando took the stage, many thought he was the surprise guest. "The Godfather" spoke with passion: "It's not my generation … but your generation's gonna catch the shit that my generation and the people before me have laid down for you … there are plenty of people … hurting. The poor people, the Indians, the white people, the blacks, the Chicanos, everybody's that's been ripped off … I'm gonna give five thousand bucks … we gotta give and give … we gotta give of our feelings." Baez followed Brando. The man from the Fairmont Hotel was noticed backstage, heading into the tuning-up trailer. Graham announced a supersession: "On bass, Rick Danko; on keyboards, Garth Hudson; on drums, Levon Helm; on guitar, Tim Drummond; on pedal-steel, Ben Keith; on harmonica and guitar, Bob Dylan!" Roar followed roar when Graham also announced Neil Young. Nearly everyone sprang to their feet to greet the Dylan-Young-Band-Doobies set. From the wings, Baez smiled approvingly. Dylan worked mostly on guitar and harmonica, but went to the piano to accompany Young's "Lookin' for a Love." He sang lead on "I Want You" and "Knockin' at the Dragon's Door" after several numbers by Young. At stage-side, Brando and Baez embraced. Other numbers were "Are You Ready for the Country," "Darker Side of Me," "Loving You," "The Weight," and "Helpless." The final encore was "Will the Circle Be Unbroken." The concert raised $200,000. As the listeners trekked home at 6 p.m., Dylan, Brando, and Graham went to dinner at the home of Francis Ford Coppola, director of *The Godfather*.

Todd Tolces in *Melody Maker*: "Simply … the most important musical event San Francisco has ever seen." He epitomized the forty-five-minute Dylan/Young set as "history." According to *After Dark*, it was "a vast efflorescence of counterculture sentiment, a harking-back to times when rock wasn't all hype and money and problems and slick showmanship … It was a great, great show, unique in many ways. The 'political' part of it is purest romance." Still, there was Dylan sharing a stage again with the obdurately political Baez and Brando, and enjoying every minute. He was hinting that he might become identified again with social action. In the early Seventies, despite his overt indifference, Dylan had been wrestling with his longing for community. His own romantic rebelliousness and social passions were cool to the point of cynicism: "The Dream is over, the Great American Dream is over ... there are guys in prison that just can't afford to get out," he told me. Perhaps he also meant the prison of his own solitude.

He wasn't ready then to envision his changes in the 1970s. "George Jackson," Bangladesh, and his appearance at the benefit for Chile in 1974 were isolated events. I don't think he had lost his social compassion; he simply wanted to run free, to drift on his own existential course, day by day. By spring 1975, he was planning the official release of his biggest "looking back" album, *The Basement Tapes*. That spring, he was ready to talk on radio with Mary Travers, however haltingly, about the past. Tour '74 had put Dylan in touch with his old music, including the music that spoke of a certain political mood. What the 1970s needed, Dylan saw, was another shot of that singular 1960s zeal. Dylan has described the Sixties as "like a flying saucer landed ... Everybody heard about it, but only a few really saw it."

After Tour '74, offers for more shows flooded in. In May 1974, Dylan and the Band were offered a million-dollar guarantee for a one-day show. Amid promoters' attempts to capitalize on Tour '74, Dylan simply went visiting. He popped up in San Francisco, with Paul McCartney and the Doobies, at the wedding of one Chick Edwards, drummer of the local band Bittersweet. In September 1974, Dylan revisited Highway 61, touring the North Country with Lou Kemp, showing his oldest children where he'd grown up. Rumors persisted that Bob was buying an apartment and other property outside Minneapolis. He visited a concert of a band he'd befriended and strongly influenced — Crosby, Stills, Nash and Young. Stills dedicated a song: "This one's for Bob." There was a CSN&Y party afterward, where Dylan played some of his new *Blood on the Tracks* material. Dylan's Tour '74 had, in Crosby's phrase, been "the ice-breaker" for the quality music his band was making. Dylan also had visited CSN&Y at the Fillmore East in June 1972.

That summer he literally had gone on record in praise of his old blues chum Ric Von Schmidt. On his *Poppy* album, Dylan's message, printed on a yellow sticker, read, in part:

his record is ... an invitation to join the glad, sad, biting, exciting, frightening, crabby, happy, enlightening, hugging, chugging world of Eric Von Schmidt ... who can sing the bird off the wire and the rubber off the tyre. He can separate the men from the boys and the notes from the noise; the bridle from the saddle and the cow from the cattle. He can play the tune off the moon. The why of the sky and the commotion from the ocean. Yes he can.

At the release of *Blood*, Dylan was socializing with people he might have written off earlier, like Dana Gillespie, the baroness-actress friend of Donovan. He once scoffed that she sang folk songs on water skis, but now he sat listening to her at New York's Reno Sweeney, with Bette Midler and David Bowie at his table. By the time he was getting *The Basement Tapes* ready for official release in July 1975, Columbia Records was promoting its prodigal-son-returned. In March 1975, both *Greatest Hits* albums had entered the lower end of the charts again and were rising fast. Some nine years after its release, *Blonde on Blonde* reentered the album charts.

Dylan was ready to spend summer 1975 walking the streets of the Village, hanging out again, almost constantly on the scene, as he had been from 1961–64. He was so omnipresent that the *Village Voice* trumpeted a page-one headline on July 14, 1975: JAMMING WITH DYLAN: WILL MACDOUGAL ST RISE AGAIN? Jerry Leichtling; "You can't spit out your window these days without hitting Dylan." Over the July Fourth weekend, the Other End on Bleecker Street became the site of "The First Annual Village Folk Festival." With many regulars out of town, the audience was small. All that week, Dylan had been seen around the Village wearing the same grubby outfit, black leather jacket, beige corduroy trousers, blue striped T-shirt. Monday night he'd jammed with Muddy Waters at the Bottom Line. Thursday, he'd joined Jack Elliott onstage at the Other End. Paul Colby had reopened the former Bitter End in June, after a year's darkness. On Saturday night, Dylan returned with Patti Smith, Tom Verlaine, and Bobby Neuwirth. Jake and the Family Jewels was the lead act. Dylan jammed backstage with Neuwirth, who announced "a surprise back-up guitarist" and dragged the reluctant guitar-picker onstage. Dylan played piano as the talented crew joined him on "Will the Circle Be Unbroken." He remained at the keyboard while Smith sang lead on "Amazing Grace," "Banks of Ohio," and "Good Night, Irene," the old Leadbelly classic. It was like a 1961 hoot. Tastes were broader now, rock had brought riches to folk, and vice versa.

Bob came in nightly with his guitar case, piles of papers, and notebooks. Phil Ochs and Dave Van Ronk staggered by. The old hassles may not have been entirely forgotten, but Dylan was trying. The next night, Dylan backed Elliott on "Pretty Boy Floyd" and "How Long Blues" and, with Neuwirth, sang a song Dylan had been working on only that afternoon.[31] After the time-honored finale, "This Land Is Your Land," the group moved next door to the Dugout, where the theme became "this drink is your drink." To Smith, Dylan seemed to be "exploding" with his new material for *Desire*. To Neuwirth, Dylan was "an audio voyeur, just listening to and watching people." A few female fans reportedly threw themselves at Dylan, but he brushed them aside. Neuwirth sensed that Dylan's scene-making was not just a momentary whim and, to keep up the momentum, organized a house band. Other musicians dropped in: Sandy Bull, Eric Kaz, Loudon Wainwright III, Mick Ronson, and T-Bone Burnett. On Neuwirth's opening night, Dylan sat in, trying out his new "Isis" and "Joey." A beaming Columbia Records man told a few people that Dylan had been down to Trenton State Prison to visit Hurricane Carter, the imprisoned boxer, and had written a song for him. The same unnamed Columbia man said Dylan was considering a Broadway show and possibly some TV work.

All of this made Dylan think about a tour of small clubs. Probably Jack Elliott suggested it, perhaps Patti Smith, perhaps Neuwirth. For a cover story in *People* on November 10, Dylan told Jim Jerome:

I didn't consciously pursue the Bob Dylan myth. It was given to me—by God. Inspiration is what we're looking for. You just have to be receptive to it ... I was locked into a certain generation. I still am. A certain area, a certain place in the universe at a certain time ... I'm not an activist. I am not politically inclined. I'm for people, people who are suffering ... Writing a song, it can drive you crazy. My head is so crammed full of things I tend to lose a lot of what I think are my best songs, and I don't carry around a tape-recorder ... We have to be able to hear that voice. I'm through listening to other people tell me how to live my life ... I'm just doing now what I feel is right for me ... For my own self.

September 10, 1975: Station WTTW's National Educational Television Studios in Chicago were taping a telecast for December 13, *The World of John Hammond* (Hammond had told me in 1972 that he and Dylan still got on well personally, that they'd recently gone to a baseball game together.) In a lecture at Hunter College just before his TV tribute was broadcast, Hammond said: "Dylan changed my life, I guess." Taping of the hour-long show, part of the second series of *Soundstage*, began at 9 p.m., but Dylan didn't appear on camera until 2 a.m., before a thinned-out audience of 150 people. Despite four heart attacks, Hammond was looking well, delighted to be honored by so many of his associates and artists. Among them were Goddard Lieberson, Benny Goodman, Jerry Wexler, former Count Basie singer Helen Humes, gospel queen Marion Williams, Sonny Terry, Hammond's son, and jazz stars Teddy Wilson, Benny Carter, Jo Jones and Red Norvo.

Dylan was rubbing the sleep from his eyes when he arrived onstage, backed by Howie Wyeth on drums, Rob Stoner on bass and back-up vocals, and Scarlet Rivera, on violin. Dylan and combo sailed into "Hurricane," jolting the tired audience. After taping "Oh, Sister" and "Simple Twist of Fate," Dylan re-taped "Hurricane," adding even more sting to his performance. His intense scowl heightened the song's anger. Before he sang "Oh, Sister," Dylan said, on camera: "I want to dedicate this to someone out there watching tonight I know. She knows who she is." To one reporter, Al Rudis, "there seemed to be blood flowing from psychic wounds throughout this short set."

Dylan left hurriedly afterwards. Observers were fascinated with the violinist in a long dress, with dark gypsy eyes and flowing hair. Some believed her to be a real gypsy Dylan had discovered walking along Second Avenue with her violin case. Some Chicagoans recognized her as Donna Shea, who had been on their local rock scene in the late 1960s. In New York, Dylan later remarked: "For all John Hammond's done for me, it was worth staying late."

Opposite: On stage with George Harrison at the Concert for Bangladesh, Madison Square Garden, August 1971.
Bottom left: Album cover *Blood on the Tracks*, 1975.
This page: Dylan as "Alias," from *Pat Garrett & Billy the Kid*, 1973.

The difference between good actors and big stars is that good actors disclose everything; big stars are mysterious.
DAVID LEAN, 1965

A work is not a series of answers, it is a series of questions … it is not the answer that enlightens, but the question.
EUGENE IONESCO

I define nothing. Not beauty, not patriotism. I take each thing as it is, without prior rules about what it should be.
DYLAN, 1965

Definition destroys … there's nothing definite in this world.
DYLAN, 1976

Above: Defining beauty in The Rolling Thunder Revue, 1975.
Left: Joan Baez in whiteface with Dylan, Rolling Thunder Revue. Dylan was pleased to be told that for Native Americans, Rolling Thunder means speaking the truth.

During those hot summer nights of 1975, the idea of a "different" tour took fire. Dylan put it this way: "We were all very close. We had this fire going ten years ago, and now we've got it burning again." Neuwirth: "It's gonna be a new living room every night. This is the first existential tour. It's a movie, a closed set. It's rock 'n' roll heaven and it's historical. It's been Rambling Jack's dream for a long time—he's the one who taught us all, and the dream's coming true."

Dylan was preparing to tape *Desire* and continuing to hang out with his Village crowd. One night at the Other End, he asked Jack Elliott if he wanted to tour with him, to "play for the people." Jack's response to the buddy he'd not seen in seven years: "Let's go!" It took planning. First, Dylan went west to see his family, then popped up in Minnesota before taping the TV tribute to John Hammond, the record producer who first recorded him. He returned to New York with ideas about a rambling, tumbling tour of the north-east, with film cameras capturing it all. It wouldn't be announced, it would just "happen." Lou Kemp, the Alaska "salmon king" from Duluth, was named tour manager, assisted by Barry Imhoff and Shelly Finkel. Jacques Levy helped with stage direction. Rob Stoner organized a backup band that included Howard Wyeth, Luther Rix, Mick Ronson, Scarlet Rivera, T-Bone Burnett, and a 19-year-old mandolin/Dobro wizard named David Mansfield. The lead singers would be Dylan, Neuwirth, Ronee Blakley, Roger McGuinn, Elliott, and Joan Baez. Dylan phoned to ask what she was doing in November. She had a tour of her own planned, but this one sounded more of a challenge. She said it was "irresistible" and she'd make it. "Diamonds and Rust." Later she described the troupe as "an incredibly happy family."

One morning in October, some twenty musicians were jamming at the Other End. More signed on: Allen Ginsberg joined the chorus, fellow-poet Peter Orlovsky enlisted as a "baggage handler," David Blue and Denise Mercedes as musicians, security people, advance men, and lighting technicians. What started as a troupe of seventy swelled to more than a hundred by Toronto. On October 22, at the Other End, David Blue was finishing his gig. Dylan sang duets with Ronee Blakley, the beauteous country singer who starred in *Nashville*. Ginsberg sang to McGuinn's guitar. "Allen, you're the king," Dylan told him.

The following night, a little surprise for Mike Porco, who was turning 61. To Mike's astonishment, four film technicians showed up at Folk City, mumbling "educational television." Under the direction of Dylan, Howard Alk, and Mel Howard, this began hundreds of hours of shooting footage. On hand were Phil Ochs, Patti Smith, Baez, Commander Cody members, Bette Midler, and Buzzy Linhart. A little after 1 a.m., Dylan's red Cadillac Eldorado cruised up to Folk City, and in loped Bob, Kemp, and Neuwirth. Dylan, as "the greatest star of all," went to the stage. He brought up Baez, and they sang "Happy Birthday" and "One Too Many Mornings." Mike grinned from wall to wall. He'd been waiting for this a long time. This was a dress rehearsal for the Rolling Thunder Revue as, by twos and more, performers took to the little stage of Folk City. Hours later, a hoarse Phil Ochs did a set of his own, some traditional songs and "Lay Down Your Weary Tune." Everyone at Dylan's table stood gaping. Dylan praised Phil when he finished. (When 35-year-old Ochs hanged himself on April 9, 1976, some said his exclusion from Rolling Thunder was the last in a long line of crushing events that gave him no way out. Ochs could not be signed on the tour because of his heavy drinking and unpredictability. His friend and eulogizer, Ed Sanders, has described Ochs's "final flameout" as a reaction to "the tyranny of booze, despair, and maddening mood swings.")

That week also saw Dylan in a Columbia studio, re-taping "Hurricane." He told two top Columbia Records executives that he wanted it rush-released. After the session, producer Don DeVito said of Dylan: "He's just totally unpredictable." All that week the troupe had been assembling at the Gramercy Park Hotel in midtown Manhattan. Over the weekend there were intensive rehearsals at a nearby studio. Two advance men had hired the Plymouth (Massachusetts) Memorial Auditorium, despite the town fathers' reportedly asking Baez not to make any political statements from the stage. On October 27, the troupe took off in three buses and some cars, most of the singers riding in a Greyhound nicknamed Phydeaux. In a few hours, they arrived at the beachside Seacrest Hotel in North Falmouth,

Massachusetts, where rehearsals continued for a couple of days. That night, Dylan sang in the hotel dining room and Ginsberg recited "Kaddish." With the pilgrims landing first in Plymouth, it seemed like the grand Bicentennial gesture, leading to that gag: "The new sound is Plymouth rock." It was Halloween too, so there were masks and games. With cameras rolling, the games became cinema. The rhetoric was flowing like a rock riff. Elliott had once worked on the rigging of the *Mayflower* replica at Plymouth. This time, Jack climbed to the top of the mizzenmast and roared, "Ahoy!" He waved down to Dylan and Ginsberg. Allen duly proclaimed: "We have, once again, embarked on a voyage to reclaim America."

Why Rolling Thunder? Dylan said he simply looked up at the sky "and heard a boom. Then, boom, boom, boom, rolling from west to east. I figured that should be the name." He appeared pleased when someone told him that to American Indians, rolling thunder means speaking truth. Along the way, a Cherokee medicine man named Rolling Thunder joined the troupe. At Providence, he was onstage stroking a feather in time to the music. On November 5, at a beach in Newport, Dr Rolling Thunder made some good medicine around a fire. He asked everyone to add private prayers. Ginsberg: "Thanks to those who brought us together, and remembrance for those who are not here." Elliott: "Oh, pray that the spirit we've generated here extends to everyone we meet on our travels." Dylan reportedly mumbled: "I pray we realize soon we are all of one soul."

Kemp's advance men were booking halls at a prodigious speed, often so fast the musicians didn't know the next stop. Handbills alone told the story. The itinerary for the autumn segment of the Rolling Thunder Revue was: October 30 and 31, Plymouth Memorial Auditorium; November 1, Southeastern Massachusetts University, North Dartmouth; 2, Lowell (Massachusetts) Technical University; 4, two shows, Providence Civic Center; 6, two shows, Springfield Civic Center; 8, University of Vermont, Burlington; 9, University of New Hampshire, Durham; 11, Waterbury (Connecticut) Palace Theater; 13, two shows, New Haven Veterans Memorial Coliseum; 15, two shows, Niagara Falls Convention Center; 17, two shows, Rochester War Memorial Coliseum; 19, Worcester (Massachusetts) Civic Auditorium; 20, Harvard Square Theater, Cambridge. Afternoon and evening shows were held on November 21 at the Boston Music Hall. Then, evening concerts: 22, Brandeis University; 24, Hartford Civic Center Arena; 26, Augusta (Maine) Civic Center; 27, Bangor (Maine) Municipal Auditorium; 29, Quebec Coliseum; December 1 and 2, Toronto Maple Leaf Gardens; 4, Montreal Forum; 7, Clinton (New Jersey) State Prison; 8, Madison Square Garden, New York, "Night of the Hurricane I."

Dylan had rarely seemed more amiable, onstage and off. Sometimes he'd disappear into a room reserved for him in the name of Keef Laundry. With such voluble sources as Baez, Neuwirth, and Ginsberg, Dylan was relieved of burdensome interviews. Jim Jerome quoted Dylan in *Creem*:

It used to be my life was very simple. It consisted of hanging around with a certain crowd and writing songs. I always had a place to write … I tried to get rid of the burden of the Bob Dylan myth for a long time, because it is a burden. Just ask anybody who is considered a star. There are certain advantages and rewards to it, but you're thinking: 'Shit, man, I'm only me.' You know, that's who I am. We are all the same. No one is on any higher level than anybody else. We've all got it within us, for whatever we want to grasp for.

Baez found Dylan easier to relate to than he'd been to her in the previous ten years. Musician Mick Ronson: "He's a super-being, from somewhere else." Steve Soles: "Dylan is a psychic, he paraphrases things I've dreamed." One troupe member: "Those looks of his onstage—there were, like, five levels to them. All meant different things … He is unbelievably subtle. There was very close physical communication between him and the musicians—like I've never seen in him before."

Grandiloquent Allen Ginsberg talked volubly, most elegiacally to Peter Chowka of *New Age Journal*:

I hadn't seen Dylan for four years. He just called me up at 4 a.m. and said: "What're you writing? Sing it to me on the telephone … OK let's go out on the road." …Rolling Thunder will be one of the signal gestures characterizing the working cultural community that will make the Seventies … wishful thinking that is also prophesy … the first gesture toward communalism … he brought his mother along … the "mysterious" Dylan had a chicken-soup Yiddish mama, who even got onstage at one point [Toronto] … Sara and his children came. Sara met Joan Baez and they all acted in the movie together and Baez brought her mother and children [sic: she has only one son, Gabriel Harris], and Jack Elliott had his daughter. So there was a lot of jumping family … Dylan is now exploring his kingdom, with a new majesty about him. He alone has the clear, clean authoritative strength to take his own monumental images, unbuild and rebuild them. This is instant teaching to a younger generation. This means he has the power to re-create America, too. All the shit he has gone through—arguments with himself—he has turned to gold. He is more a citizen than ever. And in the Bicentennial tradition, that is political, to be a hard-working citizen … There are very few moments in my experience where I have felt the heart of history touched.

From the Fourth of July weekend right on through the spring segment of Rolling Thunder, significant changes in Dylan were seen. Onstage he displayed great mobility, moving about like a cross between a Seventies rocker and a football coach, driving his "team" onward. The man in motion was not afraid to change interpretations, lyrics, stage manner, appearance. Dylan had his face painted white with pancake makeup. He dressed in multi-colored scarves and different hats. He called it all *commedia dell'arte.* At the first show in Plymouth, the back-up band's masks also recalled that sixteenth-century Italian theater form in which stock characters improvised freely. Those less historically minded saw Dylan's new face as theatrical rock *à la* Bowie or Peter Gabriel. (Dylan said the makeup helped people in the back rows to see his face.) Ever the explorer, Dylan took more "liberties" with songs from performance to performance.

There was some critical backlash. When the tour moved toward large auditoriums, Dylan was attacked for having "sold out," again. The idea of the small-scale show got lost as the cast grew and filming expenses mounted. One estimate: The first thirteen shows of RTR attracted more than 83,000 customers paying a gross ticket price of $640,000. *Variety*, always interested in money, asked: "Is Dylan Interested in Money?" Dylan riposted: "We've got seventy people … we gotta pay for. We're gonna play any place we can, but we also have a lot of expenses to meet. We're not gonna … play living rooms. It's not a nightclub show, you know." Baez was testier: "Oh, tell them to just shove it up their asses!"

Spontaneity dominated the tour, including itinerary changes, improvisation, and guest appearances. Mimi Baez, once so critical of Dylan over what she regarded as his pro-Zionism, showed up. Joni Mitchell did two New Haven shows and reappeared later. Arlo Guthrie dropped in at Springfield. Old friends David Blue, Gordon Lightfoot, and Robbie Robertson popped up. Roberta Flack was at the prison and New York concerts. Joan said she'd never seen such a spirit. Even after arduous shows, the cast would sing their way along on the bus. Joan: "We all sing and sing and laugh until we pass out. For us, it makes no difference if we just play for fifteen people or fifteen thousand." Love and kisses onstage, as well, with songs dedicated to Hurricane Carter, Kerouac, Sam Peckinpah, and Gertrude Stein. Joan told Nat Hentoff, *Rolling Stone*, January 15, 1976:

The feeling is good, because everybody has some room onstage … Bob has so powerful an effect on so many lives … I'm still deeply affected by his songs … by that presence of his. I've seen nothing like it, except in Muhammad Ali, Marlon Brando and Stevie Wonder. Bob walks into a room and every eye in the place is on him. There are eyes on Bob even when he's hiding … I used to be too hard on him … I don't expect Bob to champion my causes anymore. I've learned he's not an activist, which does not mean he doesn't care about people.

With Baez and Dylan doing eye-to-eye duets again onstage, some thought they were witnessing a romantic reunion. Dylan even asked her to sing "Diamonds and Rust," although, playfully, she wouldn't concede that it was about *him.* Her "O Brother" suggests she had learned Dylan's elliptical methods. Joan told *People*: "Dylan has been a big element in my life, and he always will be. But we are different things to each other at different times. So much for Bob." Some of the most affecting moments of the autumn tour were visible only to the camera crew. Lowell, Massachusetts: By Jack Kerouac's grave, Dylan and Ginsberg improvised a scene. Allen leafed through Kerouac's *Mexico City Blues.* Dylan told him he'd first read it in Minneapolis. At the graveside, Dylan played harmonium or guitar while Allen improvised blues. Ginsberg:

There's a giant statue of Christ described by Kerouac. Dylan got up near … the statue … and goes into this funny monologue, asking the man on the cross, "How does it feel to be up there?" … everyone sees Dylan as a Christ-figure too, but he doesn't want to be crucified. He's too smart, in a way … Dylan was almost mocking, like a good Jew might be to someone who insisted on being the Messiah, against the wisdom of the rabbis, and getting himself nailed up for it. Dylan … said: "What can you do for somebody in that situation?" I think he quoted Christ, "suffer little children," and I quoted part of "Forever Young," which is Dylan's hip, Americanese paraphrase of Christ's "Do unto others."

So there was this brilliant funny situation of Dylan ... addressing this life-size statue of Christ, and allowing himself to be photographed with Christ. It was like Dylan humorously playing with the dreadful potential of his own mythological imagery, unafraid and confronting it, trying to deal with it in a sensible way. That seemed to be the characteristic of the tour: that Dylan was willing to shoulder the burden of the myth laid on him, or that he himself created, or the composite creation of himself and the nation, and use it as a workable situation. As Trungpa would say it: "Alchemize it."

Alchemize: This metaphor of Dylan, the Alchemist, had nagged me for ten years. *Alchemy* had been a secret and blasphemous science. Jung had made a respectable term of what had once been scoffed at as a pre-scientific superstition. The alchemists were not simply trying to turn base metals into gold, but were also aiming at the perfecting of matter and of "man in fulfilling the laws of God." Jung, according to Anthony Storr:

saw alchemy as a process of inner, psychological development in the alchemist himself, and the chemical changes and new combinations as changes within the personality ... Jung regarded [alchemy] as a gigantic Rorschach test ... the projection of the psychological process of the experimenter. The alchemists, like Jung and his patients, were engaged upon a spiritual progress, search for integration and individuation.[1]

Alchemy is also a metaphor for the poetic process. Balzac, in *The Human Comedy*, wrote:

To make gold was their point of departure, but ... they were looking for something better, they wanted to find the essential molecule, they were looking for movement at its beginning.

Wallace Fowlie, discussing Mallarmé:

What the poet does ... is very close to a magical creation. In a deliberate darkness he calls up an object that has been silenced, by means of words that are allusive ... what happens next is truly magic. By the enchantment of letters ... the words begin to glow ... until the illusion they evoke is equivalent to what the eyes of a man can see in the material world ... the occupation of the poet, quite in keeping with the ancient occupation of the alchemist, is the measuring or dosage of essences ... Only the magician or the alchemist was able to apply the formula and concoct the potions.[2]

The word *alchemy* has been traced back to Noah's son Shem, or Chem. Medieval alchemists thought the Ark was the original laboratory. Rimbaud's "Alchemy of the Word" passage from *A Season in Hell* keeps the circle unbroken:

I dreamed of crusades, of unrecorded voyages of discovery, of republics with no history, of hushed-up religious wars, revolution in customs, displacements of races and continents: I believed in every kind of witchcraft ... I wrote out silences and the nights. I recorded the inexpressible. I described frenzies ... Poetic old-fashionedness figured largely in my alchemy of the word. I grew accustomed to pure hallucination: I saw quite frankly a mosque in place of a factory, a school of drummers made up of angels, carriages on roads in the sky, a parlor at the bottom of the lake; monsters, mysteries. The title of a vaudeville conjured up horrors before me. Then I explained my magic sophisms with the hallucinations of words! At the end I looked on the disorder of my mind as sacred.[3]

Back in the Rolling Thunder laboratory outside Falmouth, the two poets were improvising another scene, Allen playing the Emperor and Dylan playing the Alchemist. Ginsberg: "I enter the diner and say: 'I'm the emperor, I just woke up this morning and found out I inherited an empire, and it's bankrupt. I hear from the apothecary across the street that you're an alchemist. I need some help to straighten out karmic problems with my empire ... I just sent for a shipload of tears from Indochina, but it didn't seem to do any good. Can you help? Do you have any magic formulae for alchemizing the situation?' Dylan kept denying he was an alchemist. 'I can't help, what're you asking me for?'"

Allen continued to insist that Dylan was the alchemist who knew the secrets. Dylan had the waiter bring him crackers, ketchup, salt, pepper, sugar, milk, coffee, yogurt, and apple pie, all of which he dumped into a big aluminum pot. Allen had put down his calling card—an autumn leaf, "just like the one

Dylan pocketed in the graveyard—the leaf which runs through many of the scenes in the movie, representing, like in Kerouac's work, transiency, poignancy, regret, acknowledgments of change, death. So I threw my calling-card leaf in the pot and Dylan threw in a piece of cardboard, and then he fished out the leaf, all muddy, and slapped it down on top of my notebook, where I was taking down all the magical ingredients in his alchemical mixture. Then I said: 'Oh, I see the secret of your alchemy: ordinary object.' 'Yes,' Dylan said, 'ordinary mind.'" In his long interview with Peter Chowka for the April 1976 *New Age Journal*, Ginsberg spoke of the three marks of existence: change, suffering, and egolessness.

I don't know him because I don't think there is any him. I don't think he's got a self! Yes, he's ever-changing. He's said very beautiful, Buddha-like things ... I asked him whether he was having pleasure on the tour and he said: 'Pleasure. Pleasure. What's that? I never touch the stuff.'... He went on to explain that at one time he had had a lot of pain and sought a lot of pleasure but found that there was a subtle relationship between pleasure and pain.

One conversation led Allen to write a song, on November 1, 1975, published in *First Blues*. In "Lay Down yr Mountain Lay Down God," Ginsberg calls Dylan an alchemist. Ginsberg recounted his version of Dylan's "spiritual conversation with God," and quoted Dylan: "Anybody that's busy making elephants and putting camels through needles' eyes is too busy to answer my questions, so I came down the mountain."

In the valley below, the Rolling Thunder Revue gathered momentum. Jerry Leichtling of the *Village Voice* said of the opening Plymouth concert: "This is one of the greatest shows I've ever seen ... this tour is Dylan's masterpiece." Fans, press, and participants dubbed it "minstrel show," "medicine show," "magical mystery tour," "a floating musical crap game." Some were reminded of Joe Cocker's "Mad Dogs and Englishmen" tour, while others regarded it as a traveling electric hootenanny. Some heard echoes of Ken Kesey's Acid Test. Ginsberg told Nat Hentoff that "Dylan's getting all his mysteries unraveled," but Hentoff thought otherwise: "If he has a mania, it is for survival ... And part of the way of survival is keeping some of his mysteries damn well raveled." Jon Landau in *Rolling Stone*, January 15, 1976:

From a myth-making point of view, this is all astonishingly effective stuff. Here a man does a limited tour ... refusing to make known his itinerary, doesn't release an album, does no interviews, is actively hostile to what little press penetrates his defenses—and winds up with extraordinary amounts of acclaim and attention. This is one rock star who still knows the importance of mystery in creating art and in calling attention to the artist.

Dylan brought his troupe to halls where folk purists had once booed him. The *Worcester Gazette*: "He could do no wrong. He could have stood onstage for two hours tuning his guitar and reciting nursery rhymes and they would have loved every minute of it." In the front row sat Joseph P Kennedy III, son of the late Robert Kennedy, as Dylan said: "This song is called 'Hurricane.' If you've got any political pull at all, maybe you can help us get this man out of jail." He introduced the song at Springfield: "I hear Massachusetts is the only state that didn't vote for Nixon. Is that true?" When the listeners cheered assent, Bob replied: "Well, neither did we." John Rockwell of the *Times* was amazed at the Plymouth finale's ten-minute cheering ovation. Rockwell saw the Revue as a summation of all Dylan's musical influences plus "politics and ballads fused ... into something higher and more personal ... Rolling Thunder ... is Dylan's Bicentennial gesture to this country's true spirit."

Rolling Thunder pursued a grueling schedule of shows that were at least three and a half hours long. The first Toronto show ran an hour longer than that. At the Montreal Forum, there were 20,000 in the audience. The *Montreal Star* felt that "still, Dylan hasn't lost the sense of intimacy that seemed so important to him when the tour was conceived." There was some grumbling among the roadies and technical staff, and Baez tried to organize greater democracy within the troupe. There were problems too with the press and security. Only Ken Regan of Camera 5 and Dylan's film crew had "exclusive" photography rights. Ticket holders showed considerable irritation at being frisked by what the *Niagara Gazette* called "a goon squad." After incidents at the Niagara Convention Center, the deputy police chief conceded that the dozen Rolling Thunder security people were "rougher than necessary," but were within their legal bounds. Paul Colby to Toby Goldstein in *Modern Hi-Fi & Music*: "the last night Dylan played in the back room [of the Other End] he said he wanted to play onstage so bad he could taste it. But ... he was afraid of tape recorders ... in fact, there were two tape recorders, brought by the same guy. I spilled a glass of wine in that guy's face and threw him out … It's one of the reasons he doesn't play more often … He's leery of the public."

On November 16, at the Tuscarora Indian Reservation, north of Buffalo, Chief Arnold Hewitt received a telephone call—could the Rolling Thunder troupe drop in for a visit? Without speakers or amplifiers, troupe musicians, including Joni Mitchell and Eric Andersen, showed up at the Indians' community house. Song-swapping between his troupe and the Indians reached some intense moments. Tuscaroras did traditional songs and dances to drumbeating. While Dylan sang, a few of the younger Indian children played tag around the community house. The Rolling Thunder people and their hosts then feasted on corn soup, corn bread, and venison. All of this was filmed, including five complete concerts and assorted improvised scenes. Ginsberg saw the tour as a reaffirmation of what was actually achieved in the Sixties. He also saw the film and tour as having a dominant theme of "respect for mother-goddess, eternal-woman, earthwoman principles." Dylan told him that the film's "thread" was simply "truth and beauty." As the massed voices of the Rolling Thunder Revue sang out "This Land Is Your Land," these pilgrims who started at Plymouth Rock had another mountain to scale, Madison Square Garden.

The Hurricane Begins. How well Rubin Carter's nickname, "Hurricane," blended into Dylan's lexicon. In 1963, he wrote:

> Oh the time will come up
> When the winds will stop
> And the breeze will cease to be breathin'.
> Like the stillness in the wind
> 'Fore the hurricane begins,
> The hour when the ship comes in.[4]

Each of the 200 male and female convicts who heard Dylan and the Rolling Thunder troupe on Sunday, December 7, 1975, was waiting for some ship to come in. These prisoners at the medium-security New Jersey State Prison at Clinton listened to Ginsberg chant poems, and to Joni Mitchell, Roberta Flack, and Dylan sing.

Among the convict-listeners was a former middleweight boxer who'd been inside for nine years on a life sentence for a triple murder in Paterson, New Jersey, in 1966. Early in the morning on June 17, 1966, two black men had shot up a white working-class bar, killing the bartender and two of the three customers. A witness described the getaway car, and Carter and John Artis were found in an allegedly similar vehicle. Four months later, two small-time thieves, Alfred Bello and Arthur Bradley, testified they'd seen Carter and Artis running out of the bar. Carter and Artis were charged with the murders. In 1974, a New Jersey investigator and a *New York Times* reporter heard the two white thieves say they'd lied in fingering the two black men because the police had offered help with cases pending against them. Rubin Hurricane Carter had long insisted that he and his friend Artis were framed; a growing number of people believed him. In summer 1975, Carter had sent his autobiography, *The Sixteenth Round*, to Dylan. Bob's reaction: "I realized Hurricane and I were coming from the same place spiritually. He's a brilliant man, one of the most truthful I have ever met. He is a perfect citizen in every way. I love him as a brother. It just isn't fair. He must get out. *Today.*"

After Dylan wrote "Hurricane," collaborating on the lyrics with Jacques Levy, the boxer declared: "Words are about the most powerful drugs known to men. Bob Dylan came to prison to see me and I met a man that was for life and living, not for death and dying." In Carter, Dylan found a renewed focus for his involvement with victims and outsiders, especially black recipients of white "justice." Dylan: "I never doubted him for a moment. He's just not a killer, not that kind of man." "Hurricane" is Dylan's *J'accuse* of the American judicial system:

> How can the life of such a man
> Be in the palm of some fool's hand?
> To see him obviously framed
> Couldn't help but make me feel ashamed to live in a land
> Where justice is a game.

Now all the criminals in their coats and their ties
Are free to drink martinis and watch the sun rise
While Rubin sits like Buddha in a ten-foot cell
An innocent man in a living hell[5]

Largely through the zeal of advertising executive George Lois, the Hurricane Trust Fund was formed, and soon attracted the support of celebrities. Although Dylan was never listed on the fund's letterhead, his song and presence at two benefits gave the Carter-Artis appeal its greatest impetus. Lois had originally sought Dylan's help while Rolling Thunder was in New Haven. They planned a Madison Square Garden benefit, where a large cast of mostly black stars would support Dylan. When booking problems mounted, Dylan told Lois, "The hell with it. I'll come in with my whole revue!"

The night after the prison concert, "The Night of the Hurricane I" went to Madison Square Garden, where there were as many notables in the capacity audience as onstage. First came an hour of music from Neuwirth, Blakley, Joni, and the Rolling Thunder Revue Band. Then, for twenty minutes, the Hurricane cause was expounded. Heavyweight Muhammad Ali told the largely white audience: "You've got the connections and the complexion to get the protection." Hurricane, listening to the concert by telephone, said: "I thank you from my heart. I love you all madly." Ali swaggered with his customary feints and punches: "I know you all came here to see me, because Bob Dylan just ain't that big." John Rockwell, the *Times*: "The Carter people's desire for publicity and the Dylan people's characteristic secretiveness, inspired by the singer himself, have caused some unusual clashes … the press rebuffed by one side even as it was being encouraged by the other." Then followed nearly four hours of performances from Roberta Flack, Richie Havens, Joni and Joan, the Rolling Thunderers, and Dylan. Even *New York* magazine's Nik Cohn, usually cool toward Dylan, was impressed: "Dylan … in white-face … vagabond clown … In ten years, I'd never seen him work with more intensity … no poetical postures … he rasped and roared, he burned." During instrumental breaks, "he caromed all over the stage, stomping, rocking, as if even a moment's silence or stillness would cause him to blow sky-high." The shortened single version of the song had already made its mark. The *San Francisco Chronicle*: "One of the most convincing artistic statements of the year." The *Los Angeles Times* said Dylan had "rekindled his intensity and purpose … a return to leadership."

To the song's accompaniment, legal moves quickened. On November 6, the New Jersey Supreme Court announced it would review the appeal. A month later, Carter and Artis withdrew their application for pardon, seeking "complete vindication" in the courts and asking executive clemency pending a new trial. On January 12, 1976, the top Jersey court heard the appeal, and in March unanimously threw out the convictions, saying that a fair trial "was substantially prejudiced" because the prosecution, to bolster the reliability of its two principal witnesses, had failed to disclose evidence. Carter and Artis were freed on bail and promised a new trial.

Meanwhile, plans were afoot for a "Night of the Hurricane II." First planned for the New Orleans Superdome in December, it was moved to the Houston Astrodome on January 25, 1976. This promised to be the biggest rock benefit ever, with Dylan's troupe joined by Stevie Wonder, Stephen Stills, Ringo Starr, Dr John, Santana, Shawn Phillips, Isaac Hayes, and others. Because of strange machinations behind the promotion, this super-concert was a curious box-office fiasco, attended by 30,000, half as many as expected.

Then came the anti-climax. Just before Christmas, 1976, after the new trial's jurors had listened to seventy-six witnesses for thirty-one days, Carter and Artis were found guilty again. Bello withdrew his recantation, and all the high expectations of the previous months began to wane. Two former defense witnesses also testified that they were not with Carter at the time of the shooting. *Time*, January 3, 1977: "The judge allowed the State to argue that Carter and Artis had killed the three whites in order to avenge the murder six hours earlier of a black tavern owner whose stepson was a friend of Carter's." The new defense lawyer replied that such tactics were "a racial horror that feeds on the basest, most dirty part of all of us." Carter and Artis were led back to jail on December 21, 1976. On February 9, 1977, Carter received two consecutive and one concurrent life terms. Artis received three concurrent life terms.

The Hurricane Fund had broadened its slogan to "Freedom for All, Forever," and there were shifts in its leadership. Dylan's song continued to be played widely, rising to the Top Forty. The eyewitness named in the song, Patty Valentine, brought a suit against Dylan, Levy, Columbia Records, and Warner Bros Publishing, charging them with invasion of privacy and with presenting her "in an unfavorable light." The suit asked for a "fair and equitable share" of all money earned from the song. As so often happens, a simple cause became a morass of legal problems. The melody and the malady that inspired "Hurricane" linger on. Even if Carter and Artis should ever win their freedom on appeal, "it won't be over till they clear his name/And give him the time he's done."[6]

In November 1985, Hurricane Carter was released on bail from Rahway State Prison. Federal Judge Lee Sarokin cited "grave constitutional violations" by prosecutors. He ruled that the 1976 convictions had been based on "an appeal to racism rather than reason, concealment rather than disclosure." But Carter's nineteen-year ordeal may not be over because a third trial might be sought by the prosecution.

The White Goddess, Desire.   Another word in the Dylan lexicon is Desire, which he had invoked as early as 1964. In the eleventh of his "Outlined Epitaphs," he declared that after the storm, under a sky "constantly meanin' change," he would welcome Desire:

> *an' after it's Desire*
> *returnin'*
> *returnin' with me underneath*
> *returnin' with it*
> *never fearful*
> *finally faithful*
> *it will guide me well …*
> *never failin' …*[7]

The album named *Desire*, released in January 1976, was an eclectic musical statement, a marriage of legendary themes and contemporary meaning. It initially struck me as spare, almost rudimentary yet, beneath its simple surfaces, *Desire* has proved alive and deep, the culmination of the trilogy that began with *Planet Waves*. In some ways, this album is the real self-portrait. I began a dogged search for clues and allusions that became my voyage through the wild and unknown country of myths and dreams that have lured Dylan.

Desire was the name of a New Orleans streetcar and a western that starred Marlene Dietrich. But many poets have been lured by Desire. To Blake, it was man's ladder to the stars. In "The Question Answer'd," Blake made gratification of Desire the pivotal human impulse. Eliot's "Four Quartets" orchestrated themes that also intrigue Dylan—time, justice, roles, rebirth, redemption, and desire. Eliot wrote of "the inner freedom for the practical desire" and concluded that "only through time time is conquered." Blake illuminated his manuscripts. Eliot used footnotes. Dylan plays his cards more slyly. His brief liner notes and carefully positioned visual symbols on album jacket and songbook use the symbolism of tarot cards. Other clues lead to Robert Graves's *The White Goddess*, a complex *Historical Grammar of Poetic Myth*. Graves showed how the patriarchal structure of Judeo-Christian religion attempted to erase the ancient worship of the Goddess. Graves also maintained that Desire was crucial to poetry: "Poetry is rooted in love and love in desire, and desire in hope of continued existence." Graves advised the poet to "achieve social and spiritual independence at whatever cost," for the poet must "learn to think mythically as well as rationally."

Dylan had been "thinking mythically" since he was a boy at the movies. *Desire*, however, is a giant step forward in the breadth of his mythological thinking, moving toward a summation of themes that have long absorbed him: apocalypse, personal or societal; identity; the hero's quest for love, knowledge, redemption, liberation. He deals here with manifold myths—of justice and the outsider ("Hurricane" and "Joey"); of the woman who suffers love and offers renewal ("Isis" and "Oh, Sister"); and of life as a movie ("Romance in Durango" and "Black Diamond Bay"). Dylan has shuffled his tarot cards like a diviner, melded his old preoccupations with new, made the Egyptian oracular island of Pharos as contemporary as a TV show.

Two keynotes of the album lie in the lyrics of "Oh, Sister": "We died and were reborn and then Mysteriously saved"[8] and "Time is an ocean but it ends at the shore./You may not see me/Tomorrow."[9] Death and rebirth, and time lost, stolen, or threatened, are the Faustian questions of the alchemist who seeks spiritual perfection and redemption. Let's try to "lift the veil of Isis": The Empress tarot card on the album jacket and two other cards displayed in the song folio, the Magician and Judgment, are from the so-called Rider pack of 1910, traditional emblems redesigned by A E Waite and drawn by Pamela Colman

Smith. Waite wrote that the Empress "the fruitful mother of thousands … has been correctly described as desire and the wings thereof." Alfred Douglas, a contemporary Jungian, wrote in *The Tarot* (1973) that the Empress symbolizes an earth mother, "descendant of Demeter and Ishtar [the most popular Assyro-Babylonian goddess], patronesses of mystery cults … at which the sacred dramas of death and the renewal of life were played out." The tarot cards have positive and negative meanings. If upright, the Empress symbolizes growth; if reversed, domestic upheaval, psychic alienation, and poverty. Few myths are more pervasive than the search for the conquest of death. The Egyptian example of Isis and Osiris is invoked in the song "Isis," but resonates throughout the album.

Isis, one incarnation of the Empress, was a mother goddess, patroness of navigation, the sorrowing wife whose tears formed the Nile. She was also the redeemer whose magic mysteriously reconstituted and revived the body of her slain husband-brother, Osiris. A moon goddess identified by her heifer horns, Isis also instituted marriage. Osiris anointed her as queen of Egypt, leaving her to rule while he rambled throughout Asia to conquer without violence, disarming strange people with his gentleness, his songs, and his music-making. In Egyptian mythology, Osiris has scores of names and incarnations. One was Proteus, the oracular Old Man of the Sea, priest-king of the Pharos, gifted with the power to change his shape. Proteus, Graves tells us, married Sarah, the goddess mother of the tribe of Abraham that visited Egypt near the end of the Third Millennium. (Dylan joked on his Rolling Thunder tour of gentle conquest that "Sara" was not necessarily about his wife, perhaps about the biblical Sarah.) Pharos lore also invested the number five with magic powers, affecting festivals, architecture, even the calendar. Dylan opens "Isis" with a line about the fifth month of the year: "I married Isis on the fifth day of May,"[10] then tells a wondrous tale of a strange quest through ice-clad pyramids. But in the denouement, the poet's laconic return to the "mystical child," Isis is stranger still.

In *The White Goddess*, Graves finds the Isis-Osiris story deeply imbedded in many cultures: "the sacred king as the moon goddess's divine victim; holding that every muse-poet must, in a sense, die for the goddess whom he adores, just as the king died." Isis, sister and wife of Osiris, reconciles opposites in a "divine unity." Such relationships exist in the Finnish epic, *Kalevala*, and in Scottish ballads like "The Bobby Hind" and "Sheath and Knife." Dylan had long been searching for his ideal "twin," which heightens the sister image. Baez only confused the allusiveness when she asked in her "Oh Brother!" how *she* came to be his sister.

In "Baby Blue," Dylan had already shown awareness of the Jungian doctrine of synchronicity: "Take what you have gathered from coincidence."[11] It is scarcely coincidence that he placed on the song folio's contents page a reproduction of the 1910 tarot design of the Magician, which bears an uncanny resemblance to Dylan. The Magician card has also been called the Minstrel, the Conjurer, or the Cobbler. It once represented the traveling showman, a medicine man who told fortunes, sold quack remedies, and spread heretical ideas. Tarot expert Douglas's description of the Magician reveals a startling dual portrait of Dylan: "Half mountebank and half wise man … The Magician is forceful and self-confident, and stands alone." He is related to Prometheus, Till Eulenspiegel, Hermes, or Coyote, the Indian folk hero. Douglas thought the Magician-Prometheus figure referred to the time "when man first attained self-consciousness, 'stealing' it from the unconscious." He thus takes divine attributes, "possession of the world, but has lost sight of his soul … The Magician faces perils and temptations … on the long quest to rediscover what he has lost. His wand represents his flaming will." Above his head, a figure eight on its side stands for inspiration from "his own true Self, the spark of divinity within him." Upright, the Magician card stands for strong will, personal expansion, taking risks, initiative, adaptability, versatility, diplomacy and self-confidence. Reversed, Douglas says, the Magician becomes the Juggler, the trickster who conjures with life, delighting to observe the effect his clever sleight of hand has on lesser mortals. Then he is questing for power, not wisdom. He becomes a wizard, "the instrument of those demonic powers he sought to control." The Judgment card in the folio symbolizes rebirth, resurrection, and redemption, and has been called the card of eternal life. Douglas: "The psyche is released from the walls that imprison it, the Divine Child that rises from the tomb is the regenerated self." To alchemists this meant "the Philosopher's stone." The rising Divine Child on the Blakean Judgment card is considered "the god within," the goal of the heroic quest. That search is nearing fulfillment, and elements of the psyche have "reached full integration and are being reborn."

In a brief album-jacket poem, Dylan drops more clues. He is "On the heels of Rimbaud moving like a dancing bullet."[12] Cryptically, he writes: "Tolstoy was right."[13] Tolstoy was right about many things, but I believe Dylan was referring to *Resurrection*, his great novel of 1899 in which he advanced his belief in redemption through love. *Resurrection* is a scathing indictment of modern society in general, and the institutions of justice and the church in particular. The protagonist, Nekhlyudov, Tolstoy's alter ego, is driven by "a desire to elevate himself by joining forces with those who are most lowly." He follows a victimized prostitute to Siberia in his search for personal redemption. According to Troyat, Tolstoy's biographer: "It is not sentiment that gives rhythm and warmth to this couple's story but the denunciation of social injustice and the search for a remedy that will cure mankind's ills."

Dylan's search for redemption stretches back to *Blonde on Blonde* and *John Wesley Harding*. In everyday language, redemption means deliverance, reclamation, or salvation; in Christian terms, it is deliverance through Christ's atonement. In his 1936 essay, "Ideas of Redemption in Alchemy," Jung declared: "After the resurrection man becomes stronger and younger than he was before"—echoed in Dylan's famous line, "I'm younger than that now."[14] Jung tied the alchemist's search to the Messianic element of Hebrew prophecy, and to the myth cycles of Osiris, Orpheus, Dionysus, and Hercules, who all died and were mysteriously saved or redeemed. Jung found the epitome of artistic alchemical thinking in Goethe's Faust. What would Jung have made of Dylan's "chain with the devil" from his early Hibbing days until his redemption through love and through battling against social injustice?

Dylan's long search for redemption through alchemical identification with mythic characters culminates in *Desire*. He refers to "the songs of redemption," which Ginsberg's notes to *Desire* take as a title. Ginsberg's essay recalls that he and fellow 1950s beats dreamed of a quest for liberation, and of the marriage of poetry to music. He described *Desire* as "another great surge of prophetic feeling," hearing Hebraic cantillation in "One More Cup of Coffee." I hear Tex-Mex and *ranchero* music, and the *mélange* of flamenco and soul that Otis Redding and others explored and Van Morrison developed.

Another response to *Desire* came from W T Lhamon, Jr, in the *New Republic*: "a State of the Disunion Message ... by a man of great power, if indirect, and greater integrity, certainly, than most of the people addressing us this year." John Rockwell said in the *Times*: "some of the most wonderful music Dylan has ever made." Dave Marsh, in *Rolling Stone*, saw an important change in Dylan's attitude toward women. Jack McDonough has written that Dylan's "best poetry comes when ... modern fright and confusion and romantic questing for secret, elusive beauty meet."

Dylan's melodic resources have full sway, from the declamatory, rallying verse of "Hurricane" to the playful tune of "Mozambique," from the keening of "Sara" to the other-worldly cast of "Valley Below." "Hurricane," the album's opening track and best-known song, sets tone and texture, tolling again those freedom chimes, previewing some of the album's major themes. The Isis-Osiris relationship in "Isis," "Oh, Sister," and "Sara" continues *Desire*'s implicit struggle—against false "justice," against false love, against false labeling. Ginsberg calls them "cameo novels." Dylan's dramatic-cinematic vision was never stronger. In "Romance in Durango," with a simple chorus in Spanish, he establishes a sense of place, as he evokes palpable spacelessness in "Isis." "Durango" and "Valley Below" are of a piece, Brando-Eastwood-Dylan scripts for the man on the run.

"Joey" came in for stern criticism, which missed the point of Dylan's long fascination with the social pariah, the outsider, and the badman. Dylan can step aside and savor Joey Gallo's Cagney-like panache, reminding us that all the world's not only a stage but a screen as well. Gallo simmered up on the very streets of Little Italy that Dylan scuffed along. On the West Coast, Dylan had befriended Robert De Niro, another son of New York's mean streets. Although Gallo had read Nietzsche in stir, Dylan was probably more impressed with Gallo's being "Always on the outside/Of whatever side there was!'"[15] In jail, he was closest to black men:

> *'Cause they seemed to understand*
> *What it's like to be in society*
> *With a shackle on your hand*[16]

For all the mythical thinking on *Desire*, Dylan's old whimsy is not subdued. In "Isis," the stranger dies and the narrator hopes it isn't contagious. After endless travail and searching, the narrator is reunited with Isis. The Hemingwayesque understatement of their colloquy borders on burlesque. More whimsy surfaces in the "Black Diamond Bay" scenario, where life is again reflected in a card game. Dylan has always loved the shaggy-dog story and the confrontations of the poker game. (Baudelaire, in "Spleen," locked the Jack of Hearts and Queen of Spades in dialogue.) All the bizarre things that happen in "Black Diamond Bay" suddenly appear through a different lens when the perspective shifts in the last verse. The song's minutely observed action is instantly reduced to a news item the narrator glimpses as he idly watches TV in LA. Are we all global village idiots whom television has reduced to voyeurism, or has television so deadened us to catastrophe that we can't tell a real crisis from a fictional one? Ambiguity on all channels.

Finally, in "Sara," Dylan *seems* to be making an unabashed confessional to his wife. A plea for forgiveness and understanding, its open nostalgia stands out joltingly among Dylan's many covert, ambiguous games. After all his charades, his theatrical masks, and hide-and-seek games, he seems to say that this "Scorpio Sphinx,"[17] this "mystical wife" has an actual, as well as a mythical, identity. She is Desire incarnate. The melody and vocalizing are pained. This track became the album's most controversial. Some heard it heralding a "new Dylan" ready to stand naked, and some were just plain embarrassed by "too personal a tale."[18] Some found it riddled with banalities easy to parody, while others were touched by his naming his "Sad-Eyed Lady." On *Biograph*, Dylan declares: "I don't write confessional songs." But how can he say it in the face of "Sara" and "Abandoned Love," a "confessional song" left off *Desire*?

Desire is dominated by women deities and women colleagues. Scarlet Rivera's violin is a genuinely innovative sound, blending melancholy and exoticism. Emmylou Harris's harmony is also an important new element. (She was on the first version of "Hurricane," but Ronee Blakley sings harmony on the released version.) The women's voices against Dylan's are another experiment in texture. Although Harris is a perfectionist about intonation and polish, she acceded to Dylan's imperatives of spontaneity and urgency. Some rough-and-ready cuts were released. There is fine instrumental support from six others, most of whom were with the Rolling Thunder Revue. A very cohesive ensemble sound dominates.

Desire was unique in the presence of Jacques Levy as co-lyricist on all tracks except "Sara" and "Valley Below." Levy, a PhD in psychology, is well imbued with Jungian thinking. He's also a theatrical handyman, director of *Oh, Calcutta*, and a seasoned lyricist. He and Dylan met through Roger McGuinn, who had worked with Levy back in 1968 on a country and western musical. The two put together two dozen songs in three weeks, sixteen of which were recorded on McGuinn/Byrds albums, the best known being "Chestnut Mare." Dylan met Rambling Jacques on Bleecker Street after Tour '74. A year later, after another chance Bleecker Street encounter, Bob suggested they try to "write some stuff together." Dylan had a verse of "Isis" already written. Laughing and rapping, they worked through the night on it. At more meetings in July, things progressed so well that they went out to a Long Island retreat for three weeks in August to bang out more lyrics together, reportedly for fourteen songs. Levy suggested Joey Gallo as a theme, for he had known Gallo well during 1969, the last year of his life. Levy said that Dylan dreamed up "Valley Below" while living with gypsies in Corsica. And "Sara" had long been on his mind. He also turned to Levy for ideas for Rolling Thunder. McGuinn has attested that Levy's encouraging manner and style bring out the best in his partners.

Before arriving at his final *Desire* team, Dylan experimented with Eric Clapton, Kokomo, and the Dave Mason Band, looking for a compatible combination. Then he ran into a Lower East Side bar band, Rob Stoner and the Rebels, with whom Mick Ronson often sat in. Here Dylan found sidemen for the Rolling Thunder Band and for the final *Desire* sessions. Some of the songs' aura of search and struggle went into finding the musicians, as the credit on the album slyly attests: "This record could have been produced by Don DeVito."

The English critic and academic, Simon Frith, summarized Dylan's role: "When people dream about Dylan—and most people do—they dream of him not as a lover but as a friend. If one of his skills has been to make his private concerns public, without being mawkish or self-concerned, another has been to let us make his public world, all the songs, private, relevant to our individual concerns … Dylan sounds like a nice guy again. Someone to talk to—about the world and about ourselves."

Distant Thunder. Primarily to raise money to produce the film *Renaldo and Clara*, a second segment of Rolling Thunder was added in 1976. What I call Distant Thunder was more muted than the north-eastern tour, because the novelty and the gaze of the major media had left. After the Night of the Hurricane II at the Houston Astrodome (January 25, 1976) there was a break. The tour resumed in Florida on April 18 at the Lakeland Civic Center, the first of eight concerts during the Easter college break. By then, the backing group was calling itself Guam. They opened with a dozen songs, followed generally by Dylan doing two acoustic selections, then a set backed by Guam. McGuinn and Baez had solo stints, then Bob and Joan sang together, ending with ten or so songs from Dylan/Guam.

At the Belleview Biltmore Hotel in Clearwater, Florida, Burt Sugarman, producer of many of the shows for NBC-TV's *The Midnight Special*, videotaped the concert. A few weeks later, Dylan rejected the tape. Instead, he gave his nod to a group of documentary-makers called Top Value Television. For their show, they filmed the May 23 concert at Hughes Stadium, at Fort Collins, Colorado, broadcast on NBC-TV on September 10 as *Hard Rain*. That day also saw the live album released, with additional tapes from the Tarrant County Convention Center, Fort Worth, Texas.

The TV show was, appropriately, under raining, cloudy skies. Bob looked very tense, and what Joan later called "his viper eyes" darted around a lot. It came to be called "an anti-special," with most mainstream TV critics panning it, as "painfully artless," "a mess … a debacle." The underground *Boston Phoenix* called it "perhaps the most extraordinary and moving film of a concert ever made." Between Florida and Fort Collins, Rolling Thunder played Mobile, Hattiesburg, three cities in Texas, and Oklahoma City. The second part of Rolling Thunder ended, after a concert in Wichita, on May 25 in Salt Lake City.

Warming up for what was to become his most sustained period of visibility in the American press, Dylan provided a cover story for the most widely circulated magazine in the United States, *TV Guide*, on September 11. Since the credits of the show thanked, among others, Herman Melville and Rimbaud, Dylan explained his debts to them and to Conrad, Joyce, and Ginsberg. Asked how he imagined God, Bob replied: "I can see God in a daisy … in the wind and rain. I see creation just about everywhere. The highest form of song is prayer." (The daisy line pre-echoes his final song on *Shot of Love*, from Blake's "Auguries of Innocence": "To see a World in a Grain of Sand/And a Heaven in a Wild Flower.") Dylan had praise for the Beatles and the Stones. "And Joan Baez means more to me than a hundred of these singers around today."

Back in LA, Dylan began editing *Renaldo and Clara*. He finished a new song, "Sign Language," which Eric Clapton taped for his album *No Reason to Cry*. Phil Spector finally talked Dylan into a studio, to join backup singers on the song by Leonard Cohen and Spector, "Don't Go Home With Your Hard-on."[19]

Thanksgiving Day, 1976, was chosen as the day the Band would say a long goodbye to touring, at San Francisco's Winterland Palace. The rising director Martin Scorsese decided to direct a major film of the event, which also spawned a live album. Some of the Band had followed Bob from Big Pink to Malibu, where Robbie had a house called Shangri-La. To close out their sixteen years of hard traveling, they planned perhaps their greatest performance. With a 300-page shooting script, the director had a forty-five-member crew running seven cameras on the thirty-seven programmed songs.

The guest roster included Dr John, Joni Mitchell, Neil Diamond, Van Morrison, Neil Young, and Dylan. For visual opulence, Bill Graham rented sets from the San Francisco Opera's *La Traviata*. The 5,000 listeners not only heard a great concert but also consumed 200 turkeys and 300 pounds of salmon. The Berkeley Promenade Orchestra provided the waltzes, foreshadowing the New Romantics by a decade. Ronnie Hawkins, who had organized the Band as the Crackers in 1960, was there, and so were Bobby Charles, Paul Butterfield, Muddy Waters, and Eric Clapton.

Emmett Grogan was the MC for *The Last Waltz*. He brought on some Coast poets at intermission: Sweet William, Leonore Kandel, Michael McClure, Diane di Prima, and the dean, Larry Ferlinghetti. Robbie Robertson had only finished the signature tune, "The Last Waltz," that morning. He brought "one more friend." Dylan plugged in for "Baby, Let Me Follow You Down." Grogan said Dylan, hamming it up in a high-crowned white hat, "swaggered his lyrics" in "Hazel," "I Don't Believe You," "Forever Young," and then repeated his opener. He remained stage-center for the grand finale of "I Shall Be Released," with more stars, Ringo Starr and Ronnie Wood, joining in the jam. Scorsese, who had been on the crew of the *Woodstock* film, managed to make the movie retain a dignity rare in rock. Wrote Terry Curtis Fox in the *Village Voice*: "While ostensibly … about the Band, Scorsese's editing makes no bones about how much a Dylan event it became … Everything else disappears behind his presence. Scorsese … does nothing to hide or minimize this effect. It is not merely the best rock-concert movie ever made; it is as intensely personal as anything Scorsese has done."

Renaldo and Clara. Another film director spent most of 1977 on a film about aspects of the music life that was to be even more personal. Dylan helped edit down 240,000 feet—some 100 hours—for his film, *Renaldo and Clara*. The finished movie, running nearly four hours, became a candidate for commercial suicide. Complex, often non-communicative, it was a musical triumph but a dramatic failure. Not since *Self Portrait* were critics able to have such a field day in turning the finger-pointing toward the finger-pointer.

Dylan was most hurt by the reaction from his old neighborhood paper, the *Village Voice*. "Did you see the firing squad of critics they sent?" he asked me in summer 1978. The *Voice* published seven reviews on January 30, 1978. Karen Durbin called it "The *coup de grâce* in his de-adulation campaign," resenting his comparisons of himself to Jesus. Referring to confused scenes among Dylan, Baez, and Sara, she wrote: "Dylan could love no one like he loves himself." Richard Goldstein, like most, preferred concert scenes to the "clumsily improvised 'fictional' interludes." But he found ultimate balance, finding moments "in Altman almost as insufferable, and moments [here] as moving as anything you're likely to experience in a rock-concert film." James Walcott said the film sank so many reputations, "it's like watching the defeat of the Spanish Armada," and considered it the spiteful revenge of "an artist on his groupies." That tough professional, Pauline Kael, in the *New Yorker*, February 13, 1978, said that "despite all his masks and camouflage," he's "still the same surly, mystic tease ... more tight close-ups than any actor can have had in the whole history of movies. He's overpoweringly present, yet he is never in direct contact with us ... we are invited to stare ... to perceive the mystery of his elusiveness—his distance." Her review was headlined "The Calvary gig." Reaction in Europe was generally more favorable. Dylan courted trouble with the extensive interviews he did in the autumn and winter of 1977–78. "I talked too much about that film," he told me later, but he said it was necessary to minimize advertising costs. *Renaldo and Clara* was very much a one-man operation. Dylan not only directed but also wrote and starred in it. His Lombard Films made the work, and his own Minneapolis-based Circuit Films, in association with his brother, distributed it. Because the film was flawed, and because of years of Dylan's self-righteousness toward human flaws, it provided the ideal time for many to hit him back.

In a long interview with Jonathon Cott, who compared Dylan to Luis Buñuel, Dylan waxed lyrical and recondite with such Gallic verbal castles as: "Art is the perpetual motion of illusion. The highest purpose of art is to inspire." He made it clear that he regarded the film as being about "identity" in which "the mask is more important than the face ... about naked alienation of the inner self against the outer self." Dylan defended the work's integrity: "being faithful to the subconscious." He counter-attacked in advance: "We may be kicked right out of Hollywood after this film is released. In India, they show twelve-hour movies. Americans ... expect art to be like wallpaper with no effort ... I'm sure of my dream self. I live in my dreams. I don't live in the actual world." More variation on these themes to *Playboy* and the *New York Times*. To *Maclean's* magazine, Toronto, he said: "There's no way I should or could explain the movie ... but I can't explain 'Desolation Row' either ... Sara and Joan Baez were the same woman ... it's like a cubist painting ... Maybe there are only two or three people in the universe who are going to understand what it's about."

A two-hour version brought forward the excellent concert footage. In the full version, there were forty-seven songs on the soundtrack, twenty-two by Dylan and one each by Beethoven and Chopin. Some songs, like "Isis," "One More Cup of Coffee," and "Knockin' on Heaven's Door," are nothing less than classic. Tracks by Baez, Ronee Blakley, Roger McGuinn, and Jack Elliott shine. David Blue reminiscing about early Village days over a pinball machine was charming. Street interviews about Hurricane Carter had immediacy. But many dramatic scenes, especially those involving Dylan, Sara, and Joan, could readily lose the viewer. The single most affirmative review I've seen was by Nigel Andrews of the *Financial Times* in September 1978, after the London opening: "The mysteries exert an authentic fascination ... I shall go out on a nervous limb and say that *Renaldo and Clara* is probably the most important film of the year." It sought, he wrote, "to define a new morality, a new religion; a new sense of direction for an age which has lost faith in doctrinal Christianity."

Bitching. Not all the commentary on the Thunder/*Renaldo* experience came from the press. Some observations were made by the playwright Sam Shepard, by Joan Baez in song, and by Sara Dylan in a law court.

Shepard was already esteemed as a playwright when he joined the *Renaldo* crew to write some dialogue. Not much happened there but, in his *Rolling Thunder Logbook*, he had much, positive and negative, to record. He felt himself "a collaborator in a whirlpool." He meets Dylan, finds him "all blues" and making surrealist talk about French films. When he watched Dylan at the piano playing "Simple Twist of Fate," Shepard was touched: "Here is where it's at. The Master Arsonist. The place is smoking within five minutes … This is Dylan's true magic. Leave aside his lyrical genius for a second and just watch this transformation of energy which he carries … the kind that brings courage and hope and above all brings life pounding into the foreground … it's no wonder he can rock the nation."

The playwright began to wonder what he was doing there as the film "falls into smithereens" of random energy. "Ideas flying every which way but no play." He succumbs to the "communal giving of spirit energy through music," and sees it as an antidote to the blind adulation of the rock scene. Dylan is a "true-life Medicine Man" whose "heroism transcends being a faddist phenomenon … Because his very identity is a mystery, he pushes the question of 'who' he is into 'what' he is." Like many others, Sam Shepard found that Dylan raised more questions than answers: "What is this strange, haunted environment he creates onstage, on record, on film, on everything he touches? What world is he drawing from and drawing us all into as a result? It's right there in front of us, but no one can touch it."

In a provocative essay, "Changing Trains," in the *Threepenny Review*, Irene Oppenheim traced the curious pasts of Dylan and Shepard, using Camus's *The Myth of Sisyphus* as a guidepost on the question of how one lives without a knowledge of the meaning of existence. Camus hinted that the only stable component of the known world is an absurdist uncertainty, a dilemma that can be resolved only by one of two responses: either suicide and its metaphorical counterpart, "the deadening of consciousness, or the leap of faith"; or "remaining on that dizzying crest," balanced warily between faith and despair.

The essay found both writers sharing the self-wasting process by cannibalizing themselves for material. Right after Rolling Thunder, Shepard wrote *Suicide in B-Flat* about the death and potential rebirth of an artist. The central character is a musician being driven mad by inner voices. Oppenheim thinks both writers retreated from the crest in life-preserving moves. "Dylan, after a long flirtation, and pushed to the edge by bitter marital problems, has made a leap of faith." Shepard, "mercilessly tortured by his creative demons, has opined, in desperation for a kind of suicide." By 1984, Shepard was reborn as a writer and an actor, a Hollywood figure of stature.[20]

Joan Baez told me that she was embarrassed by some of the footage that ended up in *Renaldo and Clara*, and yet this didn't basically change her warm feelings toward Dylan. She did a little bit of mimicry of how Bob had called her in Europe at three in the morning and got her approval to let it all go as he chose to. In three songs on her late 1976 album, *Gulf Winds*, "Time Is Passing Us By," and "Sweeter for Me," and "Oh, Brother!" she sings some amazingly frank revelations of her feelings toward Dylan.

Sara had already had her say on the failing marriage with Dylan in the divorce action of 1977. How ironic that after the bitter marital strife should come the film, with Sara as another of Bob's dark-haired women. The woman had been so much a part of Dylan's life, of his retreat from stage life to be husband and father, of the shape of some of his work from *John Wesley Harding* to *Street-Legal*. The song "Abandoned Love," released officially on *Biograph* in 1985, speaks volumes about what I can only interpret as Dylan's deepest feelings of the time. By 1978, getting so deep into opening up for the press to push *Renaldo and Clara*, he opened up about marriage:

Marriage was a failure. Husband and wife was a failure, but father and mother wasn't a failure. I wasn't a very good husband … I don't know what a good husband is. I was good in some ways … and not so good in other ways. But I feel my true family relationship is up ahead of me somewhere. I'd try again. Yeah, I like comin' home to the same woman … If you fail at one job, and you pick up another job, which you like more, well then you can't consider what happened a failure. There aren't really any mistakes in life. They might seem to knock you out of proportion at the time, but if you have the courage and the ability and the confidence to go on, well, then … you can't look at it as a failure, you just have to look at it as a blessing in a way.

He said that no one in his family gets divorced and that he "figured it would last forever":

Most people … keep some contact, which is great for the kids. But in my case, I first got really married, and then got really divorced. I believe in marriage. I know I don't believe in open marriage. Sexual freedom just leads to other kinds of freedom. I think there should be a sanction against divorce. Why should people be allowed to get married and divorced so easily? … People fall in love with a person's body, with who they know, with the way they dress, with their scorecards. With everything but their real selves, which is what you need to love if you're to be happy together …

I became disillusioned about finding "the right girl"—or the right anything, for that matter. Women are sentimental. They get into that romantic thing more easily. But I see that as a prelude. Women use romance and passion to sweeten you up. A man is no more than a victim of that passion. You give me a woman that can cook and sew and I'll take that over passion any day. I'd like to find a mate. But I can't spend any time with a woman if we're not friends. If we're not friends, I don't want to get involved on a personal level.

How costly the marriage was emotionally comes through in the albums. How costly it was to prove financially is not known, but there is no doubt that the divorce settlement was expensive.

On March 1, 1977, Sara's divorce petition was filed in Superior Court in Santa Monica. She sought permanent custody of Maria, 15, and her children by Dylan: Jesse, 11; Anna, nine; Samuel, eight; and Jakob, six. She also sought child support, alimony, and court-supervised disposition of the couple's community property. Assets involved included real estate in four states, plus Dylan's holdings in publishing companies, recordings, and literary copyrights. Dylan's lawyers won a ruling to have certain legal documents closed to the public. But the British press made page-one news of the family squabbles.

Sara was granted temporary custody of the children and exclusive use of the Malibu house. The size of the settlement was among the documents hidden under the court's apron. But that it cost Dylan a very large amount of money—probably as much as $10 million, in the opinion of some observers—seems clear.

Although use of the Malibu house reverted to Dylan, it was really more of a house than a home. The famed beach colony of the stars was known for the privacy it once afforded its residents, but as its glamour spiraled, it became increasingly a fishbowl, like Woodstock. It was there that F Scott Fitzgerald once wrote in a cottage and came up with the French pun: "Honi soft qui Malibu." As the rock aristocracy succeeded the celluloid pantheon, Johnny Rivers took over the house where Greta Garbo once tried to be alone. In nearby Bel Air, the chief Beach Boy, Brian Wilson, lived in a spread that Tarzan profits had created for Edgar Rice Burroughs. Among the other rock stars who made Malibu their home were Neil Diamond, Linda Ronstadt, Mick Jagger, and Robbie Robertson.

Before the split, the Dylans had bought a relatively modest home on the Point Dome promontory from a *Los Angeles Times* columnist, on a three-acre site. In 1975, architect David Tobin undertook the remodeling, on which Dylan eventually spent more than $2 million. Tobin said he "had to keep a straight face when Bob told him he wanted a living room he could ride a horse through." Neighbors took to calling it Dylan's Taj Mahal, because it was crowned with a huge onion-shaped copper dome, which cost $16,000. There were frequent disagreements about the designs, and much revision was done. Bob and Sara moved in in late 1976. One designer on the project called it "an eclectic version of an East Coast stick and shingle house, basically American Victorian and Mediterranean. Inside it's pure New Mexico." Some neighbors were intrigued by the large outdoor polymorphous pool, and took to calling it a lake. It was heated and nestled among boulders and shrubbery. If Bob had really wanted to keep it all quiet, he never should have done an interview with a reporter from the *Chicago Daily News* at the poolside.

More land was acquired for the old homestead, until the site could hold twenty houses. The construction team lived in wigwams while the work proceeded. There were many specially crafted items, like tiled floors made in kilns on the spot. In front of the huge fireplace was a twenty-foot whale in inlaid tile. The designer said that in fifty to a hundred years, the house, "simply the nicest in Malibu, could be a historic landmark." As lavish as it was, the Malibu colony had homes that were bigger and more expensive. Dylan's comment: "One hundred years from now, I won't be judged for the house." Remarked *Time* magazine drily: "He is probably correct. One local geologist believes the mansion is already slipping into the ocean."

By the end of 1977, his family life in tatters, with various battles between him and Sara over the children still unresolved, Dylan seemed at low ebb. He was about to launch a film he anticipated would be demolished by most critics, although he nourished the hope that the audience would still support it. He made plans to undertake a world tour and another recording. It was the beginning of the end of another phase, another life, another career. With the American audience's backlash at *Renaldo and Clara*, and with the rest of the world still enthusiastic about him, it looked as if, once more, there was, for this man, no direction home.

A portrait can never be finished; it can only be abandoned.

VARIOUSLY ATTRIBUTED TO CÉZANNE, FLAUBERT, AND GIACOMETTI

The Rolling Thunder Revue reached
Lowell, Massachusetts, in fall 1975,
where they paid homage and improvised
some blues at Jack Kerouac's grave.

While Dylan scaled new heights around the world in 1978, he began to reach new depths with the American audience. In one year, he played to 115 audiences in ten countries, but encountered resistance only in his native land. As usual, some grumbles were to be heard everywhere: his look and new band suggested "the route to Las Vegas"; the new album, *Street-Legal*, sharply divided opinions. And someone's catchphrase, "the alimony tour," was picked up pervasively. No matter how it tapered off in America as Dylan played while fighting a virus, the year still seemed a strong expression of will, stamina, and artistic growth.

By the end of 1977, Dylan had signed on as his business manager Jerry Weintraub of Management III. He had worked with John Denver, Frank Sinatra, Neil Diamond, and Tom Paxton to apparently good effect. Weintraub was known for non-interference, even non-attendance at his clients' concerts. "At the time I got Jerry to manage me, I almost didn't have a friend in the world. We were working on that movie … I was being thrown out of my house. I was under a lot of pressure, so I figured I better get busy working," Dylan said.

Weintraub organized a flying squad of forty sound technicians, security people, and administrators. On the agenda were concerts in Japan, Australia, New Zealand, five countries of Western Europe, and, for the autumn, America and Canada. Dylan had recruited a new eight-piece backing band and a female gospel-style vocal trio, which yielded a radically new sound. They rehearsed seventy songs, many in startlingly new arrangements. When I asked Bob who had done the new charts, he said proudly: "There's nothing that band does that can't be worked out on my guitar. I started recruiting this band in January [1978]. It was difficult, hard. A lot of blood has gone into this band. They understand my songs. It doesn't matter if they understand me or not."

The chief novelty was the presence of an edgy, mercurial *Blonde on Blonde* texture achieved partially by Steve Douglas on saxophone and flute. David Mansfield's manic mandolin and fiddle playing was a bubbly embellishment. He wanted others as backup singers. Dylan told me: "I was determined I was never gonna have the band sing anymore. It scatters their energy and they don't come up with the hard sound I want if they also sing." Instead, a vocal trio, Helena Springs, Jo Ann Harris, and Carolyn Dennis, provided the gospel/soul backing voices.[1] Although some saw this as commercialism, they simply weren't conversant with the black music style from which it came.

The troupe began on February 20, 1978 with eleven concerts in Japan. In Tokyo and Osaka, more than 100,000 attended. Although it is the custom to react with polite restraint in the concert hall, the press reflected excitement. During two of the Tokyo gigs, Dylan recorded the *Live at Budokan* album, originally designed solely for the Japanese market. The somewhat sterile sound didn't really reflect what the tour sound was to become but, because of its immaculate pressing, the album quickly became a collector's item. So many in Europe and America were buying *Budokan* at import prices of up to $35 it was decided to remaster it in the West, with some inevitable technical losses.

A dozen well-received Australian and New Zealand concerts followed, with some hints that a 1960s level of passion was being felt on both sides of the footlights. Dylan went into a Santa Monica studio for a week in April to tape *Street-Legal*. With the momentum of the world tour, the album did well around the world, but American critics admonished him to "get a producer."

Street-Legal is one of Dylan's most overtly autobiographical albums, telling of loss, searching, estrangement, and exile. It also clearly foreshadows the Christian conversion ahead, but who among us could perceive it at that time? It is peopled by a group of narrators who are oppressed, wandering, and lonely, traveling in a foreign country of the spirit. The Tarot card imagery of "Changing of the Guard" has confounded some of the shrewdest interpreters, but it is difficult not to ascribe it either to his years with Sara or with the Band, or both. I confess the song is still an enigma to me.

But the album is generally strong on communication, rather than on code. I call attention to two minor gems and a masterwork on the album, which have not been fully appreciated: "New Pony" has a scathing blues riff on which the women's voices drive home the repeated phrase "How much longer?" out of the Bible, yet in a song that seems to be pure sexuality. "Señor (Tales of Yankee Power)" is a strong and rueful political statement that finds American foreign policy confused and unjust. More biblical language is sandwiched in between American folk language, with the reference to overturning the tables, from the passages describing Jesus and the money-changers. I hear many echoes of Robert Johnson, the blues giant, especially on "Is Your Love in Vain?" but also later in the phrase about juice running down a leg. Powerful, raw stuff amid some tenderness in "Baby Stop Crying," "True Love Tends to Forget," and "We Better Talk This Over." I hear some fine Stevie Wonder echoes on the cataloging of "No Time to Think."

But the masterwork is the final song of anguish and prophecy, a song with the sweep of "Like a Rolling Stone"—"Where Are You Tonight? (Journey Through Dark Heat)." Here we can discern the move toward Christianity, the foreshadowing of major changes after the hellish personal disorder the narrator has gone through. This is catharsis and resolution as he steals off into a troubled night with such companions as St John of the Book of Revelation. There are technical raw spots on the album, but Dylan clearly wanted to tape it red-hot and from the heart, and he had allowed himself only a week to do it before hitting the road again.

Dylan's return to Britain for six concerts at Earls Court, from June 15 to 20, really took the country by storm. The 100,000 tickets sold briskly, and it is no exaggeration to say that the whole town was talking. The method of sale had disturbed some, causing fans in London and some provincial cities to wait in line all day. Television and newspaper pictures of the weekend queues helped build the anticipation. Dylan's opening-night concert ranks in my memory as one of his greatest, a sentiment echoed in the *Daily Mail* by Ray Connolly, an often cynical commentator, who called it "the greatest concert I have ever seen."

Working with the CBS press woman Ellie Smith, an American based in London, Dylan cordially greeted the press, by twos and threes, with a kind word for most, unless they happened to break protocol by taking notes on what was said informally. I received the royal summons the second night, and was sitting in the backstage area with Michael Gray and Gabrielle Goodchild, trying to hold a conversation with Jack Nicholson, then in London with Stanley Kubrick for the filming of *The Shining*. We saw Dylan poke his nose into the enclosure, then back away. Later he explained to me: "I saw you there, but it was too emotional a thing to go in there among all those people."

When the three of us went out to chat with Bob, he was standing beside Helena Springs, and he started to tell her about the old days at Folk City and the nearby Troubadour. Clearly sensing the triumph of the evening, Bob asked me whatever happened to the Greenbriar Boys, who had topped the bill with him at Gerde's. Gabrielle got into small talk with Bianca Jagger and Michael was doing his best to say something to his idol. The idol indicated he was rushed that night and promised more time with me, so I raced off to find Ellie to make arrangements. Before I did, I told Bob the band was impressive, and asked where he had got them together. "It's about the only thing I have got together now," he said candidly.

The next night, backstage, Dylan was a bit more relaxed, and he told Gabrielle, me, and his old Woodstock friend, Happy Traum, about how England had once been so lavish with honors for Big Bill Broonzy and other black American bluesmen "when they were just working as janitors in the States." Seeing old friends in London after the post-divorce depression and the trashing of *Renaldo and Clara* by the American critics seemed to bring Bob great joy and relief. He suggested another night for supper and an interview, since he had to talk to a reporter from *L'Express*, Paris, which had a cover story planned.

We showed up at a smart Knightsbridge restaurant, San Lorenzo, where the concert promoter, Harvey Goldsmith, was hosting the crew and local staff with a dinner after the final concert. Gabrielle and I got there early, and I sized up the room. "I think he'll probably want to sit in a corner where he can watch the door," I remarked. A few minutes later, Bob walked in and headed straight for the corner table before he even saw us there. With him were singers from the gospel trio and Shusha, the Iranian-born singer-songwriter.

Dylan wanted to make it clear he was "subservient to those songs. I'm not out there as a performer underneath a dance team. The writing part is a very lonely experience, but there's strength in that loneliness. But I'm a performer too, and that's an outward thing. One is the opposite of the other, and it makes me crazy sometimes, because I can't write with the energy that I perform with. I can't perform off the energy that I write with. There just has to be time for both." Was he any more comfortable now being called a poet? "Very much so. I consider myself a poet first and a musician second." (In his first American interview of the autumn 1978 tour, he told a reporter: "I'm a musician first and a poet second.") Bob went on: "I live like a poet and I'll die like a poet. I've always liked my stuff. All you really have to please is yourself in any arena of life."

I asked him if he were able to relax on the tour. He had been going up each day to a pool in North London for a swim, he told me, and was not recognized there. How had he taken the news of Presley's death? He downed a shot of Courvoisier. "I broke down. One of the very few times. I went over my whole life. I went over my whole childhood. I didn't talk to anyone for a week after Elvis died. If it wasn't for Elvis and Hank Williams, I couldn't be doing what I do today."

At that final concert, Bob had told his audience, "I'm thinking about moving up to Liverpool." Would he consider living outside America? He told me about time spent in Corsica and France around *Blood on the Tracks*, marvelous, haunting times, with and without Sara. Would he seriously consider the expatriate life? "Yes, I would. But creatively, I couldn't live anywhere but America, because I understand the tone behind the language there. I'd love to live somewhere else, but only for a while. I lived in Mexico for three months. I wrote my fourth album in Greece, but that was an American album." He spoke with animation about "two birthdays ago" of a gypsy festival at Saintes-Maries-de-la-Mer en Carmargue, France, with all the flamenco in the air, and the wildness of Corsica. But he always brought the raging beauty back home.

"I feel at home in America," Bob continued, "because, as primitive as it is, I still can create from America. All my feelings come out of America. When you leave, you get peace. America is a very violent place, so when you leave, you get that peace to create. In America, everybody's got a gun. I've got a few of them!" It sounded like Dylan was loading up for some target practice, so I threw up the bull's-eye, the talk about "the alimony tour." Dylan replied: "The myth of the starving artist is just that—a myth!

"I earn everything I make! I'm not getting nothing for nothing. Reggie Jackson of the New York Yankees gets $3 million a year, for striking out! For every dollar I make, there's a pool of sweat on the floor. I feel we are all underpaid—my band, my singers. I put in an eight-hour day in two hours onstage." Mentioning a few of the other rock veterans "who had come through," Dylan declared: "It's a question of how much of it you can stand. How much can you stick it out."

According to Goldsmith, Dylan had originally wanted only three or four large outdoor arenas for the whole European tour, but Harvey had talked him into the six nights at Earls Court. Advance ticket sales were so great that Goldsmith undertook to convert the old Blackbushe Aerodrome, ninety minutes south of London, into a site for an audience of 100,000. When Saturday July 15 burst fair, a lot of people who hadn't bought tickets decided to spend the day in the country listening to Dylan, Eric Clapton, Joan Armatrading and others. The official police figure was 200,000, though estimates put it twenty percent higher than that. It was described as Britain's largest rock audience of all time, and even made news on American TV. Flushed with excitement, Dylan donned a top hat, which he wore throughout his three hours onstage, and sang thirty-three songs in a general mood of euphoria. As he had throughout the tour, he mostly reworked his old hits into startling new arrangements. Many were finding fresh insight into the lyrics when, as in "Tangled Up in Blue," he gave new emphasis and shape to songs long since taken for granted. As Russell Davies wrote in the *Sunday Times*, it was the best "creative re-vamping since Duke Ellington stopped coming round with savagely recycled oldies." Blackbushe soon entered the language of the British folk fan, as Woodstock had. It was more than a concert; a community, really.

By July 15, Dylan would have sung to more than 800,000 people in fifty concerts. The Continental leg of the 1978 tour took him to the Netherlands, West Germany, France, and Sweden. Still, I saw some tension, some turbulence I couldn't identify under the surface. I urged him to expand on something he'd been saying for the past year or so: "No man can fight another like the man who fights himself. Who could be a stronger enemy?"

"It's true," Bob said, "that a man is his own worst enemy, just as he is his own best friend. If you deal with the enemy within, then no enemy without can stand a chance." What was his enemy within? "Suspicion," he replied, as if he could answer all those allegations of paranoia in one word. Could he put his finger on the enemy within? Dylan laughed at my question. He pointed his index finger toward his heart. Cautiously, he continued: "It's all in those two verses of that last song." He directed me toward the mortal battle with his alter ego in "Where Are You Tonight?"

Typical of his ambiguity, the twin Dylans have so many paired faces: the Gemini polarities of strength versus weakness, kindness versus cruelty, optimism versus pessimism, life versus death, suspicion versus friendliness. It has been said by psychologists in the 1980s that the forward motion of creative people uses wide mood changes as its motor. This dialectic of internal contradiction was really a pair of matched twins locked in struggle. If any word alone can be found to characterize the contradictions in Bob Dylan, it would have to be *ambivalence*. If you're not being born, you're dying. The old "vegetation myth" told us that the death of kings fertilizes the soil for future crops, yet the "twin myth" might take that a step further, actually within one artist.

Bob nibbled at his food and kept working on the bottle of Courvoisier that was near him. He was better at small talk than I could ever remember, but he also wanted to get into the interview. "It's for your book, but you can do whatever you want to with it," he said. I teased him with his famous question, "How does it *feel*?" Dylan insisted that the ovations and rave reviews were for his work: "It's not me. It's the songs. I'm just the postman. I deliver the songs. That's all I have in this world are those songs. That's what all the legend, all the myth is about—my songs. I started writing those songs before I could walk. George Harrison told me last night I'd be singing 'It's Alright, Ma' when I'm ninety. Nobody else gives those songs life. It's up to me to do it. But those songs have a life of their own too. Jimi Hendrix sang them. Stevie Wonder, Van Morrison, and Elvis Presley have sung them …"

In the notes to *Biograph*, Dylan said he was "amazed that I've been around this long, never thought I would be" and that he tried "to learn from both the wise and the unwise, not pay attention to anybody, do what I want to do … No matter how big you think you are history is gonna rollover you. Sound like a preacher, don't I? To the aspiring songwriter and singer I say disregard all the current stuff, forget it, you're better off, read John Keats, Melville, listen to Robert Johnson and Woody Guthrie."

We can't put a price on those rhythms, cadences, and images from Bob Dylan that have re-entered our everyday speech from which he first mined, then refined them. We know Mister Jones as the arch-Philistine who is unaware that something is happening. Even though we're stuck inside Desolation Row, we keep on keeping on. There may be blood on those tracks and nothing is revealed, yet he's told us there must be some way out of here. There may be no direction home for him or for a lot of us, but with one foot on the highway and the other in the grave, we try to get outside the empty cage that holds us. Desperation and hope fight in the captain's tower, a pair of warring twins. Although it's all over now, we renew ourselves by leaving the dead behind us. We're younger than all that now. Death and rebirth. For every seven people dyin' there's seven new ones busy being born. We forget where Dylan's lines end and our own begin.

Even though he denied being in "the teachin' business," there's a world to learn by following his road, of self-made culture, of self-education. When he hopped off the subway from America's heartland in Greenwich Village, we were all looking for answers, only he probed deepest, knowing the question itself might unlock the answer. We turned to him for his vision, wit, fresh ideas, but mostly for his daring to try what hadn't been tried. Find your own answers, man, and you'll value them more, he said to us, man and woman, time and again. Even when we insisted, he didn't want to play guru. He was too skinny then to carry a cross, and too wary to let his manager carry it for him.

"There's so many sides to Dylan, he's round," said Bernard Paturel, his Woodstock friend. And he's been so many different people that this wasn't a biography of one man, but of several. "It's always lonely where I am," he said in 1966, but ten years later he said the only place he could find solitude was on a public stage. Long before Dylan met or read Robert Graves, he was following the old poet's admonition that a poet must think mythically as well as rationally. He's a disturber of the peace—ours, as well as his own.

The past could be prelude or postlude. He's already poured five lifetimes into one. He may follow Rimbaud's route, having articulated more of the language of revolt than the world was then ready for. Or he may follow Yeats's route of more seeking and more finding and even greater creativity toward old age. Knowing Dylan as much as the mystery of genius will reveal to us, he'll probably do it his own way. He always has.

The past could be a prelude or postlude.

Notes

INTRODUCTION

1 Friday, September 29, 1961.
2 Robbie Woliver, *Bringing It All Back Home*, p 80.
3 Suze Rotolo, *A Freewheelin' Time*, p 149.
4 *Guardian*, December 13, 1995.
5 Tribute dictated by Collins to ET for the Shelton memorial celebration in London on April 26, 1996.
6 Faxed tribute to ET for the memorial. See also *Society's Child*, p 62–3.
7 Writing to his sisters Ruth Kadish and Leona Shapiro, *circa* 1961, Shelton quotes a letter from Pete Seeger, "to inquire if your legal situation required financial assistance." The case is examined in *Dark Days in the Newsroom* by Edward Alwood, Philadelphia, 2007.
8 *New York Times*, December 15, 1995.
9 Laing, see "Taste-making and trend-spotting: the folk revival journalism of Robert Shelton" in *Popular Music History* 1.3 (2006), pp 307–328. Laing co-wrote *The Electric Muse* with Shelton, Karl Dallas, and Robin Denselow. The well-documented three-CD set, *Washington Square Memoirs: The Great Urban Folk Boom 1950–1970* (Rhino) offers an excellent aural history of the Shelton years.
10 From *Words International*, November 1987; reprinted in the *Telegraph*, Spring 1996.
11 Shelton in a letter to Betty Prashker, Executive Editor at Doubleday, February 12, 1979.
12 Shelton in a letter to Heather Kilpatrick, Associate Counsel at Doubleday, December 17, 1981.
13 *Ibid*.
14 Letter from James Landis, Editorial Director at Morrow, to Shelton, November 21, 1984.
15 In October 1983, Shelton was offered two alternatives: cut the manuscript to 180,000 words including addenda, or accept a $35,000 reduction in advance plus a reduced royalty and cut to only 230,000. He accepted the latter, a decision Landis described in a letter of December 5, 1984 as "a principled act." The longer a book, the higher is the cover price, which may impact on sales, hence the publisher's intransigence.
16 "Trust yourself," p 291–5 in *The Dylan Companion*, in which Shelton reflects on the publishing experience five years on.

PRELUDE

1 Carl G Jung, foreword to *I Ching*, or the *Book of Changes* (New York: Pantheon Books, 1950), p iv.
2 "Open The Door, Homer" © 1968, 1975 by Dwarf Music, renewed 1996 by Dwarf Music.
3 "Where Are You Tonight? (Journey Through Dark Heat)" © 1978 by Special Rider Music, renewed 2006 Special Rider Music
4 "Up To Me" © 1974 by Ram's Horn Music; renewed 2002 by Ram's Horn Music.
5 Letter to *Broadside* magazine, January 1964.
6 "Mr Tambourine Man" © 1964, 1965 by Warner Bros. Inc., renewed 1992, 1993 by Special Rider Music.
7 "When I Paint My Masterpiece" © 1971 by Big Sky Music, renewed 1999 by Big Sky Music.
8 "Oh, Sister" (Bob Dylan & Jacques Levy) © 1975 by Ram's Horn Music, renewed 2003 by Ram's Horn Music.
9 "It's Alright, Ma (I'm Only Bleeding)" © 1965 by Warner Bros. Inc., renewed 1993 by Special Rider Music.
10 "Advice For Geraldine On Her Miscellaneous Birthday" © 1964 Special Rider Music, renewed 1992 Special Rider Music.
11 *Another Side Of Bob Dylan*, sleeve notes, © 1973 Special Rider Music, renewed 2001 Special Rider Music.

12 "Temporary Like Achilles" © 1966 by Dwarf Music, renewed 1994 by Dwarf Music.
13 "It's Alright, Ma (I'm Only Bleeding)" © 1965 by Warner Bros. Inc., renewed 1993 by Special Rider Music.
14 *Ibid*.
15 Bob Dylan, *Tarantula*, pp 108–109.
16 *Bringing It All Back Home*, sleeve notes, © 1965 Special Rider Music, renewed 1993 Special Rider Music.
17 "Chimes Of Freedom" © 1964 by Warner Bros. Inc., renewed 1992 by Special Rider Music.
18 "Like A Rolling Stone" © 1965 by Warner Bros. Inc., renewed 1993 by Special Rider Music.
19 "Subterranean Homesick Blues" © 1965 by Warner Bros. Inc., renewed 1993 by Special Rider Music.
20 Allen Ginsberg died in 1997 at the age of 70, by which time he was regarded as America's premier poet.
21 "Subterranean Homesick Blues" © 1965 by Warner Bros. Inc., renewed 1993 by Special Rider Music.
22 "Ballad Of Hollis Brown" © 1963 by Warner Bros. Inc., renewed 1991 by Special Rider Music.
23 "11 Outlined Epitaphs" (sleeve note to *The Times The Are A-Changin'*) © 1964 Special Rider Music, renewed 1992 Special Rider Music.
24 *Ibid*.
25 "Just Like A Woman" © 1966 by Dwarf Music, renewed 1994 by Dwarf Music.
26 "11 Outlined Epitaphs" (sleeve note to *The Times The Are A-Changin'*) © 1964 Special Rider Music, renewed 1992 Special Rider Music.

CHAPTER 1

1 Bob Dylan, *Tarantula*, pp 108–109.
2 "It's Alright, Ma (I'm Only Bleeding)" © 1965 by Warner Bros. Inc., renewed 1993 by Special Rider Music.
3 "My Life In A Stolen Moment" © 1973 Special Rider Music, renewed 2001 Special Rider Music.
4 *Ibid*.
5 "North Country Blues" © 1963, 1964 by Warner Bros. Inc., renewed 1991, 1992 by Special Rider Music.
6 Music industry insider Andy Paley recalls waiting on a California course while a lone golfer sent divots flying. After a while he began chiding the hooded figure. So how was Dylan as a golfer? "Terrible, absolutely *terrible*."
7 Johnnie Ray (1927–1990), the link between Sinatra and Presley, Dylan spoke fondly of Ray in Martin Scorsese's *No Direction Home* (2005).
8 Dylan writes evocatively of the death of Hank Williams in *Chronicles*. He also contributed "I Can't Get You Off My Mind" to *Timeless: The Songs Of Hank Williams* (2001). Dylan has long been rumored to be planning his own Williams tribute album.
9 Howard Sounes' *Down the Highway* provides new information about Dylan's teenage groups.
10 John Bucklen has the earliest known recording of a Dylan original, on which the two of them can be heard performing "Little Richard" in 1958. Further Bucklen recordings were heard on the 1993 BBC TV documentary *Highway 61 Revisited*. Another Hibbing friend, Ric Kangas, taped Dylan singing "When I Got Troubles" in 1959, which can be heard on the CD soundtrack of *No Direction Home*.
11 Helstrom later spoke in further detail to Howard Sounes.
12 Dylan acknowledged Holly during his 1998 Grammy acceptance speech, recalling the Duluth show.

CHAPTER 2

1 "Like A Rolling Stone" © 1965 by Warner Bros. Inc., renewed 1993 by Special Rider Music.

2 Collins was present at Albert Grossman's Woodstock home the night Dylan finished "Mr Tambourine Man." She later released *Judy Collins Sings Dylan, Just Like A Woman* (1993).

3 "My Life In A Stolen Moment" © 1973 Special Rider Music, renewed 2001 Special Rider Music.

4 Dylan wrote affectionately of Koerner in *Chronicles*. Koerner's two albums with Tony Glover and Dave Ray *(Blues, Rags and Hollers* and *Lots More Blues, Rags and Hollers)* were released on CD in 2004.

5 Cynthia Gooding (1924–1988). Her complete 1962 radio interview with Dylan on WBAI New York—including, for the first time, Dylan's performances—was released on CD as *Folksinger's Choice* (2010).

6 Dylan spoke fondly to Scorsese of the singer Odetta (1930–2008). Awarded the National Medal of Arts in 1999, she was still performing a week before her death and had been invited to sing at the Obama inauguration.

7 Paul Nelson appeared in *No Direction Home* reminiscing about Dylan's Minneapolis days.

8 "11 Outlined Epitaphs" (sleeve note to *The Times They Are A-Changin'),* © 1964 Special Rider Music: renewed 1992 Special Rider Music.

9 Robert Shelton, *Born to Win*, p 248.

10 Woody Guthrie: *Bound For Glory*, p 57.

11 In 1952, Moses Asch (1905–1986), founder of Folkways Records, released Harry Smith's six-LP set *American Folk Song*, which Dylan heard in Minneapolis. In 1987, the Smithsonian Institution acquired Folkways from the Asch estate, and in 1999 released *Woody Guthrie, The Asch Recordings Volumes 1–4*.

12 Dylan's only official recording of Guthrie's best-known song was a curiously muted affair, which appeared on the soundtrack of *No Direction Home*. Dylan appeared on *Folkways: A Vision Shared* (1988) performing Guthrie songs with Bruce Springsteen. Springsteen guested on a further Guthrie tribute, *'Til We Outnumber Them* (2000), contributing a poignant version of "Deportees," which Dylan had so memorably performed on the 1976 *Hard Rain* TV special.

13 One of the most intriguing moments in *Chronicles* has Dylan meeting John Wayne ("he looked like a heavy piece of hauled lumber"), an encounter engineered by Bonny Beecher.

14 Tony Glover appears in Scorsese's *No Direction Home*; he also wrote the sleeve notes for *The Bootleg Series, Volume 4: Live 1966* (1998).

15 Dylan's song "Lenny Bruce" is included on *Shot of Love* (1981).

16 To date, Dylan's version of Lord Buckley's "Black Cross" (aka "Hezekiah Jones") remains officially unavailable.

17 Michael Gray has written about the significance of *Highway 61* ("the blues highway") in both his *Encyclopedia* and *Song and Dance Man III: The Art Of Bob Dylan*.

18 "My Life In A Stolen Moment" © 1973 Special Rider Music, renewed 2001 Special Rider Music.

CHAPTER 3

1 Albert Grossman (1926–1986) managed Dylan between 1962 and 1970.

2 Peter, Paul & Mary: *In The Wind* sleeve notes © 1963 Warner Bros. Records, renewed 1991 Special Rider Music.

3 "11 Outlined Epitaphs" (sleeve note to *The Times They Are A-Changin')* © 1964 Special Rider Music: renewed 1992 Special Rider Music.

4–5 *Ibid.*

6 The Clancy Brothers and Tommy Makem were key figures in the early folk revival—but are all now gone. The youngest, Liam, died in 2009. Dylan called him "the best ballad singer I ever heard." Along with Woody Guthrie, it was the Clancys of whom Dylan spoke most affectionately when interviewed for *No Direction Home*. They were also great friends with Shelton.

7 The falsetto-voiced Tiny Tim (1930–1996) was a walking encyclopedia of American popular music, and a visitor at Woodstock during 1967.

8 Mike Porco (1915–1992), early Dylan champion and a welcome guest at the second Bob Dylan Convention at Manchester in 1980.

9 At the time of writing, Izzy Young is running the Folklore Centrum in Stockholm. He appeared in *No Direction Home*, and was warmly remembered by Dylan in *Chronicles*.

10 A 1961 recording of Dylan performing "Dink's Song" eventually surfaced on the 2005 soundtrack to *No Direction Home*.

11 Dylan returned to "Poor Lazarus" during 1967, but the *Basement Tape* version cuts out after only a minute. Originally collected by Alan Lomax from a convict in 1959, the song was revived on the soundtrack of *O Brother, Where Art Thou?* (2000), after which, Lomax was able to present the freed prisoner James Carter with a royalty cheque for $20,000.

12 Dave Van Ronk (1936–2002). One of his last appearances was on Nanci Griffith's *Other Voices, Too …* (1998), on which he duetted with Eric Von Schmidt on the Dylan favourite, "He Was A Friend Of Mine."

13 Robert Shelton, *Born to Win*, p. 248.

14 Jack Elliott received the National Medal of Arts from President Clinton in 1998, and a Lifetime Achievement Award from BBC Radio 2 in 2005. *Friends Of Mine* (1998) found Tom Waits, Arlo Guthrie and Emmylou Harris, among others, paying tribute. He was the subject of a documentary, the soundtrack of which, *The Ballad of Ramblin' Jack* (2000), featured his 1961 duet with Dylan on the teen spoof "Acne."

15 Carolyn Hester was a guest at the 30th Anniversary Concert at Madison Square Garden in 1992. Her album, on which Dylan made his recording debut, was reissued on a CD with bonus tracks, as *Carolyn Hester* (1994). Hester's life with Richard Fariña, and much more besides, was covered in David Hajdu's *Positively 4th Street*.

16 Harry Belafonte was reunited with Dylan in 1985 on the charity single "We Are The World."

17 In the 1940s, Burl Ives (1909–1995) was a key mover alongside Woody Guthrie and Pete Seeger in the sourcing of folk material. He went on to act alongside James Dean and became a perennial favorite on children's radio. However, his reputation was permanently damaged in 1952, when he "named names" before the House Un-American Activities Committee.

18 "Talkin' Subway" Woody Guthrie © 1960, Ludlow Music, Inc. New York.

19 "Pretty Boy Floyd" Woody Guthrie © 1958, Sanga Music Inc. New York.

20 "Man Of Constant Sorrow" found a new audience when it appeared on the soundtrack of *O Brother, Where Art Thou?*, performed by Norman Blake, who had played with Dylan on *Nashville Skyline*.

21 "Pretty Peggy-O" ©1962 (arrangement of music and new lyric by Bob Dylan), renewed 1990 MCA.

22 *Ibid.*

23 "The House Carpenter," "He Was A Friend Of Mine," and "Man On the Street" were eventually released on *The Bootleg Series, Volumes 1–3*.

CHAPTER 4

1 "Tomorrow Is A Long Time" © 1963 by Warner Bros. Inc., renewed 1991 by Special Rider Music.

2 "11 Outlined Epitaphs" (sleeve note to *The Times They Are A-Changin'),* © 1964 Special Rider Music, renewed 1992 Special Rider Music.

3 Suze Rotolo finally broke cover in 2008 with her memoir *A Freewheelin' Time*. Besides offering insights into her life with Dylan, it is also strong on the Greenwich Village scene of which she, Dylan, and Shelton were such an integral part.

4 "Outlaw Blues" © 1965 by Warner Bros. Inc., renewed 1993 by Special Rider Music.

5 "Subterranean Homesick Blues" © 1965 by Warner Bros. Inc., renewed 1993 by Special Rider Music.

6 Bettina Jonic, *The Bitter Mirror: Songs by Dylan and Brecht* (1975).

7 Josh Dunson brought together a lot of material on the new songwriters in *Freedom in the Air: Movements of the '60s*.

8 Gil Turner, "The Great New York Newspaper Strike" © 1963, as published in *Broadside* 20. Reprinted in *Broadside*, Volume 1, Oak Publications, p 32. © 1964, *Broadside* magazine.

9 In *And a Voice to Sing With*, pp 61–63, Baez describes how Grossman brought her to meet John Hammond: "At one point, a contract was slipped across [his] big desk. They would have had me sign right then and there what I believe was an eight-year contract." Instead she chose Vanguard and Manny Greenhill, with whom her only "contract" was a handshake. But she conceded: "If I wanted to go 'big time,' Albert was the best and so was Columbia."

10 Dylan cited the painter Norman Raeben, with whom he studied in 1974, as being a great influence on *Blood On The Tracks*. In 2007, Dylan felt confident enough to hold his first gallery exhibition.

11 Dylan recalled the late Paul Clayton in the interview that accompanied *Biograph*, and later in *Chronicles*.

12 Bernice Johnson and Cordell Reagon were founder members of the Freedom Singers, who performed at the 1963 Newport Folk Festival. In February 2010 she appeared alongside Dylan before President and Mrs Obama at a concert to commemorate the role of music in the Civil Rights struggle. (*see* Chronology)

13 A five-CD box, *The Best Of Broadside 1962–1988* (2000) includes "The Ballad Of Donald White."

14 "Mixed-Up Confusion" © 1962, 1968 by Warner Bros. Inc., renewed 1990, 1996 by Special Rider Music.

15 Second only to the first single by the Quarrymen (currently in the possession of Paul McCartney), the most valuable record in pop history remains this ultra-rare stereo pressing of the original *Freewheelin'*. Currently valued at around £20,000. "John Birch," "Rambling, Gambling Willie," and "Let Me Die in My Footsteps" appear on *The Bootleg Series, Volumes 1–3*, "Rocks and Gravel" on *Live At The Gaslight 1962*.

16 "John Brown" was included on Dylan's *MTV Unplugged* (1994).

17 "I Will Not Go Down Under The Ground" is better known as "Let Me Die In My Footsteps."

18 "Only A Hobo" appears on *The Bootleg Series, Volumes 1–3*. "Talkin' Devil" has yet to be officially released.

19 "Tangled Up In Blue" © 1974 by Ram's Horn Music, renewed 2002 by Ram's Horn Music.

CHAPTER 5

1 From "A Message," Dylan's open letter to the Emergency Civil Liberties Committee after his speech to them in autumn 1963.

2 Dylan's own version of "No More Auction Block" appears on *The Bootleg Series, Volumes 1–3*.

3 Dylan recorded "Willie the Gambler" as "Rambling, Gambling Willie."

4 "11 Outlined Epitaphs" (sleeve note to *The Times They Are A-Changin'*), © 1964 Special Rider Music: renewed 1992 Special Rider Music.

5 The only change Dylan's office made to the delivered sleeve notes for *The Essential Bob Dylan* was to add Duke Ellington to the list of distinguished artists who had covered his work.

6 "Last Thoughts On Woody Guthrie" is included on *The Bootleg Series, Volumes 1–3*.

7 A clip of Dylan singing in Greenwood that day appears in *Don't Look Back*—presumably courtesy of those "TV men from New York."

8 "Playboys And Playgirls," on which Dylan duetted with Pete Seeger, appears on *Newport Broadside, Newport Folk Festival 1963* (1964). The album featured topical sleeve notes written by "Stacey Williams" (aka Robert Shelton): "The record begins with … a characteristic bit of whimsy-plus-anger from the prolific pen of Bob Dylan. He is the 22-year-old singer-poet from Hibbing, Minn., who some believe has given a major impetus to the whole topical-song development of his generation." Dylan's "Blowin' In The Wind" from the same event appeared on *The Newport Folk Festival 1963, The Evening Concerts Volume 1* (1964).

9 Joan Baez, *Daybreak*, p 84.

10 Dylan's comments to the Emergency Civil Liberties Committee were supplied to the author in a transcript the committee prepared, from its executive director, Edith Tiger.

11 From the *New Yorker* profile of Dylan by Nat Hentoff, October 4, 1964, p 64.

12 Dylan letter to *Broadside*, 1964.

CHAPTER 6

1 "Essay Towards a New Form: Jazz and Poetry" in Ralph Gleason, editor, *Jam Session: An Anthology of Jazz* (New York 1958) pp285-6

2 *Ibid.*, p 286.

3 Woody Guthrie: *Sing Out!* 17:6 (December/January), 1967–68, reprinted in *Born to Win*.

4 Newport Folk Festival program book, July 1963.

5–9 *Ibid.*

10 *Hootenanny*, column by Bob Dylan, September 1963.

11 *Ibid.*

12 *Hootenanny*, column by Bob Dylan, November 1963.

13–14 *Ibid.*

15 "The Times They Are A-Changin'" © 1963, 1964 by Warner Bros. Inc., renewed 1991, 1992 by Special Rider Music.

16–19 *Ibid.*

20 "Ballad Of Hollis Brown" © 1963 by Warner Bros. Inc., renewed 1991 by Special Rider Music.

21 *Ibid.*

22 "With God On Our Side" © 1963 by Warner Bros. Inc., renewed 1991 by Special Rider Music.

23 With Dylan's permission, the Neville Brothers added an extra verse about Vietnam when they covered "With God On Our Side" on the Daniel Lanois-produced *Yellow Moon* (1989).

24 "One Too Many Mornings" © 1964, 1966 by Warner Bros. Inc., renewed 1992, 1994 by Special Rider Music.

25 *Ibid.*

26 "North Country Blues" © 1963, 1964 by Warner Bros. Inc., renewed 1991, 1992 by Special Rider Music.

27 "Only A Pawn In Their Game" © 1963, 1964 by Warner Bros. Inc., renewed 1991, 1996 by Special Rider Music.

28 "When The Ship Comes In" © 1963, 1964 by Warner Bros. Inc., renewed 1991, 1992 by Special Rider Music.

29 *Ibid.*

30 Just before his death in 2010, William Zantzinger contributed to a BBC Radio 4 program, *The Lonesome Death of Hattie Carroll*, in which Howard Sounes interviewed those who were there in the night Hattie Carroll was assaulted, even getting to hold the cane.

31 "The Lonesome Death Of Hattie Carroll" © 1964, 1966 by Warner Bros. Inc., renewed 1992 by Special Rider Music.

32 "Restless Farewell", © 1964, 1966 by Warner Bros. Inc., renewed 1992, 1994 by Special Rider Music.

33 *Ibid.*

34 "11 Outlined Epitaphs" (sleeve note to *The Times They Are A-Changin'*) © 1964 Special Rider Music, renewed 1992 Special Rider Music.

35 From "Sweeney Agonistes" in *Collected Poems, 1909–1962*, by T S Eliot, 1936 by Harcourt, Brace & Jovanovich, © 1963, 1964 by T S Eliot. Reprinted by permission of Harcourt, Brace & Jovanovich New York and Faber & Faber, London.

36 "11 Outlined Epitaphs" (sleeve note to *The Times They Are A-Changin'*) © 1964 Special Rider Music, renewed 1992 Special Rider Music.

37–64 *Ibid.*

65 "Chimes Of Freedom" © 1964 by Warner Bros. Inc., renewed 1992 by Special Rider Music.

66–68 *Ibid.*

69 Shelton later cited "Chimes Of Freedom" as his favorite Dylan song.

70 "I Shall Be Free No.10" © 1971 by Special Rider Music, renewed 1999 by Special Rider Music.

71 "To Ramona" © 1964 by Warner Bros. Inc., renewed 1992 by Special Rider Music.

72–74 *Ibid.*

75 "My Back Pages" © 1964 by Warner Bros. Inc., renewed 1992 by Special Rider Music.

76–78 *Ibid.*

79 "I Don't Believe You (She Acts Like We Never Have Met)" © 1964 by Warner Bros. Inc., renewed 1992 by Special Rider Music.

80 *Ibid.*

81 "Ballad In Plain D" © 1964 by Warner Bros. Inc., renewed 1992 by Special Rider Music.

82–84 *Ibid.*

85 "Some Other Kinds Of Songs" (sleeve notes to *Another Side Of Bob Dylan*),© 1973 Special Rider Music, renewed 2001 Special Rider Music.

86–98 *Ibid.*

99 The 305 English and Scottish ballads collected and catalogued by Professor Francis James Child of Harvard University included "Barbara Allen," "Matty Groves," and "Geordie." They featured prominently in the early repertoire of Joan Baez, Fairport Convention and Steeleye Span, and a number appear in Harry Smith's *Anthology of American Folk Music*. The entire collection is analyzed in Child's five-volume study, *The English and Scottish Popular Ballads* (New York, 1965).

100 Robert Graves (1895–1985), English poet and novelist whose 1948 study of poetic inspiration, *The White Goddess*, Dylan has cited as an influence on his own work.

CHAPTER 7

1 "A Hard Rain's A-Gonna Fall" © 1963 by Warner Bros. Inc., renewed 1991 by Special Rider Music.

2 *Bringing It All Back Home*, sleeve notes © 1965 Special Rider Music, renewed 1993 Special Rider Music.

3 "Tombstone Blues" © 1965 by Warner Bros. Inc., renewed 1993 by Special Rider Music.

4 In 2010, Pete Karman is still writing. He can be found at karmanturn.blogspot.com.

5 IWW—Industrial Workers of the World, founded 1905.

6 Richard Fariña's article appeared as "Baez and Dylan: a generation singing out," *Mademoiselle* (August 1964), reprinted in *The Dylan Companion*.

7 "It Ain't Me, Babe" © 1964 by Warner Bros. Inc., renewed 1992 by Special Rider Music.

8 Anthea Joseph (1940–1997) remained close to Dylan and can be seen in *Don't Look Back*. She went on to work for CBS London and Joe Boyd's Witchseason Productions.

9 Philip Saville enjoyed a distinguished career in television drama, most notably directing 1982's The *Boys from the Blackstuff*. For a fuller discussion see "Bob Dylan in the Madhouse" in *The Dylan Companion*. In 2007, BBC TV screened *Dylan in the Madhouse*, a documentary on the making of the play. In 2008, BBC Radio 2 broadcast *Bob's Big Freeze*, a documentary about Dylan's first trip to the UK during the winter of 1962–3.

10 Sydney Carter (1915–2004) remains best known for his composition "Lord of the Dance."

11 The entire concert was made available on *The Bootleg Series, Volume 6: Bob Dylan Live 1964, Concert At Philharmonic Hall* (2004). Robert Shelton's original *New York Times* review is reproduced in the booklet. The CD includes four duets with Joan Baez, and further duets appear on *Joan Baez: Rare, Live & Classic* (1993), including the otherwise unavailable "Troubled And I Don't Know Why" (1963) and "Blowin' In The Wind" (1976).

12 "Advice For Geraldine On Her Miscellaneous Birthday" © 1964 Special Rider Music, renewed 1992 Special Rider Music.

CHAPTER 8

1 "Desolation Row" © 1965 by Warner Bros. Inc., renewed 1993 by Special Rider Music.

2 "Like A Rolling Stone" © 1965 by Warner Bros. Inc., renewed 1993 by Special Rider Music.

3 Calley was the US Army officer responsible for the massacre of Vietnamese civilians at My Lai in 1968.

4 Wolfgang Kayser, *The Grotesque in Art and Literature* (New York, 1963), pp 184–88.

5 *The Reader's Encyclopedia*, edited by W R Benet, © 1965 by Thomas Y Crowell Company.

6 "Subterranean Homesick Blues" © 1965 by Warner Bros. Inc., renewed 1993 by Special Rider Music.

7–8 *Ibid.*

9 Many commentators have identified the scene of Dylan flicking cue cards for "Subterranean Homesick Blues" at the beginning of *Don't Look Back* as the first pop video.

10 "She Belongs To Me" © 1965 by Warner Bros. Inc., renewed 1993 by Special Rider Music.

11 "Love Minus Zero/No Limit" © 1965 by Warner Bros. Inc., renewed 1993 by Special Rider Music.

12 "Outlaw Blues" © 1965 by Warner Bros. Inc., renewed 1993 by Special Rider Music.

13 "Mr Tambourine Man" © 1964, 1965 by Warner Bros. Inc., renewed 1992, 1993 by Special Rider Music.

14–15 *Ibid.*

16 Norman Jeffares *Profiles in Literature: W B Yeats* (Boston, 1971), p 43.

17 Gwendolyn Bays, *The Orphic Vision*, p 212.

18 "Gates Of Eden" © 1965 by Warner Bros. Inc., renewed 1993 by Special Rider Music.

19–21 *Ibid.*

22 "It's Alright, Ma (I'm Only Bleeding)" © 1965 by Warner Bros. Inc., renewed 1993 by Special Rider Music.

23–24 *Ibid.*

25 "It's All Over Now, Baby Blue" © 1965 by Warner Bros. Inc., renewed 1993 by Special Rider Music.

26–27 *Ibid.*

28 Carl G Jung, foreword to *I Ching* or the *Book of Changes* (New York, 1950), p iv.

29 *Bringing It All Back Home*, sleeve notes, © 1965 Special Rider Music, renewed 1993 Special Rider Music.

30 *Ibid.*

31 "Like A Rolling Stone" © 1965 by Warner Bros. Inc., renewed 1993 by Special Rider Music.

32 For an exhaustive analysis of the song, see Greil Marcus, *Like A Rolling Stone: Bob Dylan at the Crossroads*.

33 "Tombstone Blues" © 1965 by Warner Bros. Inc., renewed 1993 by Special Rider Music.

34 "Just Like Tom Thumb's Blues" © 1965 by Warner Bros. Inc., renewed 1993 by Special Rider Music.

35 "Outlaw Blues" © 1965 by Warner Bros. Inc., renewed 1993 by Special Rider Music.

36 The "ladies garments" quote came back to haunt Dylan in 2004 when he appeared in a television advertisement for exotic lingerie.

37 *Playboy* interview with Dylan, March 1966. For full interview, see *Dylan on Dylan*.

38 Ray Coleman (1937–1996) was Editor and Editor-in-Chief of *Melody Maker* 1970–1981. He was also a staunch Dylan fan, and employed Robert Shelton as a freelance.

39 A scene memorably captured in *Don't Look Back*.

40 In 1966, Dylan and Lennon were filmed in the back of a limo for *Eat the Document*. A transcript was printed in *Mojo* (November 1993).

41 Despite the success of "Like A Rolling Stone" in 1965, Dylan and Tom Wilson later fell out. Wilson went on to work with Frank Zappa and the Velvet Underground. He died in 1978.

42 Ewan MacColl (1915–1989), doyen of the English folk revival, wrote "Dirty Old Town" and "The First Time Ever I Saw Your Face." He famously dismissed Dylan as "a youth of mediocre talent."

43 *Don't Look Back* was on a double bill at London's ICA with "punk poet" and Dylan-lookalike John Cooper Clarke's *Ten Years in an Open Necked Shirt*.

44 The 2006 DVD release of *Don't Look Back* boasted "five additional uncut audio tracks," commentaries from D A Pennebaker and Bob Neuwirth, plus an alternate version of the "Subterranean Homesick Blues" opening.

45 *Eat the Document*, the "sequel" to *Don't Look Back*, remains "rarely shown," though some excerpts surfaced in Scorsese's *No Direction Home*.

46 In 2007 Murray Lerner brought all Dylan's 1960s Newport appearances together on a DVD—*The Other Side Of The Mirror: Bob Dylan at the Newport Folk Festival, 1963–1965*.

CHAPTER 9

1 Yevgeny Yevtushenko, *Stolen Apples* (New York, 1971), from Introduction, "Being Famous Isn't Pretty."

2 "When I Paint My Masterpiece" © 1971 by Big Sky Music, renewed 1999 by Big Sky Music.

3 Which CBS-TV tried to ban in 1967.

4 All 20 songs have been put together on a CD, *The Byrds Play the Songs of Bob Dylan* (2001).

5 The Dylan/Ramblin' Jack version of "Mr Tambourine Man" appeared on the soundtrack of *No Direction Home*.

6 Janis Ian's talent was championed by Robert Shelton. For a full account, see Ian's memoir, *Society's Child*.

7 It has since emerged that the electric overdubbing of "Sounds of Silence" was undertaken without the knowledge of either Simon or Garfunkel, CBS executives simply grafted it on using the core band from *Highway 61 Revisited*.

8 In 2001, Irwin Silber (1925–2010) reflected in *Sing Out!* on that 1964 letter: "My open letter was written at a moment when I was really disappointed. I think what I wrote, I'd stand by, but if I had to do it all over again, I don't think I would write it in the same tone and in the same way."

9 SDS, Students for a Democratic Society, founded in 1960.

10 Levon Helm drummed with the Hawks, but deeply resented the booing that greeted the 1965 electric performances. He quit Dylan's band and went to work on oil rigs in the Gulf of Mexico, returning to the Band as singing drummer in time to cut *The Basement Tapes* in 1967.

11 Dylan's performance with the Band was finally made available when *Rock of Ages* was re-released in 2001.

12 "When I Paint My Masterpiece" © 1971 by Big Sky Music, renewed 1999 by Big Sky Music.

13 "Visions Of Johanna" © 1966 by Dwarf Music, renewed 1994 by Dwarf Music.

14 *Ibid.*

15 "Pledging My Time" © 1966 by Dwarf Music, renewed 1994 by Dwarf Music.

16 *Ibid.*

17 "Visions Of Johanna" © 1966 by Dwarf Music, renewed 1994 by Dwarf Music.

18 "Temporary Like Achilles" © 1966 by Dwarf Music, renewed 1994 by Dwarf Music.

19 One of Dylan's most revealing interviews about songwriting, with Paul Zollo in 1991, was reproduced in *Dylan On Dylan* by Jonathan Cott, editor: "Being a performer, you travel the world. You're not just looking out the same window every day … Like 'yellow railroad' could have been a blinding day when the sun was bright on a railroad someplace and it stayed in my mind."

20 "Absolutely Sweet Marie" © 1966 by Dwarf Music, renewed 1994 by Dwarf Music.

21 "From A Buick 6" © 1965 by Warner Bros. Inc., renewed 1993 by Special Rider Music.

22 "Love Minus Zero/No Limit" © 1965 by Warner Bros. Inc., renewed 1993 by Special Rider Music.

23 Prefatory notes by Paul Nelson to songbook of *Blonde On Blonde* (New York, 1966), p 7.

24 Phil Spector is currently serving life imprisonment following the 2003 murder of Lana Clarkson at the same Hollywood mansion where Shelton interviewed him in 1966.

CHAPTER 10

1 Even 20 years after the event, when Shelton published his book, accepted wisdom had it that "the greatest live album never released" had been recorded at London's Royal Albert Hall. White label bootlegs had been in circulation since the late 1960s, all citing London as the location. However, doubts about the venue persisted until the official 1998 release of *The Bootleg Series Volume 4, Bob Dylan Live 1966, The "Royal Albert Hall" Concert* confirmed the recording as originating from Manchester's Free Trade Hall on May 17, 1966, 10 days before the Albert Hall concert. The subsequent five-star reviews of the set confirmed the opinion of Michael Gray, who described the shows as "the most radical, oceanic and storming electric music ever played live." For a 1999 radio documentary, *The Ghosts of Electricity*, Andy Kershaw and C P Lee attempted to track down the "Judas" shouter. Both Keith Butler and John Cordwell claimed to be the heckler—and as both men have since died, the truth may never be known. The events of that controversial 1966 UK tour, the "Judas" shout, and its aftermath, are chronicled in detail in Lee's *Like the Night (Revisited)*.

2 Victor Maimudes (1935–2001) began as Dylan's road manager in 1964, serving intermittently until 1996.

3 "Everybody around told us it wasn't working," Robbie Robertson said, looking back on those 1966 shows, "and we would tape the shows and listen to them at night—just Bob and the guys in the band—and say 'I'm sorry, but this isn't that bad!'" Interview with Patrick Humphries, *Vox* (1991).

4 Ralph J Gleason (1917–1975) was a San Francisco-based journalist and an early advocate of Dylan. In 1967 he suggested the name *Rolling Stone* as the title of a newspaper he was co-founding with Jann Wenner. In 2010 a special edition of *The Witmark Demos: 1962–1964 (The Bootleg Series Volume 9)* was made available that included a previously unknown live recording of Dylan, recorded on May 10, 1963 at Brandeis University. The tape had been in Gleason's collection for over 40 years. "It had been forgotten, until it was found last year in the clearing of the house after my mother died," said Gleason's son Toby.

5 Until 1991, the only official release by Dylan and the Hawks from the 1966 tour was a live recording of "Just Like Tom Thumb's Blues," recorded in Liverpool and issued as the B-side of "I Want You" in June 1966.

6 The French press and—to a certain extent—audiences were famously resistant to imported rock 'n' roll. In 1964 the Beatles played the Olympia, and Mark Lewisohn wrote of their residency: "The audience at this opening Olympia show was largely comprised of the Paris society set … and there was clearly little mutual affection between them and the four Liverpudlians."

7 The most exhaustive account of Dylan's rollercoaster 1966 World Tour was written by the late John Bauldie. *The Ghost Of Electricity* was privately published in 1988.

CHAPTER 11

1 From "Silence and the Poet" in *Language and Silence: Essays on Language, Literature and the Inhuman* © 1963, 1967 George Steiner. Reprinted with the permission of Atheneum Publishers New York and Faber & Faber London.

2 Pete Hamill, from liner notes to *Blood On The Tracks*. They were deleted after the first run, but were restored on the 2003 SACD reissue of the album. They appeared in the *Blood On The Tracks* songbook (London, 1975).

3 Talking to Kurt Loder in 1984 Dylan reflected: "When I had that motorcycle accident … I woke up and caught my senses, I realized that I was just workin' for all these leeches. And I didn't want to do that. Plus, I had a family and I just wanted to see my kids." See *Dylan On Dylan*.

4 Clive Davis with James Willwerth, *Clive: Inside the Record Business*, p 65.

5 *Ibid.*, p 72.

6 Dylan interview with John Cohen and Happy Traum in *Sing Out!*, October/November 1968, p 24.

7 *Ibid.*

8 In the event, the most comprehensive bootleg of the 1967 *Basement Tapes* came in 2001 with a 128-track, four-CD box set entitled *A Tree With Roots*. Various songs from the basement have also surfaced officially on *Biograph*, *The Bootleg Series* and *I'm Not There*. The most informative chronicle of the period remains Sid Griffin's *Million Dollar Bash*.

9 Gwendolyn Bays, *The Orphic Vision*, p 88.

10 "All Along The Watchtower" © 1968 by Dwarf Music, renewed 1996 by Dwarf Music.

11 Dylan interview with John Cohen and Happy Traum in *Sing Out!*, October/November 1968, p 24.

12 "John Wesley Harding" ©1968 by Dwarf Music, renewed 1996 by Dwarf Music.

13 "The Ballad Of Frankie Lee And Judas Priest" © 1968 by Dwarf Music, renewed 1996 by Dwarf Music.

14 "I Pity The Poor Immigrant" © 1968 by Dwarf Music, renewed 1996 Dwarf Music.

15 In 1997 Dylan put together a Jimmie Rodgers tribute album. (*see* Chronology)

16 "I Threw It All Away" © 1969 by Big Sky Music, renewed 1997 by Big Sky Music.

17 "Country Pie" © 1969 by Big Sky Music, renewed 1997 by Big Sky Music.

CHAPTER 12

1 A 1982 encounter with Weberman is recalled in *All Across The Telegraph: A Bob Dylan Handbook* by Michael Gray and John Bauldie, editors.

2 In the two decades it took to write his book, financial worries forced Robert Shelton to sell part of his collection. Some of these items can be seen at Seattle's Experience Music Project. At his death, everything else was donated to the Institute of Popular Music at the University of Liverpool.

3 "George Jackson" © 1971 by Ram's Horn Music, renewed 1999 by Ram's Horn Music.

4 "Watching The River Flow" © 1971 by Big Sky Music, renewed 1999 by Big Sky Music.

5 "Day Of The Locusts" © 1970 by Big Sky Music, renewed 1998 by Big Sky Music.

6 "If Dogs Run Free" © 1970 by Big Sky Music, renewed 1998 by Big Sky Music.

7 "Sign On The Window" © 1970 by Big Sky Music, renewed 1998 by Big Sky Music.

8 Dylan went on to work alongside George Harrison (1943–2001) on two Traveling Wilburys albums.

9 The fruits of those Dylan/Ginsberg sessions were finally released on a four-CD set, *Holy Soul Jelly Roll* (1994).

10 Doug Sahm (1941–1999) played with Augie Myers in the original Sir Douglas Quintet. Meyers later played on *Time Out of Mind* and *Love and Theft*.

11 A new version of *Pat Garrett & Billy The Kid* restored by the film's original editor Roger Spotiswoode, was released in 1988, but nothing more of Dylan's 'Alias' emerged.

12 "Hero Blues" © 1963 by Warner Bros. Inc., renewed 1991 by Special Rider Music.

13 "It's Alright, Ma (I'm Only Bleeding)" © 1965 by Warner Bros. Inc., renewed 1993 by Special Rider Music.

14 "Dirge" © 1973 by Ram's Horn Music, renewed 2001 by Ram's Horn Music.

15 *Ibid.*

16 "Tough Mama" © 1973 by Ram's Horn Music, renewed 2001 by Ram's Horn Music.

17 Allen Ginsberg, *First Blues, Rags and Harmonium Songs* (New York, 1975). Also, see Allen Ginsberg *Collected Poems, 1947–1980* (New York, 1985).

18 Over the years, some of the original New York recordings for *Blood On The Tracks* have emerged on various official releases including *Biograph* and *The Bootleg Series, Volumes 1–3*. The most comprehensive account of those sessions appeared in *A Simple Twist of Fate: Bob Dylan and The Making of Blood On the Tracks* by Andy Gill and Kevin Odegard.

19 Wallace Fowlie, *Rimbaud* (Chicago, 1965), p 127.

20 "Tangled Up In Blue" © 1974 by Ram's Horn Music, renewed 2002 by Ram's Horn Music.

21 *Ibid.*

22 "Simple Twist Of Fate" © 1974 by Ram's Horn Music, renewed 2002 by Ram's Horn Music.

23 *Ibid.*

24 "You're A Big Girl Now" © 1974 by Ram's Horn Music, renewed 2002 by Ram's Horn Music.

25 *Ibid.*

26 "You're Gonna Make Me Lonesome When You Go" © 1974 by Ram's Horn Music, renewed 2002 by Ram's Horn Music.

27 Wallace Fowlie, *Rimbaud* (Chicago, 1965).

28 "If You See Her, Say Hello" © 1974 by Ram's Horn Music, renewed 2002 by Ram's Horn Music.

29 "Shelter From The Storm" © 1974 by Ram's Horn Music, renewed 2002 by Ram's Horn Music.

30 *Ibid.*

31 The new song was "Abandoned Love," and this—the only known performance—was captured on tape and later released on *Biograph*.

CHAPTER 13

1 Anthony Storr, *C G Jung* (London, Fontana), p 93.

2 Gwendolyn Bays, *The Orphic Vision*, p 98.

3 *Rimbaud: Complete Works, Selected Letters*, translation, introduction, and notes by Wallace Fowlie (Chicago, 1966), pp 193–95.

4 "When The Ship Comes In" © 1963, 1964 by Warner Bros. Inc., renewed 1991, 1992 by Special Rider Music.

5 "Hurricane" (Bob Dylan & Jacques Levy), © 1975 by Ram's Horn Music, renewed 2003 by Ram's Horn Music.

6 *Ibid.*

7 "11 Outlined Epitaphs" (sleeve note to *The Times They Are A-Changin'*) © 1964 Special Rider Music, renewed 1992 Special Rider Music.

8 "Oh, Sister" (Bob Dylan & Jacques Levy) © 1975 by Ram's Horn Music, renewed 2003 by Ram's Horn Music.

9 *Ibid.*

10 "Isis" (Bob Dylan & Jacques Levy) © 1975 by Ram's Horn Music, renewed 2003 by Ram's Horn Music.

11 "It's All Over Now, Baby Blue" © 1965 by Warner Bros. Inc., renewed 1993 by Special Rider Music.

12 *Desire*, sleeve notes © 1975 by Ram's Horn Music, renewed 2003 by Ram's Horn Music.

13 *Ibid.*

14 "My Back Pages" © 1964 by Warner Bros. Inc., renewed 1992 by Special Rider Music.

15 "Joey" (Bob Dylan & Jacques Levy) © 1975 by Ram's Horn Music, renewed 2003 by Ram's Horn Music.

16 *Ibid.*

17 "Sara" © 1975, 1976 by Ram's Horn Music, renewed 2003, 2004 by Ram's Horn Music.

18 "Chimes Of Freedom" © 1964 by Warner Bros. Inc., renewed 1992 by Special Rider Music.

19 "Don't Go Home With Your Hard On" appeared on Leonard Cohen's album *Death of a Ladies' Man* (1977).

20 Besides his *Rolling Thunder Logbook*, Shepard's other major Dylan connection was as co-author of "Brownsville Girl"—the 11-minute highlight of *Knocked Out, Loaded*. Michael Gray devotes five pages of his *Encyclopedia* to the song.

POSTLUDE

1 Howard Sounes revealed that Dylan married Carolyn Dennis in June 1986. They were divorced in October 1992.

Chronology 1979-2010

1979

Dylan enters his "born again" period. In contrast to the 1978 world tour, he plays only 24 shows, all in North America, featuring exclusively religious material.

AUGUST *Slow Train Coming.*

1980

FEBRUARY Dylan wins his first Grammy—Best Male Rock Vocal Performance of 1979 for "Gotta Serve Somebody."

JUNE *Saved.*

Dylan plays a total of 68 "born-again" shows throughout the year. By November, he is also including a number of earlier songs in concert.

1981

FEBRUARY Death of guitarist Michael Bloomfield.

AUGUST *Shot of Love.*

European and American tours occupy Dylan; these include a mix of religious and secular material.

NOVEMBER First issue of UK Dylan fanzine *The Telegraph*, edited by John Bauldie.

1982

JANUARY Death of Howard Alk, cameraman on *Don't Look Back* and *Eat the Document.*

MARCH Dylan is inducted into the Songwriters Hall of Fame in New York.

JUNE Dylan joins Joan Baez onstage at Peace Sunday concert in Pasadena.

1983

NOVEMBER *Infidels.*

Dylan shoots his first promotional video for "Sweetheart Like You."

1984

Summer tour of Europe with Santana.

DECEMBER *Real Live.*

1985

JUNE *Empire Burlesque.*

JULY Dylan appears at Live Aid with Keith Richards and Ron Wood.

SEPTEMBER Dylan appears at first Farm Aid concert along with Tom Petty and the Heartbreakers.

OCTOBER *Biograph.*

NOVEMBER *Lyrics 1962–1985* published.

Columbia celebrates sales of 35m Dylan records with a party in New York. Guests include David Bowie, Pete Townshend, Billy Joel, and Neil Young.

1986

JANUARY Appears on Martin Luther King TV benefit with Stevie Wonder and Peter, Paul and Mary.

Albert Grossman dies of heart attack on flight to London.

FEBRUARY Begins Far Eastern and American tour with Tom Petty and the Heartbreakers.

MARCH Death of the Band's Richard Manuel.

Dylan receives the Founders Award from ASCAP (American Society of Composers and Performers).

JUNE Dylan marries backing vocalist Carolyn Dennis; they divorce in 1992.

AUGUST *Knocked Out Loaded.*

Dylan arrives in UK to film *Hearts of Fire.*

1987

FEBRUARY Dylan joins George Harrison and John Fogerty onstage at a Taj Mahal gig in Hollywood.

MARCH Dylan performs "Soon" at a New York gala marking fifty years since the death of George Gershwin.

JULY Six-date US tour with Grateful Dead.

SEPTEMBER European tour with Tom Petty and the Heartbreakers opens with Dylan's first dates in Israel.

1988

JANUARY Inducted into the Rock & Roll Hall of Fame by Bruce Springsteen: "The way that Elvis freed your body, Bob freed your mind."

FEBRUARY "Hurricane" Carter released from jail.

MAY Traveling Wilburys (Jeff Lynne, Tom Petty, Roy Orbison, George Harrison, and Dylan) begin recording.

Down In the Groove.

JUNE A show at Concord, California, with guitarist G E Smith is now seen as beginning Dylan's so-called Never-Ending Tour.

DECEMBER Death of Roy Orbison ("Lefty Wilbury").

1989

JANUARY *Dylan & the Dead.*

SEPTEMBER *Oh Mercy.*

OCTOBER Death of Ewan MacColl.

1990

JANUARY Toad's Place in New Haven hosts what is considered the most remarkable of *all* Dylan gigs: a four-hour show which includes covers of "Dancing In the Dark," "Help Me Make It Through the Night," and "Walk a Mile in My Shoes."

Show in São Paolo marks Dylan's South American concert debut.

Dylan is made *Commandeur de l'Ordre des Arts et des Lettres* in a ceremony at the Ministry of Culture, Paris.

MARCH At a Tom Petty and the Heartbreakers show in Los Angeles, Dylan and Bruce Springsteen appear onstage together for the first time.

SEPTEMBER *Under the Red Sky.*

OCTOBER Dylan performs at West Point Military Academy: he sings "Masters of War."

1991

FEBRUARY At the Grammys, Dylan receives a Lifetime Achievement Award presented by Jack Nicholson. His acceptance speech, carried live on TV, includes a breathtaking pause, before concluding: "My daddy… told me… 'You know, it's possible to become so defiled in this world that your own mother and father will abandon you. And if that happens,

God will always believe in your own ability to mend your own ways.' Thank you."

MARCH *The Bootleg Series, Vols 1–3*.

MAY Celebrities, including Bob Geldof and Mick Jagger, are asked what they would give Dylan for his fiftieth birthday. Robert Shelton replies: "Some film footage of how he looked thirty years ago when he hopped off a subway train in Greenwich Village after traveling in from the Midwest. It might make him smile again."

OCTOBER Dylan appears at the Guitar Greats Festival in Seville, accompanied by Richard Thompson.

1992

MARCH Death of Mike Porco.

OCTOBER Columbia hosts a thirtieth anniversary tribute at Madison Square Garden; George Harrison, Lou Reed, Eric Clapton, and Neil Young are among those who perform.

NOVEMBER *Good As I Been to You*.

1993

JANUARY Dylan performs "Chimes of Freedom" at a concert on the steps of the Lincoln Memorial marking President Clinton's inaugural.

JULY For the first time, Dylan cancels a show: in Lyon, he has a bad back.

Dylan is filmed wandering round London's Camden Lock. The footage appears as a video for "Blood in My Eye."

1994

JANUARY Ritchie Havens' version of "The Times They Are a-Changin'" used in a US TV ad for Coopers & Lybrand.

AUGUST Despite avoiding the original in 1969, Dylan appears at Woodstock II.

OCTOBER On the last night of a residency at New York's Roseland Ballroom, Dylan is joined onstage by Bruce Springsteen and Neil Young.

NOVEMBER Dylan records an appearance on MTV's *Unplugged*.

1995

JANUARY Publication of Dylan's first collection of drawings, *Drawn Blank*.

MARCH Dylan is joined onstage by Elvis Costello, Chrissie Hynde, and Carole King at the end of his residency at London's Brixton Academy.

Highway 61 Interactive CD-ROM.

APRIL *MTV Unplugged*.

JULY Opening for the Rolling Stones in France, Dylan joins the band for an encore of "Like a Rolling Stone."

AUGUST Jerry Garcia dies: "His playing was moody, awesome, sophisticated, hypnotic and subtle. There's no way to convey the loss."

SEPTEMBER Dylan appears at a concert marking the opening of the Rock & Roll Hall of Fame in Cleveland.

NOVEMBER Dylan is a surprise guest at a Frank Sinatra eightieth birthday tribute – he performs "Restless Farewell."

DECEMBER After a record-breaking 118 shows, Dylan concludes the year on dates with Patti Smith.

Robert Shelton dies at his adoptive home of Brighton, England.

1996

MAY Jakob Dylan's band the Wallflowers release *Bringing Down the Horse*, which goes on to sell six million copies.

JUNE Dylan appears at the Prince's Trust show in Hyde Park with the Who and Eric Clapton.

OCTOBER *The Telegraph* founder John Bauldie dies. "The Times They Are a-Changin'," sung by a children's choir, is used in a TV ad promoting Bank of Montreal.

DECEMBER Following the shootings in Dunblane, Scotland, in which 16 children died, Dylan gives permission for an extra verse to be added to a charity version of "Knockin' On Heaven's Door." It is a UK Number One.

1997

MAY Hospitalised with histoplasmosis, a potentially fatal heart condition, Dylan faces up to his own mortality: "I really thought I'd be seeing Elvis soon." By summer he is touring again.

JULY Dylan's own record label, Egyptian Records, releases *The Songs of Jimmie Rodgers, A Tribute*, to which Dylan contributes "My Blue Eyed Jane."

AUGUST bobdylan.com launched.

SEPTEMBER Dylan performs in Bologna before Pope John Paul II: "You don't say no to the Vatican." *Time Out of Mind* released, Dylan's first Top 10 album in nearly 20 years. It goes on to win Grammys for Best Album, Best Contemporary Folk Album and Best Male Rock Vocal, for "Cold Irons Bound."

OCTOBER Dylan receives the Dorothy and Lillian Gish Prize for making "an outstanding contribution to the beauty of the world and to mankind's enjoyment and understanding of life."

1998

MAY Dylan plays six US concerts with Joni Mitchell and Van Morrison.

OCTOBER *Bootleg Series, Vol. 4: Live 1996*

1999

JUNE Dylan and Paul Simon undertake a 32-date US tour.

For the first time, a Dylan album gets an official remix: original *Street-Legal* producer Don DeVito persuades Dylan to let him release "an accurate representation of what happened in Santa Monica at the renovated gun factory all those years ago."

SEPTEMBER *The Hurricane*, Norman Jewison's film about "Hurricane" Carter, opens. Denzel Washington stars, and Dylan's 1976 song is heard over the credits.

OCTOBER Dylan makes a surprise appearance on the US TV sitcom *Dharma & Greg*.

2000

JANUARY Dylan's mother Beatty dies, aged 84.

MARCH "Things Have Changed" from *Wonder Boys* wins Dylan the Oscar for Best Original Song.

MAY King Carl Gustav XVI of Sweden presents Dylan with the Polar Music Prize in Stockholm. The citation reads, in part: "Bob Dylan's influence as a singer-songwriter, on the development of 20th-Century popular music is indisputable."

2001

JANUARY Death of Victor Maimudes.

JULY Death of Mimi Fariña.

SEPTEMBER *Love and Theft*.

NOVEMBER Death of George Harrison ("Spike Wilbury").

2002

FEBRUARY *Love and Theft* wins a Grammy for Best Contemporary Folk Album.

Death of Dave Van Ronk.

AUGUST For the first time since 1965, Dylan plays the Newport Folk Festival, sporting a fake beard and blonde wig.

NOVEMBER *Bootleg Series, Vol. 5: Live 1975*

2003

JANUARY *Masked and Anonymous* film opens. It is written by Dylan, who co-stars alongside Mickey Rourke, Penelope Cruz and Jeff Bridges.

SEPTEMBER Release of 15 classic Dylan albums "completely remastered and available on Hybrid Super Audio CD for the ultimate audio experience."

Johnny Cash dies: "Johnny was and is the North Star. You could guide your ship by him—the greatest of the greats, then and now."

2004

JANUARY Dylan films a Victoria's Secret lingerie ad in Venice, featuring his song "Love Sick."

MARCH *Bootleg Series, Vol. 6: Live 1964*

JUNE In Scotland, Dylan receives an honorary Doctor of Music degree from the University of St Andrew's.

OCTOBER Publication of *Chronicles: Volume One*. It becomes a *New York Times* bestseller.

Publication of *Lyrics, 1962–2001*.

DECEMBER Dylan talks to *60 Minutes*, his first TV interview in 19 years. The same night he appears on *The Simpsons*.

2005

AUGUST *Bootleg Series, Vol. 7: No Direction Home*.

Death of Al Aronowitz, the New York journalist who introduced Dylan to the Beatles in 1964. Asked "is there one man who can save the world?" at a 1965 press conference, Dylan replied: "Al Aronowitz".

SEPTEMBER Martin Scorsese's documentary *No Direction Home* is screened.

NOVEMBER "Poems Without Titles," written by Robert Zimmerman while still a teenager, but signing himself "Dylan," are auctioned in New York for $78,000.

2006

Expanded version of *Don't Look Back* released on DVD.

MAY Dylan's new career as DJ begins with the first transmission of *Theme Time Radio Hour, With Your Host Bob Dylan* on XM Satellite Radio.

SEPTEMBER *Modern Times* becomes the first Dylan album to reach Number One in US since 1976's *Desire*.

Bob Dylan: The Collection, a digital box-set containing all his albums (773 tracks in total), along with 42 rare and unreleased tracks, is released on iTunes.

2007

FEBRUARY *Modern Times* is awarded the Grammy for Best Contemporary Folk/Americana Album, while "Someday Baby" wins Solo Rock Vocal Performance. It brings Dylan's Grammy total to 10.

JUNE Awarded Spain's Prince of Asturias Prize for Art.

JULY DVD release of *The Other Side of the Mirror, Bob Dylan at the Newport Folk Festival, 1963–1965*.

SEPTEMBER Opening of *I'm Not There*, Todd Haynes' film about Dylan starring Cate Blanchett, Heath Ledger and Christian Bale.

Mark Ronson undertakes the first-ever dance remix of a Dylan song, "Most Likely You Go Your Way (And I'll Go Mine)."

NOVEMBER The first gallery exhibition of Dylan's artwork opens in Chemnitz, Germany.

2008

APRIL Dylan wins a special Pulitzer Prize for music. The citation notes his "profound impact on popular music and American culture, marked by lyrical compositions of extraordinary poetic power."

OCTOBER *The Bootleg Series Vol 8: Tell Tale Signs—Rare and Unreleased 1989-2006*.

NOVEMBER Dylan visits Neil Young's childhood home in Winnipeg.

Introducing "Blowin' in the Wind" on election night, Dylan comments: "I was born in 1941. That's the year they bombed Pearl Harbor. We've been living in a world of darkness ever since. But it looks like things are going to change now."

As "arguably, the most inspirational songwriter of all," Dylan becomes the 100th artist invited by the HMV chain to select "My Inspiration." He chooses Robert Burns' "A Red, Red Rose."

2009

FEBRUARY Dylan appears with rapper Will.i.am in a Pepsi ad that is first shown during the telecast of Super Bowl XLIII, reaching a record audience of 98 million viewers. Dylan sings the first verse of "Forever Young" followed by Will.i.am doing a hip-hop version of the song's third and final verse.

"Blowin' in the Wind" is used as the soundtrack to a UK TV ad for the Co-Op.

APRIL Dylan broadcasts the 100th show in his radio series. The theme is "Goodbye" and the final record is Woody Guthrie's "So Long, It's Been Good to Know Yuh."

Together Through Life goes straight to Number One in America, making Dylan at 67 the oldest artist ever to debut at the top of that chart. The album also reaches Number One in the UK, 39 years after his previous UK chart topper, *New Morning*. Dylan is now the oldest solo artist to reach the top in the UK—unseating the previous holder, Neil Diamond.

MAY Pays £16 for the National Trust tour to visit John Lennon's Liverpool home.

JULY Tours US with Willie Nelson and John Mellencamp.

"An old scruffy man, acting suspiciously" is picked up by police in New Jersey. It turns out to be Dylan, who is believed to be looking for Bruce Springsteen's childhood home—but 22-year-old cop Kirstie Buble takes the "eccentric looking old man" in for questioning.

OCTOBER *Christmas In the Heart*. Royalties will benefit the charities Feeding America in the US, Crisis in the UK.

2010

FEBRUARY In a concert to commemorate the role music played in the civil rights struggle, Dylan performs "The Times They Are a-Changin'" at the White House. Speaking to *Rolling Stone*, President Obama said of Dylan's appearance: "Here's what I love about Dylan: He was exactly as you'd expect he would be. He wouldn't come to the rehearsal… He didn't want to take a picture with me… He came in and played 'The Times They Are a-Changin'." A beautiful rendition… Finishes the song, steps off the stage—I'm sitting right in the front row—comes up, shakes my hand, sort of tips his head, gives me just a little grin, and then leaves. And that was it… And I thought:

That's how you want Bob Dylan, right? You don't want him to be all cheesin' and grinnin' with you. You want him to be a little skeptical about the whole enterprise. So that was a real treat."

AUGUST On his radio show, Dylan announces he is "talking to a couple of car companies" about becoming their satnav voice, but added "I probably shouldn't do it, because whichever way I go, I always end up at one place—Lonely Avenue."

SEPTEMBER dylancover.com lists 31,000 covers of Dylan songs.

OCTOBER *The Witmark Demos: 1962-1964 (The Bootleg Series Vol 9).*

Acknowledgments

The author wishes to thank all copyright holders of Bob Dylan's songs and poems: Ram's Horn Music, Big Sky Music, Dwarf Music, and Special Rider Music. Also, we acknowledge permission to quote from Tarantula from Macmillan Publishing Company. For permission to quote from various writings and lyrics of Woody Guthrie, our thanks to the Woody Guthrie Children's Trust Fund. Because this book was always designed to reflect many voices commenting on the life and music of its subject, a vast number of people helped me to assemble it. Especial thanks to Liz Thomson, Gabrielle Goodchild, and Roger Ford for being the stalwart trio who helped me most directly. A variety of doors were opened up to me at the Dylan Revisited conventions in Manchester in 1979 and 1980, for which I especially thank its chief organizer, Richard Goodall. The collectors and/or discographers Steven Goldberg, Stephen Pickering, and Jacques von Son were especially helpful. I actively corresponded with a dozen academics, mostly in America, who were carrying forward multidisciplinary "Dylan Studies" in their own classrooms and research. Among those who helped me the most were Eugene Stelzig, Louis Cantor, W T Lhamon, Jr, Bill King, Jack McDonough, Belle Levenson, Suzanne MacRae, Carolyn Jane Bliss, and Betsy Bowden. I traveled many thousands of miles to research the work, and want to express my thanks for the help extended to me by the subject's mother and brother and late father. Tony Glover was especially conscientious in pulling together the chaotic, stimulating days in Minneapolis-St Paul. In New York, I was given detailed historical/emotional reconstructions by Suze Rotolo and her sister, Carla. Sis and Gordon Friesen were, as ever, generous with their recollections of the heady Broadside days. Special thanks to the author of the first serious book on Dylan, Michael Gray, for strong support over a number of years, and for his work in assembling my material on the Band, the first Australian tour, and the thorny question of bootleg recordings. For technical musical advice, thanks to the singer-guitarists Carol Crist and Barry Tomlinson. Too many editors were all too fleetingly involved on this project – a total of eleven publishers' editors and my two personal editors, Gabrielle Goodchild and Liz Thomson. I want to offer a special toast to Diane Matthews and Maggie Pringle, formerly of Doubleday & Co, and to Simon Scott, formerly of New English Library, who kept the wheels turning at crucial times. For endless rush deadlines on the manuscript typing, many thanks to Yvonne Hodson for her punctilious work. For typing and tape transcribing, Alice Robinson in Wadhurst and Emily de Souza in Hampstead. A host of friends made the "siege of Sydenham" bearable, notably Meg and David Elliott, Michael Davies, Patrick Humphries, Wendy Robin, Cathy Lloyd, Jim, Niall and Heather, Ricky and Arthur. And many thanks also to Gillian Youngs, Claire Simpson, Alison Holt, Jackie Shepcott, Gaby Landau, and Ross MacPherson.

EDITORS' ACKNOWLEDGMENTS

Carole Blake; Mitch Blank, a walking encyclopedia of Greenwich Village life and music; Dr Mike Brocken, now of Liverpool Hope, who established the Robert Shelton Archive at the University of Liverpool's Institute of Popular Music; Jasen Emmons at Seattle's Experience Music Project; David Gutman, for wise counsel; Dave Laing, for advice and guidance and for his research on Shelton's journalism; Hazel Orme; Sue Parr; Rob Strachan of the IPM; Ian Woodward, Dylan oracle. Also to Judy Collins and Janis Ian for their tributes and warm memories of Robert Shelton. Thanks also to Bill Brooke, Eleanor Brooke, Colin and Anita Davies; Jeremy Mason; Dan, Rita and Judy Paul and Marc Garrett at the Washington Square Hotel; and to the many friends and family who encouraged and supported the project. Colin and Pam Webb and the team at Palazzo; Dave Brolan for his knowledgeable photo research; David Costa/Wherefore Art for his elegant design; Charlotte de Grey for her thoughtful copy editing; and to Sonya Newland at Big Blu Books for her patience and expertise. Most of all to Robert Shelton, a friend and mentor to the Editors, who did so much to raise the standard of music journalism and biography. And to his sisters, the late Leona Shapiro and the indomitable Ruth Kadish, for their friendship and trust. Ruth, and her son, David Kadish, gave this project their blessing and, throughout, have engaged with discussion of it but never sought to interfere. We hope they feel their faith was not misplaced and that this revised edition does justice to Robert's life and work.

Select Discography

Given that Dylan's recording career is now a half-century long, this list is necessarily selective and does not seek to detail every extant recording bearing his name. At its core are the original studio albums, listed chronologically. Key "Best Of" releases are included (with notable tracks listed), but not single releases, EPs, or bootlegs. The pick of his many guest appearances can be found at the end. The (hopefully) never-ending Bootleg Series is also included, but we have listed only individual tracks unavailable elsewhere. The date in parentheses indicates the year of original release, and • indicates a live album.

This discography was compiled with reference to **bobdylan.com** *— which lists all official product, as well as a comprehensive lyric companion; the indispensable* **expectingrain.com***; and* **searchingforagem.com** *which offers up a chillingly thorough site of every official Dylan release and rarity.*

BOB DYLAN [1962]
You're No Good
Talkin' New York
In My Time Of Dyin'
Man Of Constant Sorrow
Fixin' To Die
Pretty Peggy-O
Highway 51
Gospel Plow
Baby Let Me Follow You Down
House Of The Risin' Sun
Freight Train Blues
Song To Woody
See That My Grave Is Kept Clean

THE FREEWHEELIN' BOB DYLAN [1963]
Blowin' In The Wind
Girl From The North Country
Masters Of War
Down The Highway
Bob Dylan's Blues
A Hard Rain's A-Gonna Fall
Don't Think Twice, It's All Right
Bob Dylan's Dream
Oxford Town
Talkin' World War III Blues
Corrina, Corrina
Honey, Just Allow Me One
  More Chance
I Shall Be Free

THE TIMES THEY ARE A-CHANGIN' [1964]
The Times They Are A-Changin'
Ballad Of Hollis Brown
With God On Our Side
One Too Many Mornings
North Country Blues
Only A Pawn In Their Game
Boots Of Spanish Leather
When The Ship Comes In
The Lonesome Death Of Hattie
  Carroll
Restless Farewell

ANOTHER SIDE OF BOB DYLAN [1964]
All I Really Want To Do
Black Crow Blues
Spanish Harlem Incident
Chimes Of Freedom
I Shall Be Free No. 10
To Ramona
Motorpsycho Nitemare
My Back Pages
I Don't Believe You (She Acts Like
  We Never Have Met)
Ballad In Plain D
It Ain't Me, Babe

BRINGING IT ALL BACK HOME [1965]
Subterranean Homesick Blues
She Belongs To Me
Maggie's Farm
Love Minus Zero/No Limit
Outlaw Blues
On The Road Again
Bob Dylan's 115th Dream
Mr. Tambourine Man
Gates Of Eden
It's Alright, Ma (I'm Only Bleeding)
It's All Over Now, Baby Blue

HIGHWAY 61 REVISITED [1965]
Like A Rolling Stone
Tombstone Blues
It Takes A Lot To Laugh, It Takes
  A Train To Cry
From A Buick 6
Ballad Of A Thin Man
Queen Jane Approximately
Highway 61 Revisited
Just Like Tom Thumb's Blues
Desolation Row

BLONDE ON BLONDE [1966]
Rainy Day Women # 12 & 35
Pledging My Time
Visions Of Johanna
One Of Us Must Know (Sooner

Or Later)
I Want You
Stuck Inside Of Mobile With The
  Memphis Blues Again
Leopard-Skin Pill-Box Hat
Just Like A Woman
Most Likely You Go Your Way
  (And I'll Go Mine)
Temporary Like Achilles
Absolutely Sweet Marie
4th Time Around
Obviously Five Believers
Sad-Eyed Lady Of The Lowlands

BOB DYLAN'S GREATEST HITS [1967]
Positively 4th Street (1965 single)

JOHN WESLEY HARDING [1967]
John Wesley Harding
As I Went Out One Morning
I Dreamed I Saw St. Augustine
All Along The Watchtower
The Ballad Of Frankie Lee And
  Judas Priest
Drifter's Escape
Dear Landlord
I Am A Lonesome Hobo
I Pity The Poor Immigrant
The Wicked Messenger
Down Along The Cove
I'll Be Your Baby Tonight

NASHVILLE SKYLINE [1969]
Girl From The North Country
  [with Johnny Cash]
Nashville Skyline Rag
To Be Alone With You
I Threw It All Away
Peggy Day
Lay, Lady, Lay
One More Night
Tell Me That It Isn't True
Country Pie
Tonight I'll Be Staying Here With You

SELF PORTRAIT [1970]
All The Tired Horses
Alberta #1
I Forgot More Than You'll
  Ever Know
Days of '49
Early Morning Rain
In Search Of Little Sadie
Let It Be Me
Little Sadie
Woogie Boogie
Belle Isle
Living The Blues
Like A Rolling Stone [Live 1969]
Copper Kettle
Gotta Travel On
Blue Moon
The Boxer
Quinn The Eskimo (The Mighty
  Quinn) [Live 1969]
Take Me As I Am (Or Let Me Go)
Take A Message To Mary
It Hurts Me Too
Minstrel Boy [Live 1969]
She Belongs To Me [Live, 1969]
Wigwam
Alberta #2

NEW MORNING [1970]
If Not For You
Day Of The Locusts
Time Passes Slowly
Went To See The Gypsy
Winterlude
If Dogs Run Free
New Morning
Sign On The Window
One More Weekend
The Man In Me
Three Angels
Father Of Night

MORE BOB DYLAN
GREATEST HITS [1971]
Watching The River Flow
  [1971 single]
Tomorrow Is A Long Time
  [Live 1963]
When I Paint My Masterpiece
  [Recorded 1971]
I Shall Be Released
  [Recorded 1971]
You Ain't Goin' Nowhere
  [Recorded 1971]
Down In The Flood
  [Recorded 1971]

PAT GARRETT & BILLY THE
KID [Soundtrack 1973]
Main Title Theme (Billy)
Cantina Theme (Workin' For
  The Law)
Billy 1
Bunkhouse Theme

River Theme
Turkey Chase
Knockin' On Heaven's Door
Final Theme
Billy 4
Billy 7

DYLAN (A FOOL SUCH AS I)
[1973]
Lily Of The West
Can't Help Falling In Love
Sarah Jane
The Ballad Of Ira Hayes
Mr. Bojangles
Mary Ann
Big Yellow Taxi
A Fool Such As I
Spanish Is The Loving Tongue

PLANET WAVES [1974]
On A Night Like This
Going, Going, Gone
Tough Mama
Hazel
Something There Is About You
Forever Young 1
Forever Young 2
Dirge
You Angel You
Never Say Goodbye
Wedding Song

BEFORE THE FLOOD •
[Bob Dylan/The Band 1974]
Most Likely You Go Your Way
  (And I'll Go Mine)
Lay, Lady, Lay
Rainy Day Women # 12 & 35
Knockin' On Heaven's Door
It Ain't Me, Babe
Ballad Of A Thin Man
Don't Think Twice, It's All Right
Just Like A Woman
It's Alright Ma (I'm Only Bleeding)
All Along The Watchtower
Highway 61 Revisited
Like A Rolling Stone
Blowin' In The Wind
[remaining tracks by The Band]

BLOOD ON THE TRACKS
[1975]
Tangled Up In Blue
Simple Twist Of Fate
You're A Big Girl Now
Idiot Wind
You're Gonna Make Me Lonesome
  When You Go
Meet Me In The Morning
Lily Rosemary & The Jack Of Hearts
If You See Her Say Hello
Shelter From The Storm
Buckets Of Rain

THE BASEMENT TAPES
[1975 – recorded 1967]
Odds And Ends
Million Dollar Bash
Goin' To Acapulco
Lo And Behold
Clothes Line Saga
Apple Suckling Tree
Please Mrs. Henry
Tears Of Rage
Too Much Of Nothing
Yea! Heavy And A Bottle Of Bread
Crash On The Levee (Down In
  The Flood)
Tiny Montgomery
You Ain't Goin' Nowhere
Nothing Was Delivered
Open The Door Homer
Long Distance Operator
This Wheel's On Fire
[remainder of tracks by The Band]

DESIRE [1976]
Hurricane
Isis
Mozambique
One More Cup Of Coffee
  (Valley Below)
Oh, Sister
Joey
Romance In Durango
Black Diamond Bay
Sara

HARD RAIN • [1976]
Maggie's Farm
One Too Many Mornings
Stuck Inside Of Mobile With The
  Memphis Blues Again
Oh, Sister
Lay, Lady, Lay
Shelter From The Storm
You're A Big Girl Now
I Threw It All Away
Idiot Wind

MASTERPIECES [1978
Australian Import]
Mixed-Up Confusion
  [Recorded 1962]
Just Like Tom Thumb's Blues
  [Live 1966 B-side]
Spanish Is The Loving Tongue
  [1971 B-side]
George Jackson (Big Band)
  [1971 single]
Rita May [1976 B-side]

STREET-LEGAL [1978]
Changing Of The Guards
New Pony
No Time To Think
Baby Stop Crying
Is Your Love In Vain?

345

Señor (Tales Of Yankee Power)
True Love Tends To Forget
We Better Talk This Over
Where Are You Tonight?
  (Journey Though Dark Heat)

BOB DYLAN AT BUDOKAN •
[1979]
Mr. Tambourine Man
Shelter From The Storm
Love Minus Zero/No Limit
Ballad Of A Thin Man
Don't Think Twice, It's All Right
Maggie's Farm
One More Cup Of Coffee
Like A Rolling Stone
I Shall Be Released
Is Your Love In Vain?
Going, Going, Gone
Blowin' In The Wind
Just Like A Woman
Oh, Sister
Simple Twist Of Fate
All Along The Watchtower
I Want You
All I Really Want To Do
Knockin' On Heaven's Door
It's Alright, Ma (I'm Only Bleeding)
Forever Young
The Times They Are A-Changin'

SLOW TRAIN COMING [1979]
Gotta Serve Somebody
Precious Angel
I Believe In You
Slow Train
Gonna Change My Way Of Thinking
Do Right To Me Baby (Do Unto
  Others)
When You Gonna Wake Up?
Man Gave Names To All The
  Animals
When He Returns

SAVED [1980]
A Satisfied Mind
Saved
Covenant Woman
What Can I Do For You?
Solid Rock
Pressing On
In The Garden
Saving Grace
Are You Ready?

SHOT OF LOVE [1981]
Shot Of Love
Heart Of Mine
Property Of Jesus
Lenny Bruce
Watered-Down Love
The Groom's Still Waiting At
  The Altar
Dead Man, Dead Man

In The Summertime
Trouble
Every Grain Of Sand

INFIDELS [1983]
Jokerman
Sweetheart Like You
Neighborhood Bully
License To Kill
Man Of Peace
Union Sundown
I And I
Don't Fall Apart On Me Tonight

REAL LIVE • [1984]
Highway 61 Revisited
Maggie's Farm
I And I
License To Kill
It Ain't Me, Babe
Tangled Up In Blue
Masters Of War
Ballad Of A Thin Man
Girl From The North Country
Tombstone Blues

EMPIRE BURLESQUE [1985]
Tight Connection To My Heart
  (Has Anybody Seen My Love)
Seeing The Real You At Last
I'll Remember You
Clean-Cut Kid
Never Gonna Be The Same Again
Trust Yourself
Emotionally Yours
When The Night Comes Falling
  From The Sky
Something's Burning Baby
Dark Eyes

BIOGRAPH [1985]
I'll Keep It With Mine
  [Recorded 1965]
Percy's Song [Recorded 1963]
Mixed-Up Confusion [1962 single]
Lay Down Your Weary Tune
  [Recorded 1963]
I Don't Believe You (She Acts Like
  We Never Have Met) [Live 1966]
Visions Of Johanna [Live 1966]
Quinn The Eskimo [Recorded 1967]
You're A Big Girl Now
  [Recorded 1974]
Abandoned Love [Recorded 1975]
It's All Over Now (Baby Blue)
  [Live 1966]
Can You Please Crawl Out Your
  Window? [1965 single]
Isis [Live 1975]
Jet Pilot [Recorded 1965]
Caribbean Wind [Recorded 1981]
Up To Me [Recorded 1974]
Baby, I'm In The Mood For You
  [Recorded 1962]

I Wanna Be Your Lover
  [Recorded 1965]
Heart Of Mine [Live 1981]
Romance In Durango [Live 1975]
Forever Young [Recorded 1973]

KNOCKED OUT LOADED
[1986]
You Wanna Ramble
They Killed Him
Driftin' Too Far From Shore
Precious Memories
Maybe Someday
Brownsville Girl
Got My Mind Made Up
Under Your Spell

DOWN IN THE GROOVE
[1988]
Let's Stick Together
When Did You Leave Heaven?
Sally Sue Brown
Death Is Not The End
Had A Dream About You, Baby
Ugliest Girl In The World
Silvio
Ninety Miles An Hour (Down A
  Dead End Street)
Shenandoah
Rank Strangers To Me

DYLAN & THE DEAD • [1989]
Slow Train
I Want You
Gotta Serve Somebody
Queen Jane Approximately
Joey
All Along The Watchtower
Knockin' On Heaven's Door

OH MERCY [1989]
Political World
Where Teardrops Fall
Everything Is Broken
Ring Them Bells
Man In The Long Black Coat
Most Of The Time
What Good Am I?
Disease Of Conceit
What Was It You Wanted
Shooting Star

UNDER THE RED SKY [1990]
Wiggle Wiggle
Under The Red Sky
Unbelievable
Born In Time
T.V. Talkin' Song
10,000 Men
2 x 2
God Knows
Handy Dandy
Cat's In The Well

THE BOOTLEG SERIES, VOLUMES 1–3 [1991]
Hard Times In New York Town [Recorded 1961]
He Was A Friend Of Mine [Recorded 1961]
Man On The Street [Recorded 1961]
No More Auction Block [Live 1962]
House Carpenter [Recorded 1961]
Talkin' Bear Mountain Picnic Massacre Blues [Recorded 1962]
Let Me Die In My Footsteps [Recorded 1962]
Rambling, Gambling Willie [Recorded 1962]
Talkin' Hava Negeilah Blues [Recorded 1962]
Quit Your Low Down Ways [Recorded 1962]
Worried Blues [Recorded 1962]
Kingsport Town [Recorded 1962]
Walkin' Down The Line [Recorded 1963]
Walls Of Red Wing [Recorded 1963]
Paths Of Victory [Recorded 1963]
Talkin' John Birch Paranoid Blues [Live 1963]
Who Killed Davey Moore? [Live 1963]
Only A Hobo [Recorded 1963]
Moonshiner [Recorded 1963]
When The Ship Comes In [Recorded 1963]
The Times They Are A-Changin' [Recorded 1963]
Last Thoughts On Woody Guthrie [Live 1963]
Seven Curses [Recorded 1963]
Eternal Circle [Recorded 1963]
Suze (The Cough Song) [Recorded 1963]
Mama You Been On My Mind [Recorded 1964]
Farewell Angelina [Recorded 1965]
Subterranean Homesick Blues [Recorded 1965]
If You Gotta Go, Go Now [Recorded 1965]
Sitting On A Barbed-Wire Fence [Recorded 1965]
Like A Rolling Stone [Recorded 1965]
It Takes A Lot To Laugh, It Takes A Train To Cry [Recorded 1965]
I'll Keep It With Mine [Recorded 1966]
She's Your Lover Now [Recorded 1966]
I Shall Be Released [Recorded 1967]
Santa-Fé [Recorded 1967]
If Not For You [Recorded 1970]
Wallflower [Recorded 1971]
Nobody 'Cept You [Recorded 1973]

Tangled Up In Blue [Recorded 1974]
Call Letter Blues [Recorded 1974]
Idiot Wind [Recorded 1974]
If You See Her, Say Hello [Recorded 1974]
Golden Loom [Recorded 1975]
Catfish [Recorded 1975]
Seven Days [Live 1976]
Ye Shall Be Changed [Recorded 1979]
Every Grain Of Sand [Recorded 1980]
You Changed My Life [Recorded 1981]
Need A Woman [Recorded 1981]
Angelina [Recorded 1981]
Someone's Got A Hold Of My Heart [Recorded 1983]
Tell Me [Recorded 1983]
Lord Protect My Child [Recorded 1983]
Foot Of Pride [Recorded 1983]
Blind Willie McTell [Recorded 1983]
When The Night Comes Falling From The Sky [Recorded 1985]
Series Of Dreams [Recorded 1989]

GOOD AS I BEEN TO YOU [1992]
Frankie & Albert
Jim Jones
Blackjack Davey
Canadee-i-o
Sitting On Top Of The World
Little Maggie
Hard Times
Step It Up And Go
Tomorrow Night
Arthur McBride
You're Gonna Quit Me
Diamond Joe
Froggie Went A-Courtin'

THE 30TH ANNIVERSARY CONCERT CELEBRATION • [1993]
It's Alright, Ma (I'm Only Bleeding)
My Back Pages
Knockin' On Heaven's Door
Girl From The North Country [remaining tracks by other artists]

WORLD GONE WRONG [1993]
World Gone Wrong
Love Henry
Ragged & Dirty
Blood In My Eyes
Broke Down Engine
Delia
Stack A Lee
Two Soldiers
Jack-A-Roe
Lone Pilgrim

MTV UNPLUGGED • [1995]
Tombstone Blues
Shooting Star
All Along The Watchtower
The Times They Are A-Changin'
John Brown
Rainy Day Women #12 & 35
Desolation Row
Dignity
Knockin' On Heaven's Door
Like A Rolling Stone
With God On Our Side

TIME OUT OF MIND [1997]
Love Sick
Dirt Road Blues
Standing In The Doorway
Million Miles
Tryin' To Get To Heaven
'Til I Fell In Love With You
Not Dark Yet
Cold Irons Bound
Make You Feel My Love
Can't Wait
Highlands

THE BOOTLEG SERIES, VOL. 4 – LIVE 1966 • [1998]
She Belongs To Me
4th Time Around
Visions Of Johanna
It's All Over Now, Baby Blue
Desolation Row
Just Like A Woman
Mr. Tambourine Man
Tell Me Momma
I Don't Believe You (She Acts Like We Never Have Met)
Baby Let Me Follow You Down
Just Like Tom Thumb's Blues
Leopard-Skin Pill-Box Hat
One Too Many Mornings
Ballad Of A Thin Man
Like A Rolling Stone

THE ESSENTIAL BOB DYLAN [2001]
Dignity (alt version)
Things Have Changed

LIVE 1961-2000 • [2001 Japanese Import]
Somebody Touched Me [2000]
Wade In The Water [1961]
To Ramona [1965]
The Grand Coulee Dam [1968]
Dead Man, Dead Man [1981]
Cold Irons Bound [1997]
Born In Time [1998]
Country Pie [2000]
Things Have Changed [2000]

"LOVE AND THEFT" [2001]
Tweedle Dee & Tweedle Dum

Mississippi
Summer Days
Bye And Bye
Lonesome Day Blues
Floater (Too Much To Ask)
High Water (For Charley Patton)
Moonlight
Honest With Me
Po' Boy
Cry A While
Sugar Baby

**THE BOOTLEG SERIES,
VOL. 5 – LIVE 1975 • [2002]**
Tonight I'll Be Staying Here With You
It Ain't Me, Babe
A Hard Rain's A-Gonna Fall
The Lonesome Death Of Hattie
    Carroll
Romance In Durango
Isis
Mr. Tambourine Man
Simple Twist Of Fate
Blowin' In The Wind
Mama, You Been On My Mind
I Shall Be Released
It's All Over Now, Baby Blue
Love Minus Zero/No Limit
Tangled Up In Blue
The Water Is Wide
It Takes A Lot To Laugh, It Takes
    A Train To Cry
Oh, Sister
Hurricane
One More Cup Of Coffee
Sara
Just Like A Woman
Knockin' On Heaven's Door

MASKED AND ANONYMOUS
[Soundtrack 2003]
Down In The Flood
[New version]
Diamond Joe [New version]
Dixie
Cold Irons Bound [New version]
[remaining tracks by other artists]

**THE BOOTLEG SERIES,
VOL. 6 – LIVE 1964 • [2004]**
The Times They Are A-Changin'
Spanish Harlem Incident
Talkin' John Birch Paranoid Blues
To Ramona
Who Killed Davey Moore?
Gates Of Eden
If You Gotta Go, Go Now
It's Alright, Ma (I'm Only Bleeding)
I Don't Believe You (She Acts Like
    We Never Have Met)
Mr. Tambourine Man
A Hard Rain's A-Gonna Fall
Talkin' World War III Blues
Don't Think Twice, It's All Right

The Lonesome Death Of Hattie
    Carroll
Mama, You Been On My Mind *
Silver Dagger *
With God On Our Side *
It Ain't Me, Babe *
All I Really Want To Do
[* with Joan Baez]

**THE BOOTLEG SERIES, VOL.
7 – NO DIRECTION HOME**
[2005]
When I Got Troubles
    [Recorded 1959]
Rambler, Gambler [Recorded 1960]
This Land Is Your Land [Recorded 1961]
Dink's Song [Recorded 1961]
I Was Young When I Left Home
    [Recorded 1961]
Sally Gal [Recorded 1962]
Don't Think Twice, It's All Right
    [Recorded 1963]
Man Of Constant Sorrow
    [Recorded 1963]
Blowin' In The Wind [Live 1963]
Masters Of War [Live 1963]
A Hard Rain's A-Gonna Fall
    [Live 1963]
When The Ship Comes In
    [Live 1963]
Mr. Tambourine Man
    [Recorded 1964]
Chimes Of Freedom [Live 1964]
It's All Over Now, Baby Blue
    [Recorded 1965]
She Belongs To Me
    [Recorded 1965]
Maggie's Farm [Live 1965]
It Takes A Lot To Laugh, It Takes
    A Train To Cry [Recorded 1965]
Tombstone Blues [Recorded 1965]
Just Like Tom Thumb's Blues
    [Recorded 1965]
Desolation Row [Recorded 1965]
Highway 61 Revisited
    [Recorded 1965]
Leopard-Skin Pill-Box Hat
    [Recorded 1966]
Stuck Inside Of Mobile With The
    Memphis Blues Again
    [Recorded 1966]
Visions Of Johanna
    [Recorded 1965]
Ballad Of A Thin Man [Live 1966]

**LIVE AT THE GASLIGHT
[LIVE 1962] • [2005]**
A Hard Rain's A-Gonna Fall
Rocks And Gravel
Don't Think Twice, It's All Right
The Cuckoo
Moonshiner
Handsome Molly
Cocaine

John Brown
Barbara Allen
West Texas

MODERN TIMES [2005]
Thunder On The Mountain
Spirit On The Water
Rollin' And Tumblin'
When The Deal Goes Down
Someday Baby
Workingman's Blues #2
Beyond The Horizon
Nettie Moore
The Levee's Gonna Break
Ain't Talkin'

I'M NOT THERE
[Soundtrack 2007]
I'm Not There [1967]
[remaining tracks by other artists]

**THE BOOTLEG SERIES,
VOL. 8 – TELL TALE SIGNS
(DELUXE EDITION)** [2008]
Mississippi #1 [Recorded 1997]
Most Of The Time #1
    [Recorded 1989]
Dignity [1989 Piano Demo]
Someday Baby [Recorded 2006]
Red River Shore #1
    [Recorded 1997]
Tell Ol' Bill [Recorded 2005]
Born In Time #1 [Recorded 1989]
Can't Wait #1 [Recorded 1997]
Everything Is Broken
    [Recorded 1989]
Dreamin' Of You [Recorded 1997]
Huck's Tune [Recorded 2006]
Marchin' To The City #1
    [Recorded 1997]
High Water (For Charley Patton)
    [Live 2003]
Mississippi #2 [Recorded 1997]
32-20 Blues [Recorded 1993]
Series Of Dreams [Recorded 1989]
God Knows [Recorded 1989]
Can't Escape From You
    [Recorded 2005]
Dignity [Recorded 1989]
Ring Them Bells [Live 1993]
Cocaine Blues [Live 1997]
Ain't Talkin' [Recorded 2006]
The Girl On The Greenbriar Shore
    [Live 1992]
Lonesome Day Blues [Live 2002]
Miss The Mississippi
    [Recorded 1992]
The Lonesome River
    [Recorded 1997]
'Cross The Green Mountain
    [Recorded 2002]
Duncan and Brady [Recorded 1992]
Cold Irons Bound [Live 2004]
Mississippi #3 [Recorded 1997]

Most Of The Time #2
[Recorded 1989]
Ring Them Bells [Recorded 1989]
Things Have Changed [Live 2000]
Red River Shore #2
[Recorded 1997]
Born In Time #2 [Recorded 1989]
Tryin' To Get To Heaven [Live 2000]
Marchin' To The City #2
[Recorded 1997]
Can't Wait #2 [Recorded 1997]
Mary And The Soldier
[Recorded 1993]

TOGETHER THROUGH LIFE
[2009]
Beyond Here Lies Nothin'
Life Is Hard
My Wife's Home Town
If You Ever Go To Houston
Forgetful Heart
Jolene
This Dream Of You
Shake Shake Mama
I Feel A Change Comin' On
It's All Good

CHRISTMAS IN THE HEART
[2009]
Here Comes Santa Claus
Do You Hear What I Hear?
Winter Wonderland
Hark The Herald Angels Sing
I'll Be Home For Christmas
Little Drummer Boy
The Christmas Blues
O Come All Ye Faithful (Adeste
Fideles)
Have Yourself A Merry Little
Christmas
Must Be Santa
Silver Bells
The First Noel
Christmas Island
The Christmas Song
O'Little Town Of Bethlehem

THE WITMARK DEMOS: 1962-1964 (THE BOOTLEG SERIES VOL. 9) [2010]
Man On The Street (Fragment)
Hard Times In New York Town
Poor Boy Blues
Ballad For A Friend
Rambling, Gambling Willie
Talking Bear Mountain Picnic
Massacre Blues
Standing On The Highway
Man On The Street
Blowin' In The Wind
Long Ago, Far Away
A Hard Rain's A-Gonna Fall
Tomorrow Is A Long Time
The Death of Emmett Till

Let Me Die In My Footsteps
Ballad Of Hollis Brown
Quit Your Low Down Ways
Baby, I'm In The Mood For You
Bound To Lose, Bound To Win
All Over You
I'd Hate To Be You On That
Dreadful Day
Long Time Gone
Talkin' John Birch Paranoid Blues
Masters Of War
Oxford Town
Farewell
Don't Think Twice, It's All Right
Walkin' Down The Line
I Shall Be Free
Bob Dylan's Blues
Bob Dylan's Dream
Boots Of Spanish Leather
Girl From The North Country
Seven Curses
Hero Blues
Whatcha Gonna Do?
Gypsy Lou
Ain't Gonna Grieve
John Brown
Only A Hobo
When The Ship Comes In
The Times They Are A-Changin'
Paths Of Victory
Guess I'm Doing Fine
Baby Let Me Follow You Down
Mama, You Been On My Mind
Mr. Tambourine Man
I'll Keep It With Mine

Dylan has appeared as a guest on dozens of albums since 1962; the following contain his most substantial performances.

THE CONCERT FOR BANGLADESH • [1971]
A Hard Rain's A-Gonna Fall
It Takes A Lot To Laugh, It Takes
A Train To Cry
Blowin' In The Wind
Mr. Tambourine Man
Just Like A Woman
[*2005 CD Reissue included* Love
Minus Zero/No Limit *as bonus
track*]

THE LAST WALTZ • [1978]
Baby Let Me Follow You Down
I Don't Believe You (She Acts Like
We Never Have Met)
Forever Young
Baby Let Me Follow You Down
(Reprise)
I Shall Be Released
[*2002 reissue included the bonus track*,
Hazel]

TRAVELING WILBURYS, VOL. 1 [1988]
Handle With Care
Dirty World
Rattled
Last Night
Not Alone Anymore
Congratulations
Heading For The Light
Margarita
Tweeter And The Monkey Man
End Of The Line
[*2007 CD reissue included bonus tracks,*
Maxine *and* Like A Ship]

TRAVELING WILBURYS, VOL. III [1990]
She's My Baby
Inside Out
If You Belonged To Me
The Devil's Been Busy
7 Deadly Sins
Poor House
Where Were You Last Night?
New Blue Moon
You Took My Breath Away
Wilbury Twist
[*2007 CD reissue included bonus tracks,*
Nobody's Child *and* Runaway]

ROCK OF AGES • [2001]
Down In The Flood
When I Paint My Masterpiece
Don't Ya Tell Henry
Like A Rolling Stone
[*The Band's 1972 live album, CD
reissue included previously unavailable
Dylan tracks as bonus material*]

Select Bibliography

While this bibliography is by no means exhaustive, it has been updated to include a number of titles published since the first appearance of No Direction Home *in 1986. Where previously listed books have themselves been updated, entries have been amended accordingly.*

BY BOB DYLAN
Bob Dylan Songbook, New York, 1965.
Tarantula, New York, 1971
Writings and Drawings by Bob Dylan, New York, 1973.
The Songs of Bob Dylan from 1966 Through 1975, New York, 1976.
Lyrics, 1962–2001, New York, 2004
Chronicles: Volume One, London 2004.
The Drawn Blank Series, London, 2008.
Hollywood Foto-Rhetoric: The Lost Manuscript (with photographs by Feinstein, Barry), London, 2008.
Forever Young (illustrated by Paul Rogers), London 2008.
Man Gave Names to All the Animals (illustrated by Jim Arnosky), New York, 2010

BIOGRAPHICAL
Amendt, Gunter: *Reunion Sundown: Bob Dylan in Europa*, Munich, 1985.
Cott, Jonathan (editor): *Dylan on Dylan: The Essential Interviews*, London, 2006.
Davis, Clive, with Willwerth, James: *Clive: Inside the Record Business*, New York, 1975.
Griffin, Sid: *Million Dollar Bash: Bob Dylan, The Band and The Basement Tapes*, London, 2007.
— — *Shelter from the Storm: Bob Dylan's Rolling Thunder Years*, London, 2010.
Gross, Michael and Alexander, Robert: *Bob Dylan: An Illustrated History*, London, 1978.
Hajdu, David: *Positively 4th Street: The Lives and Times of Joan Baez, Bob Dylan, Mimi Fariña and Richard Fariña*, London 2001.
Hammond, John, with Townsend, Irving: *John Hammond on Record*, New York, 1977.
Heylin, Clinton: *A Life in Stolen Moments: Bob Dylan Day by Day*, London, 1996.
Kooper, Al: *Backstage Passes: Rock 'n' Roll Life in the Sixties*, New York, 1977.
Lee, C P: *Like the Night (Revisited): Bob Dylan and the Road to the Manchester Free Trade Hall*, London 2004.
Pennebaker, D A: *Bob Dylan: Don't Look Back*, New York, 1968.
Ribakove, Sy and Barbara: *Folk-Rock: The Bob Dylan Story*, New York, 1966.
Robinson, Earl (editor): *Young Folk Songbook*, New York, 1963.
Rolling Stone (editors): *Knockin' on Dylan's Door: On the Road in '74*, New York, 1974.
Rotolo, Suze: *A Freewheelin' Time: A Memoir of Greenwich Village in the Sixties*, London, 2008.
Scaduto, Anthony: *Bob Dylan: An Intimate Biography*, London, 1996.
Schmidt, Eric von, and Rooney, Jim: *Baby Let Me Follow You Down: The Illustrated Story of the Cambridge Folk Years*, New York, 1979.
Shepard, Sam: *Rolling Thunder Logbook*, London, 2005.
Sloman, Larry: *On the Road with Bob Dylan: Rolling with the Thunder*, New York, 2002.
Sounes, Howard: *Down the Highway*, London, 2001.
Thompson, Toby: *Positively Main Street: An Unorthodox View of Bob Dylan*, New York, 1971.
Wurlitzer, Rudolph: *Pat Garrett and Billy the Kid*, New York, 1973.

DISCOGRAPHICAL
Trager, Oliver: *Keys to the Rain: The Definitive Bob Dylan Encyclopedia*, New York, 2004.

COMMENTARY
Anderson, Dennis: *The Hollow Horn: Bob Dylan's Reception in the United States and Germany*, Munich, 1981.
Barker, Derek: *Bob Dylan: The Songs He Didn't Write Under the Influence*, New Malden, Surrey, 2008.
Bauldie, John: *Bob Dylan and Desire*, Manchester, England, 1984.
— — (editor): *Wanted Man: In Search of Bob Dylan*, London, 1990.
— — and Gray, Michael: *All Across the Telegraph: A Bob Dylan Handbook*, London, 1987,
Bowden, Betsy: *Performed Literature: Words and Music by Bob Dylan*, Bloomington, Indiana, 1982.
Corcoran, Neil: *'Do You, Mr Jones?' Bob Dylan with the Poets and Professors*, London, 2002.
Day, Aidan: *Jokerman: Reading the Lyrics of Bob Dylan*, Oxford, 1988.
Denisoff, Serge: *Great Day Coming: Folk Music and the American Left*, Urbana, Illinois, 1972.

— — *Sing a Song of Social Significance*, Bowling Green, Kentucky, 1972.

— — and Peterson, Richard (editors): *The Sounds of Social Change: Studies in Popular Culture*, Chicago, 1972.

Dettmar, Kevin, J H (editor): *The Cambridge Companion to Bob Dylan*, Cambridge, England, 2009.

Dickstein, Morris: *Gates of Eden: American Culture in the Sixties*, New York, 1977.

Diddle, Gavin: *Images and Assorted Facts: A Peek Behind the Picture Frame*, Manchester, England, 1983.

Ducray, F, Manoeuvre, P, Muller, H, and Vassal, J: *Dylan*, Paris, 1978.

Fong-Torres, Ben (editor): *What's That Sound? Readings in Contemporary Music*, New York, 1976.

Frith, Simon: *The Sociology of Rock*, London, 1978.

Gans, Terry Alexander: *What's Real and What Is Not: Bob Dylan Through 1964 — The Myth of Protest*, Munich, 1983.

Gill, Andy: *Classic Bob Dylan 1962–1969: My Back Pages*, London, 1994.

— — and Odegard, Kevin: *A Simple Twist of Fate: Bob Dylan and the Making of Blood on the Tracks*, Cambridge, Massachusetts, 2004.

Goldstein, Richard: *The Poetry of Rock*, New York, 1968.

— — *Goldstein's Greatest Hits: A Book Mostly About Rock 'n' Roll*, Englewood Cliffs, New Jersey, 1970.

Gray, Michael: *Song and Dance Man III: The Art of Bob Dylan*, London, 2000.

— — *The Bob Dylan Encyclopedia*, London, 2008.

Hedin, Benjamin (editor): *Studio A: The Bob Dylan Reader*, New York, 2004.

Herdman, John: *Voice Without Restraint: Bob Dylan's Lyrics and Their Background*, Edinburgh, Scotland, 1982.

Hetmann, Frederik: *Bob Dylan: Bericht Uber Einen Songpoeten*, Hamburg, 1976.

Heylin, Clinton: *Revolution in the Air — The Songs of Bob Dylan Vol 1: 1957–73*, London, 2009.

— — *Still on the Road – The Songs of Bob Dylan Vol 2: 1974–2008*, London 2010.

Humphries, Patrick and Bauldie, John (editors): *Absolutely Dylan*, New York, 1991.

— — *The Complete Guide to the Music Of Bob Dylan*, London, 1995.

Karpel, Craig: *The Tarantula in Me: A Review of a Title*, San Francisco, 1973.

McGregor, Craig (editor): *Bob Dylan: A Retrospective*, Sydney, 1980.

Marcus, Greil: *Mystery Train: Images of America in Rock 'n' Roll Music*, New York, 1975.

— — *Stranded: Rock and Roll for a Desert Island*, New York, 1979.

— — *Invisible Republic: Bob Dylan's Basement Tapes*, New York, 1997.

— — *Like a Rolling Stone: Bob Dylan at the Crossroads*, London, 2005.

Marqusee, Mike: *Chimes of Freedom: The Politics of Bob Dylan's Art*, New York, 2003.

Marshall, Lee: *Bob Dylan: The Never-Ending Star*, Cambridge, England, 2007.

Mellers, Wilfrid: *A Darker Shade of Pale: A Backdrop to Bob Dylan*, London, 1984.

Miller, Jim (editor): *The Rolling Stone Illustrated History of Rock and Roll*, New York, 1977.

Pichaske, David R (editor): *Beowulf to Beatles: Approaches to Poetry*, New York, 1972.

— — *A Generation in Motion: Popular Music and Culture in the Sixties*, New York, 1979.

— — *Song of the North Country: A Midwest Framework to the Songs of Bob Dylan*, New York, 2010

Pickering, Stephen: *Bob Dylan Approximately: A Portrait of the Jewish Poet in Search of God*, New York, 1975.

— — *Bob Dylan Tour 1974*, Aptos, California, 1973.

Remond, Alain: *Les Chémins de Bob Dylan*, Paris, 1971.

Ricks, Christopher: *Dylan's Visions of Sin*, London 2003.

Riley, Tim: *Hard Rain: A Dylan Commentary*, New York 1993.

Rodnitzky, Jerome L: *Minstrels of the Dawn: The Folk-Protest Singer as a Cultural Hero*, Chicago, 1976.

Schmidt, Mathias R: *Bob Dylan's Message Songs der Sachziger Jahre*, Frankfurt, 1982.

Scoboe, Stephen: *Alias Bob Dylan Revisited*, Calgary, 2003.

Sheehy, Colleen J, and Swiss, Thomas: *Highway 61 Revisited: Bob Dylan's Road from Minnesota to the World*, Minneapolis, 2009.

Thomson, Elizabeth M (editor): *Conclusions on the Wall: New Essays on Bob Dylan*. Manchester, England, 1980.

Thomson, Elizabeth, and Gutman, David (editors): *The Dylan Companion*, Cambridge, Massachusetts, 2001.

Vassal, Jacques: *Electric Children: Roots and Branches of Modern Folk-Rock*, New York, 1976.

Wilentz, Sean: *Bob Dylan in America*, New York, 2010.

Williams, Don: *Bob Dylan: The Man, the Music, the Message*, New Jersey, 1985.

Williams, Paul: *Dylan — What Happened?* Glen Ellen, California, 1980.

— — *Bob Dylan: Performing Artist 1960–1973, The Early Years*, London, 2004.

— — *Bob Dylan: Performing Artist 1974–1986, The Middle Years*, London, 2004.

— — *Bob Dylan: Performing Artist 1986–1990 and Beyond*, London, 2005.

UNPUBLISHED ESSAYS AND DISSERTATIONS CITED IN THE TEXT

Bliss, Carolyn Jane: *Younger Now. Bob Dylan's Changing World and Vision*, unpublished dissertation, 1976.

Cantor, Louis: *Bob Dylan and the Protest Movement of the 1960's: The Electronic Medium is the Apocalyptic Message*, unpublished essay.

King, Bill: *Bob Dylan: The Artist in the Marketplace*, unpublished dissertation.

Levinson, Belle D: *The Deranged Seer: The Poetry of Arthur Rimbaud and Bob Dylan*, unpublished essay.
Lhamon, W T Jr: *Poplore and Bob Dylan* and *Dada Punk*, unpublished essays.
McDonough, Jack: *It Takes a Train to Cry*, unpublished dissertation.
Pichaske, David: *Perspectives on the Self—The Art of Dylan's Middle Period* unpublished essay, 1972.
Poague, Leland A: *Performance Variables: Some Versions of "It Ain't Me, Babe,"* unpublished dissertation.
Stelzig, Eugene: *Bob Dylan's Career as a Blakean Visionary and Romantic*, unpublished dissertation.

MAINLY PICTORIAL

Bob Dylan (programme book for 1978 European tour), Oxford, 1978.
Cott, Jonathon: *Dylan*, New York, 1984.
Feinstein, Barry, Kramer, Daniel, and Marshall, Jim: *Early Dylan*, New York, 1999.
Gilbert, Douglas R, with Dave Marsh: *Forever Young: Photographs of Bob Dylan*, Cambridge, Massachusetts, 2005.
Kramer, Daniel: *Bob Dylan*, Secaucus, New Jersey, 1967.
Landy, Elliot: *Woodstock Vision*, Hamburg, 1984.
Rinzler, Alan: *Bob Dylan: The Illustrated Record*, New York, 1978.
Santelli, Robert: *The Bob Dylan Scrapbook 1956–1966*, New York, 2005
Shelton, Robert (photographs by David Gahr): *The Face of Folk Music*, New York, 1968.
Williams, Richard: *Dylan: A Man Called Alias*, London, 1992.

GENERAL BACKGROUND

Allsop, Kenneth: *Hard Travellin': The Hobo and His History*, New York, 1967.
Baez, Joan: *Daybreak: An Intimate Journal*, New York, 1968.
— — *And a Voice to Sing With: A Memoir*, New York, 1987.
Bays, Gwendolyn: *The Orphic Vision: Seer Poets from Novalis to Rimbaud*, Lincoln, Nebraska, 1964.
Bradshaw, Steve: *Cafe Society: Bohemian Life from Swift to Bob Dylan*, London, 1978.
Campbell, Joseph: *Myths to Live By*, London, 1972.
Cohen, Ronald D: *Rainbow Quest: The Folk Music Revival & American Society 1940-1970*, Boston, Massachusetts, 2002.
Collins, Judy: *Trust Your Heart*, Boston, 1987.
DeTurk, David A, and Poulin Jr, A: *The American Folk Scene: Dimensions of the Folksong Revival*, New York, 1967.
Dunaway, David King: *How Can I Keep from Singing: Pete Seeger*, London, 2008.
— — with Beer, Molly: *Singing Out: An Oral History of America's Folk Revivals*, New York, 2010.
Dunson, Josh: *Freedom in the Air: Song Movements of the '60s*. New York, 1965.
Gillett, Charlie: *The Sound of the City*, London, 1970.
Graves, Robert: *The White Goddess: A Historical Grammar of Poetic Myth*, London, 1961.
Guthrie, Woody: *Bound for Glory*, New York, 1968.
Ian Janis: *Society's Child*, New York, 2008.
Laing, Dave, Dallas, Karl, Denselow, Robin, and Shelton, Robert: *The Electric Muse, The Story of Folk into Rock*, London, 1975.
Martz, Louis L: *The Poetry of Meditation: A Study in English Religious Literature of the Seventeenth Century*, New Haven, Connecticut, 1954.
Miles, Barry: *Ginsberg: A Biography*, London, 1989
Nadeau, Maurice: *The History of Surrealism*, London, 1968.
Newfield, Jack: *A Prophetic Minority: The American New Left*, London, 1967.
Oliver, Paul: *The Story of the Blues*, London, 1972.
Plowman, Max: *An Introduction to the Study of Blake*, London, 1967.
Roszak, Theodore: *The Making of a Counter Culture: Reflections on the Technocratic Society & Its Youthful Opposition*, London, 1970.
Seeger, Pete (compiler and editor): *Woody Guthrie Folk Songs*, New York, 1963.
Shelton, Robert (editor): *Born to Win: Woody Guthrie*, New York, 1965.
Weissman, Dick: *Which Side Are You On? An Inside History of the Folk Music Revival in America*, New York, 2006.
— — *Talkin' 'Bout a Revolution: Music and Social Change in America*, New York, 2010.
Wilson, Colin: *The Outsider*, London, 1956.

WEBSITES
The internet has become an invaluable forum for those interested in the life and work of Bob Dylan. Of the 15 million Dylan references on Google, these are the key sites:
bobdylan.com – *the official Dylan website*
bjorner.com/bob.htm
expectingrain.com
dylancover.com

Index